Designing Software–Intensive Systems:
Methods and Principles

Pierre F. Tiako
Langston University, USA

INFORMATION SCIENCE REFERENCE

Hershey · New York

Acquisitions Editor:	Kristin Klinger
Development Editor:	Kristin Roth
Senior Managing Editor:	Jennifer Neidig
Managing Editor:	Jamie Snavely
Assistant Managing Editor:	Carole Coulson
Copy Editor:	Lanette Ehrhardt
Typesetter:	Michael Brehm
Cover Design:	Lisa Tosheff
Printed at:	Yurchak Printing Inc.

Published in the United States of America by
Information Science Reference (an imprint of IGI Global)
701 E. Chocolate Avenue, Suite 200
Hershey PA 17033
Tel: 717-533-8845
Fax: 717-533-8661
E-mail: cust@igi-global.com
Web site: http://www.igi-global.com

and in the United Kingdom by
Information Science Reference (an imprint of IGI Global)
3 Henrietta Street
Covent Garden
London WC2E 8LU
Tel: 44 20 7240 0856
Fax: 44 20 7379 0609
Web site: http://www.eurospanbookstore.com

Library of Congress Cataloging-in-Publication Data

Designing software-intensive systems : methods and principles / Pierre F. Tiako, editor.
      p. cm.
   Summary: "This book addresses the complex issues associated with software engineering environment capabilities for designing real-time embedded software systems"--Provided by publisher.
   Includes bibliographical references and index.
   ISBN 978-1-59904-699-0 (hardcover) -- ISBN 978-1-59904-701-0 (ebook)
  1. Software engineering. 2. Computer systems. 3. Systems engineering--Data processing. I. Tiako, Pierre F.
   QA76.758.D476 2008
   005.1--dc22
                                        2008008468

British Cataloguing in Publication Data
A Cataloguing in Publication record for this book is available from the British Library.

All work contributed to this book set is original material. The views expressed in this book are those of the authors, but not necessarily of the publisher.

Table of Contents

Section I
Process Support Specification and Modeling Techniques

Chapter I
Alf Inge Wang, Norwegian University of Science and Technology, Norway
Carl-Fredrik Sørensen, Norwegian University of Science and Technology, Norway

Chapter II
Holger Giese, University of Potsdam, Germany
Stefan Henkler, University of Potsdam, Germany
Martin Hirsch, University of Potsdam, Germany
Vladimir Rubin, University of Potsdam, Germany
Matthias Tichy, University of Potsdam, Germany

Chapter III
Jaroslav Král, Charles University, Czech Republic
Michal Žemlička, Charles University, Czech Republic

Section IV
Analysis, Evaluation, and Optimization

Section V
Best Practices and Integrations

Detailed Table of Contents

Section I
Process Support Specification and Modeling Techniques

Chapter I

    Alf Inge Wang, Norwegian University of Science and Technology, Norway
    Carl-Fredrik Sørensen, Norwegian University of Science and Technology, Norway

The chapter describes the required elements to model the software process, the required external resources, and the required process support provided by a process-centered environment. The framework presents the required process support from four perspectives: at the individual level, at the group level, at the team level, and at the project level.

Chapter II

    Holger Giese, University of Potsdam, Germany
    Stefan Henkler, University of Potsdam, Germany
    Martin Hirsch, University of Potsdam, Germany
    Vladimir Rubin, University of Potsdam, Germany
    Matthias Tichy, University of Potsdam, Germany

The chapter presents modeling techniques which support the integration of several computing disciplines based on the software engineering standard UML. The authors investigate a standard for systems engineering that integrates system engineering and software engineering for requirement analysis. In addition, UML extensions that integrate traditional engineering modeling techniques, and support the implementation, verification and validation phases for embedded systems, are also presented.

Chapter III

Jaroslav Král, Charles University, Czech Republic
Michal Žemlička, Charles University, Czech Republic

The chapter proposes some solutions to implement business processes in service-oriented systems. Service orientation is one known solution enabling the reuse of legacy systems and integration of third-party products. The authors discuss subclasses of service-oriented systems. It shows how service orientation simplifies the development as it: (a) enables incremental development by using decomposition into small components; (b) supports tools for correct specification, debugging, and effective prototyping; and, (c) simplifies incremental maintenance and gradual modernization.

Section II
Requirements, Changes, and Tracability

Chapter IV

Alf Inge Wang, Norwegian University of Science and Technology, Norway
Carl-Fredrik Sørensen, Norwegian University of Science and Technology, Norway
Hien Nam Le, Norwegian University of Science and Technology, Norway
Heri Ramampiaro, Norwegian University of Science and Technology, Norway
Mads Nygård, Norwegian University of Science and Technology, Norway
Reidar Conradi, Norwegian University of Science and Technology, Norway

The chapter examines requirement analysis issues to be considered when designing and developing mobile systems. The framework described consists of a process, the characterisation of scenarios, computation of complexity indicators, and determination of nonfunctional and functional requirements. One important goal of this framework is to identify the parts that are most complex and perhaps hardest to implement in a mobile support system.

Chapter V

Gan Deng, Vanderbilt University, USA
Douglas C. Schmidt, Vanderbilt University, USA
Aniruddha Gokhale, Vanderbilt University, USA
Jeff Gray, University of Alabama at Birmingham, USA
Yuehua Lin, University of Alabama at Birmingham, USA
Gunther Lenz, Microsoft, USA

The chapter deals with distributed real-time embedded product-line architectures, which are among the most difficult software-intensive systems to develop because such systems have limited resources and must communicate via the network to meet stringent real-time quality-of-service assurance and other performance requirements. To address these challenges, the authors propose a layered and compositional architecture to modularize system concerns and reduce the effort associated with domain evolution.

Chapter VI

Ståle Walderhaug, SINTEF ICT, Norway & University of Tromsø, Norway
Erlend Stav, SINTEF ICT, Norway
Ulrik Johansen, SINTEF ICT, Norway
Gøran K. Olsen, SINTEF ICT, Norway

The chapter focuses on lifelong management of relations between artifacts in model-driven software development. Traceability is about following the status of an artifact that is part of a system. The authors show how useful traceability is in software development projects; present a generic meta-model for lifelong traceability; and propose a method for incorporating traceability in the development process.

Section III
Software Architectures and Architectural Alternatives

Chapter VII

Gerhard Chroust, J. Kepler University Linz, Austria
Erwin Schoitsch, Austrian Research Centers (ARC), Austria

The chapter introduces basic architectural alternatives as a means to make some a-priori architectural assumptions and understand their effects when designing complex software-intensive systems. The authors discuses strategic selection considerations for architectural alternatives, and investigates some cross-influences for basic architectural alternatives.

Chapter VIII

Rafael Capilla, Universidad Rey Juan Carlos, Spain
Margarita Martínez, Universidad Rey Juan Carlos, Spain
Francisco Nava, Universidad Rey Juan Carlos, Spain
Cristina Muñoz, Universidad Politécnica de Madrid, Spain

The chapter describes how the design process of virtual reality systems can be improved using detailed software architectures. Virtual reality systems are complex intensive software systems that need a lot of effort and resources during the development phase. To tackle certain problems affecting the construction of this kind of systems, the authors propose a software architecture-centric approach.

Chapter IX

Kendra M. L. Cooper, The University of Texas at Dallas, USA

Lirong Dai, Seattle University, USA

Renee Steiner, Intervoice, Inc., USA

Rym Zalila Mili, The University of Texas at Dallas, USA

The chapter presents established software architecture concepts followed by a survey of more recent approaches. The discussion includes architectural views, modularization and decomposition of the architectures, architectural styles, and architectural description languages. The survey is of interest to students, researchers and practitioners, in particular those who may be new to the area of software architecture.

Section IV
Analysis, Evaluation, and Optimization

Chapter X

Daniel G. Waddington, Lockheed Martin, USA

Nilabja Roy, Vanderbilt University, USA

Douglas C. Schmidt, Vanderbilt University, USA

The chapter reviews key techniques and technologies for analyzing the behavior of software systems via dynamic analysis: compiler based instrumentation, operating system and middleware profiling, virtual machine profiling and hardware-based profiling. The authors highlights the advantages and disadvantages of each approach with respect to measuring the performance of multithreaded systems, and demonstrates how these approaches can be combined and applied in practice.

Chapter XI

James H. Hill, Vanderbilt University, USA

Douglas C. Schmidt, Vanderbilt University, USA

John M. Slaby, Raytheon Integrated Defense Systems, USA

The chapter shows that existing techniques for evaluating the performance of component architectures are relatively complex. What is needed, therefore, are next-generation modeling tools that provide the same analysis techniques, but shield the developer from the complexity of existing tools. The authors combine system execution modeling tools with model-driven engineering technologies to address the development and integration challenges of service-oriented architecture-based enterprise software-intensive systems.

Chapter XII

Jules White, Vanderbilt University, USA
Douglas C. Schmidt, Vanderbilt University, USA
Andrey Nechypurenko, Siemens AG, Germany
Egon Wuchner, Siemens AG, Germany

The chapter deals with reducing the complexity of modeling and optimizing large systems through the integration of constraint solvers with graphical modeling tools. The authors present techniques based on integrating constraint solvers into modeling environments that can be used to address these challenges and also illuminates the complexities of leveraging constraint solvers and describes effective techniques and tools to manage the complexity they introduce.

Section V
Best Practices and Integrations

Chapter XIII

Enis Afgan, University of Alabama at Birmingham, USA
Purushotham Bangalore, University of Alabama at Birmingham, USA
Jeff Gray, University of Alabama at Birmingham, USA

The chapter shows how the requirements related to application deployment have risen and require new expertise, often not readily and easily available due to the involved complexities. This implies the need for a grid specialist who possesses deep understanding of the technology. These issues are addressed in the chapter with an introduction of a new language. The construction of this language is eased by a support tool based on metamodeling technologies.

Chapter XIV

Jeff Elpern, Software Quality Institute, Inc., USA
Sergiu Dascalu, University of Nevada–Reno, USA

The chapter presents open source development as a fundamentally new paradigm driven by economics and facilitated by new processes. The authors propose a framework for understanding the open source revolution by identifying a number of market forces driving the revolution and placing these forces within historical perspectives.

Chapter XV

Syed Ahsan, University of Engineering and Technology, Pakistan
Abad Shah, University of Engineering and Technology, Pakistan

The chapter determines and measures the data quality and its needs in data intensive domains. Data provenance has been proposed as one of the many quality metrics to determine the quality of data. So far, data provenance itself has not been investigated in detail. The mechanisms of collecting metadata to establish data provenance, the number of parameters which affect the quality of provenance, and important characteristics which must be part of any data provenance are discussed in the paper.

Chapter XVI

    Krishnakumar Balasubramanian, Vanderbilt University, USA
    Douglas C. Schmidt, Vanderbilt University, USA
    Zoltán Molnár, Vanderbilt University, USA
    Ákos Lédeczi, Vanderbilt University, USA

The chapter contributes to functional integration in distributed enterprise systems. Using a case study, the research demonstrates how metamodel composition can solve functional integration by reverse engineering an existing system and exposing it as Web services to Web clients who use these services. Metamodeling provides significant benefits with respect to automation and reusability compared to conventional integration processes and methods.

Preface

Software-intensive systems such as telecom networks, mobile systems, handheld devices, sensor networks, and command and control systems are dependable systems which can impact our daily lives and the security of our society. Therefore, their design has to encompass many important attributes, such as systems and software development processes; business process management and economic models; service-orientation and design pattern; wireless and mobile technologies; requirement engineering; component middleware and component-based design; metamodels and metadata; traceability and systems evaluation; reverse engineering and design decision; architectural trade-offs and architecture-centric design; dependability, portability and reliability; CASE tools and distributed systems; input/output models; special purpose languages and parallel processing; deterministic and probabilistic systems; data schema and data provenance metrics; program generators and grid computing, open source revolution and disruptive technology; Web services and Semantic Web; and, functional integration, seamless integration and in-silico experiments. This book addresses these attributes.

Design for software-intensive systems requires adequate methodology and tool support in order to make use of and develop very large, complex systems. Software engineering environments help reduce the design costs of sizeable and intricate software systems, while improving the quality of the software produced. This book explores complex issues associated with software engineering environment capabilities for designing software-intensive systems.

The objective of this book is to provide relevant theoretical foundations, principles, methodologies, frameworks, and the latest research findings to professors, researchers, and graduate and undergraduate students working in the fields related to computer science, software engineering, manufacturing engineering, business administration, computer engineering, electrical engineering, industrial engineering, Web technology, and information systems. In addition, the book is expected to reveal innovative capabilities for designing software-intensive systems, important guides for managers and practitioners involved in the development of very large and complex software systems.

This book differs from others in the field because it is general enough to bring together principles, methodologies, and technologies, as well as estimation and reliability in a real-world guidebook that will help software managers, engineers, and customers immediately improve their way of designing and maintaining large, complex software systems. The scholarly value of *Designing Software-Intensive Systems: Methods and Principles* is to propose new building blocks for designing software-intensive systems in a XVI chapter book comprised of five sections. Each chapter stands alone; thus, readers can focus on topics of particular interest to them.

SECTION I

Section I consists of three chapters dealing with process support specifications and design. Chapter I describes process artifacts required to support the development of large software projects. Chapter II presents modeling techniques for software-intensive systems. Chapter III shows how service orientation can be used to simplify the development of software-intensive systems.

Chapter I

"Differentiated Process Support for Large Software Projects," by Alf Inge Wang and Carl-Fredrik Sørensen, describes the required elements to model the software process, the required external resources, and the required process support provided by a process-centered environment. The framework presents the required process support from four perspectives: at the individual level, at the group level, at the team level, and at the project level. The chapter also discusses issues to be considered when planning and executing a software development process for large software projects with several levels of management. The objective of the research is to provide a guideline for evaluating tools supporting the development and management processes of large software projects.

Chapter II

"Modeling Techniques for Software-Intensive Systems," by Holger Giese, Stefan Henkler, Martin Hirsch, Vladimir Rubin, and Matthias Tichy, presents modeling principles which support the integration of several computing disciplines based on the software engineering standard UML. The chapter investigates a standard for systems engineering that integrates system engineering and software engineering for requirement analysis. In addition, UML extensions that (1) integrate traditional engineering modeling techniques with software engineering modeling techniques for the architectural design and detailed design, and (2) support the implementation, verification and validation phases for embedded systems are also presented. After outlining requirements and modeling techniques for software-intensive systems, the chapter looks into the most relevant modeling approaches involving business process engineering, software engineering, and control engineering before discussing the remaining integration problems. The chapter also discusses how to combine the UML extensions presented to provide a promising approach toward modeling of complex software-intensive systems.

Chapter III

"Service Orientation and Software-Intensive Systems," by Jaroslav Král and Michal Žemlička, proposes some solutions used to implement business processes in service-oriented systems. Service orientation is one known solution enabling the reuse of legacy systems and integration of third-party products. The chapter discusses subclasses of service-oriented systems. It shows how service orientation simplifies the development as it: (a) enables incremental development by using decomposition into small components; (b) supports tools for correct specification, debugging, and effective prototyping; and, (c) simplifies incremental maintenance and gradual modernization. Service orientation also provides management tools to support collaboration with business partners. Software-intensive systems are systems that depend on supporting software. The software is typically large and complex, and, as a rule, interacts with human users. The failure of the software implies failure of the system, usually causing substantial losses. The chapter shows that such software should be service-oriented. The interfaces of services should be well understood by users, and the services should be specific to applications and architectures. The authors present an important infrastructure of services as basic service-oriented design patterns for software-intensive systems.

SECTION II

Section II consists of three chapters exploring requirements engineering and systems development life cycle for software-intensive systems. Chapter IV examines requirement analysis issues for designing and developing mobile systems. Chapter V discusses key concepts of evolution and change in model-driven software product-line architectures. Chapter VI proposes a set of core traceability requirements for designing software-intensive systems.

Chapter IV

"From Scenarios to Requirements in Mobile Client-Server Systems," by Alf Inge Wang, Carl-Fredrik Sørensen, Hien Nam Le, Heri Ramampiaro, Mads Nygård, and Reidar Conradi, examines requirements analysis issues to be considered when designing and developing mobile systems. The framework described consists of a process, the characterisation of scenarios, computation of complexity indicators, and determination of nonfunctional and functional requirements. One important goal of this framework is to identify the parts that are most complex and perhaps hardest to implement in a mobile support system. The objective of the chapter is to provide a methodology for requirement elicitations when developing systems support for mobile workers such as craftsmen, salesmen, emergency staff, police, public transportation drivers, and service staff. A system developer with basic knowledge in software engineering will learn how to develop requirements from the initial analysis process in the development of a mobile system to the description of priority, nonfunctional, and functional requirements of the end-system.

Chapter V

"Evolution in Model-Driven Software Product-Line Architectures," by Gan Deng, Douglas C. Schmidt, Aniruddha Gokhale, Jeff Gray, Yuehua Lin, and Gunther Lenz, deals with distributed real-time embedded product-line architectures, which are among the most difficult software-intensive systems to develop because such systems have limited resources and must communicate via the network to meet stringent real-time quality-of-service assurance and other performance requirements. The chapter surveys existing technologies and categorizes them along two dimensions based on their syntax and mechanisms for supporting evolution. A representative software-intensive system is used throughout the chapter as a case study to describe how to evolve product-line architectures systematically and minimize human intervention. The chapter also describes key concepts, such as model-driven engineering, product-line architectures, and model transformations that are important for supporting evolution in large-scale software intensive systems. Difficulties faced while evolving product-line architectures include handling unanticipated requirements, satisfying existing requirements, and changing metamodels. A successful process for product-line architectures evolution must, therefore, manage such changes effectively. To address these challenges, the chapter proposes a layered and compositional architecture to modularize system concerns and reduce the effort associated with domain evolution.

Chapter VI

"Traceability in Model-Driven Software Development," by Ståle Walderhaug, Erlend Stav, Ulrik Johansen and Gøran K. Olsen, focuses on lifelong management of relations between artifacts in model-driven software development. Traceability is about following the status of an artifact that is part of a system. The paper presents the background and the state-of-the-art of traceability in software development before proposing a set of core traceability requirements. The solution proposed for traceability is based on a generic metamodel and set of service specifications that use artifacts and their relationships to derive traces models. Over all, the objectives of the chapter are to: (a) show how useful is traceability in software development projects; (b) present a generic metamodel for lifelong traceability; and, (c) propose a method for incorporating traceability in the development process and tools.

SECTION III

Section III consists of three chapters discussing architectural alternatives for software-intensive systems. Chapter VII discusses strategic selection considerations for architectural alternatives. Chapter VIII proposes a software architecture-centric approach for architecturing virtual reality systems using UML. Chapter IX proposes a survey of recent software architecture approaches.

Chapter VII

"Choosing Basic Architectural Alternatives," by Gerhard Chroust and Erwin Schoitsch, introduces basic architectural alternatives as a means to make some a-priori architectural assumptions and understand their effects when designing complex software-intensive systems. The alternatives considered in the chapter are classified according to five fundamental dimensions: time, location, granularity, control, and automation. For each dimension, several real examples are presented, discussing key properties of the choice such as elasticity and reversibility with respect to later modifications, the scope of uniformity of the system and the implication on chosen methods to accomplish the alternative. The chapter also discusses strategic selection considerations for architectural alternatives, and investigates some cross-influences for basic architectural alternatives. The analysis presented together with the specific examples and their key properties provide some insight for novices and seasoned designers and guide them during the early phases of system design.

Chapter VIII

"Architecting Virtual Reality Systems," by Rafael Capilla, Margarita Martínez, Francisco Nava, and Cristina Muñoz, describes how the design process of virtual reality systems can be improved using detailed software architectures. Virtual reality systems are complex intensive software systems that need a lot of effort and resources during the development phase. Because rigid and monolithic approaches have been often used in the past in the construction of such systems, maintenance and evolution activities become difficult tasks to carry out. Today, software architectures are used for designing more maintainable and modular systems but previous experiences in the virtual reality field didn't pay much attention to the usage of appropriate architecture descriptions. The chapter provides some guidance and potential solutions for certain design issues that can be applied to both immersive and nonimmersive virtual reality applications. To tackle certain problems affecting the construction of this kind of software intensive systems, the chapter proposes a software architecture-centric approach.

Chapter IX

"A Survey of Software Architecture Approaches," by Kendra M. L. Cooper, Lirong Dai, Renee Steiner and Rym Zalila Mili, presents established software architecture concepts followed by a survey of more recent approaches. The discussion begins with a presentation of established software architecture concepts, including architectural views, modularization and decomposition of the architectures, architectural styles, and architectural description languages. This is followed by a presentation of two well-known approaches: structured and object-oriented design. The more recent software architecture approaches included in this survey include aspect, agent, and component oriented approaches. The aspect oriented approach improves the ability to modularize capabilities, such as security, and availability in an architecture. The agent oriented approach improves the ability to model the social complexity of systems. The component oriented approach improves the ability to rapidly deploy high quality systems in order to meet new needs. In this research, each of these approaches has been proposed as a solution to a different problem. The survey is of interest to students, researchers and practitioners, in particular those who may be new to the area of software architecture.

SECTION IV

Section IV consists of three chapters describing techniques and tools to evaluate and reduce the complexity of software-intensive systems. Chapter X proposes an approach for evaluating quality of service for enterprise distributed real-time and embedded systems. Chapter XI discusses the complexity and optimization of large systems. Chapter XII reviews key techniques and technologies to analyzing the behavior of software systems.

Chapter X

"Dynamic Analysis and Profiling of Multithreaded Systems," by Daniel G. Waddington, Nilabja Roy and Douglas C. Schmidt, reviews key techniques and technologies to analyzing the behavior of software systems via dynamic analysis: compiler based instrumentation, operating system and middleware profiling, virtual machine profiling, and hardware-based profiling. Dynamic analysis is weaker and less capable when the behavioral characteristics of concern depend on a system-wide analysis such as the global thread state at a given point in time. The alternative to dynamic analysis is static analysis. The benefits of static analysis are its ability to (1) perform analysis without running the system and (2) allow inspection of all theoretically possible conditions. Although static analysis shows some promise for selected applications it cannot predict and present a complete picture of behavior for larger-scale systems. The chapter highlights the advantages and disadvantages of each approach with respect to measuring the performance of multithreaded systems, and demonstrates how these approaches can be combined and applied in practice.

Chapter XI

"Evaluating Quality of Service for Enterprise Distributed Systems," by James H. Hill, Douglas C. Schmidt, and John M. Slaby, finds out that existing techniques for evaluating the performance of component architectures are relatively complex and at the middleware infrastructure level only. What is needed, therefore, are next-generation modeling tools that provide the same analysis techniques, but shield the developer from the complexity of existing tools. The chapter describes existing techniques and tools used to evaluate the quality of service of some enterprise systems. To motivate the structure and functionality of next-generation tools, the chapter presents a service-oriented architecture case study for naval shipboard computing systems and the challenges encountered while developing and evaluating it. The main goals of this case study are to simplify the process of determining which deployment and configuration strategies will meet deadlines, and to reduce the time for integrating and testing the actual system components after they are completed. The chapter combines system execution modeling tools with model-driven engineering technologies to address the development and integration challenges of service-oriented architecture-based enterprise software-intensive systems. The research showed how an existing modeling tool could be applied to the case study presented to address integration challenges during early stages of development.

Chapter XII

"Reducing the Complexity of Modeling Large Software Systems," by Jules White, Douglas C. Schmidt, Andrey Nechypurenko and Egon Wuchner, deals with reducing the complexity of modeling and optimizing large systems through the integration of constraint solvers with graphical modeling tools. For large-scale systems, traditional modeling approaches allow developers to raise the level of abstraction used for solution specification and illuminate design flaws earlier in the development cycle. Such systems, however, have exponential design constraints, extremely large model sizes, or other complexities that make it hard to handcraft a model of a solution. For these types of challenging domains, automated design guidance based on the design constraints is needed. The chapter illustrates the specific challenges of using model-driven development tools for these types of complex domains. The chapter also presents techniques based on integrating constraint solvers into modeling environments that can be used to address these challenges and also illuminates the complexities of leveraging constraint solvers and describes effective techniques and tools to manage the complexity they introduce.

SECTION V

Section V consists of four chapters dealing with best practices and integrations in software-intensive systems. Chapter XIII proposes a domain-specific language for describing grid applications. Chapter XIV discusses market forces for understanding the open source revolution. Chapter XV presents system integration concepts for distributed enterprise systems. Chapter XV proposes mechanisms for evaluating data provenance in data intensive domains.

Chapter XIII

"A Domain-Specific Language for Describing Grid Applications," by Enis Afgan, Purushotham Bangalore, and Jeff Gray, introduces grid computing concepts and provides a taxonomy of grid users. The chapter builds on grid technologies and provides examples of grid application development and deployment through a sample scenario outlining some of the difficulties with the current grid technologies. By adopting the grid, the requirements related to application deployment have risen and require new expertise, often not readily and easily available due to the involved complexities. This implies the need for a grid specialist who possesses deep understanding of the technology. The drawback to this solution is that additional communication is necessary at the development level, which prolongs the application development in addition to possibilities to introduce errors due to miscommunication or misunderstanding. These issues are addressed in the chapter with an introduction of a new language. The construction of this language is eased by a support tool based on metamodeling technologies.

Chapter XIV

"A Framework for Understanding the Open Source Revolution," by Jeff Elpern and Sergiu Dascalu, presents open source development as a fundamentally new paradigm driven by economics and facilitated by new processes. Development theory, methodologies, processes and techniques have mostly evolved from the environment of proprietary, large-scale and large-risk software systems. The software design principles function within a hierarchical decision-making framework. Development of banking, enterprise resource and complex weapons systems all fit this paradigm. However, as this chapter describes, another paradigm for the design and implementation of software-intensive systems has emerged. The open source management structure is "flat." The development team is dispersed and works for many different organizations. The testing processes put most of the work in the user community. Judged by the methodologies of large-scale, proprietary development, open source projects look like chaos. However, the real-world results have been spectacular. The chapter proposes a framework for understanding the open source revolution by identifying a number of market forces driving the revolution and placing these forces within historical perspectives.

Chapter XV

"Quality Metrics for Evaluating Data Provenance," by Syed Ahsan and Abad Shah, determines and measures the data quality and its needs in data intensive domains. Data provenance has been proposed as one of the many quality metrics to determine the quality of data. So far, data provenance itself has not been investigated in detail. The chapter gives a literature survey of the field and discusses issues and problems of data provenance. The mechanisms of collecting metadata to establish data provenance, the number of parameters which affect the quality of provenance, and important characteristics which must be part of any data provenance are discussed in the paper. The chapter also identifies different applications of data provenance in various domains, and proposes a set of parameters and related metrics to measure data provenance. These proposed metrics can assist software researchers and practitioners to better understand and support data provenance in various domains such as software-intensive systems.

Chapter XVI

"System Integration Using Model-Driven Engineering," by Krishnakumar Balasubramanian, Douglas C. Schmidt, Zoltán Molnár, and Ákos Lédeczi, contributes to functional integration in distributed enterprise systems. With the emergence of commercial-off-the-shelf components, software integrators are increasingly faced with the task of integrating heterogeneous enterprise distributed systems built using different technologies. Although there are well-documented patterns and techniques for system integration using various middleware technologies, system integration is still largely a tedious and error-prone manual process. To improve this process, the chapter proposes that component developers and system integrators must understand key properties of the systems they are integrating, as well as the integration technologies they are applying. The chapter describes the challenges associated with functionally integrating software for these types of systems and presents how composition of domain-specific modeling languages can be used to simplify functional integration. Using a case study, the research demonstrates how metamodel composition can solve functional integration by reverse engineering an existing system and exposing it as Web services to Web clients who use these services. Metamodeling provides significant benefits with respect to automation and reusability compared to conventional integration processes and methods.

Pierre F. Tiako *is the director of the Center for Information Technology Research at Langston University (USA) and an assistant professor of computer science and information systems. He worked as a visiting professor at Oklahoma State University (OSU) before the current position. Prior to OSU, he taught computer science courses and did research at Universities of Nancy and Rennes (France), and also worked as an expert engineer at INRIA, the French National Institute for Research in Information Technology. Dr. Tiako has authored more than 50 journal and conference technical papers and coedited four proceedings volumes, resulting from services as program chair for several international conferences and workshops. He holds a PhD in software and information systems engineering from National Polytechnic Institute of Lorraine (France). Dr. Tiako is a senior member of IEEE and past chairman for IEEE Oklahoma City Computer Society.*

Acknowledgment

Publishing a scholarly book is a collective effort that involves many parties, including but not limited to the authors, the reviewers, the editor and the publisher.

Special appreciation and gratitude go to the publishing team at IGI Global, whose contributions throughout the process of the book publication have been invaluable.

I would like to specifically acknowledge the authors for sharing their valuable experiences and accumulated knowledge. Moreover, I would like to acknowledge those selected authors who, in addition to contributing to chapters in the book, have contributed as reviewers of manuscripts and played an important role in a rigorous double-blind review process.

I would like to take this opportunity and acknowledge the help of all those who were involved in the different stages of the production of this book, without whose support and assistance this effort could not have been satisfactorily completed on time and with such high quality.

Last but not least, I thank my wife, Christine, and my parents for their love, encouragement, and unfailing support throughout this project.

Pierre F. Tiako, PhD
Langston University
Oklahoma, USA
September 2007

Section I
Process Support Specification and Modeling Techniques

Chapter I
Differentiated Process Support for Large Software Projects

Alf Inge Wang
Norwegian University of Science and Technology, Norway

Carl-Fredrik Sørensen
Norwegian University of Science and Technology, Norway

ABSTRACT

This chapter presents a framework for differentiated process support in large software projects. Process support can be differentiated in different levels based on the size of the development organization and the need for coordination across different levels of the organization. We have defined four main perspectives: individual, group, team, and project level, where the framework consider essential issues when planning and executing the software development processes in organizations with different levels of management. Further, a guideline is provided that suggests what is required of process support in the various organizational levels.

INTRODUCTION

Development of large and complex software systems involves large organisations. In such working environments, it is essential to plan and coordinate the process, feed the involved developers with necessary documents, tools and files, track the process and effort, and learn from and improve the process.

Software process modeling is aimed at understanding, guiding, coordinating, automating, and improving the software process to thus improve the software quality and reduce the effort of developing software products (Wang, 2001). Many

process models and *process-centred support environments* (PSEs) have been created with the assumption that the same process support should be provided at every level in an organization (Conradi, Fuggetta, & Jaccheri, 1998; Derniame, Baba, & Wastell, 1998; Finkelstein, 2000; Fuggetta, 2000; Nitto & Fuggetta, 1998).

If we consider development of large software systems, the organisations in such projects usually involve several levels of management. Depending on the level of an organisation a person is working in, the perspective and goal of the work will vary. For a programmer, the main concern would be to have access to all necessary files, documents, and tools to carry out efficient programming. Personnel working at higher levels in the organisation would typically have other concerns like coordinating people, scheduling of the process, quality assurance, planning of activities and so forth. Thus, it is essential that the process support in such organisations reflects the levels being supported. It is also important that the way the processes are modeled is tailored for the organisational level and the characteristics of this level.

This chapter presents a differentiated process support framework that describes the elements required to model the software process, the required external resources (like tools and documents), and the required process support provided by a process-centred environment. Our framework describes the required process support from four perspectives: At the individual level, at the group level, at the team level, and at the project level. Thus, the objectives of this chapter is to give insights into essential issues to be considered when planning and executing a software development process for large software projects consisting of several levels of management. The chapter also provides a guideline for what is required of process support for the various levels of an organisation. This guideline can be used as input when evaluating tools to be used to support the development and management processes of large software projects.

BACKGROUND

This section gives an introduction to the background and the important terms used in our framework, and describes related work.

Software Process and Software Process Modeling

At a NATO Conference in Garmisch-Partenkirchen in 1968, the term **software engineering** was first introduced (Naur & Randell, 1969).

The conference discussed what was called the "software crisis" introduced by third generation computer hardware. The work within the software engineering domain has been concerned with methods, techniques, tools, programming languages, and more to face the problems in software projects like delayed products, cost overruns, and bad reliability and performance in software products. Despite the many efforts to try to solve the software crisis, we are still struggling with the same problems as they did in the sixties. Brooks (1986) argues that there is no "silver bullet" that can solve all problems in software engineering. The only way to limit the negative effects identified as the software crisis is to use best practices in the many areas of software engineering. There are no best practices that solve all problems, but in combination many issues can be eliminated. One best practice is to improve the software process itself involving all the activities necessary in developing a software product. This chapter is intended as a guideline for improving the software process at different levels in a software development organisation.

Before we take a closer look at the software process support for different levels of an organisation, it is necessary to agree on the central terminology used in this chapter. As mentioned before, the term *software engineering* covers most aspects involved when developing large software systems. According to Sommerville (1995):

Software engineering is concerned with software systems which are built by teams rather than individual programmers, uses engineering principles in the development of these systems, and is made up of both technical and non-technical aspects.

As Sommerville states, software development involves more than the technical aspects like dealing with the source code of the system. Important nontechnical aspects of developing software involve scheduling, budgeting, resource management, and so forth. In addition, the term *software process* (Lehman & Belady, 1985) is used to denote all activities performed within a software organisation.

In this perspective, *software process modeling* describes the activities of understanding and describing a given software process (Wang, 2001). Several elements have been proposed that need to be identified to describe a software process, but the most common model involves the elements *products* (a set of artefacts related to the software product), *resources* (assets, like tools or human resources needed to carry out the process), *activities* (steps of the process) and *directions* (policies, rules, and procedures that govern the activities) (Derniame et al., 1998). To be able to provide process support, the software process must be modeled. Software process modeling is, according to Høydalsvik (1997), defined as "*The activities performed, and language and tools applied, in order to create models of software development processes within a software development organisation.*"

Another term related to software process is **workflow**. Workflow is by the Workflow Management Coalition (1999) defined as "*The automation of a business process, in whole or part, during which documents, information or tasks are passed from one participant to another for action, according to a set of procedural rules.*"

The main difference between software process and workflow is that workflow focuses on business processes. However, this does not rule out the possibility to use workflow tools to support the software process.

When talking about software processes, we also often mention the term **software lifecycle** (Royce, 1987) that describes the life of a product from the initial stage to the final production and maintenance. A software lifecycle consists of several phases that a software product usually must go through: requirement specification, system design, implementation, testing and operation, and maintenance. During these phases, the required process support will vary. For the two first phases,

the main focus is on analysis and documentation. For the three last phases, the main focus is on the source code and computer system. For all these phases, various tools exist to make the software development easier.

In addition, there are other parts of the software process that are phase independent, for example, software configuration management, software cost estimation, software quality management, software process improvement, and software process technology (Wang, 2001).

The lifecycle of a software product can be organised in various ways. The classical approach is the *Waterfall model* (Royce, 1987) that describes the lifecycle as a predefined sequence of phases, where each phase has a set of defined activities. Each phase has an input and output, and the output from one phase is the input to the next. The Waterfall process is in principle linear and a succeeding phase should not start until the previous phase has been finished.

The *evolutionary development model* is another way of viewing the software development process. This approach interleaves the phases; specification, implementation and validation, and is based on rapid prototyping. A prototype is developed early in the project in cooperation with the customer and is refined until the customer is satisfied. An example of an evolutionary development model is the *Spiral Model* (Boehm, 1988) that can incorporate different development processes through separate iterations.

Agile software development models like *eXtreme Programming* (Beck, 1999) focus on being lightweight and flexible. Such model embraces short development iterations to be able to cope with upcoming changes in requirements, minimum project documentation apart from comments in source code, user involvement during development, and other best-practices. Agile methodologies fit very well for high-risk projects with unstable requirements.

A software process model gives an overview of all the required activities and how they relate to each other, documents, tools, actors, methods, techniques, standards and so forth. This chapter is not limited to process support of a specific lifecycle model, but focuses rather on the required process support independent of how the software process is modeled and carried out in detail. Thus, this chapter describes guidelines that are important to incorporate when planning and supporting a software process. This may make it easier to improve the software process, thus improving the software product.

Related Work

The framework described in this chapter divides the software process into four distinct levels. The Personal Software Process (PSP) (Humphrey, 1997) defines the software process at the individual level in a software development process. The intention of PSP was to help software engineers to do their daily work well by applying practices that work well based on experiences from the software engineering field. Further, PSP describes detailed methods for making estimates and plans, shows how software engineers can track their performance, and describes how defined processes can guide their work. The process model in PSP is described only at a high-level. The model consists of the activities Planning, Design, Code, Compile, Test, and Post-Mortem. The PSP fits very well with the individual process level described in this chapter. However, note that PSP does not say anything explicitly about coordination of developers and project management on a higher organisational level.

The Software Process Engineering Metamodel (SPEM) defines software process models and their components using UML notation (OMG, 2002). In SPEM, a software development process is usually described by a *Process role* performing an *Activity* on a *Work product*. In addition, SPEM provides modeling elements to express phases, iterations, lifecycles, steps and so forth. This means that SPEM can visualise different organisational levels

of a software process. Thus, SPEM can be used in combination with our framework to describe the software processes at different levels. However, SPEM was not made with software process enactment in mind. This means that to provide process support for a process specified using SPEM, the model has to be translated to an enactable process model language (PML).

UML4SPM is executable software PML based on UML 2.0 (Bendraou, Gervais, & Blanc, 2006). In UML4SPM PML, a software process can be represented at different hierarchical levels by using the main building blocks Process, Activity, and Action. The organisational structure can also be modeled in a hierarchical manner using the model building blocks Team and Agents. Although UML4SPM support modeling of a software process at different levels, it uses the same PML to represent all levels of an organisation. As the PML represents processes as activity-networks, collaborative activities beyond coordination are hard to represent in such PMLs (Wang, 2002).

Serendipity-II is a process management environment that supports distributed process modeling and enactment (Grundy, Apperley, Hosking, & Mugridge, 1998). The PML allows hierarchical modeling of software processes represented as process stages and subprocesses. Moreover, Serendipity-II is based on a decentralized distributed architecture that enables users to collaboratively edit process models synchronously and asynchronously. This approach enables support for autonomous suborganisations that can tailor their specific part of the process to their needs, which is essential to support different levels of a software organisation.

Kivisto (1999) describes the roles of developers as a part of a software process model for development of client-server process. Kivisto proposes a process model in three dimensions: Organisational, Technological, and Process. The organisational dimension focuses on what roles are involved in the development process and how these roles are organised. The technological dimension focuses on issues related to client-server software architecture and technology choices for such a system. The process dimension gives an overview of how the development process can be organised in phases and tasks, and the assignment of roles to specific tasks.

A taxonomy for characterising metaprocess categories with the main focus on process changes is presented in Nguyen and Conradi (1994). The taxonomy reflects the following questions to be asked concerning the metaprocess: *What* aspects of the software process are allowed to be changed, due to what reasons *(Why)*, *How* can the changes be implemented/installed and be propagated *(When)* by which roles *(Whom)*? The *Why* aspect identifies four sources for process changes: the external world, an organisation, a project environment, and individuals. The framework described in this chapter can be mapped to the individual (individual level), project environment (group and team level), and organisation (project level). Changes

in the process support will affect the processes at all levels in our framework, while modifications of the production process (the way the software is developed) would typically be mapped to the team level and below. Modifications of the metaprocess (changes and evolvement of the process model) would typically be mapped into the project level. The taxonomy described in Nguyen and Conradi (1994) is useful for analysing process changes at all four levels in our framework.

PROCESS SUPPORT IN DIFFERENT LEVELS IN A SOFTWARE DEVELOPMENT ORGANISATION

This section describes issues that must be considered when planning the process support for large software projects being organised in groups and teams (typically 20 or more people). In such software development organisations, the process

Figure 1. Overview of process support in different levels

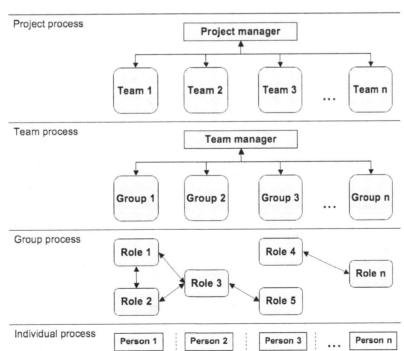

support required is very dependent on where you are in the hierarchy in the organisation. For example, the software process support needs for an individual developer is totally different from the needs of a project manager.

Our framework as detailed below, describes the software process support from four perspectives based on the organisational level, as shown in Figure 1. The *first level* in the framework focuses on the *individual process* reflecting the personal software process in the daily work. The *second level* describes group processes where two or more individual collaborate and interact. The *third level* is concerned with management of groups within a team. Finally, the *fourth level* is concerned with project management where several teams are involved. Typically for smaller projects, the team and group levels will merge.

Table 1 shows the four levels of process support required in a big software organisation. For each level, the model describes:

- **Process elements:** The required process elements needed to model the process,
- **Process relations:** The required relationships between process elements,

- **Required external resources:** The resources used by the process-centred support environment (PSE), and
- **Required process support:** The process support required at a specific organisational level.

The framework specifies interfaces that describe the input and output between levels. The uppermost interface specifies the relationships to the company and customer(s). Some activities are carried out at all levels of an organisation, for example, quality assurance and configuration management.

The rest of this section will describe each level of the framework in more detail.

Individual Process

The lowest process level in an organisation is the *individual* process level focusing on the individual tasks of a software developer. An example of a role related to this level is a programmer with typical tasks like reading documents, writing code, writing documentation, debugging code, compiling code, building code, and so forth.

Table 1. Process support in an organisation

Org. level	Process elements	Process relations	Required external resources	Required process support
Interface: Product, Experiences and knowledge, Resources, Project management rules and practice				
Project process	Teams, Team processes, Milestones	Team coordination, Assigned team(s)	Project management tools and Artefacts, Experience-/ knowledgebase, Estimation models and tools, Resource tools	Project planning, Project management, Experience exchange, Project estimation, Resource management
Interface: Input and output artefacts, Team and resources assigned, Team process state				
Team process	Groups, Group processes	Group coordination, Assigned group(s)	Team management tools and Artefacts	Team management
Interface: Input and output artefacts, Group assigned, Group process state				
Group process	Roles, Process fragments, Cooperative activities	Cooperation and coordination rules, Assigned role(s)	Cooperative tools, Configuration management and Artefacts	Coordination, Negotiation, Collaboration
Interface: Input and output artefacts, Role assigned, Process fragment state				
Individual process	Activities	Assigned activities	Tools and Artefacts	Process guidance, automation, calendar

Generally, the process of an individual actor typically consists of a set of activities related to the roles that the actor plays (an actor can play more than one role). It is very important that the process support is adaptable and configurable, making it possible for the actor to fit the work to personal preferences. The required process support is very dependent on the experience level of the individual actor. An inexperienced person would typically need process guidance to show the tasks to do next, what procedures to follow, what tools to use, where to find documentation and so forth. However, for an experienced person that knows all the basics, extensive process guidance would be a hindrance to work effectively. For the latter, it would be more useful to provide automation of repetitive tasks. Independently of the experience level of the actors, the process support should provide quick and easy access to the required tools and artefacts. The activities of the individual process should be integrated with personal digital calendars to enable activity states and deadlines to be accessible on personal computers, personal data assistants (PDAs), and mobile phones. This means that the execution environment for the process support also must be capable of communicating and utilising mobile devices and networks.

The framework presented in Table 1 identified activity as the main building block for individual process models. Another approach could be to use roles with responsibilities as the main building block. However, the most common approach is that individuals represent the daily work as a set of activities. Also, the most used process tools

for individual processes also focus on activities, like calendar software. In addition, activities or tasks are the most common output of many project-planning tools, where individuals are assigned a set of activities. This means that using activities as process model elements makes it easier to integrate with higher-level management processes and tools. In addition, because people are used to the representation of work as a set of activities and tools that represent the work as activities, it is also easier for the individuals to tailor their own processes (reschedule activities, etc.). In some cases, it can be useful to let an actor model her or his own processes. In Wang (2002), an experiment indicates that it is easier to use activity-based than role-based modeling for individual processes. This is especially true for inexperienced process modelers.

The process relation with respect to individual processes is the assign relation. A team or project manager typically assigns activities to an individual actor. In some cases, some activities must be carried out in a specific sequence, putting constraints on how the work should be carried out and how the individual process can be modified. A representation of an individual process is illustrated in Figure 2.

The process model in Figure 2 shows a collection of activities. Some of the activities have pre-order relations (the activities 1, 2, 3, 6, 7, and 8). The remaining activities have no constraints and can be carried out regardless of the state of the process.

In this chapter, we define a collection of related activities (e.g., activities related to the same

Figure 2. An individual process model

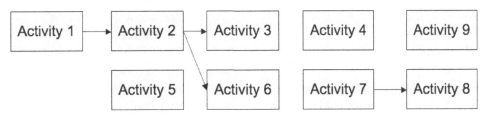

phase in the process and the same project) to be a *process fragment* (PF). The name process fragment indicates that this collection of activities is part of a larger process at a higher level of the organisation. The process of assigning activities to an individual actor in the organisation is carried out by delegating one or more process fragments to the actor. The state of the process fragment is determined by looking at the state of the activities. A process fragment is completed when all actvities in the fragment are completed.

The goal of the individual process is to produce various artefacts like requirement and design documents, source files, build files, test files and so forth. To provide a sufficient software process support at this level of the organisation, it is essential that the PSE can be integrated with production tools such as office applications, integrated development environments (IDEs), and other similar tools. The process support environment should make it easy to access all necessary tools and files, and handle configuration management.

When the individual actor initialises her/his process, the process models could either be fully specified by, for example, a team or project manager or be provided as a process template where all necessary activities are defined. For the latter, the actor must detail her/his own process to meet her/his needs and preferences. During the process enactment, the individual actor might also add, change, or delete activities depending on how the process proceeds (e.g., change of project plan, changed priorities, or changed process goals). Some PSEs might provide support for changing the process automatically or semi-automatically. It is important that the PSE is flexible enough to managing instantiation of template process fragments as well as allowing changes of the process during process enactment (Grundy et al., 1998).

Group Process

The next level in the framework is the *group* process level focusing at the cooperative aspects of the software process. Traditionally, software process modeling and enactment of software processes have been focusing on "forcing" and guiding people to work according to a specified model, where interaction between people has been coordinated through a strictly defined control/data flow. Such approaches are usually based on modeling processes as activity-networks consisting of subprocesses, activities, tasks, or operations. Cooperative aspects of the software development process have often been either eliminated or ignored because it has been hard to model cooperative activities in existing systems, or there has not been an interest for doing so. The software development processes are also human-centred processes. Cugola and Ghezzi (1998) state that "Human-centred processes are characterised by two crucial aspects that were largely ignored by most software process research: They must support cooperation among people, and they must be highly flexible."

The cooperative process involves coordination of activities carried out by several actors or roles, cooperative activities where two or more persons must participate to complete the activity, and coordination and negotiation of artefacts and resources.

At this level, *configuration management* (CM) is very important because two or more actors often will share the same resources (including files). The sharing of resources might cause conflicts where two or more actors would like to update the same data at the same time. Thus, the CM environment must be integrated with the PSE to provide support for initiating negotiation processes in case of conflicts regarding resources (e.g., files), and support for synchronising output artefacts from the process (Wang, 2000; Wang, Larsen, Conradi, & Munch, 1998).

The group process defines the synchronisation points for individual processes involving several actors. These synchronisation points represent parts of the software process where files or other resources need to be exchanged and synchronised (mainly coordination of artefact and process). In addition, the group process involves cooperative activities where two or more actors are involved. An example of such activities can be distributed brainstorming, electronic voting, collaborative authoring, and conflict management. Cooperative activities have very different characteristics compared to individual activities. While the main emphasis of the individual activities is on the activities themselves, cooperative activities are all about interaction and coordination between roles. This means that the process support for cooperative activities must provide an infrastructure to enable efficient interaction of the involved roles and to enable flexible exchange of artefacts. Note that most people working in a large software project will be involved in both individual and group processes.

The cooperative processes can be represented in many ways. However, to represent cooperative processes as a set of related activities, as described in a previous section, does not make sense because the focus is on interaction between roles. We propose two alternative approaches to represent cooperative processes at the group level.

Cooperative Software Agents

Cooperative software agents can be used to represent actors involved in cooperative activities. The cooperative agents will act on behalf of the involved actors to provide the required infrastructure for collaboration (coordination, negotiation, etc.). In Wang, Conradi, and Liu (2000), a cooperative agent framework developed to provide process support is presented. In this framework, all actors have their own workspace where they can interact and configure their agents. Agents interact on behalf of various actors in agent meeting places that represent neutral workspaces where services and artefacts can be exchanged. The collaborative aspects are supported through coordination agents, negotiation agents, and mediation agents. When software agents are used, the agent environment usually provides a set of ready-to-use agents that provide support for various collaborative tasks and that can be configured for specific user needs. If the required functionality is not supported by the predefined agents, new agents can be implemented using a high-level API. A similar approach to support group processes using software agents is described in Glaser and Derniame (1998). This approach uses agents to look for competence profiles that match the tasks to be carried out.

Role-Based Process Environments

Role-based process environments can also be used very efficiently to model and provide support for cooperative activities, for example, like the workflow system ProcessWeb (Yeomans, 1996). In ProcessWeb, all involved in the process are modeled as *roles,* and *interactions* are used to provide communication channels between roles. A role is defined by its *actions* (methods) and its *resources* (attributes). Preconditions called *"when guards"* are used to select action for enactment, and they are expressed as **if** statements. Interactions are unidirectional, asynchronously typed communication channels provided through a takeport and a giveport. A *takeport* receives data or control flow from another role, and a *giveport* sends data or control flow to another role. Similar approaches can be found in Fadlia, Said, and Nora (2005). Most role-based process modeling approaches are object-oriented and the modeling process will be similar to programming in an object-oriented programming language. This gives a very flexible and expressive PML, but it requires a certain level of expertise to handle.

A comparison of how well cooperative activities can be modeled and supported in software agents, activity networks, and role-based process environments is described in Wang (2002). The results show that activity networks are not well suited, but software agents and role-based process environments are able to represent cooperative activities very well.

In the previous section, the term process fragment was used to denote a collection of activities that represents the process for an individual actor. To model group processes, it is necessary to model the relationships between the process fragments of the individual actors as well as cooperative activities and the roles involved. *Cooperative rules* (Wang et al., 2000) can be used to define the relationships between process fragments and cooperative activities. The cooperative rules specify conditions for cooperative activities that should be initiated depending on the condition of the individual process fragments. The cooperative rules also specify how the individual processes should proceed depending on the outcome of a cooperative activity. Thus, the cooperative rules specify a loose coupling between the individual process fragments and the cooperative activities enabling federation of different PSEs for individual and group processes.

Figure 3 illustrates a group process model consisting of roles, process fragments, a cooperative activity, and cooperative rules (C1-C6). The model describes how cooperative rules describe the relationships between process fragments (individual processes) for each role and the cooperative activity. The cooperative rules are modeled as result-reaction pairs that specify the *reaction* that should be taken based on the *result* (outcome) of a cooperative activity or a process fragment. Typical reactions can be to execute, regroup, halt, change, or add a process fragment. In addition, a reaction can initiate or change cooperative activities (e.g., initiate a specified agent) or change the cooperative rules (reflective).

The cooperative rules in the process model in Figure 3 specifies that *Process fragment 1* and *3* must be completed before the cooperative activity will be executed (C1 and C2). Depending on the outcome of the cooperative activity, either *Process fragment 1* and *3* will be re-enacted (C3 and C4), or *Process fragment 2* and *4* will be initiated (C5 and C6).

In addition to provide support for cooperative activities in a PSE, it is also important for the PSE to provide access to other collaborative tools like chat-applications, collaborative editors, Wikis, discussion forums and so forth. The output of group processes is artefacts produced by the group and the individuals.

Figure 3. Group process model

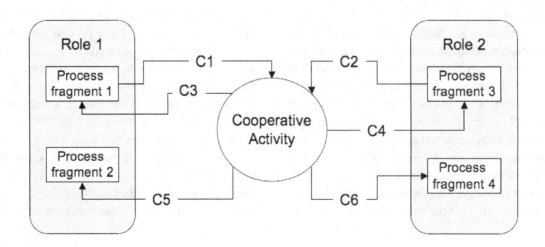

Team Process

The *team* process level is related to middle management and specific roles in a software project like a team manager. The team manager manages the development of one or more main parts of a software system within the competence of the team (e.g., security, business logic, etc.). Typical tasks at this level can be planning of group processes, assignment of group process to groups, tracking progress of the team, monitoring resource usage, and low-level quality assurance. The process support required at this level is monitoring of the ongoing processes, computation of resource usage, prediction and estimation of progress and resource usage, and creation and editing of process models. It is also essential that the team process model can integrate the group and individual process models and provide a process environment that will exchange artefacts and state changes between the individual and group processes. The main difference between the coordination and cooperation at the group and team levels is the granularity. At the group level, the cooperation between group members is tight and frequent. At the team level, the groups are independent but the coordination is still important to, for example, manage available resources and exchange project artefacts (document, source code, programs, tools, etc.). It is the team manager who is responsible for the coordination of groups. Thus, it is important that the process support provides the infrastructure and tool to support and ease this job.

Figure 4 illustrates a process model at the team level that consists of team process coordination and assigning group processes in addition to other team management activities. The group processes are coordinated through defined interfaces provided by the PSE (illustrated by the small circles). Another alternative could be to allow direct coordination between groups. This approach might cause problems because two levels of coordination must then take place at

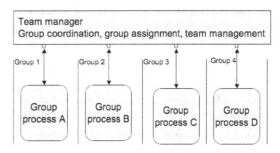

Figure 4. Team process model

the group level: coordination of individuals and coordination of groups. Another advantage by coordination groups through a team manager is that it is easier to make correct decisions about changes of the process, as this level gives a better overview of the process and the state of the different parts of the process.

The output from the team process level is the artefacts from all groups as well as the state of the team process.

Project Process

The *project* process level represents the software development process at the highest abstraction level, usually managed by a project manager. For this role, the required process support involves tools and procedures to create a project plan (project process model) for the whole project, establish and change teams and groups, assign personnel to teams and groups, estimate project resource usage, track progress of the whole project, monitor resource usage, perform company quality assurance procedures, assess and improve the development process, and so forth.

At this level it is not unusual to have external subcontractors to carry out parts of the project that require special expertise or expertise that is not present in the company. From a process support point of view, it is also likely that external subcontractors use their own process models and support environment. Thus, it is essential for the process-centred support environment to enable federation of various process model languages and tools to enable monitoring and process enactment of the whole project.

Another essential activity at the project level is to package artefacts, process models, and knowledge and experiences from completed projects that can be used as input when planning, estimating, modeling, and managing new projects. One method for harvesting experiences from completed projects is to use postmortem analysis methods (Birk, Dingsoyr, & Stalhane, 2002) like Affinity Diagram (KJ diagrams) (Scupin, 1997) and Root Cause Analysis (Straker, 1995). Affinity diagrams provide a method for carrying out a structured brainstorming focusing on successes and problems in the project. The root cause analysis investigates one particular issue found in the brainstorming process (positive or negative) to discover the causes and subcauses of the success or problem. In addition, reusable code and documents need to be identified and described with meta-information to enable search on historical information. A knowledgebase or experience-base is the most common tool to store and manage project experiences and reusable artefacts (Dingsøyr & Røyrvik, 2003).

Figure 5 illustrates a process model at the project level. A project process consists of several team processes. Some of these team processes must be carried out in a specific order (e.g., Team process 4, 2, 5, and 6). The pre-order constraints are most often caused by one team process that requires a finished product from another team process before it can start. Note also that parts of the process might be carried out by external organisations. This might implicate that this part of the process model will be expressed in a different process modeling language compared to the in-company models. Also, this part of the process model might need integration with another PSE.

The output of the project process is the final software product along with experiences and knowledge acquired during the project. The completion of a project will also release resources that can be used in new projects. The input to the project process should also be experiences and knowledge from previous projects. Further, a new project is allocated resources like people, tools, equipment, and money. Other important inputs to the project process are company policies and project management rules and practices that must be followed. These constraints will influence the way the process is organised and how the software process will be modeled.

Figure 5. Project process model

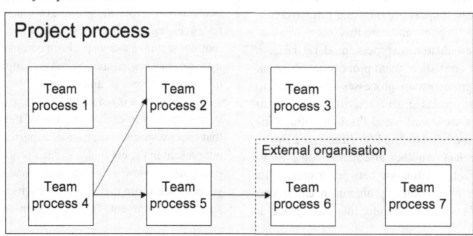

Organisational Issues

This section has so far only briefly mentioned the organisational issues that have to be taken into consideration when planning multilevel process support. This section will briefly look at organisational issues that must be taken into account.

At all levels of an organisation, people involved play different roles related to the activities they are involved in. What roles people play varies from project to project. The role also depends on the domain of the project, the company culture, and the culture of the nationalities of the people employed in the company. Kivisto (1999) describes the roles involved in the development of client-server applications to be: application developer, business object developer, database developer, end-user, team leader, project manager, quality assurancer, tester, and expert. Further, these roles are mapped into a hierarchy where the project manager is responsible for managing team leaders, and team leaders are responsible for managing the rest of the roles. This organisational decomposition fits well with the two top levels and the bottom level of our framework. For a specific project, the roles involved must be described and people that fit these roles must be found. An employee profile database can be used for this purpose to find the correct person for a specified role.

McGrath (1998) has proposed a software process modeling framework that incorporates the behavioural issues of software development. The framework has three levels: the universe of discourse (level 1), the conceptual model (level 2) and the external models (level 3). The framework includes behaviour aspects such as attitudes, opinions, beliefs, knowledge, organisational power, politics, culture, and structure. These important issues are not covered in the approach presented in this chapter.

CREATION OF A MULTILEVEL PROCESS MODEL

We propose two main approaches to create a multilevel process model for a software project: top-down and bottom-up. These two approaches are presented in this section.

Top-Down Approach

In the top-down approach, a project manager will typically first create a high level process model based on experiences from previous projects found in the knowledgebase, and the present information (constraints and resources) about the new project. This process model should at least identify the processes at the team process level. Further, the model might contain representations of group and individual processes at a coarse level. It is important that the individual and group processes are not constrained in such a way that they cannot be tailored by the process participants carrying out the processes. If the group and individual processes are modeled by a project manager (at the project level), then the process model should be described by a process template rather than an instantiated process model. If the project manager has not modeled any group or individual processes, the team manager must identify and model individual and group processes. It is also essential that the individual activities are not modeled in such a way that they cannot be altered or tailored by the process participants at the individual process level. The team manager should include sufficient content to the individual process level like activity description, necessary documents and tools, and a proposed sequence of the activities. In some cases the sequence of activities must be frozen because of coordination and synchronisation between developers. The top-down approach is suitable when the top management has a good idea of how the software is being developed in the company or the company management wants to enforce a specific way of developing software motivated by software improvement initiatives (e.g. CMM). For the latter, it is important that the project manager has a good dialogue with the people working in the teams to avoid sabotage of the process. If a process is enforced on the individual actors, they need to be motivated and know why they have to do their work in a particular way (e.g., because of quality or economical reasons).

Bottom-Up Approach

The button-up approach aims to harvest the process models by starting at the individual processes and moving upwards in the hierarchy of the software organisation. This means that the team process models will be created based on the underlying group and individual process models, and that the project process model will be created based on the underlying team process models. If no processes or process models are described or defined in the company, the bottom-up approach can be applied to create a process model that represents how the organisation is currently working. This process model can be used as a starting point to improve the process by identifying parts of the process that are cumbersome or uses unnecessary resources. However, it is likely that the process needs to be simplified to be able to model it and provide process support for it.

What Approach to Choose?

There is no clear answer if a software organisation should use the top-down or the bottom-up approach. The choice depends on the strategic goals of the organisation and on the working routines used. If the current work processes are causing several problems, a top-down approach inspired by established software development practices could be used to establish a new and more efficient way of working. If the current work processes are efficient and the employees are pleased with the way they work, a bottom-up approach should be chosen. Many organisations

are in between these two extremes. If this is the case, a combination of top-down and bottom-up can be used. To succeed in combining the two approaches, it is necessary for the different levels of the organisation to interact often and synchronise the process models to make sure they fit. This chapter can be used as a checklist of what should be considered at each level of the organisation. In addition, the chapter identifies the interfaces between the organisational levels, making it possible to provide one process model for the whole project consisting of autonomous parts.

CONCLUSION

This chapter has presented a framework that describes process support in four levels in a large software development organisation.

The *first level* is the individual level where the main focus is on the activities of individual developers and the process support they require. At this level it is important that the process support can be integrated with calendar applications running on personal computers, personal data assistants, or mobile phones. In addition, it is essential that the process support provides easy access to the required files and tools.

The *second level* is the group level where actors involved in the development process need to collaborate, and coordinate and negotiate shared resources. The process model at this level focuses on cooperative activities, cooperative rules, and the process fragments of the individual participants. The cooperative activities can be modeled and supported using software cooperative agents or role models. Because files are likely to be shared at this level, configuration management is essential. The configuration management system should be integrated to the process-centred support environment to provide process support for negotiation for shared resources.

The *third level* is the team level where the team manager coordinates the various groups in the team. The main focus at this level is team management that involves assigning work to groups, and provides the necessary infrastructure and support for intergroup coordination.

The *forth level* is the project level where the project manager initiates, manages, and finalises projects. At the end of a project, it is important that experiences, knowledge and reusable artefacts are packaged in a knowledgebase for later usage. In the initialisation phase of a new project, the knowledgebase plays a vital role when making resource estimates, modeling the process, assigning resources, and finding the reusable software components. It is also important at this level to make a heterogeneous PSE able to interact with PSEs in external organisations, as some team processes might be carried out by external resources. Finally, support for monitoring the process consisting of several teams that also might be external to the company is essential.

The main contribution of this chapter is a description of the process model elements required in a process model at each level of a software development organisation, and a description and discussion about the required process support at these levels.

FUTURE RESEARCH DIRECTIONS

Professional industrial software development organisations are always looking for ways to improve their development and project processes. One way of improving the software process is to provide the appropriate support for the process at different levels of the organisation. Most research within software process modeling assumes software development made by one company with a stable organisation and where the requirements are stable. This is not always the case.

The success of large open source projects have made open source development practices interesting to also apply within larger software organisations that perform global software development.

The ITEA COSI project (Codevelopment using inner & Open source in Software Intensive products, http://itea-cosi.org/) has observed a shift in software development, to more cooperation, new coalitions, and more collaboration with open source communities. These forms of network-enabled collaborations create new challenges for software developers (Lacotte, 2004). These new forms of development make the normal development processes less scalable and flexible because more and more of the software is harvested through reuse of internal components, through COTS, or through open source projects. In addition, a lot of the actual development efforts are outsourced, making it harder to ensure quality, productivity, and control of the software project(s).

The percentage of code actually produced locally in an organisation is decreasing, while the complexity and size of the products are still increasing. Large software companies like IBM and Sun Microsystems have made parts of their product portfolio as open source, creating precedence for how to make and publish software.

Participants in open source projects are increasingly employed by industrial companies. Many of these participants are very flexible with respect to how software is developed, and will often adapt the development practices used in the open source project.

When considering software process support for open source processes, the most important issues that must be considered are collaboration and coordination between many distributed developers and flexible and open PSEs that can be integrated with a large set of tools.

Agile methods (Abrahamsson, Warsta, Siponen, & Ronkainen, 2003) have gained much attention in recent years by moving the attention from documents and specifications to customer participation and incremental and iterative development of the products. Smaller projects are more likely to adopt agile methods, while large projects still will employ project management practices that are more heavyweight. To use agile methods in larger organisation, the main problem is to manage multiple cooperating teams that facilitate various overlapping, informal cross-team communication. Kahkonen (2004) describes an approach for introducing agile methods in large organisations. This approach was tested by Nokia with success, where the informal cross-team communication problem was solved by using communities of practices theory.

Our proposed framework is embracing these new trends by differentiating the process model and support for different levels of organisation.

REFERENCES

Abrahamsson, P., Warsta , J., Siponen , M. T., & Ronkainen, J. (2003), New directions on agile methods: A comparative analysis. In *Proceedings of the 25th International Conference on Software Engineering (ICSE'03),* Portland, OR, USA.

Beck, K. (1999). *Extreme programming explained: Embrace change.* Reading, MA: Addison-Wesley.

Bendraou, R., Gervais, M.-P., & Blanc, X. (2006). UML4SPM: An executable software process modeling language providing high-level abstracts. In *Proceedings of the10th IEEE International Enterprise Distributed Object Computing Conference (EDOC'06),* Hong Kong, China.

Birk, A., Dingsøyr, T., & Stålhane, T. (2002, May-June). Postmortem: Never leave a project without it. *IEEE Software, 19*(3), 43-45.

Boehm , B. W. (1988, May). A spiral model of software development and enhancement. *IEEE Computer.*

Brooks, F. P. (1986). No silver bullet: Essence and accidents of software engineering. In *Proceedings*

of Information Processing'86. North-Holland, IFIP.

Conradi, R., Fuggetta, A., & Jaccheri, M. L. (1998). Six theses on software process research. In *Proceedings of Software Process Technology: 6th European Workshop (EWSPT'98),* Weybridge. Springer-Verlag. LNCS 1487.

Cugola, G., & Ghezzi, C. (1998). Software processes: A retrospective and a path to the future. *SOFTWARE PROCESS—Improvement and Practice, 4*(2), 101-123.

Derniame, J.-C., Baba, B.A., & Wastell, D. (Eds.). (1998). *Software process: Principles, methodology, and technology.* Berlin: Springer-Verlag LNCS 1500.

Dingsøyr, T., & Røyrvik, E. (2003). An empirical study of an informal knowledge repository in a medium-sized software consulting company. In *Proceedings of the 25th International Conference on Software Engineering (ICSE'03),* Portland, OR, USA.

Fadila, A., Said, G., & Nora, B. (2005). Software process modeling using role and coordination. *Journal of Computer Science, 2*(4).

Finkelstein , A. (Ed.). (2000). The future of software engineering. In *Proceedings of the 22nd International Conference on Software Engineering (ICSE'2000),* Limerick, Ireland.

Fuggetta, A. (2000). *Software process: A roadmap.* In *Proceedings of the Conference on the Future of Software Engineering (ICSE 2000)* (pp. 25-34). Limerick, Ireland.

Glaser, N., & Derniame , J.-C. (1998). Software agents: Process models and user profiles in distributed software development. In *Proceedings of the 7th Workshop on Enabling Technologies Infrastructure for Collaborative Enterprises (WETICE'98),* Palo Alto, CA, USA.

Grundy, J. C., Apperley, M. D., Hosking, J. G., & Mugridge, W. B. (1998, September-October). A decentralized architecture for software process modeling and enactment. *IEEE Internet Computing, 2*(5), 53-62.

Høydalsvik, G. M. (1997). *Experiences in software process modeling and enactment.* Doctoral thesis, Department of Computer and Information Science, Norwegian University of Science and Technology, Trondheim, Norway.

Humphrey, W. S. (1997). *Introduction to the personal software process.* Information Technology for European Advancement. Addison-Wesley.

Kahkonen, T. (2004). Agile methods for large organizations—building communities of practice. *Agile Development Conference (ADC'04)*, Salt Lake City, Utah, USA.

Kivisto, K. (1999). Roles of developers as part of a software process model. In *Proceedings of the 32nd Hawaii International Conference on System Sciences.*

Lacotte, J.-P. (2004). *ITEA report on open source software* (Tech. Rep.). ITEA -

Lehman, M. M., & Belady, L. A. (1985). *Program evolution—processes of software change.* Academic Press.

McGrath, G. M. (1998, January). Behavioural issues in software engineering process modelling: A multi-paradigm approach. *Hawaii International Conference on System Sciences (HICSS).*

Naur, P., & Randell, B. (Eds.). (1969). Software engineering. In *Proceedings of the NATO Conference in Garmisch-Partenkirchen, 1968.* NATO Science Committee, Scientific Affairs Division, NATO, Brussels.

Nguyen, M. N., & Conradi, R. (1994). Classification of meta-processes and their models. In *Proceedings of the Third International Conference on Software Process*, Washington, USA.

Nitto, E. D., & Fuggetta, A. (Eds.). (1998). Process technology. *Journal on Automated Software Engineering, 5*(Special Issue).

OMG. (2002). *Software process engineering metamodel specification.* Formal/2002-11-14.

Royce, W. W. (1987). Managing the development of large software systems: Concept and techniques. In *Proceedings of WesCon, 1970.* Reprinted in Proceedings of the International Conference on Software Engineering. IEEE Computer Society Press.

Scupin, R. (1997). The KJ method: A technique for analyzing data derived from Japanese ethnology. *Human Organization, 56*(2), 33-237.

Sommerville, I. (1995). *Software engineering.* Addison-Wesley. ISBN 0-2014-2765-6.

Straker, D. (1995). *A toolbook for quality improvement and problem solving.* Prentice Hall International (UK).

Wang, A. I. (2000). Using software agents to support evolution of distributed workflow models. In *Proceedings of the International ICSC Symposium on Interactive and Collaborative Computing (ICC'2000) at International ICSC Congress on Intelligent Systems and Applications (ISA'2000)*, Wollongong, Australia.

Wang, A. I. (2001). *Using a mobile, agent-based environment to support cooperative software processes.* Doctoral thesis, Norwegian University of Science and Technology. ISBN 82-7984-172-5.

Wang, A. I. (2002). An evaluation of a cooperative process support environment. In *Proceedings of the 6th IASTED International Conference on Software Engineering and Applications (SEA2002)*, Cambridge, MA, USA.

Wang, A. I., Conradi, R., & Liu, C. (2000). Integrating workflow with interacting agents to support cooperative software engineering. In *Proceedings of the 4th IASTED International Conference on Software Engineering and Applications (SEA'2000)*, Las Vegas, NV, USA.

Wang, A. I., Larsen, J.-O., Conradi, R., & Munch, B. (1998). Improving cooperation support in the

EPOS CM System. In *Proceedings of the 6th European Workshop on Software Process Technology (EWSPT'98),* Weybridge (London), UK.

WfMC. (1999, February). *Workflow management coalition—terminology & glossary* (Tech. Rep. No. WFMC-TC-1011). The Workflow Management Coalition. Retrieved March 6, 2008, from http://www.wfmc.org/standards/docs/TC1011_term_glossary_v3.pdf

Yeomans, B. (1996). *Enhancing the World Wide Web* (Tech. Rep.). Computer Science Department, University of Manchester.

ADDITIONAL READING

The following is a list of references recommended for further reading.

Ambriola, V., Conradi, R., & Fuggetta, A. (1997, July). Assessing process-centered software engineering environments. *ACM Transactions on Software Engineering and Methodology (TOSEM), 6*(3), 283-328.

Andersson, C., Karlsson, L., Nedstam, J., Höst, M., & Nilsson, B. (2002). Understanding software processes through system dynamics simulation: A case study. In *Proceedings of the 9th IEEE Conference and Workshop on the Engineering of Computer-based Systems*, Lund, SWEDEN.

Barros, M. O., Werner, C. M. L., & Travassos, G. H. (2000, October). Using process modeling and dynamic simulation to support software process quality management. *XIV Simpósio Brasileiro de Engenharia de Software, Workshop de Qualidade de Software*, João Pessoa, Brazil.

Chatters, B. W., Lehman, M. M., Ramil, J. F., & Wernick, P. (1999, June 28-30). Modelling a software evolution process. In *Proceedings of the Software Process Modelling and Simulation Workshop*, Silver Falls, OR.

Collofello, J., Yang, Z., Merrill, D., Rus, I., & Tvedt, J. D. (1996). Modeling software testing processes. In *Proceedings of the International Phoenix Conference on Computers and Communications* (IPCCC'96), 1996.

Dean, D. L. , Lee, J. D. , Orwig, R. E., & Vogel, D. R. (1994, December). Technological support for group process modelling. *Journal of Management Information Systems, 11*(3), 43-63.

Deephouse, C., Mukhopadhyay, T., Goldenson, D. R., & Kellner, M. I. (1995, December). Software processes and project performance. *Journal of Management Information Systems, 12*(3), 187-205.

Delen, D., Dalal, N. P., & Benjamin, P. C. (2005, April). Integrated modeling: The key to holistic understanding of the enterprise. *Communications of the ACM, 48*(4), 107-112.

Estublier, J., Amiour, M., & Dami, S. (1999, March). Building a federation of process support systems. In *ACM SIGSOFT Software Engineering Notes, 24*(2), Proceedings of the International Joint Conference on Work Activities Coordination and Collaboration WACC '99.

Gary, K., Lindquist, T., Koehnemann, H., & Sauer, L. (1997, November 16-19). Automated process support for organizational and personal processes. In *Proceedings of the International ACM SIGGROUP Conference on Supporting Group Work: The Integration Challenge*, (pp. 221-230), Phoenix, AZ, USA.

Glass, R. (1999, February). The realities of software technology payoffs. *Communications of the ACM, 42*(2), 74-79.

Gopal, A., Mukhopadhyay, T., & Krishnan, M. S. (2002, April). The role of software processes and communication in offshore software development. *Communications of the ACM, 45*(4).

Gruhn, V., & Wolf, S. (1995). Software process improvement by business process orientation.

Software Process—improvement and Practice (Pilot Issue).

Kahen, G., Lehman, M. M., & Ramil, J. F. (1999, September 3-4). Empirical studies of the global software process—the impact of feedback. In *Proceedings of the Workshop on Empirical Studies of Software Maintenance (WESS-99),* Keble College, Oxford, UK.

Keating, E., Oliva, R., Repenning, N., Rockart, S., & Sterman, J. (1999). Overcoming the improvement paradox. *European Management Journal, 17(2),* 120-134.

Kellner, M. I., Madachy, R. J., & Raffo, D. M. (1999, April 15). Software process modeling and simulation: Why, what, how. *Journal of Systems and Software, 46(2/3),* 91-105.

Kueng, P., & Kawalek, P. (1997, August). Process models: A help or a burden? In *Paper presented at the Association for Information Systems 1997 Americas Conference*, Indianapolis, IN.

Lehman, M. M. (1997, April 14-15). Feedback in the software process. In *Proceedings of the Software Engineering Association Easter Workshop, SEA'97, ICSTM,* (pp. 43-49).

Lehman, M. M. (1998, April 20). Feedback, evolution and software technology—the human dimension. In *Proceedings of the ICSE Workshop on Human Dimension in Successful Software Development*, Kyoto, Japan.

Lin, C. Y., & Levary, R. R. (1989). Computer-aided software development process design. *IEEE Transactions on Software Engineering, 15(9),* 1025-1037.

Madachy, R., & Tarbet, D. (2000). Case studies in software process modeling with system dynamics. *Software Process: Improvement and Practice, 5(2-3),* 133-146.

Martin, R. H., & Raffo, D. M. (2000). A model of the software development process using both con-tinuous and discrete models. *Software Process: Improvement and Practice, 5(2-3),* 147-157.

McGrath, G. M. (1996, August 19-21). Representing organisation and management theories in software engineering process modelling. In *Proceedings of the IASTED Conference*, Honolulu, HI.

McGrath, G. M. (1997, September 28-October 2). A process modelling framework: Capturing key aspects of organisational behaviour. In *Proceedings of theAustralian Software Engineering Conference (ASWEC '97),* Sydney, Australia.

McGrath, G. M., Campbell, B., More, E., & Offen, R. J. (1999). Intra-organisational collaboration in a complex, rapidly-changing information services company: A field study. In *Proceedings of ISDSS'99*, Melbourne, Pacific Mirror Image, Melbourne, Australia, ISBN 0732620740.

Muehlen, M. Z. (2004, July-October). Organizational management in workflow applications—issues and perspectives. *Information Technology and Management, 5(3-4),* 271-291.

Mishali, O., & Katz, S. (2006, March 20-24). Using aspects to support the software process: XP over Eclipse. In *Proceedings of the 5th International Conference on Aspect-oriented Software Development*, Bonn, Germany.

Oliveira, T. C., Alencar, P. S. C., Filho, I. M., de Lucena, C. J. P., & Cowan, D. D. (2004, March). Software process representation and analysis for framework instantiation. *IEEE Transactions on Software Engineering, 30(3),* 145-159.

Paech, B., Dorr, J., & Koehler, M. (2005, January). Improving requirements engineering communication in multiproject environments. *IEEE Software, 22(1),* 40-47.

Raffo, D. M., Harrison, W., & Vandeville, J. (2000). Coordinating models and metrics to manage software projects. *Software Process: Improvement and Practice, 5(2-3),* 159-168.

Richardson, G. P., & Andersen, D. (1995). Teamwork in group model building. *System Dynamics Review, 11*(2), 113-137.

Russell, N., van der Aalst, W. M. P., ter Hofstede, A. H. M., & Wohed, P. (2006, January 16-19). On the suitability of UML 2.0 activity diagrams for business process modelling. In *Proceedings of the 3rd Asia-Pacific Conference on Conceptual Modelling,* (pp. 95-104), Hobart, Australia.

Sawyer, S., & Guinan, P. J. (1998). Software development: Processes and performance. *IBM Systems Journal, 37*(4).

Scacchi, W. (1999, June 27-29). Understanding software process redesign using modeling, analysis and simulation. In *Proceedings of the ProSim'99 Workshop on Software Process Simulation and Modeling*, Silver Springs, OR.

Sharp, A., & McDermott, P. (2001). *Workflow modeling: Tools for process improvement and application development.* Norwood, MA: Artech House.

Stelzer, D., & Mellis, W. (1998). Success factors of organizational change in software process improvement. *Software Process: Improvement and Practice, 4*, 227-250.

Verlage, M. (1996, October 16-18). About views for modeling software processes in a role-specific manner. In *Joint Proceedings of the Second International Software Architecture Workshop (ISAW-2) and International Workshop on Multiple Perspectives in Software Development (Viewpoints '96) on SIGSOFT '96 Workshops*, (pp. 280-284), San Francisco, CA, USA.

Wang, Y., & Bryant, A. (2002, December). Process-based software engineering: Building the infrastructures. *Annals of Software Engineering, 14*(1-4). J. C. Baltzer AG, Science Publishers.

Chapter II
Modeling Techniques
for Software-Intensive Systems

Holger Giese
University of Potsdam, Germany

Stefan Henkler
University of Paderborn, Germany

Martin Hirsch
University of Paderborn, Germany

Vladimir Rubin
University of Paderborn, Germany

Matthias Tichy
University of Paderborn, Germany

ABSTRACT

Software has become the driving force in the evolution of many systems, such as embedded systems (especially automotive applications), telecommunication systems, and large scale heterogeneous information systems. These so called software-intensive systems, are characterized by the fact that software influences the design, construction, deployment, and evolution of the whole system. Furthermore, the development of these systems often involves a multitude of disciplines. Besides the traditional engineering disciplines (e.g., control engineering, electrical engineering, and mechanical engineering) that address the hardware and its control, often the system has to be aligned with the organizational structures and workflows as addressed by business process engineering. The development artefacts of all these disciplines have to be combined and integrated in the software. Consequently, software-engineering adopts the central role for the development of these systems. The development of software-intensive systems is further complicated by the fact that future generations of software-intensive systems will become even more complex and, thus, pose a number of challenges for the software and its integration of the other disciplines. It is expected that systems become highly distributed, exhibit adaptive and anticipatory behavior, and act in highly dynamic environments interfacing with the physical world. Consequently, modeling as an essential design activity has to support not only the different disciplines but also the outlined new characteristics. Tool support for the model-driven engineering with this mix of composed models is essential to realize the full potential of software-intensive systems. In addition, modeling activities have to cover different development phases such as requirements analysis, architectural design, and detailed design. They have to support later phases such as implementation and verification and validation, as well as to systematically and efficiently develop systems.

INTRODUCTION

Software has become the driving force in the evolution of many systems such as embedded systems (especially automotive applications), telecommunication systems, and large scale heterogeneous information systems. These so called software-intensive systems are characterized by the fact that software influences the design, construction, deployment, and evolution of the whole system (cf. Recommended Practice for Architectural Description of Software-intensive Systems, IEEE-Std-1471-2000 (2000)).

A good example for the growing importance of software in many advanced engineering fields is automotive software. It has become an important factor in the development of modern high-end vehicles where today the size of the software grows at an exponential rate. About 70% of the innovations in these cars today are software driven and the percentage of costs due to the development of software is expected to increase from 20-25% up to 40% in the next years (cf. Grimm, 2003; Hardung, Kölzow, & Krüger, 2004). In addition, today more and more functions can only be realized by the cooperation of different control devices. This result in dramatically increasing complexity (cf. Grimm, 2003) compared to the separate control devices employed traditionally which had to fulfill a single task only.

Furthermore, the development of these software-intensive systems often involves a multi-tude of disciplines (cf. Figure 1 (a)). Besides the traditional engineering disciplines (e.g., control engineering (CE), electrical engineering (EE), and mechanical engineering (ME)) that address the hardware and its control, the system often has to be aligned with the organizational structures and workflows as addressed by business process engineering (Wirsing, 2004). The development artifacts of all these disciplines have to be combined and integrated in the software. Consequently, software engineering (SE) adopts the central role for the development of these systems.

The development of software-intensive systems is further complicated by the fact that future generations of software-intensive systems will become even more complex and, thus, pose a number of challenges for the software and its integration of the other disciplines. It is expected that systems become highly distributed, exhibit adaptive and anticipatory behavior, and act in highly dynamic environments interfacing with the physical world (Wirsing, 2004). Consequently, modeling as an essential design activity has to support not only the different disciplines but also the outlined new characteristics.

Tool support for the model-driven engineering, with this mix of composed models, is essential to realize the full potential of software-intensive systems. In addition, modeling tasks have to cover different development phases such as requirements analysis (Req.), architectural design (Arch.), and detailed design (Design). They have

Figure 1. Software-intensive systems w.r.t classical domains (cf. Figure 1 (a)), and the assignment of phases to disciplines (cf. Figure 1 (b))

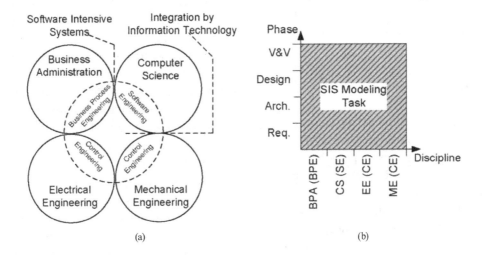

to support the phase specific modeling and analysis tasks as well as the synthesis and analysis tasks required for later phases such as implementation and verification and validation (V&V), as well as to systematically and efficiently develop systems (cf. Figure 1 (b)).

The integration of the different models used in the different disciplines is of major importance for the systematic development of software-intensive systems. Therefore, in this chapter we focus on the modeling techniques of the different disciplines involved as well as their proper integration (cf. Giese & Henkler, 2006).

We consider the different modeling options in the three main disciplines to reflect the different modeling techniques employed for software-intensive systems: UML (Unified Modeling Language), the de facto standards for software engineering, MATLAB/Simulink, the de facto standards for traditional engineering, and a number of approaches for business process engineering.

As these modeling techniques currently do not integrate the different disciplines, we fur-

ther present some approaches which support the integration based on the software-engineering standard UML. First, we sketch SysML, the proposed standard for systems engineering which integrates system engineering and software engineering for requirement analysis. In addition, we introduce MECHATRONIC UML, which integrates traditional engineering modeling techniques with software engineering modeling techniques for the architectural design and detailed design. It also supports the implementation and verification and validation phases for embedded systems.

The outlined modeling techniques will be presented by a running example taken from the Rail-Cab research project presented in the next section. After outlining the background and requirements for the modeling of software-intensive systems in the section Background, we will first look into the most relevant modeling approaches for the different involved disciplines, that is, business process engineering, software engineering, and classical engineering in the section Modeling Approaches and discuss the remaining integration problems. Thereafter, we will review approaches which bridge the remaining gaps in the different development phases in the section Integrated Modeling Approaches. The chapter closes with an outlook on future trends in the modeling of software-intensive systems in the section Future Trends and a final conclusion.

EXAMPLE

In this section, we demonstrate the modeling techniques of software-intensive systems by means of an application example. The concrete example stems from the RailCab research project (cf. Figure 2)[1], which aims at using a passive track system with intelligent, autonomous shuttles that operate individually and make independent and decentralized operational decisions. The vision of the RailCab project is to provide the comfort of individual traffic concerning scheduling and on-demand availability of transportation as well as individually equipped cars on the one hand and the cost and resource efficiency of public transport on the other hand.

The modular railway system combines modern chassis control with the advantages of the linear drive technology as employed in the Transrapid[2] to increase the passengers' comfort while still enabling high speed transportation. In contrast to the Transrapid, the shuttles from the RailCab project reuse the existing railway tracks.

Convoy

One particular problem is how to coordinate the autonomously operating shuttles in such a way that they build convoys whenever possible to reduce the air resistance and thus the energy consumption. Such convoys are built on-demand and require a small distance between the different shuttles such that a high reduction of energy consumption is achieved. When building or breaking a convoy, the speed control units of the shuttles need to be coordinated, which is a safety-critical issue and results in a number of hard real-time constraints. The behavior of a speed control unit is dependent on whether the shuttle is part of a convoy at all and it depends on the position within the convoy. The overall aim of the whole convoy is to drive with a reduced distance and to keep it on a constant level. This might be achieved by adjusting the velocity appropriately and—after reaching the required distance—holding all velocities on a constant value.

Figure 3. Logistic example

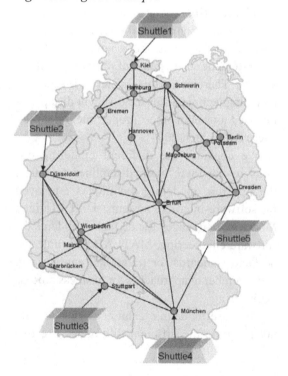

Figure 2. Application example

Logistics

Railcab shuttles transport goods and passengers between different locations. Thus, on a higher level, the logistics of a Railcab system must be specified. Activities on the logistics layer include route planning (cf. Figure 3) of a single shuttle or a number of shuttles, bidding for transport jobs and deciding whether to join or leave convoys.

In the remainder of this chapter, we will use the route planning as well as joining and leaving of convoys as examples for the workflow modeling part.

BACKGROUND

Modeling of software-intensive systems is employed for the development at rather different phases and with different intentions. Therefore, in the section Role of Modeling in the Different Development Phases, we will first review the different roles which modeling can play during the development and life cycle of a software-intensive system. These findings are then reflected and focused by presenting the most typical modeling task involved in the development of a software-intensive system in the section Typical Modeling Tasks. This provides us with a more concrete measure for the later considered modeling approaches.

Role of Modeling in the Different Development Phases

The development of software-intensive systems is divided into different phases according to design or development methodologies. The VDI guideline 2206 VDI2206 (2004) is one such example. The guideline distinguishes three major development phases (cf. Figure 4). The system model is jointly designed by the experts of the different engineering disciplines in the first phase. This phase results in a system architecture and interfaces between

Figure 4. Design methodology for mechatronic systems

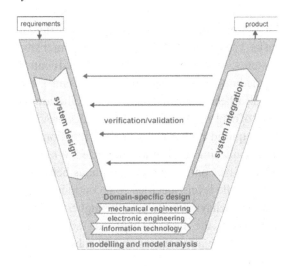

discipline-specific system elements. The next phase is called Domain-specific design in the VDI guideline 2206, although, in software-intensive systems, the models of these domains are typically not independently developed by engineers of the different disciplines. The mechanical structure is developed by mechanical engineers as well as control engineers. Control engineers also work in the electronic domain. Information technology is built both by software engineers and business process modelers. Thereafter, the different models are integrated in the final phase. Obviously, the strong separation of the different development phases is only valid for an abstract view of the development process. There are several iterations of the different design activities and a tightly integrated development by the different engineering disciplines.

Typical Modeling Tasks

In the section Role of Modeling in the Different Development Phases, the different role of modeling during the development of software-intensive systems is discussed. Here, we explain the different modeling tasks a developer has to fulfill during the different development phases.

The considered example (cf. the section Example) provides a whole collection of different tasks typical for advanced software-intensive systems. At the lowest level, sophisticated control algorithms are modeled in order to control the physical behavior of the shuttles. Above this lowest level of control algorithms, a layer which provides the required higher order control functionality and monitoring capabilities is modeled. While the lowest layer only exhibits continuous behavior, this middle levels specifies both continuous and discrete behavior. Finally, at the highest level of the system, the discrete, hard real-time coordination of the autonomous shuttle subsystems is modeled. The example provides multiple challenging development tasks: At the middle level adaptation across a layered system architecture is modeled, which may include reconfiguration of the structure and not only parameters. At the highest level, the structural reconfiguration of the system architecture is addressed and the integration of business processes for the logistics is specified.

Support for modeling is a crucial prerequisite for the development of any complex system. The developer specifies appropriate abstraction and description techniques for the specific problems at hand. At first, the structure is specified which is essential to rule the complexity of the system. Second, the common description techniques for the behavior which are state machines in the case of software engineering, some form of block diagrams for control engineering, and the activity view for business process engineering are used for specification. In addition, for requirement engineering, often a scenario view is used. As exemplified in the application example, advanced software-intensive systems further exhibit adoption. Finally, modularity is used to ensure a proper separation between different subsystems and to facilitate maintainability. The modeling tasks used in the development of software-intensive systems are described in more detail in the following paragraphs.

In early development phases, the primary task is to model discipline spanning coherencies on structural and behavioral view. Typical activities are: specifying the requirements, the structure, the behavior, the allocations, and the constraints on the system properties to support engineering analysis in early development phases. The discipline spanning development is the matter of the Systems Engineering. The specified models of the systems engineering are refined/concretized by using discipline specific modeling approaches.

For the business process engineering, an activity view as described by activity diagrams is often used. The modeling tasks are: the workflow of the logistics, the desired and the actual behavior of the developed system, the interaction with the user, the communication between agents within the organization, the assignment of tasks to different resources, the document flow within the organization and the services provided by the organization.

For the disciplines software engineering and control engineering, the type, class diagram, component/agent/block, deployment, pattern, and task view is specified, as most of them are crucial prerequisites to model complex systems. To describe complex reactive behavior, a state-machine-like notation with concepts such as hierarchical states, orthogonal states, and history is used. Another often used description technique for behavior is the scenario view provided by notations such as timing diagrams or sequence diagrams. The description of an appropriate coordination behavior at the highest level of the shuttle system would be an example where scenario-based descriptions would be helpful.

Many software-intensive systems are safety-critical systems and thus hazard analysis is mandatory. Therefore, the hazards of the system and the effects of hazard failure propagations are modeled.

A crucial prerequisite for a preimplementation validation of models is a full semantic integration of the employed visual modeling concepts and their underlying models to be able to make reasonable predictions. If a sound formal semantics exists, automated support for the analysis of the continuous and discrete behavior becomes possible. In the following, analysis support is only mentioned in the discussion of the modeling approaches as we focus on the modeling techniques in this chapter.

MODELING APPROACHES

Based on the requirements elaborated in the proceeding section, we will explain the economic perspective on complex software-intensive systems in the section Business Process Modeling, which is studied using business process modeling approaches. Then, in the section Software Engineering, we will review the capabilities provided by the Unified Modeling Language (UML)—the de facto standard for modeling in the software engineering world—and how seamlessly the modeling artifacts of the business process modeling domain can be integrated. In the section Control Engineering, we will furthermore look into the classical engineering disciplines and will outline which capabilities typical modeling approaches such as block diagrams as provided by Matlab Simulink/Stateflow offer for the development of complex software-intensive systems. This section also includes a discussion of the required integration with the software models. Finally, we will summarize our results and highlight the main challenges for the integrated modeling of software-intensive systems.

Business Process Modeling

Business process modeling is used at different stages of product development for specification, optimization, improvement, and control of business processes: It considers the *business perspective* and the *logistics* of the developed system. In this section, the modeling techniques are described with the help of the railcab examples.

First of all, we clarify the terminology used in this area. *Business process* is a collection of *activities* (both human and machine-based activities), executed in the *organization* according to certain *rules* and with respect to certain *goals*. Business processes represent the behavior of a system or the way of work in the organization: They comprise an essential part of Total Quality Management (TQM) (J.Bank, 1993), Capability Maturity Model Integration (CMMI) (CMM, 2002), and other approaches used for assessing and improving the quality of work in the organization. *Workflow* is a realization (automation) of the organizational business processes. The area of *Business Process modeling* or Workflow modeling deals with the formalisms and notations for modeling the business processes. These models can be executed by an appropriate *Workflow Management System* (WfMS) (WFMC, 1994).

It is now well-accepted that there are three basic perspectives (also called aspects) of business processes: The *control-flow* perspective describes the order in which different activities are executed. The *organizational* perspective describes the organization structure and the resources involved in the business process. The *informational* perspective describes the data (documents) and how it is propagated among different activities.

To give a feeling of business process modeling and to discuss our examples, we take a closer look at the modeling technique *Business Process Modeling Notation* (BPMN) (OMG, 2006). BPMN is a visual notation, that is, BPMN provides a Business Process Diagram (BPD), which is a diagram type designed to be used by designers and managers of business processes. A complete overview of the BPMN and its suitability to business process modeling is beyond the scope of this chapter. Therefore, we refer to Wohed, Aalst, Dumas, Hofstede, and Russell (2006) for a detailed analysis.

In Figure 5, we present a simplified example of the *shuttle transportation process*. Within this process, a route is planned, a shuttle participates in bidding against other shuttles, and then the shuttle takes the goods and passengers at the end and the shuttle carries out the transportation. First of all, we examine the *control-flow perspective* of the process, that is, we look at the order of execution of tasks[3] . The process starts with executing either the "Plan a Route" task or the "Assign a Route" task. This is modeled as an *alternative* (also called split or XOR-split) and

is syntactically represented as an X-diamond. When the route plan is obtained, the "Bid" task is carried out, and then the tasks "Take Goods" and "Enter the Shuttle" are executed *concurrently* (it is specified with the Plus-diamond). Finally, the task "Transport" finishes the process. It is worth mentioning that the "Transport" task represents the transportation *subprocess* (shown with the rectangle with plus) which includes traveling between stations, joining and leaving convoys. In the *organizational perspective*, the task "Plan a Route" is executed by a shuttle and the task

Figure 5. Shuttle transportation example (BPMN Notation)

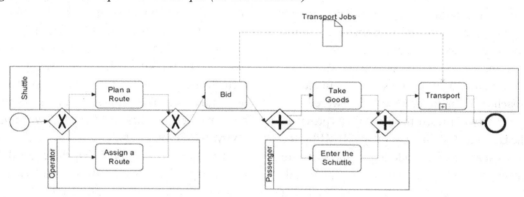

Figure 6. Client order example (BPMN Notation)

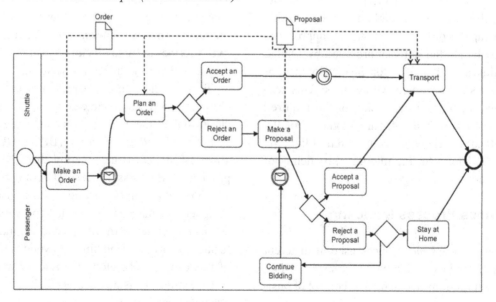

"Assign a Route" is executed by an operator: This is modeled using swim lanes. Concerning the *informational* perspective, after the bidding, the "Transport Jobs" document is created, and is then used during the transportation. This is shown in Figure 5.

Further, in Figure 6, a *client order example* is presented. This example, in contrast to the previous one, does not mostly deal with the shuttle transportation tasks, but primarily shows the *passenger's* (user's) view on the system. Before

traveling with the railcab system, the passenger places an order containing his preferred traveling time and locations: The order is processed by a shuttle and can be either accepted or rejected, depending on the availability of shuttles and the load of the transportation network. In the case of acceptance, the transportation task is carried out, otherwise the shuttle makes a new proposal to the passenger, which in its turn can be accepted or rejected by the passenger. After rejecting a proposal, passengers can either continue bidding or

Figure 7. Client order example (Petri Net)

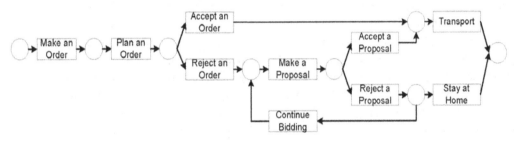

Figure 8. Client order example (UML Activity Diagram)

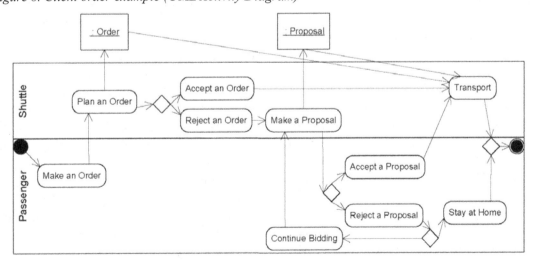

simply stay at home. Like in the previous example, the model contains the three process perspectives described above. For the control-flow, we show another way of modeling *alternatives*, using an empty diamond: Also, *merging* does not have to be modeled explicitly. For example, "Transport" and "Stay at Home" tasks are merged, but it is modeled without using a diamond. Here, we also show that different types of events can be modeled in the BPMN notation. For example, a passenger sends a message (produces "message2" event) after making an order.

Along with BPMN, established formalisms, such as *Petri Nets* (Aalst, 1998; Reisig & Rozenberg, 1998) and *High-level Petri Nets* (Aalst, Hee, & Houben, 1994; Jensen & Rozenberg, 1991) are used for the modeling and the analysis of business processes. In Figure 7, we show the control-flow perspective of the client order process modeled as a Petri net. The Petri net theory provides a bunch of analysis techniques, including reachability and deadlock analysis, analysis of process invariants and verification. However, other process modeling formalisms with less formal concepts, like *Event-based Process Chains* (EPC) (Keller, Nüttgens, & Scheer, 1992; Kindler, 2006) are widely accepted in industry. They also serve as a reference modeling technique.

Given the widespread use of *UML* as an industry modeling standard which is not restricted to software development, Activity Diagrams and Sequence and Collaboration Diagrams are applied to business engineering, process modeling and analysis. Here, we focus on UML Activity Diagrams, which can be effectively applied for modeling the dynamic behaviour of a system in general and business perspective of a system in particular. The suitability of UML 2.0 Activity Diagrams is extensively discussed in the business process modeling community (Russell, Aalst, Hofstede, & Wohed, 2006). In Figure 8, we show the client order example modeled using a UML Activity Diagram.

Discussion

In the previous section, we presented a set of business process modeling techniques. Some of them are precise, they are especially suitable for formal analysis and verification, while others are less formal, and are mainly used for discussions and collaboration between companies on the business level. For example, Petri Nets have a rather intuitive precise semantics and, thus, are suitable for formal analysis purposes. In contrast to many others diagramming techniques, they enable us to prevent ambiguities and contradictions in the models. EPCs, on the other hand, are less precise, but often used in practice and serve as a basis for such a platform as ARIS (Scheer, 2000).

On the other side, we can distinguish between modeling techniques targeted at different groups of people: Some techniques are used by business analysts and managers, others by software engineers. Nowadays, *Service Oriented Architecture* (SOA) and *Web Services* are becoming ever more important for architecting and implementing business integration and collaboration. Thereby, such Web Service *orchestration* languages as *BPEL4WS* (Arkin, Askary, Bloch, Cubera, Goland, & Kartha, 2005) have emerged recently and start playing a key role in the area of inter-organizational communication and integration. However, *BPEL* is a textual executable language targeted at *application developers. Analysts and process designers* focus more on the *BPMN* notation, which is intended to solve the problems of interoperation of business processes at the human level, rather than the process execution in the software engine. BPMN also provides a formal mapping to the BPEL4WS.

The modeling techniques emerging in the area of BPM can be compared with the help of *workflow patterns* (Aalst, Hofstede, Kiepuszewski, & Barros, 2003), which define a comprehensive workflow language functionality. As it is easy to see from our examples presented above, there are many similarities between UML Activity

Diagrams and the BPMN notation: diamonds are used for modeling alternatives, swim lanes are used for the organizational modeling, and so forth. Still, the expressive powers of these notations are different (a detailed comparison is given in Wohed et al., 2006). For example, both notations are almost equally strong in modeling the control-flow perspective, but they are different in approaching the data perspective. However, both BPMN and UML Activity Diagrams still have problems dealing with the organizational perspective. Nevertheless, elaboration of the UML-based techniques and the BPMN, and their integration with the techniques from the other domains will lead to a productive *integrated modeling* approach.

Software Engineering

The Unified Modeling Language (UML) provides a collection of notations which became the standard in model-based software engineering. The UML consists of multiple diagram types to specify architecture and behavior. Component and class diagrams are used to specify the architecture (the structure) of a system, state machines and activity diagrams are used to specify the behavior. This section will give a brief overview of these diagrams.

Component Diagrams

Complex systems are usually designed in a modular manner in order to manage their complexity. Using UML, the modular structure is specified by component diagrams. In a component diagram, multiple different component types are defined. A component type consists of required and provided interfaces. Each interface describes some features or obligations, for example, the obligation to accept and process messages or requests. Multiple interfaces are grouped in ports.

Figure 9. Example for a component

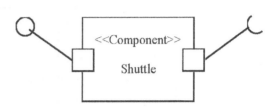

When modeling the structure of the shuttle system, as presented in the section Convoy, each shuttle is modeled as a component. In order to enable other shuttles to request the building of a convoy, the shuttle component provides an interface that accepts such request messages. Vice versa, it requires a corresponding interface in order to send requests to build convoys as well. Figure 9 shows the component type Shuttle which realizes two interfaces: The required interface is visualized by a half-circle (socket) that is connected via a solid line with its port. The port is visualized as a square at the border of the component. The provided interface is visualized as a circle (ball) which is connected with its port. The behavioral features and obligations, which are described by an interface, are not visible in the UML component diagram. They can be specified by UML protocol state machines (see below).

Class Diagrams

Class diagrams are the most common diagram found in modeling object-oriented systems. A class diagram shows a set of classes, interfaces, and collaborations and their relationships. Class diagrams are used to describe the internal architecture of components (cf. the section Software Engineering). They describe the structure that is required to realize the component's behavior, or they model the data structures which are required within the component. Figure 10 shows a cut-out of a class diagram.

Figure 10. Cut-out of a class diagram

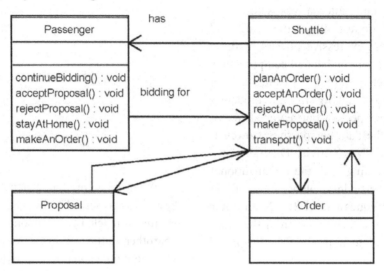

Statechart Diagrams

Statecharts diagrams are one of the diagrams in the UML for modeling the dynamic aspects of systems. A statechart diagram shows a state machine. The UML 2.0 specification proposes two kinds of state machines: A *protocol state machine* to specify the communication protocol of a port or the obligations and features of an interface and a *behavioral state machine* to specify the reactive behavior of, for example, a class or a component.

UML state machines are extensions of finite automata. Like automata models, UML state machines consist of multiple discrete states and transitions between the states. In contrast to automata, multiple discrete states can be active due to hierarchical or orthogonal states. It is possible to specify temporal behavior by using either the "after" or the "when" construct as the trigger for transitions. Both constructs specify points in time when a transition has to fire, relative to the entrance of the current state or in relation to a global clock. UML state machines consist of high-level constructs such as hierarchical and orthogonal states and deep and shallow history

mechanisms. These concepts are introduced to handle complexity.

A *protocol state machine* specifies a communication protocol. Therefore, it is associated with an interface or a port. In contrast to behavioral state machines, the protocol state machine does not specify the operations or side-effects that are executed as reactions to signals. Instead, they specify possible sequences of occurring triggers. Thus, it specifies the features and obligations of an interface or a port.

Figure 11 specifies a simple protocol for the communication between the ports Front and Rear. The call trigger callFront.start-Convoy is associated with an operation that sends the signal startConvoy via the port front. Due to the self-transition on state noConvoy, the state machine either stays in state noConvoy (for an unspecified number of steps) or switches to state noConvoy by sending the signal via port Front. The Rear state machine has to switch from state noConvoy to convoy when it receives the signal startConvoy via port Rear.

In contrast to protocol state machines, *a behavioral state machine* specifies reactive behavior. It defines how a component or a class reacts to signal

Figure 11. Example for a behavioral state machine

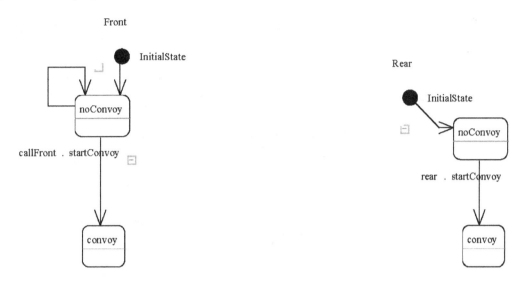

triggers or to a change of attributes. A transition is associated with a trigger (e.g., a signal), a boolean guard, and an activity. A transition, which leads from an active state to a target state, fires when the corresponding signal is raised and its guard evaluates to true. It executes an activity as effect or side-effect which consists of multiple actions. An action operates, for example, on the internal structure or sends signals to other components. States are associated with entry, do, and exit activities. They are executed on entrance or exit of the corresponding state, or they are executed while residing in the corresponding state. If a component consists of ports and interfaces whose features are specified by a protocol state machine, the behavioral state machine realizing the reactive behavior of the component has to implement the protocols specified by the protocol state machines.

Figure 12 shows a first sketch of the behavior of the Shuttle component. The state machine consists of the two (discrete) states Vel and Pos. The component switches its states when the signal toPos or toVel is raised. The activity init-VelocityController() is executed when

state Vel is entered. On entrance of state Pos, the activity initPositionController() is executed. While the system resides in this state, the activity sendPosition() is executed.

Activity Diagrams

Activity diagrams are one of the five diagrams in the UML for modeling the dynamic aspects of systems. An activity diagram is essentially a flowchart, showing the flow of control from activity to activity (cf. Figure 8).

Interaction Diagrams

We use UML 2.0 sequence diagrams *UML 2.0 Superstructure Specification* (2003, p. 435) to specify timed scenarios. UML 2.0 sequence diagrams allow us to specify durations for message transfers and lower and upper bounds for the time passed between two points on a lifeline. We can also observe the current time and reference this measurement in constraints. Upper bounds may be arbitrary sums of observations, constants and parameters, whereas lower bounds may only consist of observations and constants.

Figure 12. Example for a behavioral state machine

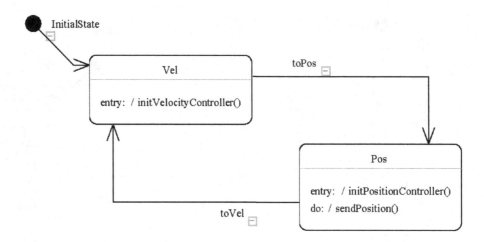

Distinguishing optional and required behavior is another important aspect of scenarios. Triggers have first been proposed as a technique for expressing conditional behavior for live sequence charts (LSC) (Harel & Marelly, 2002) and also appear in triggered message sequence charts (TMSCs) (Sengupta & Cleaveland, 2002). Assert blocks are used to describe conditional behavior of timed scenarios. Such blocks indicate a mandatory sequence of behavior that needs to be executed once the preceding steps have been observed and the block has been entered. For dealing with cases where several assertions clash, we also assign priorities to scenarios.

In order to facilitate the transition to a state-based model, state labels are explicitly added to the lifelines which represent states or sets of possible states. The labels allow us to use self-documenting state names in the generated statecharts and make it easier and much more efficient to overlay different scenarios.

Figure 13 shows an example of such a scenario with state annotations. A more detailed description can be found in Giese, Henkler, Hirsch, and Klein (2006).

Discussion

This subsection gave an overview about model-based software engineering, using UML. Standard models for the specification of structure are component diagrams and class diagrams. Behavior is modeled by state machines and activities. Especially the component diagrams provide advanced support for the specification of the architecture of complex, distributed systems. As UML was not designed for the development of software-intensive systems, it lacks description techniques for the specification of, for example, real-time behavior.

Control Engineering

Technical systems often consist of variables which change their value over time. In many cases there is a need for manipulating these variables to give them a desired behavior. Thereby, the goal is to change the variables to a given fixed value and to hold the variables at this value (e.g., the rotational speed of an engine should be 100 hertz (Hz)).

Typically, the manipulation of the variables should be done automatically as it is often not

Figure 13. A scenario (UML 2.0 sequence diagram)

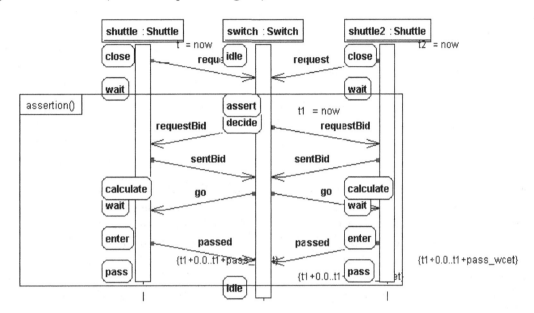

possible manually or it makes the work much easier.

As in control engineering, the focus is on the timing behavior and not on the constructive parts of the system, and the technical system is often called dynamic system. The focus of control engineering is on the modeling of a diverse range of these dynamic systems and the design of controllers that will cause these systems to behave in the desired manner (Föllinger, 2005).

In Figure 14, the principle control structure is shown. We can describe the problem of control engineering as follows: *Given the goal of a system, the controlled variable x, and the control variable y, y should customize x to reach the goal, despite the affect of disturbance z which is not completely known.* Note, *x* and *y* are elements of xr and yr. As systems with more than one control or controlled variable have the same principle problem, we consider only the variables *x* and *y*.

In principle, we can distinguish between feed-forward control and feedback control. Feed-forward control can respond more quickly to known and measurable kinds of disturbances, but cannot do much with unknown disturbances. Feed-back control deals with any deviation from the desired system behavior, but requires the system's measured variable (output) to react to the disturbance in order to notice the deviation. The inherent goal of feed-back control is to restrain or control the difference between the reference variable and the controlled variable to zero or near to zero (cf. Figure 15).

The decision of a specific controller type depends on the needed timing behavior and the needed control accuracy of the system. In the literature, it is often distinguished between three controller types: proportional (P) controller, proportional integration (PI) controller, and

Figure 14. Principle structure of control

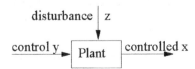

Figure 15. Feedback control

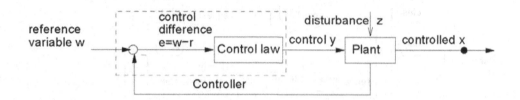

proportional integration derivative (PID) controller, which is most widely used in practice (Hahn, Philipps, Pretschner, & Stauner, 2003).

A proportional controller (p) has the effect of reducing the rise time and reduces but never eliminates the steady-state error[4]. An integral control (i) has the effect of eliminating the steady-state error, but it may affect the transient response. A derivative control (d) has the effect of increasing the stability of the system, reducing the overshoot, and improving the transient response.

Adaptive Control

Some system changes can be unpredictable and ordinary closed-loop systems may not respond properly when the input and output relation varies. Sometimes, these effects can be handled by conventional control techniques such as feed-forward control. Conservative design practices may also enable some systems to remain stable even when subjected to parameter changes or unanticipated disturbances (Isermann, Matko, & Lachmann, 1992).

Adaptive control can help deliver both stability and good response. The approach changes the control algorithm coefficients in real time to compensate for variations in the environment or in the system itself. In general, the controller periodically monitors the system input and output relation and then modifies the control algorithm. It does so by simultaneously learning about the process, while controlling its behavior. The goal is to make the controller robust to a point where

the performance of the complete system is as insensitive as possible to modeling errors and to changes in the environment.

There are two main approaches to adaptive feedback-control design: model reference adaptive control (MRAC) and self-tuning regulators (STRs). In MRAC, a reference model describes system performance. The adaptive controller is then designed to force the system or plant to behave like the reference model. Model output is compared to the actual output, and the difference is used to adjust feedback controller parameters. In STRs a self-tuning regulator assumes a linear model for the process being controlled. It uses a feedback-control law that contains adjustable coefficients. Self-tuning algorithms change the coefficients.

Reconfiguration

Until now, we have considered only a set of controllers which are all active during the whole life time. In addition, we assumed that for one task, there is one controller. For the shuttle system, for example, reconfiguration is in general required to adjust the control algorithms when shuttles build a convoy or when exploiting the context information to choose the most appropriate control strategy. A reconfiguration is needed to switch between the different roles, for example, of convoy leader and convoy follower. To enable these, requirements the purely continuous system is extended by a control logic, for example, statecharts (cf. the section Software Engineering), to decide which controller shall be active.

Figure 16. Model of the plant

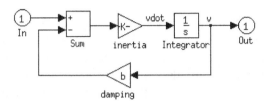

Block Diagrams

A common technique for the specification of controllers that is widely-used in different tools is the notion of hierarchical block diagrams. Block diagrams generally consist of basic blocks, specifying behavior, and hierarchy blocks that group basic and other hierarchy blocks reduce the visual complexity.

Each block has input and output signals. The unidirectional interconnections between the blocks describe the transfer of information. For example, the output signal of a basic block is fed as input signal into a hierarchy block.

Example

The de facto industry standard employing block diagrams is MATLAB/Simulink and Stateflow. Therefore, we describe our controller examples using Matlab/Simulink and Stateflow.

As described in the section Convoy, shuttles build a convoy to reduce the energy consumption. As the convoys require small distance between the shuttles, this distance must be controlled to avoid danger. In more detail this means that the velocity of the shuttle must be controlled with respect to the distance to the shuttle in front. Therefore, a shuttle which drives after another shuttle needs a distance controller and a velocity controller, while the first shuttle of a convoy only needs a velocity controller.

First, we describe the model of the plant. The model of the plant is relatively simple, as the inertia of the wheels can be neglected because of the linear drive technology, and, furthermore, it is assumed that friction, which is proportional to the shuttle's speed, is opposing to the motion of the shuttle. Then the problem is reduced with Newton's law to: $mv'+bv=u, y=v$, where m is the mass of the shuttle, v is the velocity, v' is the derivative of the velocity v, bv is the friction, u is the force of the engine, and y is the output signal (cf. Figure 16).

Now, let's take a look at how the PID controller works in this closed-loop system. Note, the difference between the desired input value and the actual output is represented by the tracking error e (cf. Figure 15). This error signal e will be sent to the PID controller and the controller computes both the derivative and the integral of this error signal. The signal u just past to the controller is now equal to the proportional gain P times the

Figure 17. PID velocity controller

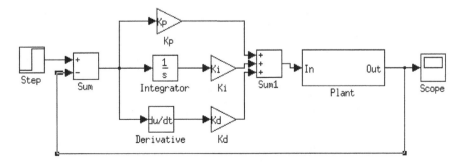

magnitude of the error plus the integral gain *I* times the integral of the error plus the derivative gain *D* times the derivative of the error. This signal *u* will be sent to the plant, and the new output *x* will be obtained. This new output *x* will again be sent back to the sensor to find the new error signal *e*. The controller takes this new error signal and computes its derivative and its integral again. This process goes on and on (cf. Figure 17).

Reconfiguration

Reconfiguration in Matlab can be modeled with conditional blocks. The decision which block is active can be realized with Stateflow and the concept of modes (Hahn et al., 2003). Figure 18 depicts the main control logic for the distance control system as a Stateflow Chart. The model consists of three states. Initially, the shuttle is in state NoConvoy. The events convoyFront and convoyRear fire the transition from state NoConvoy to state ConvoyFront or ConvoyRear. The event breakConvoy is used to cancel a convoy and to change the state back to NoConvoy. All three states are specified with a Mode, which is set when entering a state. In states NoConvoy and ConvoyFront, the control logic implements a control law for velocity control. In state Con-

voyRear, distance control is used. This is signaled by the output variable mode which is used by the underlying Simulink model containing the control laws.

Figure 19 depicts the hybrid model of the shuttle control for the distance control system as a Simulink diagram containing the control logic (top left), the control laws for distance and velocity control (middle), and a model of the physical dynamics (right). The distance control block contains both the distance controller and the velocity controller. The black bar on the right of the controller is a switch. Via the Mode input of both controller and the switch, the required controller is activated.

Discussion

To build sophisticated software-intensive systems, the capability to adapt to the given context is of paramount importance. For the shuttle system, for example, adaptation or reconfiguration is generally required to adjust the control algorithms when shuttles build a convoy or when exploiting the context information to choose the most appropriate control strategy. If also self-optimization across multiple layers should be realized, reconfigura-

Figure 18. Control logic of shuttle control

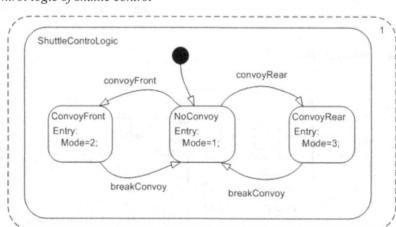

Figure 19. Hybrid model of shuttle control

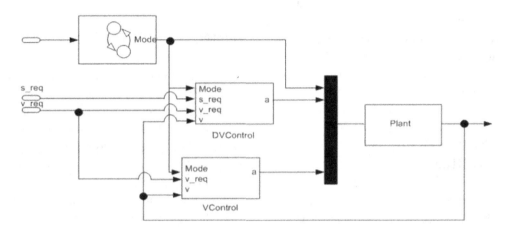

tion cross module boundaries must be possible. Otherwise, the shuttle behavior as a whole cannot take advantage of the reconfiguration options of its submodules.

In MATLAB/Simulink conditional blocks, which are only evaluated if explicitly triggered, can be used to model reconfiguration. Thus, a Stateflow diagram may be used to trigger the required elements of the currently active configuration. Besides the modeling aspects of MATLAB/Simulink, the initial focus of this tools is simulation while other capabilities have been added later or only by research approaches. For example, verification tools like CheckMate[5], which did not scale very well.

Discussion and Summary

Figure 20 shows the modeling tasks supported by the presented modeling approaches. The section Business Process Modeling shows that integration of the economic perspective on complex software-intensive systems, which is usually studied using business process modeling approaches with the modeling of the software with the de facto standard UML (cf. the section Software Engineering), is rather straightforward: Either UML activity diagrams can be used upfront for business pro-

Figure 20. Modeling tasks of standard disciplines w.r.t phases

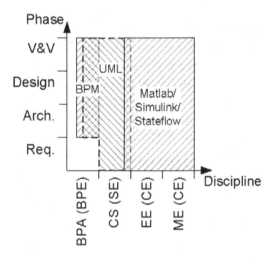

cess modeling or different notations with quite similar concepts and an additional translation step are employed.

The integration between the software world of UML and block diagrams and Stateflow in Matlab/Simulink is, in contrast, more challenging. While Stateflow and UML state machines have some commonalities, the underlying interaction paradigms are different: continuous signals and triggers in the Mathworks world and messages and events in UML. For the continuous dynamics present in Matlab/Simulink there is no equivalent in the UML world.

Thus, in the remaining sections of this chapter, we will focus on the integration of software engineering and control engineering and review solutions for it.

INTEGRATED MODELING APPROACHES

Modeling complex software-intensive systems can just be addressed in a limited manner when one of the approaches of the involved disciplines, as discussed in the last section, are employed. Therefore, a number of approaches for the modeling of software-intensive systems have been proposed which integrate their concepts. Taking the identified integration problem between software engineering and control engineering into account, the most relevant approaches are CHARON, HybridUML/HL3, HyROOM/HyCharts/Hybrid Sequence Charts, HyVisual and Ptolemy II, Masaccio and Giotto, MECHATRONIC UML, SysML, and UML (Giese & Henkler, 2006).

Unfortunately, none of these approaches address *all* development phases and their tasks (cf. the sections Role of Modeling in the Different Development Phases and Typical Modeling Tasks), from requirements engineering to real-time code generation and execution with real-time scheduling.

Consequently, we present the SysML—the upcoming standard of the OMG which focus on the early development phases—and MECHATRONIC UML—an approach which addresses the later development phases—as potential candidates for the model-driven development of software-intensive systems. We will at first review SysML in the section SysML before we will consider MECHATRONIC UML in the section MECHATRONIC UML. Finally, we will discuss the current status of the integrated modeling for software-intensive systems.

SysML

As described in the section Introduction and the section Background, software-intensive systems have an interdisciplinary character. Therefore, the system is developed by more than one discipline. The different disciplines have to be integrated to enable a successful development. Systems engineering integrates all disciplines and describes a structured development process from the conceptional phase over the production phase to the operation phase. This is called a meta discipline.

The *Systems Modeling Language (SysML)* (cf. Systems Modeling Language (SysML), 2006)[6] , is an answer to OMG's request for proposals for *UML for System Engineering (UML for SE)* (UML for System Engineering Request for Proposal, ad/03-03-41, 2003). SysML extends a subset of the UML 2.0 specification. One extension, related to the design of continuous and hybrid systems are so called *Blocks* which are based on UML's composite structured classes. They describe the fine structure of a class extended by continuous communication links between ports.

In the following, we discuss the new aspects of SysML which are useful for developing software-intensive systems.

Requirements

Functional requirements can be described with UML use case diagrams, but UML lacks the ability to describe nonfunctional requirements. Therefore, SysML defines requirements diagrams for nonfunctional requirements. The approach defines specific stereotypes for class diagrams, relations between requirements, and linking to other model elements. A requirement is defined by an unique identifier, which is a common text and must be specified by the designer or tool, and

Figure 21. Requirement of shuttle transportation

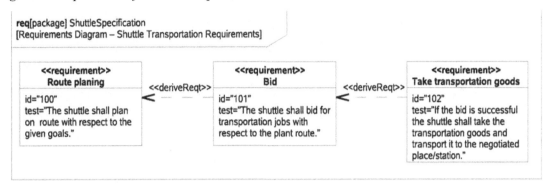

a commenting text. Operations and attributes are not allowed. Therefore, functional requirements need to be additionally specified by use cases, interfaces or scenarios.

Figure 21 shows a requirement model for the shuttle transportation based on the business process, shown in Figure 5. For the transportation process we have defined three requirements. First, a shuttle plans a route with respect to the given goals of a shuttle. If the route is planned, a shuttle shall bid to transportation jobs. As a shuttle shall bid only to transportation jobs, which could be satisfied by the planned route, requirement 101 is derived from requirement 100. The requirement Take transportation goods is derived from requirement Bid, as it describes that the shuttle shall take the transportation goods and transport it to the negotiated station. To interlink the requirement with model elements, which concern to the requirement, an association with a satisfy stereotype could be specified. For example, the activity diagram specified in the section Software Engineering satisfies the requirement Plan route.

Blocks

The Block Definition Diagram in SysML defines features of a block and relationships between blocks such as associations, generalizations, and dependencies. It captures the definition of blocks in terms of properties and operations, and rela-

tionships such as a system hierarchy or a system classification tree. The Internal Block Diagram in SysML captures the internal structure of a block in terms of properties and connectors between properties. A block can include properties to specify its values, parts, and references to other blocks. Ports are a special class of property used to specify allowed types of interactions between blocks.

SysML blocks are based on UML classes as extended by UML composite structures. Some capabilities available for UML classes, such as more specialized forms of associations, have been excluded from SysML blocks to simplify the language. SysML blocks always include an ability to define internal connectors, regardless of whether this capability is needed for a particular block. SysML Blocks also extend the capabilities of UML classes and connectors with reusable forms of constraints and multilevel nesting of connector ends.

Figure 22 shows a block diagram of shuttle. The shuttle embeds two continuous blocks, DistanceControl (dc) and VelocityControl (vc). dc has three flow ports, the required and the current distance as well as the velocity from the antecedent shuttle. These three flow ports are also specified by the shuttle block in order to make these ports visible on the shuttle level. The same modeling principles are applied to the required velocity flow port of the vc block. Further the calculated velocity of the dc block is transferred

Figure 22. Structure of shuttle system

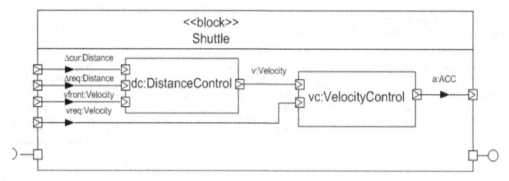

from the dc block to the vc block. Finally, the output acceleration of block vc is delegated to the superior Shuttle block. Further, the Shuttle block has a discrete in- and out- port, which are not furthermore specified.

Constraints

SysML supports the definition of parametric relationships between properties of blocks. This is called constraint block. Constraint blocks provide a mechanism for integrating engineering analysis, such as performance and reliability models, with other SysML models. Constraint blocks can be used to specify a network of constraints that represent mathematical expressions. Such constraints can also be used to identify critical performance parameter and their relationships to other parameters, which can be tracked throughout the system life cycle. Constraint blocks define generic forms of constraints that can be used in multiple contexts. For example, a definition for Newton's Laws may be used to specify these constraints in many different contexts. Reusable constraint definitions may be specified on block definition diagrams and packaged into general-purpose or domain-specific model libraries. Such constraints can be arbitrarily complex mathematical or logical expressions. The constraints can be nested to enable a constraint to be defined in terms of more

basic constraints such as primitive mathematical operators.

Figure 23 shows the constraints of the shuttle dynamics. The ShuttleDynamic constraints consists of the Acceleration, Velocity, and Distance. The Acceleration constraint block includes the constraint {F=m*a}, which is based on Newton's law, and the parameters of the constraint, F, m, and a. The Velocity constraint block describes the constraint {a=dv/dt} and the parameters a, v and t. The Distance constraint block is similar to the Velocity constraint, except the solution is the position instead of the acceleration. The application of the defined constraints is shown in Figure 24.

Activities

SysML contains constructs which extend the control in activity diagrams. In UML 2.1.1 Superstructure Specification (2006) Activities, control can only enable actions to start. SysML extend control in activity diagrams to support disabling of actions that are already executing. This is accomplished by providing a model library with a type for control values that are treated like data. A control value is an input or output of a control operator (cf. Figure 25). A control operator can represent a complex logical operation that transforms its inputs to produce an output that controls

Figure 23. Constraints of shuttle system

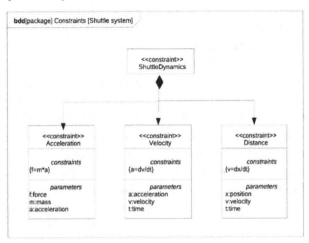

Figure 24. Applied constraints

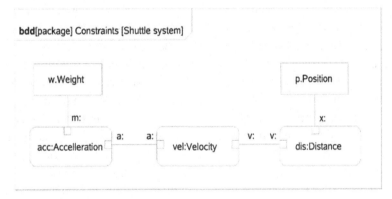

Figure 25. Activity diagram for acceleration

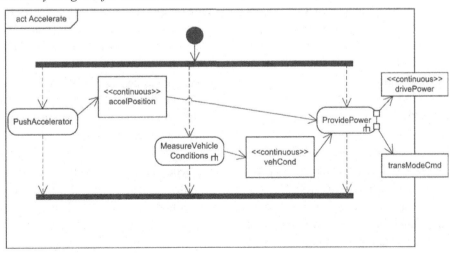

other actions (cf. Systems Modeling Language (SysML) Specification, 2006).

In Figure 25, an activity diagram of the function accelerate is shown. The accelerate function has the parallel activities PushAcclerator, MeasureVehicleCondition, and ProvidePower. PushAcclerator is connected to ProvidePower via the continuous flow accelPosition and MeasureVehicleCondition is connected to ProvidePower via the continuous flow vehCond. Based on this information, ProvidePower provides the continuous output drivePower.

Allocation

Allocation is the term used by systems engineers to denote the organized cross-association (mapping) of elements within the various structures or hierarchies of a user model. The concept of allocation requires flexibility suitable for abstract system specification, rather than a particular constrained method of system or software design. System modelers often associate various elements in a user model in abstract, preliminary, and sometimes tentative ways. Allocations can be used early in the design as a precursor to more detailed rigorous specifications and implementations. The allocation relationship can provide effective means for navigating the model by establishing cross relationships, and ensuring the various parts of the model are properly integrated (cf. Systems Modeling Language (SysML), 2006). A simple example of an allocation is the activity shown in Figure 25, which is an allocation from the block diagram shown in Figure 22.

Further Diagrams

Supported and not extended UML diagrams are sequence diagrams, state machines, and use cases. The other UML diagrams are excluded, for example, Timing Diagram, "due to concerns about its maturity and suitability for system engineering needs" (Systems Modeling Language (SysML)

Specification, 2006). Therefore, SysML lacks in supporting needed modeling tasks (cf. the section Typical Modeling Tasks) for software-intensive systems, like hybrid automata.

Mechatronic UML

The Mechatronic UML approach enables the development of software-intensive systems (cf. the section Background).

Mechatronic UML supports the specification of software structure and its changes (Becker, Beyer, Giese, Klein, & Schilling, 2006), complex real-time coordination behavior (Burmester, Giese, & Schäfer, 2005), formal verification of safety properties (Giese, Tichy, Burmester, Schäfer, & Flake, 2003) as well as hazard analysis (Giese & Tichy, 2006). In addition, the Mechatronic UML supports the modeling of control behavior by embedding controllers in the states of the real-time behavior without forfeiting the verification results (Burmester, Giese, & Hirsch, 2005).

Real-time Coordination Behavior

The real-time coordination behavior specifies the message-based communication between different mechatronic entities under hard real-time constraints. The approach starts by the specification of communication behavior in different scenarios, using Sequence Diagrams with real-time related annotations. A set of related scenarios, for example, the scenarios concerning the coordination of different shuttles in a convoy, is then used to synthesize Real-time Statecharts (RTSC) for each of the software components which take part in the scenarios. Real-Time Statecharts are an extension of UML state machines by special real-time annotations for periodic executions, real-time dependent behavior, worst case execution times, and so forth. The semantics of Real-time Statecharts are based on timed automata.

The resulting RTSCs of the different software components are combined in a so called *Real-time Coordination Pattern*. Each RTSC specifies the behavior of a certain role in a coordination

Figure 26. Real-time coordination pattern for a shuttle convoy

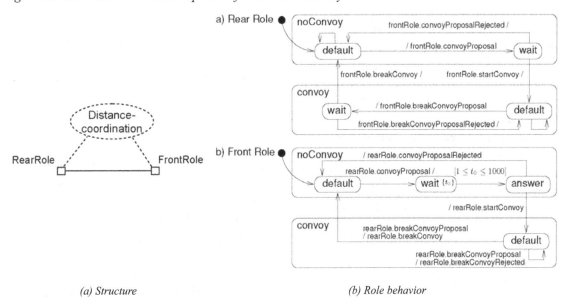

(a) Structure   (b) Role behavior

activity. In terms of the shuttle convoy example, there are roles for the first shuttle in a convoy, for the shuttles in the middle of the convoy, and for the last shuttle in the convoy. Because those coordination activities are often safety-critical, the MECHATRONIC UML supports the formal verification of the coordination patterns.

Thereafter, the component's behavior is specified by reusing and refining different role behaviors. The MECHATRONIC UML employs a refinement notion which guarantees that if a component refines a role, the verification results for the role also hold for the component. Finally, controllers are embedded into the states of the component's statechart in order to integrate the models of the control engineering domain. In the following, we will explain the different steps for the behavioral modeling in terms of the railcab convoy example.

Real-Time Coordination Patterns

In the section Software Engineering, different UML sequence diagrams are shown for different scenarios of two shuttles concerning the

coordination activities in a convoy.[7] Using the synthesis approach of Giese and Burmester (2004), the different scenarios are synthesized into two roles whose behavior is specified by Real-time Statecharts. The roles can also be directly specified by the developer without using the sequence diagrams. One role specifies the coordination behavior of the first shuttle, the other one for the shuttle at the end of the convoy (cf. Figure 26). Additionally, the characteristics of the connector (like a faulty wireless network) is also specified using Real-time Statecharts.

Initially, both roles are in state noConvoy:: default, which means that they are not in a convoy. The rear role nondeterministically chooses whether to propose building a convoy or not. After having chosen to propose a convoy, a message is sent to the other shuttle respecting its front role. The front role chooses nondeterministically to reject or to accept the proposal after max. 1000 msec. In the first case, both statecharts revert to the noConvoy::default state. In the second case, both roles switch to the convoy::default state.

Eventually, the rear shuttle nondeterministically chooses to propose a break of the convoy and sends this proposal to the front shuttle. The front shuttle chooses nondeterministically to reject or accept that proposal. In the first case, both shuttles remain in convoy-mode. In the second case, the front shuttle replies by an approval message, and both roles switch into their respective noConvoy:: default states.

For the connector between the two roles which represents a wireless network we do not apply an explicit statechart, but instead specify its QoS characteristics such as throughput, maximal delay and so forth, in the form of connector attributes. In our example, we assume that the connector forwards incoming signals with a delay of 1 up to 5 msec. The connector is unsafe in the sense that it might fail at any time, such that we set our specific QoS characteristic reliable to false.

To provide safe behavior, the following OCL constraint must hold. It demands that a combination of role states where the front role is in state noConvoy and the rear role is in state convoy is not possible. This is required because such a situation would allow the front shuttle to brake with full intensity although another shuttle drives in short distance behind, which causes a rear-end collision.

```
context DistanceCoordination inv:
  not (self.oclInState(RearRole::Main::con-
voy) and
```

```
       self.oclInState(FrontRole::Main::noCon-
voy))
```

It is shown in Giese et al. (2003) that this property holds. As mentioned there, those patterns are individually constructed and verified. After a successful verification, the patterns are stored in a pattern library.

Components

The above presented real-time coordination patterns are used in the construction of the software components. The employed component diagrams are based on UML component diagrams. Discrete components are distinguished from continuous components. The behavior of discrete components is specified using Real-time Statecharts, whereas the behavior of continuous components is specified by block diagrams for control activities. The same distinction is made for ports. The component definition supports the notion of interface statecharts (Burmester, Giese, & Oberschelp, 2005) for the specification of different port sets in different modes (states) of the component.

Discrete components simply reuse the roles and their behavior. When a developer specifies a software component, he decides in which coordination activities the component will take part. Thereafter, the appropriate roles are added to the component as ports (cf. Figure 27). The

Figure 27. Shuttle component type

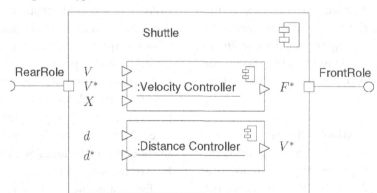

Figure 28. Real-time statechart for the shuttle component

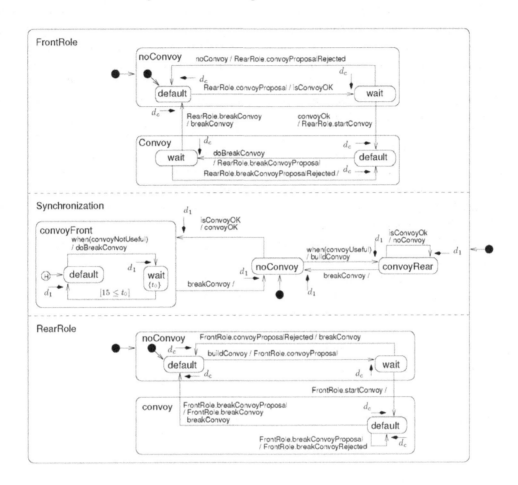

component definition also specifies which other components are contained. For our example, the shuttle component type embeds two continuous components, one for controlling the velocity of the shuttle and one for controlling the distance to another shuttle. In this example, the embedded components are feedback controllers which are developed by exports of the control engineering domain. Consequently, this model is part of multiple domains.

The role statecharts are added to the behavioral specification of the component. In this process, the role statecharts can be refined by the developer,

that is, they can be changed in a restricted way. For the shuttle example, the developer might want to ensure that a shuttle joins a convoy only as the rear or the front shuttle.[8]

Figure 28 depicts the behavior of the **Shuttle** component from Figure 27, taken from Giese et al. (2003) and extended with real-time annotations. The Real-time Statechart consists of three orthogonal states **FrontRole**, **RearRole**, and **Synchronization**. **FrontRole** and **RearRole** are refinements of the role behaviors from Figure 26 and specify in detail the communication that is required to build and to break convoys. **Synchro-**

nization coordinates the communication and is responsible for initiating and breaking convoys. The three substates of **Synchronization** represent whether the shuttle is in the convoy at the first position (**convoyFront**), at second position (**convoyRear**), or whether no convoy is built at all (**noConvoy**). The whole statechart is a refinement of both role descriptions as it just resolves the nondeterminism from the roles from Figure 26 and does not add additional behavior.

As mentioned above, components in the domain of mechatronic systems must meet real-time requirements. In the specific example, it needs not only to be specified that, for example, **RearRole** has to send a **startConvoy** message after receiving **convoyOK**, but also that this has to be finished within a specific, predictable time. Therefore, Real-time Statecharts respect that the firing of transitions consumes time and that real physical, mechatronic systems can never react in *zero time*, but always with a delay. To represent this in the model, we make use of the deadline construct.

In Figure 28 so called *deadline intervals* c and l are used to specify a minimum and a maximum duration for the time between triggering a transition and finishing its execution. For example, sending the message **convoyProposalRejected** to **RearRole** has to be finished within the time specified by c after receiving the message **noConvoy** in state **FrontRole::noConvoy::wait**. As another example for predictable timing behavior (real-time behavior) the change in **Synchronization** from **noConvoy** to **convoyFront** has to be finished within l.

For a component, which combines different patterns respective to the roles, the verified properties still hold due to the approach presented in Giese et al. (2003). Thus, components for mechatronic systems are developed in a way similar to a construction kit using several proven and verified building blocks and refine them to suit different requirements.

Figure 29. Embedding subcomponents into states of the real-time statechart

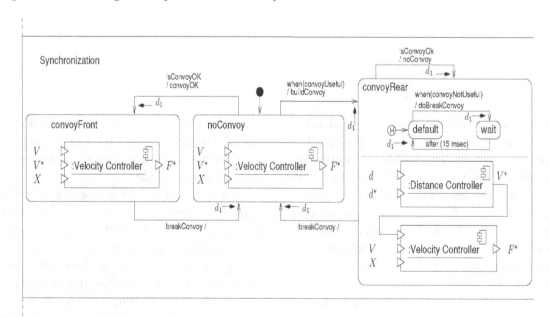

Hybrid Embedding

The component type definition of Figure 27 specifies that the shuttle component embeds two different components, the velocity controller and the distance controller. The embedded components are not always active in our example as well as in typical mechatronic systems. Which embedded components are active often depends on the current state of the software.

Consequently, the Real-time Statechart of Figure 28 is extended by embedding the active comnponents in the states of the statechart. The velocity controller is active in the convoyFront and noConvoy states, both controllers are active in the convoyRear state because the distance controllers output is fed into the velocity controller.

Adaptation of the software structure

Coordination patterns specify the coordination between different mechatronic entities. During runtime, coordinations between different groups of entities begin and end. Thus, an appropriate model must be specified which contains the information when a coordination pattern must be created and when it can be deleted. This model specifies the adaption of the software or its structure, respectively. The components and patterns formed are a structure in form of a graph. The creation and deletion of patterns as well as changes between the interconnections of components can then be formalized as graph transformations. The correctness of those software adaptations is certainly highly important for software-intensive systems. Consequently, their correctness must be formally verified.

The MECHATRONIC UML supports the specification of structures by UML class diagrams. Structural changes are specified using Story Diagrams which are a variant of UML Activity and Collaboration Diagrams based on the graph transformation formalism. The approach supports the verification of structural invariants. In the following, we will present the models for software adaptation (cf. Becker et al., 2006).

The structure of the software is specified using UML class diagrams. For the shuttle example, the class diagram (cf. Figure 30) specifies the representation of the physical entities—shuttles and tracks—and their relationships in the software of the shuttle. Tracks are short segments with room for a single Shuttle. The successor association connects them into a network. A Shuttle's position is expressed by the on association; the go association encodes physical movement toward a Track. Note that, even though we are not using attributes and are thus abstracting from the Shuttle's actual position on the Track, this level of abstraction is sufficient for designing the structural adaptation of the real-time coordination.

Figure 30. Class diagram and coordination pattern instantiation

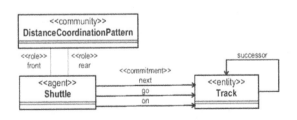

(a) Class diagram

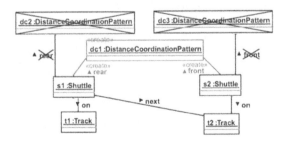

(b) Instantiation rule: creating a DistanceCoordinationPattern

Figure 31. Behavioral rules

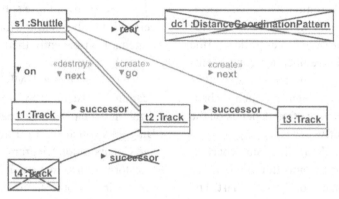

(a) Behavioral rule: Unrestricted movement for a solitary shuttle

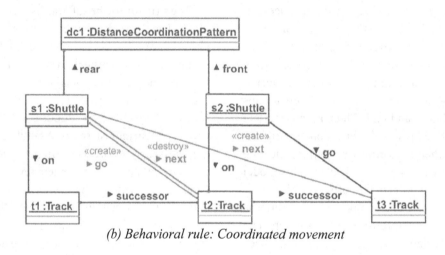

(b) Behavioral rule: Coordinated movement

Figure 32. Invariant: No uncoordinated movement of shuttles in close proximity, which would constitute a hazard

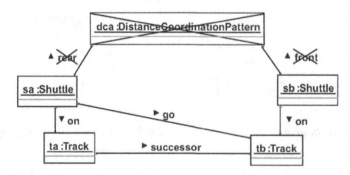

The next association represents a commitment (marked by the stereotype) to go to a specific Track. The DistanceCoordinationPattern groups two Shuttles which take on the rear respectively front *role*, again marked by stereotypes.

As mentioned above, the actual collision avoidance is realized by the DistanceCoordinationPattern. Thus, a DistanceCoordinationPattern is created once a Shuttle approaches another. The instantiation rule createDC creates a DistanceCoordinationPattern, if there is a hitherto unconnected Shuttle on a Shuttle's next Track (cf. Figure 30 (b)).

Two behavioral rules are specified: goSimple1 (cf. Figure 31 (a)) allowing a solitary (i.e., not following another Shuttle) Shuttle to move freely where no Tracks join, and goDC1 (cf. Figure (b)) which only allows the rear Shuttle in a DistanceCoordinationPattern to move, that is, go, once the front Shuttle has decided to move. These rules imply the convention that Shuttles respect the commitment expressed by their next association.

An invariant that is implied in this specification is that a Shuttle will never try to go to a Track occupied by another Shuttle without coordinating its movement, that is, making sure the other Shuttle is moving, which would constitute a hazard. Though not required for the operational correctness of the model, this implied condition (cf. Figure 32) needs to be made explicit, along with several structural constraints restricting cardinalities, in order for the specification to pass the inductive invariant checking. The correctness of this invariant is shown in Becker et al. (2006).

Modeling Failure Propagation and Hazards

If a hazard analysis is required due to safety concerns, the fact that most software-intensive systems and especially their software is made up of components and their connections can be exploited using component-based hazard analysis techniques (Grunske, 2003; Giese & Tichy, 2006; Kaiser, Liggesmeyer, & Maeckel, 2003; McDer-

Figure 33. Deployment diagram with failure propagation formulas

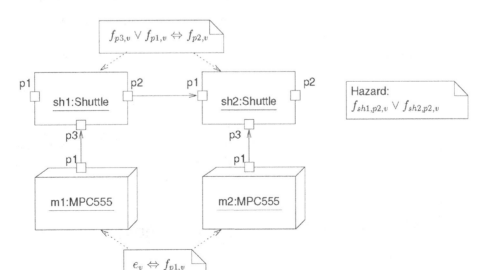

mid, 2003; Papadopoulos, McDermid, Sasse, & Heiner, 2001). The basic idea is to ease the hazard analysis by reusing already available information about failure behavior of the individual components rather than always start from scratch when performing a hazard analysis. The current approaches for component-based hazard analysis have in common that they describe the failure propagation of individual components (cf. failure propagation and transfer nets [3]). Outgoing failures are the result of the combination of internal errors and incoming failures from other components. The failure classification presented in Fenelon, McDermid, Nicolson, and Pumfrey (1994) and McDermid and Pumfrey (1994) is widely employed (as in Papadopoulos et al., 2001; Grunske & Neumann, 2002; Giese & Tichy, 2006) to distinguish different failures.

In the following, we will show how the Me- CHATRONIC UML supports the hazard analysis for the shuttle convoy scenario. Figure 33 shows the software components s1, s2 for two shuttles in a convoy. Both software components are executed on MPC555 boxes. The hazard analysis approach of the MECHATRONIC UML is based on the notion of component failure propagation (cf. fault pa-

thology, Laprie, 1992). The failure propagation is specified for each component by a boolean formula (cf. Figure 33). The boolean formula is based on boolean variables for errors e inside a component and incoming/outgoing failures f at the components' ports. In the example, a value error due to a bit-flip in the memory might occur in the hardware. Failures are propagated via the connectors between ports. This value error leads to a change of the current state from convoyFront to noConvoy in the software component. The hazard is specified by a boolean formula based on the failures f. The hazard in the example is the occurrence of a value failure due to an error in one of the hardware devices. This is a hazardous situation because one shuttle is in convoy driving mode while the other is not. In Giese and Tichy (2006), it is shown how the hazard probability is computed based on a binary decision diagram representation and the errors' individual probabilities.

Discussion and Summary

We presented first in this section how the SysML can be employed to tackle the early phases of the system development. Then, we outlined how the MECHATRONIC UML approach can be used to do the transition to the architectural and detailed design as well as automatic implementation and crucial verification and safety analysis tasks. The presented combination of two UML extensions provides a promising approach towards modeling of complex software-intensive systems. Both approaches support UML like activity diagrams. Therefore, the BPE is supported by these approaches as well as UML supports BPE (cf. Figure 34).

Figure 34. Modeling tasks of software-intensive system disciplines w.r.t phases

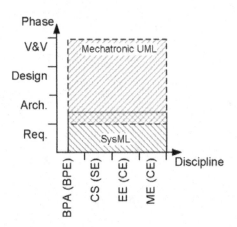

FUTURE TRENDS

The development of future generations of software-intensive systems is further complicated by the fact that these software-intensive systems will become even more complex and, thus, pose a number of challenges for the software and its integration of the other disciplines. It is expected that systems become highly distributed, exhibit adaptive and anticipatory behavior, and act in highly dynamic environments interfacing with the physical world (Wirsing, 2004). Consequently, modeling as an essential design activity has to support not only the different disciplines, but also the outlined new characteristics.

It seems that approaches with rather restricted integration concepts which restrict themselves to cosimulation will not be sufficient for the envisioned complex software-intensive systems of the future. However, it remains an open question whether integrated approaches starting from the UML such SysML or MECHATRONIC UML presented in this chapter will succeed or whether further extensions of tools such as Matlab/Simulink which are more established in the traditional engineering disciplines will dominate in the long run.

Today, in most cases the system development is approached from one or another discipline at its specific perspective, while the insights and design options the other disciplines bring into the game are not considered. Important industrial sectors with high innovation pressure such as the automotive industry already show that the importance of software and its influence grows at a high rate and that software and the capabilities of software have to be considered to develop competitive solutions. Therefore, a conceptual integration which goes beyond the composition of subsystems related to the different disciplines but target the interdisciplinary development of subsystems seems necessary. Even more ambitious visions such as cyber-physical systems[9] will require an even more fundamental conceptual integration of the different worlds.

CONCLUSION

The findings show that approaches already exists which bridge the gaps between the different disciplines and integrate the involved domains business process engineering, software engineering, and classical engineering discussed before in the section Modeling Approaches.

The modeling options for complex software-intensive systems are presented by a running example taken from the RailCab research project presented in the section Example to show the capabilities of the domain specific modeling techniques before the additional capabilities of the domain-spanning approaches are considered. The presented modeling results prove that the employed modeling techniques address most of the essential challenges as described in the section Background.

Also, some of the future trends for the modeling of software-intensive systems in the section Future Trends are already covered by the considered techniques. However, it seems that an even more tight conceptual integration will be necessary in the future, if we want to exploit the full potential of software-intensive systems.

While some of the sketched future trends for the modeling of software-intensive systems are already covered by the considered techniques, it seems that an even more tight conceptual integration has to be addressed by future research, if we want to exploit the full potential of software-intensive systems.

ACKNOWLEDGMENT

This work was developed in the course of the Special Research Initiative 614—Self-optimizing concepts and Structures in Mechanical Engineering—University of Paderborn, and was published on its behalf and funded by the Deutsche Forschungsgemeinschaft.

REFERENCES

Aalst, W. (1998). The application of petri nets to workflow management. *The Journal of Circuits, Systems and Computers, 8*(1), 21-66.

Aalst, W., Hee, K., & Houben, G. (1994). Modelling workflow management systems with high-level Petri nets. In G. Michelis, C. Ellis, & G. Memmi (Eds.), *Proceedings of the Second Workshop on Computer-supported Cooperative Work, Petri Nets and Related Formalisms,* (pp. 31-50).

Aalst, W., Hofstede, A. H. M. T., Kiepuszewski, B., & Barros, A. P. (2003). Workflow patterns. *Distributed Parallel Databases, 14*(1), 5-51.

Arkin, A., Askary, S., Bloch, B., Curbera, F., Goland, Y., & Kartha, N. (2005). *Web services business process execution language version 2.0.* WS-BPEL TC OASIS.

Becker, B., Beyer, D., Giese, H., Klein, F., & Schilling, D. (2006). Symbolic invariant verification for systems with dynamic structural adaptation. In *Proceedings of the International Conference on Software Engineering (ICSE), Shanghai, China, (pp. 21-81).* ACM Press.

Burmester, S., Giese, H., & Hirsch, M. (2005, October). *Syntax and semantics of hybrid components* (Tech. Rep. No. tr-ri-05-264). University of Paderborn.

Burmester, S., Giese, H., & Oberschelp, O. (2005, March). Hybrid UML components for the design of complex self-optimizing mechatronic systems. In J. Braz, H. Araújo, A. Vieira, & B. Encarnacao (Eds.), *Informatics in control, automation and robotics.* Springer-Verlag.

Burmester, S., Giese, H., & Schäfer, W. (2005, November). Model-driven architecture for hard real-time systems: From platform independent models to code. In *Proceedings of the European Conference on Model Driven Architecture—foun-dations and Applications (ECMDA-FA'05), Nürnberg, Germany,* (pp. 25-40). Springer-Verlag.

Fenelon, P., McDermid, J. A., Nicolson, M., & Pumfrey, D. J. (1994). Towards integrated safety analysis and design. *ACM SIGAPP Applied Computing Review, 2*(1), 21-32.

Föllinger, O. (2005). *Regelungstechnik: Einführung in die Methoden und ihre Anwendung.* Hüthig.

Giese, H., & Burmester, S. (2004, May). Analysis and synthesis for parameterized timed sequence diagrams. In H. Giese & I. Krüger (Eds.), *Proceedings of the 3rd International Workshop on Scenarios and State Machines: Models, Algorithms, and Tools (ICSE 2003 Workshop W5), Edinburgh, Scotland,* (pp. 43-50). IEE.

Giese, H., & Henkler, S. (2006, December). A survey of approaches for the visual model-driven development of next generation software-intensive systems. *Journal of Visual Languages and Computing, 17,* 528-550.

Giese, H., Henkler, S., Hirsch, M., & Klein, F. (2006, May). Nobody's perfect: Interactive synthesis from parametrized real-time scenarios. In *Proceedings of the ICSE 2006 Workshop on Scenarios and State Machines: Models, Algorithms and Tools (SCESM'06), Shanghai, China,* (pp. 67-74). ACM Press.

Giese, H., & Tichy, M. (2006, September). Component-based hazard analysis: Optimal designs, product lines, and online-reconfiguration. In *Proceedings of the 25th International Conference on Computer Safety, Security and Reliability (SAFECOMP), Gdansk, Poland,* (pp. 156-169). Springer-Verlag.

Giese, H., Tichy, M., Burmester, S., Schäfer, W., & Flake, S. (2003, September). Towards the compositional verification of real-time UML designs. In *Proceedings of the 9th European Software Engineering Conference held jointly with the*

11th ACM SIGSOFT International Symposium on Foundations of Software Engineering (ESEC/FSE-11), (pp. 38-47). ACM Press.

Grimm, K. (2003). Software technology in an automotive company: Major challenges. In *ICSE'03: Proceedings of the 25th International Conference on Software Engineering,* (pp. 498-503). Washington, DC, USA: IEEE Computer Society.

Grunske, L. (2003). Transformational patterns for the improvement of safety. In *Proceedings of the Second Nordic Conference on Pattern Languages of Programs (vikingplop 03).* Microsoft Buisness Press.

Grunske, L., & Neumann, R. (2002, October 6). Quality improvement by integrating non-functional properties in software architecture specification. In *Proceedings of the Second Workshop on Evaluating and Architecting System Dependability (easy),* San Jose, CA, USA.

Hahn, G., Philipps, J., Pretschner, A., & Stauner, T. (2003, June). Prototype-based tests for hybrid reactive systems. In *Proceedings of the 14th IEEE International Workshop on Rapid System Prototyping (RSP'03),* (pp. 78-85).

Hardung, B., Kölzow, T., & Krüger, A. (2004). Reuse of software in distributed embedded automotive systems. In *EMSOFT'04: Proceedings of the 4th ACM International Conference on Embedded Software,* (pp. 203-210). New York, USA: ACM Press.

Harel, D. and Marelly, R. (2002). Playing with time: On the specification and execution of time-enriched LSCs. In *Proceedings of the 10th IEEE international Symposium on Modeling, Analysis, and Simulation of Computer and Telecommunications Systems (MASCOTS'02)* (p. 193). Washington, DC: IEEE Computer Society.

Isermann, R., Matko, D., & Lachmann, K.-H. (1992). *Adaptive control systems.* Upper Saddle River, NJ, USA: Prentice Hall.

J.Bank. (1993). *The essence of total quality management.* Prentice Hall.

Jensen, K., & Rozenberg, G. (Eds.). (1991). *High-level Petri nets: Theory and application.* London, UK: Springer-Verlag.

Kaiser, B., Liggesmeyer, P., & Maeckel, O. (2003, October 9-10). A new component concept for fault trees. In *Proceedings of the 8th National Workshop on Safety Critical Systems and Software (scs 2003),* Canberra, Australia, (Vol. 33, pp. 37-46). Darlinghurst, Australia: Australian Computer Society.

Keller, G., Nüttgens, M., & Scheer, A. (1992). *Semantische Processmodellierung auf der Grundlage Ereignisgesteuerter Processketten (EPK).* Veröffentlichungen des Instituts für Wirtschaftsinformatik, Heft 89 (in German). University of Saarland, Saarbrücken.

Kindler, E. (2006). On the semantics of EPCs: Resolving the vicious circle. *Data Knowledge Eng., 56*(1), 23-40.

Laprie, J. C. (Ed.). (1992). *Dependability: Basic concepts and terminology in English, French, German, Italian and Japanese [IFIP WG 10.4, Dependable Computing and Fault Tolerance]* (Vol. 5). Wien: Springer-Verlag.

McDermid, J. A. (2003). Trends in systems safety: A European view? P. Lindsay (Ed.), *Seventh Australian Workshop on Industrial Experience with Safety Critical Systems and Software,* (Vol. 15, pp. 3-8). Adelaide, Australia: ACS.

McDermid, J., & Pumfrey, D. (1994). A development of hazard analysis to aid software design. In *Proceedings of the Ninth Annual Conference on Computer Assurance (compass94),* (pp. 17-25). Gaithersburg, MD, USA: National Institute of Standards and Technology.

OMG. (2006, February). *Business process modeling notation (BPMN) specification.* Retrieved March 6, 2008, from http://www.bpmn.org/ (Final Adopted Specification)

Papadopoulos, Y., McDermid, J., Sasse, R., & Heiner, G. (2001, March). Analysis and synthesis of the behaviour of complex programmable electronic systems in conditions of failure. *Reliability Engineering & System Safety, 71*, 229-247.

Recommended Practice for Architectural Description of Software-intensive Systems, IEEE-Std-1471-2000. (2000, October). 345 East 47th Street, New York, 10017-2394, USA.

Reisig, W., & Rozenberg, G. (Eds.). (1998). *Lectures on petri nets I: Basic models* (Vol. 1491). Berlin: Springer-Verlag.

Russell, N., Aalst, W., Hofstede, A., & Wohed, P. (2006). On the suitability of UML activity diagrams for business process modelling. In M. Stumptner, S. Hartmann, & Y. Kiyoki (Eds.), *Proceedings of the Third Asia-Pacific Conference on Conceptual Modelling (apccm 2006)* (Vol. 53, pp. 95-104). Hobart, Australia: ACS.

Scheer, A. (2000). *ARIS: Business process modelling*. Berlin: Springer-Verlag.

CMM. (2002, March). *Capability Maturity Model® Integration (CMMISM), Version 1.1* (Tech. Rep. No. CMU/SEI-2002-TR-012). Carnegie Mellon, Software Engineering Institute.

Sengupta, B., & Cleaveland, R. (2002, November). Triggered message sequence charts. W. G. Griswold (Ed.), *Proceedings of the Tenth ACM SIGSOFT Symposium on the Foundations of Software Engineering (FSE-10)*. Charleston, SC, USA: ACM Press.

SysML-v1.0 *Systems Modeling Language (SysML) Specification.* (2006).

UML 2.0 Superstructure. (2003). *Superstructure specification.* Document ptc/03-08-02.

UML 2.1.1 Superstructure. (2006, October). *UML 2.1.1 superstructure specification.* Document: ptc/06-10-05 (convenience document).

UML for System Engineering Request for Proposal, ad/03-03-2003 (2003), UML-RFP-03-03-28 *UML for System Engineering Request for Proposal, ad/03-03-41.* (2003, March).

VDI2206, (2004). *VDI guideline 2206—design methodology for mechatronic systems.* VDI-Verlag.

WFMC. (1994). *Workflow reference model* (Tech. Rep.). Brussels: Workflow Management Coalition.

Wirsing, M. (Ed.). (2004, May). *Report on the EU/NSF Strategic Workshop on Engineering Software-Intensive Systems.* Edinburgh, GB.

Wohed, P., Aalst, W., Dumas, M., Hofstede, A., & Russell, N. (2006). On the suitability of BPMN for business process modelling. In S. Dustdar, J. Faideiro, & A. Sheth (Eds.), *International Conference on Business Process Management (BPM 2006)* (Vol. 4102, pp. 161-176). Springer-Verlag.

Additional Reading

Burmester, S., Giese, H., Henkler, S., Hirsch, M., Tichy, M., & Gambuzza, A. (2007, May). Tool support for developing advanced mechatronic systems: Integrating the Fujaba Real-Time Tool Suite with CAMeL-View. In *Proceedings of the 29th International Conference on Software Engineering (ICSE), Minneapolis, MN, USA,* (pp. 801-804). IEEE Computer Society Press.

Burmester, S., Giese, H., Hirsch, M., Schilling, D., & Tichy, M. (2005, May). The Fujaba real-time tool suite: Model-driven development of safety-critical, real-time systems. In *Proceedings of the 27th International Conference on Software Engineering (ICSE), St. Louis, MO, USA* (pp. 670-671). ACM Press.

Burmester, S., Giese, H., Münch, E., Oberschelp, O., Klein, F., & Scheideler, P. (2007, December). Tool support for the design of self-optimizing mechatronic multi-agent systems. *International Journal on Software Tools for Technology Transfer (STTT), 8*(4), 1-16.

Freeman, P., & Hart, D. (2004). A science of design for software-intensive systems. *Communications of the ACM, 47*(8), 19-21.

Gausemeier, J., Giese, H., Schäfer, W., Axenath, B., Frank, U., & Henkler, S. (2007, August). Towards the design of self-optimizing mechatronic systems: Consistency between domain-spanning and domain-specific models. In *Proceedings of the 16th International Conference on engineering design (ICED),* Paris, France.

Giese, H., & Hirsch, M. (2005, December). *Checking and automatic abstraction for timed and hybrid refinement in Mechtronic UML* (Tech. Rep. No. tr-ri-03-266). Paderborn, Germany: University of Paderborn.

Giese, H., & Hirsch, M. (2006, January). Modular verificaton of safe online-reconfiguration for proactive components in mechatronic uml. In J.-M. Bruel (Ed.), *Satellite Events at the MODELS 2005 Conference,* Montego Bay, Jamaica, October 2-7, 2005, revised selected papers, (Vol. 3844, pp. 67-78). Springer-Verlag.

Henkler, S., & Hirsch, M. (2006, October). A multi-paradigm modeling approach for reconfigurable Mechatronic systems. In *Proceedings of the International Workshop on Multi-paradigm Modeling: Concepts and Tools (MPM'06), Satellite Event of the 9th International Conference on Model-driven Engineering Languages and Systems MODELS/UML'2006,* Genova, Italy, (Vol. 2006/1, pp. 15-25). Budapest University of Technology and Economics.

Kornecki, A. J., & Zalewski, J. (2005). Experimental evaluation of software development tools for safety-critical real-time systems. *Innovations in systems and software engineering,* (pp. 176-188).

NSF-DLS. (2003, December). *Proceedings of the NSF Workshop on Modeling and Simulation For Design of Large Software-intensive Systems: Toward a New Paradigm Recognizing Networked, Distributed and Diffuse-control Software,* Tucson, AZ.

ENDNOTES

[1] http://www-nbp.upb.de/en

[2] http://www.transrapid.de/en

[3] The term *task* is used on the modeling level, business process *activities* are instances of tasks.

[4] The steady-state error is defined as the difference between the input and output of a system in the limit as time goes to infinity.

[5] http://www.ece.cmu.edu/~webk/checkmate

[6] http://www.omgsysml.org/

[7] We consider here only a convoy of two shuttles for the sake of a clearer presentation.

[8] We consider only convoys of max. 2 shuttles to keep the example simple.

[9] http://varma.ece.cmu.edu/cps/

Chapter III
Service Orientation and Software–Intensive Systems

Jaroslav Král
Charles University, Czech Republic

Michal Žemlička
Charles University, Czech Republic

ABSTRACT

Software intensive systems are systems strongly depending on supporting software. The software is typically large, complex, and it as a rule interacts with human users. The failure of the software implies failure of the system usually causing substantial losses. Such systems are critical. The prospective redevelopment all at once of the software is no feasible solution. It is shown that such software should usually be service-oriented. The interfaces of services should be user-oriented (well understood by users and the users can use it easily). The services should be of two basic types: application services and architecture (enabling to develop an architecture) services. We present the most important infrastructure services as basic service-oriented design patterns.

INTRODUCTION

We understand as software intensive systems the systems strongly depend on supporting software. The software is typically large and the design of the systems should take into account the activities of people, the users of the system. To be more specific, the dependency of the system on its software implies that the system cannot work properly if the supporting software does not work (fails). The software is moreover so complex that

its redevelopment effort is so high and its development duration so large that the redevelopment of the entire system in "Big Bang" manner is no feasible solution. A very important but often neglected dimension of the software intensiveness is the degree of user involvement (agility) in the system and software actions and the degree of interaction of the system with real world.

All the aspects imply that the software supporting software intensive systems is a very complex high-tech engineering artifact. As such the software must be properly structured in the large. It must have a proper architecture.

The architecture should meet the following requirements:

1. The all at once (re)development of the system is too costly and time consuming so the architecture should enable a cheap seamless integration of existing (large) software artifacts like legacy systems, third party products, or newly developed artifacts.

2. The integration of the artifacts usually must not influence existing capabilities of the artifacts and their availability (but it can enhance them). It implies that the local (existing) user interfaces must be preserved, and eventually extended. These conditions enable that the exiting users of the "old" artifacts capabilities need not be aware that the integration just takes place or that the artifact has already been integrated.

3. The integrated software artifacts should be integrated with minor changes, if any, of its code to save the integration investments, to reduce the errors caused by the changes, and to reduce other undesirable effects affecting the users.

4. The integration of artifacts can be gradual (incremental). No "Big Bang" is necessary.

5. The resulting system should be easily maintainable (enhanced, extended, per partes modified).

6. It is desirable that the architecture is good for the application of modern development and integration methods (prototyping, incremental development, agile development, and the support for the overall improving software engineering quality of the new product).

7. The architecture should enable the effective implementation of the requirements of business people. An example is the support, supervision, and use of business processes offered by the system. The processes must be understood by human process users to enable online modification of the processes and commitment of business steps.

We must be aware that architecture in general means integration in the large. A change of an architecture type implies changes of the development processes. Let us remember the following analogy: Being able to lay bricks (objects or small programs) does not directly imply the ability to build good houses (large artifacts). The ability to build good houses need not imply the ability to develop good towns (large software-intensive systems).

Large technical artifacts, large software systems inclusive, cannot be reasonably developed as logical monoliths (compare power plants). Such systems must be built as compositions of quite large components and complex autonomous units. The compositions can be again composed into larger compositions, if appropriate. In software it implies that we must start with entities providing basic capabilities. In software systems the entities are usually called applications. We must have also software entities enabling communication, collaboration and orchestration of collaborating applications as well as the users and maybe real-world entities. The main, if not one and only, feasible way to implement such software systems is service orientation. Service orientation assumes that the system has a specific structure (architecture), that it has service-oriented architecture (SOA). Service-oriented (SO) paradigm and SOA are the proper solution for the majority (if not almost all) of large software (intensive) systems (Král & Žemlička, 2002).

SOA, if designed properly, simplifies solutions of many issues appearing during the specification, design, and use of software-intensive systems. In many cases, the application of SOA itself is the solution. SOA is at present the only precondition for software intensive systems to have satisfactory engineering properties.

As a service-oriented system we understand any (software) system consisting of abstract entities behaving like the services in human society (compare Open Reference Model from MacKenzie et al., 2006). Such systems should fulfill at least the following points.

1. The entities have the capability to do something. The functions provided by a capability are accessible to partners—either human beings or other services—via an interface accepting requests to perform a function (an activity) offered by the capability.

2. There can be more than one unsettled request for a capability at a time. It implies that the communication between the services is inherently asynchronous; synchronous communication is optional. The system is then a virtual peer-to-peer network in which the services are the peers mutually communicating by the exchange of messages. It implies that a message for a service must be sometimes stored in a possibly hidden data store (in a message queue Q). Q can be implemented in various ways:
    a. integrated in a software component providing the service,
    b. included in middleware, or
    c. integrated into a separate architecture service similar to data stores known from data-flow diagrams and structured design.

3. The services are permanently active (able to accept and settle requests all the time).

4. The services are used as black boxes. It suffices for the use of a service to know its interface only and any actor—service or user—able and authorized to use it can use the service.

5. As a rule there are no inherent conditions where the service resides and whether a software component is a service provider or a service requester.

Service orientation is becoming the main stream of contemporary software engineering. It is probably the deepest change in software engineering in several decades. Service orientation is one of the main reasons for the changes for the IT professional outlook (Morello, 2005). A practical experience of the authors with service orientation (Bajana et al., 2005) shows an extreme power and flexibility of service orientation even in the case of a quite small application. There are, of course, limits. It makes no sense to apply service orientation on very small software systems. We have no good modeling tools for service orientation yet. The systems like the one offered by the framework Tau 3.0 by Telelogic (Telelogic, 2008) does not seem to be appropriate enough for SOA. The standards like WS-* intended to be used in SOA are not mature enough yet. There can be problems with effectiveness or security. Main issues are, however, the necessary changes in marketing and the business strategy of software vendors and in new software development and use strategies and tactics at the side of users.

SOA is neither a matter of choice, nor the problem of a future application. It is a reality now. It can be easily verified looking at contemporary software engineering practice. SOA is crucial in many cases.

1. SOA is the only known feasible way of integration of legacy systems (e-government, health care systems, information systems of global enterprises, CRM, SCM, etc.).

2. SOA is a precondition of e-commerce.

3. SOA is a native philosophy for the development of process control soft real-time systems.

4. SOA is the only feasible way of development of large systems using agile development methods like extreme programming.

5. SOA is the way of seamless insourcing and outsourcing.

6. SOA enables incremental development and maintenance.

We can conclude that SOA is not the matter of "Why?" but of "How?". We will contribute to the answering the question "How?" and we hope that it will contribute to the answer of "Why?".

SOFTWARE CONFEDERATIONS

According to MacKenzie et al. (2006) there are three main properties of services:

1. Services can have real-world effect,
2. Services interact and communicate like real-world services, and
3. Services are visible and can be looked for by other services out all over the world, if necessary.

We discuss in the sequel a very important subclass of service-oriented systems called confederations. In confederations the constituent cooperating services know each other and they need not be looked for by the communication partners.

Software confederations (or confederations for short) occur in practice very often. In fact, the most important service-oriented systems occurring in practice are usually confederations. Examples are e-government systems, health care systems, systems of global enterprises, and so forth. Confederative architecture is a precondition of seamless outsourcing as well as insourcing of parts of software systems. It has many further engineering advantages. We believe that many failures and problems with the application of SOA are due to the fact that the systems are based on the (unnecessary) assumption that the services should be able to look for cooperation partners. We shall show that a better development philosophy for the complex systems often is to design the systems or their kernel parts as confederations. Some services of the kernel can look for the communication partners outside the kernel, or even can communicate with batch subsystems using a modernized concept of data stores. It requires, however, that there are peers providing architecture services like services (proxies or generalized adapters) providing the modification of the interfaces of other services (filtering, format transformations, etc.). We shall discuss this problem in detail below.

The main advantage of confederations is that the interfaces of the services can be proprietary, possibly a XML-based format. This attitude is often criticized not to be general enough as it does not use world-wide used standards. We believe, however, that at present such standards are universal and too programmer-oriented and therefore not user-oriented (understandable for user and based on their knowledge domains). Moreover, the great pace of the development of the standards implies that the standards are not mature yet and therefore getting obsolete too fast. The main issue is that existing standards do not support user orientation of the services.

The service-oriented systems have the following technical structure:

1. Transportation layer—middleware—providing the basic capabilities enabling the transportation of messages between services, and
2. Services able to contact the middleware by their connectors/gates. The services are at least of the following two types:
    a. Application services providing capabilities of users' domains, and
    b. Services providing the capabilities necessary for the proper work of the entire system (architecture services, for example, the proxies or adapters mentioned above).

The architecture services can play various roles, and some of them can better the interface of another service or it can enhance functions of the middleware. Services can be used as a service orchestration tool (Král & Žemlička, 2005). An application can be transformed into an application service by adding ports (gates) using appropriate plug-ins or using specific libraries. Technically, any SOA integrates autonomous software entities using an engine (middleware) enabling communication between services. The middleware can but need not be implemented using the Internet. Some functions of the middleware can be delegated to services providing some capabilities of infrastructure.

Our specification of services is a bit narrower than some specifications of SOA (compare Ang, Cherbakov, & Ibrahim, 2005; MacKenzie et al., 2006). We believe that it covers the most important variants of applications of SOA. It covers especially the integration of existing applications like existing information systems of government offices into e-government without changing their "local" capabilities.

SOURCES OF SERVICE ORIENTATION

The earliest systems, the architecture of which fulfilled almost all above mentioned properties, were the (soft) real-time process control systems written for minicomputers controlling technologies admitting intelligent interfaces. Such systems were written for operating systems providing constructs like message queue or mailbox.

This chapter is partly based on the long term experience of the authors with software intensive soft real-time systems (flexible manufacturing systems, automated warehouses, university administrative systems, health service systems, etc.). The authors have implemented several systems having main features of confederations in the 70s, 80s, and 90s. Some of them are discussed as examples below.

It can be surprising that it is rather an obstacle than advantage for the wide use of SOA, as many people think that SO is nothing new, although in the areas like global information systems it is a

completely new issue requiring new attitudes. This attitude is known as "What's new" SOA related antipattern (Ang et al., 2005). For example, many antipatterns of object orientation (Brown, Malveau, McCormick, & Mowbray, 1998) become patterns in service orientation. The most important examples are the object-oriented antipattern "Islands of Automation" and "Legacy System" (Ang et al., 2005). Easy integration of legacy systems is the main advantage of service orientation as it enables substantial savings of software investments and is in fact the only feasible way of development and maintenance of global systems. Components in service orientation are integrated differently from the approach of object orientation (Bureš & Plášil, 2004). The components (services) in SOA are loosely related and communicate asynchronously, whereas the object-oriented components usually use remote procedure call (RPC). Such communication is usually synchronous to what induces fine-grained interfaces.

The origins of service orientation are in old software intensive (soft real-time) systems. It is the reason why service orientation and service-oriented architecture are able to simplify or even solve many issues of contemporary software intensive systems.

The experience with such systems being in fact software intensive (Král & Demner, 1979, Král et al., 1987, Král & Žemlička, 2004b; see also examples given later) showed that such systems—if designed properly—were able to solve many issues of software construction:

- Seamless integration and reuse of legacy systems and third-party products—see paragraph "Front-End Gates,"
- Support for agile business processes—see paragraph "Process managers,"
- Rapid prototyping by message redirection,
- Easy integration of batch subsystems into interactive subsystems—see paragraph "Business Processes and Data Stores,"

- Autonomous development of software components that have all the main properties of software services in above sense,
- The only known feasible technique to implement e-government—see below, and
- Application of development principles that are now known from agile development (Beck , 1999; Beck et al., 2001; Král, Zemlicka, & Kopecky, 2006).

Modern tools and methods amplify existing and provide new advantages of service-oriented systems.

INTERFACES OF APPLICATION SERVICES

As application services (AS) we understand the services used as black boxes and providing some basic user problem domain capabilities. They can be encapsulated (wrapped) legacy systems, third-party products, or newly developed entities. The interfaces of application services should enable their seamless integration (orchestration) into business processes. They then provide capabilities enabling the steps of the processes. The steps must be integrated (orchestrated) into business processes that are networks of steps. The links between the processes and AS are based on the AS interfaces. The interfaces are implemented as an integral part of the AS denoted in the sequel as *G* (gate) of the software component (service).

There is a specific business issue. A step can have important business consequences—for example, losses—so due to business reasons there must be a user called *process owner* responsible for them. The owner must be able to commit or reject the step. It is therefore highly desirable that the AS interfaces are well understood by the owner, and they should mirror the user knowledge domain and language. As such the interface should be declarative (saying what rather than how to do something), and usually coarse grained and based on user knowledge domain. Such an interface is *user-oriented*.

Any change of the interface of an AS *S* implies changes in all communication partners of *S*. A crucial property of the interface of *S* is therefore its stability in time. Service-oriented interfaces are usually based on the stabilized user knowledge domains. So there is a good chance that such interfaces need not be changed frequently, if ever.

A crucial advantage of SOA, especially of confederations, is that it enables integration of legacy systems. But such systems need not have any user-oriented interface. A good solution is the use of services of a new type: front-end gates. Front-end gate is a SOA variant of an adapter.

FRONT-END GATES (LOOSELY COUPLED PROXIES OR ADAPTERS)

The interfaces of existing services need not be satisfactory, as they are usually not user-oriented. A gate *G* from Figure 1 can be even based on such emergency techniques like terminal listening. Such techniques are necessary in the case when there is no available source code of the application *A*. Even in the case that the source is available, the interface can be based on such programming concept like remote method invocation (or remote procedure call). Such interfaces can hardly be well understood or easily used by users. This is a substantial drawback. The drawback was partly avoided using SOAP protocol in the document-encoding variant.

To solve this issue we can use a solution called *front-end gates* (FEG) generalizing the concept of connectors in Enterprise Service Bus (e.g., Sonic Software, 2004). FEG can be viewed as one implementation of adapters. We believe, however, that FEG is the most powerful adapter implementation. Compare also Façade or Adapter object-oriented patterns. Front-end gates seem to be a bit more general and more flexible concept. They can be easily modified to fulfill various needs, for example, to be transformed into a portal.

Front-end gate is constructed as a new service and "inserted" between its application service and the middleware (Figure 1). The FEG is technically a standard peer of the network. If we say that a FEG is "between" an application A and the middleware, we mean that the messages are sent possibly with the help of middleware by G of A to FEG and FEG sends them—maybe transformed—to the middleware.

G is a part of the program implementing application service A. G provides access to all capabilities of A.

Figure 1 depicts the logical role of FEG. The connection between the application service A and its FEG and between the middleware and FEG can be implemented in various ways. The messages from an application service (e.g., A1) to its FEG (e.g., FEG1) can be sent via middleware. If A1 and FEG1 reside on the same computer or if they work on a distributed operating system,

they can use the tools provided by the operating system for interprocess communication.

There can be more than one FEG for a service and more than one portal for the system. The resulting service-oriented system then can have the structure from Figure 2. Different FEG of a service can be used for different groups of partners.

The development of FEG has a lot in common with the development of portals, as in both cases the task is to develop an automaton transforming k-tuples of input messages into m-tuples of output messages. We can use such tools like XSLT (W3 Consortium, 1999), XSLT 2.0 (W3, 2007) or tools or algorithms known for compiler construction. So we can conclude that the interface of (application) services can always be user-oriented, if necessary. As we can have more front-end gates for an application service, we can provide different interfaces for different groups of communicating partners.

The architecture and development pattern FEG substantially reduces the development and

Figure 1. Connection of a front-end gate

Figure 2. Multiple front-end gates

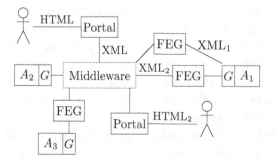

maintenance effort and costs. There are a couple of reasons for it: subsystems reusability (legacy systems, third-party products) and the reduction due to decomposition into autonomous components. Crucial is that FEG is designed as peer of the virtual peer-to-peer network too.

FEG is a generalization of the object-oriented concept of adapter, using the power of service-oriented design. It provides more complex message transformation. It can be easily modified to implement concepts of data store or user interface.

User-Oriented Interfaces, Front-End Gates, and Standards

The most important objection against user-oriented interfaces of services is based on the fact that at least nowadays and in the near future there is only a very little chance that such an interface is fully standardized. It is correct but if we want to use current universal standards, we have to give up the idea that we can use declarative, often coarse-grained interfaces and the advantages depending on it. We must moreover solve the problems related to the use of cumbersome, quickly changing and obsolete standard. A good compromise is preferable.

The use of standards like SOAP-RPC (remote procedure call) implies that we must use low-level concepts. The reward is that there are tools supporting the use of SOAP as well as such tools as WSDL, which allow obtaining of the definition of the interface in executable form, and a tool—not too successful—that allows the finding of an appropriate service. The tools are necessary in e-commerce where communication partner must in principle be looked for all over the world.

There is, however, a broad class of systems where the partners need not be looked for. The examples are e-government, health services network, global enterprises, and local authorities. In these cases, the disadvantages to have no standards can be balanced by the effects of user orientation of the services. The disadvantages can be further

reduced if the messages are in proprietary XML formats. Such messages can be encapsulated into SOAP. The result is SOAP-message encoding (SOAP-ME). SOAP-ME enables a quite good compromise, proprietary user-oriented messages with (maybe limited) possibility to look for communication partners with help of WSDL.

There can be further advantages in the future. The standardization of the user-oriented interfaces now would lead to premature standards. It will not be the case if the standards are based on the interface formats that have been used for some time. So it seems to be bearable to sacrifice standardization for some time (and associated tools as well), tune the message formats in practice and then propose the best solutions as standards.

Note that the user-oriented interfaces strongly tend to be coarse grained. It indicates (and to some degree contradicts) the recommendations from SOA Open Reference Model (MacKenzie et al., 2006) or at least indicates that there is a broad class of very important service-oriented systems for which the use of coarse-grained interfaces is essential. The possible confirmation of the statement is the success of SOAP - message encoding able to carry general XML documents.

COMPOSITE SERVICES

The front-end gates (FEG) are designed so that every FEG F enhances the interface of just one application service S. The implementation of F fulfills the requirement that all the messages for S as well as all the messages from S must pass the gate F (Figure 3). We say that we use logical view to point out that we show the connections of the provider and consumer of a message.

Assume that there are services $F, S_1, S_2, ... , S_n$ having the property that any message from an (outer) service O different from $F, S_1, S_2, ... , S_n$ to any service from $S_1, S_2, ... , S_n$ must pass F (must be sent through F) and any message from any service $S_1, S_2, ... , S_n$ for O must pass F (Figure 4).

Figure 3. Communication paths from the front-end gate F (logical view)

Figure 4. Composite service

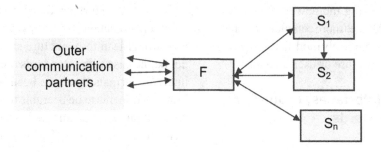

Figure 5. Process model and process control structure

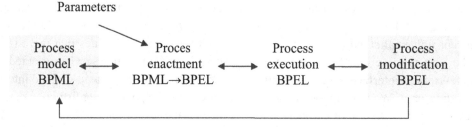

The collection of services F, S_1, S_2, ... , S_n is then called *composite service* with the head F^1.

The front-end gate generalized in this way has many properties of places in colored Petri nets (Jensen, 1997). We call it therefore *Generalized Petri Place,* as it provides more capabilities than places in colored Petri nets[2] do.

PROCESS MANAGERS

Now we can attempt to design a structure S able to control the activities of business processes, compare (Business Process Management Initiative, 2000, 2004). It is known that in peer-to-peer architectures the use of activities being "central"

should be minimized or even omitted. We shall therefore attempt to implement S not to be a part of or not to interact often with a central service (e.g., a central repository).

General schema of business process implementation (see chapter 18 in Král, 1998; Scacchi & Noll, 2005, Figures 5 and 6) is based on the following principles.

1. Every business process has its (process) owner, a person responsible for the business consequences of the process he/she owns. It implies that the owner must be able to supervise his/her business process steps and to monitor the progress of the process execution.

2. The model (definition) M of a business process P is developed; that is, P is modeled/specified. The model is written in the BPML language (Business Process Management Initiative, 2004).

3. P is enacted, that is, M is parametrized (e.g., it is stated how many products of what properties are to be produced) and transformed in a control structure C (Figure 6). Formally, the model of P in BPML is converted into C being in another language (typically BPEL; Andrews et al., 2003). More formally, the variables in M are replaced by the parameters and M slightly modified to produce C in BPEL.

4. P is executed, that is, C is used to control the actions required by P. It follows that C must store the state of the process.

5. During the execution of the process P the structure C can be modified to respond to unexpected problems and situations occurring during the process execution (rejects, failures, temporarily not available resources, and snags in process models)[3].

It is possible that C can be in some situations generated/specified directly by process owner or user, without having any model M. It is, however, usually not preferable. The points 1 and 5 imply that the interfaces of application services (possibly provided by their front-end gates) must be well understood by process owners. It is the application services that should have user-oriented interfaces, directly or via front-end gates.

If we want to implement business processes in service-oriented systems, we must decide how to represent M and C and how to implement the activities shown in Figure 6. We propose the following solution (Figure 7).

1. During the process initiation a new service (peer) P called *process manager*[4] is generated on the request of process owner. P reads the model M of the process from the process model repository or the user can generate the process model interactively. The model can be in BPML or any other process modeling language. P then uses the control structure C generated from M.

2. During execution of P, its control structure C can be online modified and the actions of P can be controlled by process owner. P communicates with services necessary to perform the steps of the process. The services performing the steps can again have their own business processes. The services can

Figure 6. Process enactment

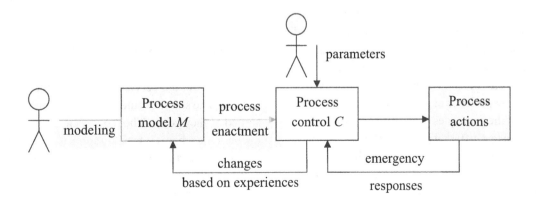

Figure 7. Implementation of business processes in SOA. Note that C can be edited from scratch (without data store of models)

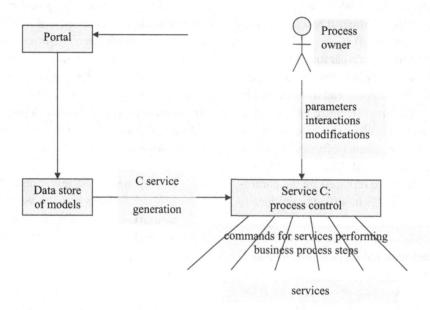

return the information about the results of their actions (OK, some problems occurred, failure) to *P*. Let us remember that it is advantageous if the communication is based on user-oriented protocol.

As the internal structure of process control service *P* is hidden behind the user-oriented formats of interfaces, *P* can use different process model (e.g., Aris (IDS Scheer), workflow (Workflow Management Coalition, 2004), BPEL (Andrews et al., 2003); even some fulltext-based description can be used here). It is very important, as the solution is less dependent on quickly changed cumbersome standards and can benefit from the experience of process owners and application of the principles of agile development. The users can use different process model techniques according their needs. Moreover, this proposal admits the application of newly developed or enhanced standards in the future.

The proposed solution reduces the intensive use of "central" services (the repository of process models) to at most one reading. We remind that such central services are often a bottleneck of the systems from the point of view of effectiveness as well as maintenance or design (compare the experience with UDDI service).

BUSINESS PROCESSES AND DATA STORES

Up to now we have not discussed the issue of how the service requests reach the services and the rules how the service selects the incoming request. The simplest rule is that the requests are settled as they come. The requests form a simple queue. This schema is broadly applied in message passing systems, especially in service-oriented systems. Often, however, a more intelligent request passing/accepting procedure is required.

Figure 8. The use of a data store to provide complex communication protocols

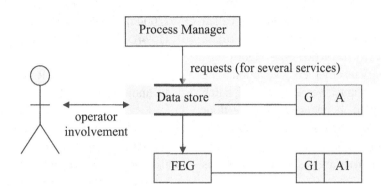

A request can be, for example, settled by several semi-equivalent services. The destination service then must be chosen by a specific procedure. It is also possible that the destination service selects itself the request for it. It can happen that a request cannot be temporarily settled. There can be optimization problems and sometime the operator involvement is required.

The data store service can be modified to implement a weaker form of the communication using the strategy publish-subscribe. Note that it can be understood as an enhancement of a communication protocol as well as a tool orchestrating the application services. In all these situations the request must be saved in a data store, selected by an algorithm (or by system operator) lately, and sent to a service to be executed.

Let us attempt to illustrate the power and flexibility of data stores and front-end gates on examples. We must take into account that in, for example, short series manufacturing and especially in technical maintenance or repairing of systems, the duration of process steps can vary, for example, due the influence of real-world processes. The services are partly interchangeable, as a request R can be settled by any service from A, B, or C, whereas similar request R can be settled

only by services B or D: This fact can depend on information known to humans only. The interface of the services need not be standardized. Implementation fulfilling such request can be based on the following way (compare some variants of the application of BizTalk by Microsoft):

1. The process manager can run several business processes in parallel,
2. The requests for application processes are sent into data store D, and
3. D selects (with an optional help of an operator) the requests to be sent to application services and then send to application services, possibly via FEG if message format transformation is necessary.

The process manager(s) then communicate(s) by a data-store service with application services in the way shown in Figure 8. Note that in this case the data store cannot be reasonably integrated into application services.

A good example of the use of data stores are information systems controlling the manufacturing of machine tool floor workshop of a medium-size enterprise producing short series products.

The enterprise level produces technological processes and generates the schedules of the processes. The collection of schedules is called floor schedule. According to several reasons (data quality, complexity of scheduling algorithms, missing data, various emergency situations) the floor schedule FS must be generated in batch mode and modified, if necessary, by the floor manager (operator). The floor schedule is generated at enterprise level by a scheduling algorithm *A*. The service requests are passed to workplaces (machine tools).

The activities of different parts of the floor (e.g., automated transport, signals from workplaces, automated interoperation warehouse) are supported by software services communicating online by exchange of messages (Figure 9). The scheduler algorithm in enterprise system was slow and it had to work in batch mode. The floor operator interpreted the schedule using flexible interface based on matrix-like structure depicting a segment of technological schedule around operation of interest and segments of the most relevant queues of operations of machine tools (Figure 10). The floor operator can easily modify the schedule using the schema from Figure 10. It suffices to change P2.y. The operator can navigate over the schedule using the interface from Figure 10.

Details can be found, for example, in Král, Cerny, and Dvorak (1987), Král & Žemlička (2004a), Král & Demner (1979), and Scheer (1994).

$sj - j$-th operation; $R.i - i$-th operation of the technologic chain R; $Pk - k$-th workplace

Such a solution is quite common. The authors have implemented it many years ago and the system was in use without any substantial maintenance until 2004 and survived several changes of the enterprise level. The floor manager interface to floor schedule is shown in Figure 10. The floor manager felt it as a comfortable support of his standard activities he had been used to. The business process restructuring was quite substantial but the related changes were at the floor level quite transparent.

Note that from technical point of view the data store service is used as a mean of integration the batch applications (scheduling) with classical "standard" service-oriented software intensive system controlling the technology of machine tool floor. The data store service containing the schedule orchestrates the coordination of the services of the floor control.

Figure 9. The structure of a flexible manufacture

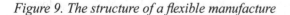

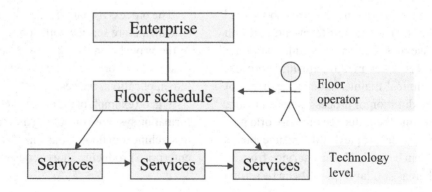

Figure 10. The floor schedule interface

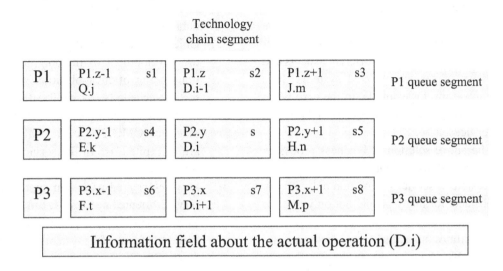

To summarize, the data store services can be used:

- To integrate batch subsystem into service oriented systems;
- To orchestrate the application services; and
- To enhance the capabilities of the middleware (e.g., by communication modes).

The service-oriented systems are often considered to be layered entities of five layers: communication, services, composite services, orchestrations, and user application layer. The issue is that some architecture services like front-end gates and generalized Petri places can provide capabilities being logically from different layers. Front end-gates can enhance communication but with a small modification they can be used to build composite services, portals, or data stores. Data stores can be used to enhance communication (e.g., to implement publish-subscribe strategy) but they can be very easily used as a powerful service orchestration tool.

ISSUES

The user-oriented interfaces of services are good for the stability of service-oriented systems and facilitate the design and control of business processes. Issues include the following.

- The interfaces of service-oriented systems must use communication formats that usually are not standardized enough yet. A proprietary XML dialect must be then designed. Such dialects are difficult to use in e-commerce (alliances) as in e-commerce the world-wide standards are preferred/necessary.
- User-oriented interfaces are coarse grained and based on user knowledge domain. They cannot contain detailed information on program structure allowing generation of a detailed framework of programs as we used to in object-oriented systems. It implies, however, that many object-oriented diagrams are of little or no use in service-oriented systems. So we can use only some

of UML diagrams for design of service-oriented systems. Examples are Use Case or Activity Diagrams. In fact, however, there are still no good tools for intuitive graphical representations of different aspects and views of service-oriented systems. It is unpleasant, for example, in the case when we need to depict various rules of data store services.

- The above solution of business processes based on process managers uses turns being feasible in service orientation only. It is an obstacle for many people not only due the fact that other diagrams must be used and sometimes no satisfactory diagrams are available[5], but also due to the fact that the basic attitudes and techniques are different. It is a consequence of the fact that service orientation is a paradigm different from the object-oriented one. There are different systems of patterns and antipatterns in both frameworks. As such the service-oriented patterns are difficult to be used by the people not familiar with service orientation. For example, there can be prejudices to apply some turns of dataflow diagrams or batch systems in service orientation.

- Service orientation is a great marketing challenge. The business strategy for the service-oriented systems must solve issues like the integration of third-party products and legacy systems, insourcing and outsourcing, and new business processes, especially for agreement negotiation.

Four different paradigms were used during the development of (large) software intensive systems:

1. Relational paradigm appropriate to be used in databases (and data tiers). Main diagrams are E-R diagrams;

2. Structured design and development used to integrate and orchestrate batch applications.

The building units were batch applications and data stores. Crucial role is played by data-flow diagrams;

3. Object-oriented paradigm to be used in the development of (monolithic) applications being often application services in service-oriented systems. The diagrams for the object-oriented paradigm are the UML diagrams (OMG, 2001). The UML diagrams are of limited use in the service-oriented framework; and

4. Service-oriented paradigm appropriate for service-oriented systems. It can be applied as an integration principle and philosophy of the development of the system infrastructure. Some UML diagrams and modified data-flow diagrams can be used; diagrams for some SOA aspects are to be invented yet.

Object orientation can be used in databases but there is no feasible solution here. Similarly, object orientation can be used in design of relation (DB) oriented systems but it usually has substantial drawbacks, especially in the area of interface and usability; unless it is combined with relational attitude (compare object-relational databases).

Service orientation is not optimal for the development of very small systems. It is feasible for many large systems, especially when existing systems must be integrated into a newly developed one.

The fact that there are four different paradigms has crucial practical consequences.

Each paradigm requires its specific techniques, marketing policies, staff skills, education, and software development processes. Service orientation and SOA is crucial for large and complex software intensive systems.

SERVICE ORIENTATION IS BOTH SIMPLE AND COMPLEX

Surprisingly enough, the main barrier of the proper use of service orientation is in its intuitive simplicity and its long term existence in a simple form in some process control systems. The architecture of service-oriented software systems (SOSS) is similar to real world (mass) service systems. Their basic principles are on abstract level quite simple. It, however, does not mean that the implementation of the principles and necessary skills are simple. The seeming simplicity of principles causes people not to be aware of risks and issues and to understand their consequences. They often think that new paradigm brings nothing essentially new and are usable to apply it properly.

Elements of service orientation have been used in batch systems often written in COBOL and real-time systems for decades. So the service orientation cannot be said to be completely new. The response of many people during the explanation of the principles of service orientation is that the principles are clear and not new. A deeper discussion and the practical activities show that a proper understanding of service orientation and skills to use them are missing. IT professionals often do not see why, where, and how to apply service orientation. An example: Many people are not able to see that SOA is the most effective way of integration of information systems of particular offices into an integrated information system of e-government. There are substantial marketing problems and problems related to business strategies of software vendors.

It was verified in practice that service orientation is a very powerful philosophy even in the case when no Web tools are used (compare the manufacturing support system described previously). But there is a prejudice that service orientation makes sense only when Web services are used (compare the flexible manufacturing system described in Král & Žemlička, 2004b, and the antipattern "SOA = Web services" from Ang et al., 2005; see also section "Business Processes and Data Stores" of this chapter).

A long term authors' practical experience show that the application of service orientation

is far from being simple. The reasons are mainly subjective; the main reason is underestimation of issues related to paradigm change. It includes:

1. The need of a deeper permanent collaboration with users, and new development processes, and form of requirement specification. It follows that IT people must be able to understand user knowledge domain (compare the need for versatility in Morello, 2005);

2. Changes in project management (iterative and especially incremental development);

3. Changes in skills and attitudes of both developers and users;

4. Resistance to changes of techniques (new tools, difference in programming techniques). Even worse: the developers often do not even see that their attitudes and skills are to be changed;

5. The need of new marketing strategies. In SOA it is possible to integrate services of different origin. It is a substantial marketing issue for software vendors. It is further open to what an optimal degree of standardization is and what standards are to be used. This issue is not only technical, but it also influences marketing; and

6. The necessity to develop tools specific for service-oriented systems, especially the modeling tools.

7. Paradigm change. Some object-oriented antipatterns are crucial patterns in service-oriented systems (Král & ·Žemlička, 2007)

CONCLUSION

The trends toward globally used software systems controlling almost everything require extremely complex software systems. It implies that almost all modern software is or is a part of software intensive systems. The only feasible way of development, use, and maintenance of the software in the software intensive systems is to apply service orientation philosophy and paradigm.

Service orientation (SO) is the only known feasible solution enabling a seamless reuse of legacy systems and integration of third-party products. SO simplifies the development as it enables the incremental development, easy and effective prototyping, agile development with user involvement supported by powerful tools for correct requirement specification[6], debugging tools, and even the effort reductions due the decomposition into small components (it is a consequence of the empirical law Effort = $c \cdot$ Length$^{9/8}$).

SO simplifies incremental maintenance and gradual modernization. SO provides new desirable capabilities for users, for example, an agile use of business processes. SO provides tools for management like easy insourcing and outsourcing, new ways for the support of cooperation with business partners like CRM and SCM and flexible cooperation with applications like Microsoft Office or OpenOffice or statistical packages like Statistica or SAS.

Last, but maybe the first: Commercial service/oriented systems and service-oriented tools like ESB, NetWeaver, and so forth, become the central paradigm of practically all software vendors. It cannot be the marketing trick only and not a buzzword only. Exceptionally, it can be a buzzword for those who are unable to use SO properly.

The service orientation is therefore the leading edge of contemporary software engineering. We believe that service orientation is the only way of development of software having all the substantial properties of high-tech products.

SO as a specific paradigm will be accepted, adopted, and governed (technically and also as a business challenge) fully in the future, although probably not in the near future. Open problems of SO adoptions are: marketing, modeling, business strategies, and education of business and IT experts. Contemporary information systems are

as rule software intensive. Our analysis as well as practice indicates that the only feasible way of their development, maintenance, and proper use is service orientation.

FUTURE RESEARCH DIRECTIONS

The future research must address the problems mentioned in the paragraph Issues. We believe that the research must start with analysis of the experiences with SOA, business experiences inclusive.

From the technical point of view it is crucial to analyze and enhance the tools used for the development of front-end gates and business managers as the techniques discussed above can be challenged by low efficiency of the tools like XSLT that moreover are not user-friendly enough.

It is also necessary to research impacts of the use of service orientation to the requirements on the professional profile of IT professionals. It is likely that the service orientation enforce some significant changes to the IT experts' curricula.

ACKNOWLEDGMENT

This research was partially supported by the Program "Information Society" under project 1ET100300517.

REFERENCES

Andrews, T., Curbera, F., Dholakia, H., Goland, Y., Klein, J., Leymann, F., et al. (2003). *Specification: Business process execution language for Web services version 1.1*. Retrieved March 6, 2008, from http://www-106.ibm.com/developerworks/library/ws-bpel/

Ang, J., Cherbakov, L., & Ibrahim, M. (2005). *SOA antipatterns*. Retrieved March 6, 2008, from http://www-128.ibm.com/developerworks/web-services/library/ws-antipatterns/

Bajana, D., Borovcová, A., Čurn, J., Fojta, R., Ignáth, Š., Malohlava, M., et al. (2005). *Výstupy projektu "Hodnocení kvality škol"* (in Czech: Outputs of the project "Evaluation of the quality of schools").

Beck, K. (1999). *Extreme programming explained: Embrace change.* Boston: Addison-Wesley.

Beck, K., Beedle, M., van Bennekum, A., Cockburn, A., Cunningham, W., Fowler, M., et al. (2001). *Agile programming manifesto.* Retrieved March 6, 2008, from http://www.agilemanifesto.org/

Brown, W. J., Malveau, R. C., McCormick, I., H.W., & Mowbray, T. J. (1998). *AntiPatterns: Refactoring software, architectures, and projects in crisis.* New York: John Wiley & Sons.

Bureš, T., & Plášil, F. (2004). Communication style driven connector configurations. *Software engineering research and applications* (Vol. 3026 of *LNCS*, pp. 102-116). Berlin: Springer-Verlag.

Business Process Management Initiative. (2000). *Business process management initiative home page.* Retrieved March 6, 2008, from http://www.bpmi.org/

Business Process Management Initiative. (2004). *Business process modeling language.* Retrieved March 6, 2008, from http://www.bpmi.org/downloads/BPML-BPEL4WS.pdf

IDS Scheer. *Aris process platform.* Retrieved March 6, 2008, from http://www.ids-scheer.com/international/english/products/31207

Jensen, K. (1997). Coloured petri nets. Basic concepts, analysis methods and practical use. *Monographs in theoretical computer science* (2nd ed.). Springer-Verlag.

Král, J. (1998). *Informační Systémy,* (in Czech: *Information systems*). Veletiny, Czech Republic: Science.

Král, J., Černý, J., & Dvořák, P. (1987). Technology of FMS control software development. In G. Menga & V. Kempe (Eds.), *Proceedings of the Workshop on Information in Manufacturing Automation,* Dresden, Germany.

Král, J., & Demner, J. (1979). Towards reliable real time software. In *Proceedings of IFIP Conference Construction of Quality Software,* North Holland, (pp. 1-12).

Král, J., & Žemlička, M. (2002). Autonomous components. In M. H. Hamza (Ed.), *Applied informatics* (pp. 125-130). Anaheim: ACTA Press.

Král, J., & Žemlička, M. (2004a). Architecture and modeling of service-oriented systems. In P. Vojtáš, M. Bieliková, B. Charon-Bost, & O. Sýkora (Eds.), *Proceedings of SOFSEM 2005 Communications,* (pp. 71-80). Bratislava, Slovakia: Slovak Society for Computer Science.

Král, J., & Žemlička, M. (2004b). Service orientation and the quality indicators for software services. In R. Trappl (Ed.), *Cybernetics and systems* (Vol. 2, pp. 434-439). Vienna, Austria: Austrian Society for Cybernetic Studies.

Král, J., & Žemlička, M. (2005). Implementation of business processes in service-oriented systems. In *Proceedings of 2005 IEEE International Conference on Services Computing* (Vol. II, pp. 115-122). Los Alamitos, CA, USA: IEEE CS Press.

Král, J., Žemlička, M., & Kopecký, M. (2006). Software confederations—an architecture for agile development in the large. In P. Dini (Ed.), *Proceedings of the International Conference on Software Engineering Advances (ICSEA'06),* (p. 39). Los Alamitos, CA, USA: IEEE CS Press.

Král, J., & Žemlička, M. (2007). Crucial patterns in service-oriented architecture. In *Proceedings of the ICDT Conference,* (p. 133). Los Alamitos, CA, USA: IEEE CS Press.

MacKenzie, C. M., Laskey, K., McCabe, F., Brown, P. F., & Metz, R. (2006, July 19). *Refer-*

ence model for service-oriented architecture 1.0, committee specification 1. Retrieved March 6, 2008, from http://www.oasis-open.org/committees/download.php/19361/soa-rm-cs.pdf

Morello, D. (2005). *The IT professional outlook: Where will we go from here?* Gartner Group.

OMG. (2001). *Unified modeling language.* Retrieved March 6, 2008, from http://www.omg.org/technology/documents/formal/uml.htm

Scacchi, W., & Noll, J. (2005). *Dynamic process enactment, discovery, and recovery.* Retrieved March 6, 2008, from http://www.ics.udi.edu/~wscacchi/Papers/New/Proposal-abridged.pdf

Scheer, A.-W. (1994). *CIM—computer integrated manufacturing: Towards the factory of the future* (3rd ed., revised and enlarged). Berlin.

Sonic Software. (2004). *Enterprise service bus.* Retrieved March 6, 2008, from http://www.sonicsoftware.com/products/sonic_esb/

Telelogic. *Tau home page.* Retrieved March 6, 2008, from http://www.telelogic.com/products/tau/

W3 Consortium. (1999). *XSL transformations (XSLT).* Retrieved March 6, 2008, from http://www.w3c.org/TR/xslt. W3C Recommendation

W3 Consortium. (2007). *XSL transformations (XSLT) Version 2.0.* Retrieved March 6, 2008, from http://www.w3c.org/TR/xslt20/. W3C Recommendation

Workflow Management Coalition. (2004). Workflow specification. Retrieved March 6, 2008, from http://www.wfmc.org/standards/docs/Wf-XML-11.pdf

ADDITIONAL READING

Adams, J., Koushik, S., Vasudeva, G., & Galambos, G. (2001). *Patterns for e-business: A strategy for reuse.* MC Press.

Allen, P. (2006). *Service orientation, winning strategies and best practices.* Cambridge, UK: Cambridge University Press.

Bieberstein, N., Bose, S., Walker, L., & Lunch, A. (2005). Impact of service-oriented architecture on enterprise systems, organizational structures, and individuals. *IBM Systems Journal, 44*(4), 691-708.

Bloomberg, J., & Schmelzer, R. (2006). *Service orient or be doomed! How service orientation will change your business.* Hoboken, NJ, USA: John Wiley.

Carter, S. (2007). The new language of business. SOA & Web 2.0. IBM Press.

Chaudron, M., van Hee, K., & Somers, L. (2003). Use cases as workflows. W. M. P. van der Aalst et al. (Eds.), *BPM 2003* (Vol. 2678 of *LNCS*, pp. 88-103). Berlin Heidelberg: Springer-Verlag.

Coenen, A. (2006). *SOA case study: Agility in practice.* Retrieved March 6, 2008, from http://www.opengroup.org/projects /soa-case-studies/uploads/40/11405/SOA_Agility_in_Practice.pdf

Erl, T. (2005). Service-oriented architecture: Concepts, technology, and design. Prentice Hall PTR.

Fielding, R. T., & Taylor, R. N. (2002). Principled design of the modern Web architecture. *ACM Transactions on Internet Technology, 2*(2),115-150.

Fuller, T., & Morgan, S. (2006). Data replication as an enterprise SOA antipattern. *Microsoft Architect Journal.* Retrieved March 6, 2008, from http://msdn2.microsoft.com/en-us/arcjournal/bb245678.aspx

Jacobs, R. (2006). Patterns of SOA.

Jones, S. (2005). Toward an acceptable definition of service. *IEEE Software, 22*(3), 87-93.

Jones, S. (2006). *SOA anti-patterns*. Retrieved March 6, 2008, from http://www.infoq.com/articles/SOA-anti-patterns

Kloppmann, M., Koenig, D., Leymann, F., Pfau, G., Rickayzen, A., von Riegen, C., et al. (2005). *Ws-bpel extension for people—bpel4people*. Retrieved March 6, 2008, from ftp://www6.software.ibm.com/software/developer/library/ws-bpel4people.pdf

Král, J., & Žemlička, M. (2005a). Architecture, specification, and design of service-oriented systems. In Z. Stojanovic, & A. Dahanayake (Eds.), *Service-oriented software system engineering: Challenges and practices* (pp. 182-200). Hershey, PA, USA: Idea Group.

Král, J., & Žemlička, M. (2005b). What literacy for software developers. In D. Carbonara (Ed.), *Technology literacy uses in learning environments* (pp. 274-287), Hershey, PA, USA: Idea Group.

Král, J., & Žemlička, M. (2006). Software architecture for evolving environment. In K. Kontogiannis, Y. Zou, & M. D. Penta (Eds.), *Software technology and engineering practice* (pp. 49-58). Los Alamitos, CA, USA: IEEE Computer Society.

Král, J., & Žemlička, M. (2007). The most important service-oriented antipatterns. In *Proceedings of the International Conference on Software Engineering Advances (ICSEA'07)*, (p. 29). Los Alamitos, CA, USA: IEEE Computer Society.

Lauesen, S. (2002). *Software requirements: Styles and techniques*. Addison-Wesley.

Margolis, B. (2007). *SOA for the business developer: Concepts, BPEL, and SCA*. Mc Press.

Marks, E., & Bell, M. (2006). *Service oriented architecture: A planning and implementation guide for business and technology*. Hoboken, NJ, USA: John Wiley & Sons.

Marks, E., & Werrell, M. (2003). *Executive's guide to Web services*. Hoboken, NJ, USA: John Wiley & Sons.

Modi, T. (2006). *SOA antipatterns*. Retrieved March 6, 2008, from http://www.ebizq.net/hot_topics/soa/features/7238.html

zur Muehlen, M., Nickerson, J., & Swenson, K. D. (2005). Developing Web services choreography standards—the case of REST vs. SOAP. *Decision Support Systems*, 40(1), 9-29.

Neill, C. J., & Laplante, P. A. (2006). Antipatterns: Identification, refactoring, and management. *Applied software engineering series* (Vol. 2). CRC Press.

O'Brien, J. A. (2004a). *Introduction to information systems* (12th ed.). McGraw-Hill.

O'Brien, J. A. (2004b). *Management information systems* (6th ed.). McGraw-Hill.

Pulier, E., & Taylor, H. (2005). *Understanding enterprise SOA*. Greenwich: Manning Publications.

Sommerville, I. (1996). *Software engineering* (8th edition). Reading, MA, USA: Addison-Wesley.

Yourdon, E. (1988). *Modern structured analysis* (2nd ed.). Prentice Hall.

Žemlička, M., & Král, J. (2004). *Legacy systems as kernel of Web services* (Tech. Rep. No. 2004/1). Prague, Czech Republic: Charles Univerity, Faculty of Mathematics and Physics, Department of Software Engineering.

ENDNOTES

1   It is obvious that for the communication partners the composite service has all the properties of services.

2   A Petri net is a network of processes and places. Processes send messages (called

colored tokens) to places. Each place can, under some conditions, consume some input tokens and send output tokens to some processes. Exact definition can be seen in Jensen (1997). Petri nets of various types are widely used in the models of parallel processes. We suppose that the similarity is of practical as well as theoretical importance.

3   Similar procedure can be used in contract-driven transactions.

4   It can be viewed as a (new function of a) portal.

5   We were faced with this problem during writing this chapter as well.

6   It is well known that requirements specification is the main cause of process failures or challenges. Compare Morello (2005).

Section II
Requirements, Changes, and Tracability

Chapter IV
From Scenarios to Requirements in Mobile Client–Server Systems

Alf Inge Wang
Norwegian University of Science and Technology, Norway

Carl-Fredrik Sørensen
Norwegian University of Science and Technology, Norway

Hien Nam Le
Norwegian University of Science and Technology, Norway

Heri Ramampiaro
Norwegian University of Science and Technology, Norway

Mads Nygård
Norwegian University of Science and Technology, Norway

Reidar Conradi
Norwegian University of Science and Technology, Norway

ABSTRACT

This chapter describes a requirement analysis framework that may be used as a tool for developing client-server systems for mobile workers. The framework concerns the initial analysis process for the development of a mobile system starting by describing scenarios of the work of mobile workers and resulting in a description of priorities both nonfunctional and functional requirements of the end-system. The framework describes a three step requirement process that includes 1) Elicit scenarios, 2) Scenario analysis, and 3) Requirement analysis. These steps will produce outputs that will be used to assess the requirements of the system. The requirement analysis process is described in detail through templates used to produce output and illustrating examples from the analysis of the development of mobile IT-support system.

INTRODUCTION

The development in mobile computing has changed the way we communicate and work. Mobile phones, smart phones, and PDAs, whose computing capacities become more and more powerful in terms of processing speed, storage capacity and operating time, have become necessary tools through functionality such as SMS, calendars, and WAP-browsers. The more powerful mobile devices have made it possible to create software systems for mobile workers that can better support and also improve their work processes. Such systems typically consist of various mobile clients connected to a server. They provide the mobile worker with information related to the running of planned tasks, and opportunities for filling in forms and reports on various locations, while being on the move.

At the same time, many wireless network technologies are also developed and deployed, for example, Bluetooth, wireless USB, wireless LAN or Universal Mobile Telecommunications System (UMTS). Many mobile devices can communicate with other electronic devices in the working environment, making it possible to make measurements and take advantage of services in the work environment through wireless communication. The environment for accessing and processing information is rapidly changing from stationary to mobile and location independent. This new work environment, called the mobile work environment, allows people to work in flexible and efficient ways.

A mobile environment is different from traditional distributed environments due to its unique characteristics such as the mobility of users or computers, the limitation of computing capacity of mobile devices, and the frequent and unpredictable disconnection of wireless networks (Forman & Zahorjan, 1994; Satyanarayanan, 1996). Therefore, development of mobile systems is different from development of distributed systems. In other words, when designing a mobile

system, we have to overcome challenges due to physical mobility of the clients, the portability features of mobile devices and the fact that the communication is wireless. Thus, it is important that these issues are examined carefully when considering the system requirements, in terms of both functional and nonfunctional requirements. As defined in Sindhgatta and Thonse (2005), (IEEE), functional requirements include all the logical and specific behaviours of a system, while nonfunctional requirements concern the overall characteristics of the system-like performance, reliability and security. Note that, in mobile systems, the nonfunctional requirements play vital roles in system development.

We have developed a requirement analysis framework that examines important issues to be considered when designing and developing such mobile systems. The framework concerns the initial analysis process in the development of a mobile system starting by describing scenarios of the work of the mobile workers[1], and resulting in a description of priority, nonfunctional and functional requirements of the end-system.

In this chapter, we will describe the MOWAHS analysis framework consisting of a process, the characterisation of scenarios, computation of complexity indicators, and determination of nonfunctional and functional requirements. One important goal of this framework is to identify the parts that are most complex and perhaps hardest to implement in a mobile support system. The framework has previously been successfully used to analyse mobile scenarios such as mobile journalists, mobile researchers and m-learning (Ramampiaro, Wang, et al., 2003) to compare their characteristics. The framework has also been used to develop a mobile IT-support system (Wang, Sørensen, et al., 2005).

Our framework is aimed at development of systems for supporting any kind of mobile workers, like craftsmen, salesmen, emergency staff, police, public transportation drivers, and service staff. For system developers, we expect that they have a basic knowledge of software engineering for he/she to be able to use our MOWAHS framework to derive the requirements. This includes knowledge of all relevant phases in a software development life cycle (e.g., the waterfall model and the like). Knowledge of UML would also be useful.

BACKGROUND

The process to identify the requirements of a mobile client-server-based system is very different from a nonmobile one. This is due to the unique characteristics of mobile environments that are the mobility of users or computers, the limitation of computing capacity of mobile devices, and the frequent and unpredictable disconnections of wireless networks. In this section, we first address the main characteristics of mobile environments, which have a strong impact on the behaviours of mobile clients and the development process of mobile systems. Later, we review work related to our MOWAHS requirement analysis framework.

The main characteristics of the mobile environments that are addressed in this section include: the mobility of clients, the limitation of wireless communications, and the resource constraints of mobile computing devices.

Physical Mobility

Mobility is the main characteristic that distinguishes the mobile environments from the traditional distributed environments. Table 1 summarizes and compares the characteristics of mobile and nonmobile environments. In traditional distributed environments, computers are stationary hosts. In mobile environments, mobile computers are continuously moving from one geographical location to another.

The mobility of a mobile host is a real-time movement. Therefore, it is affected by many environmental conditions. For example, a preplanned travel route of a mobile host can be changed because of traffic jams or weather conditions. If there is a mobile task[2] whose operations depend on the travel route of the mobile host, these operations can become invalid or extra support may being required. For example, a new route-map directory must be downloaded into the mobile host if the travel route is changed. Moreover, the movement of a mobile host can also depend on the objective of the mobile task. For example, an ambulance wants to arrive at the accident scene by selecting the shortest route within the fastest allowed speed, a bus must follow the strict timetable of a bus route, while a postman only wants to travel through each road once. During the movement, a mobile host can stop at some locations for some periods; therefore, the mobility of the mobile host includes both moving and nonmoving intervals.

Table 1. Nonmobile vs. mobile environments

	Nonmobile environments	Mobile environments
Computing hosts	Stationary sites	Mobile and nonmobile hosts
	Powerful computing capacity	Limited computing capacity of mobile hosts
	Reliable computing hosts	Less reliable computing hosts
Network connectivity	Wired and high-speed networks	Wireless, unstable, and lower-speed networks
	Reliable networks	Unreliable, error-prone, frequent and long disconnection periods

The location of a mobile host changes dynamically and frequently in accordance with the speed and the direction of the movement. The faster the mobile host moves, the more frequently the environment changes. The objective of mobile tasks may also specify the locations at which the mobile host must be in order to carry out the mobile tasks. For example, a computer technician must come to the customer locations to fix computer problems. A mobile support system must provide the utilities to manage the locations of mobile hosts (a demand which is not needed in a distributed environment). Changes of locations can cause changes in the operating environments of mobile hosts, for example, network addresses, communication protocols, mobile services, or location dependent data (Pitoura & Samaras, 1998; Ramampiaro, Wang, et al., 2003).

The behaviour of a mobile host describes the actual mobility states of the mobile host. While operating in mobile environments, the mobile host can be either in *stopped* or *moving* state. The two movement states are explained as follows:

- **Stopped:** A mobile host is said to be in the stopped state either when its movement velocity is zero, or when the location of the mobile host is not considered changing within a period of time. For example, a bus stops at a bus stop to pick up passengers, a salesman is selling products at a shopping centre, or two mobile hosts are moving close to each other.

- **Moving:** A mobile host is in the moving state either when its movement velocity has a value greater than zero, or when the location of the mobile host is considered changing over time. For example, a bus is moving along a road, or a salesperson travels to new places during the day. While in the moving state, the mobile host can continuously change its velocity and direction of movement.

Further, the behaviour of a mobile host can affect the tasks that are carried out by the mobile host, for example, a public transport vehicle needs to strictly follow a timetable. On the other hand, the movement of a mobile host may also be affected by the surrounding environmental conditions, for example, traffic jams. The movement behaviour of the mobile host demands additional support such as location management (Majumdar, Ramamritham, et al., 2003), and awareness of location dependent data (Dunham & Kumar 1998).

Mobile Devices

There are many types of mobile computing devices such as mobile phones, laptop computers, or personal digital assistants (PDAs). Mobile devices typically are smaller and lighter than stationary computers. Consequently, mobile computers have limited energy supply, limited storage capacity, and limited functionality compared to stationary computers. The characteristics of mobile computing devices are elaborated as follows.

- **Limited energy supply:** The operation of mobile computers heavily depends on the electrical power of batteries. This limited energy supply is one of the major disadvantages of mobile computing devices. The energy consumption of a mobile device depends on the power of electronic components installed on the mobile device (e.g., mobile network, CPU, display, etc.) and how these components are used (e.g., brightness of screen, reduced CPU speed, etc.). Moreover, the battery lifetime also depends on the number of applications and the application types that operate on the mobile devices (Flinn & Satyanarayanan, 1999). For example, a mobile phone can live up to 5 days, while a laptop may only be able to operate for several hours. Mobile applications that are executed on a mobile host may be interrupted or rescheduled if the mobile host is exhausting its energy supply.

- **Limited storage capacity:** The storage capacity of a mobile computer (i.e., hard disks or main memory) is much less than for a stationary computer and is harder to be expanded. Therefore, a mobile host may not be able to store the necessary data that is required for its operations in a disconnected mode (Pitoura & Samaras, 1998). Consequently, applications on mobile clients may be delayed due to data unavailability, or may require longer processing time due to frequent memory swapping operations.

- **Limited functionality:** The functionality of mobile devices is also limited in terms of the graphical user interface, the application functionalities, and the processing power. Therefore, a mobile host may be unable to perform some operations, or may require longer processing time to perform these operations. For example, the small screen of a mobile phones makes is hard or impossible to display full-size Web pages.

In the process of eliciting the requirements for a system to support mobile work, the mobile device characteristics must be taken into account. The limitations of the mobile device will naturally be a part of the nonfunctional requirement, but they will also affect the functional requirements, for example, be able to buffer information on device to save battery on network usage.

Wireless Communication

Mobile hosts communicate with other hosts via wireless networks. Compared to wired networks, wireless networks are characterized by lower bandwidth, unstable networks, disconnections, and adhoc connectivity (Schneiderman, 2002). The characteristics of wireless networks are described as follows.

- **Lower bandwidth:** The bandwidth of a wireless network is lower than for a wired network. A mobile network does not have the capacity of wired networks. For example, a mobile GSM network has bandwidth in the order of 10Kbps, a wireless local area network (WLAN) has bandwidths of 10Mbps; while gigabits (Gbps) are common in wired LANs (Schneiderman, 2002). Therefore, it may take a longer time for a mobile host to transfer the same amount of information via a wireless network than with a wired network.

- **Unstable networks:** A wireless network has high error rates, and the bandwidth of a wireless network is variable. Due to errors during data transmission, the same data packages may have to be retransmitted many times; thus, extra overhead in communication inducing higher costs. Due to the varying bandwidth, it is hard to estimate the time required to completely transmit a data package from/to a mobile host. These problems will affect the data availability of mobile hosts. As a result, the executions of applications at the mobile clients can be delayed or aborted.

- **Disconnections:** Wireless networks pose disconnection problems. Disconnection in communication may interrupt or delay the execution of transactions. Further, ongoing transactions may be aborted due to disconnections. Disconnection in communication is categorized according to two dimensions: disconnection period and disconnection rate.

  o **Disconnection period:** The disconnection period indicates how long a mobile host is disconnected. While being disconnected, the mobile host will not be able to communicate with other hosts for sharing data. Furthermore, the duration of a disconnected period of a mobile host is not always as planned; that is, it may be longer than expected. A mobile system must be able to continuously support mobile clients while a mobile host is being disconnected by caching needed data in beforehand.

o **Disconnection rate:** The disconnection rate indicates how often the wireless communication is interrupted within a predefined unit of time. The execution of mobile applications may be affected when an interruption occurs. If the applications on the mobile host are executing collaborative operations with other applications on other mobile hosts, the collaborative activities may be suspended or aborted. To cope with such problems, a mobile system must be able to support mobile transactions to resume at or recover from previously interrupted points.

• **Adhoc connectivity:** The wireless network technologies introduce a new way to support direct and nearby communication among mobile hosts, called *any-to-any* or *mobile peer-to-peer* communication (Flinn & Satyanarayanan, 1999; Ratner, Reiher, et al., 2001). For example, two mobile hosts can directly share information via the support of Bluetooth or infrared technologies (Pradhan, Lawrence, et al., 2005). The characteristics of this peer-to-peer communication are: unstructured (i.e., adhoc), short-range, and mobility dependent (Ratner, Reiher, et al., 2001; Le & Nygård, 2005).

The issues high-lighted above concerning wireless communication is mainly related to nonfunctional requirements, but some aspects will also affect the functionality in the system like transaction support to handle disconnections.

Operations of Mobile Clients

The operational behaviour of mobile hosts depends on the availability of mobile resources such as network connectivity and battery energy. We distinguish two operational modes for mobile hosts in mobile environments: *interactional and isolation*. These operational modes of mobile hosts are explained as follows:

• **Interactional.** When a mobile host is sharing data with other hosts, it is said to be in the interactional mode. The two essential prerequisite conditions for the interactional mode are: (1) the mobile host is operational, and (2) network connectivity is available. It is not necessary that the mobile host connects to other hosts all the time. This may help the mobile host to save battery energy and reduce the communication cost. However, in the interactional mode, communication channels between the mobile host and other hosts must always be available and present whenever needed.

• **Isolation.** When a communication channel between a mobile host and other hosts is not available, the mobile host is disconnected from other hosts and is said to be in the isolation mode. There are many factors that contribute to disconnections of a mobile host; for example, the mobile host moves out of the wireless communication range, network services are not available, or the mobile host is running out of energy.

The behaviour of mobile hosts also illustrates the correlations among the different characteristics of mobile environments. Disconnection in communication may be the result of the movement of mobile hosts or the limitation of mobile resources. When mobile hosts communicate with others via short-range wireless network technologies, for example, infrared, Bluetooth or wireless LAN, the communication will be disconnected if the mobile hosts move outside the communication range. Mobile hosts may be disconnected more frequently and for shorter periods, that is, seconds or minutes, when they move in and out of the shadows of physical obstructions such as high buildings. The disconnection periods may also be longer, that is, hours or days, when mobile hosts stay in some locations within which the wireless network service is not available. Further, a mobile host may volunteer to disconnect if its supplied energy is running out.

Related Work

Scenario analysis is used in requirement engineering (Sutcliffe 1998), and thus the use of scenarios is not novel. The novel part is the focus on mobility issues in the requirement engineering process. Thus, this section will outline research that is related to characterisation of mobile scenarios that support development, that is, requirement analysis and design, of mobile applications. Many research papers on mobile work have proposed a support system for specific mobile work scenarios, resulting in the development of tailor-made systems (Sindhgatta & Thonse, 2005; Florio & Deconinck, 2002). Other papers (Forman & Zahorjan, 1994; Satyanarayanan, 1996; Zimmerman, 1999) have attempted to give an overview of the characteristics of mobile computing based on state-of-the-art technology. However, to our knowledge, there is no other similar characterisation framework for mobile works.

Satyanarayanan (1996) identifies four constraints of mobile computing concerned with limited resources, physical security (e.g., theft), communication and durability issues. Another approach is proposed by Forman and Zahorjan (1994) who examine three basic features of mobile computing including wireless communication, mobility and portability. These two approaches provide different ways of addressing mobility issues. The former focuses on connectivity issues, while the latter deals with Quality of Service (QoS), such as network bandwidth and device durability. There are several disadvantages of these proposals. First, the strong connection among these features of mobile computing has not been addressed. Second, how these features impact the operation of mobile clients, that is, mobile works, has not been discussed.

Rakotonirainy (1999) discusses current and future technologies (e.g., CORBA and mobile IP) adaptable to mobile computing environments. For this, he presents a scenario revealing the limitations of the current technologies. Although characteristics of mobile work may be derived from this approach, it does not provide a comprehensive framework for characterising mobile work environments.

Kangas and Kinnunen (2005) have argued and demonstrated that the most important aspect of the design process for mobile applications is the usability of the final products. This means that important features such as applied technologies and contextual design must be taken into consideration (otherwise, the developers may not know enough about the real needs or expectations of the end clients). Maccari (1999) also presents an example of requirement engineering challenges in the mobile telephone industry due to the complex mobile phone architecture and its corresponding performance. The author argues that requirement engineering for mobile telephones is a collaborative task and has to cope with many issues, such as protocols and technology standards. Further, the limitations of wireless devices, such as network connectivity and speed, imply important challenges that developers have to deal with. However, the author has not shown how developers can be supported to be aware of these factors.

Zimmerman (1999) suggests a MOBILE framework for determining when mobile computing technology should be used to solve challenges related to mobility. This framework focuses on current technology and software development trends in mobile computing. Further, some common scenarios are discussed, including news reporting and hotel operations. The framework provides a useful overview of support needed for specific mobile environments. However, the framework does not provide any guidelines for how to analyse or design systems for mobile support.

Designing applications for mobile platforms is more challenging than traditional software design (Holtzblatt, 2005). Holtzblatt presents a contextual design method, where customer centring plays a major role, for mobile applications. In this customer-centred design methodology, the users' situation, that is, the tasks, operating conditions, and device capacities, must be taken into account. However, this method is mainly focusing on the mobile devices, while other challenging factors like client mobility or network issues have not been fully addressed.

Raptis, Tselios, et al. (2005) have proposed a context-based design framework for mobile applications. In this framework, context is defined in four dimensions: system, infrastructure, domain and physical context. The authors have discussed in detail how such context factors impact the design decisions of mobile applications. Furthermore, the paper addresses how developers should take into consideration such context information. The disadvantage of the proposal is that the context is too coarse-grained to be useful. For example, the clients are either fixed or mobile. In our characterisation framework, we apply more fine-grained levels for the mobility of clients, that is, our framework ought to be more suitable for mobile application development.

The related work discussed above mainly focuses on the technical aspects of mobile computing. Our framework investigates mobile computing from another point of view, by focusing on the mobile scenarios to be supported and the identification of various system complexities introduced by the scenarios. In addition, our framework focuses on software support for mobile works and identifies issues that are not directly related to mobility, like process and transactional infrastructure. This is especially useful in design and development of systems for mobile work environment.

MOWAHS REQUIREMENT ANALYSIS FRAMEWORK

This section describes the MOWAHS requirement analysis framework. The starting point for using this framework is a mobile scenario. Using the mobile scenario, we can derive requirements based on an analysis of the tasks and roles described by the scenario. Identification and specification of requirement is useful with respect to the design and development of systems to support for mobile work.

The first question is, however, what minimum knowledge is required, or how much knowledge is expected to use the framework. To answer this question, the underlying assumption is that a user of the framework must have basic knowledge of software engineering to be able to use the MOWAHS framework to derive requirements. This includes knowledge of all relevant phases in a software development life cycle (e.g., the waterfall model, the spiral model, RUP, etc.). Knowledge of UML would also be useful.

The second question concerns the completeness of the scenarios. What is lacking when deriving requirements from the scenarios? To be able to produce a complete requirement specification, scenarios that cover all relevant aspects (also the nonmobile parts) are needed. However, this cannot be guaranteed with our framework due to following:

- The scenario description may be subjective and could be dependent on the person that performs the description; and
- Our focus is mainly on mobility; thus the framework will normally not include aspects not related to mobility.

Further, the produced requirements are not formal; thus, two developers will rarely produce identical requirements. However, this is not the ultimate goal of the framework. Rather, it emphasises on highlighting different aspects of the scenario to get as complete requirements as possible (with focus on mobility aspects). The framework is, thus, meant to act as a guideline for developers to extract requirements from scenarios. This means that the main contributions relate to the process of producing requirements and comprehensive checklists useful for developers to identifying requirements.

Before the MOWAHS requirement analysis framework is described in detail, a scenario that will be used as an example for the rest of the chapter is introduced to illustrate how the framework can be applied to a scenario.

The scenario is based on experiences from an IT-support organisation that wanted to look into the possibilities of introducing mobile clients to its existing Web-based system to support its daily work. A typical working day for the IT-support organisation consists of buying new hardware and software, installing new hardware and software, updating hardware and software, and assisting users with various problems concerning hardware

and software. A nonmobile system was used to manage incoming requests form users sent by e-mail or filled out using Web forms. The system supported assignment of incoming tasks to various persons within the organisation. The clients of the system were running on a Web browser on a standard PC, and the IT-staff could read through their assigned tasks, look at the task history, change states, write reports and so forth. The main goal of the Web-based system was to maintain information about incoming requests during the lifetime of a specific task. In the following sections, first the theory of the requirement analysis method will be presented followed by an example of how the method can be used illustrated with the scenario described in this paragraph.

Requirement Analysis Process

The high-level process of our framework consists of three main steps, as shown in Figure 1.

Figure 1. High-level process

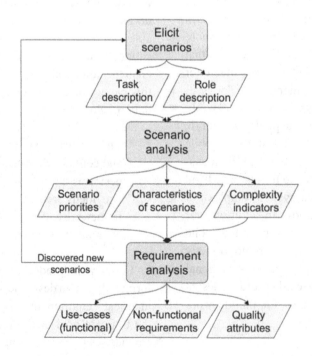

In the *first* step, *elicit scenarios*, the mobile workers' daily routines are described. This description will typically involve several roles and result in a description of both roles and tasks of the mobile workers.

The *second* step, *scenario analysis*, goes through the tasks described in the first step using a set of predefined mobile task characteristics. The results of this step are priorities of the tasks from the first step, characteristics of all tasks, and a set of computed complexity indicators.

The *third* and last step, *requirement analysis*, uses the results from the two previous steps to produce nonfunctional and functional requirements of the end-system. The following sections describe each step of our method by introducing the main concepts followed by an example of practical usage based on the scenario described in beginning of this section.

Step 1: Elicit Scenarios

The elicitation step can be carried out using various approaches depending on the type of work for which to develop a system and the type of company or organisation. One approach is to interview various mobile workers and the people working with back-end support. Another approach is to observe the mobile workers over time and then carry out interviews about daily routines. In this phase, it is important to identify and describe all roles involved in the mobile work, as well as people working with economy, inventory, project planning, customer service and so forth.

In our framework, a scenario contains a collection of mobile work task descriptions and role descriptions. A scenario is given a name along with a short description of the theme and process goal. The roles are described by a name and a short description of responsibilities.

The next step is to describe all tasks part of the scenario along with assignment of responsible roles to each task. A task is described by name, description, responsible role, precondition to start

the task, postcondition to complete the task, and dependencies. The pre- and post-conditions are divided into three parts:

- **Location:** The worker must be in a specific place before or after completion of a task,
- **Resources:** Resources that must be in place before or will be available after completion of the task, and
- **Tasks:** Tasks that must be completed before starting the current task or tasks that can start after completing the current task.

The *tasks'* pre- and post-conditions define the horizontal relationships among tasks. The dependency part of the task description is used to identify dependencies on other roles and tasks in the scenario. This includes task composition that describes vertical relationships among tasks (hierarchical process model) and instantiation of roles (number of people involved in the task). A template for a task description is shown in Table 2.

Some parts of the task template above might not be applicable and will then be filled out with NA (Not Applicable).

Example:
Various persons from the IT-support organisation introduced in the beginning of this section are interviewed to elicit their daily routines. The first step then is to describe the scenario as indicated above. (see Box 1)

From the description above, it is obvious that the role *support engineer* is the only one involved in mobile tasks. Thus, the rest of the example will focus on the support engineer. For this role, the following tasks have been identified: *set up new computer*, *upgrade computer*, and *assist user*. In this example, we will focus on the task *assist user*. In Table 3, a task description of the task *assist user* is presented.

The task description is based on information acquired from interviewing the IT-staff. Note that

Table 2. Task description template

Task name	<unique task name within a scenario>
Priority	<from very low (1) to very high (5)>
Responsibility	<responsible role>
Description	<short description of the task>
Precondition	*Location*: <location requirement to start the current task> *Resources*: <resource requirement(s) to start the current task> *Tasks*: <task(s) to be completed to start the current task>
Postcondition	*Location*: <location when completing the current task> *Resources*: <resource(s) available after completing the current task> *Tasks*: <task(s) allowed to be started after completing the current task>
Dependencies	*Other roles*: <other role(s) involved in the task> *Agents*: <number of people involved in the task> *Parent task*: <relationship to parent task> *Child tasks*: <relationships to child tasks>

Box1.

> **Scenario**:
> *Name*: Mobile IT-support
> *Description*: Describes the mobile aspects of IT-support work processes
>
> **Roles**:
> *Name*: Support manager
> *Description*: Responsible for managing the IT-support including assigning tasks to IT-support staff
>
> *Name*: Support desk
> *Description*: Responsible for registration of user inquires and solving problems that can be solved remotely using a computer
>
> *Name*: Support engineer
> *Description*: Responsible for solving problems concerning hardware and software at specific locations (computer labs, offices, etc.)

Table 3. Task description–Assist user

Task name	Assist user
Priority	Very high (5)
Responsibility	Support engineer
Description	Help users to solve computer problems, like malfunctioning mouse, keyboard, software, etc.
Precondition	*Location*: Must be at user's location (office, lab) *Resources*: Information or equipment dependent on user problem *Tasks*: User has reported problem, task assigned to support engineer
Postcondition	*Location*: NA *Resources*: Solution report (electronic), changed task state *Tasks*: NA
Dependencies	*Roles*: None *Agents*: 1 *Parent task*: NA *Child tasks*: Find user/equipment, show task information, solve problem, report solution, change task state

in order to specify the child tasks, the task *assist user* had to be decomposed into subtasks that describe necessary steps to carry out the task.

Step 2: Scenario Analysis

The scenario analysis can be used in several ways. The analysis can be used as a checklist for issues one should consider when making computer support for mobile work. Further, it provides a more careful examination of the requirements for making a system to support mobile scenarios. This examination will produce requirement indicators to identify, for example, complex parts of the system, type of client device, type of network, and services needed. In addition, the framework can be used to identify interfaces between a mobile client and back-end systems and indicate information requirements for the mobile worker.

Table 4. MOWAHS characteristics

Characteristic	Possible values	Description
General		
G1. Decomposable	(1 No, 5 Yes)	Composed of subtasks?
G2. Part of sequence	(1 No, 5 Yes)	Order dependencies with other tasks?
G3. Preplanned	(1 Planned, 3 Partial, 5 Adhoc)	To what degree planned in beforehand?
G4. Data synchronisation	(1 Never, 3 After end, 5 Duration)	When update data with other tasks?
G5. Data exchange rate	(1 Never, 3 Once, 5 Many)	How often will the task exchange data with other tasks within its lifetime?
Information		
I1. Info content	(1 Text, 3 Graphics, 5 Multimedia)	Complexity of info required/produced?
I2. Info streaming	(1 NA, 3 Discrete, 5 Continuous)	Does the task require streaming of data?
I3. Freshness of data required	(1 NA, 2 Day, 3 Hour, 4 Min, 5 Real-time)	How fresh must data received from a server be to execute the task?
I4. Freshness of data produced	(1 NA, 2 Day, 3 Hour, 4 Min, 5 Real-time)	How fresh must data received by a server and produced by the task be?
I5. Data transmission	(1 NA, 2 Slow, 3 Medium, 4 Fast, 5 Very fast)	What is the expected transmission speed required to execute the task?
Location		
L1. Location dependent	(1 No, 5 Yes)	Must be executed at a specific location?
L2. Require services at location	(1 No, 5 Yes)	Require electronic services at the location?
L3. Produce services at location	(1 No, 5 Yes)	Produce electronic services at the location?
L4. Location report	(1 No, 5 Yes)	Must report the current location to a server?
L5. Route constraint	(1 No, 5 Yes)	Must follow a specific route when moving?
Time		
T1. Event-triggered	(1 No, 3 Partial, 5 Yes)	Is the task triggered by an event?
T2. Time constraint	(1 No, 3 Partial, 5 Yes)	Must the task be executed at a specific time?
T3. Temporal coordination	(1 No, 3 Partial, 5 Yes)	Must the task be timed with other tasks?
T4. Task resumption	(1 No, 3 Partial, 5 Yes)	Can the task be halted for later to be resumed from where it left off without a restart?
T5. Task lifetime	(1 Sec, 2 Min, 3 Hour, 4 Day, 5 Week)	What is the expected lifetime?

The characteristics are divided into four main categories:

- **General characteristics** that specify task structure and organization,
- **Information characteristics** that specify how information and data is used by a task,
- **Location characteristics** that specify how a task depends on a geographical location, and
- **Time characteristics** that specify the temporal properties of a task.

For each of the four main categories, there are five questions related to the category. Thus, there are 20 questions to be answered for every task described in Step 1: Elicit scenarios. Table 2 shows the 20 characteristics used in the scenario analysis of tasks described in a mobile scenario.

To carry out the scenario analysis, the following procedure should be performed.

- For each role; list the tasks
- For each task:
  a. Assign task priority (1-5; 1 is least important and 5 is most important)
  b. Characterise the task using the characterisation questions (as shown in Table 4 above)
  c. Calculate the requirement indicators for the task

Table 5. Complexity indicators

Indicator	Characteristic	Explanation
General Task Indicator (GTI)	Average of G1-G5	A high GTI score indicates that the underlying process and transactional infrastructure (e.g., workflow system) must be advanced.
Information Complexity Indicator (ICI)	Average of I1-I5	A high ICI score indicates that the end-system must cope with complex information presentation, management and transmission. The ICI can also be used to select the appropriate hardware and software to be used as a mobile client and server.
Location Complexity Indicator (LCI)	Average of L1-L5	A high LCI score can indicate that the end-system must be location-aware, include Geographic Information System (GIS) functionality, and use a mobile client suitable for mobility in terms of weight, size, battery power, etc.
Time Complexity Indicator (TCI)	Average of T1-T5	A high TCI score indicates that time management and coordination of tasks, and advanced transactional support might be necessary. In addition, the TCI also indicates the level of performance and availability required.
Network Connectivity Indicator (NCI)	Average of G3, G4, G5, L4 and T1	The NCI indicates the level of connectivity between the mobile client and the server. It determines the required networking capabilities of the mobile client. Further, it indicates nonfunctional requirements for the system such as reliability and latency.
Network Speed Indicator (NSI)	Average of I3-I5	A high NSI score means that the transmission speed and quality of service must be high between the mobile client and supporting servers. The NSI also indicates what wireless network technology can be used for the end-system.
Energy Consumption Indicator (ECI)	Average of I5, L1, L2, L3 and T5	A high ECI score means that it is likely that the mobile client device to complete the task will consume much energy.
Transaction Support Indicator (TSI)	Average of G3, G4, G5, T1, T4 and T5	The TSI describes the need for flexible/advanced transactional support. A high TSI score indicates that the transactional support must go beyond ACID transactions.
Mobility Indicator (MI)	Average L4 and L5	The MI indicates how much mobility is involved. The MI is useful for determining the complexity of the environment the mobile client will operate in, e.g., variation in wireless networks. A high MI will affect the choice of equipment (device) and tools necessary to accomplish the task.
Task Complexity (TC)	Average of all characteristics of a task	The TC indicates the complexity of one task. The TC is useful for finding the most complex task that should have the most attention in a further examination.

To measure the different characteristics, an ordinal scale (1-5) is used. High values indicate higher complexity in terms of system requirements, while low values indicate lower complexity. Many of the characteristics do not use the full scale, but only the values 1, 3 and 5, or simply 1 and 5 to get a uniform representation of extreme values. We are aware that it is mathematically fuzzy to calculate average values on the ordinal scale, but we have found the usage of extreme values valuable for discovering complexity in specific areas of the scenario. From the scores of the 20 characteristics in the framework, indicators can be computed that help analysing the mobile scenario and thus prioritising and extracting nonfunctional and functional requirements (see Step 3: Requirement analysis). The indicators are an average of selected characteristics related to certain complexity aspects. The indicators are described in Table 5.

Because the indicators are averages of the characteristics, the provided values can be used for suggesting complexity for certain properties. The actual numbers are used to compare the complexity of different tasks to identify which tasks that require more attention in the following requirement analysis, and the design and implementation of the end-system. In addition, the values of the indicators will identify particular areas concerned with nonfunctional requirements that must be carefully managed, for example, network connectivity and speed, energy consumption, or location management.

Example:

In this step of the process, the focus is on going through the scenario. For the IT-support scenario, we had to go through a characterisation of all the tasks for the roles *support manager, support desk* and *support engineer*. Here we will focus on the role *support engineer*. To illustrate how to carry out the characterisation, we will demonstrate how to determine the score for three characteristics, namely *G1 Decomposable, L1 Location dependent* and *T5 Task lifetime* for the task *assist user*.

G1: *Is the task assist user composed of sub-tasks?*
Answer: If we look at dependencies/child tasks in the task description, we clearly see that this task is decomposable.
Score: 5 (Yes).

L1: *Must the task assist user be executed at a specific location?*
Answer: If we look at the precondition/location in the task description, we see that the *support engineer* must be at the location of the user.
Score: 5 (Yes).

T5: *What is the expected lifetime of the task assist user?*
Answer: In this case, the task description does not say anything about the duration of a task. To get this information, the IT-support staff may be asked about the expected time for assisting a user.
Score: 3 (Hour).

We will now use the results from characterising the three tasks *set up new computer, upgrade computer* and *assist user* for the role *support engineer* to calculate the requirement indicators (see Table 5). The results of the calculations of the requirement indicators are shown in Table 6.

The *assist user* task has the highest scores or equally high scores for all the indicators compared to the other two tasks. This means that this task is probably the most complex with respect to mobile client, mobile network, and back-end support. This also means that it is the task that is most important to analyse more in detail because it will likely cause most challenges when designing the system in terms of mobile support for both nonfunctional and functional requirements.

Step 3: Requirement Analysis

The final step of the process is to identify and structure the nonfunctional and functional requirements of the end-system. It relies on results

Table 6. Requirement indicator scores from the IT-support scenario

Requirement Indicator	Set up new computer	Upgrade computer	Assist user
General Task Indicator (GTI)	2,2	2,6	3,4
Information Complexity Indicator (ICI)	2,4	3,4	3,4
Location Complexity Indicator (LCI)	2,6	2,6	3,4
Time Complexity Indicator (TCI)	3,0	3,0	4,0
Network Connectivity Indicator (NCI)	2,2	2,2	5,0
Network Speed Indicator (NSI)	2,0	3,7	3,7
Energy Consumption Indicator (ECI)	2,5	2,5	3,3
Transaction Support Indicator (TSI)	2,3	2,3	4,5
Mobility Indicator (MI)	3,0	3,0	3,0
Task Complexity (TC)	2,6	2,9	3,6

from the two previous steps. The result of this step is a collection of nonfunctional and functional requirements. Parts of the functional requirements are found by decomposing tasks from the scenario description. The decomposed tasks can be used as an input for a new iteration (back to step 1), where these tasks are further described, characterised and analysed.

The ISO9126 taxonomy (International Organization for Standarization, 2001) describes six main quality characteristics of a software system: functionality, maintainability, portability, usability, reliability and efficiency. Some nonfunctional requirements in mobile systems are difficult to directly map onto ISO9126. The nature of mobile systems is very dependent on the execution environment, for example, mobile device capabilities, network infrastructure and availability, power availability, and the physical environment. The execution environment affects how the system architecture (both hardware and software) is designed to operate in a mobile setting with nondeterministic properties. For example, the mobile device capabilities relate to functionality, portability, usability, reliability and efficiency in ISO9126. It is, however, difficult to map the mobility properties onto the taxonomy.

Nonfunctional requirements: The mobile device

Table 7 shows how device requirements are addressed in the MOWAHS analysis framework. These nonfunctional requirements need to be considered in all mobile systems. The nonfunctional requirements for a mobile device is determined by going through all the requirements in the table one by one, looking at the associated characteristics and indicators for the given requirement. If the characteristics and indicators related to a requirement indicate high complexity, this should be translated into, for example, high CPU speed, or high memory usage.

Some of the issues will require adaptation strategies with respect to hardware and software heterogeneity. Others related to informational and computational requirements force one to consider computational distribution and information mobility not normally specified in nonmobile systems. Issues like load balancing should also be considered to off-load computations (using cyber foraging) on a mobile device to a server to save battery, CPU, memory and communication costs. Note that the characteristics and indicators must be considered as help on the way to specifying the nonfunctional requirements.

Table 7. Framework mapping onto device requirements

Requirement	Issues	Characteristics	Indicators
CPU	Speed	I1, I2, I5	ICI, NSI, ECI
Memory	Size and speed (primary, secondary)	I1, I2, I3, I4, I5	ICI
Graphics hardware	3D, video, speed	I1	None
Audio	Speakers, earphone, loudness	L1, L2, L3, T2, T3	LCI, TCI
Notification	Vibration, alarm, ring tone, low energy	L1, L2, L3, T2, T3	LCI, TCI, ECI
Network support	Type (BT, WiFi, 3G, GPRS), handover, session mobility	G4, G5, I2, I5, T2	NCI, NSI
Screen	Resolution, colour, lightness	I1	None
Battery capacity	Lifetime wrt. CPU, screen, communication, graphics, audio	I5, L1, L2, L3, T5	ECI
Input device	Modal / Nonmodal	None	None
Location-detection	GPS, network detection	L1, L2, L3, L4, L5	LCI
Weight and size	Portability	I1, I5, L1, L2, L3, T5	LCI, ECI

Example:

Consider again the *assist user* task (because this was the task with the highest complexity scores) from the IT-support scenario and the following nonfunctional requirements for the mobile device: *memory*, *network support* and *location-detection*.

Requirement: *Memory*

Indicator: ICI (Information Complexity Indicator)

Reasoning: If both characteristics and indicators are available for a requirement, indicators should be used (because indicators are computed from the characteristics). The ICI score for the *assist user* task was 3,4 (see Table 6) and just above average for a task. This means the expected memory usage of the application is about average, and we do not need a mobile device with the highest requirements in terms of memory.

Requirement: *Network support*

Indicators: NCI (Network Connectivity Indicator), NSI (Network Speed Indicator)

Reasoning: The scores of the *assist user* task for NCI and NSI were (see Table 6) 5,0 and 3,7 respectively. These results indicate the highest value of required connectivity for the device.

Thus, it is important that the wireless networks supported by the mobile device always are available in various locations. If the *support engineer* only should work within office buildings where WiFi is available, it is sufficient that the mobile device has support for WiFi. However, if there is a mixture of networks available that varies from building to building where the IT-support organisation is responsible, it is important that the mobile device supports various networks and automatic handover processes from one wireless network to another.

Requirement: *Location-detection*

Indicator: LCI (Location Complexity Indicator)

Reasoning: The LCI score of the task *assist user* was 3,4 and a bit above average. This means that location-aware services should be considered. It is also possible to look at some of the characteristics to clarify this issue for example L1 (Is the task location dependent? - see Table 4). From the precondition of the task description in Table 3, it is obvious that the task *assist user* is location dependent. This means that the mobile device must support some kind of location detection, for example, GPS, base station triangulation, and so forth.

Nonfunctional requirements: The network

Table 8 shows how network requirements are addressed in the MOWAHS analysis framework. A mobile system must deal with issues related to network availability and quality of service (QoS). Knowledge of network coverage and QoS can be used to predict which information should be managed and stored on the mobile device and which information should be managed and stored on a back-end system.

In addition to the nonfunctional requirement described above, other issues like device heterogeneity and client software requirements (like portability) should be addressed (but is not covered in this chapter). Further, nonfunctional requirements for the back-end systems must be addressed and analysed.

An example of how network requirements are elicited is not presented in this chapter, as it is carried out in the same way as for mobile device requirements described above.

**Functional requirements:
Starting from the role and task descriptions**

A starting point for capturing the functional requirements using the MOWAHS analysis framework is the scenario descriptions (role and task descriptions). To carry out the requirement elicitation, all the tasks in the scenario must be analysed with respect to system boundaries; that is, establish use-cases of the end-system. In this process, the tasks are decomposed into a set of steps that describe the basic functionality to be provided by the 1) mobile client or 2) the back-end system. The roles will identify stakeholders and use-case actors. The requirement analysis can be used in combination with the scenario-based requirements analysis method described in Sutcliffe (1998).

Table 8. Framework mapping onto network requirements

Requirement	Issues	Characteristics	Indicators
Bandwidth	Transfer speed	G5, I3, I4, I5	NSI
Latency	Performance, delay	G4, I2, I3, I4 (L2, L3), T3	ICI
Availability	Coverage, connectivity, reliability	G4, L1, L2, L3, L4, L5, T3	LCI, NCI
Cost	Transfer cost	G5, I1, I2, I5, L2, T5	NSI

Figure 2. Use-case diagram of the task assist user

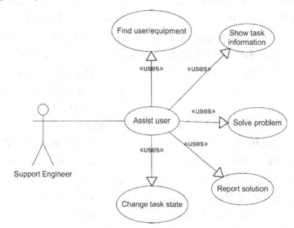

Example:

Consider the task *assist user* from the IT-support scenario: This task is decomposed into the following child tasks: *find user/equipment, show task information, solve problem, report solution,* and *change task state.* These child tasks can be directly considered as use-cases. The *support engineering* will thus be the use-case actor. Use cases derived from the task *assist user* are shown in Figure 2.

The requirement analysis process can be further elaborated by analysing the identified use-cases. In use-case *find user/equipment,* the following functional requirements can be derived:

- **FR1:** The system needs to store or update information about users and equipment with unique ID;

- **FR2:** The system needs to store or update location information related to user or equipment ID;

- **FR3:** The system needs to provide functionality to locate user or equipment;

- **FR4:** The system needs functionality to map user or equipment onto problem task;

- **FR5:** The system needs to provide functionality to show location of user or equipment; and

- **FR6:** The system needs to provide functionality to show route information to user or equipment.

Functional requirements:
Starting from the requirement indicators

Another way of using the MOWAHS analysis framework to identify functional requirements is to use the values of the requirement indicators. The indicators themselves cannot directly be used to derive functional requirements, but the indicators may imply areas of functionality that must be looked into or supported to provide system support for the scenario being analysed. Table 9 shows a mapping between indicators and functional requirements. To use the table, one should check if some of the indicators in the table have high scores. If this is the case, the functional requirement linked to these indicators ought to be considered in the end-system.

Example:

Again we go back to our IT-support scenario focusing on the task *assist user* and the two functional requirements areas *network management* and *transaction management.*

Requirement: *Network management*
Indicator: NCI (Network Connectivity Indicator)
Reasoning: The NCI score for the *assist user* task has the highest value 5,0 (see Table 6). This means that connectivity is very important for the end-system. In terms of functional requirements, this might include data buffering management (in

Table 9. Framework mapping into functional requirements

Requirement	Issues	Indicators
Workflow infrastructure	Provide a process support infrastructure	GTI
Multimedia management	Provide support for advanced GUI, audio/video playback, multimedia streaming	ICI
Context management	Provide support for location-aware/context-aware information and services	LCI
Time management	Provide support for task arbitration and coordination, task scheduling and task planning	TCI
Network management	Provide support for network services required	NCI
Storage management	Provide support for storage management (cyber foraging vs. local storage vs. communication)	NSI/ECI
Transaction management	Provide support for transaction management and infrastructure	TSI

case of a network failure), automatic handover between various networks without loosing data, caching of data and so forth.

Requirement: *Transaction management*
Indicator: TSI (Transaction Support Indicator)
Reasoning: The TSI score for the *assist user* task has a very high value 4,5 (see Table 6). This indicates that the end-system most likely should provide support for transactions beyond standard ACID (Ramampiaro & Nygård, 2004), for example, support for long transactions, updating or viewing the same data on several mobile devices as well as the back-end system concurrently.

CONCLUSION

This chapter has presented a requirement analysis framework useful for analysing mobile work scenarios to implement systems supporting mobile users. It describes the process with steps starting with a vague description of a scenario, and then detailing the scenario description through definition of roles and tasks. These tasks are then analysed according to 20 characteristics, and 10 complexity indicators are calculated. The final step elicits nonfunctional and functional requirements based on knowledge from the previous steps.

Our discussion shows the limitations of our framework with respect to coverage of nonmobile types of requirements. The framework might be used as a tool in any software process life cycle. We believe it provides important input and knowledge in the development of systems to support mobile users. Further, although our framework has been tested against real-world scenarios, and that it has been implemented, there are room for other improvements. As such, our future work includes validating the MOWAHS framework within mobile software system design environments. This will allow us to reveal all-important aspects that we have to take into account, in addition to those our framework already covers.

FUTURE RESEARCH DIRECTIONS

In the recent years, the fact that mobile software systems have become larger and more complex has been widely recognised. Such systems increasingly involve interaction between various mobile devices and interfaces, various servers, and even services offered by legacy systems. Thus, it becomes more important to carefully analyse requirements for such systems, especially requirements related to mobile environments. Having this in mind, we believe that our requirement analysis framework will be even more useful for future design and development of mobile systems. In addition, we recognise the increasing need for computer support for mobile occupations. Despite the fact that our framework does not cover all aspects of requirement analysis of a software system, we believe it plays an important role for highlighting mobile issues.

Another recent observed trend is that sensors have become smaller (e.g., use of nanotechnology), cheaper and widespread (Satyanarayanan, 2003). Sensors combined with the rising numbers of activators (or triggers), give new opportunities and challenges for new types of mobile applications. Such applications will utilise the state of the environment around the user to provide services that are relevant to current task, time, location and situation. Our framework can be used to analyse parts of emerging scenarios (e.g., issues related to location and time). The framework can be extended and adapted to also handle new aspects and issues that arise with new technologies.

Currently, service-oriented computing and service-oriented architectures are considered as suitable approaches for designing and developing mobile applications and services. Our mobile characterisation framework can be useful in terms of providing context information of mobile clients. This can enhance the availability and reliability of the provided mobile services.

The proposed process can be regarded as agile by the use of scenarios, and iterative and incremental analysis. Because tasks have been given priorities, the priorities can be used to manage and plan implementation and deployment of functionality in the system. Our process is based on collaboration between the stakeholders, but do not explicitly define this collaboration. The method can be used as part of other software processes like eXtreme Programming (XP) and RUP.

REFERENCES

Dunham, M. H., & Kumar, V. (1998). Location dependent data and its management in mobile databases. In *Proceedings of the Database and Expert Systems Applications (DEXA) Workshop.*

Flinn, J., & Satyanarayanan, M. (1999). Energy-aware adaptation for mobile applications. In *Proceedings of the Symposium on Operating Systems Principles (SOSP).*

Florio, V. D. & Deconinck, G. (2002). On some key requirements of mobile application software. In *Proceedings of the International Conference on Engineering of Computer-based Systems (ECBS 2002).*

Forman, G. H., & Zahorjan, J. (1994). The challenges of mobile computing. *Computer, 27*(4), 38-47.

Holtzblatt, K. (2005). Customer-centered design for mobile applications. *Personal and Ubiquitous Computing, 9*(4), 227-237.

IEEE IEEE-Std 830 1993 IEEE Recommended Practice for Software Requirements Specifications.

International Organization for Standarization. (2001). *ISO/IEC Standard 9126: Software engineering--product quality,* part 1, ISO.

Kangas, E., & Kinnunen, T. (2005). Applying user-centered design to mobile application development. *Communications of the ACM (CACM), 48*(7), 55-59.

Le, H. N., & Nygård, M. (2005). A mobile affiliation model for supporting mobile collaborative work. In *Proceedings of the Workshop on Ubiquitous Mobile Information and Collaboration Systems (UMICS).*

Maccari, A. (1999). The challenges of requirements engineering in mobile telephones industry. In *Proceedings of the 10th International Conference and Workshop on Database and Expert Systems Applications (DEXA '99).* Springer-Verlag.

Majumdar, R. K., Ramamritham, K., & Xiong, M. (2003). Adaptive location management in mobile environments. In *Proceedings of the International Conference on Mobile Data Management (MDM 2003).* Melbourne, Australia, ACM Press.

Pitoura, E., & Samaras, G. (1998). *Data management for mobile computing.* Kluwer Academic.

Pradhan, S., Lawrence, E., & Zmijewska, A. (2005). Bluetooth as an enabling technology in mobile transactions. In *Proceedings of the International Symposium on Information Technology: Coding and Computing (ITCC 2005).*

Rakotonirainy, A. (1999). Trends and future of mobile computing. In *Proceedings of the 10th IEEE International Workshop on Database and Expert Systems Applications.* Florence, Italy: IEEE CS Press.

Ramampiaro, H., & Nygård, M. (2004). CAGIS-Trans: Providing adaptable transactional support for cooperative work--an extended treatment. *Information Technology & Management (ITM) Journal, 5*(1-2), 23-64.

Ramampiaro, H., & Wang, A. I., et al. (2003). Requirement indicators derived from a mobile characterisation framework. In *Proceedings of the IASTED International Conference on Applied Informatics (AI'2003).* Innsbruck, Austria: Acta Press.

Raptis, D., & Tselios, N. K., & Avouris, N. M. (2005). Context-based design of mobile applications for museums: A survey of existing practices. In *Proceedings of the 7th Conference on Human-computer Interaction with Mobile Devices and Services*. Salzburg, Austria: ACM Press.

Ratner, D., & Reiher, P. L., Popek, G. J., & Kuenning, G. H. (2001). Replication requirements in mobile environments. *Mobile Networks and Applications (MONET), 6*(6), 525-533.

Satyanarayanan, M. (1996). Fundamental challenges of mobile computing. In *Proceedings of the fifteenth annual ACM Symposium on Principles of Distributed Computing* (pp. 1-7). Philadelphia.

Satyanarayanan, M. (1996). Fundamental challenges in mobile computing. In *Proceedings of the 15th Annual ACM Symposium on Principles of Distributed Computing*. Philadelphia, PA: ACM Press.

Satyanarayanan, M. (2003). Of smart dust and brilliant rocks. *IEEE Pervasive Computing, 4*(2), 2-4.

Schneiderman, R. (2002). *The mobile technology question and answer book: A survival guide for business managers*. American Management Association.

Sindhgatta, R., & Thonse, S. (2005). Functional and non-functional requirements specification for enterprise applications. *Product focused software process improvement (PROFES 2005)*. Berlin/Heidelberg: Springer-Verlag.

Sutcliffe, A. (1998). Scenario-based requirements analysis. *Requirements Engineering, 3*(1), 48-65.

Wang, A. I., & Sørensen, C.-F., et al. (2005). Using the MOWAHS characterisation framework for development of mobile work applications. *Product focused software process improvement (PROFES 2005)*. Berlin/Heidelberg: Springer-Verlag.

Zimmerman, J. B. (1999). *Mobile computing: Characteristics, business benefits, and the mo-bile framework* (Tech. Rep. No. INSS 690 CC). University of Maryland European Division.

ADDITIONAL READING

The following is a list of references we recommend for further reading.

Aoyama, M. (2005). Persona-and-scenario based requirements engineering for software embedded in digital consumer products. In *Proceedings of the 13th IEEE International Conference on Requirements Engineering (Re'05)*. IEEE Computer Society.

Bohn, J. (2006). Prototypical implementation of location-aware services based on super-distributed RFID tags. *Architecture of computing systems (ARCS 2006)*. LNCS 3894. Springer-Verlag.

Burns, M. (2006). Utilizing scenarios for user testing of mobile social software. In *Proceedings of the CHI 2006 Workshop on Mobile Social Software*.

Chung, L., Nixon, B., Yu, E., & Mylopoulos, J. (2000). *Non-functional requirements in software engineering*. Boston: Kluwer Academic.

Dunham, M. H., Helal, A., & Balakrishnan, S. (1997). A mobile transaction model that captures both the data and movement behavior. *Mobile Networks and Applications, 2*(2), 149-162.

Følstad, A., & Rahlff, O. W. (2002). Basic user requirements for mobile work support systems—three easy steps. In *Proceedings of the ER/IFIP8.1 Workshop on Conceptual Modelling Approaches to Mobile Information Systems Development (MobIMod 2002)*.

Goguen, J., & Linde, C. (1993, January 4-6). Techniques for requirements. Elicitation. In *Proceedings of the 1st IEEE International Symposium on Requirements Engineering (RE'93)*, San Diego, CA, USA, (pp. 152-164).

Gregoriades, A. (2005). Scenario-based assessment of nonfunctional requirements. *IEEE Transactions on Software Engineering, 31*(5), 392-409.

Haumer, P., Pohl, K., & Weidenhaupt, K. (1998). Requirements elicitation and validation with real world scenes. *Software Engineering, 24*(12), 1036-1054.

Lee, V., Schneider, H., & Schell, R. (2004). *Mobile applications: Architecture, design, and development.* HP Professional Books/Prentice Hall.

Lindgaard, G., Dillon, R., Trbovich, P., White, R., Fernandes, G., Lundahl, S., & Pinnamaneni, A. (2006). User needs analysis and requirements engineering: Theory and practice. *Interacting with Computers, 18(*1), 47-70.

Manaouer, A. B., Shekhar, A., & Liang, Z. Y. (2004). A generic framework for rapid application development of mobile Web services with dynamic workflow management. In *Proceedings of the 2004 IEEE International Conference on Services Computing (SCC'04).* IEEE CS Press.

Maiden, N., & Robertson, S. (2005). Developing use cases and scenarios in the requirements process. In *Proceedings of the 27th international Conference on Software Engineering (ICSE 2005).* ACM Press.

Maiden, N., Seyff, N., Grunbacher, P., Otojare, O., & Mitteregger, K. (2006). Making mobile requirements engineering tools usable and useful. In *Proceedings of 14th IEEE International Requirements Engineering Conference (RE'06),* (pp. 29-38). IEEE CS Press.

Mummert, L.B., Ebling, M.R., & Satyanarayan, M. (1995). Exploiting weak connectivity for mobile file access. In *Proceedings of the Fifteenth ACM Symposium on Operating Systems Principles.* ACM Press.

Nakamura, H. (2001). A development scenario for ubiquitous networks: Viewed from the evolution of IT Paradigms. *NRI Papers, 26,* 1-9.

Seyff, N., Grunbacher, P., Maiden, N., & Tosar, A. (2004). Requirements engineering tools go mobile. In *Proceedings of the 26th International Conference on Software Engineering.* IEEE CS Press.

Sommerville, I., & Sawyer, P. (2000). *Requirements engineering: A good practice guide.* John Wiley.

Sutcliffe, A. (1995). Scenario-based requirements analysis. *Requirements Engineering Journal, 3*(1), 48-65.

Yacoub, S. M., Cukic, B., & Ammar, H. H. (1999). Scenario-based reliability analysis of component-based software. In *Proceedings of the 10th International Symposium on Software Reliability Engineering (ISSRE 99).* IEEE CS Press.

ENDNOTES

[1] A mobile worker is defined as a person that has to change location/context to perform his/her work.

[2] A mobile task describes a working task of a person with a mobile occupation, like a traveling salesman.

Chapter V
Evolution in Model–Driven Software Product–Line Architectures

Gan Deng
Vanderbilt University USA

Jeff Gray
University of Alabama at Birmingham, USA

Douglas C. Schmidt
Vanderbilt University USA

Yuehua Lin
University of Alabama at Birmingham, USA

Aniruddha Gokhale
Vanderbilt University USA

Gunther Lenz
Microsoft, USA

ABSTRACT

This chapter describes our approach to model-driven engineering (MDE)-based product line architectures (PLAs) and presents a solution to address the domain evolution problem. We use a case study of a representative software-intensive system from the distributed real-time embedded (DRE) systems domain to describe key challenges when facing domain evolution and how we can evolve PLAs systematically and minimize human intervention. The approach uses a mature metamodeling tool to define a modeling language in the representative DRE domain, and applies a model transformation tool to specify model-to-model transformation rules that precisely define metamodel and domain model changes. Our approach automates many tedious, time consuming, and error-prone tasks of model-to-model transformation, thus significantly reducing the complexity of PLA evolution.

INTRODUCTION

Software *product-line architectures* (PLAs) are a promising technology for industrializing software-intensive systems by focusing on the automated assembly and customization of domain-specific components, rather than (re)programming systems manually (Clements & Northrop, 2001).

A PLA is a family of software-intensive product variants developed for a specific domain that share a set of common features. Conventional PLAs consist of *component frameworks* (Szyperski, 2002) as core assets, whose design captures recurring structures, connectors, and control flow in an application domain, along with the points of variation explicitly allowed among these entities.

PLAs are typically designed using *scope/commonality/variability* (SCV) analysis (Coplien, Hoffman, & Weiss, 1998), which captures key characteristics of software product-lines, including: (1) *scope*, which defines the domains and context of the PLA, (2) *commonalities*, which name the attributes that recur across all members of the product family, and (3) *variabilities*, which contain the attributes unique to the different members of the product family.

Motivating the Need for Model-Driven Software Product-Line Architectures

Despite improvements in third-generation programming languages (such as C++, Java and C#) and runtime platforms (such as CORBA, J2EE and Web Services middleware), the levels of abstraction at which PLAs are developed today remains low-level relative to the concepts and concerns within the application domains themselves, such as manually tracking the library dependency or ensuring component composition syntactical

and semantic correctness. A promising means to address this problem involves developing PLAs using *model-driven engineering* (MDE) (Schmidt, 2006), which involves systematic use of models as key design and implementation artifacts throughout the software lifecycle. MDE represents a design approach that enables description of the essential characteristics of a problem in a manner that is decoupled from the details of a specific solution space (e.g., dependence on specific OS, middleware or programming language).

As shown in Figure 1, MDE-based PLAs help raise the level of abstraction and narrow the gap between the problem space and the solution space of software-intensive systems by applying the following techniques:

- **Domain-specific modeling languages:** A *DSML* (Gray et al., 2007) consists of *metamodels* and *model interpreters*. A metamodel is similar to the grammar corresponding to a programming language that defines a semantic type system that precisely reflects the subject of modeling and

Figure 1. Using DSMLs and domain-specific component frameworks to enhance abstraction and narrow the gap between problem and solution space of software-intensive systems

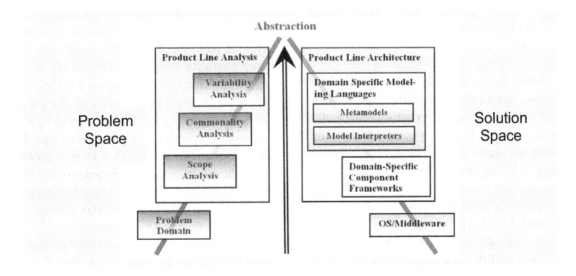

exposes important constraints associated with specific application domains. Model interpreters can read and traverse the models, analyze them, and help create the executable system based on these models. DSMLs help automate repetitive tasks (Gray, Lin, & Zhang, 2006) that must be accomplished for each product instance, including generating code to glue components or synthesizing deployment and configuration artifacts for middleware platforms and the underlying operating systems (Balasubramanian et al., 2006).

- **Domain-specific component frameworks:** Through SCV analysis, object-oriented extensibility capabilities are often used to create domain-specific component frameworks, which factor out common usage patterns in a domain into reusable platforms (Clements & Northrop, 2001). These platforms, in turn, help reduce the complexity of designing DSMLs by simplifying the code generated by their associated model interpreters and addressing the product-line specific functional and systemic concerns, including quality of service (QoS) concerns, such as latencies, throughput, reliability, security, and transactional guarantees. Throughout the rest of the chapter we use the two terms "domain-specific component frameworks" and "component frameworks" interchangeably.

MDE helps software developers explore various design alternatives that represent possible configurations for a specific instance of the product family. For example, a product instance ultimately needs to be deployed into a specific target running environment, where all software components must be deployed and mapped to available hardware devices and configured properly based on the specific software/hardware capabilities of the devices. If the PLAs are intended for use with different hardware devices, however,

the mappings between the software components and hardware devices cannot be known *a priori* when the software PLAs are developed. Instead of analyzing every product instance individually and manually writing source code or scripts repetitively for every different target execution environment, an MDE-based approach to PLA deployment and configuration automates such repetitive and labor-intensive tasks by integrating domain knowledge and expertise into metamodels and model interpreters. Hence, a DSML infuses intelligence into domain models, which helps address many "what if" problems, such as "what glue code or configuration scripts must be written if the product is to be deployed into an environment with XYZ requirements?" These "what if" scenarios help developers understand the ramifications of design choices of software-intensive systems at a higher level of abstraction than changing source code manually at the implementation level.

Challenges with Evolution of Model-Driven Software Product-Line Architectures

Although an MDE-based approach helps improve productivity of software-intensive systems by raising the level of abstraction through composition of DSMLs and domain-specific component frameworks, it is hard to evolve software PLAs by incorporating new requirements. Examples of such requirements include using new software platforms or applying the current PLA in a new use case that may impose a different set of concerns than those handled by the current PLA. Consequently, in addition to assisting in the exploration of design alternatives among product instances, an MDE-based PLA technology must also address the *domain evolution problem* (Macala, Stuckey, & Gross, 1996), which arises when existing PLAs must be extended or refactored to handle unanticipated requirements.

Depending on the scopes of the DSMLs and domain-specific component frameworks, unanticipated requirements can be either functional requirements or nonfunctional requirements, or both. For example, consider an MDE-based PLA that is available on two different component middleware technologies, such as Enterprise Java Beans (EJB) (Sun Microsystems, 2001) and CORBA Component Model (CCM) (OMG, 2006). A goal of a DSML that supports PLA is to selectively use the technologies within a product instance based on the system requirements. The metamodel of the DSML must define proper syntax and semantics to represent both component middleware technologies. With domain evolution, if the CCM technology must be replaced by another emerging middleware technology such as Web Services, the MDE-based PLA must evolve accordingly to satisfy the new requirements, that is, new syntax and semantics must be introduced into the metamodel and new domain-specific component frameworks must be developed based on the emerging Web Services technology.

Unfortunately, adding new requirements to MDE-based PLAs often causes invasive modifications to the PLAs in the DSMLs and component frameworks if DSMLs and component frameworks were not initially designed to be extensible to incorporate such new requirements. Conventional MDE tools do not handle the domain evolution problem effectively because they require significant handcrafted changes to existing PLAs, at both the component framework level and the DSML level. The domain evolution problem is particularly hard because the coupling of architecture and infrastructure concerns often *crosscut* the component framework layer and the DSML layer (Deng, Lenz, & Schmidt, 2005) within a PLA.

Moreover, changes made on metamodels in a PLA often invalidate existing domain models based on previous versions of the metamodels (Sprinkle & Karsai, 2004), which makes the evolution process of model-driven software PLAs hard. Other examples of this problem occur in programming language or object-oriented

framework design, where changes to a grammar or class hierarchy for a programming language or framework may introduce errors in existing legacy source code (Klusener, Laemmel, & Verhoef, 2005). Another example is schema evolution in a database, where changes to a database schema may render the contents of the database useless (Roddick, 1992). Just like legacy source code and contents of database, domain models are crucial assets of an organization, so they must be handled well during the metamodel evolution process.

From these observations, there are many complexities involved when MDE-based software PLAs need to evolve. Although software developers can manually update their metamodels, domain models, and component frameworks for small-scale systems, this approach is clearly tedious, time consuming, error-prone, and nonscalable for software-intensive systems.

Solution → Systematic PLA Evolution with Automated Domain Model Transformation

To address these challenges, a layered and compositional architecture is needed to modularize system concerns and reduce the effort associated with domain evolution. With the help of this architecture, different layers of PLAs can evolve systematically and tool supported domain model evolution also becomes feasible. The overall approach can be characterized in the following ordered steps:

1. The first step deals with component framework evolution. Because component frameworks provide core functionalities to the product instances, they have the most direct impact on the PLAs. As a result, whenever PLAs need to incorporate new requirements, component frameworks must first be refactored. To reduce the impact of such evolution outside the component frameworks, the key point is using pattern-oriented software

architecture (Gamma, Helm, Johnson, & Vlissides, 1995; Schmidt, 2000).

2. The second step deals with metamodel evolution. Because metamodels are used to define type systems of particular domains based on proper language syntax, a language can be decomposed into smaller units to localize the evolution impact, and allow such smaller units to be composed to form the new metamodel.

3. The third step deals with the domain model transformation. This step applies automated model transformation techniques to specify model-to-model transformation rules that define metamodel changes. The application of automated model transformation alleviates many tedious, time consuming, and error-prone tasks of model-to-model transformation to reduce the complexity of PLA evolution. In particular, when an existing DSML in a PLA is changed, the domain models defined by this DSML can be migrated automatically to the new DSML by applying a set of model transformation rules.

While the three-step approach above could be applied to any model-driven software PLAs, this chapter focuses on distributed real-time embedded (DRE) PLAs, which are among the most difficult software-intensive systems to develop because such systems have limited resources and must communicate via the network to meet stringent real-time quality-of-service (QoS) assurance and other performance requirements. A representative software-intensive DRE system is used throughout the chapter as a case study to describe how to evolve PLAs systematically and minimize human intervention. Along with presenting the approach for domain evolution of MDE-based PLAs, the chapter also describes key concepts, such as model-driven engineering, product-line architectures, and model transformations that are important for developing and evolving PLAs for large-scale software-intensive systems.

The remainder of this chapter is organized as follows: We first evaluate related work that supports evolution of software PLAs for DRE systems and compare it with our approach. Then, we describe a conceptual architecture of MDE-based PLAs for DRE systems and define the key elements in this architecture as background of this chapter. After that, we introduce a representative case study of a PLA for avionics mission computing used throughout the chapter. Then, we describe the challenges involved when facing evolving model-driven PLAs and present the solutions to address these challenges. Lastly, we present our concluding remarks and lessons learned.

RELATED WORK

This section surveys the technologies that provide solutions to MDE-based software PLA evolution for software-intensive systems. The related work has been categorized along two dimensions based on the syntax of the modeling mechanism the software PLA evolution relies on, that is, a graphical based modeling approach or a text-based modeling approach.

Graphical Modeling Approaches

A UML metamodel for software PLA evolution (Mens & D'Hondt, 2000) has been developed based on the concept of an *evolution contract*. The idea of an evolution contract is that when incremental modifications and evolution of software artifacts are made on a software product line, a formal contract must be defined between the provider and the modifier. The purpose of the contract is to define the evolution behavior formally. A UML metamodel has been defined to capture the formal evolution contract. This offers a generic MDE-based mechanism for dealing with unanticipated evolution. By documenting model evolution through formal models, incompatibilities or undesired behavior across different modeling artifacts can be detected when models are upgraded, or when different software developers independently make changes to the same or related parts of a model. This approach allows conflicts to be detected regardless of the specific kind of model that is under consideration. The approach has been integrated into third-party CASE tools, such as IBM Rational Rose (IBM, 2007).

KobrA (Atkinson et al., 2002) is another approach based on UML for component-based software PLAs that support model-driven representation of components. In this method, evolution management in software PLAs is divided into three activities, that is, configuration management, change management, and maintenance planning. Configuration management in KobrA is a static method for bringing together different artifacts within a PLA. Change management consists of techniques to evaluate evolution requests. The use of appropriate formal change operators to evolution requests assists in traceability within change propagations in a PLA. Maintenance planning is responsible for constructing infrastructure for the change and configuration management activities. The idea of KobrA is based on a change-oriented model, that is, new versions are obtained from changes applied to some artifacts in the product line. To support the evolution in KobrA, the *evolution graph* technique (Atkinson et al., 2002) is proposed to capture version histories of different artifacts of the PLA and trace the dependencies.

Another technique similar to the evolution graph is called *design decision tree* (DDT) (Ran & Kuusela, 1996), which is a formal approach to incrementally document, refine, organize and reuse the architectural knowledge for software design. The formalism is a hierarchical organization of design patterns that is a partial ordering of design decisions put in the context of the problem requirements and the constraints imposed by earlier decisions. This model integrates architectural knowledge of software design into a software development process. A DDT contains system-wide design information in a form that can be used to analyze change requests and determine their impact on system structure. Because the tree is maintained throughout the lifecycle of a PLA, it can be used as the main repository of design knowledge (Karhinen & Kuusela, 1998). Such a repository can be used to analyze the impact of new requirements to the existing requirement space and to investigate the changes that different implementation strategies may cause to the system structure, which makes it possible to classify different options and to react to them and analyze their architectural implications.

Summary

The related work described above adopts a domain-independent modeling technique to capture the software PLA evolution requirements either explicitly or implicitly. Our approach is similar to these related works in the sense that they all provide visualization capabilities through graphical modeling tools for PLAs. Our approach, however, uses a domain-specific modeling technique that adds additional abstractions representing domain concepts to the modeling languages that are not available in general-purpose domain-independent modeling languages such as UML. DSMLs thus require less effort and fewer low-level details to specify a given system (Tolvanen & Kelly, 2005).

Text-Based Modeling Approaches

Architectural Description Language (ADL) is an important technique in this dimension that facilitates software PLA evolution. The Mae environment (Hoek, Mikic-Rakic, Roshandel, & Medvidovic, 2001), for example, uses ADL to facilitate incremental evolution by capturing all changes made to any architectural elements within a PLA. A key concept in the Mae environment is a system model that allows architectural concepts and configuration management to be mapped with each other through ADL syntax, that is, the ADL allows users to describe what and how the changes should be made to the model. The essence of the approach lies in the use of this model to integrate change management concepts (such as revisions, variants, and configurations) with architectural concepts (such as components, connectors, subtypes, and styles) through ADL descriptions. By mapping the generic system model onto a specific ADL, the design analyses of a software PLA and its evolution can be adapted for the purpose of maintaining the consistency of the architectural configurations captured by the model.

Similar to the idea of the Mae environment, the Koala Component Model (Ommering, Linden, Kramer, & Magee, 2002) also uses ADL to explicitly describe the architecture and provides a platform-centric approach to the design of PLAs for consumer electronics software. Specifically, the Koala Component Model allows variability options to be modeled explicitly via a property mechanism. Using a third-party versioning system, Koala can be used to capture the evolution of a PLA.

XADL (Dashofy, Hoek, & Taylor, 2003) is an XML-based ADL that is constructed from a set of extensible XML schemas. XADL also defines a set of associated libraries that provide a programmatic interface to XADL documents, and provide runtime facilities to create, store, and modify XADL documents. XADL and its associated libraries provide three important benefits for the purposes of supporting software PLA evolution: (1) the core of the XADL language supports variability in both space and time; in XADL, variabilities of artifacts are a natural and integral part of the language, (2) the language can be extended, which allows individual activities in the lifecycle to be able to attach additional information, and (3) the library provides a generic interface to easily access XADL documents, which supports the rapid construction of new tools supporting PLA evolution.

Summary

The related work described in this section all use text-based languages (such as structural languages or XML) to either explicitly capture the PLA evolution activities, or implicitly associate the evolution requirements with actual software components. Our approach is similar to this dimension of the related work in the sense that PLA evolution can be captured through the software PLA architecture itself, rather than through a separate dedicated language.

Hybrid Approaches

Some technologies span both text-based and graphical-based approaches. A well-known example in this category is called QVT (Query/View/Transformation) (OMG, 2005b), which is the OMG standard for model-to-model transformations. This technology provides a standard language to transform UML or custom model types from one type to another. It accepts XML Interchange (XMI) (OMG, 2005b) as input and output. Typical usage scenarios include automating transformation of a high-level design model into a more detailed model, transforming a UML model into a custom data model, or transforming one custom model type into another. The core benefits of this feature set are a standards-based language to express common model transformations with traceability, which provides repeatable results.

Summary

The specification of QVT defines both graphical syntax and textual syntax for the transformation language, but so far there lacks a full implementation of the specification. Moreover, while QVT is restricted to only XMI to XMI transformations, our approach does not have this restriction, so it can exploit any internal representation of the DSMLs.

MDE-BASED PRODUCT LINE ARCHITECTURE FOR DRE SYSTEMS

This section introduces an architecture of a MDE-based product line architecture for software-intensive DRE systems, focusing on the design concepts, common patterns, and software methodology. An MDE-based design and composition approach for DRE systems entails the combination of DSMLs with reusable component frameworks. Figure 2 illustrates the high-level design principles and an overall architecture of an MDE-based PLA solution for software-intensive DRE systems that exploits a *layered* and *compositional* approach. This architecture takes advantage of layering and composition design principles (Krueger, 2006) to make the associated PLAs easier to develop and evolve than *ad hoc* approaches.

As shown in Figure 2, the PLA architecture is based on a core set of COTS middleware and OS platforms, component frameworks and domain-specific modeling languages. The right side of the figure shows the technologies available to implement the design artifacts on the left

side. For example, the "Generator Technology" shown on the right can be used to build model interpreters that automatically generate code to bridge the gap between models and component frameworks.

The remainder of this section introduces and defines key terms and concepts in the architecture shown in Figure 2.

Commercial-Off-The-Shelf (COTS) middleware and OS platforms

COTS middleware and OS platforms provide the infrastructure upon which DRE systems run. Many DRE systems are based on OS platforms with real-time scheduling capabilities. Examples of such OS platforms include *VxWorks* (Wind River Systems, 1998), *Timesys Linux* (Timesys, 2002), and *Windows CE* (Microsoft, 2007). Middleware is an enabling technology that allows multiple processes running on one or more machines to interact across a network. Middleware can be further decomposed into multiple layers (Schmidt, 2002), such as those shown in Figure 3 and described below:

Figure 2. MDE-based product-line architecture for DRE systems

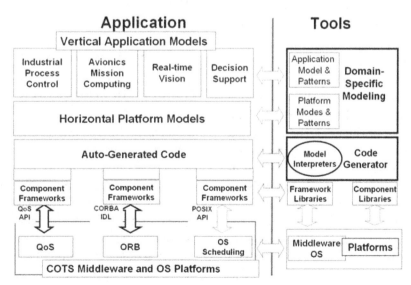

Figure 3. OS, middleware, DSML and application layer relationships

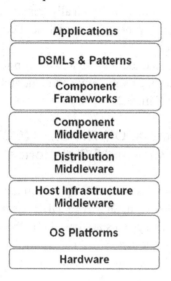

- **Host Infrastructure Middleware:** The host infrastructure layer resides directly atop the operating system and provides a set of higher-level APIs that hide the heterogeneity of different operating systems and network protocols. The host infrastructure layer provides generic services to the upper middleware layers by encapsulating functionality that would otherwise require much tedious, error-prone, and nonportable code, such as socket programming and thread manipulation primitives. Examples of such middleware include ACE (Schmidt, 1993), Real-time Java (Bollella et al., 2000) and Rocks (Zandy & Miller, 2002).
- **Distribution Middleware:** The distribution layer resides atop the host-infrastructure layer and provides high-level programming abstractions, such as remote object operations. Using the distribution layer, a developer can write a distributed application in a similar way to a stand-alone application. CORBA 2.x (OMG, 2003), DCOM (Microsoft, 2000), Java RMI (Sun Microsystems, 2000) and Data Distribution Service (DDS) (OMG, 2004a) are the main solutions to distribution middleware.

- **Component Middleware:** The component middleware layer resides atop the distribution middleware layer and adopts the component-based software engineering approach (Heineman & Councill, 2001) to allow maximum reuse of software components. Component middleware also provides mechanisms to configure and control key distributed computing aspects, such as connecting event producers to event consumers and managing transactional behavior, separate from the functional aspects of the application. Examples of component middleware platforms include Enterprise Java Beans (EJB) (Sun Microsystem, 2001) and OMG Corba Component Model (CCM) (OMG, 2005a).

Because many DRE systems require a loosely-coupled distribution architecture to simplify extensibility, COTS middleware typically provides event-driven publish/subscribe communication mechanisms, which help reduce ownership costs by defining clear boundaries between the components in the application. Such mechanisms reduce dependencies and maintenance costs associated with replacement, integration, and revalidation of components. COTS middleware and OS platforms are designed to maintain the commonality, portability, reusability, and applicability of software for different domains.

Component Frameworks

Component frameworks provide reusable domain-specific building blocks for PLAs of DRE systems. As illustrated in Figure 3, component frameworks reside atop COTS middleware and OS platforms. The key difference between component frameworks and component middleware is that the latter is domain independent while the former is domain-specific. Component frameworks define "semicomplete" applications that embody domain-specific object structures and functionality to raise the level of abstraction at which the software product instance is composed, and offer product-line specific environments to capture the variabilities. Components in such a framework coordinate with each other to provide core functionalities for a family of related applications. Complete applications can be composed by inheriting from or instantiating framework components.

Examples of component frameworks include the Boeing Bold Stroke product line architecture (Schulte, 2003) in the avionics mission computing domain and Siemens Building Technology APOGEE product line architecture (Siemens, 2007) in the building automation domain. For example, the Boeing Bold Stroke PLA supports many Boeing product variants using a component-based platform. The Boeing Bold Stoke PLA supports systematic reuse of mission computing functionality and is configurable for product-specific functionality and execution. The philosophy of component frameworks is to develop reusable components that are well-defined and have specific use contexts and variability points, which helps reduce the effort associated with using low-level middleware interfaces or OS APIs.

Domain-Specific Modeling Languages (DSMLs) and Patterns

DSMLs and patterns facilitate the model-based design, development, and analysis of DRE systems.

Figure 4 shows how DSMLs and patterns can be combined with component frameworks to build product instances. A DSML can represent either a vertical application domain model (specific to concerns within a specific industry or domain) or a horizontal model (generic to concerns that span several domains).

Vertical application domain models address the problems arising within a particular domain, and they are often modeled in a platform-independent manner (Frankel, 2003). Examples of such vertical application domains include industrial process control, telecommunications, and avionics mission-critical systems. Some DSML examples developed for vertical domains include the *Saturn Site Production Flow* (SSPF), which is a manufacturing execution system serving as an integral and enabling component of the business process for an automotive factory (Long, Misra, & Sztipanovits, 1998). Another example is the *Embedded System Modeling Language* (ESML) (Karsai, Neema, Abbott, & Sharp, 2002), which models mission computing embedded avionics applications in the Boeing Bold Stroke PLA.

Horizontal platform domain models are also called platform-specific models (Frankel, 2003). A platform-specific model is a model of a system that is linked to a specific technological platform (e.g., a specific middleware platform, operating system or database). An example of a DSML for horizontal platforms is the *Rhapsody* modeling environment (iLogix, 2006), which allows application generation for embedded software platforms

Figure 4. Integration of domain-specific modeling and component frameworks

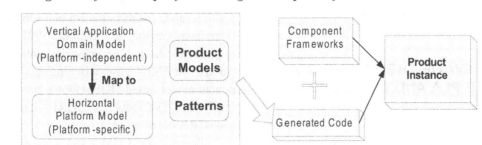

based on many real-time operating systems. Other examples of DSMLs for horizontal platforms include the *Platform Independent Component Modeling Language* (PICML) (Balasubramanian et al., 2005a) and J2EEML (White, Schmidt, & Gokhale, 2005), which facilitate the development, deployment, and configuration of QoS-enabled component-based DRE systems based on CCM and EJB, respectively.

The main idea is that it should be possible to use a model transformation technique to transform vertical application domain models to a horizontal platform domain model. Regardless of whether the DSMLs target horizontal or vertical domains, *model interpreters* can be used to generate various artifacts (such as code and metadata descriptors for deployment and configuration), which can be integrated with component frameworks to form executable applications or simulations. Key advantages of using DSMLs and patterns in PLAs are to rigorously capture the key roles and responsibilities of a product instance and help automate repetitive tasks that must be accomplished for each product instance.

In summary, an MDE-based PLA for software-intensive systems must be based on an architecture that adheres to well-documented principles of architectural design with a clear separation of commonalities and appropriate provisions for incorporating variations by integrating vertical/horizontal DSMLs, component frameworks, middleware and OS platforms. In this architecture, MDE technologies are used to model PLA features and glue components together; for example, they could be utilized to synthesize deployment artifacts for standard middleware platforms (Balasubramanian et al., 2006).

OVERVIEW OF THE BOEING BOLD STROKE PLA AND EQAL MDE TOOL

This section introduces a case study based on a real-time avionics mission computing product line called Boeing Bold Stroke and describes the structure and functionality of the *Event QoS Aspect Language* (EQAL) MDE tool based on this product line. The Boeing Bold Stroke PLA supports many Boeing product variants (e.g., F/A-18E, F/A-18F, F-15E, and F-15K) using a component-based publish/subscribe pattern (Gamma et al., 1995). The EQAL MDE tool is intended to reduce many complexities associated with the integration, deployment and configuration of different implementations of publish/subscribe mechanism. The Bold Stroke PLA and its associated models in EQAL will serve as the case study throughout this chapter.

Overview of Boeing Bold Stroke Product Line Architecture

Figure 5 illustrates the Boeing Bold Stroke PLA (Sharp, 1999), which was developed by Boeing in the mid-1990s to support systematic reuse of avionics mission computing functionality and is configurable for product-specific functionality (such as heads-up display, navigation, and sensor management) and execution environments (such as different networks/buses, hardware, operating systems, and programming languages) for a variety of military aircraft. Bold Stroke is a very complex framework with several thousand components implemented in several million lines of C++ code.

The Boeing Bold Stroke architecture contains a set of event-driven component-based component frameworks built atop (1) The ACE ORB (TAO) (Schmidt, Levine, & Mungee, 1998), which implements key Real-time CORBA (OMG, 2005a) features, and (2) TAO's Real-time Event Service (Harrison, Levine, & Schmidt, 1997), which implements the publish/subscribe architectural pattern. Bold Stroke uses a Boeing-specific component model called PRISM (Roll, 2003), which implements a variant of the CORBA Component Model (CCM) atop TAO.

Following the CCM specification, PRISM defines the following types of ports, which are

Figure 5. Boeing bold stroke product line architecture

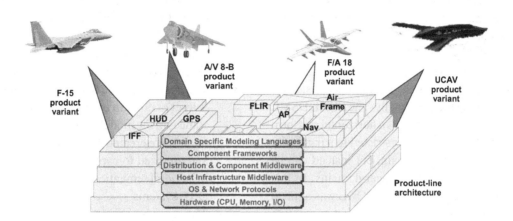

named interfaces, and connection points components used to collaborate with each other:

- **Facets**, which define named interfaces that process method invocations from other components.
- **Receptacles**, which provide named connection points to facets provided by other components.
- **Event sources and event sinks**, which indicate a willingness to exchange event messages with one or more components via event channels.

Bold Stroke is a representative PLA for DRE systems in the real-time avionics mission computing domain. Its event-driven communication architecture employs a control flow/data flow (Sharp, 1999) principle, where control flow represents the movement of execution through a software system, while the data flow represents the movement of data through a software system. Depending on requirements, different product variants in the Boeing Bold Stroke PLA may require different levels of QoS assurance for event communication, including timing constraints,

event delivery latency, jitter, and scalability. Even within the same product variant, different levels of QoS assurance must be ensured for different communication paths, depending on criticality of the data. For example, the communication path between a collision radar component and the LED display component must have much more stringent timeliness deadline requirements than regular GPS components and navigation display components.

To alleviate the complexity in provisioning the event-driven publish/subscribe services and their QoS assurance in the Boeing Bold Stroke PLA, we designed an MDE-based tool called the Event QoS Aspect Language (EQAL) that can automate and simplify the integration of publish/subscribe services into QoS-enabled component-based systems.

Overview of the EQAL MDE Tool

One core part of the EQAL MDE tool is the EQAL DSML (Edwards, Deng, Schmidt, Gokhale, & Natarajan, 2004), which is implemented using the Generic Modeling Environment (GME) (Lédeczi, Nordstrom, Karsai, Volgyesi, & Maroti, 2001).

The GME is a toolkit that supports the development of DSMLs. The EQAL DSML provides an integrated set of metamodels, model interpreters, and standards-based component middleware that allow DRE system developers to visually configure and deploy event-driven communication mechanisms in DRE systems via models instead of programming them manually. The EQAL DSML is an example that supports a horizontal platform domain; that is, it is not restricted to a particular vertical application domain, but instead can be leveraged by multiple vertical domains. In this case study, we describe how EQAL was applied to the Bold Stroke avionics mission computing PLA.

As shown in Figure 6, EQAL is a layered architecture that supports several types of abstractions, which are subject to change stemming from domain evolution as explained below:

- The *bottom layer* in the architecture is the EQAL Runtime Framework, which is a portable, OS-independent middleware framework based on light-weight CCM (OMG,

Figure 6. EQAL MDE tool architecture

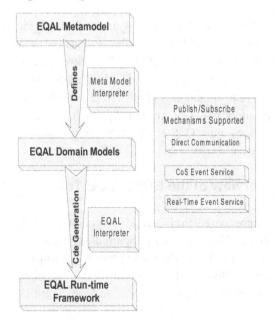

2004b). The EQAL Runtime Framework provides an extensible way to deploy various event-driven publish/subscribe mechanisms, including a two-way event communication mechanism based on direct method invocation instead of using a mediator channel.

- The *middle layer* in the EQAL architecture is a set of domain models that represent instances of the modeled DRE systems. These models are created using the EQAL DSML and are used to capture the structural and behavioral semantic aspects of event-driven DRE systems.

- The *top layer* of the EQAL architecture consists of a metamodel that enables developers to model concepts of event-driven DRE systems, including the configuration and deployment of various publish/subscribe services. This layer also contains several model interpreters that synthesize different types of configuration files that specify QoS configurations, parameters, and constraints, such as the threading model for event dispatching, event filtering configuration, and event channel federation configurations (Edwards et al., 2004). The EQAL interpreters automatically generate publish/subscribe service configuration files and service property description files needed by the underlying EQAL Runtime Framework and selected middleware.

As shown in Figure 7, EQAL allows DRE system deployers to create and synthesize publish/subscribe QoS configurations and deployments via graphical models (i.e., EQAL domain models) that are much easier to understand and analyze than hand-crafted code. During the modeling phase, EQAL ensures that dependencies between configuration parameters are enforced by declaring constraints on the contexts in which individual options are valid (e.g., priority-based thread allocation policies are only valid with component event connections that have assigned

Figure 7. Code generation from EQAL domain model

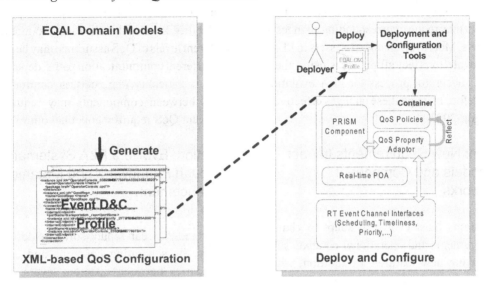

priorities). EQAL can then automatically validate configurations and notify users of incompatible QoS properties during model validation, rather than at component deployment and runtime. The generated XML-based QoS configuration and deployment descriptors can then be fed into deployment and configuration runtime tools to deploy and configure the components and real-time event channels within the Boeing Bold Stroke.

SUPPORT MDE-BASED PLA EVOLUTION WHEN FACING DOMAIN EVOLUTION

This section examines the following challenges associated with evolving MDE-based PLAs:

1. Challenges stemming from capturing new requirements into existing MDE-based PLAs for DRE systems.
2. Challenges stemming from migrating existing domain models with MDE-based PLA evolution.

For each challenge, we explain the context in which the challenge arises and identify key problems that must be addressed. Many of these challenges also exist in MDE-based PLAs for DRE systems, so they are not limited solely to event-driven DRE systems as described in our case study. In the remainder of this section, we first discuss the challenges and solutions associated with domain-specific component framework evolution and DSML evolution, then the challenges and solutions associated with domain model evolution.

Challenges Stemming from Capturing New Requirements into Existing MDE-based PLAs for DRE Systems

Context

Evolution is a natural occurrence in software development and an inevitable part of the software PLA lifecycle (Chapin, Hale, Kham, Ramil, & Tan, 2001). The changes may be initiated to correct, improve, or extend assets or products. Because assets are often dependent on other assets, changes to one asset may require corresponding changes in other assets. Moreover, changes to assets in PLAs can propagate to affect all products using these assets. A successful process for PLA evolution must therefore manage these changes effectively (McGregor, 2003).

Problem: New Requirements Impact Metamodels and Component Frameworks

DRE systems must evolve to adapt to changing requirements and operational contexts such as supporting new features. In addition, when some emerging technologies become sufficiently mature, it is often desirable to integrate them into existing PLAs for DRE systems. Figure 8 shows different affected scopes caused by such evolution.

In our Boeing Bold Stroke case study, for example, depending on system requirements, different product variants in the Bold Stroke PLA may require different levels of QoS assur-

ance for event communication, including timing constraints, event delivery latency, jitter, and scalability. Even within the same product variant, different levels of QoS assurance may be required for different communication paths, depending on system criticality (e.g., certain communication paths between components may require more stringent QoS requirements than others).

Solution: Evolve a PLA Systematically Through Framework and Metamodel Enhancement.

A layered PLA can reduce software design complexity by separating concerns and enforcing boundaries between different layers. Because different layers in a PLA need to interact with each other through predefined interfaces, to integrate new requirements into a PLA, all layers must evolve in a systematic manner. This evolution can be generalized to the following three steps:

1. **Component framework evolution.** As discussed earlier, frameworks are often built atop middleware and OS platforms to

Figure 8. Challenges stemming from adding new requirements into model-driven software PLAs

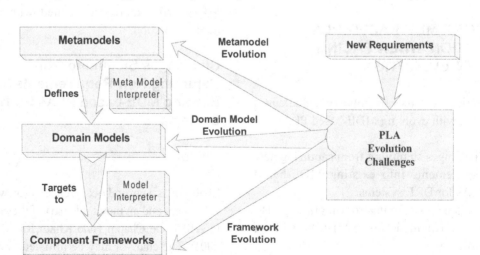

provide the runtime environment of DRE systems. As a result, whenever a DRE system must evolve to adapt to new requirements, component frameworks are often affected because they have direct impact on the system.

2. **DSML evolution.** DSML metamodels and interpreters are often used to capture the *variability* and *features* of DRE systems to expose different capabilities for different product variants. As discussed previously and shown in Figure 2, typically the DSMLs for vertical application domains have a higher level of abstraction than DSMLs for horizontal platform domains. These lower level DSMLs are built atop domain-specific component frameworks and are often used to glue different component framework entities together to form a complete application. Therefore, the evolution of lower level DSMLs should be performed after framework evolution is completed.

3. **Domain model evolution.** The DSML metamodel defines a type system to which domain models must conform. Because the changes to the metamodel of a DSML often invalidate the existing domain models by redefining the type system, domain model evolution must be performed after the DSML evolution.

In the remainder of this section, we further elaborate the solution approach and describe how it applies to our case study.

Component Framework Evolution

Component frameworks consist of a set of core reusable components that can be configured using well-defined interfaces. In order to capture the commonalities of software PLAs, one must formulate a set of usage patterns. The component frameworks encapsulate these usage patterns and provide reusable libraries that contain wrapper façades for the underlying implementation classes

and shield component developers from tedious and error-prone programming tasks associated with lower-level details. Component frameworks are typically designed by analyzing various potential problems that the frameworks might address and identifying which parts of each solution are the same and which areas of each solution are unique through the SCV analysis.

The first step is to define the domains (i.e., the problem areas a framework addresses) and the context of the framework. The next step is to define the attributes that recur across all members of the family of products based on the framework. The final step is to describe the attributes unique to the different members of the family of products. The SCV analysis requires extensive knowledge about the domain and the PLA requirements so one can reason what parts of the system should be implemented by the framework (commonalities) and what parts of the system should be specialized in subclasses or parameters (variabilities). To implement such design usually requires effective and skillful use of programming language features, such as templates and virtual functions, in conjunction with design patterns (Gamma et al. 1995).

Applying the Solution to the EQAL Case Study
In our EQAL case study, the scope is to design a framework to simplify the event communication between the event sources and event sinks of PRISM components. The commonality in this scope is straightforward, that is, every software product instance should implement an event-driven publish/subscribe pattern. The variability of the EQAL Runtime Framework results from different concrete service types that provide different interfaces and different QoS mechanism for the event communication, as shown in Figure 9. Because different real-time publish/subscribe services depend on different representations of real-time QoS properties, the EQAL Runtime Framework implements the adapter pattern that converts a service-independent representation

of real-time properties into a service-specific representation.

The benefits of EQAL's design are twofold: (1) component developers need not concern themselves with peculiar configuration interfaces, and (2) no matter what changes occur to the underlying publish/subscribe services, the interface exposed to components does not change. The EQAL Runtime framework also implements the strategy pattern to enhance the extensibility by allowing new publish/subscribe services to be easily plugged-in. This design results in a pluggable publish/subscribe service implementation that is interchangeable and extensible, and enables all event communication mechanisms supported by EQAL to provide the same interface, yet can also be configured with different strategies and QoS configurations even facing the domain evolution of adding new publish/subscribe service types.

DSML Evolution
The core component in the DSML is the metamodel. To help understand the context of

domain evolution, Figure 10 presents a matrix of several evolution tasks that require automated assistance to manage the various dependencies among metamodels, instance models, and corresponding source code. As shown at the top of Figure 10, a metamodel represents a modeling language definition that is instantiated to represent end-user intentions in a specific domain. Elements in the instance models (middle of figure) have metatypes that are specified in the metamodel. A vertical transformation (i.e., a transformation that goes across abstraction layers) exists between the instance models and the legacy source code at the bottom, which represents updates that are needed in one artifact that are triggered by a change at a different layer of abstraction. Correspondingly, horizontal transformation occurs at the same layer of abstraction to address changing requirements (i.e., the Δ at each layer represents a horizontal transformation).

To simplify the evolution of DSMLs, the reusability of metamodels is crucial when the domain becomes complex. Ideally, a metamodel

Figure 9. Component framework architecture of EQAL

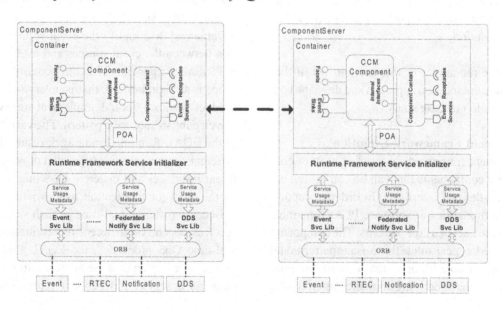

can be developed based on a set of reusable (usually smaller) metamodel units, with different units capturing different aspects in the domain of interest. For example, these metamodel units might include different variations of signal flow, finite state machines, data type specifications, and petri-nets. The unified metamodel can then extend these units and glue them together. This technique is called *compositional metamodeling* (Karsai et al., 2004), and the main motivation of this technique is to make metamodels more scalable and easier to evolve.

Composition metamodeling provides a capability for reusing and combining existing modeling languages and language concepts. When changes need to be made in the metamodel units to reflect a better understanding of the given aspect in the domain, such changes can be propagated automatically to the metamodels that utilize them. Furthermore, by precisely specifying the extension and

composition rules, models specified in the original domain language can be automatically translated to comply with the new, extended and composed, modeling language. Another important benefit of compositional modeling is its ability to add new capabilities while simultaneously leveraging prior constraints and model generators of existing DSMLs. Thus, it is ideal for evolving existing DSMLs to address new requirements.

Applying the Solution to the EQAL Case Study
EQAL is implemented within GME, which offers the compositional modeling capability. When new publish/subscribe services are integrated, a new DSML can be designed within GME and import the old EQAL metamodel as a reusable "library." Apart from being read-only, all objects in the metamodel imported through the library are equivalent to objects created from scratch. Because the new publish/subscribe services share

Figure 10. A matrix of evolution activities within DSMLs

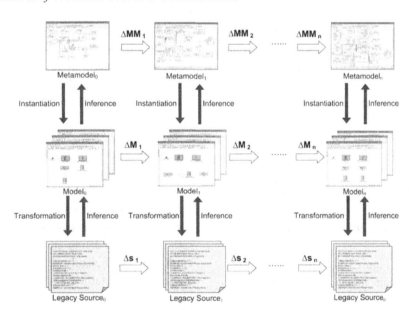

ΔMM: The changes made to the metamodels
ΔM: The changes reflected in the domain models
ΔS: The changes reflected in the legacy source

119

much commonality between the existing publish/subscribe services that EQAL already supports, when the old EQAL metamodel is imported as a library, subtypes can be created and instances from the metamodel library can refer to library objects through references.

Challenges Stemming from Migrating Existing Domain Models with MDE-Based PLA Evolution

Context

The primary value of the MDE paradigm stems from the models created using the DSML. These models specify the system from which the executable application can be generated or composed. Changes to the system can be modeled and the resulting executable model is thus a working version of the actual system. Unfortunately, if the metamodel is changed, all models that were defined using that metamodel may require maintenance to adapt to the semantics that represent the system correctly. Without ensuring the correctness of the domain models after a change to the domain, the benefits of MDE will be lost. The only way to use instance models based on the original metamodel is to migrate them to use the modified metamodel. During this migration process, we must preserve the existing set of domain model assets and allow new features to be added into domain models; ideally, with as little human intervention as possible.

Problem: Existing Domain Model Evolution Techniques Require Excessive Human Intervention

As illustrated in Figure 11, to preserve the existing set of domain model assets, old domain models must be transformed to become compliant with the changed metamodel. In the MDE research community, particularly in the DSML community, research has been conducted on us-

ing model transformation to address metamodel evolution (Sprinkle et al., 2003, Gray et al., 2006, Jouault & Kurtev, 2006). The underlying structure of models, particularly visual models, can be described by graphs. Model transformation research has therefore often been conducted in the context of graph transformation. In particular, recent research (Balogh & Varro, 2007; Vizhanyo, Agrawal, & Shi, 2004) has shown that graph transformation is a promising formalism to specify model transformations rules.

Most existing model transformation techniques, however, require the transformation be performed *after* the domain metamodel has changed. For example, when an old metamodel is modified and a new metamodel based on it is created, the model transformation must consider both the old metamodel and new metamodel as input, and then manually specify the model transformation rules based on these two metamodels by using a transformation specification language provided by the transformation tool. Although such a design approach could solve the model transformation problem, it introduces additional effort in specifying the model transformation rules, even if the metamodel evolution is minor (e.g., a simple rename of a concept in the metamodel). This additional effort is particularly high when the metamodels are complex, because the transformation tool must take both complex metamodels as input to specify the transformation.

Solution: Tool-Supported Domain Model Migration

To preserve the assets of domain models, our approach is to integrate *model migration* capabilities into the metamodeling environment itself. This approach is sufficiently generic to be applied to any existing metamodeling environment. A description of the change in semantics between an old and a new DSML is a sufficient specification to transform domain models such that they are correct in the new DSML. Moreover, the pat-

Figure 11. Domain model evolution problem

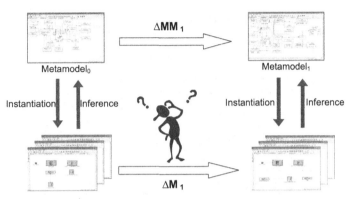

$\triangle$MM: The changes made to the metamodels

$\triangle$M: The changes reflected in the domain models

tern that specifies the proper model migration is driven by the change in semantics and may be fully specified by a model composed of entities from the old and new metamodels, along with directions for their modification.

Below we describe how syntactic and semantic based model transformation approaches can be integrated to address the domain model migration problem.

Integration of Syntactic-Based and Semantic-Based Domain Model Evolution

The purpose of a DSML metamodel is to properly define the syntax and semantics to precisely describe software-intensive systems at a higher level of abstraction. As a result, both the syntax and the semantics of a metamodel can be affected when it is migrated from one version to another version. Consequently, to migrate a source domain model to the destination model, we must deal with both the syntax aspect and the semantics aspect.

Based on the characteristics of metamodel change, we have classified 8 atomic types of metamodel changes, as shown in Table 1. From this table, we can see that the all "additions" (addition of new type, new attribute or new association

between types) to the metamodel will not affect the domain models because the target metamodel is a *superset* of the source metamodel and all the relationships of the source metamodel will still be preserved. On the other hand, other types of metamodel changes including all "deletion" and "modifications" will result in unavoidable domain model change because the target metamodel is no longer a *superset* of the source metamodel.

These results provide intuition into the problem of domain model evolution. In some cases, the semantics can be easily specified. For example, if the metamodel designer deletes an atom called "foo" in the metamodel and creates a new atom called "bar" we can then specify the semantics of the change as:

replace(Atom("foo") -> Atom("bar"));

Syntactic metamodel changes, however, can often affect semantic changes, which result in a highly challenging task in model migration, that is, *semantic migration*. Semantic migration requires that the meaning of the old domain models be preserved after the transformation and that the new domain models conform to the entire set of static constraints required in the new domain.

Table 1. How atomic types of metamodel changes will affect domain models

Type of Metamodel Changes		Domain Model Change Required?
Additions		
1	Addition of new type	No
2	Addition of new attribute of a type	No
3	Addition of association between types	No
Deletions		
4	Deletion of an existing type	Yes
5	Deletion of an attribute of a type	Yes
6	Deletion of association between types	Yes
Modifications		
7	Replacing one type with another type	Yes
8	Replacing one association with another	Yes

For model migration, we generalized two approaches to perform model transformation with semantic migration. In the first approach, given two *distinct* metamodels, source metamodel and destination metamodel, we can perform a transformation that converts the source models in entirety to the destination models. This means that a complete set of rules is needed to convert each entity in the models. In the second approach, we create a *unified* metamodel (*old + new*), such that both old and new domain models are valid. Developers can then write transformation specifications that convert those parts of the model belonging to the source part of the paradigm to equivalent models in the destination part of the paradigm.

We have found that the second approach is much cleaner and user-friendly than the first approach because it requires much less human effort. In particular, in this second approach, after the unified metamodel is formulated, we can use an "SQL-like" declarative language that allows one to query and change the model to define model transformation rules. The *Embedded Constraint Language* (ECL), used by the C-SAW GME plug-

in (Gray, Bapty, Neema, & Tuck, 2001), is such a language. ECL is a textual language for describing transformations on visual models. Similar to the Object Constraint Language (OCL) defined in OMG's UML specification, ECL provides concepts such as collection and model navigation. In addition, the ECL also provides a rich set of operators that are not found in the OCL to support model aggregations, connections, and transformations. ECL is a declarative language that allows one to specify the formal transformation rules of the syntax translator to capture the semantic migration.

In previous work, we showed how ECL can be used to accomplish several model transformation tasks (Gray et al., 2006). As an input language to C-SAW, ECL can support aspect modeling, as well as the ability to scale a base model to a larger model with replicated structures. Figure 12 illustrates an input source model being transformed by an ECL transformation rule to generate a new target model. An example of using ECL to handle the domain model migration in our case study is described in the next subsection.

Applying the Solution to the EQAL Case Study

In an old version of the EQAL metamodel there is a modeling object type called "`EventChannelGateway`," which can be used to federate different event channels together (Edwards et al., 2004). The definition of such a modeling element in a metamodel is similar to defining a class in C++ or Java. With domain evolution, this `EventChannelGateway` object type needs to be defined as an *abstract base* type (similar to the *abstract base* class concept in C++ or Java), and two new derived types called `IIOPGatway` and `UDPGateway` are defined in order to configure different underlying transport protocols between event channels. An issue arises regarding the type assignment of `EventChannelGateway` elements; depending on the context, these elements could be migrated to either the type of `IIOPGatway` or `UDPGateway`. In cases like these, it is quite challenging to discover the semantics of the change, that is, the semantics of

the model elements cannot be deduced from the syntax. To require that such algorithms provide actual semantic migration capabilities necessitates human input because semantic changes in metamodels cannot be captured through syntactic changes alone.

Figure 13 shows the BasicSP application scenario (Balasubramanian et al., 2005b) in the Boeing Bold Stroke PLA. We use the BasicSP scenario as an example to showcase the problems encountered when evolving PLAs for component-based DRE systems and motivate the need of ECL for model transformation. In this figure, two component instances named `BMDevice` and `BMClosedED` are connected with each other through a real-time event channel provided by TAO's Real-time Event Service. An event channel consists of one `RTEC_Proxy_Consumer` module and `RTEC_Proxy_Supplier` module, which could be configured with various QoS settings, such as event dispatching threading models, priority configuration and periodic event processing configurations. Consider a domain

Figure 12. Model transformation using the ECL (Gray et al., 2006)

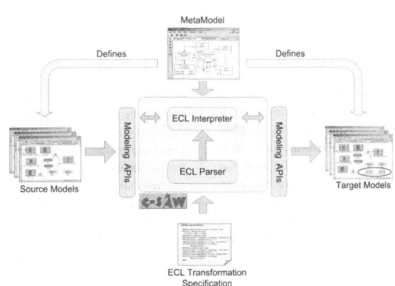

Figure 13. EQAL configuring real-time event service between two components

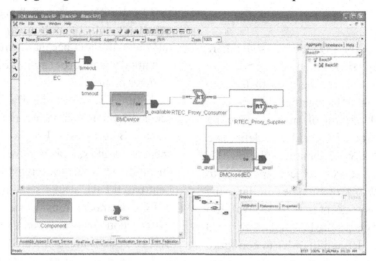

evolution scenario, where the Real-time Event Service is not the desired choice for a particular Bold Stroke product variant, so it must be replaced with the TAO Federated Notification Service. In this case, the current domain model of Figure 13 will become invalid and must be migrated to the new EQAL DSML that supports the configuration of TAO's Federated Notification Service.

With ECL, a model transformation rule can be defined to accomplish the model migration task noted above. In the ECL, a strategy represents a transformation rule that is applied to a specific location of a model. A query can be written in the ECL to define a collection of models that need to be transformed, and a strategy can be invoked on the collection. The strategy in Box 1 speci-fies the desired model migration. The semantic meaning of this transformation is straightforward, that is, line 1 declares the strategy based on the ECL syntax; lines 4-10 find the interested model elements and their associations that are based on TAO's Real-time Event Service; line 11 removes the found model elements, and lines 13-20 replace these model elements and associations with TAO's Federated Notification Service. (see Box 1)

CONCLUSION

Change is a natural and inevitable part of the soft-ware-intensive system lifecycle. The changes may be initiated to correct, improve, or extend assets or products. Because assets are often dependent on other assets, changes to one asset may require corresponding changes in other assets. Moreover, changes to assets in PLAs can propagate to affect all products using these assets.

To use MDE-based PLA technologies ef-fectively in practice requires practical and scal-able solutions to the *domain evolution problem*, which arises when existing PLAs are extended or refactored to handle unanticipated require-ments or better satisfy existing requirements. For example, changing metamodels in a PLA often invalidates models based on previous versions of the metamodels. Although software developers can manually update their models or components developed with a previous metamodel to work with the new metamodel, this approach is clearly tedious, error-prone, and nonscalable. A success-ful process for PLA evolution must therefore manage these changes effectively.

Box 1.

```
1.  strategy ChangeToFNS() {
2.      declare FNS_Proxy_Consumer, FNS_Proxy_Supplier : model;
3.
4.      // Find interested model elements…
5.      if(atoms()->select(a | a.kindOf() = "RTEC_Proxy_Consumer")->size() >= 1) then
6.
7.      //get the RTEC_Proxy_Consumer model element
8.      //and its connections
9.      …
10.     //delete the RTEC_Proxy_Consumer model element
11.     RTEC_Model.deleteModel("RTEC_Proxy_Consumer", "RTEC_proxy_consumer");
12.
13.     //add the FNS_Proxy_Consumer model
14.     FNS_Proxy_Consumer:= addModel("FNS_Proxy_Consumer", "FNS_proxy_consumer");
15.     FNS_Proxy_Consumer.setAttribute("Reactive", "1");
16.     FNS_Proxy_Consumer.setAttribute("LockType", "Thread Mutex");
17.
18.     //add the connections
19.     RTEC_Model.addConnection("Event_Source_Proxy_Consumer", event_source, FNS_Proxy_Consumer);
20.     RTEC_Model.addConnection("Proxy_Supplier_Event_Sink", FNS_Proxy_Consumer, event_sink);
21.
22.     //do similar to the FNS_Proxy_Supplier model
23.     …
24.     endif;
25. }
```

To rectify these problems, this chapter describes a layered and compositional architecture to modularize system concerns and reduce the effort associated with domain evolution. This chapter illustrates via a case study how systematic evolution with three ordered steps can maintain the stability of domain evolution against MDE-based software PLAs, and how structural-based model transformations help reduce human effort by automatically transforming existing domain models based on metamodel-based rules.

The following is a summary of lessons learned from our experience in evolving product-lines using MDE tools:

- **DSMLs and component frameworks are highly synergistic:** An MDE approach expedites PLA development with the proper integration of DSMLs and component frameworks. The component frameworks help shield the complexities of the design and implementation of modeling tools, and decouple many aspects of concerns

between the modeling tools and the executable systems. In our case study, if the publish/subscribe service type is the only missing or changing concern in the Boeing Bold Stroke PLA (which is typical in our case), little new application code must be written, yet the complexity of the generation tool remains manageable due to the limited number of well-defined configuration "hot spots" exposed by the underlying infrastructure. Likewise, when component deployment plans are incomplete or must change, the effort required is significantly less than starting from the raw component middleware without MDE tool support.

- **Declarative-based model transformation alleviates transformation effort:** Structural-based model transformations help maintain the stability of domain evolution of MDE-based DRE systems by automatically migrating domain models. A declarative-based model transformation language like ECL is an ideal approach in such a case. The case study presented in this chapter highlights the ease of specification and the general flexibility provided by the transformation engine.

- **Testing and debugging of transformation specification is still hard:** Transformation specifications, such as those used to specify the transformation strategy in this chapter, are written by humans and prone to error. To improve the robustness and reliability of model transformation, there is a need for testing and debugging support to assist in finding and correcting the errors in transformation specifications. Ongoing and future work on ECL focuses on the construction of testing and debugging utilities to ensure the correctness of ECL transformation specifications.

All software in this chapter can be downloaded from our Web sites. The EQAL framework is shipped as part of the CIAO and is available at http://download.dre.vanderbilt.edu. The EQAL DSML is available at http://www.dre.vanderbilt.edu/cosmic/. C-SAW is available at http://www.cis.uab.edu/gray/research/C-SAW/.

FUTURE RESEARCH DIRECTIONS

This section discusses the future trends in the areas of MDE and component middleware, and how together they are impacting MDE-based PLAs, particularly for DRE systems.

Emerging Interest in Domain-Specific Modeling

The interest and adoption of DSMLs over the past decade has surged. Strong support for basic research has been committed by the large European Union ModelWare and ModelPlex projects, which are funded at 30M Euros (ModelWare Project, 2006). Metamodeling tools that support

DSM continue to emerge from both commercial and open source projects (e.g., Microsoft's DSL Toolkit (Microsoft, 2006) and the Eclipse Modeling Project (Eclipse, 2007)), as well as numerous academic research projects (e.g., Vanderbilt's Generic Modeling Environment (GME, 2007)). Initial success stories from industry adoption of DSM have been reported: The newly created DSM Forum (DSM Forum, 2007) serves as a repository of several dozen successful projects (mostly from industry, such as Nokia, Dupont, Honeywell, and NASA) that have adopted DSM. Over the past 5 years, the annual DSM workshop at OOPSLA (52 international participants in 2007) provides a venue for reporting experiences in DSM research and practice.

Future Research Directions of MDE Tools for DRE Systems

MDE has already played an important role in the assembly, configuration and deployment lifecycle stages of today's DRE systems. We envision next generation MDE tools will seamlessly integrate all lifecycle stages of software product lines, including requirement management, functionality specification, QoS specification, system partitioning and implementation, component assembly and packaging, system configuration, system planning and analysis and runtime system management. With such seamless integration, models will become vital artifacts in all aspects of software PLA development lifecycle, and sophisticated model transformation techniques will bridge the gap between models in different lifecycle stages. The need for seamless integration of models across the lifecycle is driving the need for integration across a collection of different modeling tools, where each offers some advanced capability not found in another tool. The need for tool integration will continue to heighten the role that model transformation plays as the key enabler of model sharing (Sendall & Kozaczynski, 2003).

Future Research Directions of Component Middleware for DRE Systems

The success of component middleware technologies has resulted in DRE systems created by customizing pre-existing COTS components rather than creating them from scratch. The increased use of pre-existing components shifts the focus from development to configuration and deployment of COTS components. With more COTS components provided by different vendors, the capability of *heterogeneous* deployment becomes a challenging task to evolve today's DRE systems.

Future component middleware technologies will enable rapid development of adaptive large scale DRE systems to accommodate changing operating environments. To facilitate the development of large-scale DRE systems, component middleware must support the agility in business service provisioning within and across organizations while ensuring the quality of service. The combination of these two techniques will finally enable software PLA developers to capture and represent adaptability of DRE systems at the business level and automatically translate this business adaptability into component and process adaptability.

As PLAs become more complex, they will be adopted into software-intensive systems of very large-scale, as typified by the focus of Ultra Large-Scale systems (Ultra Large-Scale, 2007). In such cases, it is not unrealistic to imagine the PLAs using multiple different middleware platforms. To accommodate these requirements demands new investigation in deployment and configuration across heterogeneous middleware platforms. This heterogeneity also adds to the challenges in provisioning QoS end-to-end for these PLAs. All these require novel modeling capabilities that can abstract away the heterogeneity.

We envision these future research directions will greatly simplify the development of MDE-based PLAs and make next generation DRE systems more robust.

ACKNOWLEDGMENT

This was supported in part by an NSF CAREER award (CCF-0643725).

REFERENCES

Atkinson, C., Bayer, J., Bunse, C., Kamsties, E., Laitenberger, O., Laqua, R., et al. (2002). *Component-based product line engineering with UML*. Addison-Wesley.

Balasubramanian, K., Balasubramanian, J., Parsons, J., Gokhale, A., & Schmidt, D.C. (2005a, March). A platform-independent component modeling language for distributed real-time and embedded systems. In *Proceedings of the 11th IEEE Real-Time and Embedded Technology and Applications Symposium*, San Francisco, CA, (pp. 190-199).

Balasubramanian, K., Gokhale, A., Lin, Y., Zhang, J., & Gray, J. (2006, June). Weaving deployment aspects into domain-specific models. *International Journal on Software Engineering and Knowledge Engineering, 16*(3), 403-424.

Balasubramanian, K., Krishna, A., Turkay, E., Balasubramanian, J., Parsons, J., Gokhale, A., & Schmidt, D.C. (2005b, April). Applying model-driven development to distributed real-time and embedded avionics systems *International Journal of Embedded Systems, special issue on Design and Verification of Real-Time Embedded Software*.

Balogh, A., & Varro, D. (2007). The model transformation of the VIATRA2 framework. *Science of Computer Programming (Special Issue on Model Transformation)*.

Bollella, G., Gosling, J., Brosgol, B., Dibble, P., Furr, S., Hardin, D., & Turnbull, M. (2000). *The real-time specification for Java*. Addison-Wesley.

Buschmann, F., Meunier, R., Rohnert, H., Sommerlad, P., & Stal, M. (1996). *Pattern-oriented software architecture—a system of patterns*. John Wiley & Sons.

Chapin, N., Hale, J., Kham, K., Ramil, J., & Tan, W. (2001, January). Types of software evolution and software maintenance. *Journal of Software Maintenance: Research and Practice*, 3-30.

Clements, P., & Northrop, L. (2001). *Software product-lines: Practices and patterns*. Addison-Wesley.

Ultra large-scale systems: The report. (2007). CMU Technical Report. Retrieved March 7, 2008, from http://www.sei.cmu.edu/uls/

Coplien, J., Hoffman, D., & Weiss, D. (1998, November/December). Commonality and variability in software engineering. *IEEE Software*, *15*(6), 37-45.

Dashofy, E.M., Hoek, A., & Taylor, R.N. (2002, May). An infrastructure for the rapid development of XML-based architecture description languages. In *Proceedings of the 24th International Conference on Software Engineering*, Orlando, FL, (pp. 266-276).

Deng, G., Lenz, G., & Schmidt, D.C. (2005, October). Addressing domain evolution challenges for model-driven software product-line architectures (PLAs). In *Proceedings of the MoDELS 2005 Workshop on MDD for Software Product-lines: Fact or Fiction?*, Montego Bay, Jamaica.

DSM Forum. (2007). *From domain-specific modeling forum*. Retrieved March 7, 2008, from http://www.dsmforum.org/tools.html

Eclipse Modeling Project. (2007). Retrieved March 7, 2008, from http://www.eclipse.org/modeling/

Edwards, G., Deng, G., Schmidt, D.C., Gokhale, A., & Natarajan, B. (2004, October). Model-driven configuration and deployment of component middleware publisher/subscriber services. In *Proceedings of the 3rd ACM International Conference on Generative Programming and Component Engineering*, Vancouver, Canada, (pp. 337-360).

Frankel, D.S. (2003). *Model driven architecture: Applying MDA to enterprise computing*. John Wiley & Sons.

Gamma, E., Helm, R., Johnson, R., & Vlissides, J. (1995). *Design patterns: Elements of reusable object-oriented software*. Addison-Wesley.

GME. (2007). *Generic modeling environment*. Retrieved March 7, 2008, from http://escher.isis.vanderbilt.edu/downloads?tool=GME

Gray, J., Bapty, T., Neema, S., & Tuck, J. (2001). Handling crosscutting constraints in domain-specific modeling. *Communications of the ACM*, *44*(10), 87-93.

Gray, J., Lin, Y., & Zhang, J. (2006, February). Automating change evolution in model-driven engineering. In D. Schmidt (Ed.), *IEEE Computer*, *Special Issue on Model-driven Engineering*, *39*(2), 51-58.

Gray, J., Tolvanen, J., Kelly, S., Gokhale, A., Neema, S., & Sprinkle, J. (2007). Domain-specific modeling. In P. Fishwick (Ed.), *CRC handbook on dynamic system modeling*. CRC Press.

Heineman, G.T., & Councill, W.T. (2001). *Component-based software engineering: Putting the pieces together*. Addison-Wesley.

Harrison, T., Levine, D., & Schmidt, D.C. (1997, October). The design and performance of a real-time CORBA event service. In *Proceedings of OOPSLA*, Atlanta, GA, (pp. 184-200). ACM.

Hoek, A., Mikic-Rakic, M., Roshandel, R., & Medvidovic, N. (2001, September). Taming architectural evolution. In *Proceedings of the 8th*

European Software Engineering Conference (held jointly with 9ᵗʰ ACM SIGSOFT International Symposium on Foundations of Software Engineering), Vienna, Austria, (pp. 1-10).

IBM. (2007). *Rational software.* Retrieved March 7, 2008, from http://www-306.ibm.com/software/rational/

iLogix. (2006). *Rhapsody.* Retrieved March 7, 2008 from http://www.ilogix.com/sublevel.aspx?id=284

Jouault, F., & Kurtev, I. (2006, April). On the architectural alignment of ATL and QVT. In *Proceedings of ACM Symposium on Applied Computing* (pp. 1188-1195). Dijon, Bourgogne: France.

Karhinen, A., & Kuusela, J. (1998, February). Structuring design decisions for evolution. In *Proceedings of the Second International ESPRIT ARES Workshop,* Las Palmas de Gran Canaria, Spain, (pp. 223-234). Springer-Verlag.

Karsai, G., Maroti, M., Lédeczi, A., Gray, J., & Sztipanovits, J. (2004, March). Composition and cloning in modeling and metamodeling. *IEEE Transactions on Control System Technology, Special Issue on Computer Automated Multiparadigm Modeling, 12*(2), 263-278.

Karsai, G., Neema, S., Abbott, B., & Sharp, D. (2002, August). A modeling language and its supporting tools for avionics systems. In *Proceedings of the 21st Digital Avionics Systems Conference,* (Vol. 1, pp. 6A3-1-6A3-13).

Klusener, S., Laemmel, R., & Verhoef, C. (2005). Architectural modifications to deployed software. *Science of Computer Programming, 54,* 143-211.

Krueger, C.W. (2002, August). Variation management for software production lines. In *Proceedings of the Second International Conference of Software Product Lines,* SPLC 2, San Diego, CA, (pp. 37-48).

Lédeczi, Á., Nordstrom, G., Karsai, G., Volgyesi, P., & Maroti, M. (2001). On metamodel composition. In *Proceedings of the 2001 IEEE International Conference on Control Applications,* Mexico City, Mexico, (pp. 756-760).

Long, E., Misra, A., & Sztipanovits, J. (1998, August). Increasing productivity at Saturn. *IEEE Computer, 31*(8), 35-43.

Macala, R.R., Stuckey, L., & Gross, D. (1996, May). Managing domain-specific, product-line development. *IEEE Software, 14*(13), 57-67.

Mens, T., & D'Hondt, T. (2000, March). Automating support for software evolution in UML, *Automated Software Engineering, 7*(1), 39-59.

McGregor, J.D. (2003). *The evolution of product-line assets* (Tech. Rep. No. CMU/SEI-2003-TR-005m ESC-TR-2003-005).

Microsoft Corporation. (2000). *Microsoft COM technologies DCOM.*

Microsoft Corporation. (2006). *Microsoft domain-specific language (DSL) tools: Visual studio 2005 team system.* Retrieved March 7, 2008, from http://msdn.microsoft.com/vstudio/teamsystem/workshop/DSLTools

Microsoft Corporation. (2007). *Windows embedded CE 6.0.* Retrieved March 7, 2008, from http://www.microsoft.com/windows/embedded/

ModelWare Project. (2006). Retrieved March 7, 2008, from http://www.modelware-ist.org/

OMG. (2002, April). *MOF 2.0 query/views/transformations RFP.* OMG document ad/2002-04-10.

OMG. (2003, July). *The common object request broker: Architecture and specification.*

OMG. (2004a, December). *Data distribution service.* OMG document, formal/04-12-02.

OMG. (2004b).*Light-weight CORBA component model.* OMG document, ptc/04-06-10.

OMG. (2005a, January). *Real-time CORBA specification*. OMG document, formal/05-01-04.

OMG. (2005b, November). *MOF QVT final adopted specification*. OMG document, ptc/05-11-01.pdf.

OMG. (2006, April). *CORBA component model*. OMG Document formal/2006-04-01 ed.

Ommering, R., Linden, F., Kramer, J., & Magee, J. (2002, March). The Koala Component Model for consumer electronics software. *IEEE Computer*, *33*(3), 78-85.

Ran, A., & Kuusela, J. (1996, March). Design decision trees. In *Proceedings of the Eighth International Workshop on Software Specification and Design*, (p 172).

Roddick, J.F. (1992). Schema evolution in database systems: An annotated bibliography. *SIGMOD Record, 21*(4).

Roll, W. (2003, May). Towards model-based and CCM-based applications for real-time systems. In *Proceedings of the International Symposium on Object-oriented Real-time Distributed Computing (ISORC)*, Hokkaido, Japan, (pp. 75-82).

Schmidt, D. C. (1993). The ADAPTIVE communication environment: An object-oriented network programming toolkit for developing communication software. *Concurrency: Practice and Experience*, *5*(4), 269-286.

Schmidt, D. C. (2002, June). Middleware for real-time and embedded systems. *Communications of the ACM, 45*.

Schmidt, D.C. (2006, February). Model-driven engineering. *IEEE Computer*, 25-32.

Schmidt, D.C., Levine, D., & Mungee, S. (1998, April). The design and performance of real-time object request brokers. *Computer Communications, 21*, 294-324.

Schulte, M. (2003, May). Model-based integration of reusable component-based avionics system. In *Proceedings of the Eighth IEEE International Symposium on Object-oriented Real-time Distributed Computing (ISORC'05)* (pp. 62-71). Seattle, WA.

Sendall, S., & Kozaczynski, W. (2003, September-October). Model transformation—the heart and soul of model-driven software development. *IEEE Software, 20*(5), 42-45.

Sharp, D. (1999, October). Avionics product line software architecture flow policies. In *Proceedings of the 18th IEEE/AIAA Digital Avionics Systems Conference (DASC)*, St Louis, MO.

Siemens. (2007). Retrieved March 7, 2008, from http://www.us.sbt.siemens.com/bau/products/default.asp

Sprinkle, J., Agrawal, A., Levendovszky, T., Shi, F., & Karsai, G. (2003, April). Domain model translation using graph transformations. In *Proceedings of the Conference on Engineering of Computer-based Systems*, Huntsville, AL, (pp. 159-167).

Sprinkle, J., & Karsai, G. (2004, June). A domain-specific visual language for domain model evolution. *Journal of Visual Languages and Computing, 15*(3-4), 291-307.

Sun Microsystems. (2000). *Java remote method invocation specification*, revision 1.5, JDK 1.2, Oct. 1998.

Sun Microsystems. (2001). *Enterprise JavaBeans specification*. Retrieved March 7, 2008, from java.sun.com/products/ejb/docs.html

Szyperski, C. (2002). *Component software: Beyond object-oriented programming*. Addison-Wesley.

Timesys. (2002). *Predictable performance for dynamic load and overload*. Retrieved March 7,

2008, from www.timesys.com/prodserv/whitepaper/Predictable_Performance_1_0.pdf

Tolvanen, J.P., & Kelly, S. (2005). Defining domain-specific modeling languages to automate product derivation: Collected experiences. In *Proceeding of the 9th Software Product Line Conference*, Rennes, France, (pp. 198-209).

Vizhanyo, A., Agrawal, A., & Shi, F. (2004, October). Towards generation of efficient transformations. In *Proceeding of the ACM International Conference on Generative Programming and Component Engineering*, Vancouver, Canada, (pp. 298-316).

White, J., Schmidt, D.C., & Gokhale, A. (2005, October). Simplifying autonomic enterprise Java Bean applications via model-driven development: A case study. In *Proceedings of the 8th International Conference on Model Driven Engineering Languages and Systems*, Montego Bay, Jamaica, (pp. 601-615).

Wind River Systems. (1998). *VxWorks 5.3*. Retrieved March 7, 2008, from ww.wrs.com/products/html/vxworks.html

Zandy, V. C., & Miller, B. P. (2002, September). Reliable network connections. In *Proceedings of the Eighth Annual International Conference on Mobile Computing and Networking*, (pp. 95-106).

ADDITIONAL READING

Batory, D. (2006). Multilevel models in model-driven engineering, product lines, and metaprogramming. *IBM Systems Journal, 45*(3), 527-540.

Bézivin, J. (2001, July 29-August 03). From object composition to model transformation with the MDA. In *Proceedings of the 39th international Conference and Exhibition on Technology of Object-oriented Languages and Systems*, Washington, DC, (p. 350).

Bézivin, J. (2005). On the unification power of models. *Software and Systems Modeling, 4*(2), 171-188.

Billig, A., Busse, S., Leicher, A., & Süß, J. G. (2004, October 18-22). Platform independent model transformation based on triple. In *Proceedings of the 5th ACM/IFIP/USENIX International Conference on Middleware*, New York, (Vol. 78, pp. 493-511). New York: Springer-Verlag.

Bosch, J. (2000). *Design and use of software architectures: Adopting and evolving a product-line approach*. ACM Press/Addison-Wesley.

Buck, J., Ha, S., Lee, E.A., & Messerschmitt, D.G. (1991). Ptolemy: A framework for simulating and prototyping heterogeneous systems. *International Journal on Computer Simulation, 4*, 155-182.

Czarnecki, K., Antkiewicz, M., & Kim, C. H. (2006, December). Multi-level customization in application engineering. *Communications of the ACM, Special Issue on Software-Product Line Engineering*.

Czarnecki, K., & Helsen, S. (2003, October). Classification of model transformation approaches. In *Proceedings of the 2nd OOPSLA'03 Workshop on Generative Techniques in the Context of MDA*, Anaheim, CA.

Durán, A., Bernárdez, B., Genero, M., & Piattini, M. (2004, October). Empirically driven use case metamodel evolution. In *Proceedings of 7th International Conference Unified Modeling Language: Modeling Languages and Applications*, Lisbon, Portugal, (pp. 1-11).

Fairbanks, G., Garlan, D., & Scherlis, W. (2006, October). Design fragments make using frameworks easier. *ACM SIGPLAN Notices, 4*(10).

Greenfield, J., Short, K., Cook, S., & Kent, S. (2004). *Software factories: Assembling applica-*

tions with patterns, models, frameworks, and tools. John Wiley & Sons.

Gokhale, A., Balasubramanian, K., Balasubramanian, J., Krishna, A., Edwards, G.T., Deng, G., et al. (2007). Model driven middleware: A new paradigm for deploying and provisioning distributed real-time and embedded applications. In M. Aksit (Ed.), *Elsevier Journal of Science of Computer Programming: Special Issue on Model Driven Architecture.*

Gokhale, A., Schmidt, D. C., Natarajan, B., & Wang, N. (2002, October). Applying model-integrated computing to component middleware and enterprise applications. *The Communications of the ACM Special Issue on Enterprise Components, Service and Business Rules, 45.*

Gore, P., Schmidt, D.C., Gill, C., & Pyarali, I. (2004, May). The design and performance of a real-time notification service. In *Proceedings of the 10th Real-time Technology and Application Symposium* (pp. 112-120). Toronto, CA.

Gray, J., Bapty Neema, T., & Tuck, J. (2001, October). Handling crosscutting constraints in domain-specific modeling. *The Communications of the ACM.*

Johnson, R.E. (1997, October). Frameworks = (components + patterns). *Communications of the ACM, 40*(10), 39-42.

Ledeczi, A., Bakay, A., Maroti, M., Volgysei, P., Nordstrom, G., Sprinkle, J., & Karsai, G. (2001, November). Composing domain-specific design environments. *IEEE Computer,* 44-51.

Lenz, G., & Wienands, C. (2006, July 6). *Practical software factories in .NET.* Apress.

Pohl, K., Bockle, G., & Linden, F., van der. (2005). *Software product line engineering.* Berlin, Heidelberg, New York: Springer-Verlag.

Schmidt, D.C., Stal, M., Rohert, H., & Buschmann, F. (2000). *Pattern-oriented software architecture: Concurrent and networked objects.* John Wiley & Sons.

Sztipanovits, J., & Karsai, G. (1997, April). Model-integrated computing. *IEEE Computer,* 110-112.

Tourwé, T., & Mens, T. (2003, September). Automated support for framework-based software evolution. In *Proceedings of the International Conference on Software Maintenance,* (p. 148). Washington, DC: IEEE Computer Society.

Chapter VI
Traceability in Model–Driven Software Development

Ståle Walderhaug
SINTEF ICT, Norway & University of Tromsø, Norway

Erlend Stav
SINTEF ICT, Norway

Ulrik Johansen
SINTEF ICT, Norway

Gøran K. Olsen
SINTEF ICT, Norway

ABSTRACT

This chapter introduces a tracability solution for use in a model-driven software development approach. It argues that a trace model based on a provided traceability metamodel will provide a flexible solution for all types of artifacts to be traced througout the lifetime of a software system. The proposed traceability solution is demonstrated in the BusCatcher example where traces are established and analyzed. The authors hope that the metamodel and solution design can assist researchers and tool vendors in the development of unified trace models and services for model-driven software development approaches. Only then can the full potential of traceability be achieved.

INTRODUCTION

Developing an information system implies the creation, usage and modification of a large number of *artifacts*. An *artifact* can be defined as any object or work product in the software lifecycle and can take the form of a document, a requirement, a use case diagram or source code (Ramesh & Jarke, 2001). All artifacts involved in a system development process are related to some of the other artifacts through some kind of dependency relations, for example, *uses*, *implements*, *rationale*, *tests*. As the software systems are being developed, managed, maintained or extended, there is a need to trace and control these relations to maintain a complete documentation and ensure system consistency.

Traceability is about following the status of an artifact that is part of a system. Traceability information can improve the control of software quality and the development process. Software development processes such as the IBM Rational Unified Process (RUP) and RUP for Systems Engineering (Cantor, 2003) can utilize and facilitate traceability solutions. For instance, the Metrics set proposed by Espinoza (Espinoza, Alarcon, & Garbajosa, 2006) can be used to analyze the traceability solution and will provide valuable information to measure the system quality using, for example, the "Measurement and analysis" process area of Capability Maturity Model Integration (CMMI) (Carnegie Mellon University/Software Engineering Institute). However, this demands that the traceability information is captured, stored and made available for the actors involved in the development process.

Model-driven software development (MDSD) is a relatively new software engineering methodology that is getting much attention from the Software Engineering (SE) community. In MDSD, the architects and developers seek to represent all artifacts as model elements that have attributes, behavior, and relationships to other model elements. There is a common understanding in the MDSD community that a traceability solution should be integrated in the development and maintenance process (Desfray, 2003), but as of today there is no common way of sharing traceability information between the tools involved in the process(Aizenbud-Reshef, Nolan, Rubin, & Shaham-Gafni, 2006; Letelier, 2002). This leads to the problem statement addressed in this chapter:

How can (trace) relations between the artifacts involved in a MDSD project be established, used and managed in order to improve control over the quality of artifacts throughout the lifetime of a software system?

This problem can be further broken down into three subproblems:

- Artifact tools must create traceability information;
- Transformation information must be shared with other tools; and
- Services must be specified to improve software development process.

This chapter proposes a generic solution for traceability in MDSD that offers a metamodel and set of service specifications that is meant to cover both the specification and appliance of traceability. The core of the proposed traceability solution is a generic metamodel which can be used by a traceability manager to build a model of which artifacts and relations to trace, and which information to include in the traces. Further, the solution defines a set of extensions to the generic traceability metamodel. These extensions predefine reusable artifact and relation trace types, and are considered to be of common interests for various appliers of traceability. The predefined semantics of the extensions enable the development of tools with more predefined traceability support, and can also simplify and guide the development of trace models.

The objectives of this chapter are to:

- Show the usefulness of a shared traceability solution in (model-based) software development projects;
- Present a generic traceability solution for lifelong artifact traceability;
- Propose a method for incorporating traceability into the development process and tools; and
- Demonstrate the use of traceability services in an example.

The next section presents the background and the state of the art of traceability in software development. Then, a set of core traceability requirements and services are specified before a complete traceability solution is described. The described solution is used in a trivial example to demonstrate traceability concepts and services before remarks on future trends and concluding remarks are given.

BACKGROUND

Traceability in Software Development

Traceability is a concept that has been mainly used to manage requirements in software development projects. Early work on identifying problems on incorporating traceability into systems development was done by Gotel and Finkelstein (1994). In 2001, Ramesh and Jarke published the highly referenced article "Towards Reference Models for Requirements Traceability." Following an empirical approach they defined reference models for traceability links between various development tasks, and applied these in several use cases and incorporated the models into some tools. They define a simple model that is comprised of three layers: a metamodel defining which traceability models that can be defined; a set of reference traceability models that can be customized; and a database of actual traces, recorded under the chosen models. In this metamodel, four basic link types (i.e., Dependency, Satisfies, Rationale and Evolves-To) are specified, and links are grouped into "product-related" and "process-related" link types. From the work on reference models and tools, they conclude that *"the uptake of these models, if accompanied by appropriate management support and user attitudes, may indeed yield substantial benefits in terms of quality as well as efficiency, leading to improved software quality."*

There are many definitions of traceability (Champeau & Rochefort, 2003; Letelier, 2002; Ramesh & Jarke, 2001), and in this chapter a revised version of the one found in Aizenbud-Reshef

et al. (2006) is used. The definition is focused on traceability in software system development: *Traceability can be defined as the ability to track any relationship that exists between artifacts involved in the software-engineering life cycle.* The definition comprises all products created in the software development process, and the succeeding deployment and maintenance phases. And, the traceability information will have to be available during the whole lifetime of a software product, also after the deployment phase.

Aizenbud-Reshef et al. (2006) present the state of the art on traceability. They found that most traceability tools that are available focus on requirements tracing, to ensure that all requirements are tested and implemented. The actual trace information is stored either as a part of the artifact itself, or in an external repository. Compromise solutions that store traceability information inside the artifact and export some parts of it to an external repository have been implemented and tested. The main benefit from having an external repository is that it allows for sharing of traceability information between tools. However, an external traceability information storage solution requires a unique identification of all artifacts that are involved and a standardized way of representing the trace information.

During the lifetime of a software system, the relationships between artifacts will gradually erode because of subsequent revisions, bug-fixes and changes in requirements and design. The software development process should include management of traceability information. In a survey on traceability models in 32 projects from six IT companies, Gills found that traceability was paid special attention to in 53% of the cases, medium attention in 22% and 25% paid no attention. Despite the positive look on traceability, only 18% used a special tool for managing traceability information (Gills, 2005).

There is a common understanding that a traceability solution that is accessible with up to date information will provide valuable services to the project managers, software developers and IT maintenance consultants. The information will assist in controlling the quality of the software artifacts and the process of developing them, and can be valuable input to system and project quality measuring techniques. Aizenbud-Reshef states that:

A well-defined, automated method of accomplishing traceability would be of value in any domain, on any project with any methodology. (Aizenbud-Reshef et al., 2006)

Integration of Traceability into Development Tools

Traceability information can improve the control of software quality and the development process if the information is available to those who need it. According to Ramesh (Ramesh & Jarke, 2001), the U.S. Department of Defense spends about 4% of its IT costs on traceability. A well-functioning tool and process would improve the quality of trace information and reduce the costs of obtaining it.

Model-Driven Software Development (MDSD) (Stahl & Völter, 2006), including Model Driven Architecture (MDA) (Kleppe, 2003; Mellor, 2004; Miller & Mukerji, 2003) from the Object Management Group (OMG)(Object Management Group (OMG)), has the potential of improving the creation, use and management of traceability information. MDSD seeks to represent all artifacts involved in the development process as formal modeling elements using a formal language such as the Unified Modeling Language (UML) (Object Management Group (OMG), 2005). The modeling elements have attributes and operations, and are related to each other by some kind of association or dependency link. These dependencies are explicitly stored and can be considered as valuable traceability information. To create executable software, MDSD makes use of model transformation and code generation techniques.

During this process, traceability information can be captured and stored (Bondé, Boulet, & Dekeyser, 2006; Ivkovic & Kontogiannis, 2004; Jouault, 2005).

To improve the MDSD tool support for traceability, Letelier presents a metamodel for requirements traceability based on UML. The metamodel is provided as a UML Profile that he demonstrates in a simple project using a RUP(IBM, 2007) software development process. Letelier states that there are no appropriate tools for requirements traceability, and that a traceability solution must allow for specification of the attributes and their possible values for each selected type of artifact. UML profiles is also used by Champeau and Rochefort to represent a conceptual UML traceability model that includes both requirements and other model elements (Champeau & Rochefort, 2003). They also state that there is a need for a flexible navigation and query mechanism for trace relations, but that there is no tool support for this.

Many MDSD tools are available, both commercially and under GPL license. Traceability is an essential part of MDSD (Desfray, 2003) and future versions of MDSD tools will provide functions for capturing and sharing traceability information.

The Traceability Problems

Traceability is widely accepted as a valuable mechanism in software engineering. There are, however, limited support for sharing and using traceability information across software tools. With the growing popularity of MDSD and code generation, many initiatives have addressed the traceability in MDSD, but there is still a need for a unified traceability scheme:

There is a lack of a commonly accepted traceability definition further than the term definition, a standard way of specifying traceability among items, and a traceability type classification; besides, conflicts among a number of approaches exists.

As a result traceability-schemes implementation in tools lacks of generality and exchangeability. (Limón & Garbajosa, 2005)

Aizenbud-Reshef et al. identifies the lack of integration among the various environments and tools that need to share traceability information as one of the main challenges in traceability(Aizenbud-Reshef et al., 2006). A necessary step toward better integration is the definition of a standard traceability metamodel, which should provide for customization and support extensibility mechanisms. In addition, a standard format for exchanging traceability information is needed, as well as the ability to uniquely identify artifacts across space and time. There is also a need for providing richer semantics. One approach is to allow users to add attributes to relationships, and another is to provide a predefined standard set of relationship types. An optimal solution should provide a predefined link metamodel, allow customization, and allow extensibility to define new link types(Aizenbud-Reshef et al., 2006; Arkley, Mason, & Riddle, 2002; Ramesh & Jarke, 2001; Walderhaug, Stav, Johansen, & Aagedal, 2006). One approach for a system solution is to keep all artifacts in a metadata repository. Such a solution, although attractive from the traceability point of view, is less appealing to tool vendors because it requires tight integration and strong coupling. A compromise solution leaves the responsibility for the management of artifacts to the tool while keeping some replicated artifact information in a shared repository.

In order to be applied actively during the development process and achieve the benefits described by Ramesh and Jarke, traceability information must be created without increasing the workload on the developers. The usability aspect of a traceability solution was investigated by Arkley et al. (2002). They present the result of a recent study in one company where they addressed the problem of applying traceability tools. Their find-ings shows that data entry is considered a burden and that documentation often is inaccessible or out of date, making it impossible to create valid traceability information.

Another problem related to traceability of artifacts in MDSD is model synchronization. This problem is outside the scope of this chapter, but is essential to a viable traceability solution for MDSD. As the development artifacts are altered or modified due to evolution or maintenance activities, inconsistencies may occur, especially if the artifacts are created and maintained by different tools. Much research work is being done on this issue (Ivkovic & Kontogiannis, 2004; Paige & Shaham-Gafni, 2006), and because of the complexity of the problem it will not be discussed in this chapter.

TRACEABILITY AS A TOOL IN SOFTWARE SYSTEM DEVELOPMENT AND MANAGEMENT

Trace information about the artifacts document how different artifacts—ranging from requirements to final code—are created, modified, deleted, and related, as well as the rationale for decisions during the development process. Trace information can be useful to improve the control of quality during all phases of the lifecycle of a system, from requirement gathering, through design, implementation, deployment, and to maintenance of a system.

The relationships between artifacts are dependent of the context in which they are used. A software engineering use context includes factors such as involved stakeholders and the development phase. Each stakeholder may have a different view of the relations and their strength (Ramesh & Jarke, 2001), for example, a project manager may have a completely different understanding of a relation between two artifacts than a system designer. The use of traceability information varies with the development phase. Typical development phases and use scenarios include:

- **Planning:** An example is decisions regarding the system development that will be used as rationale in the succeeding phases. A decision or agreement should be related to its origin, for example, a specific meeting or request from a stakeholder.
- **Design:** An architect may need to link a functional component specification to a requirement using "implements" or "satisfies" relationships, expressing dependency between two logical software components.
- **Implementation:** using model transformation and code generation there is a need to capture the relationships between source and target.
- **Testing/deployment:** Traceability information can be used to check that all requirements are "satisfied" by one or more artifacts in the system. A coverage analysis of requirements and "satisfied-by" relationships can be used.
- **Maintenance:** If one software component fails or not performs according to specification, a maintenance engineer can use traceability information to identify errors or bottlenecks.
- **Upgrade/change:** If a new feature should be added, or an existing feature changed, using an impact analysis service will provide useful information about the complexity of implementing the change or upgrade.

In the following section the overall requirements for a traceability solution is specified. The requirements are followed by a definition of the roles that interact with a traceability solution and the artifacts they operate on. Finally, the services required by the defined roles are described.

Requirements to a Traceability Solution

A prerequisite for providing traceability services to the actors in a development process is that necessary trace information is captured according to an appropriate trace model and made available for inspection and analysis. A complete traceability solution must address these issues:

- The model that describes which and how artifacts can be traced should be possible to adapt to the development project's needs.
- The trace information must be continuously collected during the whole lifecycle of the system.
- It must be possible to collect the trace information without too much additional work for the developer. Trace information should mainly be captured automatically by the tools.
- In MDSD, transformations are used to generate artifacts, and thus transformations are likely sources for automatically generated trace information. A risk with automatic capture is producing overwhelming amounts of irrelevant trace information, and thus limiting what is captured to what can actually be useful is a challenge that should be addressed by a traceability solution. This implies that a traceability solution should support definition of exactly which information to trace for the target system.

Table 1 shows a set of generic requirements for a traceability solution based on the definition of traceability given in the previous section.

Roles and Artifacts

Before presenting the services to be provided by a traceability solution, it is necessary to define the roles and artifacts that are involved in the process. A role in this context can be filled by one or more

Table 1. Requirements to a traceability solution

Requirement Group	Requirement Description
Artifact types to be traced	It shall be possible to decide what artifact types shall be traced. A traceability solution must be easy to configure for new artifact types. The most common artifact types (e.g., requirements, use cases; components interfaces, packages, test cases; class files) should be preconfigured.
Artifact trace to generate	It shall be possible to decide what information shall be traced for each artifact of a specific type. Specified information may both include artifact type specific information (e.g., artifact id., version id.) and artifact type independent information (e.g., time when trace occurred, who caused the trace). It shall be possible to specify in what situations trace information shall be generated (e.g., when an artifact was created, accessed, changed, deleted).
Artifact identifier	Any generated trace information shall uniquely be associated to some traceable artifact, and that traceable artifact shall uniquely be identified.
Relations between artifact trace to generate	It shall be possible to decide what information shall be traced for some relation between two artifacts of some specific types. Specified information may both include artifact relation specific information (e.g., target artifact is a transformation type x of source artifact), and artifact type independent information (e.g., same as for artifact trace). It shall be possible to specify allowed cardinalities for source and target artifact types. It shall be possible to specify in what situations trace information shall be generated (e.g., when a relation was created, removed).
Change management	This concerns the impact changes of artifacts (create, change, delete) will have on relations that exists for the artifacts. The traceability shall support functionality to control relation trace associated with artifacts, based on events (e.g., create, change, delete) or situations (e.g., attribute x equals y) that occur to the artifacts. Management of relations may be a combination of manual and automatic control.
Version management	This concern supports baselining of artifacts. A baseline is defined by a subset of all artifacts within a specified context where each included artifact has a unique version (i.e., a snapshot from its lifecycle/history). The traceability functionality concerning this is to trace artifacts including their version identification, and to be able to identify these artifacts based on version identification.
Automatic or manual control of trace generation	Generation of trace information shall be possible to control manually or automatically. Automatically generation of trace is triggered by events (e.g., a relation trace shall be generated when an artifact of a specific type is created) or situations (e.g., a specific trace attribute value being stored is invalid and a specific trace shall indicate this) related to occurrence of trace information or values of trace information, or by time related aspects (e.g., generate a specific trace reported at a specific time). Manual generation of trace information can be done from inside the artifact tool or using a standalone traceability tool having that has access to both the artifact tool and trace repository data storage.

stakeholders, and also one stakeholder can have multiple roles. The roles defined are:

- **Developer:** during development the developer performs different operations on the system being traced, such as creating, modifying, and deleting development artifacts. During these operations, the traceability solution captures trace information automatically or through manual input from the developer, based on the definitions of the trace model being used for the system. A developer can also be a *Trace user*.

- **Trace user:** uses the collected trace information. Stakeholders that have this role typically include project manager, test manager and developer.
- **Traceability manager:** defines the trace model for the system, which is used by the traceability system to determine what trace information to capture, and how to capture it.
- **Tool supplier:** implements the traceability metamodel in the tools comprising the traceability system, and enhances or makes adapters for modeling, transformation and

other development tools to use the traceability metamodel to generate trace information automatically or by manual input.

These roles work on artifacts at different meta-levels. Three types of artifacts are defined:

1. **Traceability metamodel:** provides the framework for the definition of trace models. The *tool supplier* implements support for a certain *traceability metamodel*.
2. **Trace model:** defines exactly what information will be traced for a system. The *Traceability Manager* uses the *Traceability metamodel* to define which types of traces that can be created, and what information the traces should include. The complete definition constitutes the *Trace model*.
3. **Trace:** represents the actual trace information collected for a system. The trace information uses the types of traces that are defined in the *Trace Model*. Both the *Developer* and the *Trace User* will use the *Trace* artifact.

Each of the defined roles will use tools during their usage and definition of the traceability system. In addition to regular modeling and development tools, transformation tools will have a central role in MDSD. When the developer uses a transformation tool (e.g., to perform a model-to-model, or model-to-text transformation), the tool should use the definitions provided in the trace model to determine what trace information to generate during transformations. Regular development tools, such as modeling tools, should also use the trace model to, for example, automatically generate trace for operations performed by the user. This document defines the metamodel and interfaces that tools need to use or implement in order to interact with the traceability system solution.

Figure 1 describes the set of roles involved in usage and definition of a traceability solution, and identifies the artifact each of these will use or create.

Traceability Management Services

The roles defined in the previous section use different services on the traceability solution. The *Tool Supplier* will use the *Traceability Metamodel* when implementing an adapter or a module for interfacing the traceability solution.

Figure 1. Traceability roles and artifacts in a traceability solution

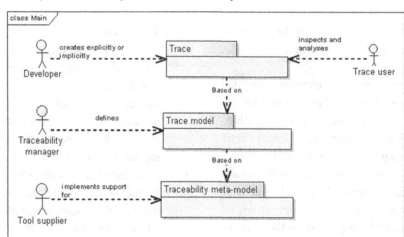

The metamodel provides information about the structures and concepts that the traceability solution is built on.

The *Traceability Manager* needs services for the management of the *Trace Model*. The major parts of a *Trace Model* will most likely be reused between projects, but it should be possible to add new types of artifacts and attributes thereof to the *Trace Model*.

The *Developer* will use create *Traces* according to the *Trace Model* and will need services that enables correct structure, semantics and storage of these. Explicit *trace* creation such as manually specifying an *implement* relation between a *Requirement* and a *Java Class* will require a special service.

Traceability User Services

The services offered to a *trace user* by a Traceability Solution can be grouped into three parts: inspection, analysis and reverse engineering (see Figure 2).

- **Trace inspection:** The purpose of trace inspection is to allow the trace user to inspect trace information to get a better understanding of (parts of) the system and its development, both during development and maintenance. Trace inspection functionality should include the ability to visualize, navigate, and query traces. This allows the trace user to answer questions such as: why was this design selected for an artifact (rationale), how was this artifact generated (e.g., source, mapping, tool) and which transformations where applied, which component(s) covers this requirement, and so forth.

- **Trace analysis:** Through trace analysis the trace user can determine specific properties of a system and find parts of a system that needs further attention. Analysis is done using a set of standard queries on the system which can be performed manually or automatically. The analysis functionality can utilize the mechanisms used for inspecting traces to display and navigate the results. As shown in Figure 2, three types of

Figure 2. Traceability services offered to the trace user

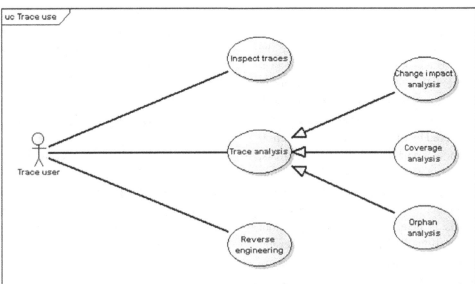

trace analysis have been identified to be of particular interest to the trace user: change impact analysis, coverage analysis, and orphan analysis. Each of these is described in the following.

- **Change impact analysis:** One use of trace information is to determine the impact a change to an artifact will have on other artifacts. The results of a change impact analysis can be used to estimate the cost, resources and time required to perform the change, or even to determine if the change can be allowed or realized at all. The trace use could in this case be presented with a list of artifacts that may need to be updated if the change is carried out. As the change can have impact on multiple levels of the system, the analysis need to follow relations between artifacts for multiple levels of depth. An example of use of this functionality would be that the trace user starts by selecting one specific artifact to be deleted, and is then prompted for which of the relation types defined between this artifact and related artifacts to include in an impact analysis. The system would identify all artifacts that are related to the selected artifact, directly or indirectly, through any relation of the specified relation types.

- **Coverage analysis:** Through coverage analysis, the trace user can determine the degree to which some artifacts of the system are followed up by other artifacts in the system. A typical example is to check the degree to which a set of requirements are covered by the design and implementation, for example, to follow up on progress, (re)allocate resources within the development project, identify bottlenecks in the development, and so forth. The coverage analysis is determined by checking that trace relations that should exist are present. Coverage analysis can also be useful during development of, for example, model to text

transformations. By performing a coverage analysis on a source model it is possible to see if all parts of the model have been utilized in the model transformation. If the number of "unused" model elements are high, this may indicate that the transformation has an undiscovered potential of generating more code from the models (Olsen & Oldevik, 2007).

- **Orphan analysis:** Orphan analysis is used to find artifacts that are orphaned with respect to some specified trace relations. The analysis should be able to find single orphaned artifacts, but also isolated groups of artifacts with trace relations of the specified types only internally in the group. An example is analysis to find artifacts that is not related to any of the requirements of the system, which, for example, could be used to discover components no longer needed because requirements have been changed or deleted, or to discover "gold plating," features added without any need identified in the requirements.

- **Reverse engineering:** the trace user wants to rebuild a source artifact from a target artifact and trace information through a reverse transformation. In a model to text transformation scenario, the UML model with all its dependencies can be rebuilt from a Java source file using trace information stored in a repository.

A TRACEABILITY SOLUTION

In the previous section a three-layered architecture for traceability solution was presented with the stakeholder roles working on the different layers (Figure 1). This architecture can be used directly in the design of a traceability solution. With reference to Figure 3:

Figure 3. Traceability packages overview

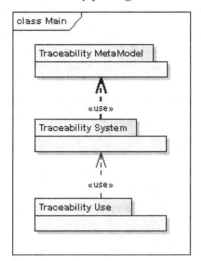

- The Traceability MetaModel package defines the Traceability MetaModel artifact;
- Instantiations of classes in the Traceability MetaModel package define the Trace Model artifact; and
- Instantiations of the classes of the Traceability System package define the Trace artifact(s).

In this section, a traceability solution architecture addressing the requirements specified is presented. The solution consists of three main packages on three different metalevels. Figure 3 shows a schematic presentation of the three-layered architecture.

In the following, each metalevel package is described by its classes and relationships.

Traceability Metamodel

A metamodel is a way of describing information about information and is a common way of defining concepts in MDSD. The Traceability metamodel should define the concepts required to define trace models for target systems, including:

- How traceable artifacts shall be defined;
- How a trace relation shall be defined;
- How to manage trace relations between artifacts; and
- How to maintain artifact trace relation consistency.

The use of a metamodel is well supported in the literature. Ramesh et al. (2001) states that it is a widely accepted concept that a traceability repository will comprise at least three layers: the traceability metamodel, the traceability reference models and finally the database with the actual trace information.

The *Traceability Metamodel* (Figure 4) package includes four main metaclasses:

- **TraceModel** is the Traceability users' mean to define their own traceability needs. TraceModel specifies which model artifacts that can be created (TraceableArtifactType), and which traces of model artifacts (ArtifactTraceType) and relations between model artifacts (RelationTraceType) that can be created. TraceModel is used by TraceRepository and related classes as a definition of how the actual trace model looks like and thereby how it shall be applied.
- **TraceableArtifactType** defines the mapping of a specific model artifact type to a corresponding traceable artifact type. The model artifact type is the type for the actual modeling elements that shall be traced and must have a corresponding traceable artifact type definition in the trace model. The TraceableArtifactType represents the model artifact type in the traceability system solution, that is, the traced model artifact is not stored in the TraceRepository.
- **ArtifactTraceType** defines a specific trace type for some TraceableArtifactType. The definition may, for example, specify what attributes shall be traced and what actions

to be executed when a trace related to this artifact type occur.

- **RelationTraceType** defines a specific trace type for a certain relation between a source and a target artifact type. The definition may, for example, specify what attributes shall be traced and what actions to be executed when a trace related to these artifact types occur. For example, a trace between a UML UseCase model and a UML Activity Model may include other attributes than a trace between a requirement and a UML UseCase model.

A *Trace Model* can be reused by different traceability systems (*TraceRepositories*) When defining the trace model, it is important to take into consideration the use context for the trace model to be defined, because artifacts or traces using the same definitions may be applied within different context (Aizenbud-Reshef et al., 2006). The following context related aspects are identified:

- **Stakeholders:** Stakeholders are the users of traceability. Different stakeholders may use different artifacts and trace links, or they may use the same but maybe with different semantics and importance. Example stakeholders are: Authorities, Owner, Producer, Developer, Customer and User.

- **Lifecycle phase:** Lifecycle phases identify different periods in time that are closely related to both use of traceability and to relevance for different stakeholders. As for stakeholders, different lifecycle phases may have relevance for different artifact and link types, or the same artifact and link types but maybe with different semantics and importance. Example lifecycle phases are: Prestudy, Requirement, Development, Implementation, Test, Installation, Use and Maintenance, and Decommission.

- **Granularity level:** Granularity level specifies the degree of detailing that the traces shall have. Granularity level is also an aspect that is closely related to the different stakeholder needs concerning traces use. Example granularity aspect types can be: Time, Confidence, Logical grouping and Aggregation level.

Applying traceability for its intended purpose—generation of trace information—requires that specifications of what shall be traced must have been done. This can be obtained by defining one or more trace models using the traceability structure presented in the previous section (i.e., instantiation of the *Trace Model* class and its related classes). In principle, the traceability definition may have been left completely generic, meaning that any specification about what shall be traced

Figure 4. UML class diagram of the traceability metamodel

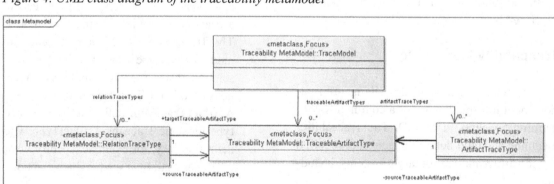

is left to the users. The advantage with that would be that no restrictions or limitations for what is possible to trace has been set, while the main disadvantage would be that no standardization of actual traces is defined. It is therefore considered to be of common interest to define some standard specializations with predefined semantics which can be applied in trace models. Of course, it is up to the users to decide if these extensions are used or not in a particular usage scenario.

Such common extensions must be used according to their semantically rich descriptions. The predefined semantics of the extensions enable the development of tools with more predefined traceability support, and can also simplify and guide the development of *Trace Models*. The main criteria for selection of the extensions are that they are of interest to MDSD, and that they cover a set of traceability requirements that have been identified by potential users. Some examples of *RelationTraceType* extensions are:

- **Realization:** The trace between two artifacts where target implements the complete or parts of the source artifact. Examples of source artifacts can be UML classifiers such as classes, methods and use cases, while target artifacts can be UML classifiers such as classes and methods, or source code.
- **Transformation:** The trace of a transformation from source to target artifact.
- **Rationale:** A trace between two artifacts where the source is the rationale or justification for the target artifact. Example: used from a quality requirement to a design choice.
- **Verification:** A trace between two artifacts where the source is a verification for the target. Example: A JUnit that tests the behavior of a Java Class.

A more extensive list including common extensions of artifact trace types and relation trace types can be found in Johansen, Stav, Walderhaug, and Aagedal (2006).

Traceability System

The *Traceability System* package uses the metaclasses and relationships defined in *Traceability MetaModel*. Using the metamodel ensures that the system conforms to a common concept for creating and managing trace information. Figure 5 shows the classes in the *Traceability System* package:

- **TraceRepository** is responsible for managing generated trace information, which is constituted by the collection of TraceableArtifact, ArtifactTrace and RelationTrace entities.
- **TraceableArtifact** defines the type to be instantiated when a traceable artifact shall be traced. A TraceableArtifact refers a corresponding TraceableArtifactType defined in the trace model.
- **ArtifactTrace** defines the type to be instantiated when a specific trace related to a traceable artifact occurs. An ArtifactTrace refers to a corresponding ArtifactTraceType defined in the trace model.
- **RelationTrace** defines the type to be instantiated when a specific trace related to a relation between two related traceable artifacts occurs. A RelationTrace refers to a corresponding RelationTraceType defined in the trace model.
- **TraceSession** is a session administrator when traceability is provided to users as a service. Using traceability implies a successful logon from a user that establishes a communication session between the user and the traceability service. This session will be managed by a TraceSession entity, and the session will last until explicitly disconnected. Multiple users may use traceability simultaneously, and each user will be assigned a TraceSession entity. As trace information is regarded as a historical log describing the lifetime of artifacts, and

Figure 5. UML class diagram of the traceability system package

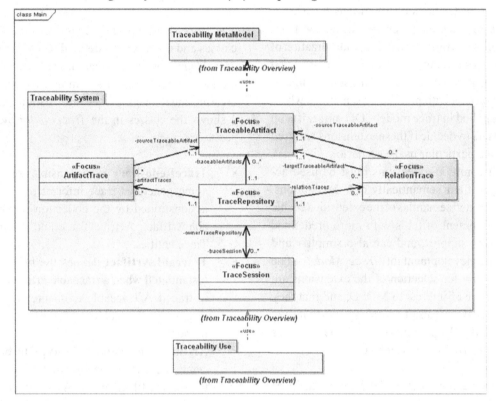

is not information that will be changed, consistency is not a concern even during concurrent use of multiple users.

Traceability Use

The Traceability Use classes must be implemented in an artifact tool in order to interface the Traceability System through the Trace Session. Two types of classes should be implemented:

- TraceClient is the client side definition of the traceability system solution. The traceability system solution definition implies a clean client/server structure where all initiatives are initiated from the client and no initiatives are initiated from server side. This implies that client side definitions are left empty because the traceability system has no dependencies to the clients.

- TraceSubscriber is the client side representation of a Subscribe/Notification service. Initiation of a subscription at client side must include a reference to a TraceSubscriber entity to be used for serving notifications received from server side. It is a client concern how TraceSubscriber is defined internally, but the interfacing to environments (i.e., to the server side) must be defined.

TRACEABILITY IN PRACTICE

Process for Using the Traceability Solution

The first step to set up a traceability system solution is to define what needs to be traced and how. This is defined in the *Trace Model*. The *TraceModel* is used by *TraceRepository* and its related classes as

Figure 6. UML class diagram of the traceability use package. The TraceSubscriber and TraceClient use the interfaces implemented by the TraceSession class in the traceability system. The diagram shows the operations on the interfaces to illustrate the functionality provided by the traceability system through the TraceSession.

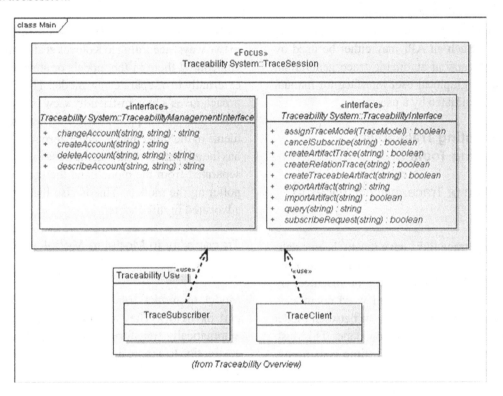

a definition of how the actual trace model looks like and thereby how it shall be applied (Figure 5). The trace model specification consists of three main tasks, each of which includes the identification of entity types and the detailed specification of these. The steps are:

1. Specification of traceable artifact types, for example, UML Model, textual descriptions (such as source code);
2. Specification of artifact and relation trace types, for example, Refine, Transformation, Evolves_to, Rationale, Generation, Justifies, Modifies, Uses, Implements, Owns, Executes and Validates; and

3. Specification of actions, for example, versioning of specific documents.

The first step is to identify which traceable artifact types are of relevance. These correspond to the model artifacts that shall be traced. The next step is to specify which traces shall be generated for these artifacts. These are defined by the artifact trace types which specify some trace for a specific traceable artifact type, and the relation trace types which specify some trace for the relation between two artifact types. There may be defined multiple artifact and relation trace types for the same traceable artifact type. The final step is to specify actions if relevant for use.

Action specifications must be related to defined traceable artifact types and artifact and relation trace type definitions.

Trace information, represented by the entity types described above, is generated by using an API provided by the *Traceability System* (see Figure 6). Such an API may either be used by some tool causing automatic trace generation, or by some graphical user interface for manual generation initiated by a user.

Implementing Traceability in Modeling Tools

Integration of Traceability Services in Tools

In the past, trace links have mostly been established manually by the different persons involved in the development process, for instance, by creating trace links between word documents and use-case model elements or between model elements and implementation code. This task has been known as difficult, time consuming, and very often a source to errors both when it comes to the establishment of new links and keeping the existing links updated and consistent (Egyed, 2004).

Following an MDSD approach and utilizing model transformations makes it possible to generate an extensive amount of these trace links explicitly or implicitly in the transformation specification. By implicit, we mean that some transformation tool, for example, MOFScript (Oldevik, Neple, Grønmo, Aagedal, & Berre, 2005), populates a trace model automatically when a transformation is executed. By explicit, we mean that additional trace code must be inserted into the transformation. This can be achieved in two ways; by writing the trace code each time or running a higher order transformation on the transformation model. The latter approach is used in the Atlas Transformation Language (ATL) (Jouault, 2005).

The final adopted OMG standard MOF Models to Text Transformation Language also requires that the ability to explicitly create trace blocks in the code is present (Object Management Group (OMG), 2006).

Storing the established trace links can be done in two ways, according to Kolovos et al., either by embedding them in the models or storing them externally in a separate new model. The first approach gives a human-friendly view of the trace links, but it only supports trace links between elements in the same model. The external approach has the advantage of having the trace information separated from the model, and therefore avoids polluting the models. This is also the approach advocated in this chapter.

Traceability in Model to Model Transformation

Model to model transformations are a vital part in MDSD. They are, for example, used to automatically transform models at one level of abstraction to a more detailed level (PIM to PSM transformations). During such a transformation many new artifacts are generated and trace links are needed to keep track of the relations between the source and target elements, and to perform, for example, change impact analysis on one level and see how the changes will propagate through the models.

In QVT Request for Proposals (RFP) issued by OMG in 2002, traceability is an optional requirement (Object Management Group (OMG), 2002) The specification describes three model transformation languages that can be used; Relations, Core, and Operational Mappings. In the Relations and Operational Mappings languages, trace links are created automatically without user intervention. In the Core Language, a trace class must be specified explicitly for each transformation mapping. The QVT Operational implementation provided by Borland is one implementation that has this support, but the implementation is, however, not ideal because it does not store the trace model as an external file that can be interexchanged between different tools (Kurtev, Dee, Goknil, & Berg, 2007).

Atlas Transformation Language (ATL) is another model to model transformation language that supports this functionality. ATL is an official Eclipse M2M Project (The Eclipse Foundation, 2007a) and has a large user community. The transformation specifications that are written in ATL have a model representation and can be used as source to a HOT transformation that inserts trace specific code into the transformation. This is achieved by running a *"TraceAdder"* transformation on the already existing transformation specification. It also supports the storage of a separate trace model that represents the relationship between source and target elements (Jouault, 2005).

Traceability in Model to Text Transformation

Several model to text languages exist, and some of them have support for traceability. In the MOF Models to Text Transformation Standard(Object Management Group (OMG), 2006), traceability is defined to be explicitly created by the use of a trace block inserted into the code, as illustrated below.

```
[trace(c.id()+ '_definition') ]
 class [c.name/]
 {
 // Constructor
 [c.name/]()
 {
 [protected('user_code')]
 ; user code
 [/protected]
 }
 }
[/trace]
```

This approach provides user-defined blocks that represent a trace to the code generated by the block. This is specifically useful for adding traces

to parts of the code that are not easily automated. A drawback of the approach is a cluttering of the transformation code. It should be noted that there currently are no available implementations of the OMG standard at this time, but it will be provided as an Eclipse m2t project (The Eclipse Foundation, 2007b) component in the near future (first release scheduled for June 2007).

A complementary approach, as taken in MOF-Script, is to automate the generation of traces based solely on model element references. MOFScript is a model to text transformation tool and language. It can be used to generate text from EMF-based models. The transformation implementation contains references to model elements that should be substituted in the generated text. The references to model elements are the basis of MOFScript traceability. Any reference to a model element that is used to produce text output, results in a trace between that element and the target text file. The granularity is from model element to line and column in the text file (Oldevik & Neple, 2006; Olsen & Oldevik, 2007).

MOFScript also supports the notion of unprotected blocks. These blocks are created with the use of the *unprotect* keyword in the transformation code, as illustrated in the transformation code for operations below.

```
self.ownedOperation->forEach(o:uml.Operation){
'\n 'o.visibility' void ' o.name'(){'
unprotect{
 ' //User code here for operation'
}
' }\n'
}
```

The resulting code (if the transformation has been executed on a UML class "Book" containing an operation "printAuthor()") is shown below. It represents the unprotected block as comments containing a *#BlockStart* and a *#BlockEnd* and an identifier for the source model element. Trace links have also been created from the model element class Book's features "visibility" and "name" to the location in the generated Java file and can be obtained from the trace model.

```
public void printAuthor(){
  //#BlockStart number=4 id=_MeMJULEPEdu-Ve-
pu7rgPLg
//User code here for operation
      //#BlockEnd number=4
}
```

Between the block comments, the user can insert or remove code, and the changes will be preserved the next time the transformation is run. All the traces that have references to the file after the block will also be generated in accordance with their new position in the file. The block comment tag (here *'//'*) is controlled by environment settings and can be changed to match the target language.

Both model to model and model to text trace links can be incorporated in a traceability solution as described in this chapter.

As we see from the above sections on model transformation traceability, an extensive amount of trace link is possible to generate automatically. It is possible to connect both MOFScript and ATL to the trace solution described in this chapter through so called adapters.

Sharing Traceability Information Between Tools

The proposed traceability solution assumes an external traceability repository and a client-server use pattern. An artifact tool must communicate with the Traceability Repository on a shared network and implement an adapter that uses the API provided by the TraceSession class (see Figure 6). Complete specification of the API can be found in Johansen et al. (2006). The Trace-Client and TraceSubscriber classes have been proposed as classes to be implemented in the artifact tool. Figure 6 shows these classes along with the interfaces provided through the TraceSession class. Artifact tools can implement the

traceability adapter differently; as an integrated feature or as a separate tool with its own user interface. However, the adapter needs to use the same TraceModel as the traceability repository and follow the procedure for use.

A developer using a tool (e.g., Artifact Tool 1) will send updated traceability information from the tool to the trace repository in an automatic or manual manner. To avoid trace information overflow, an automatic approach should be configured to only send trace information on certain events such as upon check-in in version control systems or initiation of tool build processes. Figure 8 shows the sequence of updating trace information for an artifact in a trace repository.

Traceability Example: BusCatcher System

To demonstrate the use of the proposed traceability solution, this section presents a trivial example. The example system, called BusCatcher, provides bus information services to bus passengers using mobile devices (e.g., cell phones). The main service offered by the BusCatcher system is *to give updated bus information to the passenger based on the passenger's current location (a bus stop).*

In this example system, the user (passenger) uses a mobile terminal such as a cell phone to access the bus schedule. The information can be accessed using SMS or MMS services:

- **SMS:** Send a SMS to the <BusCatcher Number> with information about your current location and destination
- **MMS:** Take a picture of a barcode located at the bus stop, and send it to the <BusCatcher Number>. The barcode is decoded at the server side to an ID which maps to the location and destination info.

In both cases the system will return updated information on when the next busses for the user's destination can be expected at the current location.

Figure 7. UML component diagram showing an example of two artifact tools communicating traceability information with an external traceability repository

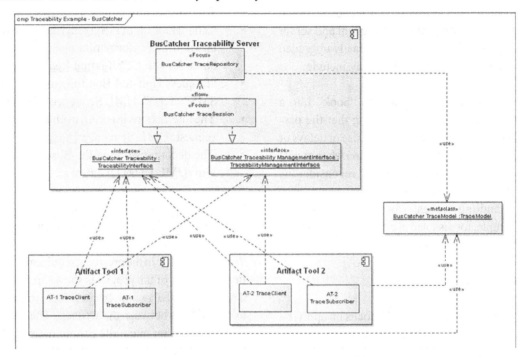

Figure 8. UML interaction diagram showing the BusCatcher developer working with Artifact Tool 1 that sends trace information to the BusCatcher trace repository

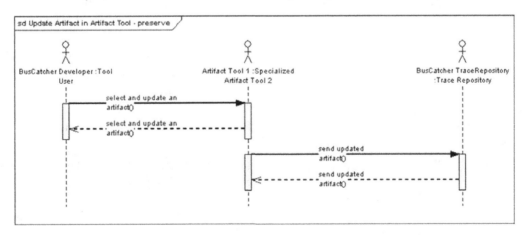

BusCatcher Requirements

The system should support multiple software and hardware platforms on both the client and server side. The system should also be easily upgraded and extended. Future services may include:

- Allowing the passenger to "book" into a corresponding bus, ensuring that the passenger will catch the bus in case of delays or providing updated information when events occur where the user should reconsider the travel plan; and
- Handling requests for assistance, for example, for disabled users needing assistance to get on the correct bus.

BusCatcher TraceModel

The example is presented with focus on applying analysis services on the trace information. This implies that the specification of the *Trace Model, TraceableArtifacts, RelationTraces and Artifact-Traces* may be incomplete for other purposes. The BusCatcher *TraceModel* is defined below. To increase legibility, only simple examples of attributes being traced are included in the specification.

BusCatcher Trace Creation

In the prestudy, requirements and design phases of the system development process, the following *TraceableArtifacts* are created (the *TraceableArtifactType* underlined):

- "BusCatcher Pre-Study Report.doc": <u>Text Document</u>
- "BusCatcher UML Main UseCase": <u>UML Use Case Model</u>
- The activities performed to request a bus-schedule using the BusCatcher MMS Service: <u>UML Activity Diagram</u>.
- Three functional requirements

- "The BusCatcher System must provide updated bus information using SMS" "F.1.1": <u>Textual Requirement</u>
- "The BusCatcher System must provide updated bus information using MMS and barcodes" "F.1.2": <u>Textual Requirement</u>
- "Request Updated Bus Information Using SMS" "F.1.3": <u>UML Sequence Diagram</u>
- The interactions involved in a bus-schedules request: <u>UML Sequence Diagram</u>
- The decomposition of the BusCatcher system: <u>UML Class Diagram</u>

A description of the created *RelationTraces* and *ArtifactTraces* is not provided in detail. A summary of the trace information created in the *TraceRepository* in the prestudy, requirements and design phases of the project is shown in Figure 9. The *RelationTraces* and *ArtifactTraces* are shown as dotted lines between the artifacts. These traces are created either manually or automatically by a tool. The label indicates their trace-type.

BusCatcher Trace Analysis

This section shows a trivial analysis of the BusCatcher trace information. The example provided is too small to illustrate the full power of trace analysis, but the concept is the same independent of the project size and the amount of trace information available.

Requirements Coverage Analysis

Query: Find if all requirements are implemented or satisfied in the design artifacts.

There are three requirements defined in the requirements phase: F.1.1-3. From Figure 9 we see that F.1.3 is not implemented in any of the (two) design artifacts as there is no *implementation* relation from the F.1.3 requirement. This means that the details specified in F.1.3. are not necessarily implemented or satisfied.

Table 2. BusCatcher TraceableArtifactTypes

TraceableArtifactTypes	Description
Text_Document	To trace, for example, a Microsoft Word document. Traceable attribute for the Word document includes version, creation date, owner and filename and file size.
UML_UseCase_Model	To trace a UML Use Case model. Traceable attributes include UML_version, UseCase name, its origin model, the tool-ID, the XMI string representing the UseCase and the XMI version used
UML_Activity_Diagram	To trace a UML Activity Diagram the UML version, the XMI string and version, and the diagram's path and origin would be stored
Textual_Requirement	To trace a requirement specified textually, the requirement name, the owner, requirement specification, its condition, related constraints and the creation date would be stored
UML_Class_Diagram	To trace a UML Class Diagram, the UML version along with the XMI string and path/origin would be stored
UML_Sequence_Diagram	To trace a UML Sequence Diagram the UML version along with the XMI string and path/origin would be stored
UML_Interface	To trace a UML Interface
UML_Class	To trace a UML Class

Table 3. BusCatcher RelationTraceTypes

RelationTraceTypes	Description
Text_2_UseCase_Rationale	To store trace information about the rationale relation between a text document and a UML UseCase Model. The trace would include information about the source version and owner, as well as the target UML version, tool-ID and a rationale description. In addition, information about whether this is an automatic or manually created trace along with creation date and tool used would be stored
UseCase_2_Activity_Realization	To store trace information about the realization relation between a UML Use Case Model and a UML Activity Diagram. Trace attributes stored would include source and target UML version, source and target tool-ID, and the names of the usecase and activity diagrams
UML_Activity_2_Sequence_Refinement	To store trace information about the refinement relation between a UML Activity Diagram and a UML Sequence Diagram
UseCase_2_Text_Req_Rationale	To store trace information about the rationale relation between a UseCase Model and a Textual Requirement
Text_Req_2_Interface_Implements	To store trace information about the implements relation between a Textual Requirement and a UML Interface
UML_Interface_2_Class_Implements	To store trace information about the implements relation between a UML Interface and UML Class

Table 4. BusCatcher ArtifactTraceTypes

ArtifactTraceTypes	Description
Text_Document_Version	This is an artifact trace type that enables versioning of MS Word files. The parameters that can be traced include the file version, who created the new version, a comment and the new document date
Text_Requirement_Version	To store trace information about a specific version of a Textual Requirement
UML_Sequence_Version	To store trace information about a specific version of a UML Sequence Diagram

Figure 9. Summary of the BusCatcher traceable artifacts and relation traces

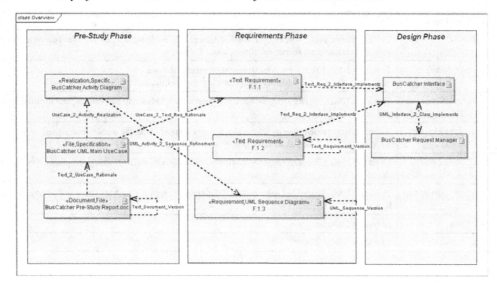

Requirements Orphan Analysis

Query: Check if all requirements are based on a documented need, that is, there is a rationale for all requirements.

From Figure 9 we see that:

- **F.1.1:** Rationale from main use case which is based on (rationale) the prestudy report.
- **F.1.2:** No rationale.
- **F.1.3:** A refinement of the activity diagram which is a realization of the main use case which again has a rationale in the prestudy report.

Change Impact Analysis

Query: Find all artifacts that are affected if the "BusCatcher Activity Diagram" is updated

The query will result in two direct relationships that should be inspected: the realization trace from the "BusCatcher Main UseCase" and the refinement trace to the "F.1.3 UML Sequence Diagram."

Indirect links to the "BusCatcher Pre-Study Report.doc" and any previous versions of the F.1.3 requirement can also be provided. The depth of analysis should be specified in the query.

FUTURE RESEARCH DIRECTIONS

Traceability information can provide valuable information for quality measurement mechanisms and project management processes. The history has shown that many software development projects overrun costs (Jorgensen & Molokken-Ostvold, 2006) and there is a need to improve the management processes and tools.

The popularity of MDSD is growing, and with the increasing tool support for the Model Driven Architecture (MDA) (Mellor, 2004; Miller & Mukerji, 2003) approach from OMG(Object Management Group (OMG)), the use of model transformation and code generation will increase. Traceability is a central feature in MDSD, and tool vendors are implementing traceability support in their new versions. More research is needed on how to share traceability information between tools in an effective manner.

All available model-driven development tools based on MOF are using XMI for model information storage. One way to integrate traceability into MDSD is using XMI import and export. Plug-ins are available for some tools such as Objecteering, and can be developed for Eclipse-based tools using the provided plug-in development framework from Eclipse.

This chapter presents a metamodel and a system solution for lifelong traceability of artifacts in software development projects. The solution is primarily specified for model-driven development projects using models as the primary artifacts, but the metamodel supports tracing of any kind of artifact involved in the development process. The presented traceability solution requires specification of a *Trace Model* and setup of a *Trace Repository* before it can be used in a project. The *TraceRepository* and the artifact tools, such as a UML modeling tool or a requirements specification tool, must interface with and conform to a common *TraceModel*. The *TraceModel* specifies what can be traced and how. Much of the traceability systems that are available today suffer from the fact that they require a significant amount of manual operation. Very often traceability is omitted because of the initial effort required. This will most likely also be the case if a *TraceModel* must be created for each development project. However, a MDSD project will use standardized (e.g., UML 2.0) models that will not differ much between projects, although the models are extensible. For a company, a small number of *TraceModels* will satisfy all traceability needs in the projects. A standardization process on trace models with predefined link types such as *implements, extends, rationale, evolves_to*, would be a big step toward a common schema for traceability in model-driven software development.

A key point when it comes to sharing traceability information between tools in a development project is how to integrate with the tools. The proposed solution offers a well defined interface provided to the artifact tools through the *TraceSession* class. Details can be found in Johansen et al. (2006) and Walderhaug et al. (2006). Initiatives working on traceability plug-in development are needed and should be harmonized through a standardization process of trace models.

Aizenbud-Reshef et al. (2006) states about traceability solutions that "An optimal solution should provide a predefined link metamodel, allow customization, and allow extensibility to defined new link types." The traceability solution proposed in this chapter satisfies these requirements and will form a valuable basis for implementation of traceability solutions in the software development businesses.

CONCLUSION

In MDSD it is important to trace relations between artifacts, and also between artifacts created and stored by different artifact tools. A common way of implementing a traceability solution in MDSD is needed. The solution presented in this chapter provides a flexible metamodel that can be customized to support a project's traceability needs. The use of a generic *TraceModel* can reduce the initial efforts of establishing the traceability solution in the projects.

The process of creating traceability information was presented in terms of model transformation. The artifact tools can automatically or manually create information that can be shared with other artifact tools using a common *TraceModel* and a shared repository. A common external repository holding the trace information opens for analysis services that can improve the control of the development process and provide better information, for example, resource use estimation of upgrades and maintenances procedures.

All software development projects need to consider traceability of artifacts to manage and control the development process. The trend is that requirements traceability is incorporating more types of artifacts to cover the complete software development process through the whole life-cycle. Using the proposed analysis services in the BusCatcher example, we demonstrated that simple analysis mechanisms can reveal important information using traceability information. In a large software project, such analysis services can mean the difference between success and failure.

REFERENCES

Aizenbud-Reshef, N., Nolan, B. T., Rubin, J., & Shaham-Gafni, Y. (2006). Model traceability. *IBM Systems Journal, 45*(3), 515-526.

Arkley, P., Mason, P., & Riddle, S. (2002, September). Position paper: Enabling traceability. In *Paper presented at the 1st International Workshop in Traceability in Emerging Forms of Software Engineering (TFFSE)* (pp. 61-65). Edinburgh, Scotland.

Bondé, L., Boulet, P., & Dekeyser, J.-L. (2006). Traceability and interoperability at different levels of abstraction in model-driven engineering. In *applications of specification and design languages for SoCs* (pp. 263-276).

Cantor, M. (2003, August). Rational unified process for systems engineering--part1: Introducing RUP SE Version 2.0. *The Rational Edge: E-zine for the Rational Community.*

Carnegie Mellon University/Software Engineering Institute. (2007, June 30). *Capability maturity model integration (CMMI).* Retrieved March 7, 2008, from http://www.sei.cmu.edu/cmmi/

Champeau, J., & Rochefort, E. (2003, October 21). Model engineering and traceability. In *Paper presented at the UML 2003 SIVOES-MDA Workshop*, San Francisco, CA, USA.

Desfray, P. (2003). *MDA—when a major software industry trend meets our toolset, implemented since 1994*: SOFTEAM.

Egyed, A. (2004). Resolving uncertainties during trace analysis. In *Paper presented at the Proceedings of the 12th ACM SIGSOFT Twelfth International Symposium on Foundations of Software Engineering* (pp. 3-12). Newport Beach, CA, USA.

Espinoza, A., Alarcon, P. P., & Garbajosa, J. (2006). *Analyzing and systematizing current traceability schemas* (pp. 21-32).

Gills, M. (2005, November 8). Survey of traceability models in IT projects. In *Paper presented at the European Conference on Model Driven Architecture - Traceability Workshop 2005*, Nuremberg, Germany.

Gotel, O. C. Z., & Finkelstein, C. W. (1994). *An analysis of the requirements traceability problem* (pp. 94-101).

IBM. (2007). *Rational unified process (RUP).* Retrieved March 7, 2008, from http://www-306.ibm.com/software/awdtools/rup/

Institute of Electrical and Electronics Engineers. (1991). IEEE standard computer dictionary. A compilation of IEEE standard computer glossaries. *IEEE Std 610.*

Ivkovic, I., & Kontogiannis, K. (2004). Tracing evolution changes of software artifacts through model synchronization. In *Paper presented at the Proceedings of the 20th IEEE International Conference on Software Maintenance* (pp. 252-261).

Johansen, U., Stav, E., Walderhaug, S., & Aagedal, J. (2006). *Modelware - traceability metamodel and system solution* [D1.6-4]. Trondheim: SINTEF.

Jorgensen, M., & Molokken-Ostvold, K. (2006). How large are software cost overruns? A review of the 1994 CHAOS report. *Information and Software Technology, 48*(4), 297-301.

Jouault, F. (2005, November 8). Loosely coupled traceability for ATL. In *Paper presented at the European Conference on Model Driven Architecture - Traceability Workshop 2005*, Nuremberg, Germany.

Kleppe, A. (2003). *MDA explained: The model driven architecture™: Practice and promise.*

Kolovos, D. S., Paige, R. F., & Polack, F. A. C. (2006, July). On-demand merging of traceability links with models. In *Paper presented at the European Concerence on Model Driven Architecture Traceability Workshop (ECMDA-TW)*, Bilbao, Spain.

Kurtev, I., Dee, M., Goknil, A., & Berg, K. V. D. (2007). Traceability-based change management in operational mappings. In *Paper presented at the ECMDA Traceability Workshop (ECMDA-TW)* (pp. 57-87). Haifa, Israel.

Letelier, P. (2002, September). A framework for requirements traceability in UML-based projects. In *Paper presented at the Proceedings of the 1st International Workshop on Traceability, co-located with ASE 2002* (pp. 32-41). Edinburgh, Scotland, UK.

Limón, A. E., & Garbajosa, J. (2005, November 8). The need for a unifying traceability scheme. In *Paper presented at the European Conference on Model Driven Architecture - Traceability Workshop 2005*, Nuremberg, Germany.

Mellor, S. J. (2004). *MDA distilled: Principles of model-driven architecture.*

Miller, J., & Mukerji, J. (2003). *MDA guide version 1.0.1* [omg/2003-06-01]. Object Management Group (OMG).

Object Management Group. (OMG). Retrieved March 7, 2008, from http://www.omg.org/

Object Management Group. (OMG). (2002). *Request for proposal: MOF 2.0 query/views/transformations RFP* [OMG document ad/2002-04-10]. Object Management Group (OMG).

Object Management Group. (OMG). (2005). *UML 2.0 superstructure FTF Rose model containing the UML 2 metamodel.* Object Management Group (OMG).

Object Management Group. (OMG). (2006). *MOF models to text transformation language final adopted specification* [ptc/06-11-01]. Object Management Group (OMG).

Object Management Group. (OMG). (2007). *Object management group (OMG).* Retrieved March 7, 2008, from http://www.omg.org/

Oldevik, J., & Neple, T. (2006, July). Traceability in model to text transformations. In *Paper presented at the European Conference on Model Driven Architecture Traceability Workshop (ECMDA-TW)*, Bilbao, Spain.

Oldevik, J., Neple, T., Grønmo, R., Aagedal, J., & Berre, A.-J. (2005, November 7-10). Toward standardised model to text transformations. In *Paper presented at the Model Driven Architecture (Foundations and Applications, First European Conference, ECMDA-FA 2005)* (pp. 239-253). Nuremberg, Germany.

Olsen, G. K., & Oldevik, J. (2007). Scenarios of traceability in model to text transformations. In *Paper presented at the Third European Conference on Model Driven Architecture Foundations and Applications (ECMDA'07)* (pp.144-158). Haifa, Israel.

Paige, R., & Shaham-Gafni, Y. (2006). *D1.5 model composition: Development of consistency rules* [Modelware D1.5].

Ramesh, B., & Jarke, M. (2001). Toward reference models for requirements traceability. *IEEE Transactions on Software Engineering, 27*(1), 58-93.

Stahl, T., & Völter, M. (2006). *Model-driven software development: Technology, engineering, management.* Chichester: John Wiley.

The Eclipse Foundation. (2007a). *Eclipse model to model (M2M).* Retrieved March 7, 2008, from http://www.eclipse.org/m2m/

The Eclipse Foundation. (2007b). *Eclipse model to text (M2T).* Retrieved March 7, 2008, from http://www.eclipse.org/modeling/m2t/

Walderhaug, S., Stav, E., Johansen, U., & Aagedal, J. (2006, July). Towards a generic solution for traceability in MDD. In *Paper presented at the European Conference on Model Driven Architecture Traceability Workshop (ECMDA-TW),* Bilbao, Spain.

ADDITIONAL READING

For more information on traceability in model-driven software development, the authors recommend the following literature (in alphabetical order):

Aizenbud-Reshef, N., Nolan, B. T., Rubin, J., & Shaham-Gafni, Y. (2006). Model traceability. *IBM Systems Journal, 45*(3), 515-526.

Arkley, P., Mason, P., & Riddle, S. (2002, September). Position paper: Enabling traceability. In *Paper presented at the 1st International Workshop in Traceability in Emerging Forms of Software Engineering (TFFSE),* Edinburgh, Scotland.

Bondé, L., Boulet, P., & Dekeyser, J.-L. (2006). Traceability and interoperability at different levels of abstraction in model-driven engineering. *Applications of specification and design languages for SoCs* (pp. 263-276).

Champeau, J., & Rochefort, E. (2003, October 21). Model engineering and traceability. In *Paper presented at the UML 2003 SIVOES-MDA Workshop,* San Francisco, CA, USA.

Desfray, P. (2003). *MDA–when a major software industry trend meets our toolset, implemented since 1994.* SOFTEAM.

Espinoza, A., Alarcon, P. P., & Garbajosa, J. (2006). *Analyzing and systematizing current traceability schemas.*

Gills, M. (2005, November 8). Survey of traceability models in IT projects. In *Paper presented at the European Conference on Model Driven Architecture—traceability Workshop 2005,* Nuremberg, Germany.

Gotel, O. C. Z., & Finkelstein, C. W. (1994). *An analysis of the requirements traceability problem.*

Ivkovic, I., & Kontogiannis, K. (2004). Tracing evolution changes of software artifacts through model synchronization. In *Paper Presented at the Proceedings of the 20th IEEE International Conference on Software Maintenance, 2004.*

Johansen, U., Stav, E., Walderhaug, S., & Aagedal, J. (2006). *Modelware—traceability metamodel and system solution [D1.6-4].* Trondheim: SINTEF.

Jorgensen, M., & Molokken-Ostvold, K. (2006). How large are software cost overruns? A review of the 1994 CHAOS report. *Information and Software Technology, 48*(4), 297-301.

Jouault, F. (2005, November 8). Loosely coupled traceability for ATL. In *Paper presented at the European Conference on Model Driven Architecture—traceability Workshop 2005,* Nuremberg, Germany.

Kolovos, D. S., Paige, R. F., & Polack, F. A. C. (2006, July). On-demand merging of traceability links with models. In *Paper presented at the European Conference on Model Driven Architecture Traceability Workshop (ECMDA-TW),* Bilbao, Spain.

Kurtev, I., Dee, M., Goknil, A., & Berg, K. V. D. (2007). Traceability-based change management in operational mappings. In *Paper presented at the ECMDA Traceability Workshop (ECMDA-TW),* Haifa, Israel.

Letelier, P. (2002, September). A framework for requirements traceability in UML-based projects. In *Paper presented at the Proceedings of the 1st International Workshop on Traceability, co-located with ASE 2002*, Edinburgh, Scotland, UK.

Limón, A. E., & Garbajosa, J. (2005, November 8). The need for a unifying traceability scheme. In *Paper presented at the European Conference on Model Driven Architecture—traceability Workshop 2005*, Nuremberg, Germany.

Oldevik, J., & Neple, T. (2006, July). Traceability in model to text transformations. In *Paper presented at the European Conference on Model Driven Architecture Traceability Workshop (ECMDA-TW),* Bilbao, Spain.

Oldevik, J., Neple, T., Grønmo, R., Aagedal, J., & Berre, A.-J. (2005, November 7-10). Toward standardised model to text transformations. In *Paper presented at the Model Driven Architecture (Foundations and Applications, First European Conference, ECMDA-FA, 2005),* Nuremberg, Germany.

Olsen, G. K., & Oldevik, J. (2007). Scenarios of traceability in model to text transformations. In *Paper presented at the Third European Conference on Model Driven Architecture Foundations and Applications (ECMDA'07),* Haifa, Israel.

Ramesh, B., & Jarke, M. (2001). Toward reference models for requirements traceability. *IEEE Transactions on Software Engineering, 27*(1), 58-93.

The Eclipse Foundation. (2007). *Eclipse model to model (M2M).* Retrieved March 7, 2008, from http://www.eclipse.org/m2m/

The Eclipse Foundation. (2007). *Eclipse model to text (M2T).* Retrieved March 7, 2008, from http://www.eclipse.org/modeling/m2t/

Section III
Software Architectures and Architectural Alternatives

Chapter VII
Choosing Basic Architectural Alternatives

Gerhard Chroust
J. Kepler University Linz, Austria

Erwin Schoitsch
Austrian Research Centers (ARC), Austria

ABSTRACT

When designing a complex software-intensive system it is unavoidable to make some a-priori basic assumptions about its architecture. We introduce so-called basic architectural alternatives as a means to guide these decisions and to understand their effects. These alternatives are classified according to five fundamental dimensions (enactment time, location, granularity, control, and automation and task distribution). For each dimension we describe some six typical, real examples of such an alternative. For each example we indicate fundamental properties of that alternative: elasticity with respect to later compromises, reversability of the choice (with resonable effort), uniformity requirements with respect to the different elements of in the system, and applicability of the chosen method accross the dimension. Finally, we discuss synergistic or contradictive effects of alternatives with respect to others. We hope that this analysis, together with the specific examples and their key properties, provide some insight for novices and seasoned designers and guides them during the early phases of system design.

INTRODUCTION

Essential Difficulties in Engineering Software-Intensive Systems

The character of software applications has changed considerably in the past decades. Initially, standalone applications for well-understood and manually well-established tasks were implemented, like bookkeeping, warehouse-management, ledger, statistics, and so forth. Software was merely a dedicated tool for faster data processing. Gradually, more sophisticated and challenging tasks were tackled. This emerged for several reasons: Users (especially business users) detected more and more interesting applications in which computers could be usefully employed to open up new business applications; these applications showed an increasing amount of complexity. The advent of Internet (from 16 million users in 1996 to 1.1

billion users in 2006 (Internet World Stats, 2007)) and global commerce provided even more (software-supported) business opportunities, calling for more and more sophisticated software-intensive systems (e-commerce, e-business, e-learning, etc.). These new systems called for more 'intelligent' software being able to handle an increasing amount of data with increased speed.

At the same time software has also made dramatic in-roads into all kinds of technical equipment, replacing conventional mechanical and electro-mechanical subassemblies. Software moved more and more from pure "data processing" to "automation and control." This is shown also by the fact that besides IFIP, the International Federation for Information Processing, a second international organization, IFAC, the International Federation for Automation and Control was founded and both organizations still exist in parallel. Both areas are inherently different with respect to their treatment of process control, and automation is also concerned with real-time applications.

Recent market research shows that 90% of innovation in the automotive industry is expected to come from electronics by 2010 (IBM, 2005). These applications are usually summarized by the term 'embedded system' (cf. Wikipedia-English, 2005, embedded system) and establish the next step of evolution of computer control systems. They are special-purpose computer-controlled electro-mechanical systems in which the computer is completely encapsulated by the device it controls or completely integrated in its environment ("hidden" computing). In many cases it is not a single-task system but is integrated in a network of (co-operating) embedded systems interacting with their environment. An embedded system has specific requirements and performs pre-defined tasks, unlike a general-purpose personal computer. In both cases high financial investments and the lives of many people depend on these systems. The latest evolution is characterized by putting intelligence (machine perception, situation aware-

ness, computer vision, machine learning) on top of networks of embedded systems in order to enable them to behave autonomously as a system. The terms "embedded intelligence" or "ambient intelligence" are used for these systems. The failure of these systems can have and often has considerable financial, social and health consequences. In these cases we speak of software-intensive embedded systems. The challenges of this domain are excellently described in Broy (2006).

The design of such software-intensive, dependable, embedded systems becomes more and more difficult. This is shown by many critical analyses of the success rate of software-intensive systems (Charette, 2005; Glass, 2006; Standish Group, 2006). Despite some progress as documented since 1994 by the Chaos Report of the Standish Group there are still, after decades of process improvement and evaluation, only 34% of projects "successful" (within time, cost, and functional appropriate), 51% "challenged" (completed, but with severe time or cost overrun, or functionally degraded), and still 15% a disastrous failure. For safety-related or safety critical applications, the 51% are not only an annoyance (as may be in the entertainment sector) but a thread to humans and economy.

Many approaches to the problem have been suggested: Rigid rules for the development processes via process models and their assessment and improvement (CMM (Humphrey, 1989), SPICE (ISO/IEC, 2005), etc.), rigid elicitation of the requirements (Boehm, Grünbacher, & Briggs, 2001), and Agile process development (Beck, 2000) brought considerable improvement. We also think that the provision of an appropriate architecture considerably increases the chance of a successful project and its longevity. Under the slogan of architecture-centered design, this approach has lately gained some visibility (Georgas, Dashofy, & Taylor, 2005; Keller & Wendt, 2003).

A key to a successful design is the creation of an acceptable architecture (ESD Architecture Committee, 2004; Blaauw, 1972; Brooks, 1965; Zemel, 1994).

Many authors stress the need to decide early on certain key architectural decisions (Clements, 1995b; Hordijk, Krukkert, & Wieringa, 2004) about what is often called 'architectural primitives,' 'architectural style,' 'design patterns,' 'chunks of architectural design' (Bass, 2007), 'design alternatives' (Bass, 2007; Mehta & Medvidovic, 2005; Maruyama & Smith, 1977; Kazman, Klein, & Clements, 2000; Software Engineering Institute, 2007) and so forth.

They also point out that changing such architectural decisions later is very difficult, very costly and often too late. Wood and Agogino (2005) state that "the initial phase of the design process—conceptual design—sets the stage for all downstream activities. Decisions made during conceptual design can account for as much as 80% of the life cycle costs of the design." An additional problem stems from the fact that nowadays many systems, especially embedded systems, can be classified as *wicked systems* in the terminology of Hermann Kopetz (Kopetz, 1997). Their implementation is more complicated than the class of *environment systems*, as introduced by Lehman (Lehman, 1980, 1985); see section 'A Hierarchy of System Complexity' for details.

A key problem of the development of wicked systems (besides all other difficulties like size, complexity, ill-definition etc.) is that they often have the unpleasant property of *the problem they are trying to solve cannot be specified without some concept of its solution* (Kopetz, 1997).

This means that a system designer has to base these concepts on few, often very vague, and unreliable pieces of information that can be gathered about the intended system.

The situation is aggravated by the fact that these concepts usually will find their way into the inherent, basic structure of the system and establish there what ISO 9126 (ISO/IEC, 2001a) calls the 'design quality.' It is defined as *"the quality represented in the core parts or backbone of the software design."* By necessity these initial architectural decisions (broad as they may be) will

restrict the breadth of feasible/acceptable final solutions (Kopetz, 1997).

Due to the complexity of these future systems we also have to expect problems in understanding the interdependencies and interaction of individual features (Meadows, Meadows, Zahn & Millig, 1969). These interactions might even give rise to *emergent properties* (Brunner, 2002; Fiadeiro, 1996; Meehl & Sellars, 1956), that is, properties which are not present in any of the system's subsystems and only appear due to certain structural configurations of the new system (cf. ESD Architecture Committee, 2004). Their usually unexpected emergence may invalidate predictions about functionality and behavior (Chroust, 2002a, 2002b; Baas & Emmeche, 1997; Pessa, 1998), because the various choices may 'collide' with one another and have synergistic or contradicting effects (see section 'Examples of Aggregated Influences in Systems Engineering').

Lacking sufficient information on the adequate solution for the problem and also on the badly understood effects of features the system designers have to base their architectural decision on the concepts to be chosen on their overall knowledge, experience and intuition in order to create a reasonable initial solution to be later refined and modified to a certain extent.

The better initial 'intuitive' conceptual architectural choices are, the faster a feasible solution can be found. This statement complements the statement about "wicked systems" as defined by Kopetz: For a wicked system *the problem cannot be specified without some concept of its solution (Kopetz, 1997).*

Starting from the wrong architectural assumptions wrong initial decisions will not only lengthen the development process; under today's pressing economic demands of time-to-market and cost, reversing and redirecting the basic architectural decisions in a project is usually not possible. The consequence is that a project either continues with an inappropriate basic architectural design ('design quality') or the project has to be abandoned, with the negative consequences of a decision of this kind. The literature and professional journals report on many of such unsuccessful projects (Standish Group, 2006).

A Hierarchy of System Complexity

The increase in complexity of software-intensive systems seems to be inherent in the software industry. The increase is partially due to the wish to enhance/improve systems by adding more features and functionality in an evolutionary way (Noppen et al., 2002), as predicted by Lehman's second Law (Lehman, 1996). In other cases completely new business ideas also create complex systems from the beginning (e.g., the German Road Pricing System, the new U.S. Air Traffic Control System in the eighties, the Social Security Accounting System of Styria (Austria)). Some of these systems ended in disaster due to inappropriate initial architectural decisions.

Lehman proposed a hierarchy of such systems (Lehman, 1980, 1985) based on their complexity, which was later extended by Kopetz (1997) and Chroust (2004):

- **S-system (Specification system):** "S-type software addresses problems that are formally defined and specified. Programs derived from this kind of specifications can, and normally will, be required to be correct, in the full mathematical sense of the term, relative to that specification" (Lehman, 2005, p. 3.). A typical example is the allocation of number plates to cars. The rules and procedures are well known and the system has to fulfil them.

- **P-system (Problem system):** "This [class] was originally defined as a program that solved an abstract, though not well-understood or precisely stated, problem. A formal specification could not or was not, therefore, developed. Correctness proofs, as required for type S, are meaningless" (Lehman, 2005,

p. 3.). In this case a solution which solved (at least largely) the problem was acceptable. A typical example is the simulation of traffic. The system fulfils its purpose if the predicted traffic flow corresponds to reality, irrespective of the actual algorithms chosen.

- **E-system (Environment system):** This class characterizes "computing applications, systems and software that operate in or interact outside the artificial world of the model embedded in the software. They address problems or activities or execute in what is colloquially termed the real world....The designation *E* [for environment] was selected because...such systems must continuously be evolved in accordance with changes in the real world "(Lehman, 2005, p. 3.). Very often it is the application of these systems themselves which changes the environment respectively the behavior of the elements in the system. Industrial automation and control systems as well as simple embedded systems belong in most cases to this type of systems. A typical example is the control of traffic (traffic lights, etc.) according to the expected traffic forecasted by the simulation. Drivers very soon at least believe they can beat the system by choosing different routes or changing their behavior, respectively.

- **W-systems (Wicked systems):** These systems show (beyond E-systems) the following disturbing properties: they are large and complex, the problem cannot be expressed in a well-defined form, isolating the problem from the environment causes the problem to collapse or to disappear, there is no termination rule, and there is always a better solution. Solutions are not correct or wrong but only better or worse, there being no well-defined test for a successful solution. Even if the solution passes all tests according to the requirements/specifications there are still sufficient possibilities for the system to fail because complex real world systems with mutual interactions between system and environment (in both directions) tend to have always incomplete requirements and thus incomplete specifications. Additionally, *the problem cannot be specified without some concept of its solution* (Kopetz, 1997). Most networked embedded systems with critical controls and Ambient Intelligence systems belong to this class. An example for a wicked system would be the use of the outcome of the traffic simulation (see P-system) for suggesting (or enforcing) routing of cars in order to reduce both route length and fuel consumption.

Today's information systems show a continuous growth in complexity, ascending on the scale of system complexity. The reasons is that all the 'simple' systems (S-type and largely also P-type) have already been implemented (many times over). Today, the information and communication technology allows more imaginative solutions for new problems (e.g., e-market, e-business, artificial intelligence, sophisticated control in many domains, ambient assisted life systems, smart systems at home, in health care, infotainment, etc.) and globalization pushes us to more complex solutions.

The Need for a System Architecture

The growth of systems with respect to complexity and size, together with increased expectations in their usefulness for our lives/environment and the ever-growing demands to satisfy customers creates the need to make the structure of the systems more transparent and systematic, both with respect to the internal organization (in order to ease development and maintenance) and the external view provided for the users. These requirements (together with some further properties) impact the definition of the *system architecture* as specified very early in the life cycle (specifically in the concept phase as identified in Table

1 and in Kossiakoff and Seet (2003)) by defining a so-called system architecture. One of the oldest, and still quite valid definitions of system architecture (actually looking at computers only, hence 'computer architecture') is found in Brooks (1962). He stated:

Computer architecture, like other architecture, is the art of determining the needs of the user of a structure and then designing to meet those needs as effectively as possible within economic and technological constraints. Architecture must include engineering considerations, so that the design will be economical and feasible; but the emphasis in architecture is on the needs of the user, whereas in engineering the emphasis is on the needs of the fabricator.

This concept has been taken further into 'abstract architectures' by Zemanek (1980).

In Wikipedia-English (2005, system architecture) we find: *The software architecture of a program or computing system is the structure or structures of the system, which comprise software elements, the externally visible properties of those elements, and the relationships between them.* This definition is consistent with the one given in Keilser (2006): *A software architecture describes the structure of a solution set to a problem space.* This definition stresses the applicability of an architecture to more than one problem by describing a set of possible solutions.

Thus system architecture provides high-level abstractions of description of coarse-grained structures, connections, data elements, their interfaces, and their configurations. The system composition patterns and constraints on architectural elements comprise the architectural styles. A system architecture reaps additional benefits when it is established as a basis for a whole family of systems with shared characteristics now called 'product line' (Mehta & Medvidovic, 2005; Hoyer, 2007). The original trigger for Brooks' definition was a planned computer family, the famous IBM

System/360 (Amdahl, Blaauw, & Brooks, 1964).

The basic architecture as defined at the beginning of a project can be changed later only with great effort and cost. It establishes what ISO/IEC 9126 (ISO/IEC, 2001a) calls 'design quality.'

Although the architecture should finally be 'one whole' it is actually created by an aggregation of many small decisions, which have to be made individually and in agreement and consistency with other such decisions. We also know that the architecture itself undergoes refinement from very rudimentary basic decisions to the final level of granularity needed for the further steps in the development process.

BACKGROUND: SYSTEM ENGINEERING

System Development: Process and Product

The creation of software-intensive systems is the domain of systems engineering (ISO/IEC, 2006a; Kossiakoff & Seet, 2003; Thome, 1993; Wymore, 1993): *"Systems engineering is an interdisciplinary approach to evolve and verify an integrated and optimally balanced set of product and process designs that satisfy user needs and provide information for management decision making"* (DeFoe, 1993). Software itself is only a part of a software-intensive system, providing one or several software subsystems for the whole system. Software Engineering (Endres & Rombach, 2003; ISO/IEC, 2001b; McDermid, 1991) (Sommerville, 2007) is concerned with providing these software subsystems. It is an interdisciplinary concerted team effort, involving many specialists from various disciplines like hardware, electrical, mechanical, chemical engineering, economics and human factors (Wikipedia-English, 2005, systems engineering). It is a human intensive and a collaborative team effort. Table 1 shows the life cycle stages of systems engineering according to (ISO/IEC,2006a).

Table 1. System engineering development stages according to IEC 61508-98 (IEC, 1998)

Life Cycle Stage	Purpose
CONCEPT	Identify stakeholders' needs Explore concepts Propose viable solution
DEVELOPMENT	Refine system requirements Create solution description Build system Verify and validate system
PRODUCTION	Integrate components and subsystems Produce system Inspect and test
UTILIZATION	Operate system to satisfy users' needs
SUPPORT, MAINTENANCE	Provide sustained system capability
RETIREMENT, DISPOSAL	Store, archive or dispose of the system

The development of wicked systems is not essentially different from other system developments as standardized by ISO/IEC 15288(ISO/IEC, 2006a) (see Table 1). For wicked systems the concept phase, however, is of special importance because here the foundation for the final system is laid down. In the concept phase it is necessary to assess and understand the *stakeholder needs* which will, by necessity, be vague and ill-defined (otherwise, we would not have a wicked system in the first place).

With the activity *Explore concepts* the need for early-up understanding of the possible basic architectural alternatives and their influences and consequences comes into consideration. The activity *Propose viable solution* has to decide on one or more sets of compatible, adequate basic architectural alternatives. This activity also implies an initial choice. This choice has to be based on the aggregated properties of the system to be implemented. In this stage, obviously, predicting the final properties from the chosen architectural alternatives can be performed to a limited extent. This makes it necessary to understand the consequences of the various basic architectural alternatives and also to consider their cross-influences, see section 'Examples of Aggregated Influences in Systems Engineering.'

Different solution concepts will usually compete with one another and will contain different and opposite basic architectural alternatives. This makes it necessary to make some strategic, higher-level decisions based on global, strategic considerations (see section 'Strategic Selection Considerations for Basic Architectural Alternatives').

Properties of Software-Intensive Systems

At the time of conceptualization of the system (Concept Phase) it is not possible to make comprehensive statements of the final properties of the system. Only some initial estimates are possible. In this contribution, we will consistently use the term *"property"* knowing that several other terms are also used like "characteristic" (ISO/IEC 2001a) or "attribute" (Laprie et al., 1992; ISO/IEC, 2006a; DeFoe, 1993) of systems as listed in various standards (ISO 9126 (ISO/IEC, 2001a, 2006b; Project Management Institute, 2005; IEC, 1998). We have aggregated the properties found in these documents as far as they can meaningfully be considered at the early stage of concept creation. We have identified a few so-called fundamental properties by aggregating the existing characteristics from other standards (see section 'Fundamental Properties of Software-intensive (Embedded) Systems'). The main sources for this aggregation are described in the subsequent sections. They relate to the following five classifications as show in section 'Product Quality Properties' to section 'Project Oriented Properties.'

Product Quality Properties

Following ISO/IEC 9126 (ISO/IEC, 2001a) and its successor ISO/IEC 25010 (ISO/IEC, 2006b)

the key properties of a product (they are called 'characteristics' in these standards) are defined as seen from an engineering point of view. They define main properties, each having several sub-properties:

- **Functionality:** The capability of the software product to provide functions which meet stated and implied needs ... Sub-properties are: suitability, accuracy, interoperability, security, compliance
- **Reliability:** The capability of the software product to maintain a specified level of performance ... Sub-properties are: maturity, fault tolerance, recoverability, compliance
- **Usability:** The capability of the software product to be understood, learned, used and attractive to the user ... Sub-properties are: understandability, learnability, operability, attractiveness, compliance
- **Efficiency:** The capability of the software product to provide appropriate performance, relative to the amount of resources used, ... Sub-properties are: time behavior, resource utilisation, compliance
- **Maintainability:** The capability of the software product to be modified. Modifications may include corrections, improvements or adaptation of the software to changes in environment, in requirements and functional specifications. Sub-properties are: analysability, changeability, stability, testability, compliance
- **Portability:** The capability of the software product to be transferred from one environment to another. Sub-properties are: adaptability, installability, co-existence, replaceability, compliance

Dependability Properties

With the growth of the field of dependable computers, especially in safety critical controls, certain key attributes gain special importance. To some extent they are already covered by the ISO9126

(ISO/IEC, 2001a) but need special attention which is for example, the intention of IEC 61508-98/00 (IEC, 1998). There is no full consent yet. An extended set of dependability attributes follows (Laprie et al., 1992; Redmill, 1988; Schoitsch, 2003b; Sonneck & Schoitsch, 2003). The compound term "dependability" is the central notion. It consists of availability, reliability, safety, security (confidentiality, integrity, authenticity), maintainability, and survivability:

- **Dependability:** The collective term for availability performance and its influencing factors: reliability performance, maintainability performance and maintenance support performance (IEC, 1990, IEC TC 56). The term was extended (Laprie et al., 1992; van der Meulen, 2000, 1995) to cover all principal characteristics in connection with safety-related systems: "Trustworthiness of a computer system such that reliance can be justifiably placed on the service it delivers." Thus, dependability is an umbrella term for a set of sub-properties: availability, maintainability, reliability, safety, security (including confidentiality, integrity, authenticity), and survivability (robustness).

- **Availability (Readiness for use):** The ability of a functional unit to be in a state to perform a required function under given conditions at a given time instance or over a given time interval, assuming that the external resources are provided (ISO/IEC, 1996).

- **Maintainability (Easiness of maintenance):** From a hardware/software systems perspective, this includes more than just the preservation of the status quo of a system (as in ISO/IEC, 1996). It includes enhancements and modifications to perform new/additional functions to fulfil new requirements, for example, upgrades and adaptations (Arthur, 1988; Sommerville, 2007). In the system context (and context of the dependability definitions of Laprie et al., 1992) it can be

defined as *"The ease with which a (software, hardware) system or component can be modified to correct faults, improve performance or other attributes, or adapt to a changed environment* (IEEE, 1990; for details, see Redmill, 1989; Schoitsch, 1997).

- **Reliability (Continuity of service):** The probability that an item can perform a required function under given conditions for a given time interval (IEC, CENLEC). The ability of a functional unit to perform a required function under given conditions for a given time interval (ISO/IEC, 1996).

- **Safety (freedom from unacceptable risk):** Freedom from (likelihood of) those conditions that can cause death, injury, occupational illness, or damage to or loss of equipment or property, or damage to the environment (Department of Defense, 1993).

- **Security:** Dependability with respect to unauthorized access or information handling (deliberate (malicious) interaction!). Normally, sub-properties to be included are availability, confidentiality, integrity and authenticity of information.

- **Survivability:** (capability to withstand a hostile environment) The capability of a system to avoid or withstand a hostile environment without suffering an abortive impairment of its ability to accomplish its designated mission (van der Meulen, 2000; Department of Defense, 1992). This includes any kind of impairment especially from the environment, including security attacks and so forth.

Further essential properties are:

- **Fault tolerance:** The ability of a functional unit to continue to perform a required function in the presence of faults or errors (IEC, 1998).

- **Risk:** (combination of probability of concurrency and severity of harm): The combination of frequency, or probability, and the consequence of a specific (or combination of) hazardous events (IEC, 1998).

- **Hazard:** a potential source of harm (IEC, 1998).
- **Predictability**: The ability to provide a correct forecast of the behavior of a system or component in space and time under given conditions for all foreseeable operational states (in dependable embedded real-time systems, it normally means that the behavior in space and time can be statically defined beforehand by proper configuration of the system).
- **Responsiveness:** The ability of a functional unit to react to a given event according to requirements, and under stated conditions (generalized from Redmill, 1989).
- **Timeliness ("in time"):** Ability of a system or component to perform its required function before its deadline.
- **Robustness:** Capability of a system to withstand hostile environment, intended or unintended malicious (mis-)use. Robustness can be seen as a combination of reliability, survivability, safety and security).

Quality in Use Properties

With the growing number of nontechnical people interfacing with these systems, their satisfaction gains importance. These properties take only the viewpoint of the user into account. They are dependent on the product quality properties and the dependability properties for systems, but are a set of properties in their own right. They are explicitly addressing the view of the product *"in a specified context of use"* (ISO/IEC, 2001a; Redmill, 1988), that is, depending on the kind of use which may, for the same product, be different for different types of users. A second, very important aspect is "public acceptance," because the interaction of embedded systems with everyday life often leads to problems from "uneasy feelings"

of users (not exactly knowing what a systems does, or being confronted with unexpected system behavior because of misinterpretation by users or deployers ("dangerous surprise")) and, finally, to severe public concerns ("big brother"). The key properties following ISO/IEC 9126 and ISO/IEC 25010 as seen by a user of the product are:

- **Effectiveness:** The capability of the software product to enable users to achieve specified goals with accuracy and completeness in a specified context of use.
- **Productivity:** The capability of the software product to enable users to expend appropriate amounts of resources in relation to the effectiveness achieved in a specified context of use. Relevant resources can include time to complete the task, the user's effort, materials or the financial cost of usage.
- **Safety:** The capability of the software product to achieve acceptable levels of risk of harm to people, business, software, property or the environment in a specified context of use. Risks are usually a result of deficiencies in the functionality (including security), reliability, usability or maintainability.
- **Satisfaction:** The capability of the software product to satisfy users in a specified context of use. Satisfaction is the user's response to interaction with the product, and includes attitudes toward use of the product).

Systems Engineering-Oriented Properties

The INCOSE report (DeFoe, 1993) proposes to "evaluate each [design] alternative against the requirements and the effectiveness criteria [and to] determine the alternative that provides the best weighted value combining." Without any further definition the following properties of a system are listed: **effective, efficient, safe, reliable, producible, testable, maintainable, easy to learn**.

Project-Oriented Properties

Besides influencing the properties of a final product, most choices of alternatives also have considerable influence on the properties of a project (development time, effort, etc.). According to the Project Management Institute (2005) the most influential characteristics are:

- **Functionality:** The capability of the software product to provide functions which meet stated and implied needs (ISO/IEC, 2001a);
- **Effort:** The number of labor units required for completing the project work (Project Management Institute, 2005);
- **Duration:** The total number of work periods (not including holidays or other nonworking periods) required to complete a scheduled activity or work breakdown structure component. Usually expressed as workdays, workweeks, or workmonths. Sometimes incorrectly equated with elapsed time (Project Management Institute, 2005);
- **Quality:** The degree to which a set of inherent characteristics fulfills requirements (Project Management Institute, 2005);
- **Budget:** The approved estimate for (financial) cost, time, or any other resource of the project, of any workbreakdown structure component, or of any scheduled activity (Project Management Institute, 2005); and
- **Risk:** An uncertain event or condition that, if it occurs, has a positive or negative effect on a project's objectives (Project Management Institute, 2005).

These properties do not directly contribute to a system's properties and are not identical to those of section 'Product Quality Properties' to section 'Quality in Use Properties' because they express another viewpoint. They are, however, highly influential in deciding what properties of a product are 'affordable,' which again will influence the choice of alternatives (see section 'Strategic Selection Considerations for Basic Architectural Alternatives').

Fundamental Properties of Software-Intensive (Embedded) Systems

In the concept phase a designer will be interested in the effects of different choices of alternatives on the resulting overall product properties at the *system level*. Obviously, no detailed statements about the properties of the resulting system are helpful and therefore cannot be made.

We have therefore reduced the set of product properties as presented in section 'Properties of Software-intensive Systems' and aggregated them into a few properties which we believe can be estimated early in the concept phase and are helpful and influential with respect to the final product. We ignore in this context the differences between new development and maintenance.

In the list below we have also indicated which of the characteristics are closely related to the fundamental properties.

For some properties, no mapping could be made, mainly because in the concept phase no meaningful predictions can be made. The chosen fundamental properties are:

- **Complexity:** The term 'complex system' has no precise definition but can often be taken to mean a system with many strongly-coupled degrees of freedom (Wikipedia-English, 2005, complexity; Dörner, 1996). Complexity is taken to be the source of many problems in systems design and usage. Laird and Brennan (2006, p. 55) distinguish structural complexity ('the quality of interconnectedness'), conceptual complexity ('the difficulty of understanding') and computational complexity ('the complexity of the computation being performed).

In functional safety standards such as the generic safety standard IEC 61506 (IEC, 1998), complexity is one of the most used terms, but only defined for "low complexity systems" (all others are of "high complexity") because then certain simplifications are allowed. In van der Meulen (1995, 2000) and IEEE (1990), and according to ISO SC7 WAG 9, complexity is roughly defined as "the degree to which a software (but this may be applied to systems in general) has a design or implementation that is difficult to comprehend and verified by simple measures." In the upcoming ISO WED 26262 (Automotive Functional Safety) the term is being reconsidered at the moment.

(IEC, 1998) defines the notion of *low complexity safety-related system* as a safety-related system in which: a) the failure modes of each individual component are well defined; and b) the behavior of the system under fault conditions can be completely determined.

Complexity is the driving force for many of the attributes of systems, both with respect to usage and development.

Other properties strongly influenced by this property (see section 'Properties of Software-intensive Systems'): adaptability, analysability, changeability, composability, functionality, installability, interoperability, learnability, operability, predictability, quality, replaceability, testability, understandability, and usability.

- **Flexibility:** The quality of being adaptable or variable (Wikipedia-English, 2005, flexibility). In many instances, it is desirable that the choices for the system do not preclude later changes and modifications too much, leaving the system flexible for later modification concerning the quality of being adaptable or variable. Flexibility covers several properties which are important both with respect to longevity and maintainability.

Other properties strongly influenced by this property (see section 'Properties of Software-intensive Systems'): adaptability, changeability, co-existence, maintainability, portability, productivity, quality, and replaceability.

- **Dependability:** "The capability of the software product to maintain a specified level of performance when used" (ISO/IEC, 2006b, clause 6.2). In the context of this paper we take a very broad view and summarize under this term many aspects where the users 'depend' on a system (see also IEC, 1998; Laprie et al., 1992; Schoitsch, 2003a, and also section 'Dependability Properties'). Dependability is strongly related to survivability.

Other properties strongly influenced by this property (see section 'Properties of Software-intensive Systems'): accuracy, availability, confidentiality, effectiveness, fault tolerance, maturity, predictability, productivity, quality, recoverability, reliability, responsiveness, robustness safety, satisfaction, security, and stability timeliness.

- **Survivability:** In the context of this chapter, we take a very broad view and summarize many ways a system has to 'survive' in awkward situations under this property. Strictly speaking dependability and survivability describe different aspects. The common denominator is that the system can survive dangers and attacks (external as well as internal ones). In this sense, the user can expect the system to be available and provide the expected services in a reliable way, that is, that the system is capable of maintaining a specified level of performance when used/consumed (ISO/IEC, 2006b, clause 6.2). Thus, this property overlaps 'dependability' in many aspects or is part of it.

Other properties strongly influenced by this property (see section 'Properties of Software-intensive Systems'): availability, dependability, fault tolerance, integrity, maturity, predictability, quality, recoverability, reliability, robustness safety, stability security, and timeliness.

- **Time consumption:** ISO/IEC 25000 defines 'time consumption' as *the capability of the software product to provide appropriate response and processing times and throughput rates when performing its function ...* (ISO/IEC, 2006b, clause 6.4.2) In general, this is strongly related to the time consumption. If we base this on the elapsed time (the time it takes the system to perform a task) a large part of the implications is covered. If people work in parallel, this will be subsumed as effort and will be considered with respect to the project-oriented parameters.

  "Time" is very often considered just as "resource," to be considered under resource utilization. Some properties of time (e.g., unilateral extension), however, induce separate treatment.

  Other properties strongly influenced by this property (see section 'Properties of Software-intensive Systems'): duration and efficiency.

- **Resource utilization:** The capability of the software product to use appropriate amounts and types of resources when the software performs its function under stated conditions (ISO/IEC, 2006b, clause 6.4.1).

  Other properties strongly influenced by this property (see section 'Properties of Software-intensive Systems'): efficiency, time consumption, adaptability, and maintainability.

- **Ease of use:** This is a very fuzzy notion and can only be estimated intuitively. Ease of use is of key importance with respect to quality in use.

  Other properties strongly influenced by this property (see section 'Properties of Software-intensive Systems'): attractiveness, efficiency, functionality, satisfaction, suitability, and understandability.

It should be noted that the property 'functionality ' (see section 'Product Quality Properties') and the project-oriented properties (see section 'Project-oriented Properties') are not included in the lists above. They are considered to be, rather, inputs or constraints for the total project. They relate to a different concern, the engineering of the total system. They will be discussed in section 'Strategic Selection Considerations for Basic Architectural Alternatives.' The properties discussed above are rather concerned with (high-level) architectural design and implementation decisions once the project itself is understood.

BASIC ARCHITECTURAL ALTERNATIVES

The Notion of Basic Architectural Alternatives

One can say that in the field of engineering *the essence ... is making intelligent trade-offs between conflicting parameters* (Lucky, 2006). We often find trade-offs between two opposite, often incompatible alternatives for a design: for example, you can design a system for extreme flexibility or for extreme resistance to change. Each has its advantages and disadvantages. For example, the Internet, based on the original DARPA-network (Plasser & Haussteiner, 2005), was designed for maximizing the communication between scientists and at the same time minimizing the effects of disruption of the connections (including catastrophes and war action as demonstrated by the 9/11-attacks). This decision causes today's problem with security and there is no quick and easy remedy at this time.

As a simplistic and prototypical example of such a basic alternatives we will take the popular saying: *"You can't keep the cake and eat it."* The cake example is typical for a large class of these alternatives. Typically, keeping the cake for (much) later might imply a different technology for eating it, because it might have dried out (e.g., by dipping into coffee).

An example from software engineering is the initial choice for a new programming language *to design it for being compiled or being interpreted* (Gries, 1971). This choice has major consequences for syntax and semantics and probably cannot be fully reversed later (at least not in both directions).

We suggest calling these basic conceptual decisions 'basic architectural alternatives' (Chroust, 2004, 2005) because they identify essentially diametrically opposite ends of a spectrum of alternatives. Due to their very basic nature, they characterize the alternative choices to be made at the start of the system design of a wicked system (section 'A Hierarchy of System Complexity').

In comparison to the approaches provided by other authors (e.g., Bass, 2007; Clements, 1995b; Hordijk et al., 2004; Mehta & Medvidovic, 2005; Maruyama & Smith, 1977; Wood & Agogino, 2005; Zdun & Avgeriou, 2005) we concentrate on the identification of the truly basic underlying patterns. Following Keilser (2006) they would be "conceptual patterns."

We understand that describing these alternatives in their abstracted, essential form is only part of the real-world design process where trade-offs and modifications are often possible and needed. We understand that the final architecture might be able to improve good decisions and ameliorate suboptimal decisions. These basic architectural alternatives can be seen as an analogy to architectural patterns (Alexander, Ishikawa, & Silverstein, 1977; Keilser, 2006) and software patterns (Buschmann, 1994; Gamma, Helm, Johnson, & Vlissides, 1995; Gomaa, Menasce, & Shin, 2001; Laplante & Neill, 2006). They are also similar to the cultural differences of societies described by Hampden-Turner and Trompenaars (2000).

We believe that by isolating and describing these alternatives together with their essential properties, implications, consequences and interactions, system designers (both newcomers and seasoned ones) will be helped and guided to make better initial conceptual decisions by clearly understanding the different options available and their interaction and interdependence, thus providing some support for the necessary intuitive decisions by the designer. What distinguishes this approach from other approaches is that they are arranged in pairs of completely opposite behavior. They are essential, prototypical and somewhat hypothetical extremes of the design, abstracted from real-world designs. They can be considered either as basic conflict pairs or basic trade-off pairs.

Dimensions of Basic Architectural Alternatives

Basic architectural alternatives relevant for software-intensive systems can be groups into five dimensions. Each dimension describes a continuous spectrum between two opposite extremes. The conceptual endpoints of the individual dimensions actually designate the (often infeasible) or impractical ends of a spectrum. A good system designer will make a reasonable compromise and choose a certain intermediate position (see the discussion of the placement of Etruscan villages with respect to their distance to the sea in Piatelli and Bianchi, 1998).

Alternatives can be associated with different dimensions (time, space, etc.; see section 'Dimensions of Basic Architectural Alternatives.') The Time Dimension is perhaps the most easily understood dimension: A certain task can be performed prior to the need or when the need arises.

For these dimensions many examples can be given (see section 'Specific Examples of Basic Architectural Alternatives'). More than one Basic Architectural Alternative can be found within such a dimension. Therefore, we order the identified alternatives according to the relevant dimension. In some instances, the same alternative can be associated with more than one dimension. This is noted specially. We also recognize that probably many more of these alternatives exist. Obviously, these choices have a multidimensional cost function associated with them, which depends on many other properties of the system: performing a certain task later might make it less risky due to more information, but also more costly due to rising manpower costs; having material in a central place might reduce the redundant stock but might increase transport costs, and so forth.

Section 'Dimensions of Basic Architectural Alternatives' identifies major dimensions of basic architectural alternatives. In section 'Specific Examples of Basic Architectural Alternatives,' examples are shown from system engineering and some of the trade-offs involved in making the choices are discussed.

We can classify the alternatives according to the dimension in which the variation occurs (Figure 1). The assignment to the chosen dimensions is somewhat up to interpretation, as shown in Table 7. The dimensions below seem to be the most basic ones in current information systems.

- **Enactment time (reactive-proactive):** WHEN should a foreseen action be performed, either proactively when the necessary action is known (or suspected) or when the actual need arises (see section 'Enactment Time (on-demand-proactive)')?
- **Location (local-remote):** WHERE should needed data, and programs (and functionality) be placed (see section 'Location (local-remote)')?
- **Granularity (coarse-fine):** HOW MANY/ MUCH should be accessed/handled in one step (see section 'Granularity (coarse-fine)')?
- **Control (central-distributed):** WHO or WHAT has the responsibility for leading the interaction? WHERE should control be located (see section 'Control (central-distributed)')?
- **Automation and Task Distribution (human-automatic):** TO WHAT DEGREE is

a tasks automated (see section 'Automation and Task Distribution (human-automatic)')? This includes the question of whether or not a certain task is to be performed by a human being or by a computer.

Most of the described individual alternatives (see section 'Specific Examples of Basic Architectural Alternatives') can be summarized under more than one dimension, depending on the particular view, as shown in section 'Multiple Classification' and Table 7.

These dimensions have been isolated from a wealth of candidates; some of the more interesting candidates were:

- **Optimistic/pessimistic approach:** seems to be rather a general strategy of the choice of the alternatives (see section 'Optimistic vs. Pessimistic Updating.')
- **Project and technical risk:** this is a pervasive concept and rather a strategic guideline for making the choice between alternatives (PMI Risk Management Specific Interest Group, 2002; Redmill, 1988; Schoitsch, 1997) and so forth.
- **Synchronicity:** this was regarded as a consequence of the sequencing control action (see section 'Control (central-distributed)'). section 'Check-and-do vs. Try-and-abort'
- **Resource constraints:** This is a consequence of the question as to how many resources can be used. Finally, we thought that this is closely related to the question of granularity (how much/many) of something may/have to be used. This is a critical issue in embedded systems.

Observations on Basic Architectural Alternatives

Looking at the different alternatives (see section 'Dimensions of Basic Architectural Alternatives') several observations can be made (some of them we relate again to our cake example).

Figure 1. Dimensions of architectural alternatives

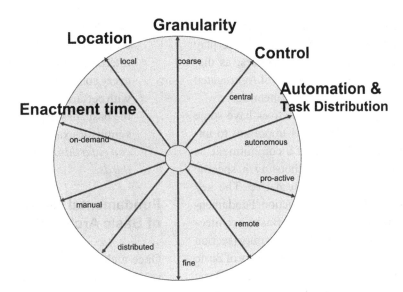

1. Especially in the software business almost everything 'can be done,' if one is willing to spend enough resources. We will, however, restrict all considerations to approaches which are called *AGARP, "as good as reasonably practical"* and ignore outlying approaches. *" ALARP,"* denoting *"as low as reasonably practicable"* was coined in IEC (1998) and is a basic principle in safety-related systems, because 100% safety cannot be achieved. A detailed discussion of "tolerable Risk and the "ALARP" principle is given in Redmill and Dale (1997, chapter 8.7).

2. The choice of an alternative has strong, often irreversible influence on the properties of the final system, for example, *once eaten, the cake is gone!*.

3. Many of the alternatives are not symmetric; choosing an alternative at one time precludes a change of mind later, for example, *you can keep the cake today and eat it tomorrow*, but not vice versa.

4. In real life the extreme positions are usually not taken but some compromise with some trade-offs will have to be found, which choose a 'middle way' with more or less bias toward the originally chosen alternative, for example, *eating a third of the cake and keeping the other two thirds*. The initial bias, however, will still be seen in the final system.

5. If circumstances change, a different choice could be better, for example, *keeping a cake if one is not hungry.*

6. Changing the alternative might involve a change in methods/technology. A given action can be performed at some point in time or much later. Postponing an action might, however, involve a different method or technology. *You can cross the lake in winter on foot if it is frozen, but crossing it in half a years time you need some other means (e.g., swimming or boating).*

7. The wrong combination of choices might result in a suboptimal system.

8. Alternatives are usually neither orthogonal to one another nor independent from one another. This means that a systems engineer additionally has to consider the interplay between several of these choices, as discussed in section 'Examples of Aggregated Influences in Systems Engineering.'

9. basic architectural alternatives have some inherent properties. It is important to understand 'how much of a commitment' is actually made when choosing a specific Basic Architectural Alternative. The key properties are elasticity (section 'Fundamental Elasticity Property of Basic Architectural Alternatives') and uniformity (section 'Fundamental Uniformity Property of Basic Architectural Alternatives'). For each Basic Architectural Alternative, we will identify the relevant Basic Property.

10. When considering modifying initial basic architectural alternatives, one has also to consider the cost of doing so.

Fundamental Elasticity Property of Basic Architectural Alternatives

It is important to know at the start of a project how elastic a certain choice still is with respect to later modifications. The elasticity can be considered in two ways: whether a compromise between the extreme positions is possible *(can one eat half a cake and keep half a cake)* and if one can go back on one's decision later *once the cake is eaten, you cannot 'keep it' anymore"!)*. The following alternatives can be distinguished (section 'Specific Examples of Basic Architectural Alternatives'):

- **Dichotomic:** Some alternatives are strictly 'either-or,' there is no possibility for a compromise 'in the middle' (*"One cannot be 30% pregnant"*);
- **Flexible:** In some instances, an initial choice can be relaxed by bringing in some aspects

of the other alternative. This flexibility can be complete in the sense that one can completely reverse the situation or only to a limited amount. Typically, the compiler/interpreter alternative is flexible because every compiler can (and actually is) supplied with certain interpretative components, but the basic design has to stay compilative. A simplistic example of this distinction is: *you can eat a third of the cake and keep the two thirds.*

Fundamental Reversibility Property of Basic Architectural Alternatives

Once a choice is made, it is helpful to know if such a decision can later be taken back. For many alternatives the reversibility is asymmetric, being possible in one direction but not in the other. We distinguish:

- **Reversible:** The choice can be taken back and another choice made. One has to consider, however, that reversing a choice usually induces certain costs *for example, you may decide to keep the cake for tomorrow, but a few hours later you may decide to eat it.*
- **Irreversible:** Once made, the choice cannot be taken back: *Once the cake is eaten, the option for keeping does not exist anymore.*
- **Semi-reversible:** Very often, we find the case that one of the two extreme positions can be taken back but the other not. *Eating or keeping a cake is such an example.*

Fundamental Uniformity Property of Basic Architectural Alternatives

The choices made usually affect many elements, and—in many instances—are different for the individual elements. This property describes which elements have to conform to the same choice of alternative. Does the choice of an alternative in one subsystem of the considered system imply or require the same alternative to be chosen in other subsystems or not? Here we have to distinguish four cases of stringency:

- **No uniformity:** There is no necessity for different subsystems to follow the same alternative as any other subsystem. Typically, you can use storage management for some variables and garbage collection (Mössenböck, 2002) for the rest. *Simplistically, of two owners of a cake the one can eat his piece now while the other keeps it.*

- **Scope uniformity:** Within the scope of the subsystem of a system the same alternative has to be chosen for *all* of its subsystems. In a hierarchically layered computer system, for example, it is not possible to have a compilative approach when the next higher level is interpretative (Chroust, 1989) but several compilative levels may follow one another (see also 'scope conserving evaluation,' and Chroust, 1971). *Simplistically, there is no point in delivering a pair of skis, one for cross-country skiing and the other one for alpine skiing.*

- **Peer-level uniformity:** (Merriam-Webster, 1996, peer) defines a peer as "one that is of equal standing with another." In our case, it will mean that subsystems or elements identified to be equal in some respect should have the same Basic Architectural Alternative chosen. The peerage could be the same hierarchical level (leaves vs. inner nodes of a tree), thus having "horizontal uniformity," and being the same "distance" from real hardware or of the same type (e.g., in parameter passing all single elements might be treated differently from structured elements (Wikipedia-English, 2005, Evaluation strategy)). *Simplistically: two carriages of the same train have to go in the same direction, but other carriages may take different routes.*

- **Complete uniformity:** Within the total system for all elements (as far as applicable) the same alternative has to be chosen.

In Figure 2 when under a peer-level uniformity regime (when considering the type) a1, a2, b1, b2, b3 and c2 would be subjected to the same alternative, while under scope uniformity a1, a2, a3 and a4 would have to apply the same alternatives.

Fundamental Method Applicability Property of Basic Architectural Alternatives

In some instances, the method can stay the same between the selected dimensions, while in other instances the method has to change. Typically, fetching the value of variables can be performed at different times (section 'Enactment Time (on-demand-proactive)') but still using the same method. Some methods are only applicable to one of the alternatives. *For example, storage management vs. garbage collection (section 'Enactment Time (on-demand-proactive)') need different methods.* Again, a simplistic example is: *you can eat the cake now* or *you can eat it in a year's time, but probably you will have to use a different method, for example, grinding it to crumbs.*

For the scope of this discussion, we will just identify two cases:

- **Same method applicable:** Meaning that you *can* use the same method, but not necessarily need to use the same method.
- **Different method necessary:** Inherently, a different method has to be taken.

SPECIFIC EXAMPLES OF BASIC ARCHITECTURAL ALTERNATIVES

In this section we list, sorted by the identified dimensions, basic architectural alternatives of systems engineering.

Figure 2. Uniformity

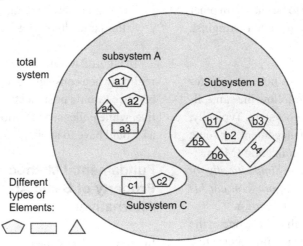

Enactment Time
(On-Demand-Proactive)

We know that not every action has to be performed immediately after its identification. One of the essential decisions for an action is as to *when* it should be enacted, assuming that it has to be enacted sometime. The action could be performed on recognizing the potential need to perform it (*proactive*) immediately (as soon as possible), it may be more advantageous to delay it, or it could be postponed until the last minute (*on demand*), actually reacting to the immediate request. With respect to the fundamental properties of the software-intensive system, the influence of the Enactment-time-Dimension can be sketched as in Table 2. One of the essential decisions for an action is as to *when* it should be enacted. The action can be performed as early as possible, as soon as it is identified as potentially necessary. This is also known as "eager execution" and is related to "work ahead"-scenarios (Phillips, 1988). This usually allows to devote more time to the action, allowing a more thorough work process, with the uncertainty that the work might prove unnecessary. The alternative is to wait until the actions

is really needed (*"on demand"* or *"just-in-time"*). In this case, an action is performed only when really required and at the last moment, but that might be at a very awkward moment. High-speed computers prefetch data in order to avoid costly fetches or even page faults later. This entails the risk of sometimes being wrong and having to throw away the result of some work. Especially, paging systems with their comparatively high penalty of not having the needed page available immediately have created a wealth of methods to anticipate which information is needed next.

Major reasons for delay can be:

- During a time-critical action no time should be "wasted" on lower-priority tasks, especially if there will be some slack time later to do the work.
- At a later time there might be more accurate information available to perform a task in a better way.
- Resources might be cheaper later.
- Complexity increases for prefetching.
- Run time performance is increased when a value is actually needed, but decreased for the start up of the model.

- Wasted effort increases in the case of prefetching.
- In embedded systems, sometimes processor speed can be reduced if there is no demand, resulting in saving of energy (which may be a critical resource).

Computation of Functions vs. Table Look-Up

In order to compute mathematical values (e.g., trigonometric functions) all necessary values could be precomputed and stored in a table (needing considerable memory) or the requested value could be computed whenever needed, using considerable ad-hoc time.

Fundamental Properties of this Alternative:

- Flexible (e.g., using interpolation for values between looked-up values)
- Semi-reversible (despite the availability of a look-up table one can compute a function, but not vice versa)
- No uniformity
- Different method necessary (table look-up or computation)

Search vs. Systematic Archiving

Retrieval of archived information and documents is one of the major problems of administrations. In the past, the problem was approached by establishing elaborate, time consuming index-

Table 2. Enactment time—effects

Effects on system properties	Usual consequences of proactive execution on system properties
complexity	• Complexity increases if data available have to be stored until they can be used • Complexity increases because pro-activity usually has to consider several future cases (e.g., like in a compiler (section 'Interpretation/Compilation') or formal verification (section 'Testing vs. Formal Verification') • Complexity decreases at the point of actual decision if the decisions have already been made (e.g., table look up) • Complexity decreases if it allows to handle several items by one action (see section 'Granularity (coarse-fine)')
flexibility	• Flexibility increases because the actions can be performed at a convenient point of time between the earliest point and the deadline
dependability	• Dependability increases with proactive behavior because actions can be verified/validated ahead of actual need
survivability	• Survivability increases because bottlenecks can be avoided by proactive behavior • Proactive behavior (e.g., early binding of resources (variables)) my detect insufficient resources (e.g., memory) prior to execution time and avoid safety critical situations
time consumption	• Time consumption increases when a value is actually needed, and not available • The initial overhead (typically for computing the look-up table (section 'Computation of Functions vs. Table Look-up'), for compilation (section 'Interpretation/Compilation'), or for indexing (section 'Search vs. Systematic Archiving')) increases time consumption for start-up of operations • On-demand binding decreases time consumption at startup time but increases time consumption when a value is actually needed
resource utilization	• Potentially wasted effort for unnecessary proactive actions • Increased storage utilization to store proactively produced data
ease of use	• Proactive (optimistic) updating is more convenient initially by accessing objects, which might be the overriding concern in development (*'do not hinder creativity'*) but backfires at the end when (parallel) changes to the same object have to be consolidated

ing systems (often several of them) and hoping that—when need arises—the information efficiently can be found using these indices. Today, often electronically readable information can be stored essentially unordered *(chaotic)* and un-indexed. Elaborate search engines will "waste" some (unnoticeable) extra time for retrieval but will also find items for which no index has been generated. A typical example is chaotic storage management (e.g., the Amazon company).

Fundamental Properties of this Alternative:

- Dichotomic (it only makes sense, if the whole store is indexed or searched)
- Semi-reversible (one can always perform a search)
- Complete uniformity
- Different method necessary

Binding of Variables: Latest-Earliest

Memory space has to be allocated to a program's variables ('binding of variables'). Allocation can be completed *before* the program starts ('statically'), using considerable memory space, even for variables which might not be used at all. Alternatively, binding can be performed 'dynamically' when storage for the variable is actually needed at the price of perhaps valuable (or even critical) time to be lost, or critical resources to be exhausted (memory). Therefore, for safety critical systems avoiding dynamic binding is highly recommended! Binding can also be done at several convenient points in between: at compile time, when the program is linked with other programs or when the program is loaded into the computer system (Franz, 1997).

Fundamental Properties of this Alternative:

- Flexible (individual variables can be bound early or late)

- Reversible (the preferences can be changed)
- No uniformity
- Same method applicable

Interpretation/Compilation

The programming languages we need/want (e.g., problem-oriented languages) cannot be directly executed on the existing hardware. It is necessary to *translate* these high-level language statements into the primitive control statements of the hardware. This translation might be completely transparent to the user (Holmes, 1997). This translation can essentially be performed in two ways (Figure 3):

- Translate the *complete program* at once and execute it later (*'compilation,'* Gries, 1971; Rechenberg, 1993), or
- Translate *one statement* (a 'minimally meaningful expression of the language') at a time, execute it and then translate the next statement (*'interpretation,'* Flynn, 1979; Mackrodt, 1981).

For computer programs the major difference is the much higher speed of execution of a compiled program (due to the fact that most of the tests and decisions can be done beforehand and that a compiler, "seeing" the complete program, can do many optimizations an interpreter with its limited "view" is unable to do). On the other hand, a compiler is much more complicated to write (it has to anticipate all possible combinations of program constructs) and additionally tracing back a run-time error to the relevant source program is more difficult.

Pure interpretation is not applicable to all high-level language constructs. Some of them (e.g., Ada (Barnes, 1980; van, 1984) and PL/I (Lucas & Walk, 1969)) need some "look ahead" and more than one pass. The basic trade-off is whether you invest a lot of work front-up in order to speed up the ultimate processing, or whether you are willing to pay a little each time you enact the program.

Both compilation and interpretation have their specific advantages. The basic trade-off is whether considerable effort is invested beforehand (writing a compiler and executing the compiler to translate the programs) or one is willing/forced to expend some small amount of additional effort each time a higher-level language statements is executed interpretatively.

Fundamental Properties of this Alternative:

- Flexible (most compiled code contains interpretative subparts)
- Semi-reversible (compiled code at one level can be interpreted at a lower level, but not vice-versa)
- Scope uniformity (within a scope mixing does not make sense)
- Different method necessary (interpretation is different from compiling)

Garbage Collection vs. Storage Management

Many systems create intermediate objects (occupying memory) which are not needed after task termination. There are two ways to handle this:

- Record each created object and remove it when not needed any more. In the programming language PL/I (Walk et al., 1968) these were called 'controlled' variables and had to be explicitly requested and explicitly released; and
- Leave the unused objects 'unconnected' (and often 'unaccessible') in the system and at appropriate times (usually when there is little work to do) eliminate *all* superfluous objects via the so-called "garbage collection" (Mössenböck, 2002). System requirements like safety influence potential choices of such alternatives: for safety critical systems, the first alternative is recommended.

Fundamental Properties of this Alternative:

- Dichotomic ('partial garbage collection' cannot meaningfully be performed)

Figure 3. Compiler and interpreter

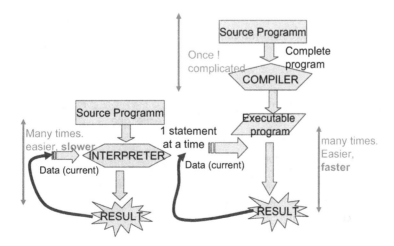

- Semi-reversible (one can always perform storage management for some elements, despite the general garbage collection)
- No uniformity (one can perform garbage collection and controlled access in parallel, but not for the same variable)
- Different method necessary

Testing vs. Formal Verification

On endeavouring to establish the correctness of a program, basically, two approaches are (within limits) available: At the time of writing a program an attempt could be made to ascertain its correctness by formally defining and verifying it (which is very expensive and theoretically not fully possible (Agresti, 1986; Bowen & Hinchey, 1995)). As an alternative one could wait until the program is finished and then try to show the correctness of its execution by inspections (Gilb & Graham, 1993), by testing (which is also very expensive and theoretically not fully possible), or by other verification/validation methods.

Fundamental Properties of this Alternative:

- Flexible (one even can apply both methods)
- Reversible (one can switch between the methods)

- No uniformity (one can apply both methods in parallel)
- Different method necessary

Error Detection vs. Error Prevention

The expected probability of an error (Sommerville, 2000, chapter 16) to take place (e.g., 2 users updating the same element, a hardware error to occur) can be evaluated in an optimistic or pessimistic fashion. Assuming that everything will run well will induce relying on detecting errors and on ex-post repair (at unknown cost) while the pessimistic view (e.g., assuming Moore's Law) will invest a-priori in an attempt to prevent problems by checking, see 'foolproofing,' Nakajo, 1985).

Fundamental Properties of this Alternative:

- Flexible (both methods can be applied, partial error prevention and detection are possible)
- Reversible (both methods can be applied)
- No uniformity (both methods can be applied)
- Different method necessary

Figure 4. Checkout vs. access and consolidation

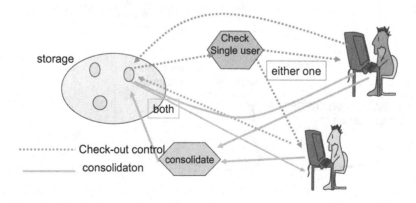

Optimistic vs. Pessimistic Updating

When working on some common objects (e.g., several developers working on the same set of modules in a larger development project) parallel changes of the same detail cannot be accepted.

Access can be permitted to one user at a time, using a 'check-out/check in' procedure with an appropriate locking mechanism. Alternatively, all users can be permitted to access and change modules in parallel. In a subsequent 'consolidation process' inconsistencies are detected and a consistent clean-up is initiated. Commercial databases prefer the first approach, while software engineering environments often apply the second approach in order to avoid the bottleneck at check-out time, optimistically assuming a low probability of truly conflicting changes (Kurbel & Schnieder, 1994). The choice between check-in/check-out vs. consolidation (or alternatively 'validate first and if okay give permission' vs. 'perform first and check for potential collisions afterwards') obviously depends on the probability of conflicts on individual items within a module. Thus, it also relates to the module size or the number of modules per user.

Fundamental Properties of this Alternative:

- Flexible (one can use a coarse exclusion rule and check the remaining potential collisions afterwards)
- Irreversible (on an element level)
- No uniformity (one can mix the methods on a case by case basis).
- Different method necessary

Location (Local-Remote)

Global commerce and cooperation tend to keep data and resources in different places (Figure 10). The placement of data or work is a critical decision which has strong impact on performance

of an information system, but often must be decided without having good data on amount and access requirements of future data. This dimension is closely related to the 'Control Dimension' (section 'Control (central-distributed)') with the distinction that in this section the location of 'resources' is considered and while in section 'Control (central-distributed)' the focus is on the control of activities.

With respect to the fundamental properties of the software-intensive systems, there is a significant difference between considering the properties from a local point of view or from the viewpoint of the whole system. The influence of the Location Dimension can be sketched as in Table 3.

Remote Function Call vs. Program Fetch

In computer networks, programs can be stored anywhere. Execution of such programs can either be performed in the remote environment ('remote job entry') or programs can first be fetched in order to execute them locally (Figure 5). The advantage of local access has to be compared to the effort of fetching programs and keeping redundant copies (Adler, 1995).

Fundamental Properties of this Alternative:

- Dichotomic (a single subsystem is either local or remote)
- Reversible (the allocation can be changed any time)
- Scope uniformity (subsystems of a remote system should preferably also be remote and vice versa)
- Same method applicable

Embedding vs. Linking, Copying vs. Pointing

Remote data can be brought to the attention of the user either by having a pointer or a link to the

Table 3. Location—effects

Effects on system Properties	Usual consequences for remoteness
Complexity	• communication, data exchange, is more complex • synchronization of data can become a real problem • parallel computing needs a more complex synchronization mechanism • localization of functions increases performance
Flexibility	• local flexibility is higher, overall flexibility is reduced
Dependability	• local dependability is increased, global dependability is decreased • parallel execution implies more problems with deadlock, etc. • migrated functions are usually more secure and safe from modifications (Chroust, 1989)
Survivability	• the parallel execution resulting from remoteness induces more problems with deadlock, etc. • migrated functions are usually more secure and safe from modifications (Chroust, 1989)
Time Consumption	• remoteness needs more time for access, communication, and coordination, but less duration time if tasks are distributed reasonably • remoteness often offers better performance • parallel computing in total needs more total time
Resource Utilization	• embedding needs storage on the receiving side • parallel computing in total needs more storage
Ease of Use	• local access is much easier • access to remote resources is more complicated and is less secure • functional distribution increases performance

Figure 5. Remote function call vs. program fetch

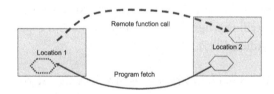

remote location or by bringing the data physically to the user (imbedding or copying) (Adler, 1995). This choice could also be interpreted as a choice *when* the data are fetched (prefetch or just-in-time, i.e., pre-hoc or ad-hoc).

Fundamental Properties of this Alternative:

- Dichotomic (either linking or embedding on a per unit basis)
- Reversible

- No uniformity (each element can be handled differently)
- Different method necessary

Linear vs. Parallel Execution

A task can be executed in a linear fashion or alternatively (if possible) split into several parallel streams to be executed in parallel (Chen, 1971), often in a networked fashion. The advantages of Parallel Execution are a major decrease in elapsed time, permitting larger computation tasks in reasonable time (e.g., 'grid computing,' IBM Corp., 2004) but at the cost of increased complexity and at the price of having to handle synchronization (Kuck, 1977).

Fundamental Properties of this Alternative:

- Flexible (the amount of parallelism can be chosen)
- Reversible (the amount of parallelism can be changed)

- No uniformity (each potentially parallel code can be handled differently)
- Same method applicable

Vertical Migration (Near To/Remote From Hardware Level)

A computer system consists of many layers of service, each lower level supporting the higher levels with certain services (see ISO's Open Systems Interconnection Reference Model of ISO/IEC Standard 9834). A certain task (program) can be performed on many of these levels, achieving different trade-offs with respect to speed, ease of implementation and change, and so forth. Programs near the hardware level execute very fast and are safe from many security attacks, but are difficult to write and to change. In the other extreme programs on the application-oriented levels are written, understood and changed more easily, at the price of vulnerability and (comparative) slowness. In computer architecture the term 'vertical migration' (Chroust, 1989, p.115-150) and also (Chroust, 1980a, 1980b; Richter, 1980) (Stockenberg & van Dam, 1978) has been used

to describe the transfer of some system function from one architectural level (e.g., the level of the programming interface) to some higher or lower level (e.g., the level of the hardware circuits); see Figure 6.

Fundamental Properties of this Alternative:

- Flexible (selected function can be migrated)
- Reversible (one can use both the migrated function and the non-migrated version even on a case by case basis)
- Scope uniformity (subsystems of a migrated function better be also migrated)
- Different method necessary (different code, because running on different platforms)

Granularity (Coarse-Fine)

In many cases, a strategy relies on a good choice of the granularity of the partitioning of the domain of activity. In the extreme case it could be the whole domain, or the smallest meaningful element (similar to having a bound encyclopedia or a loose-leaf edition). By this dimension, we summarize

Figure 6. Vertical migration

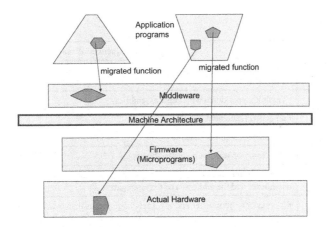

alternatives which distinguish themselves by the granularity ("size") of the items treated as one, for example, size of a portion of storage, size of a unit of work, and so forth. Either exactly the needed items can be fetched (from some storage medium) or also some 'neighboring' items can be fetched in the hope of needing them later (Figure 8).

With respect to the fundamental properties of the software-intensive system, the influence of the Granularity Dimension can be sketched as in Table 4.

Lock Size (Small-Large)

Granting unique access rights to a collection of data (Figure 7) can be done in a coarse-grained fashion easing administration, but which increases the chances of creating a bottleneck situation and preventing many other users from access (Kemper & Eickler, 1997). Alternatively, access rights can be granted for single elements, making both administration and simultaneous access to several elements more complicated and increasing the danger of deadlocks (Silberschatz, Galvin, & Gagne, 2002, p. 217); see also the transaction concept (Silberschatz et al., 2002; Kemper & Eickler, 1997).

Fundamental Properties of this Alternative:

- Flexible (the lock size has to be handled in a flexible way)
- Reversible (the algorithms to define the lock size can easily be changed)
- No uniformity
- Same method applicable

Accessing Multiple Remote Data (Many-Few)

When operating on remote data the complete data set or a large portion of it can be copied/transferred from the remote location to the location of processing, knowing that only a fraction of the data will actually be used and at the same time perhaps excluding other users from use. Alternatively, only the needed minimum data can be copied/transferred, knowing that more re-fetches will be necessary later resulting in an overall higher effort. Paging systems (Silberschatz et al., 2002, p. 267; Tanenbaum, 1995) are essentially based on the former strategy (Figure 8). If data items are dependent on each other, the situation becomes more complex because individual fetches require more complex locking mechanisms.

Table 4. Granularity—effects

Effects on system properties	Usual consequences of coarseness
Complexity	• administrative effort for the *whole assembly* usually decreases • administrative effort *within the assembly* usually decreases
Flexibility	• flexibility goes down with larger assemblies
Dependability	• no general statement possible
Survivability	• no general statement possible
Time consumption	• "efficiency of scale" arguments often apply
Resource utilization	• more resources are needed for storing the aggregates themselves, less resources are needed for the indexes and the addresses of the aggregates
Ease of use	• it is easier to administer and use a few large pieces than many small pieces, assuming that the resources are sufficient and that decomposition was well done

Figure 7. Size of locked area

Figure 8. Granularity

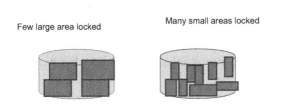

Few large area locked   Many small areas locked

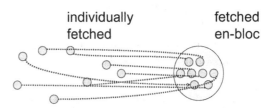

individually fetched   fetched en-bloc

Fundamental Properties of this Alternative:

- Flexible (the amount of elements has to be handled in a flexible way)
- Reversible (the algorithms can easily be changed)
- No uniformity
- Same method applicable

Choice of Page Size (Large-Small)

In a paging system, the immediately accessible storage is divided into so-called pages (Silberschatz et al., 2002, p. 267) and (Tanenbaum, 1995). Each page can be independently removed to and fetched from backup storage. A larger page size reduces the administrative effort to maintain the page lists and the addressing system at the price of having more irrelevant data in the immediately accessible storage (Figure 7) and more users being excluded from accessing those data.

Fundamental Properties of this Alternative:

- Flexible
- Irreversible (usually the page size, once chosen, is fixed. The page size, due to the need of addressing, has considerable impact on size of address registers, instructions, etc.)
- Complete uniformity (for the complete computer system)
- Same method applicable

Module Size (Big-Small)

For various reasons, systems have to be divided into individual components (Höltta, Suh, & de Weck, 2005; Myers, 1976; Parnas, 1972). There are two diametrically different trends: divide the system into the smallest possible modules, usually making these small elements easy to design and handle, but at the price of having numerous individual modules, which pose a communication and interface problems, or divide the system into a few large subsystems which are in themselves complex but provide simple, easy interfaces (Schulz, 1990).

From experience, we know that the complexity of a module grows over-proportionally with its size which induces a small module size. On the other hand, a system of many modules (each of low complexity) has an over-proportional growth of connection complexity. The quantitative situation is shown in Figure 17. An interesting observations made by Höltta et al. (2005) is that despite all the advantages of modularization as always proclaimed by its exponents, there are also detrimental effects when designing large complex airplanes; see also section 'Aerospace Industry: Modularity and other System Properties.' Modularization should result in modules of reasonable functionality in system context (which is more important than just "size"); otherwise one could, in the extreme, consider each machine code statement as a "small module."

Fundamental Properties of this Alternative:

- Flexible (has to be chosen individually, depending on the function to be implemented)
- Reversible (with strong limits due to the functionality of a module)
- Peer uniformity (basically, no uniformity is required because each subsystem could be treated differently, but in the interest of a uniform handling of items on the same level, the peer uniformity seems appropriate)
- Same method applicable

Sequential vs. Pseudo-Parallel Execution

For multiuser systems without real parallel processing capability a 'simulation' is provided by *time-sharing* systems (Silberschatz et al., 2002). Each user is allotted a certain amount of processing time and then another user gets permission for processing (Figure 9). Too small slots carry the burden of considerable fixed system overhead due to housekeeping like initialization and allocation of resources ("thrashing"). Too large slots generate user dissatisfaction due to the need to wait longer.

Fundamental Properties of this Alternative:

- Dichotomic (in the sense that if no mechanism for time sharing is provided it cannot be added later)
- Semi-reversible (a timeshared system can be run without time-sharing but not vice versa)
- Scope uniformity (only a certain uniformity makes sense)
- Different method necessary (timesharing functionality must be provided, and has strong implications on the way the execution mechanism is constructed)

CISC vs. RISC

In the past, considerable speed differences existed between the circuitry of the central processing unit (then in semiconductor technology) and main memories (then still using considerably slower technology like magnetic core and discs). The appropriate strategy was to fetch/store a large amount of data during each computer step in order to conserve fetch time. As a consequence, powerful and complex instructions were needed for handling the large amount of data, resulting in a "*C*(omplex) *I*(nstruction) *S*(et) *C*(omputer)" (Stallings, 1986; Williams & Steven, 1990). When

Figure 9. Timesharing principle

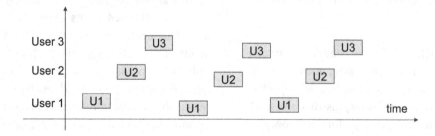

memory technology achieved the same technology and speed as the central processing unit "*R*(educed) *I*(nstruction) *S*(et) *C*(omputers)" were created with simple, less powerful instructions. RISC-technology implies complex, time-consuming compilers due to larger semantic differences between the instructions of the problem-oriented programming languages and the (less powerful) instructions of the RISC hardware (Chroust, 1992).

Fundamental Properties of this Alternative:

- Flexible (the amount of complexity/reduction in the instruction set be chosen freely)
- Reversible (Compilers can be changed easily. To a limited extent, the instruction set can be changed later, typically in microprogrammed machines (Chroust, 1992; Husson, 1970), but not in real hardware. A true CISC machine it will never become a RISC machine).
- Scope uniformity (basically, no uniformity is required because each instruction could be treated differently, but in the interest of a uniform system scope uniformity seems appropriate)
- Different method necessary (different codes and therefore different programs)

Data Sensitivity

One of the key parameters of designing a radar system (Lucky, 2006) is the sensitivity as to how fine-grained the recognized images are. Obviously, complexity increases with higher sensitivity and processing speed is reduced and so forth. In addition (see section 'Data Sensitivity ') the danger of random patters identified as objects also rises.

Fundamental Properties of this Alternative:

- Flexible (the sensitivity can be varied to a certain degree, at least into the direction of lower sensitivity)

- Semi-reversible (a reduction of sensitivity can be easily achieved, a great increase is usually precluded due to physical properties of the various components)
- Scope uniformity (in a certain limited area mixed sensitivity does not make much sense)
- Different method necessary (usually dramatic changes of sensitivity require heavy changes in equipment, computers, antennas, etc.)

Control (Central-Distributed)

In a computer system, the responsibility for concerted actions can be assigned in different ways. In the domain of communication and distributed embedded systems a major decision is the placement (distribution) of functions (see section 'Location (local-remote)') and of control. We have to note that this is a truly basic design decision because, of natural and technical reasons, very high dependability requirements cannot be met by single or central hardware (the limit is about 10^{-5} failures/h). Higher dependability (e.g., SIL4 with the 10^{-9} failures/h challenge) can only be met by redundancy and diversity means, that is, distributed control architectures (Kopetz, 1997; IEC, 1998; Schoitsch, 1997).

With respect to the fundamental properties of the software-intensive system, the influence of the Control Dimension can be sketched, as in Table 5.

Centralized vs. Networking

In today's distributed, often global networks, control can either be located in a single location or distributed over many locations (Figure 10). Different properties are associated with these choices, typically ease and speed of control and update. Lower access costs favour distribution, while problems of consistency, synchronization, and networking costs favour centralized solutions. As catastrophes (like 9/11 in New York) have proven, highly decentralized systems are more

Table 5. Control dimension

Effects on system properties	Usual consequence of distributed control
complexity	• distributed control makes communication and transmission more complex
flexibility	• flexibility on the local level is higher
dependability	• on the local level dependability is higher • on the global level dependability of communications is lower due to longer and vulnerable command lines and problematic protocols • dependability of a distributed system is higher than of a centralized one in case architectural paradigms (redundancy/diversity, time-triggered predictable protocols) are properly used
survivability	• local level survivability depends on the dependency on the central structure • on the global level survivability of the total system is lower due to longer and vulnerable command lines and often complex protocols • if failure of individual nodes is not fatal, but compensated, survivability of the total network is also higher (it is a system architecture issue to consider redundancy of nodes and protocols)
time consumption	• for the local nodes time consumption is lower
resource utilization	• no conclusive statement possible • in safety-related embedded systems resource consumption is lower due to the configuration requirements to guarantee the deadlines and predictable behavior
ease of use	• locally considerable ease of use can be achieved due to short communication lines (compensated by reasonable user interfaces) • familiarity with the local habits improves ease of use

Figure 10. Centralized vs. networking

Location A1, A2, A3, ...

Location B

 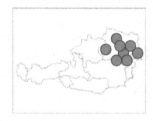

likely to survive, a consideration which already stood at the beginning of the DARPA-network, the starting point for the World Wide Web (Plasser & Haussteiner, 2005). On the other hand, security is more difficult to implement in a widely distributed system with many access points.

Fundamental Properties of this Alternative:

*   Flexible (the amount of (de)centralization can be chosen and changed)
*   Reversible (all decisions can be reversed)
*   Scope uniformity (makes sense, although not strictly necessary)

- Different method necessary (with respect to communication, cooperation, etc.)

Polling vs. Interrupt

A classic decision with respect to a communication protocols is who should be in control of an interaction. The requester(s) can periodically *poll* the supplier(s) about the availability of data or the supplier(s) can offer this information via *interrupt* (Figure 11). Polling is easier to program and—seen from the requestor—allows for more control, but cannot cater for preemption of tasks. This is necessary in real-time systems and in systems with an arbitrary large number of suppliers. Interrupting another process is an asynchronous event and causes more administrative work, is more difficult to program, more error-prone, and unpredictable. In safety-related networked embedded systems, a variant of polling systems exists, so-called time-triggered protocols. Fixed time-slots are assigned to nodes, and a global time is defined. These are the only means to guarantee deadlines and a predictable behavior beforehand (Kopetz & Bauer, 2003) and are therefore highly recommended in the new draft of IEC 61508 (as expressed in the Austrian comment by Schoitsch). The approach is similar to a push/pull approach (Hauswirth & Jazayeri, 1999).

Fundamental Properties of this Alternative:

- Dichotomic (there is no 'middle' way)

Figure 11. Polling vs. interrupt

- Irreversible (both methods need specific routines, especially interrupt mechanisms cannot easily be added later)
- Scope uniformity (producer and consumer must obey the same protocol)
- Different method necessary

Check-and-Do vs. Try-and-Abort

A typical example of 'try and abort' is CSMACD "Carrier Sense Multiple Access Collision Detect" (Zoebel & Albrecht, 1995) which is a typical optimistic protocol for communication of many equal modules. At any time a module may put data on the common and shared data bus to send to another modules. If there is no other module sending, everything goes well. In the other situation, the systems detects (by recognizing invalid codes on the bus) that more than one module is sending. All modules stop their send operation and restart the sending of the complete message after a randomly chosen time again. In the case that the load on the system is light and messages are not too long, this protocol works well.

For transactions, a similar approach is valid. A system can check whether all resources for a safe execution of a transaction are available (and lock them) before performing a transaction. Alternatively, it can perform the transaction keeping all results in a temporary storage. When the transaction has been completed the system checks whether all conditions are fulfilled and then commits the changes; otherwise the results are abolished and the status of the system is rolled back (Silberschatz et al., 2002, p. 240).

Fundamental Properties of this Alternative:

- Dichotomic (there is no middle way)
- Semi-reversible (checking can usually be provided without too much effort, try-and-abort is difficult to add later)
- Scope uniformity
- Different method necessary

Master/Slave vs. Democratic

Assigning control to one communication partner is usually simpler and more straightforward. This partner is in command and regulates the behavior of the other(s).

An obvious advantage is the simplicity and straightforwardness of this approach, while a major disadvantage is the vulnerability of the system to failure (by a disabled master, the master becoming the bottleneck, or the danger of unfairness). The democratic case is much more difficult to program due to potential anomalies in voting system; see (Kramer, 1990; Zdun & Avgeriou, 2005, p. 142). This situation is similar to the 'centralized vs. distributed' alternative (section 'Control (Central-Distributed)'.

Fundamental Properties of this Alternative:

- Dichotomic (within on decision domain)
- Irreversible (due to the need to establish the necessary protocols)
- Peer uniformity
- Different method necessary

Direct vs. Indirect Addressing

Addressing storage can be done by explicitly providing the whole address or by having the address in some intermediate storage (e.g., a register). Usually, this alternative is used in a flexible mode b composing the address from several sources. An example is the addressing mechanism of the IBM /360 family (Figure 12). The trade-offs are described and discussed by Amdahl and Brooks (1964). Zdun and Avgeriou (2005, p. 138) give a more formal description of indirection.

Fundamental Properties of this Alternative:

- Flexible (the proportion between directly and indirectly supply parts of an address can be chosen)
- Irreversible (due to early freezing of instructions sets)
- Peer uniformity (the peers are usually instructions of the same type)
- Different method necessary

Automation and Task Distribution (Human-Automatic)

The distribution of tasks (and the responsibility for their consequences) is an important decision which goes beyond technical and feasibility considerations and has strong ramifications with respect to usability, job satisfaction and public acceptance of a system (e.g., the Vienna Metro system operates fully automated, but in order to

Figure 12. Register usage in IBM System/360

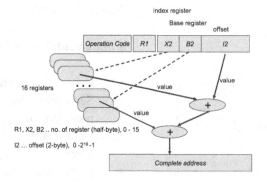

provide a feeling of trust and comfort to users, the trains are manned with an operator). At a NATO conference on dependability, as reported by Schoitsch, the question was brought up "Do we need the driver any longer?" when discussing the evolving option of autonomous road vehicles. A participant from the aircraft industry asserted that "in aircrafts one does not really need the pilot." Many systems (and there are examples like fully automated metro systems) are performing better than any human controlled one. What is even more important, in certain domains the full potential of automation, like platooning cars on highways, crash avoidance systems and so forth, cannot be exploited if human overruling becomes the rule.

Decisions of distributing tasks between humans and machines are often made unconsciously, and even worse, without any profound considerations. Often, only that part of a task which cannot reasonably be automated is left for the human being to perform.

As a consequence holistic, task-oriented units of human work are often not found. At the same time automated tasks often ignore the need for overruling by human decision making for unexpected situations.

These examples demonstrate the complexity of the problem: Only by a very thorough analysis (IEC, 1998) of the system requirements and scenarios can a proper decision be made which control tasks can be taken away from humans and which not, and this situation will change with further progress in software technology, especially in car automation, traffic management and human adaptation to new systems (Schoitsch, 2005). This complex area is still an issue for future research.

With respect to the fundamental properties of the software-intensive system, the influence of the Automation and Task Distribution Dimension can be sketched, as in Table 6.

Control of Car Driving (Human-Computer)

According to the basic "Vienna Convention" 1968, Art. 8, 13, defining the principles of how a motor vehicle (and even a horse coach!) has to be built: *"the driver (or coachman) always has to have full control over the vehicle"*. This becomes more and more violated by modern electronic systems in the car, like advanced driver assistance systems, electronic stability systems, ABS and so forth, which may lead to unexpected behavior. Still, the driver has full liability. DEKRA, the German licensing authority for cars, claimed (Dekra, 2006) that neither legal nor validation

Table 6. Automation and task distribution

Effects on system properties	usual consequences of full automation
complexity	• complexity has to be higher, because humans tend to 'absorb' complexity by applying common sense and context dependent error correction
flexibility	• flexibility in responding to the "real world" is lost due to the rather strict formal requirements for programming machines
dependability	• machines usually are more dependable in the mechanical sense of the word (i.e., verification) while less dependable when judgement etc., is involved (validation)
survivability	• survivability is reduced due to the inferior error correction mechanisms of machines
time consumption	• usually the automated process is faster
resource utilization	• no meaningful comparison possible
ease of use	• in general humans work better with humans, machines often better with other machines

nor licensing rules have been adapted properly to cope with this situation!

The Vienna Convention requires the driver to be able to overrule the electronic control system. The automatic system takes over control only under the condition that based on timing and environmental conditions the driver is unlikely to reach a safe state.

Street traffic seems to be far more complex than track-oriented systems (trains, airplanes!), and there are examples in which control systems in prototype cars failed due to unexpected situations in which humans would have reacted more adequately. For example, a prototype crash avoidance system was programmed to follow the car in front at a given distance depending on speed. Then, suddenly, an overtaking third car squeezed into the gap between the original two cars. Because the overtaking car was faster (of course!) and replaced the original one from the viewpoint of the sensors of the prototype car, the latter's control system speeded up thinking that the car before it had increased speed. Because of this mistaken situation-awareness, the situation became absolutely critical (a reasonable driver would have reduced speed for a moment to allow the other car to squeeze into the gap!).

Fundamental Properties of this Alternative:

- Flexible (sharing of tasks can be changed easily)
- Reversible (the sharing can easily be changed)
- Peer uniformity (similar functions should have similar types of control)
- Different method necessary

Short-Term–Long-Term Safety-Critical Decisions

In many technical systems (Laprie, 1990), we have a separation of concerns: safety critical short term actions are fully automated (e.g., pressure valves and temperature control at critical values in chemical reactors of chemical plants). Control mechanisms allowing more time and differentiated decisions are delivered to humans (operators), who get the information and warnings in time and have, for example, the duty to decide in a safe and cost-effective manner (e.g., not to immediately switch off a complex process). The decision of which actor is allowed to decide what is part of the system design is in itself a highly subtle decision which can only partially be based on criteria like the criticality of the considered process and the presumed experience of the user/operator (Littlewood & Wright, 1997).

Fundamental Properties of this Alternative:

- Flexible (the proportion can be chosen)
- Irreversible (it is very difficult to re-allocate safety-critical control decisions)
- Complete uniformity (basically no uniformity is required because each case could be treated differently, but in the interest of a uniform safety situation complete uniformity is necessary)
- Different method necessary

Overriding Safety-Critical Machine Decisions by Humans

An electronic interlocking system is usually fully automated. Especially for high speed trains, the speed control is supervised in a manner that by missing timely reaction of the driver an automatic emergency action is taken. A railway is designed as a fail-safe system. Stopped trains are considered safe. To guarantee safe operation the entry to a track segment occupied by another train is blocked by a signal and its control mechanism. Nevertheless, there are exceptional situations like construction works, equipment out of order (under repair), shunting movements in stations and so forth, where relaxations of the strict rules are necessary to keep the system operational. In this case, rules have to be defined as to how humans can take over responsibility: communicating with the driver-station master, moving slowly manually in range of sight and so forth.

Fundamental Properties of this Alternative:

- Flexible (the amount of human influence can be chosen)
- Semi-reversible (due to the requirement of human override, switching to human decision making is easy, in the other direction very difficult and sometimes technologically too complicated)
- Scope uniformity (within one scope the same level of control and overriding should be provided)
- Different method necessary

Work-Sharing in Office Work (Manual-Automatic)

The investigation of optimal work sharing and support of humans in office work has been an ongoing research topic for more than 3 decades (Eason, Domodaran, & Stewart, 1974; Mumford & Sackman, 1974) and has to be re-evaluated with every new technological advance in office automation. The basic rule should be *software ergonomics* (Schulz, 1990), that is, that the computer is here to serve and adapt to humans and not vice versa. This is a good example for "undesired" task sharing: Who adapts to what? Because humans are much more flexible, they tend to adapt to the most curious and impracticable computer behaviors and interfaces and to find "work-arounds."

Various studies have shown the influence of computer support (Burgess, 2000; Henry & Stone, 1995; Hirschheim, 1986; Wimmer, 2000), often under the label of 'Office Automation' or 'Electronic Performance Support Systems' (Banerji, 1995; Chroust, 2000).

A general trend goes into increasing both the support with respect to technology and also via

more intelligent tools. Automation as a trend is only partially reversible, both due to new procedures and loss of know how of manual processing and also due to the lack of noncomputerized files, once a system has been converted.

Fundamental Properties of this Alternative:

- Flexible (initially the division of labour can be decided)
- Irreversible (once the manual system has been abolished, there is (almost) no way back)
- Scope uniformity (basically no uniformity, but in the desire for seamless communication a certain pressure to uniformity arises)
- Different method necessary

Software Agents

A software agent is a piece of software that acts for a user or other program in the relationship of an agency. Such "action on behalf of" implies the authority to decide when (and if) action is appropriate. The idea is that agents are not strictly invoked for a task, but activate themselves (Wikipedia-English, 2005, software agent). Here we, too, find a sharing of intelligent tasks between humans and machines. Behaving *on behalf of a human being* provides numerous questions in technical respect (Bic, Fukuda, & Dillencourt, 1996; Chen, Houston, & Nunamaker, 1996), legal (Sonntag, 2002), and sociological (Miller, 2004; Payr & Trappl, 2004).

Fundamental Properties of this Alternative:

- Dichotomic (as long as the agent operates)
- Reversible (the mandate for the agent can be withdrawn)
- No uniformity (different tasks can be assigned to agents or not)
- Different method necessary

Table 7. Classification of alternatives, X ..prime dimension, x .. alternate dimension

Architect. Alternative section 'Specific Examples of Basic Architectural Alternatives'	Enactment Time	Location	Granularity	Control	Automation +Task Distribution
Computation of functions vs. Table look-up	X	x	x	x	
Search vs. Systematic Archiving	X	x		x	x
Binding of Variables	X				
Interpretation/Compilation	X		x		
Garbage Collection vs. Storage Management	X		x	x	
Testing vs. Formal Verification	X			x	x
Error Detection vs. Error Prevention	X			x	x
Optimistic vs. Pessimistic Updating	X		x		x
Remote Function Call vs. Program Fetch		X		x	
Embedding vs. Linking/Copying vs. Pointing		X		x	
Linear vs. Parallel Execution	x	X	x	x	
Vertical migration		X		x	
Lock Size	x		X		
Accessing Multiple Remote Data	x		X		
Choice of Page Size			X		
Module Size			X		
Sequential vs. Pseudo-parallel Execution	x		X	x	
CISC vs. RISC			X		
Data Sensitivity			X		x
Centralized vs. Networking		x		X	
Polling vs. Interrupt	x			X	
Check-and-do vs. Try-and-abort	x			X	
Master/Slave vs. Democratic		x		X	
Direct vs. Indirect Addressing	x	x		X	
Control of Car Driving	x	x		x	X
Short-time—Long-time Safety-Critical Decisions	x			x	X
Overriding Safety-Critical Machine Decisions by Humans	x	x		x	X
Work-sharing in Office Work		x	x	x	X
Software Agents	x	x		x	X

Multiple Classification

Most of the alternatives can be assigned to more than one class. Table 7 shows some of these overlaps, and how some of the examples in this chapter could also be classified.

BASIC ARCHITECTURAL ALTERNATIVES AND THE DESIGN OF REAL SYSTEMS

Designing a whole system in the spirit of Systems Engineering (see section 'System Development: Process and Product') requires the consideration of many aspects and *their interaction*. This is demonstrated by the fact that the basic architectural alternatives can be classified according to different dimensions (depending on the main focus of the observer; see Table 7) and by the additional fact that there are strong interrelations, synergies and conflicts with respect to the effects on the properties of the whole system.

Strategic Selection Considerations for Basic Architectural Alternatives

Beyond the product properties, as discussed in the previous sections, any systems engineering project has additionally to consider the interplay with other chosen alternatives. The essential properties are shown in section 'Project Oriented Properties.' These will limit the choice of basic architectural alternatives.

With respect to designing real systems (DeFoe, 1993) inter alia gives the following advice:

- Maintain a "need based" balance among the often conflicting criteria.
- Select criteria that are measurable (objective and quantifiable) and express them in well known, easily understood units. However, important criteria for which no measure seems to exist must still be explicitly addressed.
- Use trade-offs to show the customer the performance, cost, schedule, and risk impacts of requirements and solutions variants.

For a real system this advice can be answered by identifying, choosing and evaluating the basic architectural alternatives. A typical method for evaluating an architecture is ATAM (Architecture Trade-off Analysis Method), developed at SEI (Kazman et al., 2000). It has one specific phase, the Analysis Phase, in which the architect discusses different architectural approaches in detail, identifies business and quality needs based on requirement documents, generates a quality attribute tree, and analyses proposed architectural approaches in order to come to a decision.

The following observations can be made:

- The individual choices are not independent from one another but have considerable cross-influences, impacting other choices. Some of them enforce one another, others diminish the effect of them, a typical situation which is described in (Senge, 1990); see also section 'Cross-Influences of Basic Architectural Alternatives.'
- Each of these choices with respect to basic architectural alternatives directly or indirectly influences several cost drivers (development time, execution time, development cost, future orientation, sustainability, etc.) and the totality of basic architectural alternatives therefore has to be chosen in the light of optimization of the total system.
- The totality of the chosen basic architectural alternatives contribute to the 'next higher' function (cost, complexity, implementation effort, etc.). In systems design these 'higher' functions have to be optimized. A typical example is the division of a system into components and the resulting complexity; see 'modularity' in section 'Granularity (coarse—fine)' and Figure 17. Reducing the size of the components reduces the complexity of the individual module at the price of increasing the complexity of interconnections. Due to the nonlinear growth of the influence of the parameters, a picture as in Figure 17 results, which has an optimum somewhere between the extremes.
- Any optimization has always to take into account the *whole* system and avoid sub-optimization.
- Beyond the influence on measurable technical parameters the designed systems have also to be *understood (also intuitively!) and operated* by humans. This means that an effort must be made for similar choices in a consistent manner in order to allow the human users to build their mental models of the total system.

- What finally counts are the overall properties of the system. It is necessary to look for *emergent properties* (Chroust, 2002b, 2003; Baas & Emmeche, 1997; Pessa, 1998). They can be the result of interactions between different basic architectural alternatives and can have a strong influence on the properties of the resulting system; see section 'Cross-Influences of Basic Architectural Alternatives.' Some of such emergent properties are completely unexpected. Mullins (2006) reports that establishing the video-observed collector-machines for the pay-as-you-enter parking fees for the City Center of London also deterred criminals. On the other hand, some alternatives are completely ruled out, for example, by dependability requirements (safety, security of embedded systems).

The success of a software-intensive system, especially of a wicked system, largely depends on an appropriate choice of *all* relevant basic architectural alternatives. Besides the technical considerations on the fundamental properties (see section 'Fundamental Properties of Software-intensive (Embedded) Systems') additional factors are considered which are to a large part outside the realm of the project. Such decisions might even promote suboptimal systems (from an individual project's standpoint) which, however, optimize a supersystem or a system family. They depend on the general attitude of the system designer. The key factors below have a strong influence in which direction a product should tend, that is, which alternatives are preferred. The evaluation of these key factors is, however, outside of the scope of this contribution. Some of the key factors are:

- **Planning horizon:** The planning horizon is the amount of time one will look into the future when making decisions.
- **Willingness to take risks:** In the case of conceptualization of the system, most variables carry a large margin of uncertainty, which usually increases with the planning horizon. The risk-taking culture of the company will show strong influence.
- **Optimistic/pessimistic outlook:** In many instances the best strategy depends on the (often unknown) statistical distribution of the favorable and unfavorable cases (see section 'Enactment Time (on-demand—pro-active)'). More precisely, it is an assumption about the chances that the desirable situation will prevail (e.g., despite multiple access of a data base no double update of the *same* data field). Many of the basic architectural alternatives can be seen as a choice between optimism and pessimism.
- **Desired flexibility:** It is known that added flexibility carries a higher initial cost. Together with the consideration of the planning horizon the feasible (and affordable) flexibility has to be estimated.
- **Technological dynamics:** The impact and thus the choice of basic architectural alternatives depends also on the existing/coming-up technology by influencing the importance of certain properties. Typically, in classical software-intensive systems (but still not in embedded systems!) storage consumption is now a minor factor as compared to some 25 years ago.
- **Safety/security considerations:** Not only safety, but increasingly security and the mutual influence of security on safety, and vice versa, considerably influence the choice of basic architectural alternatives and very often rule out certain alternatives for technical, legal or acceptability reasons.
- **Market and competition:** Market and competition (the marketing window) have a strong influence on the desired/optimal time-to-market. Various trade-offs in system engineering offer themselves to reduce time-to-market, especially by reducing requirements like safety, reliability, security, and so forth, with the risk of future problems.

The concept of good-enough-quality (Musa, 2006) is a reasonable guidance in making these decisions.

- **Development considerations:** Additional considerations come from the production environment. Questions like tradition of methods and tools, qualification of personnel, and available resources and budget, but also global project considerations like product line approaches have to be considered (Hoyer, 2007; Clements & Northrop, 2002).

- **Maintenance considerations:** The expected maintenance activities, typically due to changes in market, competition, technology, regulations and user expectation also have a strong influence.

Cross-Influences of Basic Architectural Alternatives

In the previous section, we have discussed certain basic choices of Architectural Alternatives and the related trade-offs. All basic architectural alternatives have a greater or lesser influence on other Alternatives as discussed in section 'Dimensions of Basic Architectural Alternatives.' Obviously, given the number of dimensions and the multitude of individual alternatives, only very general statements can be made, as shown in Table 8.

Aggregated Contributions to System Properties

Some observations can be made as to how the basic architectural alternatives of different dimensions have generic effects on various fundamental properties. Some of them show synergistic influences while others show contradicting effects. Complexity and ease of use are ambivalent, possibly synergistic, possibly contradictory. For example, increase of ease of use usually implies increase in resource utilization.

The necessary application of many basic architectural alternatives bears as a consequence, that the resultant fundamental properties (section

Table 8. Interdependence of alternative dimensions

Dimension	Enactment Time	Location	Granularity	Control	Automation and Task Distribution
Enactment Time	—	proactive actions allow to move work/data to different locations	proactive actions allow *aggregating* more elements and coarser granularity	proactive actions allow to distribute control	proactive actions favour human planning and decision making
Location	Remoteness could hinder on-demand enactment	—	remote locations tend to favour finer granularity	remote locations favour distributed control	remote locations allow bringing the work to the users (not vice versa)
Granularity	finer granularity eases on-demand enactment	finer granularity eases remoteness	—	finer granularity allows more distributed control	fine granularity contradicts human needs for a holistic view and work
Control	central control favours proactive enactment	distributed communication protocols tend to favour remoteness	distributed control favours lower granularity	—	distributed control favours human satisfaction and work
Automation and Task Distribution	automation favours on demand enactment	no clear preference	human work favours coarser granularity in a holistic work environment	distributed control is preferred for human decision, but insufficient in emergency	—

Figure 13. Mutual influences on basic properties

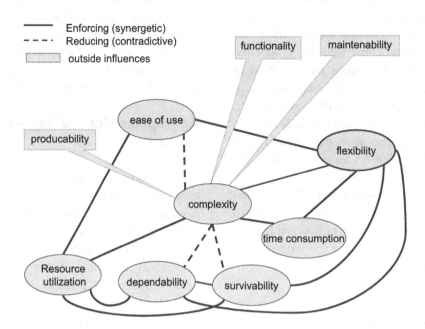

'Fundamental Properties of Software-intensive (Embedded) Systems') superimpose one another interacting not in an easily predictable way (see Figure 16) to yield the final properties of the system.

First of all, we have to observe that these cross-influences can be of an *enforcing (synergistic)* or of a *reducing (contradictory)* effect, as known from systems theory (see Figure 14 and Figure 15). Senge (1990) provides some interesting discussion on these phenomena. He states that in practical life any enforcing behavior will, after a certain time, be limited by some reducing effect which effectively limit the further increase caused by the first effect. The two effects are usually connected by (at least one) common variable (e.g., market success will be limited by exhausting the market, etc.). When considering the aggregated effects of various specific Basic Architectural Alternative, it is necessary to discuss their basic behavior with respect to specific system properties depending on where along the Basic Architectural Alterna-

tive dimensions they are positioned. Following de Weck and Jones (2005), we usually expect to have one of two basic forms of the curve: small-is-more or large-is-more (see Figure 14). In reality, the curve could have many different forms (concave, convex, saddle point, etc.), but we expect them to be either non-decreasing or not-increasing without any change in between.

In the simplest case, we have two contributing Alternatives (Ra and Rb) which both depend on an independent variable P, the essential parameter of this scenario. Actually, this could be any parameter and it is not necessarily directly connected to the system. Typically "module size" is a 'by-product' of some other considerations (see Figure 17). Rs is the sum of both contributions (Ra and Rb). We have to note that our assumption of a simple sum is another simplification.

We can identify two basic types of behavior:

- **Type MIB (middle is best):** Figure 14 shows a typical idealized minimum situation as it has already been discussed for the case of module size in Figure 17 (see section ,Module Size (big-small) and section 'Information Systems: Software Modularization'). This can also be found as a standard example in software engineering text books (e.g., Schulz, 1990; Myers, 1976).

- **Type EIB (extreme is best):** The other situation is depicted in Figure 15. In this case, both Alternatives enforce one another's influence on the fundamental properties and there is no 'minimal point.' For example, the trade-off between driver behavior and safety systems for cars was already discussed in section 'Control of Car Driving(human—computer).' In context of the alternatives provided by "Automation and Task Distribution" (section 'Automation and Task Distribution (human—automatic)') a maximum of human control combined with a maximum of automation of a safety back-up system only acting in case of emergency would be an EIB solution with maximum user satisfaction at the extreme (the user wants safety and freedom).

Experience teaches us that the curve will not go to infinity but will flatten out (a sigmoidal function) or even go back due to the effect of some other (not considered) influences.

The terms "MIB (middle is best)" and "EIB (extreme is best)" were chosen in analogy to the terms chosen by de Weck and Jones (2005) ("small is best" and "large is best") in order to characterize aggregated effects of system properties.

Both scenarios only depict idealized cases. In a practical situation, any complicated curve can result, even for seemingly innocent monotone increasing/decreasing functions (see Figure 16) with 'reasonable' assumptions concerning their behavior.

Following Lehmann (2005), we also know that there is no absolute prediction of the resulting properties of a system design. One cannot even generate a taxonomic list of *all* relevant properties. In practice there is fortunately only a small set of properties which are of prime interest, but they will be different for different systems and application domains. Some of these properties

Figure 14. Balancing effects of architectural alternatives (Type MIB: Middle is best)

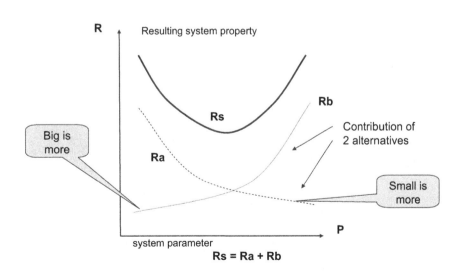

$$Rs = Ra + Rb$$

Figure 15. Enforcing effects of architectural alternatives (Type EIB: Extreme is best)

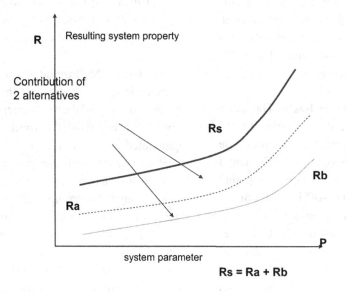

Figure 16. Nonmonotone sum of monotone properties

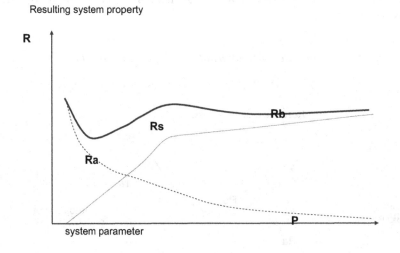

will appear as emergent properties (emergence) (Baas & Emmeche, 1997; Brunner, 2002; Pessa, 1998). Emergent properties depend strongly on the structure of the system, which is practically unknown in the early design phase.

These observations mean that no general prediction is possible, even in the simple case of two basic architectural alternatives, let alone for a collection of them. The examples below (section 'Examples of Aggregated Influences in Systems Engineering') therefore only describe a few 'well-behaved' situations in order to show some basic interactions between basic architectural alternatives.

EXAMPLES OF AGGREGATED INFLUENCES IN SYSTEMS ENGINEERING

The previous section considered individual basic architectural alternatives along the dimensions as described in section 'Dimensions of Basic Architectural Alternatives.' When designing a complete system, it is necessary to consider how these individual Alternatives contribute to the final attributes of the system (e.g., to weight, cost, complexity). At the same time it must be taken into account how a specific choice of one Basic Architectural Alternative may preclude or predefine other choices. A typical example is given in section 'Information Systems: Software Modularization,' where the need to provide the complete functionality makes the number of modules a function of the size of the individual modules (which implies added complexity). Some of these considerations are discussed in section 'Aerospace Industry: Modularity and other System Properties' and also in ESD Architecture Committee (2004). In this section, we give some examples of the cross-influences of different interesting Architectural Alternatives with respect to some important systems properties. These descriptions go beyond the very general discussion in section

'Cross-Influences of Basic Architectural Alternatives' insofar that certain examples of concrete combinations of basic architectural alternatives are discussed and the combined effect on specific fundamental properties is shown.

As discussed in section 'Specific Examples of basic architectural alternatives' these basic architectural alternatives show large differences with respect to the properties above. The choice of an alternative not only directly influences the final system properties (see section 'System Development: Process and Product') but often also influences strongly the available options for other alternatives and dimensions, sometimes in an undesirable way.

Especially in the area of dependable systems the fact that attributes of dependability (mainly reliability, safety and security) are NOT independent from each other and that the degree of interdependency (and severity of the trade-offs between them) depends on the system and its requirements (with respect to internal and external bidirectional interactions with the environment) causes problems in unexpected or unusual situations (see section 'Railway Service Availability: Overriding Safety or Security Measures').

Information Systems: Software Modularization

A classical example (Schulz, 1990) is the choice of module size: choosing a very small module size makes the modules easy to implement and to handle due to their low complexity. As a consequence, numerous modules are to be created which by necessity have many interfaces, thus increasing complexity of communication. Choosing a large module size increases the intramodule complexity but reduces communication complexity. Due to the nonlinear growth of the resulting complexity (Figure 17), the optimum is somewhere between the extremes.

With respect to the general pattern of Figure 14, we can make the following mapping:

Figure 17. Tradeoff between number of modules and size of modules

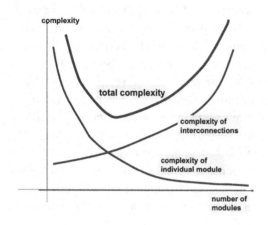

Figure 18. Interrelation between technical and human failures

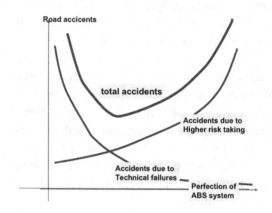

- Rs: Complexity of the system
- P: Number of modules
- Ra: Complexity due to module size
- Rb: Complexity due to interconnections
- Type: MIB

Car Safety: Over-Relying on Safety Measures

If people rely too much on the control systems support, they adapt their behavior and behave in a more risky manner than before. This becomes dangerous when the system is performing at its limits and an unexpected situation takes place. Then the driver will no longer be able to control the situation. It should be added that the comparison is not quite fair: The independent variable P is in one case the *actual* perfection of the ABS-system while in the case of the driver it is the *perceived* perfection of the ABS-system. Similar considerations can be made for the installation of traffic lights, traffic sign warnings and so forth. Nevertheless, from a holistic systems point of view, the example is correct.

With respect to Figure 14 we can take the following interpretation of the variables:

- Rs: Total number of accidents
- P: Perfection of an ABS-system

- Ra: Number of accidents related to (technical) perfection of the ABS-system
- Rb: number of accidents related to taking on the higher risk taking due to a perceived perfection of the ABS-system
- Type: MIB

Car Automation: Road Safety vs. Human Satisfaction

Another aspect is covered by the "full safety automation" vs. "user satisfaction" dilemma in car automation. The user (driver) wants to have full control over the vehicle, but on the other hand accidents with severe consequences are not what the driver wants. A dependable, fully automated safety-back-up system in the car which only acts in case of emergency would allow the driver to fully expand his driving capabilities until the limit, would satisfy both requirements: maximum user satisfaction with maximum automation (only in case the driver wants to commit suicide with his car these arguments won't hold).

With respect to Figure 14, we can take the following interpretation of the variables:

- Rs: User satisfaction (increases with both, freedom to drive to limits and safety)

- P: Degree of control (machine/human)
- Ra: User satisfaction by freedom to drive to limits (human)
- Rb: User satisfaction by perfection of the safety back-up system (machine)
- Type: EIB ("both is best")

Railway Service Availability: Overriding Safety or Security Measures

There are trade-offs between all attributes, especially between reliability, availability, security and safety. For example, a system with a fail-safe state is safe in this state, but may be no longer available and therefore the service becomes unreliable. This is the case for a railway which has to continue operation even in case of an unsafe state, for example, a damaged signal. The same holds for security: a system of highest security level is often very difficult to use ("no access" vs. "free access"). On the other hand, safety requirements may imply relaxing of security, for example, doors of secure area to be opened in case of fire to allow evacuation. This requirement may, on the other hand, be misused by a malicious attacker causing a fire alarm in order to misuse the (planned) security relaxation for illegal intrusion. Additionally, implemented security in control systems for doors and windows may become dangerous when it locks in the human. Some years ago a minister in South-east Asia had to be released by brute force from his heavy plated car when he was locked in because of a security measure; the simulation was life critical because in the meantime the temperature rose beyond 50 degrees within the car.

With respect to Figure 14, we can take the following interpretation of the variables:

- Rs: Total security/safety of system
- P: Strictness of enforcement
- Ra: Insecurity due to inability to leave
- Rb: Security due to inaccessibility
- Type: MIB

Software Systems: Trashing

In a time-sharing system (Randell, 1997) the productivity of a user is reduced by waiting for his/her time-slot to be called again and by the portion of the time a system needs for house-keeping, essentially task switching (see also Figure 9). Short time-slots reduce waiting time, but at the same time increase house-keeping time consumption.

With respect to Figure 14, we can take the following interpretation of the variables:

- Rs: Unproductivity of the user
- P: Size of time slots
- Ra: Amount of productive time (not used for house keeping)
- Rb: Amount of time waiting for the next assigned time slot
- Type: MIB

Information Systems: Password Security vs. Ease of Use

It is known that longer, more complex passwords decrease the chance of their detection and thus decrease the vulnerability of a system. On the other hand, complex passwords are difficult to remember but should be easily on hand for the user. Thus, if the passwords get too complex, the users by necessity have to note them down somewhere (don't forget that most IT-users have a multitude of different passwords) where a password can also be found by hackers.

With respect to Figure 14, we can take the following interpretation of the variables:

- Rs: Vulnerability of the system
- P: Complexity of the password
- Ra: Vulnerability due to complexity of the password
- Rb: Vulnerability due to potential detection of a recorded password
- Type: MIB

Information Systems Access: Enhanced Security vs. Ease of Use

The password issue was already discussed in section 'Information Systems: Password Security vs. Ease of Use.' There are other, stronger means to make information access secure, that is, biological identification like by finger print. These stronger authentication means are easier to use, so both is best (easier to use and stronger authentication) to increase security (reduce vulnerability) of information access. Although this is a quantitative and noncontinuous variable, the systematics are the same.

With respect to Figure 14, we can take the following interpretation of the variables:

- Rs: Nonvulnerability (in this case security) of the system
- P: Strength of authentication
- Ra: Nonvulnerability due to the strength of authentication
- Rb: Nonvulnerability due to ease of use (therefore used)
- Type: EIB

Aerospace Industry: Modularity and Other System Properties

When designing large systems (e.g., airplanes) a basic tenet was (and is) that modularity helps to improve design speed and effort, and thus reduces design cost, due to the many advantages of modularity. Hölttä et al. (2005) shows that too much modularization often results in a suboptimal product with respect to some parameters relevant for operational costs (like weight, size, etc.). Thus, with respect to the aggregates influences, we could show the effects by considering the effort to design (reduced by modularity) vs. the effort to operate (increased by modularity). Due to the basic advantages of modularity, we also expect a 'MIB' curve; see Figure 14.

With respect to Figure 14, we can take the following interpretation of the variables:

- Rs: Total life-time cost of product
- P: Amount of modularization (low to high)
- Ra: Design cost
- Rb: Operating cost
- Type: MIB

Radar: Data Sensitivity

Increased sensitivity of radar not only implies higher cost and effort both with respect to hardware and software, but it entails another problem, caused by certain interaction with the purpose of the radar. It is usually desirable to increase the radar's sensitivity, measured by the probability of recognizing existing targets (true positives). As sensitivity goes up, the probability of reporting things that don't exist (false positives) increases (Lucky, 2006).

With respect to Figure 14, we can take the following interpretation of the variables:

- Rs: Correctness of detection (false negatives vs. false positives)
- P: Sensitivity of radar
- Ra: Amount of false negatives (things not detected)
- Rb: Amount of false positives (nonexisting things detected)
- Type: MIB

Networking: Connectivity vs. Security

Being connected to a computer network entails certain security risks (malware). The perfect precaution is to disconnect oneself, but this means also giving up on all advantages. The value of a network increases with the number of participants, but also more participants might create malware (Lucky, 2006).

With respect to Figure 14, we can take the following interpretation of the variables:

- Rs: Value of being connected
- P: Number of persons one is connected to
- Ra: (Negative) value of taking the security risk
- Rb: Value of being connected
- Type: MIB or EIB (depending on actual values of Ra and Rb)

Computer Architecture: IBM System /360

When specifying a new computer generation as a computer family back in the 1960's, one of IBM's first steps was to clearly state what was meant by 'computer architecture' (Amdahl & Brooks, 1964; Blaauw, 1972; Husson, 70; Chroust, 1980c). It was also possible to define the system properties and create the design largely independently from specific hardware restrictions. Thus, it was possible to define the computer architecture in an abstract form and leave the implementation to the hardware engineers and the microprogrammers. Amdahl and Brooks (1964) detail many of the decisions and trade-offs made and incorporated into the IBM System /360 architecture. The issues discussed are on a low machine-oriented level. Some of the considered trade-offs were: register machine vs. stack machine (Myers, 1977), character size (4, 6, 7 or 8 bit), word markers vs. length parameter in instruction, and so forth. Because the design was for a computer family of a wide range of performance, the user profiles of different customer (sizes) were also taken into the considerations.

A typical discussion was on the length of computer words: Having longer words increased performance but at the same time wasted (at that time) valuable storage and internal bus width.

With respect to Figure 14, we can take the following interpretation of the variables:

- Rs: Total value of storage and performance
- P: Size of computer word
- Ra: (Negative) value of wasting storage
- Rb: Value of performance
- Type: MIB

CONCLUSION

In this chapter, we have introduced the concept of *basic architectural alternatives* of systems design as an aid to make early architectural decisions. They become increasingly important in the very early conceptual phases of systems design, especially for so-called wicked systems (Kopetz, 1997). During the initial concept phase, the fundamental properties of the final system are established. These initial decisions will to a large extent define what ISO 9126 calls the *design quality* (ISO/IEC, 2001a). It is very difficult, often impossible, to make considerable changes to these early decisions later. The problem is aggravated by the fact that these decisions in most cases have to be based on incomplete, fuzzy, and unreliable facts. Additionally, there is usually not enough time to evaluate several alternative designs in parallel or one after the other.

It is therefore important for the designing engineers to know about available alternatives, intuitively understand their system consequences (Mehta & Medvidovic, 2005; Clements, 1995a) and choose them accordingly. Special attention must be put on their cross-influences with respect to enforcing (synergistic) or reducing (contradicting) effects of multiple basic architectural alternatives in order to be able to design a stable and sustainable initial architectural concept for the system to be created and to avoid crucial mistakes.

We have attempted to identify basic architectural alternatives along five dimensions in order to show commonalities between groups of alternatives and differences between alternatives belonging to different dimensions.

Analyzing their effects on system properties in isolation and then relating this analysis to their interaction and their aggregated effect on the whole system allows to teach these basic architectural alternatives and their properties and thus improve choices at the initial stage of system design. For beginners, this might be a great help and for seasoned designers this still might give some insight, allowing them to move from a 'guts feeling' approach to some more substantial know-how.

We have classified these basic architectural alternatives along the following five dimensions:

- **Enactment time:** WHEN should a foreseen action be performed, either proactively when the necessary action is known (or suspected) or when the actual need arises? (see section 'Enactment Time (On-Demand-Proactive)')
- **Location:** WHERE should needed data and programs (or their functionality) be placed? (see section 'Location (Local-Remote)')
- **Granularity**: HOW MANY/MUCH should be accessed/handled in one step? (see section 'Granularity (Coarse-Fine)')
- **Control**: WHO or WHAT has the responsibility for leading the interaction? WHERE should control be located? (see Section 'Control (Central-Distributed)')
- **Automation and Task Distribution**: TO WHAT DEGREE are the tasks automated? This includes the question whether a certain task is to be performed by a human being or by a computer (see section 'Automation and Task Distribution (Human-Automatic)'

For each dimension, we have listed several examples from the domain of software-intensive systems. Depending on the specific point of view, however, the allocation is not unique, as we have shown in Table 7.

By providing an initial catalogue of such basic architectural alternatives, we believe that this is useful in providing students and novices in the systems field with initial ideas and concepts.

As an initial step we have discussed the 'pure cases' (ESD Architecture Committee, 2004) knowing that reality is quite more complicated and involved. In general basic architectural alternatives associated with one dimension also influence properties of alternatives of other dimensions (Table 8).

We can make several observations with respect to the basic architectural alternatives:

- Alternatives have to be chosen with consideration of their influence on *fundamental system properties* (cost, complexity, dependability, implementation effort, etc.).
- While the different alternatives can be described independently, they contribute to the *same overall* systems properties. Any optimization has always to consider the *whole* system and avoid suboptimization.
- The systems design has to optimize the resulting (over all) system properties.
- The wrong combination of several alternatives might result in a suboptimal system.
- The individual choices are not independent from one another but have considerable cross-influences, reducing the available choices for other alternatives.
- A disturbing observation is that the combination of different alternatives has interesting and often surprising additional effects ('emergent properties') of the systems.
- The real world does often behave in an unexpected or even intended malicious manner, and the system under control and the control system (IEC, 1998; Schoitsch, 2005) have to take this into account.

Returning to the proverb *"you can't keep a cake and eat it,"* it can be said that it is helpful to understand the consequences of keeping/eating, knowingly making the choices in such a way as to get the most out of it, whatever the situation and the preferences are.

FUTURE TRENDS

The dynamics of the IC-technologies, the high demand on sophisticated systems supporting a growing global business and global communication together with the need for both time-to-market with largely unknown new application fields, especially in the area of "embedded systems," will bring new challenges to the system development community (Broy, 2006; Schoitsch, 2005).

In the future there will be more *wicked systems*. The reason is that less complex systems will evolve into more complex systems ('evolutionary systems') and also that the application domains we engage in will become more complex and involved. All these challenges are additionally exacerbated by the growth in international, global interaction and business and the reduced time-to-market for competitive reasons. Thus, systems engineering will encounter more and more wicked systems and at the same time will given less time for reflection and evaluation.

As a consequence, the need for having to start with *some concept of the solution* is rising, but demanding ever better initial approximations for the final solution. As a consequence, being able to identify the relationship between basic architectural alternatives and fundamental properties will be a basis to find better approximations to the final solution. For the future, we see a need for further theoretical investigations of the dimensions of basic architectural alternatives. This would include both an attempt to study their 'general' properties in more detail, together with their interaction and cross-dependencies. It could also mean a redefinition and re-allocation of some of the dimensions, perhaps even introducing more dimensions.

On the practical side it would mean identifying and explaining better the existing basic architectural alternatives and trying to identify their impact on one another and on system parameters. Of special interest would be a kind of 'feature clash analysis,' identifying forbidden or unfavorable combination of different basic architectural alternatives, similar to the ATAM-methodology (Kazman et al., 2000).

A third objective could be a catalogue of basic architectural alternatives for students and novices in Systems Engineering helping them to see the full realm of possibilities, making them aware of possible alternatives and showing the consequences of such choices.

This research would come closer to the old engineering dream of 'property driven system design,' that is, deriving a high-level system architecture based on the desired properties of the system to be created. This would mean a better analysis and understanding of how (total) system properties can be derived from adequate basic architectural alternatives available to the designers.

What we need are system engineers with a broad view of systems in mind, taking holistic approaches to solve real-world problems, taking into account that the real world is somehow "fuzzy" and requires a high degree of fault tolerance (including technical, natural environment and human behavior).

The concepts presented here hopefully will help to ease the conceptualization of such systems by presenting an ontology of basic architectural alternatives, helping systems engineers to build increasingly more valuable systems in less time and with a smaller margin of error.

FUTURE RESEARCH DIRECTIONS

This chapter is an initial step into the systematization of basic architectural alternatives in the field of systems engineering well-understood, well-analyzed alternatives (similar to software patterns). Given the current state of systems engineering, its youth and the dynamics of the field, this chapter by necessity had to leave many questions unanswered. These questions should be the basis for further research. The growth of imbedded and security critical systems together with the growing time pressure for their development makes this approach even more important.

A final goal is a catalogue of basic architectural alternatives together with their properties, advantages, disadvantages and their interdependence. This would give valuable guidance to systems engineers. In the sequel, we will sketch some needed and promising research directions.

- Which further examples of basic architectural alternatives do exist, also looking into other, neighboring fields like mechanical engineering, software engineering and so forth?

- Are the dimensions defined in this chapter really the basic ones; are they orthogonal; are there additional ones?

- During the early phases of systems engineering what are key system properties of interest, especially for the user (quality in use), for system development (project management), and for system evolution (maintenance)?

- Are the quality characteristics (= system properties) described in ISO/IEC 9126 sufficient/necessary for the early phases especially in view of the changing focus of systems engineering (embedded systems, distributed systems, software-intensive systems, component-based systems)?

- Is there some generalized dependency between the different dimensions due to some (hidden) common parameters?

- Which further examples of the interaction of different basic architectural alternatives do exist?

- How could one classify these interactions (diminishing, enforcing, neutral, etc.)

- Can one predict in some way the effect of changing an basic architectural alternative along a dimension with respect to choices for other basic architectural alternatives? Can one make qualitative or quantitative predictions?

- How can the aggregated value of the system characteristics caused by different architectural choices be estimated (note that this is a general problem of system construction from components)?

- How can one recognize/analyze emergent system properties due to different basic architectural alternatives? What is the interplay between these emergent properties and human behavior?

- Given a specification of overall system properties, can one come up with some procedure (at least a heuristic one) to optimize choices of alternatives?

- Given that many of these basic architectural alternatives also strongly interact with human behavior and human psychology, can we predict human reactions with respect to (preferences) of these alternatives?

Many of the questions listed above require a systemic approach, a consideration of the *whole* product and its environment (business, security, human, etc.) and the multilevel interactions between basic architectural alternatives. It is expected that in the future systems engineering will need a much closer intertwining with systems theory, both for absorbing its result and for posing new questions.

REFERENCES

Adler, R. (1995). Emerging standards for component software. *IEEE Computer, 28*(3), 68-77.

Agresti, W. (1986). *New paradigms for software development.* North Holland: IEEE Computer Society Press.

Alexander, C., Ishikawa, S., & Silverstein, M. (1977). *A pattern language—towns, buildings, construction.* New York: Oxford University Press.

Amdahl, G.M., Blaauw, G., & Brooks, F. (1964). Architecture of the IBM system/360. *IBM Journal of Research and Development, 8*(2), 87-97.

Arthur, L. (1988). *Software evolution—the software maintenance challenge.* John Wiley.

Baas, N., & Emmeche, C. (1997). *On emergence and explanation.* Retrieved March 7, 2008, from http://www.nbi.dk/~emmeche/coPubl/ 97d. NABCE/ExplEmer.html (2001-11-22)

Banerji, A. (1995). Electronic performance support systems. In *Proceedings of the International Conference on Computers in Education (ICCE '95).*

Barnes, J. (1980). An overview of ada. *Software—Practice and Experience, 10,* 851-887.

Bass, L. (2007). *Reasoning about software quality attributes.* Retrieved March 7, 2008, from http://www.sei.cmu.edu/architecture/reasoning_about.html

Beck, K. (2000). *Extreme programming explained—embrace change.* Longman Higher Education.

Bic, L. F., Fukuda, M., & Dillencourt, M. (1996). Distributed computing using autonomous objects. *IEEE Computer, 29*(8), 55-61.

Blaauw, G. (1972). Computer architecture. *El. Rechenanl., 14*(4), *154. also: Hasselmeier H., Spruth W.G. (Eds.), Rechnerstrukturen, Oldenbourg München* (pp. 14-35).

Boehm, B., Grünbacher, P., & Briggs, B. (2001, May-June). Developing groupware for requirements negotiation: Lessons learned. *IEEE Software,* 46-55.

Bowen, J., & Hinchey, M. (1995). Ten commandments of formal methods. *IEEE Computer, 28*(4), 56-63.

Brooks, F. J. (1962). Architectural philosophy. In W. Buchholz (Ed.), *Planning a computer System—Project STRETCH* (pp. 5-16). McGraw-Hill.

Brooks, F. (1965). The future of computer architecture. In W. A. Kalenich (Ed.), *Information processing (Proceedings IFIP Congress)* (pp. 87-91). Washington, DC: Spartan Books, London: Macmillan.

Broy, M. (2006). The 'grand challenge' in informatics: Engineering software-intensive systems. *IEEE Computer, 39*(10), 72-80.

Brunner, K. (2002, April). What's emergent in emergent computing? In R. Trappl (Ed.), *Proceedings of EMCSR 2002: European Meeting on Cybernetics and Systems Research,* Vienna, Austria, (pp. 189-192).

Burgess, V. (2000). Changing nature of electronic performance support systems. Retrieved March 24, 2008, from *http://scholar.coe.uwf.edu/students/ vburgess/ChangingEPSS/tsld001.ht*m

Buschmann, F. (1994). *Pattern oriented software architecture—a system of patterns.* John Wiley & Sons.

Charette, R. (2005). Why software fails. *IEEE Spektrum, 92*(9), 36-43.

Chen, T. (1971, January). Parallelism, pipelining and computer efficiency. *Computer Design,* 365-372.

Chen, H., Houston, A., & Nunamaker, J. (1996). Towards intelligent meeting agents. *IEEE Computer, 29*(8), 63-70.

Chroust, G. (1971). Scope conserving expression evaluation. In *Proceedings of IFIP Congress,* (pp. 509-512).

Chroust, G. (1980a). Orthogonal extensions in microprogrammed multiprocessor systems. In G. Chroust & J. R. Mühlbacher (Eds.), *Firmware, microprogramming and restructurable hardware: Proceedings of the IFIP Working Conference,* (pp. 185-190). Linz: North Holland Publishing Company.

Chroust, G. (1980b). Orthogonal extensions in microprogrammed multiprocessor systems: A chance for increased firmware usage. *EUROMICRO Journal, 6*(2), 104-110.

Chroust, G. (1980c). Programme chairman's preface. In G. Chroust & J. R. Mühlbacher (Eds.), *Firmware, microprogramming and restructurable hardware: Proceedings of the IFIP Working Conference,* (pp. vii-viii). Linz: North Holland Publishing Company.

Chroust, G. (1989, February). *Mikroprogrammierung und Rechnerentwurf.* Oldenbourg: Springer-Verlag.

Chroust, G. (1992). *Modelle der Software-Entwicklung—Aufbau und Interpretation von Vorgehensmodellen.* Oldenbourg: Springer-Verlag.

Chroust, G. (2000, September). Electronic performance support systems—challenges and problems. In P. Kopacek (Ed.), *Proceedings of Computer Aided Systems Theory—EUROCAST'99,* Vienna, (pp. 281-284). Springer-Verlag.

Chroust, G. (2002a, September). Emergent properties in software systems. In C. Hofer, & G. Chroust, (Eds.), *Proceedings of IDIMT-2002: 10th Interdisciplinary Information Management Talks,* Zadov, (pp. 277-289). Verlag Trauner Linz.

Chroust, G. (2002b, April). System properties under composition. In R. *Trappl (Ed.), EMCSR 2002: Proceedings of the European Meeting on Cybernetics and Systems Research, Vienna,* (pp. 203-208). Austrian Society for Cybernetic Studies.

Chroust, G. (2003, February). The concept of emergence in systems engineering. In C. Hofer & G. Chroust (Eds.), *The eleventh Fuschl conversation.* Vienna: ÖSGK, Reports of the Austrian Society for Cybernetic Studies.

Chroust, G. (2004). The empty chair: Uncertain futures and systemic dichotomies. *Systems Research and Behavioral Science, 21*, 227-236.

Chroust, G. (2005). Dichotomic architectural patterns in systems engineering. *IFSR 2005—the new roles of systems sciences for a knowledge-based society (Paper No. 20121).* Jaist Press (CDROM).

Clements, P. (1995a). From subroutines to subsystems: Component-based software development (pp. 7-15). In *American Programmer, 8(*11), and A.W. Brown, (Ed.), *Component-based software engineering.* IEEE Computer Society.

Clements, P. (1995b, April). Understanding architectural influences and decisions in large-system projects. In *Proceedings of the First International Workshop on Architectures for Software Systems,* Seattle, WA, (p. 13).

Clements, P., & Northrop, L. (2002). *Software product lines—practices and patterns.* Reading, MA: Addison-Wesley.

de Weck, O., & Jones, M. B. (2005). Isoperformance: Analysis and design of complex systems with desired outcomes. *Systems Engineering, 9*(1), January 2006, 45-61.

DeFoe, J. (1993). *An identification of pragmatic principles of systems engineering* (Final report). *INCOSE.* Retrieved March 24, 3008, from nhp.at.fortnet.org

Dekra (2006, October 25-26). In Proceedings of the Autotest Conference, Stuttgart, Germany.

Department of Defense. (1992, January). *Military standard 973: Military standard for configuration management* (Tech. Rep.). Washington, DC: Department of Defense.

Department of Defense. (1993, January). *Military standard 882c: Standard practice for system safety program requirements* (Tech. Rep.). Washington, DC: Department of Defense.

Dörner, D. (1996). *Die Logik des Mißlingens—Strategisches Denken in komplexen Situationen.* sachbuch-9314, rororo Verlag, Hamburg.

Eason, K., Domodaran, L., & Stewart, T. (1974). Interface problems in man-computer interaction. In E. Mumford & H. Sackman (Eds.), *Human choice and computers* (pp. 91-105). North Holland Publishing Company.

Endres, A., & Rombach, D. (2003). *A handbook of software and systems engineering—empirical observations, laws and theories.* Reading, MA: Addison-Wesley/Pearson.

ESD Architecture Committee. (2004). The influence of architecture in engineering systems. *MIT-eds, engineering systems monograph* (p. 30).

Fiadeiro, J. (1996). On the emergence of properties in component-based systems. In *Proceedings of AMAST96.* Springer-Verlag.

Flynn, M. H. L. (1979, February). *A theory of interpretive architectures: Ideal language machines.* CA: Stanford University Computer Systems Lab., TR 170.

Franz, M. (1997). Dynamic linking of software components. *IEEE Computer, 30*(3), 74-81.

Gamma, E., Helm, R., Johnson, R., & Vlissides, J. (1995). *Design patterns—elements of reusable object-oriented software.* Reading, MA: Addison-Wesley.

Georgas, J. C., Dashofy, E. M., & Taylor, R. N. (2005). Architecture-centric development: A different approach to software engineering. *Crossroads, 12*(4), 6.

Gilb, T., & Graham, D. (1993). *Software inspection.* Reading, MA: Addison-Wesley.

Glass, R. L. (2006). The standish report: Does it really describe a software crisis? *Communications of the ACM, 49*(8), 15-16.

Gomaa, H., Menasce, D. A., & Shin, M. E. (2001). Reusable component interconnection patterns for distributed software architectures. *ACM SIGSOFT Software Engineering Notes, 26*(3), 69-77.

Gries, D. (1971). *Compiler construction for digital computers.* New York: John Wiley.

Hampden-Turner, C., & Trompenaars, F. (2000). *Building cross-cultural competence—how to create wealth from conflicting values.* Yale University Press.

Hauswirth, M., & Jazayeri, M. (1999). A component and communication model for push systems. In *Proceedings of ESEC/SIGSOFT FSE,* (pp. 20-38).

Henry, J. W., & Stone, R. W. (1995). Computer self-efficacy and outcome expectancy: The effects on the end-user's job satisfaction. *SIGCPR Comput. Pers., 16*(4), 15-34.

Hirschheim, R. A. (1986). The effect of a priori views on the social implications of computing: The case of office automation. *ACM Computer Survey, 18*(2), 165-195.

Holmes, N. (1997). Converging on program simplicity. *IEEE Computer, 30*(12), 134ff.

Hölttä, K., Suh, E., & de Weck, O. (2005, August 15-18). Tradeoff between modularity and performance for engineered systems and products. In *Proceedings of the International Conference on Engineering Design, ICED05,* Melbourne, (p. 14). Canberra: Institution of Engineers Australia.

Hordijk, W., Krukkert, D., & Wieringa, R. (2004). *The impact of architectural decisions on quality attributes of enterprise information systems: A survey of the design space* (Tech. Rep. No. TR-CTIT-04-48). Centre for Telematics and Information Technology, University of Twente, Enschede.

Hoyer, C. (2007). *ProLiSA—an approach to the specification of product line software architectures.* Doctoral thesis, J. Kepler University Linz.

Humphrey, W. (1989). *Managing the software process.* Reading, MA: Addison-Wesley.

Husson, S. (70). *Microprogramming—principles and practices.* Englewood Cliffs, NJ: Prentice Hall.

IBM Corp. (2004). *IBM GRID computing.* Retrieved March 25, 2008, from http://www-1.ibm.com/grid/,

IBM (Ed.). (2005). *Valeo and IBM to collaborate for automotive software development.* Retrieved March 25, 2008, from http://www-03.ibm.com/solutions/plm/doc/content/news/announcement/1346122113.html

IEC (Ed.). (1990). *International electrotechnical vocabulary (IEV): Dependability and quality of service* (chap. 191, Tech. Rep. No. IEC 60050(191):1990). IEC: International Electronic Commission.

IEC. (1998). *ISO/IEC 61508, Part 1-7: Functional safety of electric/electronic/programmable electronic systems* (Tech. Rep.). IEC: International Electronic Commission.

IEEE. (1990). Standard glossary of software engineering terminology, IEEE standard 610.12. *IEEE software engineering standards collection (Spring ed.).*

ISO/IEC. (Ed.). (1996). *Information technology—vocabulary—part 14: Reliability, maintainability and availability* (Tech. Rep. No. ISO/IEC 2382-14:1996). International Organization for Standardization.

ISO/IEC. (2001a). *Software engineering—product quality—part 1: Quality model* (Tech. Rep. No. ISO/IEC 9126-1:2001). International Organization for Standardization.

ISO/IEC. (2001b). *Software engineering body of knowledge (SWEBOK)* (Tech. Rep. No. DTR 19759). International Organization for Standardization.

ISO/IEC. (2005, September). *Information technology—software process assessment—part 6: An exemplar system life cycle process assessment model* (Tech. Rep. No. ISO/IEC-15504-6). International Organization for Standardization.

ISO/IEC. (2006a, January). *Systems engineering—system life cycle processes* (Tech. Rep. No. ISO/IEC 15288:2006, wd.1). International Organization for Standardization, ISO/IEC JTC 1/SC 7/WG 7.

ISO/IEC. (2006b). *Software engineering: Software product quality requirements and evaluation (SQuaRE) quality model* (Tech. Rep. No. ISO/IEC WD 25010). International Organization for Standardization.

Kazman, R., Klein, M., & Clements, P. (2000). *Atam:sm method for architecture evaluation* (Tech. Rep. No. SEI, CMU/SEI-2000-TR-004, ESC-TR-2000-004).

Keilser, S. (2006). *Software paradigms.* New York: John Wiley-Interscience.

Keller, F., & Wendt, S. (2003, April). Fmc: An approach towards architecture-centric system development. In *Proceedings of the 10th IEEE International Conference and Workshop on the Engineering of Computer-Based Systems (ECBS'03)*, (p. 173).

Kemper, A., & Eickler, A. (1997). *Datenbanksysteme—Eine Einführung.* Oldenbourg: Springer-Verlag.

Kopetz, H. (1997). *Real-time systems—design principles for distributed embedded application.* Boston/Dordrecht/London: Kluwer Academic.

Kopetz, H., & Bauer, G. (2003). The time-triggered architecture. *IEEE Special Issue on Modeling and Design of Embedded Software.*

Kossiakoff, A., & Seet, W. (2003). *Systems engineering—principles and practice.* New York: Wiley Series in Systems Engineering and Management, Wiley Interscience.

Kramer, J. M. J. (1990). The evolving philosophers problem: Dynamic change management. *IEEE Transactions on Software Engineering, 16*(11), 1193-1306.

Kuck, D. (1977). A survey of parallel machine organization and programming. *ACM Computing Surveys, 9*(1), 29-58.

Kurbel, K., & Schnieder, T. (1994). *Integration issues of information engineering based i-case tools.* Working Papers of the Institute of Business Informatics, University of Münster (No. 33). Retrieved March 25, 2008, from http://www. wi.uni-muenster.de/inst/arbber/ab33.pdf

Laird, L., & Brennan, M. (2006). *Software measurement and estimation—a practical approach.* New York: Wiley Interscience, IEEE Computer Society.

Laplante, P., & Neill, C. (2006). *Avoiding anti-patterns at work can help you sleep at night. Centredaily.com.* Retrieved March 25, 2008, from http://www.centredaily.com/ mld/centredaily/news/opinion/14078324.htm? template=contentModules/printstory.jsp

Laprie, J. (1990). On the assessment of safety-critical software systems. In F. R. Valette,, P. A. Freeman, & M. C. Gaudel (Eds.), *Proceedings of the 12th Internat. Conference on Software Engineering,* (p. 222). IEEE Computer Press.

Laprie, J.-C., Avizienis, A., Kopetz, H., Voges, V., & Anderson, T. (Eds.). (1992). *Dependability—basic concepts and terminology.* Springer-Verlag.

Lehman, M. (1980). Programs, life cycles, and laws of software evolution. *Proceedings of the IEEE, 68*(9), 1060-1076.

Lehman, M. B. L. (Ed.). (1985). *Program evolution—processes of software change.* APIC Studies in Data Proc. No. 27, Academic Press.

Lehman, M. M. (1996). Laws of software evolution revisited. In *Proceedings of the European Workshop on Software Process Technology,* (p. 11). IEEE Computer Society.

Lehman, M. M. (2005). The role and impact of assumptions in software development, maintenance and evolution. In *Proceedings of the 2005 IEEE International Workshop on Software Evolvability,* USA. IEEE Computer Society.

Littlewood, B., & Wright, D. (1997). Some conservative stopping rules for the operational testing of safety-critical software. *IEEE Trans SwE, 23*(11), 673-683.

Lucas, P., & Walk, K. (1969). On the formal description of pl/i. *Annual Review in Automatic Programming, 6,* Part 3, 105-182.

Lucky, R. (2006, November). Impossible trade-offs. *IEEE Spectrum,* p. 52.

Mackrodt, W. (1981). Considerations on language interpretation for microprocessor systems. *Microprocessing and Microprogramming, 7,* 110-118.

Maruyama, K., & Smith, S. (1977). Analysis of design alternatives for virtual memory indexes. *Communications of the ACM, 20*(4), 245-254.

McDermid, J. (Ed.). (1991). *Software engineer's reference book.* Butterworth-Heinemann Oxford.

Meadows, D., Meadows, D., Zahn, E., & Millig, P. (1969). *Die Grenzen des Wachstums—Bericht des Club of Rome zur Lage der Menschheit.* Bertelsmann.

Meehl, P., & Sellars, W. (1956). The concept of emergence. In H. Feigl & M. Scrive (Eds.), *Minnesota studies in the philosophy of science: The foundations of science and the concepts of psychology and psychoanalysis* (Vol. 1, pp. 239-252). University of Minnesota Press.

Mehta, N. R., & Medvidovic, N. (2005). Composing architectural styles from architectural primitives. In *ESEC/FSE-11: Proceedings of the 9th European Software Engineering Conference held jointly with the 11th ACM SIGSOFT International Symposium on Foundations of Software Engineering,* (pp. 347-350). New York: ACM Press.

Merriam-Webster, I. (Ed.). (1996). *Webster's new encyclopedic dictionary.* Black Doc and Leventhal.

Miller, C. (Ed). (2004). Human-computer etiquette: Managing expectations with intentional agents. *Communications of the ACM, 47*(4).

Mössenböck, H. (2002). Automatische Speicherbereinigung. In P. Rechenberg & G. Pomberger

(Eds.), *Informatik-Handbuch, 3. Auflage, Kap. D12.6.* Hanser-Verlag.

Mullins, J. (2006, July). Ring of steel. *IEEE spectrum* (pp. 5-7).

Mumford, E., & Sackman, H. (Eds.). (1974). Human choice and computers. In *Proceedings of the IFIP Conference on Human Choice and Computers,* Vienna. Amsterdam: North Holland Publishing Company.

Musa, J. (2006). *More reliable software faster and cheaper: An overview of software reliability engineering.* Osborne/McGraw-Hill.

Myers, G. (1976). *Software reliability—principles and practices.* New York: John Wiley & Sons.

Myers, G. (1977). The case against stack-oriented instruction sets. *CAN, 6*(3), 7-10.

Nakajo, T. K. H. (1985). The principles of fool-proofing and their application in manufacturing. *Reports of Statistical Application Research JUSE, 32*(2), 10-29.

Noppen, J., et al. (2002). Optimizing software development policies for evolutionary system requirements. In *Proceedings of the First International Workshop on Unanticipated Software Evolution (USE'02),* Malaga, Spain, (p. 10).

Parnas, D. (1972). On the criteria to be used in decomposing systems into modules. *Communications of the ACM, 15*(12), *1053.*

Payr, S., & Trappl, R. (Eds.). (2004). *Agent culture—human-agent interaction in a multicultural world.* Mahwah, NJ: Lawrence Erlbaum.

Pessa, E. (1998). Emergence, self-organisation, and quantum theory. In G. Minati (Ed.), *Proceedings of the First Italian Conference on Systemics, APOGEO Scientifica,* (pp. 59-79).

Phillips, R. (1988). State change architecture: A protocol for executable process models. In C. Tully (Ed.), *Representing and enacting the software process: Proceedings of the 4th International Software Process Workshop, May ACM Software Engineering Notes,* (Vol. 14, No. 4., pp. 129-132).

Piatelli, M., & Bianchi, N. (1998). Maritime Etruscian cities: A systemic approach for explaining their sites. In G. Minati (Ed.), *Proceedings of the First Italian Conference on Systemics, APOGEO Scientifica,* (pp. 273-292).

Plasser, E., & Haussteiner, I. (2005, June). *What made the Internet work—a review of interrelations, intentions and the success of the ARPA initiative and its implications for a key technology* (Rep. No. 8). Austria: Publication of the Institute for Systems Engineering and Automation, J. Kepler University Linz.

PMI Risk Management Specific Interest Group. (2002). *The new PMBOK risk management concept.* The New PMBOK Risk Management Concept. Retrieved March 25, 2008, from http://www.heartlandits.com/Newsroom/PMI/New%20PMBOK%20%20Risk%20pz#256,1

Project Management Institute (PMI). (2005). *A guide to the project management body of knowledge (PMBOK) (*3rd ed., Tech. Rep.). Philadelphia, PA, USA: PMI.

Randell, B. (1997). *Operating systems: The problems of performance and reliability.* 40 Years of Computing at Newcastle—the first paper on dependability, SRM/311. Retrieved March 25, 2008, from http://www.cs.ncl.ac.uk/events/anniversaries/40th/webbook/dependability/os1/os1.html

Rechenberg, P. (1993). Compilers. In D. Morris & B. Tamm (Eds.), *Concise encyclopedia of software engineering (pp. 59-64).* Pergamon Press.

Redmill, F. (Ed.). (1988). *Dependability of critical computer systems 1, EWICS TC7 guidelines 1 (Documentation, system requirements, development and (V&V).* UK: Elsevier Science.

Redmill, F. (Ed.). (1989). *Dependability of critical computer systems 2: Design, assessment, maintenance and modification, EWICS TC7 Guidelines 2*. UK: Elsevier Science.

Redmill, F., & Dale, C. (Eds.). (1997). *Life cycle management for dependability*. London: Springer-Verlag.

Richter, L. (1980). Vertikale Migration—Anwendungen, Methoden und Erfahrungen. In K. H. Hauer & C. Seeger (Eds.), *Tagung "Hardware für Software", Konstanz* (pp 9-28). Springer-VerlagTeubner.

Schoitsch, E. (1997). Managing maintenance and change. In F. Redmill (Ed.), *Life cycle management for dependability* (pp. 163-188). London: Springer-Verlag.

Schoitsch, E. (2003a). Dependable embedded systems—vision und roadmap. In G. Fiedler & D. Donhoffer (Eds.), *Mikroelektronik 2003, Wien*. ÖVE Schriftenreihe, Wien, Nr. 33.

Schoitsch, E. (2003b, January). Embedded systems—introduction. *ERCIM News,* (52), 11.

Schoitsch, E. (2005). Design for safety and security. *Cyberspace security and defense: Research issues* (Vol. 196). Springer NATO Science Series.

Schulz, A. (1990). Software-Entwurf—Methoden und Werkzeuge. *2., verbesserte Aufl., Handbuch der Informatik, Oldenbourg 1990*.

Senge, P. (1990). *The fifth discipline—the art and practice of the learning organisation*. New York: Doubleday/Currency.

Silberschatz, A., Galvin, P., & Gagne, G. (2002). *Operating system concepts*. New York: John Wiley, 6. Auflage.

Software Engineering Institute (Ed.). (2007). *The architecture tradeoff analysis method (ATAM)*. Retrieved March 25, 2008, from http://www.sei.cmu.edu/architecture/ata_method.html

Sommerville, I. (2000). *Software engineering* (6th ed.). Reading, MA: Addison-Wesley. Sommerville, I. (2007). *Software engineering* (8th ed.). Reading, MA: Addison-Wesley. Sonneck, G., & Schoitsch, E. (2003). *AMSD deliverable D2.1., part ii: R+D top-level synthesis of DES—roadmaps—final deliverable* (Tech. Rep.). Seiberdorf, Austria: Seibersdorf Research.

Sonntag, M. V. (2002). Legal aspects of mobile agents with special consideration of the proposed Austrian e-commerce law. In *Cybernetics and Systems 2002: Proceedings of the 16th European Meeting on Cybernetics and Systems Research*, (pp. 153-158). Vienna: Austrian Society for Cybernetic Studies.

Stallings, W. (Ed.). (1986). *Reduced instruction set computers—tutorial*. Computer Society Press.

Standish Group. (2006). *The chaos report 2006* (Tech. Rep.). Standish Group.

Stockenberg, J., & van Dam, A. (1978). Vertical migration for performance enhancements in layered hardware-firmware-software systems. *Computer, 11*(5), 35-50.

Tanenbaum, A. (1995). *Distributed operating systems*. Englewood Cliffs, NJ: Prentice Hall.

Thome, B. (Ed.). (1993). *Systems engineering—principles and practice of computer-based systems engineering*. Chichester-New York: John Wiley.

van, D. L. P. S. R. (1984). Development environments and run-time support in ada. In P. Depledge (Ed.), *Software engineering for microprocessor systems* (pp. 133-140). London: P. Peregrinus.

van der Meulen, M. (1995). *Definitions for hardware/software reliability engineers*. Rotterdam.

van der Meulen, M. (2000). *Definitions for hardware/software safety engineers*. London: Springer-Verlag.

Walk, K., Alber, K., Bandat, K., Bekic, H., Chroust, G., Kudielka, V., et al. (1968, June). *Abstract syntax and interpretation of pl/i* (Tech. Rep. 25.082). Vienna, Austria: IBM Laboratory.

Wikipedia-English. (2005). *Wikipedia, the free encyclopedia.* Retrieved March 25, 2008, from http://en.wikipedia.org/wiki/

Williams, F., & Steven, G. (1990). How useful are complex instructions?—a case study using the Motorola M68000. *Microprocessing and Microprogramming, 29*(4), 247-259.

Wimmer, M. A. (2000, October). *Designing interactive systems: Key issues for a holistic approach.* Doctoral thesis, Kepler University Linz, Austria.

Wood, W., & Agogino, A. (2005). Decision-based conceptual design: Modeling and navigating heterogeneous design spaces. *Transactions of the ASME, 127,* 2-10.

Wymore, W. A. (1993). *Model-based systems engineering.* Boca Raton, London, Tokyo: CRC Press.

Zdun, U., & Avgeriou, P. (2005). Modeling architectural patterns using architectural primitives. In *OOPSLA '05: Proceedings of the 20th Annual ACM SIGPLAN Conference on Object Oriented Programming, Systems, Languages, and Applications,* (pp. 133-146). New York: ACM Press.

Zemanek, H. (1980). Abstract architecture: General concepts for systems design. In D. Bjoerner (Ed.), *1979 Copenhagen Winter School, Proceedings,* (pp. 1-42). Berlin: Springer-Verlag, Lecture Notes in Computer Science (No. 86).

Zemel, T. R. W. (1994). The role of software architectures in mega-system development. In M. M. Tanik, W. Rossak, & D. E. Cooke (Eds.), *Software systems in engineering* (pp. 74-85). New Orleans, LA/New York: The American Society of Mechanical Engineers Engineers.

Zoebel, D., & Albrecht, W. (1995). *Echtzeitsysteme—Grundlagen und Techniken.* Bonn, Germany: Internat. Thomson Publ.

ADDITIONAL READING

The interdisciplinarity of this chapter suggest to split suggested readings into different fields. Note that publications listed in the body of the chapter are not repeated here.

Systems Engineering, System Properties, System Design

(Abran et al., 2004) (Banker et al., 1993) (Blackburn & Scudder, 1996) (Boehm et al., 2000) (Boehm, 1983) (Brooks, 1986) (Crnkovic et al., 2002) (Jabir & Moore, 1998) (Pfleeger, 2001) (Pressman, 1994) (Rechtin, 1997) (Treleaven, 1982)

Architecture and Architectural Concepts

(Hordijk et al., 2004) (MacLean, 1989) (Zemanek, 1980)

Programming, Programming Languages and Translation

(Aho & Ullman, 1972) (Gamma et al., 1995) (Sammet, 1969)

Quality Issues

(Bach, 1997) (ISO/IEC, 2004) (ISO/IEC, 2004) (Sanders & Curran, 1995) (Voas, 2001)

Dependable, Critical, Embedded Systems

(Bowen, 2000) (Barbacci, 1996) (Barbacci et al., 1997) (Debelack et al., 1995) (ISO/IEC (ed.),

1996) (ISO/IEC (ed.), 1996) (Kopetz, 1997) (Lee & Anderson, 1990) (van der Meulen, 1995) (Myers, 1976) (Redmill & Anderson, 1993), (Redmill & Rajan, 1997) (Schoitsch & Gerstinger, 2007),

Human-Computer Interaction

(Arbaoui et al., 1999) (Banathy, 1996) (Chroust, 2007) (Chroust, 2005) (Curtis, 1981) (Heckel, 1984) (Rajlich et al., 2001) (Sujan et. al. 2006) (Sujan et. al., 2002)

Systems Theory

(Bertalanffy, 1968) (Checkland & Scholes, 1990) (Francois, 2004) (Klauninger, 2002) (Klir, 2001) (Minati & Pessa, 2002) (Yolles, 2002)

Listing of Additional Reading References

Abran, A., Moore, J., Bourque, P., Dupuis, R., & Tripp, L. L. (2004). *Guide to the software engineering body of knowledge: 2004 version* (Tech. Rep. No. DTR 19759). International Organization for Standardization.

Aho, A., & Ullman, J. (1972). *The theory of parsing, translation, and compiling* (Vol. I). Parsing. Prentice Hall.

Arbaoui, S., Lonchamp, J., & Montangero, C. (1999). The human dimension of the software process. In J.-C. Derniame, D. Ali Kaba, & D.G. Wastell (Eds.), *Software process: Principles, methodology, and technology* (pp. 165-200). New York: Springer-Verlag.

Bach, J. (1997). Good enough quality: Beyond the buzzword. *IEEE Computer, 30*(8), 96-98.

Banathy, B. (1996). *Designing social systems in a changing world.* New York: Plenum Press.

Banker, R., Datar, S. M., Kemerer, C., & Zweig, D. (1993). Software complexity and maintenance costs. *Communications of the ACM, 36*(11), 81-94.

Barbacci, M. (1996). Survivability in the age of vulnerable systems. *IEEE Computer, 29*(11), 8.

Barbacci, M., et al. (1997). *Steps in an architecture tradeoff analysis method: Quality attribute models and analysis* (Tech. Rep. No. CMU/SEI-97-TR-29). Software Engineering Institute, Carnegie Mellon University.

Bertalanffy, L. (1968). *General system theory—foundations, developments, applications.* New York: George Braziller.

Blackburn, J., & Scudder, G. (1996). Improving speed and productivity of software development: A global survey of software developers. *IEEE Transactions on SW Engineering, 22*(12), 875-885.

Boehm, B. (1983). Seven basic principles of software engineering. *Journal of Systems and Software, 3,* 3-24.

Boehm, W., et al. (2000). *Software cost estimation with COCOMO II* (1st ed.). Prentice Hall PTR.

Bowen, J. (2000). The ethics of safety-critical systems. *Communications of the ACM, 43*(28), 91-97.

Brooks, F. (1986). No silver bullet—essence and accidents of software engineering. In H. J. Kugler (Ed.), *Proceedings of Information Processing 86, IFIP Congress*, (pp. 1069-1076).

Checkland, P., & Scholes, J. (1990). *Soft systems methodology in action.* Chistester: John Wiley.

Chroust, G. (2005, September). Mutual influences of society's paradigm and information and communication technologies. In *Proceedings of the 49th Annual Conf of ISSS: The Potential Impacts of Systemics on Society,* Mexico, (pages file 05-09, pp. 1-18). ISSS 2005 (CDROM).

Chroust, G. (2007). Software like a courteous butler—issues of localization under cultural diversity. In *Proceedings of the ISSS 2007,* Tokyo.

Crnkovic, I., Larsson, S., & Stafford, J. (2002). Component-based software engineering: Building systems from components at 9thh IEEE conference and workshop on cb-systems. *Software Engineering Notes, 27*(3), 47-50.

Curtis, B. (Ed.). (1981). *Human factors in software development*. IEEE Computer Society Press.

Debelack, A., Dehn, J., Muchinsky, L., & Smith, D. (1995). Next generation air traffic control automation. *IBM Systems Journal, 34*(1), 63-77.

Francois, C. (2004). *International encyclopedia of systems and cybernetics* (2nd ed., 2 Volumes). Munchen: K.G.Saur.

Gamma, E., Helm, R., Johnson, R., & Vlissides, J. (1995). *Design patterns—elements of reusable object-oriented software*. Reading, MA: Addison-Wesley.

Heckel, P. (1984). The elements of friendly software design. *Warner Books.*

Hordijk, W., Krukkert, D., & Wieringa, R. (2004). *The impact of architectural decisions on quality attributes of enterprise information systems: A survey of the design space* (Tech. Rep. No. TR-CTIT-04-48). Centre for Telematics and Information Technology, University of Twente, Enschede.

ISO/IEC (Ed.). (1996). *Information technology—vocabulary—part 14: Reliability, maintainability and availability* (Tech. Rep. No. ISO/IEC 2382-14:1996). International Organization for Standardization.

ISO/IEC. (2004). *Fdis 15504-1 information technology—process assessment—part 1: Concepts and vocabulary* (Tech. Rep. No. ISO/IEC JTC 1/SC 7/WG 10).

ISO/IEC. (2004). *ISO 25000: Software and systems engineering: Software product quality requirements and evaluation (square)* (Tech. Rep.). International Organization for Standardization.

Jabir & Moore, J. (1998). A search for fundamental principles in software engineering. *Computer Standards and Interfaces, 19*(2), 155-160.

Klauninger, B. (2002, April). Causality and emergence. In R. Trappl (Ed.), *Proceedings of EMCSR 2002: European Meeting on Cybernetics and Systems Research, Vienna.*

Klir, G. J. (2001). *Facets of systems science, IFSR Internet: Series on systems science and engineering* (Vol 15, 2nd ed.). New York, Boston, Dordrecht, London, Moscow: Kluwer Academic/Plenum.

Kopetz, H. (1997). Echtzeitsysteme. In P. Rechenberg & G. Pomberger (Eds.), *Informatik-Handbuch* (pp. 689-602). Munchen: Carl Hanser Verlag.

Lee, P., & Anderson, T. (1990). *Fault tolerance: Principles and practice*. Wien: Springer-Verlag.

MacLean, A. Y. R. M. M. T. P. (1989). Design rationale: The argument behind the artifact. In *Proceedings of CHI'89,* Austin, TX.

Minati, G., & Pessa, E. (Eds.). (2002). *Emergence in complex, cognitive, social, and biological systems*. New York: Kluwer Academic/Plenum.

Myers, G. (1976). *Software reliability—principles and practices*. New York: John Wiley & Sons.

Pfleeger, S. L. (2001). *Software engineering: Theory and practice* (2nd ed.). Prentice Hall.

Pressman, R. (1994). Software engineering: A practitioner's approach. New York: *McGraw-Hill.*

Rajlich, V., Wilde, N., Buckellew, M., & Page, H. (2001). Software cultures and evolution. *IEEE Computer, 34*(9), 4-27.

Rechtin, E. (1997). The synthesis of complex systems. *IEEE Spectrum, 34*(7), 51-55.

Redmill, F., & Anderson, T. (Eds.). (1993). *Safety critical systems: Current issues, techniques and standards*. London: Chapman and Hall.

Redmill, F., & Rajan, J. (1997). *Human factors in safety-critical systems*. Oxford: REED Educational and Professional Publ., ISBN 0-7506-2715-8.

Sammet, J. (1969). *Programming languages: History and fundamentals*. Englewood Cliffs, NJ: Prentice Hall.

Sanders, J., & Curran, E. (1995). *Software quality.* England: Addison-Wesley.

Schoitsch, E., & Gerstinger, A. (2007). Special session: Dependable embedded systems. In *Proceedings of INDIN 2007: 5th IEEE International Conference on Industrial Informatics*, (Vol. 2, pp. 965-1008).

Sujan M. A., et al. (2006) Qualitative analysis of dependability argument structure. In D. Besnard, et al. (Eds.), *Structure for dependability: Computer-based systems from an interdisciplinary perspective* (pp. 269-290). London: Springer-Verlag.

Sujan, M. A., Rizzo, A., & Pasquini, A. (2002). Contradictions and critical issues during system evolution. In *Proceedings of the 2002 ACM Symposium on Applied Computing*, Madrid, Spain, (pp. 711-715). New York: ACM Press.

Treleaven, P. B. D. H. R. (1982). Data-driven and demand-driven computer architecture. *Computing Surveys, 14*(1), 93-143.

van der Meulen, M. (1995). *Definitions for hardware/software reliability engineers.* Rotterdam.

Voas, J. (2001). Composing software component "ilities." *IEEE Software, 18*(4), 16-17.

Yolles, M. (2002). *Management systems.* Pitman.

Zemanek, H. (1980). Abstract architecture: General concepts for systems design. In D. Bjoerner (Ed.), *Proceedings of the 1979 Copenhagen Winter School,* (pp. 1-42). Berlin: Springer-Verlag. Lecture Notes in Computer Science (No 86).

Chapter VIII
Architecting Virtual Reality Systems

Rafael Capilla
Universidad Rey Juan Carlos, Spain

Margarita Martínez
Universidad Rey Juan Carlos, Spain

Francisco Nava
Universidad Rey Juan Carlos, Spain

Cristina Muñoz
Universidad Politécnica de Madrid, Spain

ABSTRACT

Virtual reality systems are a kind of complex software systems that need a lot of effort and resources during its development phase. Because rigid and monolithic approaches for these systems have been used in the past, maintenance and evolution activities become difficult tasks to carry out. Today, software architectures are used for designing more maintainable and modular systems, but previous experiences in the virtual reality field didn't pay much attention to the usage of appropriate architecture descriptions. In this chapter we describe how the design of virtual reality systems can be improved with software architectures. Our main goal is to provide guidance in the design of virtual reality systems that can be reused for similar applications. A software architecture-centric approach is proposed and used to tackle certain problems that affect the construction of this kind of software intensive systems.

INTRODUCTION

Software-intensive systems engineering focus on the development and maintenance of large complex systems. We can give several types of examples of such systems belonging to different domains, such as: banking, health care, government, real-time systems, entertainment, simulators, embedded systems, and virtual reality applications.

In this kind of application, the size, complexity, and design issues become critical compared to less complex systems, and the challenges for the design of software intensive systems can be manifold. Pohl (2003 p. 1) emphasizes two of them: "the increasing complexity and the increasing need to adapt to a fast changing technology and environment." The increasing complexity, cost and design time in software intensive systems are based on observable factors like, for instance, the increase in functionality, an increasing demand of the quality needs, and software mass customization which leads to the existence of hundreds of software systems/versions. Thus, maintenance operations and software configuration management activities becomes complex, consuming tasks. In addition, the need for adaptation demanded by organizations to change their products and processes must respond to new technologies and business opportunities. In other cases, certain software intensive systems must use a specific software platform or special hardware devices (e.g., virtual reality systems).

Organizations are increasingly demanding interaction between software systems. In general, modeling software-intensive systems often involves several disciplines and techniques such as software engineering, control engineering or virtual modeling, and several hardware and software technologies have to be combined to build the target system. For instance, visual model-driven approaches (Burmester, Giese, & Henkler, 2005) like Mecatronic UML or the Systems Modelling Language (SysML, 2006) are interesting alternatives to be considered.

To address some of the problems mentioned before, the mission of this chapter is the description of the development of virtual reality systems. Prior to this, we will discuss some modeling approaches from other authors and afterwards we will propose to use modern design techniques like software architectures, rather than other monolithic design approaches. We will illustrate important modeling issues that may affect the construction of these systems (e.g., the influence of quality attributes in the rendering process) and how software architectures can help to solve certain design problems. Also, we employ well-known design patterns and architecture styles as reusable chunks of architectural knowledge that are of common use in the construction of software architectures. In this chapter, we will use the Unified Modeling Language 2.0 standard (UML 2.0: Booch, Rumbaugh, & Jacobson, 2005) for describing the architecture of such systems. At the end, we will provide the lessons learned and the conclusions.

BACKGROUND

The main challenge of a virtual reality (VR) system is to simulate the real world in a virtual environment, making it real for the users who are immersed in it. A virtual reality system has special characteristics that differ from other types of applications. Some of these characteristics introduce a factor of complexity in the development of such applications. For instance, immersive VR systems need special hardware devices (e.g., head-mounted display, 3D haptics, etc.), which are used to provide the interaction between the user and system. This multimodal interaction often complicates the design of graphical user interfaces. Moreover, the presence of the user in the virtual scene results key for many VR systems where virtual users (i.e., an avatar) interact and manipulate virtual objects in the same way as they do in the real life.

The development of virtual reality systems often takes a lot effort for building the virtual world, and the modeling process requires different techniques and skills that have to be addressed. In the virtual reality domain, we can have different types of applications, depending of the degree of immersion of the user in the virtual scene. The traditional classification divides virtual reality applications into immersive and nonimmersive systems. In addition, some of them could be distributed across different machines. One example of highly immersive systems is those CAVE-based systems (Cave Automatic Virtual Environment). In a CABE system the virtual scene is projected in the floor and walls, and the user experiments a high degree of immersion using the virtual world. During the creation of this virtual world, tridimensional (3D) development techniques are carried out, but these modeling tasks consume a lot of effort during the design activity. In the lower level of abstraction, complex graphic operations (e.g., object collision, 3D rendering) are enacted by specialized graphic engines. In addition, quality and real-time requirements like CPU usage and memory consumption become key aspects for the success of the system.

One of the main problems that may appear during the construction of a virtual reality application is the usage of monolithic design approaches (both at design and code levels), which impede its proper evolution over time. This lack of flexibility exhibited by many virtual reality systems is one of the main problems that we need to solve in order to reduce the development and maintenance effort. Another important issue specific to virtual reality applications, refers to the organization of the tridimensional objects in the virtual scene. A proper organization of the scene-graph containing the 3D objects has impact in low level graphic operations (e.g., redrawing the virtual scene or during the initialization of the virtual world). All these issues have to be addressed during the design phase and software architectures play an important role here.

Software architectures have been extensively used for more than 20 years to represent the design of modern software systems. Architectures are mainly described by means of a set of components and connectors (Shaw & Garlan, 1996), and they are usually built under an iterative process in which several design decisions are made before the final design is finished. The aim of the design process is to produce the architecture documentation which comprises different architectural views (Bass, Clements, & Kazman, 2003) that describe different points of view that represent the interest of different stakeholders. From an architecture perspective, many virtual reality systems don't provide a detailed software architecture and only coarse-grained approaches with little detail are described. To support our approach, we discuss some architecture approaches of existing virtual reality systems.

Software Architectures of Existing VR-Systems

Not many software architectures for virtual reality systems can be found in the literature. Most of them are poorly described because the details are not properly reflected in the design. Therefore, the challenge to reproduce a similar system becomes a difficult task when the architecture doesn't reflect the design decisions made in the past. Moreover, virtual reality developers find serious difficulties to implement the target application from architectures poorly described. We can give several examples of this.

Schöntage and Eliëns (1999) mention some problems that appeared in the construction of distributed virtual reality systems. They provide four architectural styles for classifying object-oriented software for distributed environments. The DIVA Distributed Architecture Visualization (Schönhage, van Ballegooij, & Eliëns, 2000) uses architectural patterns (Buschmann, Meunier, Rohnert, Sommerland, & Stal, 1996) to describe the architecture (Schönhage & Eliëns, 2000)

Figure 1. Architecture of the Dragon virtual reality system (Julier, King, Colbert, Durbin, & Rosenblum, 1999)

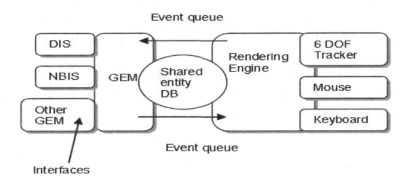

of distributed VR systems. Another example is Dragon (Julier, King, Colbert, Durbin, & Rosenblum, 1999), which is a real-time battlefield visualization virtual environment, composed by two major subsystems: the *rendering engine* (RE) and a *generic entity manager* (GEM). The main subsystems of the Dragon's architecture are described at a very high level in Figure 1.

The rendering engine (RE) draws the virtual environment, processes the user input and creates requests and events that are sent to the GEM subsystem. GEM is responsible to collect data from external sources and represent them under a common format. Both subsystems interact through a pair of unidirectional event queues and a shared entity database. DIS (Distributed Interactive Simulation) and NBIS (Joint Maritime Command Interaction) are interfaces of the system. The architecture of Figure 1 only reflects a context diagram in which the main modules are described, but not the detailed architectural decisions made in the design. In addition, this context diagram of the Dragon systems doesn't use standard design notations like UML to communicate other architecture views (e.g., static or dynamic views) which can be interesting for other stakeholders involved in the system development.

Software architectures can facilitate the challenge for building large-scale virtual environments, and important issues like scalability and

synchronization between the entities of a distributed virtual reality system have to be addressed. The DEVA3 distributed architecture (Pettifer, Cook, Marsh, & West, 2000) represents an example in which the distribution, shared entities, simultaneous number of users, and an execution environment are key issues that must be properly described using an architecture approach. Other examples can be found in Alexandre and Medioni (2001), Fernando, Murray, Tan, and Wimalaratne (1999), and Hua, Brown, Gao, and Ahuja (2003), but as in the previous cases, the lack of a well detailed system structure limits the reconstruction of similar virtual reality applications and provides little insight for developers.

Other experiences focus on the architectures for specific virtual reality devices, like tracking, which is an indispensable part of any virtual reality and augmented reality application. Reitmayr and Schamalstieg (2001) describe the open software architecture (OpenTracker) for different tasks belonging to tracking input devices and for the processing of multimodal input data in virtual environments and augmented reality systems. The OpenTracker system provides a flexible way of hardware setups compared to what is typically offered by virtual reality development packages. Because the core classes of the OpenTracker architecture are not well described in the design, the stakeholders interested in it may experiment some difficulties to understand the proposed design. Traditionally, research prototypes in the virtual reality and augmented reality fields do not emphasize software architecture, and contributions in this area are particularly welcome. For instance, in Reicher, MacWilliams, Brügge, and Linder (2003), the authors state this problem and they propose a reference architecture (i.e., a high level architecture description that represents the main standard parts and its relationships of a family of similar systems in a given domain) for augmented reality systems. A detailed map of the relationships between approaches for subsystem implementation is given, but important standard parts of the component description are not provided. In addition, the authors mention the importance for desired quality attributes that affect the construction of the architecture. As opposed to other approaches in which the architecture of a virtual reality system focuses on low level entities like graphic engines as well as the interaction with special hardware devices, the model presented in De Antonio, Ramirez, Imbert, and Aguilar (2005) goes a step beyond because it describes the business logic of an intelligent virtual environment (a multi-agent system) using a software architecture. The major components and subsystems of the target application are described, but some missing points like the attributes and methods of the multi-agent architecture are not explicitly addressed.

Compared to simple architecture descriptions for augmented reality systems (e.g., see Gelenbe, Husain, & Kaptan, 2004), a more accurate study is conducted in Brügge (2004), which describes an overview of the augmented reality research landscape from the perspective of software architecture, and in particular the ARVIKA architecture. The study provides in-depth descriptions of individual architectures, a reference architecture for comparing augmented reality systems and a classification of architectural approaches used to address typical problems in the augmented reality application domain. It states also the importance

for quality attribute evaluation, and architectural evaluation methods have been used to rank which quality requirements are important for such systems. As an example, the performance of a virtual reality system may depend on the complexity of the scene needed to be displayed, or the latency of tracking and rendering is considered important in almost all virtual reality systems (e.g., the maximum limit of 10ms was given several times). The definition of significant quality attributes and requirements is a major issue of interest. Blach, Landauer, Rösch, and Simon (1998) mention some of the requirements architectures must fulfil (e.g., modularization, extensibility, device independence) as a practical guide to support the design process of modern VR systems. As a result, one of the main outcomes reported is a reference architecture that supersedes existing augmented reality designs that can be mapped to specific software components in the augmented reality field. Another advantage is the definition of flexible and maintainable architectures rather than using rigid approaches. On the other hand, it seems necessary to detail such architecture descriptions with specific variation points that can extend the level of flexibility of the proposed designs. The reference and software architectures discussed in Brügge (2004) provide a better description with respect to past proposals because different architectural views (Kruchten, 1995) are explicitly addressed (e.g., logical view, development view), and also because the architecture describes all levels of a classical augmented reality application. We mean with this that the low level graphic system, the user input and output, and the business logic level of the target system, which are explicitly detailed through UML classes and component diagrams. Figure 2 shows a partial view of the ARVIKA architecture.

The description of the elements of figure 2 is as follows. The user input sybsystem includes any input made by the user as a mean to a control the system which is generally achieved through different input devices. The *user output* subsys-

Figure 2. Partial view of the ARVIKA architecture mapped onto reference architecture (Brügge, 2004)

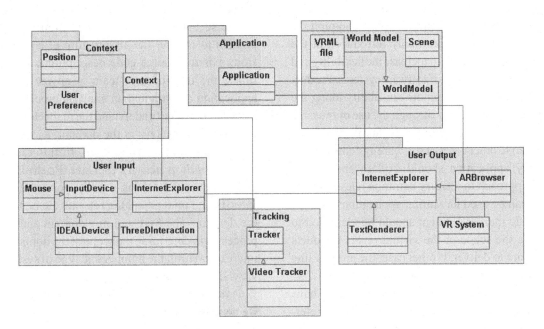

tem is a human machine interface that can be achieved through several channels as text, voice, or sound, but 3D graphics output represents the most important output of the system. The *context* subsystem uses a context manager for collecting different types of context related with the user (e.g., user preferences, current situation). The *world model* subsystem stores and provides information about the world of the user, which is represented in various formats such as a VRML model. The *tracking* subsystem is introduced due to its important in some kind of virtual reality systems like, for instance, augmented reality applications. Tracking can be achieved with several techniques (e.g., video tracker). Finally, the *application* subsystem represents a particular virtual reality application. The detailed description of the packages of the ARVIKA architecture can be examined in Brügge (2004). One missing point in the architecture of Figure 2 is that attributes and methods are not depicted, so the details still remain at a high level.

The experiences already discussed follow, in many cases (except the last two), a monolithic approach that complicates the development of large scale virtual environments because rigid architectures may block important quality attributes such as *maintenance, reusability* and *extensibility,* among others (Oliveira, Crowcroft, Slater, & Brutzman, 1999). From the software architecture perspective, the low degree of modularity exhibited by certain VR system architectures doesn't facilitate the representation and implementation of adequate variation points, which are commonly used to introduce the necessary flexibility demanded by modern software designs to address evolution problems. The usage of design patterns in some of the approaches presented before clearly benefits the construction of virtual reality systems for two main reasons. First, they use standard and proven design solutions to model the design issues of such complex systems. Second, they increment the level of modularity and reusability by organizing the different pieces in systems that tend to follow a monolithic approach. Complementary to this, virtual reality could benefit from product line architectures, as they are able to exploit the variability that is commonly introduced at the design and code level to increase the flexibility and configurable options of software systems. Product line architectures promote reusability along the entire product family through the use of reusable assets that are shared by all the family members. Similar to other types of software systems, virtual reality application should explore and exploit this approach to identify common relevant parts that can be used for similar applications. Also, a specific market segment should be identified to define the scope of the virtual reality products we want to deliver. If other case, the product line approach will not have too much sense.

The experiences previously discussed have highlighted the need to count with detailed reference and software architectures for virtual reality applications. In order to overcome the design and modeling issues described in the approaches already discussed, the remainder of this chapter deals with potential solutions that extend and improve the issues mentioned previously.

ARCHITECTING VIRTUAL REALITY APPLICATIONS

The approach presented in this chapter is based on a previous work described in Capilla and Martínez (2004), where a software architecture for an immersive virtual reality was developed. Before describing our case study, we will discuss some architecture development strategies and modeling issues that can be applied to the construction of virtual reality systems.

Architecture Development Approaches

Two fundamental approaches can be taken for building the architecture of a software system.

Software architectures can be developed from scratch following a top-down approach or using a reverse engineering process (bottom-up approach) to recover the architecture of a system from existing source code descriptions. Sometimes, the development team is novice in the application domain and an analysis process has to be carried out to understand the main elements and parts that belong to the domain, as well as their relationships among them. In this case, a *domain analysis* activity (Schäfer, Prieto-Díaz, & Matsumoto, 1994) is usually performed to identify and understand the relevant elements of the domain. The first step in a domain analysis process is to determine the scope of the domain of interest and limit the number and type of systems we want to analyze.

After the domain scoping activity is done, we need to identify and understand the relevant elements which are typical in a virtual reality application. For instance, virtual reality systems use special hardware devices to allow the interaction with the user and the system. In the lower level of abstraction, understanding how graphic engines work could be an interesting issue, but is not the main concern of virtual reality application developers. Also, because graphic and rendering engines are often supported by the software environment in which the virtual reality system runs. The remainder of the functionality belongs to the business logic of a particular application, but some key elements are typical of virtual reality systems. For instance, defining the scene-graph for organizing the 3D objects in the virtual world is a classical problem that has to be reflected in the domain model and in the architecture Also, virtual users (i.e., avatars), sensors for detecting certain events like object collision, and processing events for reacting to the user inputs, constitute relevant parts that have to be depicted. In this subactivity, the availability of documentation and domain experts constitute important knowledge sources for the success of the domain analysis process. The result of the domain analysis process is a domain model representing the most relevant elements (and their relationships among them) of the domain. Often, this domain model is the starting point to build the architecture of a system or set of similar systems.

Many times the information of a domain analysis process is not enough, and we need to validate our domain model and the architecture with data obtained from existing applications. In this case, a *reverse engineering* process used to recover the high level description of a software system from low level assets (e.g., source code). Thus, combining both approaches, we can produce a more accurate and refined architecture of the system. In addition, because VR systems can be written in several languages (VRML, C, C++, OpenGL, and FreeVR), similar concepts with different terminology can be implemented in different ways using different programming languages (e.g., VRML nodes can be associated to Java 3D objects; Nadeau, 1999). Therefore, we need to map and abstract similar concepts in order to avoid any overlapping of concepts and terminology. Furthermore, source code analysis from virtual reality systems shows interesting information that can be modeled as UML classes (e.g., physical properties affecting the objects in the scene, like the color, shape and texture, among others). Another interesting result is the classical structure of a typical virtual reality application. In virtual reality systems, the device initialization section, the instructions for loading a virtual world, the definition of virtual observers to provide different points of view in a virtual scene, and the rendering loop that processes the functionality, are key elements that are commonly used. All this information should be gathered to properly understand the typical structure of virtual reality systems.

Modeling Virtual Reality Systems

Virtual reality systems have special features that make them different from other kinds of systems.

In this section, we illustrate some issues that describe the particularity of these systems and which modeling solutions can be provided.

a. **The Scene-graph problem:** All virtual reality systems have to manage a particular virtual world which is displayed to the user who interacts with the system by means of special hardware devices. During the system initialization, the database containing the structure of the virtual world has to be loaded. Because of the number of objects, its main parts (e.g., faces, edges, hidden and visible parts, etc.), the materials and textures, the virtual effects we can applied in the scene, and so forth, the database containing this virtual world is about several Megabytes, and the initial loading time can take several minutes. Moreover, when the user interacts with the system, the objects have to be re-arranged in the scene and the rendering process for redrawing the objects in the virtual scene may need certain time, mostly depending on the hardware performance. This problem can be influenced when quality requirements are required for a particular system (e.g., a real-time flight simulator system) that needs to increase its performance. To tackle this issue, we have to define the best object hierarchy (i.e., the scene-graph) for arranging the objects in the scene, and several alternatives are possible. Most of virtual reality environments offer the possibility to define groups of objects (i.e., group nodes) that logically organize a set of tridimensional objects in the scene. This technique is used to reduce the loading time needed during the initialization of the system or in rendering operations. Also, defining which objects will be hidden or visible is another mechanism used to increase performance. The question that arises is to know the number and type of group nodes we need to define, as well as which objects will be visible or not. The type of the virtual reality application we want to develop may define this issue, but in principle we can consider the following alternatives.

1. **No group nodes:** The scene graph is formed by a root node and in some cases one or two object groups (some virtual reality environments have predefined object groups representing the database system, e.g., the Multigen paradigm has one root node (db) and two predefined group nodes, g1 and g2). In this case, all the 3D objects will hang from a single root node or from one object group node.

2. **Group nodes at all levels of the hierarchy:** In this case, we define group nodes at all levels of the hierarchy. The main problem with this approach is that we can lose the control of the number of group nodes or even relate objects that have no logical relationship between them.

3. **Group nodes for objects logically related:** The third possibility defines group nodes for the intermediate levels of the object hierarchy and only for those objects logically related. For instance, if we are modeling a 3D house, we can define one group node for the external view of the house and another group for the internal view, and the objects belonging to both views will hang from their parents previously defined. Objects under the same parent will share kinds of relationship or behavior. As an example, we can group objects that have the same type of movement or those that have to be lighted at a given moment.

It is easy to imagine that the third possibility seems to be the most balanced one because it offers a combination between the number of objects and the group nodes. The issue now is to know which would be the best configuration for defining the object groups. To know this, we can carry out some simulation for the target system and measure the loading time for each different configuration of the hierarchy. Another factor that strongly influences the organization of the scene-graph is the order of the objects in the hierarchy. Those 3D objects that are visible in the scene should be placed before in the object hierarchy. The same applies for the group nodes. By doing so, the rendering engine will display the virtual scene in less time because visible objects are displayed first, then hidden ones. The last issue that might impact the organization of the scene-graph is the definition of the number of faces, edges or textures for each single object. A significant reduction of the number of faces, edges, and textures, for instance, will reduce the time spent by the graphic engines to render the scene (i.e., the depth of the scene-graph is smaller). Figure 3 describes three alternatives for organizing the scene-graph in a virtual reality application.

The first alternative to Figure 3 describes one root node (root node 1) and one group node group from which the virtual objects and their basic parts (faces, edges) hang on. In Figure 3, alternative (a) doesn't provide object group, while alternative (b) defines group nodes at all levels of the hierarchy, some of them containing related objects, whereas some of them do not. Finally, alternative (c) introduces significant group nodes for objects logically related which have the same parent. We have shown three different ways to structure the database hierarchy containing the virtual world. By doing this we can avoid large hierarchies that are very time-consuming during the execution of the system. Reducing the polygons (i.e., faces) count by removing hidden polygons and replacing complex shapes with simple outlines is another way to cut the depth of the scene-graph. As stated by some vendors, a good rule of thumb is to reduce the number of polygons for each level of detail to 60% of the original.

Figure 3. Different alternatives for organizing the scene-graph of the 3D objects in virtual reality applications

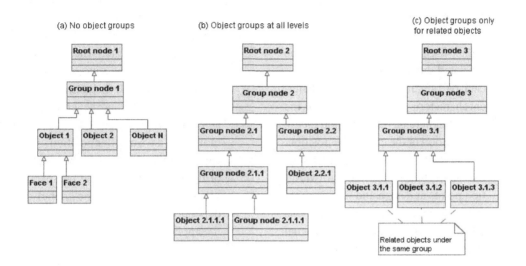

b. **Architecture variation points:** We understand by architecture variation point an area of a software system affected by variability. Variation points are usually introduced at the design and code levels to reflect different possibilities or configurations that allow a high degree of flexibility for implementing and configuring a software system. System requirements can be specified in terms of system features, and these features (usually represented using a feature tree) are described by means variation points. Software variability is used to delay the design decisions to the latest time in which the variability is realized (i.e., binding time; Fritsch, Lehn, & Strohm, 2002). The representation of the variation points can be done using proprietary notations or using some UML mechanisms (Dobrica & Niemelä, 2003), like stereotypes, attributes and tagged values. In general, UML suffers of a more precise notation for representing all variability issues, but for a high level description, UML class diagrams can be annotated with variability information. Nevertheless, none of the architectures of the virtual reality systems examined in the *background* section introduced variability in their designs. Because variation points provide a way to produce flexible architectures (widely used in product line architectures; Bosch, 2000), it can be used to avoid rigid architectures that impeded a proper evolution of the system. A clear advantage of using this approach is to produce similar virtual reality applications that could share common part. To achieve this goal, we need to know where variability occurs in the system, how to characterize the variation points, and which variability mechanism we will use to implement the variation points in the code. We can provide several examples where variation points can be applied.

1. **Initialization of VR devices:** Many virtual reality systems use multimodal interaction combining several input and output devices. Because each device has a different initialization

procedure, we can use variation points to determine the type of device and then call the appropriate initialization routine.

2. **Virtual effects:** Different virtual effects are widely used (e.g., sound, lights, fog), and each effect must be activated during run-time. Moreover, each particular effect may have different characteristics like, for instance, the type of light (e.g., infinite, spot, local), the duration of the effect, the position, and so forth. All these characteristics can be explicitly modeled with variation points at design and implementation to provide configurable options during run-time. For instance, a virtual user walking inside a building may activate the lights depending on his/her position. UML classes can define these variation points as a way to decouple the particular characteristics of each single effect from the conditions of the scene in which that effect is activated.

3. **Motion models**: Many virtual reality applications provide different types of motion models for the users who are immersed in the scene. Depending of the specific hardware device used, users may have different degrees of freedom to perform different types of movements. For instance, virtual users can walk to different positions with different speed or maybe they can fly inside the cockpit of a flight simulator system with several degrees of freedom (DOF nodes in the scenegraph). Variation points may provide the selection of a particular motion model with their own characteristics. Free and user-defined motion models represent different movement alternatives. Figure 5 shows an example of

variation points defined in UML class attributes to specify different types of motions.

c. **Event processing:** Another characteristic is the detection of events that may happen during the interaction with the system. These events can be generated when objects change their position in the virtual scene or even when objects collide. In gaming applications (e.g., a war game where several players fight against themselves), avatars are constantly moving to have a better position where they can shoot the enemy, and the point of view of the observers (e.g., the perspective of a virtual user inside in the scene) changes depending on the conditions simulated in the application. This situation leads to continuously compute the new position and to re-arrange the objects in the scene to show a different perspective. Such events can be described at design time with appropriate classes representing the events and the responses generated during the execution of the system. In other cases like object collision, the virtual reality environment computes the new situation of the object after the collision, and such event is managed by the current environment. A way to detect collisions is to use sensors to detect certain events. For instance, we could determine the position of a virtual user walking inside a building and then activate a particular effect when the user is near a certain point or to avoid the collision with a fixed object. In mechanical engineering, virtual applications can detect the deformation of virtual objects and then reduce the pressure of the virtual glove used to manipulate the object. We can think in an infinite number of situations where events may happen, but we cannot represent all of them under the same design. Unfortunately, we cannot provide a more precise architectural solution for this problem, but decoupling the event process-

Figure 4. UML classes use variation points to decouple the specification of virtual effects from the current context

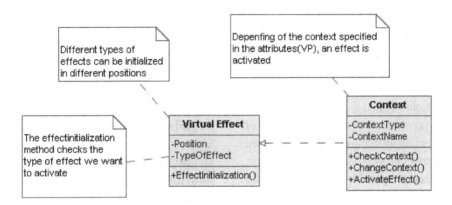

Figure 5. Variability for specifying different types of motion models and speed ranges for the players in the virtual scene

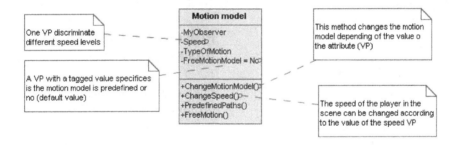

ing from the sensors needed, we can offer a flexible alternative to avoid a monolithic approach. Also, variation points can be used to discriminate different categories of events.

d. **Distributed VR applications:** Finally, some virtual reality systems (e.g., gaming applications or war simulation systems) are distributed applications where several users interact at the same time. Distributed aspects have to be taken into account to define which nodes will behave as a master and which ones as slaves. Virtual reality development environments use specific packages

and libraries for configuring distributed applications and creating communicating objects that are used to send/receive data and synchronization information. These libraries are usually built on top of a communication environment in which certain parameters like the transport protocol used (TCP, UDP), the port, and the definition of the master and the slaves hosts are configurable options. Also, during the initialization of the system, the master and the slaves have to be synchronized to communicate the changes from the master to the slaves in the visual simulation and then redraw the virtual scene. Variation points could be defined to configure the distribution parameters used by the system.

To this point we have described some of the design problems that may arise during the development of a virtual reality system, as well as some potential solutions that can be used. Current software environments aimed for building complex virtual reality applications provide a variety of high quality technical features that can be used in the development process. As you can imagine, no single architecture provides a general solution for all the cases, but the design issues discussed before provide some guidance for building more maintainable virtual reality systems. To refute what we said, in the next section, we describe how we carried out the construction of a small immersive real world virtual reality application, and the problems we encountered during the construction of the system.

BUILDING A VIRTUAL REALITY CHURCH SYSTEM

The last section of this chapter illustrates the issues discussed before based on a case study belonging to a real immersive virtual reality system developed in 2004, which consists of the development of virtual church that implements a virtual tour guide inside the church. The VR church system is a tourist information system for the cultural heritage of a small village in the north of Spain and displays the 3D model of the church that can be virtually visited. The application shows the internal and the external views of the church and the user can visit the interior part, as well as learn the history of the monument through specific information text points located at strategic places.

The previous experience of the authors concerning the development of virtual reality systems and software architectures is as follows. One of the authors has at least more than 6 years of experience architecting software systems, while another author worked as a senior system analyst for more than 15 years. Both authors participated in the analysis and design activities and they spent around 2 months doing this, but none of them worked before building virtual reality systems. In addition, another author has 3 years of experience in designing virtual reality systems, in particular the user interface and the usability concerns. Finally, the fourth author is a senior developer who carried out the implementation activities of the church system and the modeling tasks of the virtual world.

In next subsections, we describe how we enacted the architecting process for the virtual church, the problems we found, and the solutions we provided. We will detail all the steps we carried out to provide the reader a detailed perspective of what was done.

Process for Architecting Virtual Reality Systems

The process for building and architecting a virtual reality system doesn't differ too much from the development of other systems, except the modeling of the virtual world and the usage of special hardware devices. Prior to the description of the detailed steps we did for architecting the virtual church, we provide an overview of the process for architecting software systems in general.

a. **Analysis of the target domain:** Because the virtual reality domain was new for most the authors, we analyzed the target domain. The analysis of a given domain can be enacted from two different but complementary approaches. A top-down approach, usually known as domain analysis, which analyses the relevant elements, features, and the relationships between the elements to produce a domain model. This domain model can be used as the basis for building the architecture of the system. Domain analysis frequently requires the participation of domain experts, as well as examining existing documentation to understand the main concepts of the domain. In those cases where the domain analysis activity is not enough to fully understand a particular domain or when the outcome of the domain analysis activity has to be validated, a bottom-up approach has to be carried out. This bottom-up approach includes processes like reverse engineering or architecture recovery, and existing systems are analyzed, often with some (semi)automatic tool support, to extract relevant information which is used to produce a high level description of the system from the lower one. The combination of top-down and bottom-up approaches can produce a more accurate description of the problem domain. In this chapter we carried out both approaches. In other cases where the domain is well-known, it is unnecessary to perform such activities.

b. **Analysis of architecture requirements:** This is a classic in all software systems which are performed before design time. Functional and nonfunctional requirements are elicited from the problem description as well as other specific application or hardware requirements. More specifically, architecture requirements are a subset of the system requirements, determined by architectural relevance. Once we have determined the system context and its scope, the business goals are translated into use cases and used to document functional requirements. In addition, system quality attributes are specified as nonfunctional requirements, which may impact at levels of the architecture with a particular significance in the quality of the final system.

c. **Architecting phase:** Architecting concerns with the creation of the software architecture for a specific system by exploiting its common parts with reuse purposes. The architecture is created and documented using the following subactivities:

c.1. **Reuse of architectural knowledge:** Existing codified design patterns and reference models are (re)used for guiding the initial steps of the architecture construction process and taking into account the architecture requirements. In addition, if a domain model exists, it can be used as the preliminary view of the architecture. Otherwise, the architect will start building the architecture from scratch. In our case, we used a basic domain model obtained from the combination of the domain analysis and reverse engineering activities.

c.2. **Building the reference architecture:** In certain domains it seems useful to count with a reference architecture which constitutes the base of the future software architecture. Existing knowledge from step c.1 (e.g., patterns, styles, domain models) can be reused. In our case and because we didn't find good architecture models for the VR church system we decided to build a reference architecture.

c.3. **Architecture refinements:** Architectures are not built in a single step and several iterations are often carried out to refine the architecture until the final design is achieved. For each of the iterations, several design decisions are made.

c.4 **Architecture customization:** The outcome of this step is to produce a tailored version of the architecture according to the system requirements. This task involves a customization process that refines the previous designs, and exploiting the commonalities and variability of the architecture.

d. **Architecture evaluation and assessment:** Sometimes it is possible to count with more than one candidate architecture for the same goal. The selection of the best alternative depends on the level of quality we need to achieve, and quality attributes drive an evaluation process in which the best candidate architecture will be selected. This evaluation can be carried out during the development of the architecture for deciding between several alternatives for a particular intermediate architectural product. Several evaluation methods can be used for this goal.

e. **Architecture validation:** This phase involves people from outside the architecting team that performs an objective assessment to ensure to which degree the architecture fulfills the requirements. Scenarios are commonly used to assist the assessment process. In other cases an architecture compliance checking process is used to validate the architecture against an existing system or prototype.

f. **Architecture documentation:** This last step is common to all software engineering projects and is used for documenting the products generated during the development phases. Documenting the architecture should not only comprise the final architecture, but also all the intermediated products generated in the process, as well as the design decisions that led to them. In addition, and because different stakeholders may have a different perspective of the system, different architecture views should be recorded and explicitly documented.

Figure 6 illustrates the ordered sequence of the steps previously discussed, which will be described in detail in next subsections.

The activities described before summarize the steps which are usually carried out during

Figure 6. Architecting activities and processes for building software systems. Reverse engineering and domain analysis activities can be optionally carry out.

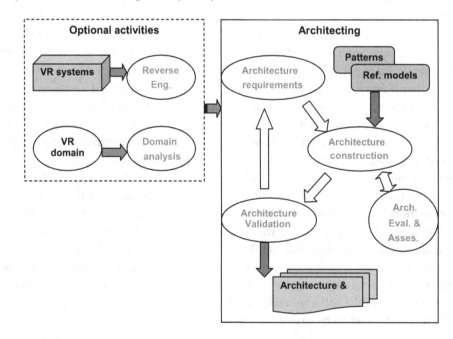

any architecting process. The level of expertise of the architects involved in the project is a factor to decide if some of these steps can be skipped or not and the number of iterations needed.

Analysis of the Virtual Reality Domain

Because most of the authors were novice in the virtual reality systems domain and before building the software architecture, we had to analyze the characteristics of the target domain as well as analyze the main characteristics of some VR systems. The strategy we selected to achieve the proposed goal was twofold. On the one hand we carried out a domain analysis process to understand the domain of interest. On the other hand we examined some source code from sample virtual reality applications to validate the results of the domain analysis process.

Domain analysis is used to understand and to identify the most important elements and their relationships in a given domain. The knowledge sources for executing the domain analysis process were obtained from experts in the domain as well as from existing documentation (e.g., existing technical books and Web pages of VR system construction, technical manuals from VR platforms). We interviewed three experts in the domain and we examined existing documentation to identify the relevant elements of the domain. As a result, we extracted a large list of elements (e.g., 3D objects, textures, virtual effects, avatars, etc.) and relationships. Both architects spent around 3 weeks collecting and organizing all the domain vocabulary to produce a preliminary domain model.

In order to validate the outcome of the domain analysis process, we examined existing source code from small virtual reality applications. In particular, we analyzed the following applications implemented in different languages: 5 VRML, 3 Java 3D, 4 C + OpenGL + FreeVR applications and 2 Multigen's Vega examples from the Multigen's

paradigm. We analyzed both immersive and non-immersive systems, but we didn't consider CAVE systems (Cave Automatic Virtual Environment is a visualization device where images are projected in the floor and walls) because they need a highly cost infrastructure not affordable for everybody. Also, we didn't include virtual reality engines because it is not the main focus for virtual reality application developers, and also because low level graphic operations are supported by specific development/platform environments. Reverse engineering tools can be used to analyze the source code and produce basic UML class models, but we decided to perform a manual inspection of the virtual reality applications because all the systems we analyzed were small and because we didn't find reverse engineering tools for VRML and FreeVR code. For instance, one of the results we obtained from the analysis activity is the typical structure of a Multigen's application, which served as a template for describing many virtual reality systems. Figure 7 shows some of the relevant parts of a typical Multigen's system.

One of the architects guided the analysis process of the source code, which was performed by two additional senior developers. This task took a bit more than 2 weeks and we used the results to validate the information defined in the domain model.

For instance, properties of the tridimensional objects and textures are classical elements used in VR systems that were identified in the domain analysis process and validated during the code inspection task. Figure 8 shows a brief portion of code of two virtual reality applications that match some of the elements identified in the domain analysis process. Tridimensional objects (e.g., a cube), materials, and properties of the 3D object like shape, appearance, or events were identified.

The domain model we obtained was the basis for the construction of the reference architecture and software architecture for the virtual church application, but prior to this, we analyzed the

Figure 7. Typical stucture of a Multigen's virtual reality application

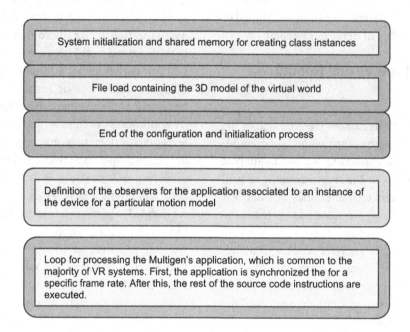

System initialization and shared memory for creating class instances

File load containing the 3D model of the virtual world

End of the configuration and initialization process

Definition of the observers for the application associated to an instance of the device for a particular motion model

Loop for processing the Multigen's application, which is common to the majority of VR systems. First, the application is synchronized the for a specific frame rate. After this, the rest of the source code instructions are executed.

Figure 8. Source code sample from two virtual reality systems

```
Group {
    children [
        DEF SENSOR TouchSensor {
        }
        DEF SELECT Switch {
            whichChoice 0
            choice [
                Group {
                    children IS inactive
                }
                Group {
                    children IS active
                }
RollOver {
inactive [
    Shape {
        appearance Appearance {
            material Material {
                diffuseColor 0.5 0.5 0.5 }
        }
DEF OFF_Z Script {
    eventIn SFBool bool_in
    eventOut SFInt32 choice_out
    url "vrmlscript:
    function initialize() {
        choice_out=0;
    }
```

```
/* initialize FreeVR routines */

vrStart();

/* set up the FreeVR library functions */
vrSetFunc(VRFUNC_ALL_DISPLAY,
vrCreateCallback(draw_world, 0));
/* do world simulation */
vrSleep(10000000); /* 10 seconds */
/* close up shop */
vrExit();
exit(0); }

void draw_world(void)
{
/* set the polygon shading parameters */
glShadeModel(GL_SMOOTH);
/* clear the screen */
glClearColor(0.0, 0.0, 0.0, 0.0);
glClearDepth(1.0);
glClear(GL_COLOR_BUFFER_BIT|GL_DEPTH_BUF-
FER_BIT);
/* draw a blue cube */
glColor3ub(100, 100, 255);
glTranslatef(-2.0, 1.0, -6.0);
draw_cube();
```

(a) VRML code
(b) C code with OpenGL and FreeVR routines

requirements for the target system to accommodate the final architecture to the customer needs. Also, quality requirements were considered before delivering the final architecture.

System Requirements

All software systems are built from a set of software requirements that represent the customer needs. The requirements specification document constitutes the starting point before any architecting process. In this section, we will not provide an extensive requirements list for the virtual reality church system because we preferred to concentrated on how the architecting activity and the solutions provided can be carried out. Instead, we will give an overview of the types of requirements identified and its relationship within to the construction of these systems.

Virtual reality systems usually include requirements specific of this kind of application. Such requirements mainly belong to the virtual world modeling and to the use of special hardware devices. As Table 1 shows, a big number of modeling requirements were identified for the virtual church system. The complexity of the virtual scenes, the degree of the realism needed, the interaction between the user and the 3D objects, and the visualization capabilities demanded, produces an extensive list of requirements related to such tridimensional modeling activities. This is true because virtual world designers need to spend a

Table 1. Type of requirements identified for the VR-church system

Requirement type	Number of requirements identified
Functional	28
Nonfunctional	5
Modeling requirements for the virtual scene	62
Hardware and platform-specific	6

lot of effort in this task in order to achieve the necessary degree of realism. The requirements for modeling the virtual world have a direct impact in the architecture because they organize the virtual objects in the scene, while functional requirements might impact the selection of appropriate classes and variation points used for building and configuring similar systems. In addition, nonfunctional requirements can be associated to:

- Hardware and platform requirements because of special graphical capabilities required;
- The performance of the system during rendering operations; and
- Usage of special hardware devices exclusively of virtual reality systems.

Moreover, distributed virtual reality applications may have impact in the number and type of the hardware nodes required for supporting the distribution feature, where several virtual users interact in the virtual scene at the same time (e.g., gaming applications). Because the virtual reality church application is a standalone system, no distribution requirements were defined. Once the requirements phase was completed, we started the architecting process, as we explain in next subsection.

Architecting Process

Software architectures are usually built under a set of project iterations in which intermediate architectural products. Each architectural solution represents a more refined design respect to its predecessor until the final architecture is delivered. One of the reasons for this work is to make explicit the transition to a modular architecture in that follows an object-oriented approach implemented, which is reflected in some parts of the UML diagrams that describe the architecture for the virtual reality church. The architecting task was performed by two architects who spent 3 weeks producing the final design.

First iteration: During the first iteration, the early design decisions made tried to decompose the architecture according to the typical structure of a virtual reality system, and a three layered architecture was used to organize the main functional parts. The higher layer represents the user interface that supports the interaction with the special hardware devices as well as the output displayed to the user. The middle layer represents the business logic of the target system, and the lower layer describes the engines for processing graphic operations.

Because architectures are often are combination of heterogeneous architectural patterns and styles, the layer architecture style was combined with Model-View-Controller (MVC) pattern to decouple the functionality offered by the user input (the Controller), the output (the View) and the logic of the application (the Model). The variety of hardware devices and initialization procedures are supported by means of the Controller class, which defines appropriate variation points implemented in the attributes and class methods. Also, another UML class was used to specify the different views a virtual reality system may offer. Figure 9 shows the first version of the architecture as explained.

The lower layer of the architecture was described using a pipe and filter architecture style for connecting the different graphic engines (not shown in Figure 9). To this point, we have to mention that we will focus only on the two higher layers of the architecture. The lowest layer will be considered a black box and its functionality will be supported by the current platform/environment because virtual reality engines are not the main concern for application developers. Therefore, we prefer to concentrate on those design issues that affect the construction of typical virtual reality applications. For the sake of simplicity, in the next architecture iterations we will only depict the higher abstraction levels of the architecture. The attribute DeviceType is used as a variation point to discriminate the type of the device in use, which is passed as a parameter to the initialization() method aimed for controlling the start-up of a particular device.

Figure 9. First intermediate architecture for the virtual church, which combines a three-layered style with the MVC pattern

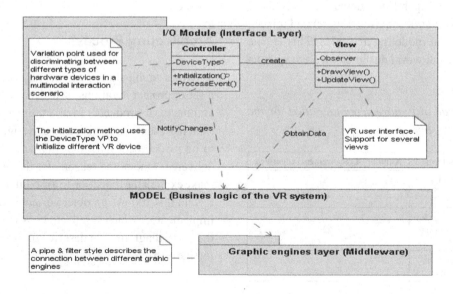

Second iteration: In the second iteration, we refined the architecture of Figure 9, adding more functionality to the middle layer in the form of UML packages and classes. The classes introduced in the architecture are the following. The package so-called 3DObjects comprises a set of classes that define a particular object hierarchy, which is needed by all virtual reality systems to represent the tridimensional objects in the scene. All virtual reality systems organize their objects in a particular hierarchy where some of these objects (and the faces that compose the objects) can be displayed or not. One root node organizes the hierarchy from the highest level to the lowest. Object groups can be defined to group logically similar objects. In addition to the object hierarchy, each particular system can define their own tridimensional effects, which are represented by the 3D Effects class. In the model, each single effect is described by a class which specifies its attributes and methods. Figure 10 represents the refine version of the previous architecture.

Figure 10. Second version of the architecture as a refinement of the previous design to include part of the functionality specified in the Model layer

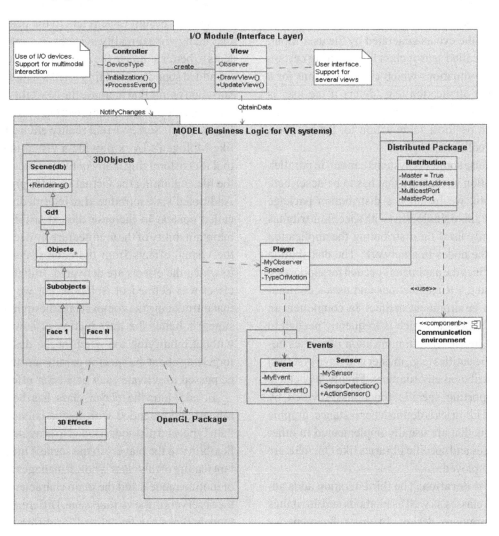

Furthermore, virtual reality systems use avatars to represent the virtual users in the scene. To support this we have introduced the player class. Players may have a different point of view in the virtual scene depending on where the observer is located. Some typical attributes used by the player are the speed and the type of the motion model (e.g., walk, fly).The attributes Speed and TypeOfMotion of the player class act as variation points for defining different speeds for the avatar and for selecting a new motion model when needed. This second attribute is particularly important to make the class more reusable for other types of virtual reality applications that might employ a different type of movement. Finally, the events package contains appropriate classes for handling the events generated by the user input, and a so-called sensor class for detecting certain events or situations which can be relevant for a particular application (e.g., detect if the user is approximating to a certain object in the scene and then perform some action to, for instance, avoid a collision).

Because some VR systems can run in parallel, distribution is a feature that has to be described. Therefore, we included a distribution package that contains a single class with specific attributes commonly used for distributing the application across the nodes in a network. The distribution class defines the parameters needed for supporting distributed VR applications and uses a communication environment artifact 8a component in the UML design) which is frequently needed to support low level communication processes between the entities (e.g., master and slave systems) in a distributed environment. Finally, a package for supporting specific functions provided by external libraries is defined. For instance, graphic functions that are usually implemented in other languages and specific libraries like OpenGL are often employed.

Third iteration: The third iteration adds additional classes as well as methods and attributes to the previous design. In this refinement we tried to exploit the commonality and variability of the system by introducing variation points at different parts of the architecture. The design decisions made in this level are mostly related to functional requirements, and the variation points introduced are used to increase the flexibility of the design. Figure 11 shows the reference architecture obtained in this step. The object hierarchy represented in the 3D objects package doesn't vary too much from its predecessor, except that we have introduced object groups for grouping related objects. As discussed in a previous section, these groups will have a strong impact in the organization of the virtual world as well as in the performance requirement.

Another design issue refers to the possibility that many virtual reality systems use special effects to better simulate the real world. In our case, we added sound and lighting effects with specific variation points that increase the flexibility for the configurable options of the effect (e.g., position for lights, type). Some virtual reality environments like Multigen's Lynx provide a visual interface tool for customizing many of these effects before the file containing the virtual world is produced. Additionally, we introduced an intermediate class called context to increase the extensibility and maintainability of the architecture by decoupling the virtual effects from the context conditions in which the effects are activated. Initially, each effect was defined in isolation, but we noticed that introducing the context class the architecture supports better the introduction of new effects without modifying too much of the design and forgetting about the specific parameters that have be passed to activate each particular effect.

In addition, the player class has been also refined and extended with new attributes (e.g., PathType) and methods needed to provide greater flexibility to the players in the scene. One important feature of this class is how it manages the type of motion models and the main characteristics of the observers in the virtual scene. Different motion models types can be defined for different types

Figure 11. Reference architecture for virtual reality systems

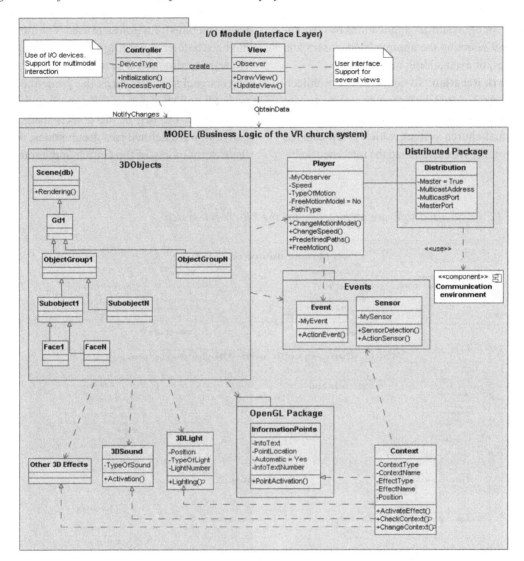

of applications (e.g., a flight simulator where the pilot uses a motion model that simulates the flight inside the cockpit).

Finally, the OpenGL package is used to display certain information on the virtual scene overlapping some of the virtual objects. This package includes now a class with specific attributes and methods for a particular functionality of the virtual church system. The aforementioned class activates text information points at specific locations inside the church, but it could also be reused for similar tourist applications. Several design decisions have been made to produce the architecture of Figure 11, which is the result of all the decisions made.

Also, some microrefinements for each single iteration were made affecting a particular class, method, or attribute. For instance, one small intermediate product was generated for connecting the virtual effects with the context class to provide the necessary flexibility for adding more effects in the future. This reference architecture can also be used for other similar applications by customizing and selecting the appropriated classes and packages, or even adding new ones.

Fourth iteration: To conclude the architecting process, we used the reference architecture of Figure 11 to produce the software architecture for the virtual church system, which is represented by Figure 12. We customized the reference architecture according to the system requirements and taking into account some additional features of the development environment used. The hierarchy has been tailored according to the particular world we want to simulate. The scene-graph of the 3D objects package introduces the predefined root node (db) of Multigen and the group node (gd1) from which the rest of the objects hang. Basically, we have defined two group nodes, one for the external view of the church and another for

Figure 12. Customized software architecture for the VR church system

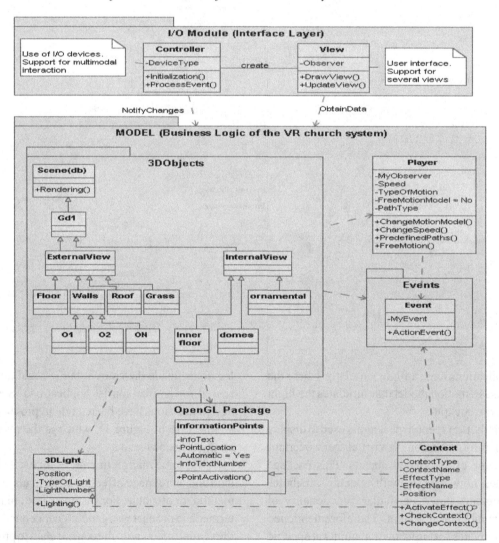

the internal view. Additional group nodes were added for grouping related objects belonging to the internal view (e.g., church benches, ornamental objects), but due to space reasons only a partial view of the hierarchy is shown. Each particular application may define their own object hierarchy, but the essence of this architecture piece (not explicitly documented before from the architecture point of view) is to reuse the object hierarchy for similar applications.

The lighting virtual effect was included in the final architecture, but we removed the virtual sound effect because it was not a system requirement. The OpenGL package is used to implement the text information points during the virtual tour, and a specific UML class has been included for this (i.e., InformationPoints class). Taking a look to the classes specified in the Events package, we didn't use any sensors, so we decided to remove it from the final design. The same applies for the distribution package because the VR church system is a standalone application, as defined in the requirements, and no distribution is required. The player class, used to define the observers for the virtual tour inside the church, contains the motion model employed during the visit, and implements the way in which the virtual user walks inside the church. Also, the variation points introduced in this class allow the user of the system to change the speed of the avatar, even to start and stop the visit at a certain point; read a particular information point; or even take a detailed view of the church from a specific location. As a summary, the reference architecture has been tailored and adapted for the virtual reality church system and according to the functionality specified in the system requirements. The architecting process took 4 iterations and 15 design decisions were made. Several alternatives were considered for some the decisions and also we evaluated the pros and cons (i.e., the implications) for each of the alternatives. According to the alternatives and to the requirements, the best decisions were selected for producing the final architecture.

Architecture Evaluation

During the architecting phase, several design decisions have to be made as part of the decision-making activity, but before selecting the best choice it often happens that we need to evaluate several alternatives before the final decision is selected. An evaluation process has to be carried out to determine the best design alternative or even to select between two or more candidate architectures. Different architectural evaluation methods like ATAM, SAAM or ARID (Clements, Kazman, & Klein, 2002) have been proposed and used in different case studies to prove that the architectural design decisions made, in particular for quality attributes, were the right ones. Nevertheless, virtual reality systems require, in many cases, simulation tasks to check the validity of the proposed design solutions. In our case we evaluated the architecture of the VR systems in two different ways. First, we did a pre-evaluation of the scene-graph. We modeled three different examples of small virtual worlds of the church belonging to the three alternatives described in Figure 3, and we measured the loading and rendering times. As a result, we discarded the first two possibilities and we decided to introduce object groups. In addition, we evaluate two additional alternatives, including object groups to know which configuration worked better according to the distribution of the objects under the groups. Two main object groups, one for the external object and one for the internal ones, and 14 intermediate group nodes were defined. Also, we limited the number of visible objects and faces to increase the performance of the loading time of the database object. The best configuration was that with 50% of polygons compared to the original design. In this particular case, we reduced the number of faces of the columns inside the church and we used simple textures for the floor and walls. This simulation task was quite important to meet the performance quality requirement.

Second, we evaluated the suitability of the variation points defined in the architecture to obtain modular and customizable routines compared to existing systems. The variability mechanism we applied was twofold: configuration directives in a separate file and function parameters with ranges of allowed values for each parameter representing the variation points defined in the architecture. The realization of the variation points in the code demonstrated that the initial configuration options, as well as the configurable run-time choices, increased the flexibility implemented in the system. Such configurable options increased the perception of that architects respect to the future maintenance of the system.

Architecture Views and Documentation

The design of every modern software system includes an architecture which has to be documented as a way to communicate this to other stakeholders. Because different stakeholders may be interested in different architectural views (Kruchten, 1995), software architectures are usually described by a set of viewpoints or view types (Clements, Bachman, Bass, Garlan, Ivers, Little, et al., 2003) which represent the interests of the different stakeholders. In the case of complex software systems, more than one architectural view is frequently needed to offer different perspectives for the variety of stakeholders involved in the development process. All these views belong to the architecture documentation, which can be shared and communicated to others. In addition and depending on each particular project, but not all the architecture views are needed. In our case study, we believed the following three architectural views (according to Hofmeister, Nord, & Soni, 2000), were needed to describe the architecture of the virtual church.

- **Conceptual view:** It describes the logical view of a software system and the main relationships between its components. We have represented this view using UML 2.0 classes and packages and depicted with the MagicDraw UML 10.5 tool. This conceptual view, including the intermediate products and the final architecture, is documented in Figures 9, 10, 11, and 12.

- **Module view:** An implementation diagram of the system describes the principal modules of the system. One module may correspond in the conceptual view to one or more components (e.g., classes) and connectors. Figure 13 describes the main modules and the relationships and dependencies among them. Two independent components initialize the virtual devices and load the database containing the virtual church. The component that loads the virtual church world uses an application definition file (ADF) which contains a description of some configuration parameters of the virtual world. The main loop of the program controls the remainder of the functionality of the application and continuously renders the scene to update the changes performed, for instance, the modification of the user's speed, lighting effects, or the appearance of information points. We can also see a specific component that implements the OpenGL graphic routines which is used by the information point component to display the text information points in the scene. As a result, the architect provides a view closer to the developer's perspective in such a way that the program can be structured in individual which gives a modular view of the system.

- **Execution view**: UML sequence diagrams (see Figure 14) are used to describe the behavior of a software system. In our case study, we believe describing the sequence of activities and interactions that happen during run-time in the virtual church system provides an interesting perspective to understand how virtual reality systems work. This

Figure 13. Component diagram showing the main modules that implement the functionality of the virtual church system

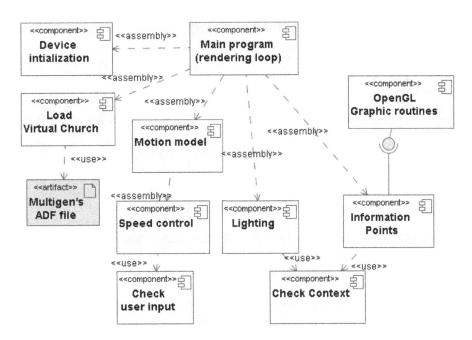

view provides insight to the stakeholders interested in it about the dynamic aspects of the system and gives a broader perspective to the other views that are more focused on structural and static properties. As we can see in Figure 14, at the beginning of the execution time, the devices and the virtual church are initialized and the user starts the virtual tour by pressing one of the buttons of the 3D mouse or tracker. The virtual scene is continuously rendered during the virtual tour because the avatar changes its position as it walks inside the church. During the visit staring in the central aisle of the church, the position of the user is checked to know when the virtual lights have to be activated or not. In addition and depending on the position of the user or when an ornamental object or historic place appears in front of the user, the system activates and displays the text information points indicating where

the user is and providing useful historical information to the visitor. By pressing the buttons of the mouse (or tracker) the user can stop and start the visit or increment the speed of the avatar. At the end, the visit terminates with one text information point indicating that the visit has finished.

Because the VR church is not a distributed system it didn't seem necessary to provide the deployment view of the system. Rather than this and complementary to the traditional architectural views, we have added a "new" view, so-called the **decision view** (Dueñas & Capilla, 2005) for documenting the design decisions and the rationale used to motivate the decisions made. This view crosscuts other existing architectural views and increases the value of the architectural documentation when architecture recovery processes are needed to replay to decisions made. We documented the decisions using the ADDSS tool

Figure 14. Sequence diagram that shows the interaction between the runtime entities during the virtual tour

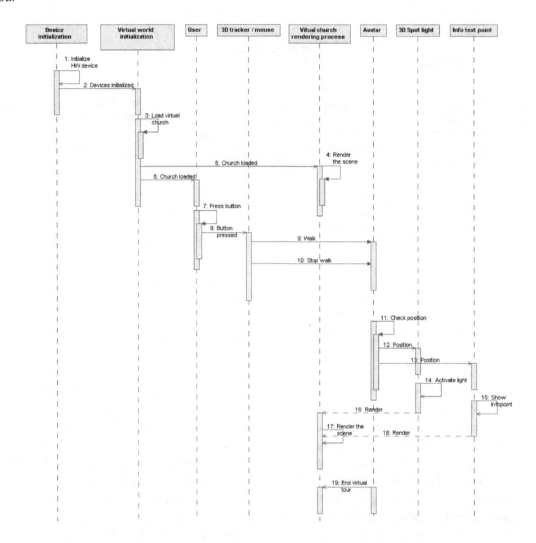

(Architecture Design Decisions Support System) as described in Capilla, Nava, Pérez, and Dueñas (2006). The current version of ADDSS generates automatically PDF documents containing the decisions made, the architectural products and the requirements, in such a way that traceability links between requirements and architectures can be established. Other approaches for documenting architectural views can be found in Clements, Bachman, Bass, Garlan, Ivers, Little, et al. (2003), as well as a more modern approach in Rozanski and Woods (2005).

As opposed to the traditional architecture views, the decision view doesn't have a particular graphical description because it represents and documents the design decisions made in the other views. These decisions and the rational that guides them are stored as a free text describing each single decision or combined with design patterns. Thus, no graphical description can be provided for this "decision view." The overall set of UML diagrams serve as a guide for developers to implement the main issues specified in the requirements, in particular the conceptual view of the architecture which explicitly describes the UML classes with attributes and methods and their relationship among them. The perception of virtual reality designers is that UML provides a good description for showing different architecture views with different degrees of detail that makes the system more understandable.

DISCUSSION

The experience in building the virtual reality church systems was at the same time successful and exciting, because most of the authors dealt with new challenges like architecting and implementing the user input with special hardware devices, and the modeling issues of the virtual world, which took a lot of time. In addition, defining and implementing the variation points for the virtual reality system was not easy at the beginning because the target language is mixed with OpenGL routines. The variability introduced in the architecture provided a greater flexibility to the system, in particular for the virtual visit inside the church. During the implementation phase, one key aspect of the virtual tour was to control both the speed of the avatar (not too slow and not too fast), the input using the mouse or tracker to start and stop the movement of the avatar, and in particular to compute the exact coordinates indicating the position of the avatar in order to avoid a collision with other virtual objects inside the church (e.g., benches, columns, etc.). In general, we believe that the specification of the routes and paths of virtual users consumes an important part of the implementation and testing phases. In our experience, we had to test several times to see which path was the right one to achieve a

complete visit to all the historical places of the church. In other cases, the user will miss some important information during the visit.

Other discussion from the lessons learned is as follows. First, we would like to discuss the convenience for using or not using UML as modeling language for describing the architecture of VR systems. In favor of this, we have to say that UML is a modeling language for software engineering which has been widely accepted by the software engineering community as a common vehicle for describing and communicating the architecture of systems. Other notations can be employed, but the benefit of using a standard is clear. In contrast we have to mention that UML is not powerful enough to describe all the modeling issues with enough detail, in particular those related to the description of the variability in the system. Moreover, UML was not designed to support and describe the decisions and the rationale that lead to a particular architecture.

Another issue refers to the modeling problems that have been addressed and solved in our case study. Some of the initial decisions we made led to produce a first version of the architecture that was too rigid. Therefore, we had to refactor some parts of the design to make it more flexible and adaptable against future changes. More specifically, and as an example, the variation points introduced in the attributes and methods of the UML classes, and the decoupling made in the UML classes for adding new virtual effects by only adding the class specific for that effect produced a more architectural architecture which seemed easy to maintain. Also, the selection of the best object hierarchy according to quality requirements represents a clear example of how we solved certain design issues specific to the construction of virtual reality systems as well as how UML helped us to document these issues which has not been documented before with enough degree of detail suing a software architecture approach.

Some additional details refer to the variation points defined in the architecture for handling the diversity of options specified in the requirements. For instance, part of the variation points can be modeled and configured using the Multigen's lynx tool. The remainder variations points were realized at code level using "if then else" constructions and function parameters that are activated depending on the context conditions and initial settings. Thus, virtual reality systems use the context information to activate (manually or automatically) the appropriate choices. This increases the flexibility of the system as well as the user's satisfaction. The evaluation of these variation points was done during the testing phase and also interviewing the users about the usability and satisfaction levels using the virtual church system. In summary, architects and developers can benefit using UML for documenting with enough degree of detail complex intensive systems, because it offers a modern description language able to represent most of the issues specified in the requirements. Other approaches used in the past could more or less produce similar descriptions, but one disadvantage is that such descriptions often do not follow a modern standard and also because the details are not explicitly shown in the design, and large text descriptions are needed to substitute the poorly documented graphic descriptions.

CONCLUSION

The construction of complex software-intensive systems needs a lot of effort during the development phase. The case of the design of virtual reality systems covered in this chapter differs from other types of software systems for two main reasons.

The first reason refers to the effort spent for modeling complex virtual worlds. Virtual games and complex simulator systems are examples that involve big teams with different skills during several months. The second reason comes from the programming issues associated to special hardware devices to provide the necessary inter-

action with the virtual world. The complexity of some of these special devices and the possibility for having multimodal user-input may complicate the development issues.

The topics covered in this chapter have tried to provide some guidance for designers and developers that have to deal with this class of systems. We have addressed some design problems specific to VR systems development using well-known architectural techniques and patterns that can be used to solve certain design issues like the scenegraph problem. Because software architectures have been proven as a successful technique to avoid monolithic approaches used in the past, we encourage the introduction of variation points in virtual reality systems development to facilitate the construction of similar applications. As a concluding remark we can say that software intensive systems still need a large amount of effort and interdisciplinary teams able to provide appropriate solutions for the variety of design and implementations issues, which many times are restricted by current development platforms.

FUTURE RESEARCH DIRECTIONS

The variety of technologies involved in the development of software-intensive systems needs an integration effort to combine the diversity of hardware and software technologies. The interoperability with emerging technologies in the Internet era (e.g., Grid computing) and the need for large scale systems, often distributed across different locations, constitutes a critical factor of success in the today's system development. Software architectures constitute the cornerstone for describing any successful software system, and the definition of evolvable architectures and architectures for interoperability is part of the ISIS (Integration of Software Intensive Systems) initiative (http://www.sei.cmu.edu/isis/) which seems an interesting approach to consider.

The virtual reality application domain covered in this chapter requires specific architectural solutions tailored for these kind of systems. For instance, the scene-graph problem and the multimodal interaction with special immersive hardware devices are clear examples we have addressed. Moreover, the right architecture has to meet its quality requirements and there is a need to count with simulation facilities already integrated with existing virtual reality development environments in order to test better the appropriateness of the proposed design solutions.

Because the development of virtual reality systems needs to bridge the gap between design and implementation, new design issues are needed. In this way, research on new architectural patterns for virtual reality systems is welcome. Another issue refers to count with specific tool support for the description and customization of the variation points that represent alternatives and customizable options of the target system, and software variability has been proven as an important modeling technique to produce system families under strong time to market conditions. Related to the variability of software systems, product line engineering (Bosch, 2000) approaches can also be considered as an interesting approach for building future virtual reality systems, by putting stronger emphasis on reuse as well as on the variability modeling for building similar products as a way to reduce the effort spent for each single application.

From a different perspective, domain-specific languages seem to be important for virtual reality development because many of the current environment and platforms are proprietary solutions, and virtual reality applications have special modeling characteristics that differ from other type of systems. Thus, domain-specific languages can play an important role for defining specific characteristics, in particular for modeling tridimensional worlds.

The popularity of recent research topics like service-oriented architectures for Internet ap-plications, is another research issue to explore. Some recent approaches try to introduce this ar-chitectural approach to the development of remote virtual reality systems, such as, for instance, in the telemedicine domain. This kind of tele-im-mersion for sharing virtual environment (Dang, Cheng, Jin, Yang, & Wu, 2005) can exploit the benefits of using Web services remotely to transfer the immersion experience to far locations under a distributed context.

Finally, the use of COTS (Common Off-the Self) components and open source software tech-nologies is an interesting alternative to explore for offering a different alternative to existing proprietary solutions.

REFERENCES

Alexandre, R.J. F., & Medioni, G. G. (2001). A modular software architecture for real-time video processing. In *Proceedings of the 2nd International Workshop on Computer Vision Systems*, (pp. 35-49).

Bass, L., Clements, P., & Kazman, P. (2003). *Software architecture in practice* (2nd ed.). Addison-Wesley.

Blach, R., Landauer, J., Rösch A., & Simon, A. (1998). A highly flexible virtual reality system. *Future Generation Computer Systems Special Issue on Virtual Environments 14*(3), 167-178.

Booch, G., Rumbaugh, J., & Jacobson, I. (2005). *Unified modeling language user guide* (2nd ed.). Addison-Wesley.

Bosch, J. (2000). *Design & use of software architectures*. Addison-Wesley.

Brügge, B. (2004). *Study on software architectures for augmented reality systems: Report to the AR-VIKA Consortium* (Tech. Rep. No. TUM-I0410). Germany: Technische Universität München.

Burmester, S., Giese, H., & Henkler, S. (2005). Visual model-driven development of software intensive systems: A survey of available tools and techniques. In *Proceedings of the Workshop of Visual Modeling for Software Intensive Systems*, (pp. 11-18).

Buschmann, F., Meunier, R., Rohnert, H., Sommerland, P., & Stal, M. (1996). *Pattern-oriented software architecture: A system of patterns*. New York: John Wiley & Sons.

Capilla, R., & Martínez, M. (2004). Software architectures for designing virtual reality applications. In *Proceedings of the European Workshop on Software Architectures* (EWSA 2004) (LNCS, pp. 135-147).

Capilla, R., Nava, F., Pérez, S., & Dueñas, J.C. (2006). A Web-based tool for managing architectural design decisions. In *Proceedings of the First Workshop on Sharing and Reusing Knowledge*, ACM Digital Library, Software Engineering Notes (Vol. 31, No. 5, pp. 1-8).

Clements, P., Bachman, F., Bass, L., Garlan, D., Ivers, J., Little, R., et al. (2003). *Documenting software architectures*. Addison-Wesley.

Clements, P., Kazman, R., & Klein, M. (2002). *Evaluating software architectures*. Addison-Wesley.

Dang, G, Cheng, Z.Q., Jin, S.Y., Yang T., & Wu, T. (2005). A service-oriented architecture for tele-immersion. In *Proceedings of the IEEE International Conference on E-technology, E-commerce, and E-services (EEE 2005)*, Hong Kong, China, (pp. 646-649). IEEE Computer Society.

De Antonio, A., Ramirez, J., Imbert., R., & Aguilar, R.A. (2005). A software architecture for intelligent virtual environments applied to education. *Rev. Fac. Ing. Universidad de Tarapaca, 13*(1), 47-55.

Dobrica, L., & Niemelä, E. (2003). Using UML notational extensions to model variability in product line architectures. In *Proceedings of the International Workshop on Software Variability Management, ICSE'03*, Portland, OR, USA, (pp. 8-13).

Dueñas, J.C., & Capilla, R. (2005). The decision view of software architecture. In *Proceedings of the 2nd European Workshop on Software Architecture (EWSA 2005)*, (pp. 222-230). LNCS 3047, Springer-Verlag.

Fernando, T., Murray, N., Tan K., & Wimalaratne, P. (1999). Software architecture for constraint-based virtual environment. In *Proceedings of the ACM International Symposium on Virtual Reality Software and Technology (VRST'99)* (pp. 147-154), London, UK.

Fritsch, C., Lehn A., & Strohm, T. (2002). Evaluating variability implementation mechanisms. In *Proceedings of the International Workshop on Product Line Engineering (PLEES'02)*, (pp. 59-64). IESE Report N° 056.02/E, 2002.

Gelenbe, E., Husain, K., & Kaptan, V. (2004). Simulating autonomous agents in augmented reality. *The Journal of Systems and Software, 74*, 255-268.

Hofmeister, C., Nord, R., & Soni, D. (2000). *Applied software architecture*. Addison-Wesley.

Hua, H., Brown, L.D., Gao, C., & Ahuja, N. (2003). A new collaborative infrastructure: SCAPE. In *Proceedings of IEEE Virtual Reality'03* (pp. 171-179).

Julier, S., King, R., Colbert, B., Durbin J., & Rosenblum, L. (1999). The software architecture of a real-time battlefield visualization virtual environment. In *Proceedings of IEEE Virtual Reality* (pp. 29-36). Houston, TX, USA.

Kruchten, P. (1995). Architectural blueprints. The 4+1view model of software architecture. *IEEE Software, 12*(6), 42-50.

Nadeau, D.R. (1999). Building virtual worlds with VRML: IEEE computer graphics and applications. *IEEE Computer Graphics (IEEECS)*, *19*(2), 18-29.

Oliveira, M., Crowcroft, J., Slater, M., & Brutzman, D. (1999). *Components for distributed virtual environments (VRST'99)*, London, UK, (pp. 176-177).

Pettifer, S., Cook, J., Marsh, J., & West, A. (2000). DEVA3: Architecture for a large-scale distributed virtual reality system (VRST'2000). ACM Press, 33-40, Seoul, Korea.

Pohl, K. (2003). Challenges for the design of software-intensive systems: Handling complexity and the two-way alignment between the business (problem) and the solution (software). In *Proceedings of the Workshop on the Science of Design*, Airlie Center, Dulles, VA, USA. Retrieved March 11, 2008, from http://www.cs.virginia.edu/~sullivan/sdsis/Program/Klaus%20Pohl.pdf

Reicher, T., MacWilliams, A., Brügge, B., & Linder, G. (2003). Results of a study on software architectures for augmented reality systems. In *Proceedings of the 2nd IEEE and ACM International Symposium on Mixed and Augmented Reality (ISMAR'03)*. IEEE.

Reitmayr, G., & Schmalstieg, D. (2001). An open software architecture for virtual reality interaction. In *Proceedings of VRST'01*, Banff, Alberta, Canada. ACM.

Rozanski, N., & Woods. E. (2005). *Software systems architecture*. Addison-Wesley.

Schäfer, W., Prieto-Díaz R., & Matsumoto, M. (1994). *Software reusability*. Ellis Horwood.

Schönhage B., & Eliëns, A. (1999). From distributed object features to architectural styles. In *Proceedings of the Workshop on Engineering Distributed Objects (EDO'99), International Conference on Software Engineering (ICSE)*, Los Angeles, CA, USA.

Schönhage, B., & Eliëns, A. (2000). Information exchange in a distributed visualization architecture. In *Proceedings of the Shared Concept Space of Distributed Objects Applications (DOA'00)*, Antwerp, Belgium.

Schönhage, B., van Ballegooij, A., & Eliëns, A. (2000). 3D gadgets for business process visualization. In *Proceedings of the International Conference on the Virtual reality Modeling Language and Web 3D Technologies*, Monterrey, CA, USA.

Shaw, M., & Garlan, D. (1996). *Software architecture*. Prentice Hall.

SysML. (2006). *Systems modeling language*. Retrieved March 11, 2008, from http://www.sysml.org/

ADDITIONAL READING

Alexander, C. (1979). *The timeless way of building*. Oxford University Press.

Azuma, R., Baillot, Y., Behringer, R., Feiner, S., Julier, S., & MacIntyre, B. (1999). Recent advances in augmented reality. *IEEE computer graphics and applications* (pp. 34-47). IEEE Computer Society.

Balzer, R. (1998). Wrapping COTS products to achieve large scale reuse. In *Proceedings of the 2nd European Reuse Workshop*, Madrid, Spain, (pp. 93-96).

Bass, L., Klein, M., & Bachmann, F. (2002). Quality attribute design primitives and the attribute driven design method. In *Proceedings of the 4th International Workshop on Product Family Engineering*, (pp. 169-186). Springer-Verlag, LNCS 2290.

Bauman, J. (2002). The perfect architecture is non-optimal. In *Proceedings of the 4th International Workshop on Product Family Engineering*, (pp. 248-257). Springer-Verlag, LNCS 2290.

Becker, M., Geyer, L., Gilbert A., & Becker, K. (2002). Comprehensive variability modelling to facilitate efficient variability treatment. In *Proceedings of the 4th International Workshop on Product Family Engineering*, (pp. 294-303). Springer-Verlag, LNCS 2290.

Bowman, D.A., & Hodges, L.F. (1999). Formalizing the design: Evaluation and application of interaction techniques for immersive virtual environments. *Journal of Visual Languages and Computing, 10*(1), 37-53.

Brooks, F.P. (1999).What's real about virtual reality. IEEE computer graphics and applications. *IEEE Computer Society*, 16-27.

Cohen, P., McGee, D., Oviatt, S., Wu, L., & Clow, J. (1999). Multimodal interaction for 2D and 3D environments. IEEE computer graphics and applications. *IEEE Computer Society*, 10-13.

Dikel, D.M., Kane, D., & Wilson, J.R. (2001). *Software architecture: Organizational principles and patterns*. Prentice Hall.

Gabbard, J.L., Hix, D., & Swan, J.E. (1999). User-centered design and evaluation of virtual environments. IEEE computer graphics and applications. *IEEE Computer Society*, 51-59.

Gamma, E., Helm, R., Johnson, R., & Vlissides, J. (1995). *Design patterns*. Addison-Wesley.

Hartling, P., Just, D., & Cruz-Neira, C. (2001). Distributed virtual reality using Octopus. In *Proceedings of IEEE Virtual Reality*, Yokohama (Japan), (pp. 53-60). IEEE Computer Society.

IEEE Recommended Practice for Architectural Description of Software-intensive Systems, IEEE Std. 1471-2000. (2000). Software Engineering Standards Committee, IEEE Computer Society.

Kim, G. (2005). *Designing virtual reality systems: The structured approach*. Springer-Verlag.

Lu, T., Lin, M., & Lee, C. (1999). Control mechanism for large-scale virtual environments. *Journal of Visual Languages and Computing, 10*(1), 69-85.

MacWilliams, A., Reicher, T., Klinder, G., & Bruegge, B. (2004). Design patterns for augmented reality systems. In *Proceedings of the International Workshop on Exploring the Design and Engineering of Mixed Reality Systems (IUI 2004)*, (pp. 64-71).

Medvidovic, N., Rosenblum, D.S., Redmiles, D.F., & Robbins, J.E. (2002). Modeling software architectures in the unified modeling language. *ACM Transactions on Software Engineering and Methodology, 11*(1), 2-57.

Poupyrev, I., Tan, D.D., Billinghurst, M., Regenbrecht, H., & Tetsutani, N. (2002). Developing a generic augmented-reality interface. IEEE Computer Society. *Computer, 35*(3), 44-50.

Reicher, T., MacWilliams, A., & Bruegge, B. (2003). Towards a system of patterns for augmented reality systems. In *Proceedings of the International Workshop on Software Technology for Augmented Reality Systems*, Tokyo, Japan.

Reitmayr, G., & Schmalstieg, D. (2001). An open software architecture for virtual reality interaction. In *Proceedings of ACM VRST'01*, Alberta, Canada.

Walczak, K., & Cellary, W. (2003). X-VRML for advanced virtual reality applications. *IEEE Software, 36*(3), 89-92.

Watson, B., Walker, N., Woytiuk, P., & Ribarsky, W. (2003). Maintaining usability during 3D placement despite delay. In *Proceedings of IEEE Virtual Reality*, (pp. 133-140).

Wilson, J.R., Eastgate, R.M., & D'Cruz, M. (2002). Structured development of virtual environments. In Netlibrary (Ed.), *Handbook of virtual environments: Design, implementations and applications* (pp. 353-377).

Zhai, S., & Woltjer, R. (2003). Human movement performance in relation to path constraint—the law of steering in locomotion. In *Proceedings of IEEE Virtual Reality*, (pp. 149-156).

Chapter IX
A Survey of Software Architecture Approaches

Kendra M. L. Cooper
The University of Texas at Dallas, USA

Lirong Dai
Seattle University, USA

Renee Steiner
Intervoice, Inc., USA

Rym Zalila Mili
The University of Texas at Dallas, USA

ABSTRACT

This chapter presents a survey of software architecture approaches. It is intended for a broad audience of students, practitioners, and researchers, in particular those who may be new to the area of software architecture. The chapter begins with a brief history of software architecture as a discipline. This is followed by a survey of established and emerging software architecture approaches. In the section on established approaches software architecture concepts are presented, which include software architecture views, decomposition strategies, description languages, and patterns; overviews of two established approaches (structured design and object-oriented design) are provided. In the section on emerging approaches, agent-, aspect-, and component-oriented approaches are included. For each of these approaches an overview, survey of the literature in the area, and a discussion are presented. The discussion includes current research issues in the community. The conclusions provide a summary of the chapter; future research directions follow.

INTRODUCTION

Software engineering has a number of established activities used in developing systems including requirements engineering, designing the software at multiple levels of abstraction, implementing, testing, and so forth. One of the design activities is to create a software architecture, which realizes the functional and nonfunctional requirements for the system. Today, a software architecture is generally understood to be a collection of components, which have externally visible properties (i.e., the provided services, performance characteristics, fault handling, shared resource usage, etc.) and the relationships among the components (Abowd, 1998; Clements, 2003; IEEE 1471, 2000; Shaw & Garlan, 1996). The concept of software architecture is beyond the algorithms and data structures of the computation and focuses on designing and specifying the overall system's gross organization and global control structure; protocols for communication, synchronization, and data access; assignment of functionality to design elements; physical distribution; composition of design elements; scaling and performance and selection among design alternatives.

The discipline of software architecture has its roots in the early work of Dijkstra (1968) and Parnas (1972), where the importance of well structured, or modularized, system was described. The term architecture was used by Brooks and Iverson in the 1960s (1969); they defined it as the "conceptual structure of a computer...as seen by the programmer." This work has made a clear distinction between the description of what each module should do and its implementation, a distinction that remains in place today. As the discipline matured, topics within software architecture have received substantial attention, including the definition of architectural styles, or patterns, architecture description languages, and approaches to analyze software architectures. A broad survey of the history of the discipline is available in Shaw and Garlan (2006), providing a

valuable organization and presentation of software architecture work. Due to its breadth, however, more recent architectures are not included (e.g., aspect-oriented architecture) or receive light treatment (e.g., agent- and service-oriented). This chapter proposes a complementary comparison, which surveys more recent approaches in more depth. Established approaches and three newer approaches (aspect-oriented, agent-oriented, and component-oriented architecture) are included. The three newer approaches have been selected based on the research interests of the authors; the survey is not exhaustive and could be extended in the future to include additional approaches, for example, supporting the design of dynamically adaptable systems.

Each of these emerging approaches included in the survey has been proposed to offer a distinct improvement to the established approaches. The aspect-oriented approach improves the ability to modularize capabilities, such as security, availability, and so forth, in an architecture that would typically crosscut many parts of a more traditional design; this improves the maintainability of the design. The agent-oriented approach improves the ability to model the social complexity of systems, as modern systems may need to operate in distributed environment composed of diverse, interacting business organizations that have their own goals and strategies. The component-oriented approach improves the ability to rapidly deploy high quality systems in order to meet the needs of quickly changing business environments. The approaches included in the survey for these emerging software architecture approaches have been selected because they provide a (standardized) reference model, a novel software architecture solution, or a software architecture methodology. This survey is expected to be of interest to students, researchers and practitioners, in particular those who may be new to the area of software architecture.

The remainder of this chapter is structured as follows. Established and recent approaches to software architecture are presented. The discussion on established software architecture approaches begins with a presentation of established software architecture concepts, including architectural views, modularization and decomposition of the architectures, architectural styles, and architectural description languages. This is followed by a presentation of two well-known approaches: structured- and object-oriented design. The recent approaches in the survey include agent-oriented, aspect-oriented and component-oriented. Conclusions and directions for future research are presented in the final two sections.

ESTABLISHED SOFTWARE ARCHITECTURE APPROACHES

Software architecture has been evolving as a discipline for over 40 years and is now an established activity in software engineering. The topic is covered in general software engineering books (Breugge, 2003; Pfleeger, 2006; Pressman, 2005; Sommerville, 2006) and a historical survey on the evolution of software architecture as a discipline is available (Shaw & Garlan, 2006). Although this discipline has been maturing, there are a large number of definitions for software architecture. For example, the IEEE Standard 1471 (IEEE 1471, 2000; Maier, Emery, & Hilliard, 2001) describes the software architecture as "the fundamental organization of a system, embodied in its components, their relationships to each other and the environment, and the principles governing its design and evolution." This standard is technology-free and does not propose concrete solutions for how to architect a software system. It does, however, provide a set of software architecture concepts with recommended practices. The standard places a strong emphasis on the relationships between stakeholders, their concerns and relevant architectural viewpoints. A definition that builds upon the IEEE's definition and considers the role of abstraction (i.e., externally visible properties)

in an architecture and multiple architecture views (structures of the system) has been proposed (Bass, Clements, & Kazman, 2003): "The software architecture of a program or computing system is the structure or structures of the system, which comprise software elements, the externally visible properties of those elements, and the relationships among them." Having multiple views is necessary to represent different, but related, characteristics of the architecture, such as the structure, behavior, and so forth. The composition of the structures into larger subsystems and the rationale for selecting a particular solution also need to be captured in the architecture. Recurring architectural problems have been recognized and solutions have been captured as reusable patterns. The notations used to represent the software architecture have also been investigated. Architecture description languages are languages specifically designed to formally represent a software architecture, more specifically, the components and their interactions. The formal representations support the rigorous verification and simulation of the architecture. Viewpoints (or views), decomposition strategies, patterns, and architecture description languages are now established concepts in software architecture; each of these is discussed below. In addition, two approaches to architecting a system are presented: structured and object-oriented design. Structured design dominated the discipline in the 1970s to the early 1990s; object-oriented design from the 1990s to the present.

Software Architecture Concepts

Software Architecture Views

To help manage the complexity of the software architecture and recognizing that a single definition of a software architecture is not adequate for all of the stakeholders, Krutchen (1995) proposed the use of multiple, concurrent views (Table 1). According to Krutchen's "4+1" View approach, the software architecture distinguishes between the logical, process, deployment, development, and use case views. Every view can have its own unique structure.

The logical view provides a decomposition of the system into subsystems and defines their interfaces. The subsystems collaborate to realize the system's requirements, which are captured in use cases. The process view of a system's architecture encompasses the threads and processes that form the system's concurrency and synchronization mechanisms. The performance, scalability and throughput of the system's architecture are considered here. The implementation view represents the components used to assemble and release the physical system. This view focuses on configuration management and software builds/releases. The deployment view shows the processing nodes (i.e., hardware) on which the system executes. This view focuses on the distribution and communication among the nodes. The use case view models the behavior of the system as seen by its external stakeholders, for example, end users.

Recently, an alternative set of views has been proposed (Clements et al., 2002). The three views are the module, component and connector, and the allocation. The module view is a structural view of the architecture, comprising the code modules such as classes, packages and subsystems in the

Table 1. "4+1" views of the architecture (Krutchen, 1995)

View	Description
Logical	defines the decomposition of and interactions among subsystems
Process	defines concurrency and synchronization mechanisms
Deployment	defines the mapping of the software onto processing nodes (hardware) and their interactions
Development	Defines the software's static organization in the development environment
Use Case	Scenarios (instances of use cases) are defined to help discover architectural elements and validate the architecture

design. It also captures module decomposition, inheritance, associations and aggregations. The component and connector view describes the behavioral aspects of the architecture. Components are typically objects, threads or processes, and the connectors describe how the components interact. Examples of connectors include sockets, middleware (e.g., CORBA), and shared memory. The allocation view shows how the processes in the architecture are mapped to hardware and how they communicate (e.g., using networks, databases, etc.). It also captures a view of the source code under configuration management and who is responsible for the modules of code.

Decomposition Strategies

The decomposition of a system can be accomplished using a variety of techniques. Five approaches to decompose a system, presented in Wasserman (1996), are functional, event, data, outside-in, and object-oriented. These decomposition approaches can be used alone or in combinations. Several of the strategies base the decomposition of the system using an external, more interface driven approach (event, data, outside-in). An event-oriented approach uses events, for example, signals from sensors, to modularize the components. An outside-in approach uses user input to modularize the components. A data-oriented approach uses the format and content of external data, for example, provided by a database, to modularize the components. Each subsystem is decomposed to provide more detailed explanations. For example, in a data-oriented decomposition, the high-level components describe the more general data structures; lower-level components define the data elements and their relationships. The remaining two approaches, functional and object-oriented, are less focused on decomposing the system based on external entities. These approaches focus on providing capabilities by using a functional or an object-oriented decomposition. In the functional decomposition, each subsystem is decomposed and provides more detailed explanations of the functional capabilities it provides. In the object-oriented decomposition, classes of objects and their relationships are used to modularize the components.

Architecture Patterns

As software architecture has matured, recurring architectural problems have been identified and solutions have been proposed and cataloged as architectural patterns (Buschmann, Meunier, Rohnert, Sommerlad, & Stal, 1996). The problem-solution pair documents that exist are well-proven design experience that can be re-used, not only by experts, but by less experienced people as well. Architectural patterns identify and specify abstractions that are above the level of single classes and instances or of component. They provide a common vocabulary that improves the architects' ability to communicate and understand the system; they also provide a means of documenting the software architecture. Architecture patterns help in the construction of software with defined properties, for example, maintaining the consistency between cooperating components or providing transparent peer-to-peer interprocess communication. As architecture patterns can be used like building blocks, high quality software architectures for complex software can be assembled rapidly.

Architectural patterns (Buschmann et al., 1996) have been grouped and presented in four categories: structure, distributed systems, interactive system and adaptable systems (Table 2).

A pattern is specified by describing its components and their responsibilities in addition to their relationships and collaborations. The elements of a pattern definition include: name, context, problem, forces, solution, strategies, benefits and drawbacks and related patterns. Part of the Layers architectural pattern, based on Buschmann's definition (Buschmann et al., 1996) is presented in Box 1 as an example.

Table 2. A catalog of architectural patterns (Buschmann, 1996)

Category	Pattern
Structure	Layers Pipes and Filters Blackboard
Distributed Systems	Broker
Interactive Systems	Model-View-Controller Presentation-Abstraction-Control
Adaptable Systems	Reflection Microkernel

Box 1.

Name: Layers
Context: A large system that requires decomposition.
Problem: A system has a mix of high-level (e.g., complex graphical user interface) and low-level (e.g., reading sensor data) issues. Requests typically move from high level to low level; responses flow in the opposite direction.
Forces:
Parts of the system should be replaceable.
Interfaces should be stable.
Changes in one part of the system should not ripple to other parts.
Similar responsibilities should be grouped together to improve understandability and maintainability.
Complex components may have to be decomposed.
Crossing component boundaries reduces performance.
Parts of the system should be straightforward to allocate to teams for design, implementation and testing (internal or external).
Solution: Structure the systems into groups of components that form layers. The lowest layer is numbered 1; the top layer is N. The upper layer uses services of the layer below it. For example, Layer N uses the services of Layer N-1, Layer N-1 uses Layer N-2, and so forth.
...

New patterns continue to be proposed as problems and their solutions are distilled by experts. For example, patterns have recently been proposed for architecting adaptable, agent, aspect, component, and service-oriented systems (Birov, 2004; Muller, Braun, & Kowalczyk, 2005; Parsons, Rashid, Telea, & Speck, 2006; Stal, 2006).

Architecture Description Languages

Architects need to describe and reason about the software architecture they are developing. Semiformal languages, such as the Unified Modeling Language (UML) (OMG, 2004) have been used to model software architecture. UML is a well-known modeling language, used for specifying, visualizing, constructing, and documenting designs of software systems. UML provides graphical notations to express the design of software systems with semiformal syntax and semantics, and an associated language, the Object Constraint Language (OCL), for expressing logic constraints. Due to the semiformal foundation of the language, UML does not support the rigorous analysis of the software architecture for errors with automated tool support (e.g., type-checkers, model-checkers, etc.). The analysis of the software architecture is important, as errors detected earlier in the software development lifecycle require less time and cost less to correct. A software architecture captured in UML needs to be manually reviewed by experts. This is a time consuming activity that is costly and prone to human error.

Architecture description languages (ADLs) and their toolsets have been proposed as solutions to this problem. ADLs can be used to formally represent a software architecture, more specifically the components and their interactions; their toolsets can aid in analyzing the architecture for errors using verification and simulation techniques. Numerous ADLs have been proposed, including Rapide (Luckham et al., 1995), Armani (Monroe, 1998), Æmilia (Balsamo, Bernardo, & Simeoni, 2002), Wright (Allen, 1994), Aesop (Garlan, Allen, & Ockerbloom, 1994), and ACME (Garlan, Monroe, & Wile, 1995), an ADL interchange language. Recent surveys of ADLs are available (Clements, 1996; Fuxman, 2000); a framework for classifying and comparing ADLs has also been proposed (Medvidovic & Taylor, 2000). Three key elements are available in ADLs: components, connectors, and configurations. A component is a unit of computation or a data store. A connector is used to model interactions among components and rules that govern those interactions. A configuration is a graph of components

and connectors that describe the structure of the software architectural.

The work in Clements (1996) summarizes common features discovered in the ADLs they surveyed. The ADLs had a graphical syntax, provided support for modeling distributed systems, handled data and control flows as interconnection mechanisms, could represent hierarchical levels of detail, could instantiate multiple instances of templates to quickly copy substructures, and provided support for the application engineer (many with upfront analytical capabilities).

Software Architecture Approaches

Structured

Structured design is an early family of methodologies used to architect a system. These techniques use a functional decomposition strategy to define the overall structure and behavior of a system. The origins of structured design are in the early 1970s at IBM, led by Edward Yourdon, Larry Constantine, Glenford Myers and Wayne Stevens. Numerous variations have been proposed, and comprehensive surveys of structured design techniques are available (Page-Jones, 1988; Yau & Tsai, 1986; Wieringa, 1998). This family of design approaches dominated the community until the early 1990s. The approach by Yourdon and Constantine (1979) is a classic example.

The structured design approach by Yourdon and Constantine consists of the following high-level steps (Yau & Tsai, 1986). First, the flow of data in the system is identified and represented in a data flow graph. Second, the incoming, central, and outgoing transform elements and identified and factored out to form a hierarchical program structure, or high-level design. This design is represented using a structure chart. Third, the structure chart is refined and optimized. Last, the logic for each module in the structure chart is developed.

The structure charts illustrate the following information about a system in a visual format:

- Functional decomposition of a system into named modules,
- Top-down hierarchy and organization of modules,
- Links between modules, and
- Flow of data, control and exception information.

Modules in a structure chart represent sequences of program statements. The graphic symbol is a box; each module has a unique name, or identifier. Directed arcs from a calling module to a called module show the structure of the software. Input and output parameters are provided as labels near the arcs. Open circles at the parameter arrow tail denote data and closed circles show control. Repetitions, or loops, are indicated with an arc that starts and ends in one module box; the arc crosses the called modules involved in a loop. A diamond at the bottom of a module box indicates a decision point in the design.

As object-oriented programming languages gained popularity in the mid 1980s (e.g., Ada, C++), the structured design approaches did not provide a clean mapping from the design to the implementation. Functionally decomposed designs needed to be remapped into an object-oriented implementation. Object-oriented design techniques were proposed to provide a simple, clear mapping from the design to the implementation.

Object-Oriented

The object-oriented paradigm is a more recent family of methodologies used to architect a system. These techniques modularize objects and their relationships to define the overall structure and behavior of a system. The origins of object-oriented design are in the 1980s, led by Abbott (1983) and Booch (1983). Numerous variations

have been proposed; surveys in Capretz (2003) and Wieringa (1998) consider over 20 approaches. This family of design approaches currently dominates the community. A widely-used approach to architect a system is the Rational Unified Process (RUP) (Kroll & Krutchten, 2003; Rational Unified Process Workbench, 2007).

RUP is a comprehensive, object-oriented software engineering process model, which is based on a set of software development principles and best practices. The set of principles and best practices includes: develop software iteratively, manage requirements, visually model software (using UML), verify software quality, and control changes to software. RUP is an architecture-centric approach, which incorporates the "4+1" views (Krutchen, 1995) and promotes the use of a component-based architecture. The use of a component-based architecture creates a system that is easily extensible, intuitively understandable and promotes software reuse.

RUP is based on a set of building blocks, or content elements, describing what is to be produced, the necessary skills required and the step-by-step explanation describing how specific development goals are achieved. These building blocks are organized in an iterative process that has four phases: inception, elaboration, construction and transition. The main building blocks, or content elements, include roles, work products, and tasks. The roles define a set of related skills, competencies, and responsibilities, such as a designer. The work products include the documents and models produced while working through the process. The tasks describe a unit of work assigned to a role. Within each iteration, the tasks are categorized into engineering disciplines (business modeling, requirements, analysis and design, implementation, test, deployment) and supporting disciplines (configuration and change management, project management, environment).

The architecture is defined and refined iteratively in the analysis and design discipline, primarily during the elaboration and construction phases. The analysis and design discipline defines a set of activities; the principal ones include:

- Defining a candidate architecture,
- Analyzing the behaviors identified in the requirements, and
- Designing the components of the system.

The main artifact used to document the software architecture is called the Software Architecture Document (SAD). It is used to gather and communicate all of the architectural decisions made during the elaboration phase. A template for this document is available (IBM, 2007); it is structured around the "4+1" views of the architecture.

EMERGING SOFTWARE ARCHITECTURE APPROACHES

Agent-Oriented Software Architecture

Multi-agent System (MAS) combine local behavior, autonomy, mobility and distributed decision-making to form efficient and flexible architectures. Furthermore, MAS consists of agents acting and reacting within an environment made up of a set of passive objects that can be perceived, created, destroyed and modified by agents. Whether or not, and to what extent agents cooperate is defined in the agent itself; however, the whole point of MAS is so agents can form emerging relationships with other agents in order to satisfy their desires (Mili, 2004).

The following definitions are integral to understanding agent systems:

- **Agent:** An agent is a computer system that is situated in some environment, and that is capable of autonomous action in this environment in order to meet its design objectives (Wooldridge, 2002).

- **Environment:** In situated MAS, the environment is an active entity with its own processes that can change its own state, independent of the activity of the embedded agents (Weyns, Parunak, & Michel, 2005).

- **Multi-agent system (MAS):** A MAS is a system that consists of a number of agents, which interact with one another. Agents interact on behalf of users with different goals and motivations. To successfully interact, they require the ability to cooperate, coordinate, and negotiate with each other (Wooldridge, 2004).

- **Multi-agent simulation system (MASS):** A computer simulation is the discipline of designing a model of an actual or theoretical physical system, executing the model on a digital computer and analyzing the execution output. A MASS is a computer simulation specifically for MAS (Drogoul, Vanbergue, & Meurisse, 2003; Fishwick, 1996).

Agent-oriented architectures take advantage of object-oriented principles such as encapsulation, data protection, and abstraction. However, there are characteristics that can best be represented using agent orientation, such as sociality, cooperation, communication, mobility, and self-interest. For example, communication needs are sometimes best served using an event-based or implicit invocation method which is not present in pure object-oriented systems. Agents are more autonomous than objects because they represent a whole, whereas objects are generally a part. Agents have more flexible behavior and are reactive, proactive and social, whereas objects do not possess these qualities. Also, agents have at least one thread of control; objects are not required to have a thread at all.

AOSE methodologies, based in OO (i.e., Gaia (Zambonelli, Jennings, & Wooldridge, 2003), Message (Evans et al., 2001), and MaSE (DeLoach, 2006)), have attempted to extend the principles

Figure 1. Genealogy of proposed methodologies (Sudeikat, Braubach, Pokahr, & Lamersdorf, 2004)

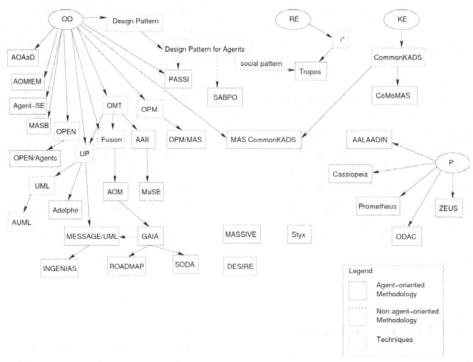

with processes and notation that address agent specific concepts.

Overview of Agent-Oriented Approach

The agent-oriented paradigm was born from several different disciplines namely, artificial intelligence, social science, and software engineering. Given the multidisciplinary beginnings of the technology, it should be no surprise that methodologies to support agent-orientated systems are just as diverse. Agent methodologies have evolved from object orientation, requirements engineering, knowledge engineering and procedural methodologies (Figure 1).

Survey of Agent-Oriented Architecture Approaches

In this section, we present a general architecture and several specific agent-oriented architecture approaches.

Agent Technologies

Many agent architectures are based on a standard specified by the Foundation for Intelligent Physical Agents (FIPA) (FIPA, 2005). FIPA is an IEEE Computer Society standards organization that promotes agent-based technology and the interoperability of its standards with other technologies. The FIPA abstract architecture (Figure 2) and the FIPA Agent Management Reference Model (Figure 3) are core concepts for FIPA.

Likewise, a key concept to FIPA and agent-oriented systems is the Agent Lifecycle (Figure 4). It serves as a reference as to why other non-agent-oriented methodologies are insufficient to fully describe the complexities of MAS.

Another strong concepts in many MAS and represented in some methodologies is described in the literature especially works by Ferber. In Ferber (1999) and Ferber and Michel (1996), Ferber presents an agent-environment model based on the principles of influences and reaction. Once agents execute actions, they produce

Figure 2. FIPA Abstract Architecture and Relationship with Concrete Architecture Elements (FIPA, 2007)

Figure 3. FIPA agent management reference model (FIPA, 2007)

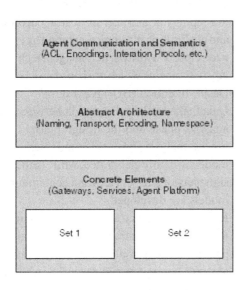

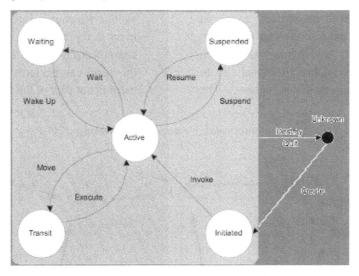

Figure 4. Agent lifecycle (FIPA, 2007)

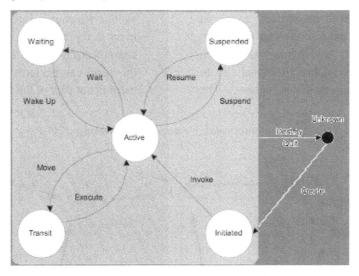

influences that are synchronously communicated to the environment. The environment interprets these influences, reacts to them, and changes its state. The new state is then synchronously communicated to the agents. In this manner, all agents have the same information about the environment at the same time.

Many of the methodologies use UML and AgentUML (AUML) as their notation. AUML began as the result of collaboration between FIPA and the Object Management Group (OMG) (Bauer, Muller, & Odell, 2001). Their goal was to increase industry acceptance for agent technology while leveraging UML whenever possible. AUML was intended to serve as a notation for agent concepts that could not be modeled concisely using only UML. Typical concepts that are difficult to model in UML include the following:

- Organization-based concepts such as roles and membership
- Agent goals
- Communication and collaboration among multiple entities
- Active, dynamic behavior

Agent-based Software Architecture Methodologies

- **Gaia:** Gaia is an organizational-based methodology with an object-oriented influence (Zambonelli et al., 2003). This means that emphasis is placed on defining agents in terms of the organizations that they form and the roles they hold in that organization. This organizational structure results in an architecture that resembles Figure 5. The

general purpose of organizations is to allow agents to work collectively to achieve some common community goal.

The Gaia architects pay particular attention to keeping the architecture abstract in order and not limiting the implementation by tying it too closely with a particular agent technology (e.g., agents which are based on a Belief Desire Intention (BDI) paradigm).

Gaia makes a clear distinction between the analysis phase and the design phase. During the analysis phase, roles and interaction models are fully elaborated, while in the design phase agent services and acquaintance models are developed.

Recently, Gaia has added the environment to its primary abstractions in the analysis phase. The environment is treated as an abstract computational resource in which it is made available to the agents for sensing, affecting and consuming (i.e., Ferber influence/reaction model). To facilitate the agent/environment interaction, the environment is represented as a list of resources characterized by the type of actions that the agent can perform on it. The environment is not part of the architectural design

Figure 5. Multiagent systems as computational organizations (Jennings, 2001)

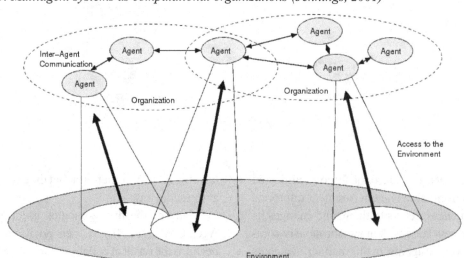

phase because it is considered too related to the underlying technology and, according to the Gaia team, to design it properly would break the proposed generality of the architecture.

- **MESSAGE/UML:** MESSAGE (Methodology for Engineering Systems of Software Agents) (Evans et al., 2001) is a methodology with an object-oriented influence that covers both analysis and design phases of the development lifecycle. The notation used in MESSAGE is based on UML and AUML as appropriate.

  MESSAGE is also organizational-based, but also includes in its core concepts that of an InformationEntity and a Message. An InformationEntity is simply an object which encapsulates data, while a Message is an object communicated between agents that requires an action to be taken by both the sender and receiver. The InformationEntity

is the closest entity to the concept of environment for MESSAGE: it has no responsibilities but contains partial information about the state of the system.

In the analysis phase, MESSAGE defines the following views which are not completely orthogonal but have overlapping subsets of entity and relationship concepts:

- o Organization view (OV)
- o Goal/Task view (GTV)
- o Agent/Role view (AV)
- o Interaction view (IV)
- o Domain view (DV)

During analysis, these views are refined in an iterative approach. A sample Interaction diagram is shown in Figure 6.

- **MaSE:** The MaSE (Multiagent Systems Engineering) methodology provides a multi-step process for developing MAS (Deloach, 2006). During analysis, use cases and application goals/subgoals are defined as well as agent interactions and their roles. With

Figure 6. MESSAGE sample interaction diagram

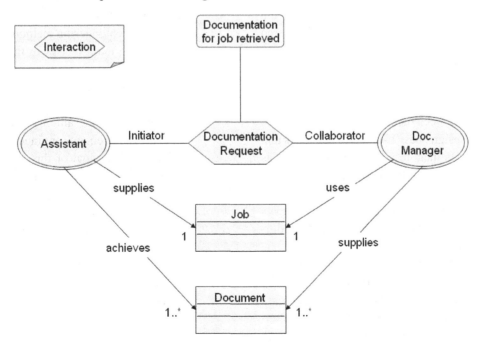

the results of the analysis phase as input, the design phase produces agent classes and agent interaction protocols. However, while it allows for the definition of roles, MaSE does not define any higher organizational abstraction. Because there are no organizational abstractions, the design phase cannot produce any organizational structure; therefore, the definition of the organization is implicitly derived from the analysis phase. This makes MaSE suitable only for closed agent systems. The developers of this methodology are "investigating techniques to allow multiagent teams to design their own organization at runtime" (DeLoach, 2006). This would allow the system to be dynamic, and able to handle more complex scenarios.

The analysis phase of MaSE is responsible for producing a set of roles that can service system level goals. This process includes three steps:

o **Capturing goals:** This involves extracting goals from the requirements document.

o **Applying use cases:** In this step, the goals produced by the previous step are refined into use-cases.

o **Refining roles:** This final step produces a Role Model, which describes system roles and the communication between them.

The design phase takes roles and tasks and converts them to a form that can serve as input to the implementation phase. It is composed of the following four steps:

o **Construction of agent classes:** Agents and their relationships are defined during this step.

o **Constructing conversations:** This step produces the communication design for agents. Conversations are modeled as a pair of finite state automata and are similar to concurrent tasks.

o **Assembling agent classes:** During this step, detailed agent class diagrams are produced.

o **Deployment design:** This step defines the system configuration with respect to the quantity of agents, types of agents, and the deployment platform.

MaSE has several open research items. One topic is to provide a mechanism for agent/environment communication. Currently, there is no provision for an environment as a primary abstraction or for communicating with agents. Another open topic is to make provisions for dynamic organizations. Organizations are currently fixed and agents tend to maintain limited roles and have little ability to alter the roles.

• **Tropos:** The Tropos methodology has a strong basis in the organizational metaphor for BDI agents (Bresciani, Petrini, Giorgini, Giunchiglia, & Mylopoulos, 2004). A concept which sets Tropos apart is the strong emphasis on the early requirements analysis phase. Tropos sees that phase as crucial to developing agent systems. This emphasis is expected given that Tropos is derived from requirements engineering methodologies. There are five main phases in the Tropos methodology:

o **Early requirements:** This phase is unique to the typical software engineering lifecycle, although it is known to the requirements engineering community. The goal of this phase is to determine the domain stakeholders, model them as actors and determine their dependencies. A dependency could be goal-, plan- or resource-related.

o **Late requirements:** In this phase, the system is added to the conceptual model and dependencies are defined for all functional and nonfunctional requirements.

o **Architectural design:** This phase takes as input the deliverables from the requirements phases to produce a system specification.

o **Detailed design:** This phase specifies the agent's capabilities and interactions.

o **Implementation:** This is a typical software engineering implementation phase which takes as input the detailed design and produces a functioning system.

While Tropos uses an organizational metaphor, it does not define organizational rules. This tends to make the implementation difficult because it is left up to the developer to decide what the rules should be. In this way, the analysis phase trivializes the importance of global rules in MAS.

Discussion on Agent-Oriented Architecture Approaches

Four agent oriented architecture approaches have been presented here along with general concepts that are regarded as standard in the agent community. The approaches have varying degrees of emphasis on the organizational metaphor but all agree it is a necessary part in defining a successful architecture for MAS.

Since MAS combine local behavior, autonomy, mobility and distributed decision-making to form efficient and flexible architectures, they stand to become the natural successor to object orientation. Also, given that agents cooperation is defined in the agent itself and, agents can form emerging relationships with other agents in order to satisfy their desires, agent orientation is well suited to system where non-deterministic behavior is desired.

However, given the relative newness of this paradigm, there are many research topics open. One topic involves the acceptance of the environment as a primary abstraction in MAS. Gaia is

the only presented approach that considers the environment a primary abstraction however; the community is beginning to realize that separating the environment and agent concerns is an important part of the evolution of MAS. Although, this concept is gaining wider acceptance, many issues still need to be solved. For example, AUML has no notation specifically for the environment.

Furthermore, agent orientation is in its childhood if not its infancy and there are many opportunities to utilize these methodologies to create a flexible and dynamic system that could drive an industry to develop new products based on, and supporting this, technology.

Aspect-Oriented Software Architecture

Overview of Aspect-Oriented Approaches

Aspect-oriented programming (AOP) is a new programming technique, which is proposed to deal with increasing various kinds of design concerns that cannot be captured (i.e., modularized) cleanly within source code in object-oriented programming (OO) (Elrad, Filman, & Bader, 2001). An example of such concern is "logging," which is frequently used in distributed applications to aid system debugging. One typical scenario of using logging is tracing function calls at the beginning and end of each function body. This could result in the logging functionality crosscutting all classes that have at least one function. Other crosscutting concerns include error handling, performance optimization, memory management, and so forth. Associated costs of tangled code include that they are difficult to understand and change, they increase with the size of the system, and consequently, the system maintenance cost becomes huge. The idea of AOP is that a software system is better programmed by separately specifying the various concerns (properties or areas of interest) of the system, and then relying on mechanisms in the underlying AOP environment to weave or compose these concerns together into a coherent system (Elrad et al., 2001). In AOP, core functionalities of the system (i.e., those that can be cleanly modularized) are implemented in an object-oriented language (e.g., Java) and crosscutting concerns are separated into single units called aspects. Finally, both the OO code and aspects are combined into a final executable form using an aspect *weaver*. An aspect encapsulates behaviors that affect multiple classes into reusable modules, and as a result, this increases both reusability and maintainability of source code.

AspectJ is one aspect-oriented programming language available. Components of AspectJ include join points, pointcuts, and advices. An aspect example in AspectJ is presented in Figure 7. In AOP, join points represent well-defined points. Pointcut is a language construct that picks out a set of join points based on defined criteria. Advice is used to define additional code to be executed before, after, or around join points. An aspect class includes a set of pointcuts and advices.

The issue of separation of concerns does not only appear in the implementation stage of the software development lifecycle. Recently, much attention has been focused on how to build nonfunctional requirements into software systems from the beginning. In general, nonfunctional requirements are constraints on various attributes of functions or tasks a system must support. Examples of nonfunctional requirements are performance, security, reliability, usability,

modifiability and so forth (Keller, Kahn, & Panara, 1990). As an early phase of the software lifecycle, it is widely recognized that decisions made at the architecture design stage have a strong impact on the quality of the final product (Shaw & Garlan, 1996). Hence, to provide a positive impact on the realization of a system's nonfunctional requirements, these requirements need to be designed and analyzed in architecture designs. However, many nonfunctional requirements, such as performance, security, and so forth, are global requirements and their design tends to crosscut many design elements at the architecture design level. This crosscutting reduces the established metrics for a "good" object-oriented design, as it decreases cohesion and increases coupling. A significant result of this is the object-oriented design with the crosscutting elements, which is more difficult to maintain and extend over time.

The positive results obtained by researches on aspect-oriented programming during the last few years are promoting the aim to export AOP ideas to the design of nonfunctional requirements in software architectures. The integration of architecture design and aspect orientation has been realized as one of the promising approaches to deal with the problem of crosscutting concerns modeling (Filman, Elrad, Clarke, & Aksit, 2005; Krechetov, Tekinerdogan, Garcia, Chavez, & Kulesza, 2006). With aspect-oriented architecture, a system's tangling concerns (e.g., nonfunctional

Figure 7. An AspectJ example

```
public aspect MyAspect {
        public pointcut sayMethodCall (): call (public void TestClass.sayHello() );
        public pointcut sayMethodCallArg (String str): call (public void TestClass.sayAnyThing (String)) && args(str);
        after(): sayMethodCall() {
            System.out.println("\n TestClass." + thisJoinPointStaticPart.getSignature().getName() + " end..."); }
        before(String str): sayMethodCallArg(str) {
            if (str .length() < 3) { System.out.println ("Error: I can't say words less than 3 characters");
12:  return; }
13: } }
```

requirements) are encapsulated in model element called an *aspect*. Subsequently, a *weaving* process is employed to compose core functionality model elements (those realize the system's functional requirements) with these aspects, thereby generating a complete architecture design. Integration of aspect orientation into software architecture would make the design and analysis of complex systems an easier task, while the costs of system development and maintenance would be reduced and software reusability would be improved. In summary, the benefits of aspect-oriented architecture include:

- Aspect-oriented approaches facilitate the process of capturing nonfunctional requirements in an architecture design by providing architects with a new model element *aspect*; while such properties are relatively difficult to be encapsulated within object-oriented model elements such as classes, operations, and so forth.
- With aspect orientation, aspects can be added into an architecture design one at a time. Multiple aspect models may be generated, and each of such models can be developed independently.
- When facing changes, aspect-oriented architecture approaches are more cost-effective, as aspect models are created and evolved relatively independently. This reduces the complexity of understanding, changing, and analyzing of design models, and in turn, decreases maintenance time and cost.
- As nonfunctional requirements are encapsulated in individual aspects, aspect-oriented architecture approaches in a large degree promote software reusability, which can also help reduce the development cost in the long run.

Survey of Aspect-Oriented Architecture Approaches

- **Formal design analysis framework:** Formal design analysis framework (FDAF) (Cooper, 2005; Dai, 2005), is an aspect-oriented approach proposed to support the design and automated analysis of nonfunctional properties for software architectures. In FDAF, nonfunctional properties are represented as aspects. At the architecture design level, aspect is either a property that permeates all or part of a system, or a desired functionality that may affect the behavior of more than one architecture design elements, such as security aspects. Security aspects, including data origin authentication, role-based access control, and log for audit, have been defined in FDAF. The definition of these security aspects uses UML diagrams (OMG, 2004). The definition for a security aspect includes its static view and dynamic view. The static view of a security aspect is defined using UML class diagram, presenting the attributes and operations that need to be used in order to include the desired functionality in a system. It may also include OCL invariants, preconditions, and postconditions regarding the weaving constraints of the security aspect. The dynamic view of a security aspect is defined in UML sequence diagram, describing the dynamic behavior of the security aspect, including the information about when and where to use the operations defined in the security aspect's static view. Architecture designs are documented using UML class diagram and swim lane activity diagram in the FDAF. FDAF also proposes a UML extension to support the modeling of security aspects in UML. The extension assists architects in weaving an aspect into a design and updating an aspect in a design. The syntax and semantics for this UML extension have been defined. FDAF uses a set of existing formal analysis tools to automatically analyze a UML architecture design that has been extended with security aspects. The automated analysis of an extended UML architecture design in existing formal analysis tools is achieved by formalizing part of UML into a set of formal languages that have tool support. The translation into a formal language with existing tool support leverages a large body of work in the research community. The formalization approach used is the translational semantic approach. In translational semantics, models specified in one language are given semantics by defining a mapping to a simpler language that is better understood. Algorithms for mapping extended UML class and swim lane activity diagrams to a set of formal languages have been defined, verified with proofs, and implemented in FDAF tool support, and thus automated translation from UML to this set of formal languages are realized. Formal languages that UML can be formalized in FDAF for the analysis of security properties include Promela and Alloy, where Promela's analysis tool is used to analyze data origin authentication and log for audit security aspect design and Alloy's analysis tool is used to analyze role-based access control security aspect UML design. The example system selected in FDAF is the Domain Name System (DNS), which is a real-time, distributed system. The three security aspects data origin authentication, role-based access control, and log for audit have been modeled in the DNS, where data origin authentication is used to ensure the source of data, role-based access control is used to ensure the access control of the DNS database, and log for audit is used to log DNS messages.

- **COMQUAD component model:** A component model (Göbel, Pohl, Rottger,

& Zschaler, 2004) is presented to enable the specification and runtime support of nonfunctional aspects in component-based systems. A clear separation of nonfunctional requirements and functionally motivated issues is provided. This is achieved by extending the concepts of the existing component-based systems Enterprise JavaBeans (EJB) and CORBA Components (CCM). Nonfunctional aspects are described orthogonally to the application structure using descriptors, and are woven into the running application by the component container acting as a contract manager. The container implicitly instantiates component specifications and connects them according to the current requests. The election of actual implementations depends on the particular client's nonfunctional requirements. This technique also enables adaptation based on the specific quantitative capabilities of the running system. In the component model, Sun's Enterprise JavaBeans (EJB) and the Object Management Group's (OMG) CORBA Component Model (CCM) are extended with the following concepts:

- o The specification of nonfunctional issues,
- o Container-managed instantiation and connection of component implementations based on the specific quantitative capabilities of the system, and
- o Streaming interfaces.

The design notation selected is the UML 2.0 component diagrams. Different levels of instantiation are proposed for a component: (functional) component specification, component implementation, installed component, and component instance. Nonfunctional requirements are associated with component implementations: There can be multiple implementations of the same functional component specification. Each implementation provides the same functionality, but may have different non-functional requirements. These properties are described using potentially multiple profiles, which represent the operational ranges of the component implementation. The deployer installs component implementations on a component container. There may be multiple installed components for the same implementation, differing only in the setting of configuration parameters. Prior to actual service usage, clients have to contact the desired component's home interface to obtain an instance. The component container then calculates the required component instance network according to the specified interrelationships. Subsequently, installed components are instantiated. For each component specification, the container chooses an implementation from the set of deployed implementations, based on their nonfunctional requirements and the current client's nonfunctional requirements. The resulting component network instances are designed to serve exclusively one client's requests, thus providing the notion of a session that encapsulates all nonfunctional contracts and resource reservations of a client connection.

- **Integrated aspect-oriented modeling approach for software architecture design:** An aspect-oriented modeling approach (Krechetov et al., 2006) is presented for software architecture design. This approach focuses on the modular representation of aspects at the software architecture design, and provides an attempt to integrate the best practices of the existing aspect-oriented architectural approaches in a single general-purpose modeling language. The aspect-oriented architecture modeling approach is based on UML. The integration is based on a systematic comparison of four modeling techniques: PCS Framework (Kande, 2003), AOGA (Kulesza, Garcia, & Lucena,

2004), TranSAT (Barais, Cariou, Duchien, Pessemier, & Seinturier, 2004), and CAM of DAOP-ADL (Pinto, Fuentes, & Troya, 2005). In the approach, a set of aspect-oriented modeling concepts are provided. These concepts are aspect, component, point-cut, advices, static and dynamic crosscutting, aspect-component relation, and aspect-aspect relation. Here, an aspect is a concern that crosscuts many architectural units. The visual representation of aspect is a stereotyped UML component. A component is typically a container of crosscutting concerns at the architectural level and the UML component notation is used to represent a component. The use of aspect interfaces is proposed to capture the crosscutting influence of the aspectual components. It captures the notion of pointcuts and advice at the architectural models. For the representation of aspect interfaces the features of three different approaches are combined: crosscutting interfaces from AOGA, evaluated interface from DAOP-ADL (CAM), and the point-cut labels from TranSAT. The notion of crosscutting interface is an extension to the notion of interfaces in UML, in which point-cut labels capture the crosscutting nature on how an aspect affects the other architectural components. It also allows for abstracting the different ways in which different programming languages and detailed design modeling languages implement composition. The crosscutting interface with point-cut labels is presented as an UML stereotyped interface with method names being the point-cut labels. Thus, if an aspect has a crosscutting interface attached, this means it operates on certain points in the execution flow bound to the point-cut labels of the crosscutting interface. It is also possible to leave the crosscutting interface empty (no point-cut labels bound), and postpone the point-cut specification until later development stages.

Both point-cut and advices are represented as subcomponents. A point-cut may be a subcomponent of the aspect, realizing the composition rules (or point-cuts) for the crosscutting interface, basing on the point-cut labels. An advice may be modeled as a subcomponent, which gets a delegation from the enclosing aspect (UML delegation connector) to realize the advice for the crosscutting interface. For the dynamic crosscutting modeling the integrated approach supports *point-cut* and *advice* concepts. To model the static crosscutting the following available concepts from the observed approaches are combined: *Introduction* element from PCS Framework and the *crosscutting interface* to *component* relation from AOGA. The "crosscuts" unidirectional association between a *crosscutting interface* of an *aspect* and a *component* is stated to indicate that there is a static crosscutting within the component structure. For a detailed specification of the static crosscutting an *introduction* subcomponent of the aspect can be used. It abstracts the structural changes that are necessary for a target component to hold the *crosscutting interface* contract. Aspect-component relation is a binding of an aspect to a component. For the purpose of an encapsulation of binding details, an association class or association tagged values may also be provided for the aspect-component relation. Finally, the inheritance and precedence relation from the PCS Framework are used to define the "abstract" aspects that may be detailed and refined by successors, and for setting aspect priorities. In UML this is modeled as *generalization* and "dominates" navigable binary association, respectively.

- **Re-QoS management approach:** The approach (Tesanovic, Amirijoo, Bjork, & Hansson, 2005) presents a method for developing reconfigurable feedback-based QoS management for real-time systems,

denoted as Re-QoS. By combining component-based design with aspect-oriented software development, this approach enables handling of crosscutting nature of QoS policies, as well as evolutionary design of real-time systems and QoS management architectures. The Re-Qos provides three types of aspects: QoS policy aspects, QoS task model aspects, and QoS composition aspects. The QoS policy aspects adapt the system to provide different QoS management policies. The QoS task model aspects adapt the task model of a real time system to the model used by different QoS policies. There can be a number of aspects defined to ensure enrichment or modifications of the task model, so that the resulting task model is suitable for different QoS or applications needs. The QoS composition aspects facilitate the composition of a real-time system with the QoS-related components. Once the QoS management is developed according to Re-QoS, all developed aspects and components implementing a plethora of different QoS management policies and algorithms, are grouped into a so-called QoS aspects package. By adding a QoS aspect package to an existing system without QoS guarantees, it is possible to use the same system in unpredictable environments where performance guarantees are essential. Furthermore, by exchanging aspects within the QoS aspect package one can tailor the QoS management of a real-time system based on the application requirements. In order to provide a method that is application-, domain-, and system-independent, Re-QoS is proposed to be applicable to a large class of real-time systems across different applications, and that the QoS architecture is flexible in that QoS policies can be exchanged and modified depending on the application requirements. The method achieves this by defining a set of requirements that a real-time system needs to fulfill in order to apply the Re-QoS method, and utilizing aspect-oriented software development, together with component-based development in Re-QoS. Aspects allow one to overcome the problem of QoS policies employed in existing methods are metric-centric, thus to enable the exchange of the controlling metric by simply weaving appropriate aspects into the controllers. The approach has been applied to an example system, a component-based embedded real-time database, called COMET.

- **Aspectual software architecture analysis method:** The Aspectual Software Architecture Analysis Method (ASAAM) (Tekinerdogan, 2003) is proposed with the aim to explicitly identify and specify architectural aspects and make architectural aspects transparent early in the software development life cycle. Similar to the notion of aspect at the programming level, concerns that cannot be easily localized and specified in individual architectural components are called architectural aspects. The ASAAM is an extension and refinement to the Software Architecture Analysis Method (SAAM). The extensions of ASAAM to SAAM include explicit mechanisms for identifying architectural aspects and the related tangled component. Similar to SAAM, the method ASAAM takes as input a problem description, requirements statement and architecture descriptions. Besides developing candidate architecture and scenarios, ASAAM consists further of the following steps: candidate architecture development to provide an architecture design that will be analyzed with respect to the required quality factors and potential aspects; develop scenarios from various stakeholders; individual scenario evaluation and aspect identification, here, scenarios are firstly categorized into direct and indirect scenarios. The scenario evaluation also searches for potential archi-

tectural aspects. A set of heuristic rules are defined to further classify scenarios into direct scenarios, indirect scenarios, aspectual scenarios and architectural aspects. Aspectual scenarios are derived from indirect or indirect scenarios and represent potential aspects; scenario interaction assessment and component classification, the goal of this step is to assess whether the architecture supports an appropriate separation of concerns. This includes both noncrosscutting concerns and crosscutting concerns (i.e., aspects; refactoring of architecture, a refactoring of the architecture can be done using conventional abstraction techniques, such as design patterns, or using aspect-oriented techniques). The architectural aspects and the tangled components are explicitly described in the architecture. In ASAAM a set of heuristic rules to categorize scenarios into direct scenarios, indirect scenarios and architectural aspects are defined. The heuristics rules are expressed using conditional statements in the form of in the form of IF <condition> THEN <consequent>. Here, direct scenarios describes a scenarios that can directly perform the provided scenarios; indirect scenario describes a scenario which requires some changes to the component that it interacts; aspectual scenario is a direct or indirect scenario which is scattered over different architectural component and which cannot be captured in one component; and architectural aspect is a well-defined concern transformed from an aspectual scenario based on the domain models resulted from a domain analysis process. After scenarios have been classified, ASAAM focuses on scenarios at individual components. ASAAM delivers the following types of components: cohesive component, which is a component that is well defined and performs semantically close scenarios; composite component, which is a component consisting of several subcomponents that each performs semantically set of scenarios; tangled component, which is a component that performs an aspectual scenario which is either directly or indirectly performed by the component; and ill-defined component, which is a component that includes semantically distinct scenarios, but which cannot be decomposed or does not include an aspectual scenario. After architectural aspects and related tangled components are identified, this information will be used to redesign the given architecture in which the architectural aspects are made explicit. This is briefly discussed in ASAAM using software architecture description languages or using a visually modeling language to represent aspects in the architecture.

Discussion on Aspect-Oriented Architecture Approaches

Five representative aspect-oriented architecture approaches have been presented here. All these five approaches have proposed the problem of crosscutting concerns at the architecture level and tried to adopt aspect orientation to this level. Such crosscutting concerns are nonfunctional requirements in some approaches (e.g., FDAF, COMQUAD Component Model, Integrated Aspect-oriented Modeling Approach for Software Architecture Design), or QoS attributes in others (e.g., Re-QoS Management Approach). In all five approaches, these crosscutting concerns are called as aspects in the architecture level. While ASAAM focuses on identifying crosscutting concerns as architectural aspects from problem description, requirements statement and architecture descriptions, other four approaches put more attention on how to specify the relationships between aspects and functional components (i.e., functionalities can be localized) in an architecture design. This part can be referred as the aspect weaving at the architecture level. The design notation used by

majority aspect-oriented architecture approaches (e.g., FDAF, COMQUAD Component Model, Integrated Aspect-oriented Modeling Approach for Software Architecture Design, ASAAM) is UML, where in FDAF, an architecture design in UML is further translated into formal specifications to automatically analyze aspects.

It is evident that using the aspect-oriented architectural approach to deal with crosscutting concerns at the architecture level is a promising area. However, there are still some issues that remain to be solved in this field, for example, standards on aspect modeling, such standards could help practitioners specify architectural aspects and weaving aspects into an conventional design; the visualization of aspect weaving algorithms at the architecture design level, which would facilitate the process of adding aspects into an architecture design and extracting aspects out of an architecture design; and finally, automated code generation from an aspect-oriented architecture design, which leads to the problem of how to map the aspect modeling elements at the architecture level to aspect implementation mechanisms (i.e., a point-cut in AspectJ language).

Component-Oriented Software Architecture

Overview of Component-Oriented Approaches

The need to rapidly develop large-scale, high quality software intensive systems has led researchers to investigate component-based software development as a solution. This approach is based on the idea that software systems can be developed by selecting appropriate off-the-shelf components and then assembling them with a well-defined software architecture (Szyperski, 1998). Because the components have already gone through the time consuming activities to specify, design, implement, test, and document their capabilities, the premise is that buying the components is a better decision, especially with respect to development time and quality, in comparison to building the capabilities from scratch. Component technologies (e.g., CORBA, Enterprise JavaBeans, .NET) have emerged as alternative approaches to improve the reuse of components. In addition, more general component-based software architecture methodologies have been proposed in the literature.

Survey of Component-Oriented Approaches

Component Technologies

Component technologies have evolved as a means to improve the reuse, and consequently improve the productivity gains achieved using encapsulation and abstraction in the object-oriented paradigm (Cai, Lyu, Wong, & Ko, 2000; Emmerich, 2000; Pour, 1998). In component technologies, the components are used to isolate and encapsulate specific functionalities and offer them as services in such a way that they can be adapted and reused without having to change them programmatically. The goal is to provide a mechanism by which developers can build applications by composing components, with well defined interfaces, rather than the traditional approach of developing new or modifying existing components. By acquiring components from third-party providers, the process of development becomes less time consuming, the level of implementation abstraction is raised, and the software quality is improved, as the components have previously been deployed and hardened over time. Component technologies have been proposed by the OMG, Sun Microsystems, Inc., and Microsoft, Inc.

o **OMG:** The OMG has proposed the Object Management Architecture (OMA), which provides guidance on how the standardization of component interfaces can be used to create a plug-and-play, distributed component software environment (OMG, 1995). The OMG has proposed standards to support this architecture, including the Common Object Request Broker (CORBA), which enables open interconnection of components that can be implemented in different languages and executing on different platforms (OMG, 2004). Initially proposed in 1991, CORBA has evolved to define a set of invocation interfaces (dynamic invocation, interface description language stubs, object request broker interface), object adapters, and the object request broker. CORBA services, including naming, notification, trading, security, and so forth, have been standardized in addition to two CORBA facilities, internationalization and time, and mobile agents. Recently, Real-time CORBA, Lightweight CORBA and COBRA/e standards have been made available by the OMG to support the development of real-time, resource constrained, and embedded system development.

o **Sun Microsystems, Inc.:** Sun Microsystems, Inc. has proposed two component models: JavaBeans and Enterprise JavaBeans. Java-Beans is a nondistributed component model for the Java 2 Platform, Standard Edition (Sun Microsystems, Inc., 1997). The components, called JavaBeans, are reusable software programs that can be developed and assembled to create applications. The specification describes the application programming interfaces and semantics for intercomponent event registration, event delivery, recognition and use of properties, customization and persistence. Its purpose is to support the issues found in assembling components to develop an application using a visual, builder tool. The JavaBeans component model is general purpose, as it can be used to develop a wide variety of applications. Subsequently, standards to support the creation of more sophisticated JavaBeans components and applications with more seamless integration in their runtime environment (i.e., desktop, Web browser, etc.) have been made available: the extensible runtime containment and services protocol, the drag and drop subsystem for the Java Foundation Classes, and the JavaBeans activation framework.

Enterprise JavaBeans (EJB) is a component model proposed by Sun for the Java 2 Platform, Enterprise Edition (JCP, 2006). EJB is a specification that defines a scalable service framework in which components, called EJBs, can be portably deployed in distributed environments. The EJB component model has been proposed to handle the needs of transactional business applications, in particular the middle-tier/server side. An EJB architecture is typically composed of an EJB server and EJB clients. The server has EJB containers, which provide run-time services (e.g., support for concurrent data access, security, etc.). The containers have EJB components, which encapsulate the business logic for the application. The containers automatically provide services to all enterprise beans. This model allows developers to focus on the business logic, as the framework provides the infrastructure support for transactions, state management, and deployment time attributes. The EJB specification integrates seamlessly with the CORBA standard.

o **Microsoft, Inc.:** Microsoft, Inc. has proposed the Component Object Model (COM) technology family and the service-oriented .NET Framework. For new development, Microsoft recommends using the .NET Framework. The family of COM technologies includes the original COM, Distributed COM (DCOM), and COM+ (Microsoft COM, 2007). The original COM technology was proposed in 1993; it defines how to create reusable components and link com-

ponents together to build applications. The components are in binary format, providing language independence. They can only be accessed through their interface; the binary representation of a COM interface is specified in the standard. The DCOM is a protocol that enables components to communicate directly over a network in a reliable, secure, and efficient manner. It supports multiple network transports, including Internet protocols such as HTTP. The DCOM technology uses proprietary formats, not open standards such as Extensible Markup Language (XML) and Simple Object Access Protocol (SOAP). The Microsoft Transaction Server (MTS), which provides support for transactions, scalability services, connection management, and point-and-click administration, has been integrated with COM and DCOM to create COM+. COM+ is the standard in this technology family that supports the development of distributed, secure, scalable enteprise applications.

The .NET Framework, introduced in 2003, provides the ability to quickly build, deploy, manage, and use connected, security-enhanced solutions with Web services (Microsoft .NET, 2007). The framework is composed of the Common Language Runtime (CLR) environment and a class library. The CLR is a virtual machine provides important services such as security mechanisms, memory management, exception handling, and so forth. The class library is a rich collection of precoded solutions, including user interfaces, data access, database connectivity, cryptography, Web application development, numeric algorithms, and network communications. Programmers use these libraries in combination with their own code to create applications. The .NET Framework uses open standards such as XML and SOAP.

Component-based Software Architecture Methodologies

o   **Evolutionary process for integrating COTS-based systems:** The Software Engineering Institute (SEI) has presented this framework to meet the challenges of building, fielding, and supporting component-based business solutions (Albert & Brownsword, 2002). EPIC is a comprehensive, tailored version of the RUP that meets the challenges of building, fielding, and supporting COTS component-based business solutions. A component is defined (Kroll & Krutchten, 2003) as *a nontrivial piece of software: a module, package, or subsystem that fulfills a clear function, has a clear boundary, and can be integrated into a well-defined architecture.* In UML, a COTS component is represented as a physical and replaceable part of the system that provides a set of interfaces and typically represents the physical packaging of classes, interfaces, and collaborations.

The EPIC approach simultaneously defines and makes trade-offs among four *spheres of influence*: the stakeholders' needs and their business processes (i.e., more traditional RE, analysis), the components currently available in the marketplace, the architecture and design of the system under development, and programmatics and risks. The trade-offs are considered in each iteration. As iterations progress and decisions are negotiated, the solution space becomes smaller, knowledge of the solution accumulates, and stakeholder buy-in increases. As a result, the components available in the marketplace are re-examined in each iteration to determine if they are suitable. While leveraging the Rational Unified Process (RUP), the EPIC project investigates the design, evolution, and management of COTS-based systems as well as evaluation techniques for assessing the suitability of COTS products and COTS-based program risks.

The milestones, workflows, activities, artifacts, terms, and descriptions from the RUP are reused or modified as needed; new process elements are added. For example, new artifacts to characterize the component marketplace include the market segment information, component dossier (for each component that is considered), and the component screening criteria and rationale. For each new artifact, EPIC provides a guideline that describes the purpose of the information gathered, key questions to answer, the information needed, and techniques to use.

EPIC has been used as the basis for the IBM RUP for COTS Package Delivery plug-in (IBM RMC, 2007). For example, templates for the COTS inception, elaboration, construction, and transition iterations are defined. Under each of these, the activities are refined into subactivities and ultimately tasks. Each task has properties that can be instantiated, including the guidelines. The guidelines are left empty in the plug-in to provide flexibility. The guidelines are targeted in this work as a way to introduce agility into the process.

o   **Model-based architecting and software engineering:** This is a unified approach that considers four types of models for a system: success, process, product and property (Boehm, 2000: Boehm, Port, Abi-Antoun, Egyed, 1998). The models must be consistent with one another and well-integrated. The success models are considered first. If, for example, a success model is to "Demonstrate a telepresence system in 18 months," this requirement constrains the other success models and determines many aspects of the product model (architecture must easily shed lower-priority features to meet schedule), the process model (design to meet the schedule), and various property models (only portable and reliable enough to achieve a successful demonstration). MBASE is consistent with the use of COTS components (Boehm, 2000).

Property models are invoked to help verify that the project's success models, product models, process models, and property levels or models are acceptably consistent. This is recommended at two particular life cycle process milestones. The first milestone is the Life Cycle Objectives milestone. Here, the basis for a business commitment to proceed at least through an architecting stage is verified. This involves verifying that there is at least one possible architecture and there is a choice of COTS/reuse components that is feasible to implement within budget and schedule constraints, to satisfy key stakeholder win conditions, and to generate a viable investment business case. The second milestone is the Life Cycle Architecture milestone. Here, the basis for a sound commitment to product development is verified. The verification considers the selected system architecture with specific COTS and reuse commitments. These must be feasible with respect to budget, schedule, requirements, operations concept and the business case. The key life-cycle stakeholders are identified and critical risk items are eliminated.

o   **COTS-aware requirements engineering and software architecture:** The COTS-aware Requirements Engineering and Software Architecture (CARE/SA) approach is characterized as goal-oriented, agent-oriented, knowledge-based, and has a defined methodology, or process (Chung & Cooper, 2004; Cooper, 2005; Ma, Cooper, & Chung, 2006). From a workflow perspective, the CARE/SA process has the following high level activities: Define System Agents, Define System Goals (with COTS), Define Software Requirements (with COTS), De-

fine the Software Architecture (with COTS), and Maintain the COTS Repository. In this approach, the roles include the requirements engineer (RE), software architect (SA), and component engineer (CE). The activity to Define the Architecture (with COTS) is decomposed into activities to select architectural styles or patterns, define, establish traceability, analyze, correct, verify, integrate, and baseline the subsystems. Each of these is described briefly below.

The SA selects one or more architectural styles or patterns to define the overall structure of the solution. At this point, an architectural outline is established in which the overall structure of the system is identified but not explicitly defined. Once the architectural styles are selected, the SA defines the subsystems of the architecture. For example, if a layered style is used, then each layer is a subsystem that need to be defined in terms of the capabilities it provides (i.e., meets specific functional requirements), its interfaces, and its constraints (i.e., meets specific nonfunctional requirements). The SA establishes the traceability between the requirements and the subsystems. The SA analyzes each subsystem description for internal consistency and then verifies it with respect to the system goals and software requirements. The SA identifies errors of commission (conflicting, incorrect, and redundant capabilities, interfaces, or constraints) and omission (missing capabilities, interfaces, or constraints).

Once the subsystems are verified, the SA determines if COTS components are available that may provide the capabilities, match the interfaces, and match the constraints. Earlier in the CARE/SA process, potential matches are identified when the goals and the requirements for the system under development are defined. If components are already identified, then the SA determines if one or more of the components are a match for the current definition of the architecture. If one or more components are a good match, then the SA selects a component. If there is not a good match, then the SA has several options. The SA may a) determine the impact of selecting one of the possible components on the architecture; b) consult with the CE and request a search for additional components; c) consult with the RE and determine if the requirements can be modified; or d) develop the subsystem from scratch.

Once subsystems are defined, they need to be integrated and verified. When subsystems are nested (i.e., one subsystem is composed of other subsystems) the analysis may proceed top down, bottom up, or middle out. Once integrated, the new subsystem is analyzed, corrected, and verified. The SA and CM baseline the verified, integrated architecture and places it under configuration management.

The CARE/SA approach uses a knowledge base (repository) that is populated with components. The descriptions of the COTS components are stored and maintained at two levels of abstraction: their goals (softgoals and hardgoals) and their detailed specifications (functional and nonfunctional). The goals provide high-level descriptions of the functional and nonfunctional capabilities of a component; they contain information like that found on marketing brochures for products. The description provides enough information for a reader to determine if the product appears to have the potential for use and warrants further investigation. The product specifications are the detailed descriptions of the functional and nonfunctional characteristics of a component; they contain information like that found on the technical product specifications or data sheets for a product. A rich set of attributes are stored and maintained for a product

specification including name, functional overview, domain, vendor, vendor evaluation, version number, operating system, memory requirements, and so forth.

Discussion on Component-Oriented Architecture Approaches

Component technologies have been proposed to improve the reuse and improve productivity in software development. Components are used to isolate and encapsulate specific functionalities and offer them as services that developers can compose into systems. The OMG, Sun Microsystems, Inc., and Microsoft, Inc. have proposed alternative component models over the last decade. The OMG has proposed the OMA and a collection of CORBA standards. Sun Microsystems, Inc., has proposed JavaBeans and Enterprise JavaBeans for the Java 2 Standard and Enterprise Editions, respectively. Microsoft has proposed two models. The COM family of technologies (including COM, DCOM, and COM+) and, more recently, the .service-oriented NET Framework.

Component-based software architecture methodologies have also been proposed. EPIC is a tailored version of the RUP that considers the procurement of COTS components throughout the development lifecycle. This approach simultaneously defines and makes trade-offs among four *spheres of influence*: the stakeholders' needs and their business processes (i.e., more traditional RE, analysis), the components currently available in the marketplace, the architecture and design of the system under development, and programmatics and risks. MBASE provides a high level framework based on the use of four models: success, process, product, and property. The success models are considered first and constrain the other models. The software architecture is defined as one of the elements in the product model. The CARE/SA approach considers two early activities in the software development lifecycle: requirements and software architecture. In the activity to define the software architecture, the software architecture iteratively defines a software architecture and then matches, ranks, and selects COTS components from a repository.

Research trends in this area include investigating software architecture methodologies that support the development of component-based dynamically adaptable systems; this broad category includes systems with service-oriented architectures. In addition, the modeling and analysis of software architectures for component-based systems that realize nonfunctional, or quality of service attributes, remains a challenging and difficult problem in the community.

CONCLUSION

Established software architecture concepts are presented in this chapter, followed by a survey of more recent approaches. Over the last 40 years, the community has reached a general understanding of what a software architecture is and has defined a set of concepts, including views, patterns, and architectural description languages. The more recent software architecture approaches included in this survey include agent-, aspect-, and component-oriented approaches. Each of these approaches has been proposed as a solution to a different problem. Agent-oriented approaches have been proposed to provide a means to model complex social interactions among strategic entities that can make decisions and their interactions with their environment. Aspect-oriented approaches have been proposed to provide a way to encapsulate capabilities that crosscut the design, such as many nonfunctional capabilities like security, and so forth. As aspects can be added (i.e., woven) into an architecture one after another, they can ease the development of the design. The encapsulation of the aspects improves the design's maintainability. Component-oriented approaches have been proposed to improve the reuse, and consequently improve the

productivity gains achieved using encapsulation and abstraction in the object-oriented paradigm. Here, components are the basic building block; systems are composed by selecting and integrating components with well-defined interfaces, rather than the traditional approach of developing new or modifying existing components.

FUTURE WORK DIRECTIONS

As discussed in the subsections on agent-, aspect-, and component-oriented development, there are important research topics to investigate in the future. In the agent community, open research issues include how to model the environment as a first class entity and the agents' interactions with it. Notations and techniques are needed to support this. In the aspect community, open research issues include developing standards that could help practitioners specify architectural aspects and weaving aspects into a conventional design; the visualization of weaving algorithms at the architecture design level; and the automated code generation from an aspect-oriented architecture design. In the component community, open research issues include software architecture methodologies that support the development of component-based dynamically adaptable systems; this broad category includes systems with service-oriented architectures. In addition, the modeling and analysis of software architectures for component-based systems that realize nonfunctional, or quality of service attributes, remains a challenging and difficult problem in the community.

In the future, it would be very interesting to extend this survey to include dynamically adaptable system architecting approaches. The environments in which software are executing today have increased considerably in complexity, and software may need to adapt themselves at run-time to changes in the security level, CPU utilization, memory usage, and so forth. Autonomous adaptable systems are needed in a wide variety of domains. For example, unmanned autonomous vehicles are needed in remote or hazardous conditions in submersible, aerospace, and military/police systems. Studies on the development of autonomous adaptable systems for Web servers and wireless multimedia have been presented in the literature in addition to collaborative learning environments, medical, and manufacturing applications. The new approaches to develop such systems are diverse, including biologically inspired approaches (e.g., based on immune or neurological systems), agent-based, grid-based systems, service-oriented approaches, and so forth. Currently, however, there is limited work presented from a design perspective (Cooper, Cangussu, & Wong, 2007; Huang, Garlan, & Schmerl, 2004).

These self adapting systems present challenging new (re)design issues. As a system's behavior is nondeterministic, the execution environment must be monitored for changes. In addition, the state of the system must be reasoned about in the context of its changing environment; the system needs to be able to adapt without human intervention. Ideally, the system should be able to predict violations (e.g., to avoid a memory constraint violation) in advance, as this gives the system time to adapt before a violation occurs. Research is needed to provide rigorous modeling and analysis techniques for these complex systems. For example, interesting problems include how to extend agent-, aspect-, and component-oriented techniques to support the design and analysis of dynamically adaptable systems.

REFERENCES

Abbott, R.J. (1983, November). Program design by informal English descriptions. *Communications of the ACM, 26*(11), 882-894.

Abowd, G. (1998). Analyzing development qualities at the architecture level: The software architecture analysis method. In L. Bass, P. Clements, & R. Kazman (Eds.), *Software architecture in practice*. Addison-Wesley.

Albert, C., & Brownsword, L. (2002). *Evolutionary process for integrating COTS-based systems (EPIC) building, fielding, and supporting commercial-off-the-shelf (COTS) based solutions* (Tech. Rep. No. CMU/SEI-2002-TR-005).

Balsamo, S., Bernardo, M., & Simeoni, M. (2002). Combining stochastic process algebras and queueing networks for software architecture analysis. In *Proceedings of the ACM International Workshop on Software and Performance*, (pp. 190-202).

Barais, O., Cariou, E., Duchien, L., Pessemier, N., & Seinturier, L. (2004). TranSAT: A framework for the specification of software architecture evolution. In *Proceedings of the Workshop on Coordination and Adaptation Techniques for Software Entities, ECOOP 2004*.

Basili, V.R., & Boehm, B. (2001, May). COTS-based systems top 10 list. *Computer, 34*(5), 91-95.

Bass, L., Clements, P., & Kazman R. (2003). *Software architecture in practice* (2nd ed.). Addison-Wesley.

Bauer, B., Muller J.P., & Odell, J. (2001). Agent UML: A formalism for specifying multiagent interaction. In P. Ciancarini & M. Wooldridge (Eds.), *Agent-oriented software engineering* (pp. 91-103). Berlin: Springer-Verlag.

Birov, D. (2004). Aspects pattern oriented architecture for distributed adaptive mobile applications. In *Proceedings of the International Conference on Computer Systems and Technologies (E-learning),* (pp. 1-6).

Boehm, B. (2000). Requirements that handle IKIWISI, COTS, and rapid change. *IEEE Computer, 33*(7), 99-102.

Boehm, B., Port, D., Abi-Antoun, M., & Egyed, A. (1998). *Guidelines for the life cycle objectives*

(LCO) and the life cycle architecture (LCA) deliverables for model-based architecting and software engineering (MBASE). TR USC-CSE-98-519, USC-Center for Software Engineering.

Booch G. (1983). *Software engineering with Ada.* Menlo Park, CA: Benjamin/Cummings.

Buschmann, F., Meunier, R., Rohnert, H., Sommerlad, P., & Stal, M. (1996). *Pattern-oriented software architecture. A system of patterns* (Vol. 1). John Wiley & Sons.

Bresciani, P., Perini, A., Giorgini, P, Giunchiglia, & Mylopoulos, J. (2004). Tropos: An agent-oriented software development methodology. *Journal of Autonomous Agents and MultiAgent Systems, 8,* 203-236.

Breugst, M., Choy, S., Hagen, L., Hoft, M., & Magedanz, T. (1998). Grasshopper—an agent platform for mobile agent-based services in fixed and mobile telecommunications environments. *Software agents for future communication systems.* Springer-Verlag.

Brooks, Jr., F.P., & Iverson, K.E. (1969). *Automatic data processing, System/360 edition.* New York: John Wiley & Sons.

Cai, X., Lyu, M., Wong, K., & Ko, R. (2000). Component-based software engineering: Technologies, development frameworks, and quality assurance schemes. In *Proceedings of the Seventh Asia-Pacific Software Engineering Conference,* (pp. 372–379).

Capretz, L. (2003). A brief history of the object-oriented approach. *SIGSOFT Software Engineering Notes, 28*(2), 1-10.

Chung, L., & Cooper, K. (2004, June 22). COTS-aware requirements engineering and software architecting. In *Proceedings of the International Workshop on Systems and Software Architecting,* Las Vegas, NV, (pp. 57-63).

Clements, P. (1996). A survey of architecture description languages. In *Proceedings of the 8th International Workshop on Software Specification and Design,* (pp. 16-25).

Clements, P., Bachmann, F., Bass, L., Garlan, D., Ivers, J., Little, R., et al. (2002). *Documenting software architectures: Views and beyond.* Addison-Wesley.

Cooper, K., Cangussu, J., & Wong, E. (2007). An architectural framework for the design and analysis of autonomous adaptive systems. In *Proceedings of the 31st Annual International Computer Software and Applications Conference.*

Cooper, K., Dai, L., & Deng, Y. (2005). Performance modeling and analysis of software architectures: An aspect-oriented UML based approach. *Journal of Science of Computer Programming, System and Software Architectures, 57*(1), 89-108.

Cooper, K., Ramapur, C., & Chung, L. (2005). *Component aware techniques (CAT) A COTS-aware requirements engineering and software architecting approach (CARE/SA): Defining system level agents, goals, requirements, and architecture (version 4).* UTDCS-24-05. The University of Texas at Dallas, Department of Computer Science.

Courtney, R.E., & Gustafson, D.A. (1990). Evolution of architectural design representations. In *the Proceedings of the 1990 Symposium on Applied Computing,* (pp. 381-384).

Dai, L. (2005). *Formal design analysis framework: An aspect-oriented architectural framework.* Doctoral dissertation, The University of Texas at Dallas.

DeLoach, S. (2006). Engineering organization-based multiagent systems. In A. Garcia et al. (Eds.), *Proceedings of the 4th International Workshop on Software Engineering for Large-Scale Multi-Agent Systems, (SELMAS'05),* (pp. 109-125). Berlin: Springer-Verlag.

Dijkstra, E. (1968). Go to statement considered harmful. *Communications of the ACM*, 11(3), 147-148.

Drogoul, A., Vanbergue, D., & Meurisse, T. (2003). Multi-agent based simulation: Where are the agents?. *Lecture Notes in Computer Science, 2581*, 1-15.

Elrad, T., Filman, R.E., & Bader, A. (2001). Aspect-oriented programming: Introduction. *Communications of the ACM, 44*(10), 29-32.

Emmerich, W. (2000). *Engineering distributed objects*. John Wiley & Sons.

Evans, R., Kearney, P., Caire, G., Garijo, F., Gomez Sanz, J., Pavon, J., et al. (2001). *MESSAGE: Methodology for engineering systems of software agents*. EURESCOM.

Ferber J. (1999). *Multi-agent systems: An introduction to distributed artificial intelligence*. Addison-Wesley.

Ferber, J., & Michel, F. (1996). Influences and reaction: A model of situated multiagent systems. In *Proceedings of the 2nd Annual Conference on Multi-agent Systems*. AAAI Press.

Filman, R., Elrad, T., Clarke, S., & Aksit, M. (2005). *Aspect-oriented software development*. Addison-Wesley.

FIPA. (2007). *The Foundation for Intelligent Physical Agents home page*. Retrieved March 11, 2008, from http://www.fipa.org/specs/fipa00001/SC00001L.pdf

Fishwick, P. (1996, February). Computer simulation: Growth through Extension. *IEEE Potential*, 24-27.

Fuxman, A. D. (2000). *A survey of architecture description languages* (Tech. Rep. No. CSRG-407).University of Toronto, Canada: Department of Computer Science.

Garlan, D., Allen, R., & Ockerbloom, J. (1994). Exploiting style in architectural design environments. In *Proceedings of SIGSOFT '94: Foundations of Software Engineering*, (pp. 175-188).

Garlan, D., Monroe, R., & Wile, D. (1995). *ACME: An architectural interconnection language* (Tech. Rep. No. CMU-CS-95-219). Carnegie Mellon University.

Göbel, S., Pohl, C., Röttger, S., & Zschaler, S. (2004). The COMQUAD component model: Enabling dynamic selection of implementations by weaving non-functional aspects. In *Proceedings of the Third International Conference on Aspect-Oriented Software Development*, (pp. 74-82).

Huang, A., Garlan, D., & Schmerl, B. (2004). Rainbow: Architecture-based self-adaptation with reusable infrastructure. In *Proceedings of the First International Conference on Autonomic Computing (ICAC'04)*, (pp. 276-277).

IBM Rational Unified Process Software Architecture Document Template. (2007). Retrieved March 11, 2008, from www.128.ibm.com/developerworks/rational

IEEE Std 1471-2000. (2000). *IEEE recommended practice for architectural description of software-intensive systems*.

Jatlitebean Web pages. (2007). Retrieved March 11, 2008, from http://waitaki.otago.ac.nz/JATLiteBean

Java Community Process (JCP). (2006, May). *Enterprise JavaBean specification version 3.0*. Retrieved March 11, 2008, from www.jcp.org

Jennings, N.R. (2001, April). An agent-based approach for building complex software systems. *Communications of the ACM, 44*(4), 35-41.

Kande, M. (2003). *A concern-oriented approach to software architecture*. Doctoral dissertation, Lausanne, Switzerland: Swiss Federal Institute of Technology (EPFL).

Keller, S., Kahn, L., & Panara, R. (1990). Specifying software quality requirements with metrics. In R. Thayer & M. Dorfman (Eds.), *Tutorial: System and software requirements engineering* (pp. 145-163). IEEE Computer Society Press.

Krechetov, I., Tekinerdogan, B., Garcia, A., Chavez, C., & Kulesza, U. (2006). Towards an integrated aspect-oriented modeling approach for software architecture design. In *Proceedings of the Workshop on Aspect-oriented Modeling, Aspect-oriented Software Development.*

Kroll, P., & Krutchten, P. (2003). *The rational unified process made easy.* USA: Addison-Wesley.

Krutchen, P. (1995). Architectural blueprints: The "4+1" view model of software architecture. *IEEE Software, 12*(6).

Kulesza, U., Garcia, A., & Lucena, C. (2004). Towards a method for the development of aspect-oriented generative approaches. In *Proceedings of the Workshop on Early Aspects, OOPSLA.*

Luckham, D.C., Kenney, J.J., Augustin, L.M., Vera, J., Bryan, D., & Mann, W. (1995). Specification and analysis of system architecture using Rapide. *IEEE Transactions on Software Engineering, 21*(4), 336-354.

Ma, W., Cooper, K., & Chung, L. (2006). Component-aware systems architecting: A software interoperability perspective. In *Proceedings of the 5th International Workshop on System/Software Architectures*, Las Vegas, NV, USA.

Maier, M., Emery, D., & Hilliard, R. (2001). Software architecture: Introducing IEEE standard 1471. *Computer, 34*(4), 107-109.

Martin, J., & Finkelstein, C. (1981). *Information engineering.* Carnforth, England: Savant Institute.

Medvidovic, N., & Taylor, R. (2000). A classification and comparison framework for software architecture description languages. *IEEE Trans-actions on Software Engineering, 26*(1), 70-93.

Microsoft .NET Framework. (2007). Retrieved March 11, 2008, from msdn2.microsoft.com

Microsoft Component Object Model (COM). (2007). Retrieved March 11, 2008, from msdn2. microsoft.com

Mili, R.Z., Steiner, R., & Oladimeji, E. (2004). Abstract architecture of agent-environment systems. *Multiagent and Grid Systems, 2*(4).

Mili, R., Zalila, Z., Daescu, O., Zhang, K., Steiner, R., Oladimeji. E., & Xue, P. (2004). *Prediction and visualization of large scale distributed multi-agent systems.* The University of Texas at Dallas: Department of Computer Science.

Monroe, R.T. (1998). *Capturing software architecture design expertise with Armani* (Tech. Rep. No. CMU-CS-98-163). Carnegie Mellon University: School of Computer Science.

Muller, I., Braun, P., & Kowalczyk, R. (2005). Design patterns for agent-based service composition in the Web. In *Proceedings of the Fifth International Conference on Quality Software*, (pp. 425-430).

Object Management Group. (1995). *OMG object management architecture guide version 3.0.* Retrieved March 11, 2008, from www.omg.org

Object Management Group. (2004). *OMG common object request broker architecture: Core specification version 3.0.3.* Retrieved March 11, 2008, from www.omg.org

Object Management Group. (2004). *OMG unified modeling language specification version 2.0.* Retrieved March 11, 2008, from www.omg.org

Page-Jones, M. (1988). *Practical guide to structured systems design.* Englewood Cliffs, NJ: Prentice Hall.

Parnas, D. (1972). On the criteria to be used in decomposing systems in modules. *Communication on the ACM, 15*(12), 1053-1058.

Parsons, D., Rashid, A., Telea, A., & Speck, A. (2006, February). An architectural pattern for designing component-based application frameworks. *Software—practice and Experience, 36*(2), 157-90.

Pinto, M., Fuentes, L., & Troya, J.M. (2005). A dynamic component and aspect platform. *The Computer Journal, 48*(4), 401-420.

Pour, G. (1998). Component-based software development approach: New opportunities and challenges. In *Proceedings of the Technology of Object-oriented Languages*, (pp. 375-383).

Rational Unified Process Workbench. (2007). Retrieved March 11, 2008, from http://www-306. ibm.com/software/rational

Shaw, M., & Garlan, D. (1996). *Software architecture: Perspectives in an emerging discipline.* Prentice Hall.

Shaw, M., & Garlan, D. (2006). The Golden Age of software architecture. *IEEE Software*, 31-39.

Stal, M. (2006, March-April). Using architectural patterns and blueprints for service-oriented architecture. *IEEE Software, 23*(2), 54-61.

Sudeikat, J., Braubach, L., Pokahr, A., & Lamersdorf, W. (2004). Evaluation of agent-oriented software methodologies—examination of the gap between modeling and platform. In *Proceedings of the Fifth International Workshop on Agent-Oriented Software Engineering, (AOSE).*

Sun Microsystems, Inc. (1997, March). *JavaBeans 1.01 specification.* Retrieved March 11, 2008, from www.java.sun.com

Szyperski, C. (1998). *Component software: Beyond object-oriented programming.* New York: Addison-Wesley.

Tekinerdogan, B. (2003). ASAAM: Aspectual software architecture analysis method. In *Proceedings of the Workshop on Early Aspects:*

Aspect-oriented Requirements Engineering and Architecture Design, held in conjunction with the AOSD Conference.

Tesanovic, A., Amirijoo, M., Björk, M., & Hansson, J. (2005). Empowering configurable QoS management in real-time systems. In *Proceedings of the Fourth International Conference on Aspect-oriented Software Development*, (pp. 39-50).

Wasserman, A.I. (1996, November). Toward a discipline of software engineering. *IEEE Software, 13*(6), 23-31.

Weyns, D., Parunak, H. V. D., & Michel, M. (Eds.). (2005). Environments for multiagent systems: State-of-the-art and research challenges. In *Post-Proceedings of the First International Workshop on Environments for Multiagent Systems, Lecture Notes in Computer Science,* (Vol. 3374).

Wieringa, R. (1998, December). A survey of structured and object-oriented software specification methods and techniques. *ACM Computing Surveys, 30*(4), 459-527.

Wooldridge, M. (2002). An introduction to multi-agent systems. *An introduction to multi-agent systems.* John Wiley.

Wooldridge, M. (2004). America's school on agents and multiagent systems. In *Proceedings of AAMAS'04.*

Yau, S.S., & Tsai, J. (1986, June). A survey of software design techniques. *IEEE Transactions On Software Engineering, SE-12*(6), 713-721.

Yourdon, E., & Constantine, L. (1979). *Structured design.* Englewood Cliffs, NJ: Prentice Hall.

Zambonelli F., Jennings N., & Wooldridge, M. (2003, September). Developing multiagent systems: The Gaia methodology. *ACM Transactions on Software Engineering and Methodology, 12*(3).

ADDITIONAL READING

Chitchyan, R., Rashid, A., Sawyer, P., Garcia, A., Pinto Alarcón, M., Bakker, J. et al. (2005). *Survey of aspect oriented analysis and design approaches*. University of Lancaster, Lancaster, UK: AOSD Europe.

Clarke, S., & Baniassad, E. (2005). *Introduction to aspect-oriented analysis and design*. Addison-Wesley.

Dai, L., & Cooper, K. (2007). A survey of modeling and analysis approaches for architecting secure software systems. *International Journal on Network Security, 5*(2), 187-198.

Dobrica, L., & Niemel, E. (2002). A survey on software architecture analysis methods. *IEEE Transactions on Software Engineering, 28*(7), 638-653.

Ferber, J. (1999). *Multi-agent systems: An introduction to distributed artificial intelligence*. Addison-Wesley.

Gomez-Sanz, J., Gervais, M., & Weiss, G. (2004). A survey on agent-oriented oriented software engineering research. *Methodologies and software engineering for agent systems: The agent-oriented software engineering handbook* (pp. 33-62). Kluwer Academic.

Heineman, G., & Councill, W. (2001). *Component based software engineering: Putting the pieces together*. Addison-Wesley.

Kazman, R., Bass, L., & Klein, M. (2006). The essential components of software architecture design and analysis. *Journal of Systems and Software, 79*(8), 1207-1216.

Kiselev, I. (2003). *Aspect-oriented programming with AspectJ, computer languages, Sams*.

Lange, C., Chaudron, M., & Muskens, J. (2006, March-April). In practice: UML software architecture and design description. *IEEE Software, 23*(2), 40-46.

Mahmood, S., Lai, R., & Kim, Y.S. (2007, April 18). Survey of component-based software development. *Inst. of Engineering and Technology Software Journal, 1*(2), 57-66.

Rinard, M., Salcianu, A., & Bugrara S. (2004, November). A classification system and analysis for aspect-oriented programs. *ACM SIGSOFT Software Engineering Notes, 29*(6), 147-158.

Szyperski, C. (1998). *Component software: Beyond object-oriented programming*. New York: Addison-Wesley.

Weiss, G. (Ed.). (1999). *Multiagent systems: A modern approach to distributed artificial intelligence*. MIT Press.

Wooldridge, M. (2001). *An introduction to multiagent systems*. John Wiley.

Section IV
Analysis, Evaluation, and Optimization

Chapter X
Dynamic Analysis and Profiling of Multithreaded Systems

Daniel G. Waddington
Lockheed Martin, USA

Nilabja Roy
Vanderbilt University, USA

Douglas C. Schmidt
Vanderbilt University, USA

ABSTRACT

As software-intensive systems become larger, more parallel, and more unpredictable the ability to analyze their behavior is increasingly important. There are two basic approaches to behavioral analysis: static and dynamic. Although static analysis techniques, such as model checking, provide valuable information to software developers and testers, they cannot capture and predict a complete, precise, image of behavior for large-scale systems due to scalability limitations and the inability to model complex external stimuli. This chapter explores four approaches to analyzing the behavior of software systems via dynamic analysis: compiler-based instrumentation, operating system and middleware profiling, virtual machine profiling, and hardware-based profiling. We highlight the advantages and disadvantages of each approach with respect to measuring the performance of multithreaded systems and demonstrate how these approaches can be applied in practice.

INTRODUCTION

Microprocessors execute code as a sequential flow of instructions. Most contemporary operating systems support multitasking, which allows more than one program to execute simultaneously. Multitasking is achieved by dynamically scheduling different executions to the available processors over time (sometimes referred to as time slicing).

The unit of logical flow within a running program is a thread. Although the exact definition of a thread can vary, threads are typically defined as a lightweight representation of execution state. The underlying kernel data structure for a thread includes the address of the run-time stacks, priority information, and scheduling status. Each thread belongs to a single process (a process requires at least one thread). Processes define initial code and data, a private virtual address space, and state relevant to active system resources (e.g., files and semaphores). Threads that belong to the same process share the same virtual address space and other system resources. There is no memory protection between threads in the same process, which makes it easy to exchange data efficiently between threads. At the same time, however, threads can write to many parts of the process' memory. Data integrity can be quickly lost, therefore, if access to shared data by individual threads is not controlled carefully.

Threads have traditionally been used on single processor systems to help programmers implement logically concurrent tasks and manage multiple activities within the same program (Rinard, 2001). For example, a program that handles both GUI events and performs network I/O could be implemented with two separate threads that run within the same process. Here the use of threads avoids the need to "poll" for GUI and packet I/O events. It also avoids the need to adjust priorities and preempt running tasks, which is instead performed by the operating system's scheduler.

With the recent advent of multicore and symmetric multiprocessor (SMP) systems, threads represent logically concurrent program functions that can be mapped to physically parallel processing hardware. For example, a program deployed on a four-way multicore processor must provide at least four independent tasks to fully exploit the available resources (of course it may not get a chance to use all of the processing cores if they are occupied by higher priority tasks). As parallel processing capabilities in commodity hardware grow, the need for multithreaded programming has increased because explicit design of parallelism in software is now key to exploiting performance capabilities in next-generation processors (Sutter, 2005).

This chapter reviews key techniques and methodologies that can be used to collect thread-behavior information from running systems. We highlight the strengths and weaknesses of each technique and lend insight into how they can be applied from a practical perspective.

Understanding Multithreaded System Behavior

Building large-scale software systems is both an art and an engineering discipline. Software construction is an inherently iterative process, where system architects and developers iterate between problem understanding and realization of the solution. A superficial understanding of behavior is often insufficient for production systems, particularly mission-critical systems where performance is tightly coupled to variations in the execution environment, such as load on shared resources and hardware clock speeds. Such variations are common in multithreaded systems where execution is affected directly by resource contention arising from other programs executing at the same time on the same platform. To build predictable and optimized large-scale multithreaded systems, therefore, we need tools that can help improve understanding of software subsystems and help avoid potential chaotic effects that may arise from their broader integration into systems.

Multithreaded programs are inherently complex for several reasons (Lee, 2006; Sutter & Larus, 2005), including: (1) the use of nondeterministic thread scheduling and pre-emption; and (2) control and data dependencies across threads. Most commercial-off-the-shelf (COTS) operating systems use priority queue-based, preemptive thread scheduling. The time and space resources a thread needs to execute on an operating system are thus affected by:

- Thread priority, which determines the order in which threads run;

- Processor affinity, which defines the processors that the thread may run on;
- Execution state, which defines whether the thread is ready, waiting, or stopped; and
- Starvation time, which is caused by system delay during peak load periods.

Switching execution context between multiple threads results in an execution "interleaving" for each processor in the system. In a single-processor system, there is only one stage of scheduling: the choice of deciding which runnable thread to execute next. Systems that have multiple cores or SMP processors require an additional stage that maps the threads ready to run on to one of many possibly available cores, as shown in Figure 1.

Even if we know exactly how long each thread will have access to the processor (which ignores any form of priority-driven pre-emption and interthread dependency), the number of feasible interleavings that can occur in the system are staggering. For example, using the criteria in Figure 1, which has only four independent threads, each with eight execution quanta, there are 10^{17} possible interleavings for just one processor! Server-based systems with hundreds of threads and tens of processors are now common. Over the next decade

we expect tera-scale systems will have hundreds of cores (Intel Corporation, 2006b).

Approaches to Extracting Multithreaded Behavioral Characteristics

There are two basic approaches to behavioral analysis: static and dynamic. Static analysis inspects the underlying constituents of a system without executing any program (Jackson & Rinard, 2000). It therefore requires some "model" of the system or implementation artifact that is correlated directly with expected behavior. For example, analysis of program source code is considered a form of static analysis. This type of analysis has the advantage that it can be performed without running the system. In particular, it can explore dimensions of behavior that are hard to stimulate through manipulation of program input.

Static analysis tools typically construct program execution models, potentially through reverse engineering. These models can then be analyzed to derive and ensure behavioral characteristics. Model checking (Clarke, Grumberg, & Peled, 2000) is a static analysis technique that is often applied to multithreaded programs to

Figure 1. Interleavings caused by 1-stage and 2-stage scheduling

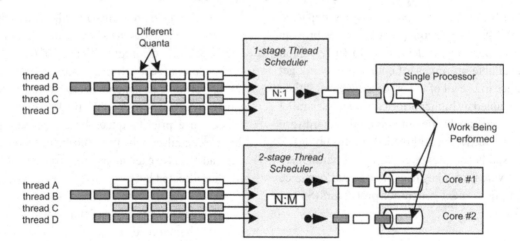

explore all feasible interleavings exhaustively to ensure correctness properties, such as absence of deadlock and livelock (Rinard, 2001). This approach can check all feasible paths of execution (and interleavings) and thus avoid leaving any behavior unchecked.

In practice, model checking is computationally expensive and limited in its applicability, due to the vast number of feasible interleavings a large multithreaded system may exhibit. Other forms of static analysis, such as automated checking of design intent (Greenhouse, 2003) and program analysis driven theorem proving (Freund & Qadeer, 2003), have also been applied to multithreaded systems to ensure correct behavior. Each approach trades off analytical thoroughness and computational cost. Static-analysis techniques typically do a good job of modeling relative time and temporal ordering. They do not, however, model—and thus cannot reason about—absolute (wall-clock) time.

The only practical approach to behavioral analysis that can incorporate aspects of absolute time is dynamic analysis, also known as profiling. Profiling is inspection of behavior of a running system. An advantage of this approach is that it can measure aspects of the system and know that they are exactly representative of the system. Approaches to profiling can be classed as either active or passive. Active profiling requires that the application or system being measured explicitly generates information about its execution. An example of active profiling is the user of compiler-based probe insertion, where the application makes callbacks to the trace collection engine to record execution behavior. Conversely, passive profiling relies on explicit inspection of control flow and execution state through an external entity, such as a probe or modified runtime environment. Passive profiling typically does not require any modification of the measured system, but is harder to implement and may require specialized tracing hardware.

Profiling (whether active or passive) collects precise and fine-grained behavioral data from a running multithreaded systems, which can be coupled with off-line analysis to help summarize and reason about observed results. The collected data is thus accurate and representative of system execution, as long as the overhead of the measurement has not unduly influenced the results. Profiling can also only provide behavioral data for control paths that actually execute, so successfully applying profiling tools depends largely on analyzing multiple runs of the program that test all relevant paths in the system. This coverage can be achieved through careful selection of stimuli (e.g., input data) to the system, as well as through artificial fault injection.

Profiling is limited, however, to the inspection of behavior that can be made to run by appropriate stimulation of the system, for example, through selection of input. This limitation means that profiling is more useful for behavior analysis in circumstances where a sampling of behavior is sufficient. For example, profiling is useful for optimizations that aim to improve performance on statistically frequent paths of execution. Profiling is thus not well suited to ensure correct behavior in a system when only one execution in a million can lead to system failure.

Both static analysis and dynamic analysis have their advantages and disadvantages. Advanced behavioral analysis solutions (Nimmer & Ernst, 2001; Waddington, Amduka, DaCosta, Foster, & Sprinkle, 2006) commonly use a combination of static and dynamic analysis to provide a more complete picture of system behavior. The remainder of this chapter presents and evaluates general approaches to profiling within the context of multithreaded systems. We examine the type and scale of behavioral data that can be collected dynamically from running systems and review state-of-the-art profiling tools and methodologies available today that operate at various levels of abstraction, including the operating system, virtual machine, and middleware levels.

BACKGROUND

Behavioral analysis is the examination and understanding of a system's behavior. Within the context of computing systems, behavioral analysis can be applied throughout the software lifecycle. The role of behavioral analysis—and the benefits it brings—vary according to how it is applied and the point in the life cycle to which it is applied. At a broad level, behavioral analysis supports assurance, optimization, diagnosis and prediction of software-system execution. Table 1 shows the relationship between these roles and different stages of software development.

Nondeterministic Behavior in Multithreaded Systems

Systems that behave according to classical physics, including electronic computers that are based on the von Neumann architecture, are deterministic in a strict sense. Actually predicting the behavior of a computing system, however, is fundamentally connected with the ability to gather all necessary information about the start state of the system. In most cases this is impractical, primarily due to very long causal chains (sequences of interrelated effects) and environmental interactions (i.e., input) that are hard to model and predict. In this chapter, we define determinism as the ability to predict the future state of a system. We therefore consider computer systems as generally being nondeterministic because we cannot practically predict the future state of the system. Accurate predictions would require a complete understanding of the start state, as well as prediction of environmental variables, such as user interaction and environmental effects (e.g., temperature sensitivity).

Most enterprise-style computing systems today demonstrate nondeterministic behavior. Key sources of nondeterminism in these systems include distributed communications (e.g., interaction across a network to machines with unknown state), user input (e.g., mouse/keyboard), and dynamic scheduling (e.g., priority-based with dynamic priority queues). These activities and actions typically result in a system whose execution behavior is hard to predict a priori.

A prominent cause of nondeterminism in multithreaded systems stems from the operating system's scheduler. The choice of which logical thread to execute on which physical processor is derived from a number of factors, including thread readiness, current system load (e.g., other threads waiting to be run), priority, and starvation time (i.e., how long a thread has been waiting to be run). Many COTS operating systems use complex scheduling algorithms to maintain appropriate timeliness for time-sensitive tasks and also to achieve optimal use of processing resources. From

Table 1. Roles of behavioral analysis in software-systems development

Role	Lifecycle Stage	Purpose
Assurance	Design, Implementation, Testing	Ensuring correct functionality and performance
Optimization	Implementation	Ensuring optimal use of computing resources
Diagnosis	Integration, Testing	Determining the conditions that lead to unexpected behavior
Prediction	Maintenance	Assessing how program modifications and integration will affect system behavior

the perspective of behavior analysis, however, these types of scheduling algorithms make static prediction of scheduling outcome infeasible in practice. Certain properties, such as absence of deadlock, can be checked effectively using static analysis because all possibilities can be explored explicitly. However, other properties, such as the absolute time taken to execute given functionality, can only be assessed practically using runtime profiling.

Behavioral Characteristics Relevant to Multithreaded Programs

Certain elements of behavior result from, and are thus pertinent to, the use of multithreaded programming. Table 2 describes some different characteristics that are commonly specified and

measured in real-time and safety-critical systems. These are the types of characteristics that can be analyzed using the profiling tools and technologies discussed in this chapter.

To provide a sense of the necessary sampling scale (i.e., frequency of events) in today's COTS-based systems, we performed a number of simple experiments to gather some system measures. Understanding the expected sampling rates is useful to understanding the viability and impact of different profiling techniques. Our experimentation is based on measurements taken from Microsoft Windows XP, running on a dual-processor, hyper-threaded (Intel Xeon 2.8 GHz) system, executing a stress-test Web client/server application. The measurements were taken using both Windows performance counters and the on-chip Intel performance counters. Table 3 shows the results.

Table 2. Common characteristics of multithreaded systems

Behavioral Characteristic	Description
Synchronization overhead	The additional processing time incurred by the use of synchronization mechanisms, such as mutexes, semaphores, and condition variables. Different mechanisms and topologies (e.g., inter- and intra-processor) typically have different overhead.
Task latency and jitter	The time between a thread being released (e.g., by a lock being freed) and regaining access to the processor. The task jitter is the observed variation in latency.
Task execution quanta	The length of time a thread executes for before either yielding access explicitly, or by being pre-empted by the operating system scheduler.
Unsafe memory access	Data that is being shared between threads must be controlled carefully to avoid data corruption due to the inability to modify data in one atomic action. To ensure the integrity of shared data is maintained, appropriate synchronization mechanisms must be used.
Priority inversion	Priority inversion occurs when a lower priority task is preventing a higher priority task from executing by being unable to execute and thus release a resource required by the higher priority task. A common solution to the priority inversion problem is for the lower priority to temporarily inherit the higher (waiting) priority so that it can release the resource.
Deadlock and livelock	Deadlock is a cyclic dependency between two or more threads. For example, thread A is waiting for a resource R1 from thread B before it will give up R2, and thread B is waiting for resource R2 from thread A before it will give up R1. In this condition both threads are blocked and cannot progress. Livelock is a similar condition to deadlock, except that the interdependent threads cause each other to perform an infinite amount of work before becoming free.
Effective parallelism	Effective parallelism is a measure of the ability of threads to perform work over time. For example, threads that do not have data interdependencies have a very high effective parallelism, whereas threads that are "lock-stepped" by a single shared resource have a low effective parallelism.
Worst-case execution time	Worst-case execution time (WCET) relates to task latency and jitter caused by load on the system. WCET is the maximum time a given thread or set of threads takes to perform some function. This measure is invaluable in building real-time systems that must adhere to strict deadlines.

Table 3. Example metric ranges

Category	Metric	Range
Processor	Clock Rate	2,793,000,000 Hz *
	Micro-ops Queued	630,000,000 uops/second *
	Instructions Per Second	344,000,000 instructions/second *
	L2 Cache Reads	65,000,000 reads/second *
Thread Scheduling	Number of Threads	500 total count
	Context Switch Rate	800-170,000 switches/sec
	Thread Queue Length	0-15 total count
	Scheduling Quanta	20-120 ms
System Resources	System Calls	400-240,000 calls/sec
	Hardware Interrupts	300-1000 interrupts/sec
	Synchronization Objects	400-2200 total count

* per logical processor

The data listed in Table 3 is comprised primarily of finer-grained metrics that occur at very high frequencies in the lower levels of the system. Of course, less frequent "application-level" events are also of interest in understanding the behavior of a system. For example, rare error conditions are often of importance. The data in Table 3 shows that the frequency (and therefore quantity) of measurable events can vary significantly by up to nine orders of magnitude. Because the impact of measurement is scaled proportionally, analysis methodologies that work well for low-frequency events may not do so for higher-frequency events.

Challenges of Multithreaded System Profiling

The remainder of this chapter focuses on the realization and application of runtime profiling on multithreaded systems. Profiling multithreaded systems involves addressing the following key challenges:

- Measurement of events at high frequencies—Events of interest typically occur at high frequency. The overhead and effect of measurement on the system being measured must be controlled carefully. Without careful control of overhead, results become skewed as the process of measurement directly alters the system's behavior.

- Mapping across multilevel concepts—Threads can be used at multiple levels of a system. For example, threads can exist in the operating system, virtual machine, middleware, and in the application (lightweight threads and fibers). Virtual machine and application-layer threads can map to underlying operating system threads. Extracting the mapping between thread representations is inherently hard because in many cases the mappings are not one-to-one and are even adjusted dynamically.

- Extraction of complex interactions—Threads represent the fundamental unit of execution in a software system and are inherently interdependent. Their interactions are facilitated through the sharing of system resources, such as memory, file, and devices. Determining which resources are the medium of thread interaction is inherently hard because measuring events on all of the resources in the system is not feasible due to excessive instrumentation overhead.

- Interpolation between raw events and broader properties—Deriving the behavior of a system requires more than simple collection of event data. Raw event data (i.e., data collected directly from low-level execution activities) must be used to build a composition of behavior that can be more readily analyzed by engineers. Abstraction and collation of data is a key requirement in deriving properties of synchronization that exist in multithreaded systems.

Research in the area of multithreaded software profiling and analysis has made some inroads into these challenges. In this chapter, we review the state-of-the-art in tools and techniques, some of which are commercial products and others that are research prototypes, and discuss how they try to address some of the challenges described above.

COMPILER-BASED INSTRUMENTATION TECHNIQUES

The most common approach to runtime profiling is to modify the code that executes so it explicitly generates trace information. A wide array of techniques can be used to generate this information, applied at different stages of the program code lifecycle, as shown in call-outs A to D in Figure 2.

Source-Code Instrumentation

Instrumenting source code manually is impractical in large systems. Instrumentation can be automated, however, through source-to-source transformation. Metaprogramming frameworks, such as Proteus (Waddington & Yao, 2005), TXL (Cordy, Halpern, & Promislow, 1991), Stratego (Visser, 2001) and DMS (Baxter, 2004), enable modifications to source code before it is com-

Figure 2. Different points of code modification

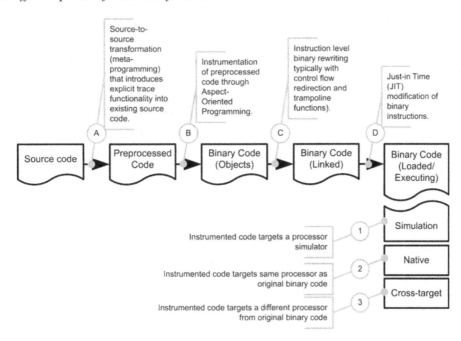

piled or preprocessed (Figure 2, label A). These metaprogramming frameworks provide a programming language that can be used to define context-sensitive modifications to source code. Transformation programs are compiled into applications that perform rewriting and instrumentation of source, which is given as input. Source code can also be instrumented just before it is compiled in a form of preprocessing (Figure 2, label B). Aspect-oriented programming (Spinczyk, Lohmann, & Urban, 2005; Kiczale, Hilsdale, Hugunin, Kersten, Palm, & Griswold, 2001) is an example of preprocessed code modification.

Applying instrumentation to source code—as opposed to applying it to binary code—makes it easier to align trace functionality with higher-level, domain-specific abstractions, which minimizes instrumentation because the placement of additional code is limited to only what is necessary. For example, to measure the wait times of threads that are processing HTTP packets received from a network in a given application, developers could instrument only those wait calls that exist in a particular function, as opposed to all wait calls across the complete program. Definition of the context (function and condition) is straightforward in a metaprogramming or aspect-programming language. The following excerpt illustrates an AspectC++ (Spinczyk et al., 2005) rule for such an example.

Given the original code:

```
#include <stdio.h>
#include <pthread.h>
```

```
pthread_mutex_t * mute;
int count = 0;

int main() {
    pthread_mutex_init(mute, NULL);
    pthread_mutex_lock(mute);
    count = 1;
    pthread_mutex_unlock(mute);

    ReadPacket();
    return 0;
}

void ReadPacket() {
    /* code that we wish to instrument */
    pthread_mutex_lock(mute);
    pthread_mutex_unlock(mute);
}
```

The following AspectC++ aspect defines a rule that inserts calls to function TraceEvent() after each call to pthread_mutex_lock that exists within function ReadPacket (expressed through a join-point filter). (Box 1)

The result of "weaving" (i.e., performing source-to-source transformation) the above source code is the following. The weaving process has defined additional classes and inline functions to support the specified trace functionality. It has also redirected control flow according to the trace requirement (after call to function). (Box 2)

Aspect-oriented programming and other forms of source-to-source transformation are useful for selective and precise instrumentation of source code. Modification of source code is portable with respect to different processor architectures. The performance impact of the measurement is often minimal because instrumentation is customized and only inserted where absolutely necessary.

Box 1.

```
aspect TraceAspect {
    advice call("% pthread_mutex_lock(...)") && within("% ReadPacket(...)") : after()
    {
        TraceEvent();
    }
};
```

Box 2.

```
#ifndef __ac_fwd_TraceAspect__
#define __ac_fwd_TraceAspect__
class TraceAspect;
namespace AC {
    inline void invoke_TraceAspect_TraceAspect_a0_after();
}
#endif

…

#line 1 "main.cc"
#include <stdio.h>
#include <pthread.h>

pthread_mutex_t * mute;

int main()
{
    pthread_mutex_init(mute, NULL);
    pthread_mutex_lock(mute);
    pthread_mutex_unlock(mute);

    return 0;
}

/* Function generated by aspect weaver to call the "trace" aspect
    after calls to pthread_mutex_lock */

inline int __call__ZN10ReadPacketEv_0_0 (::pthread_mutex_t * arg0) {
    AC::ResultBuffer< int > result;
    ::new (&result) int (::pthread_mutex_lock(arg0));
    AC::invoke_TraceAspect_TraceAspect_a0_after ();
    return (int)result;
    }

void ReadPacket()
{
    __call__ZN10ReadPacketEv_0_0 (mute);
    pthread_mutex_unlock(mute);

}
…
class TraceAspect {

    public:
        static TraceAspect *aspectof () {
            static TraceAspect __instance;
            return &__instance;
        }
        static TraceAspect *aspectOf () {
            return aspectof ();
        }

    public:
        void __a0_after()
        {
```

continued on following page

Box 2. continued

```
            printf("TRACE");
        }
};

namespace AC {
    inline void invoke_TraceAspect_TraceAspect_a0_after () {
    ::TraceAspect::aspectof()->__a0_after ();
    }
}
```

Instrumentation can be performed in the same order of time that is needed to compile the code. Source-code instrumentation is ideal for coarse-grained event tracing, particularly where the trace criteria must be related to application-level abstract events that are hard, if not impossible, to detect at the instruction level. Nevertheless, source-code instrumentation is target language dependent and can also be problematic when dealing with language idiosyncrasies, such as language preprocessing and syntactic variations.

Static Binary-Code Instrumentation

An alternative approach to adding event-tracing functionality to source code is to modify compiled binary code directly. Many compilers, such as GNU GCC, and profiling tools, such as Rational Purify and Quantify (IBM Corporation,

2003), can compile code with additional profiling instrumentation and also to link with pre-instrumented runtime libraries. For example, applying the command line options -pg, -ftrace-arcs, and -ftest-coverage, to the GNU GCC compiler produces binary code that is instrumented with additional functionality that traces the count of function calls and basic blocks executed in the program. The following excerpts show the basic profiling instrumentation produced by the GNU GCC compiler for this example C source code:

```
void foo(){
    if(i<10)
        i++;
    else
        i=0;
    return;
}
```

Box 3.

```
08048373 <foo>:
 8048373: 55                          push  %ebp
 8048374: 89 e5                       mov   %esp,%ebp
 8048376: 83 3d 78 95 04 08 09        cmpl  $0x9,0x8049578
 804837d: 7f 08                       jg    8048387 <foo+0x14>
 804837f: ff 05 78 95 04 08          incl  0x8049578
 8048385: eb 0a                       jmp   8048391 <foo+0x1e>
 8048387: c7 05 78 95 04 08 00       movl  $0x0,0x8049578
 804838e: 00 00 00
 8048391: c9                          leave
 8048392: c3                          ret
 8048393: 90                          nop
```

Box 4.

```
080488da <foo>:
 80488da:    55                              push    %ebp
 80488db:    89  e5                          mov     %esp,%ebp
 80488dd:    e8  62  fd  ff  ff              call    8048644 <mcount@plt>
 80488e2:    83  3d  00  a2  04  08  09      cmpl    $0x9,0x804a200
 80488e9:    7f  16                          jg      8048901 <foo+0x27>
 80488eb:    ff  05  00  a2  04  08          incl    0x804a200
 80488f1:    83  05  38  a2  04  08  01      addl    $0x1,0x804a238
 80488f8:    83  15  3c  a2  04  08  00      adcl    $0x0,0x804a23c
 80488ff:    eb  18                          jmp     8048919 <foo+0x3f>
 8048901:    c7  05  00  a2  04  08  00      movl    $0x0,0x804a200
 8048908:    00  00  00
 804890b:    83  05  40  a2  04  08  01      addl    $0x1,0x804a240
 8048912:    83  15  44  a2  04  08  00      adcl    $0x0,0x804a244
 8048919:    c9                              leave
 804891a:    c3                              ret
```

The generated assembly code (x86) without instrumentation is shown in Box 3.

The generated assembly code (x86) with instrumentation is shown in Box 4.

The first highlighted (80488dd) block represents a call to the profiling library's mcount() function. The mcount() function is called by every function and records in an in-memory call graph table a mapping between the current function (given by the current program counter) and the function's parent (given by return address). This mapping is typically derived by inspecting the stack. The second highlighted block (80488f1) contains instructions that increment counters for each of the basic blocks (triggered by the -ftrace-arcs option).

Profiling data that is collected through the profiling counters is written to a data file (gmon.out). This data can be inspected later using the GNU gprof tool. Summarized data includes basic control flow graph information and timing information between measure points in code. The overhead incurred through this type of profiling can be significant (over 60%) primarily because the instrumentation works on an "all or nothing" basis. Table 4 shows experimental results measuring the

Table 4. Slow-down incurred by GNU GCC profiling

Test	No profiling	With profiling	% Slow Down
Numeric Sort	812.32	498.2	38.67
String Sort	103.24	76.499	25.90
Bitfield	4.35E+08	1.65E+08	62.11
FP Emulation	73.76	52.96	28.20
Fourier	15366	15245	0.79
Assignment	24.292	9.77	59.78
Huffman	1412.7	1088.7	22.93
Neural Net	18.091	12.734	29.61
LU Decomp	909.76	421.48	53.67

performance impact of the GNU GCC profiling features. Tests were performed by running the BYTEmark benchmark program (Grehan, 1995) on a 3.00 GHz Intel Pentium-D running Redhat Enterprise Linux v4.0. It is possible, however, to enable profiling on selected compilation units, thereby minimizing instrumentation costs.

This type of code instrumentation is termed static because the code is modified before execution of the program (Figure 2, label C). COTS compiler-based instrumentation for profiling is generally limited to function calls and iteration counts. Another more powerful form of static binary instrumentation involves the use of a set of libraries and APIs that enable users to quickly write applications that perform binary rewriting (Hunt & Brubacher, 1999; Larus & Schnarr, 1995; Srivastava & Eustace, 1994; Romer, et al., 1997; Hollingsworth, Miller, & Cargille, 1994).

The following capabilities are typical of binary rewriting libraries:

- Redirection of function calls and insertion of trampoline functions that execute the originally called function;
- Insertion of additional code and data; and
- Control and data-flow analysis to guide instrumentation.

The following code illustrates the use of control-flow analysis and insertion of additional code through the Editing Executable Library (EEL) (Larus & Schnarr, 1995), machine-independent, executable editing API: (Box 5)

EEL code "snippets" encapsulate of pieces of code that can be inserted into existing binary code. They are either written directly in assembly language (which makes the instrumentation ma-

Box 5.

```
nt main(int argc, char* argv[])
{
 executable* exec = new executable(argv[1]);
 exec->read_contents();
 routine* r;

 FOREACH_ROUTINE (r, exec->routines())
     {
     instrument(r);
     while(!exec->hidden_routines()->is_empty())
         {
         r = exec->hidden_routines()->first();
         exec->hidden_routines()->remove(r);
         instrument(r);
         exec->routines()->add(r);
         }
     }

 addr x = exec->edited_addr(exec->start_address());
 exec->write_edited_executable(st_cat(argv[1], ".count"), x);
 return (0);
}

void instrument(routine* r)
{
 static long num = 0;
 cfg* g = r->control_flow_graph();
```

continued on following page

Box 5. continued

```
bb* b;

FOREACH_BB(b, g->blocks())
    {
    if (1 < b->succ()->size())
        {
         edge* e;

        FOREACH_EDGE (e, b->succ())
            {
            // incr_count is the user-defined code snippet
            e->add_code_along(incr_count(num));
            num += 1;
            }
        }
    }
r->produce_edited_routine();
r->delete_control_flow_graph();
}
```

chine dependent) or written using a higher-level language that is compiled into assembly. To graft snippet code into existing code, each snippet identifies registers used in the snippet that must be assigned to unused registers.

Dynamic Binary-Code Instrumentation

An alternative to static binary instrumentation is dynamic instrumentation. Dynamic instrumentation, implemented as Just-in Time (JIT) compilation, is performed after a program has been loaded into memory and immediately prior to execution (Figure 2, label D). Dynamic instrumentation has the advantage that profiling functionality can be selectively added or removed from the program without the need to recompile: Trace functionality is only present when needed. Moreover, dynamic instrumentation can be applied reactively, for example, in response to some event in the system, such as processor slow down. Dynamic instrumentation is particularly useful for facilitating conditional breakpoints in code, for example, Buck and Hollingsworth (2000) show that this approach is 600 times more efficient than conventional trap-based debug breakpoints.

The Paradyn work from the University of Wisconsin, Madison (Miller, Callaghan, Cargille, Hollingsworth, Irvin, & Karavanic, 1995) was designed specifically for measuring the performance of parallel programs. Paradyn uses dynamic instrumentation to apply trace functionality according to a set of resource hierarchies, as shown in Figure 3 (shaded nodes represent an example focus, all spin locks in CPU#1, in any procedure). Entities within the resource hierarchies effectively represent the scope of the current tracing functionality.

Buck and Hollingsworth expanded the dynamic instrumentation element of Paradyn in their Dyninst work (Buck & Hollingsworth, 2000). Dyninst provides a C++ API and a set of run-time libraries that allow users to build tools for modifying dynamic binary code. It attaches to loaded binaries that are either already running or that are explicitly loaded by the Dyninst run-time. Once attached to an executable, tools written using the Dyninst API (termed mutators) can be used to modify the binary image directly in memory.

Dyninst works by adding "trampolines" into the target binary at selected positions, shown in

Figure 3. Paradyn sample profiling criteria

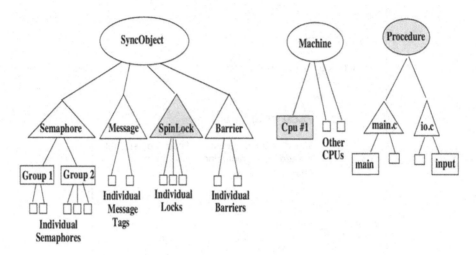

Figure 4. Dyninst trampoline architecture

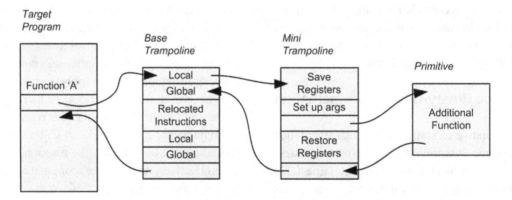

D. Branch instructions are inserted into the target program, at user-defined positions, to redirect control flow into the base trampoline. Base trampolines are instantiated for each instrumentation point in the target code. Each contains pre- and post- branching to global primitives (called for all processes) and local instrumentation primitives (called only for the specific instrumentation point). Base trampolines also include the original code that was displaced from the target, which is also executed.

Dyninst's thread abstraction allows developers to associate instrumentation with specific threads that are running in the system, which is a necessary part of their selective profiling scheme. With this approach the overhead of instrumentation is incurred up-front in modifying the binary image. After the image has been modified, the only overhead is the cost of trampolining and the additional instructions imposed by the instrumented primitives.

Snippet code (the code which is being added to the target image) is created using the DyninstAPI to dynamically assemble variable declarations, expressions, and so forth. The following excerpt illustrates how the Dyninst API can be used to create a global counter variable and an expression that increments it. (Box 6)

Dyninst is designed to target the native processor; the modified instructions target the actual underlying hardware. Other work, such as Pin (Luk et al., 2005), Dixie (Fernandez, Ramirez, Cernuda, & Espasa, 1999), DynamoRIO (Bruening, 2004), and Valgrind (Nethercote, 2004), have pursued the use of JIT cross-compilation so that the modified binary code can be executed on an emulated (i.e., virtual) machine architecture. Targeting a virtual machine provides more control and the ability to inspect low-level details of behavior, such as register and cache activity. It also does not necessarily imply translation across different instruction set architectures (ISA). In most instances, the virtual machine uses the same ISA as the underlying host, so that while hooks and interceptors can be put in place, the bulk of the code can simply be passed through and executed by the host.

The Pin program analysis system (Luk et al. 2005) is an example of dynamic compilation targeting a virtual machine architecture using the same ISA as the underlying host. As shown in Figure 5, the Pin system consists of:

- Instrumentation API, which is used to write programs that perform dynamic interception and replacement;
- JIT Compiler, which compiles and instruments the bytecode immediately before execution;
- Code cache, which caches translations between the target binary and the JIT compiled code;
- Emulation unit, which interprets instructions that cannot be executed directly; and
- Dispatcher, which retrieves and executes code from the code cache.

To analyze a program's behavior (multithreaded or not), Pin users must write a program that performs dynamic instrumentation. Pin provides an API based on the ATOM API (Srivastava & Eustace, 1994) that shields programmers from idiosyncrasies of the underlying instruction set and allows passing of context information, such as register contents, to the injected code as parameters. Pin programs typically consist of analysis and instrumentation elements. The basic building blocks for defining instrumentation points are machine instructions, basic blocks, procedures, images, and applications. For example, the C++ code below shows the use of the Pin API to instrument the target code with trace functions each time `sleep()` is invoked.

Box 6.

```
// create a global int variable in the address space of the application
//
BPatch_variableExpr * intCounter = appThread->malloc(*appImage->findType("int"));

// create an expression that increments counter variable
//
BPatch_arithExpr addOne(BPatch_assign, *intCounter, BPatch_constExpr(1));
```

Figure 5. The Pin software architecture

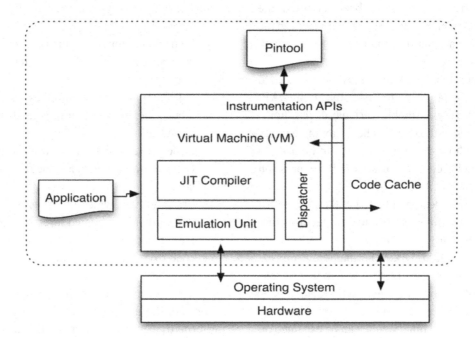

First, a replacement function is defined with the same signature as the function that is being replaced (in this example `sleep()`). (Box 7)

A callback function `ImageLoad()` is used to intercept binary-image loads that are executed by the target application. The Pin API can then be used to obtain the function that will be replaced with the new tracing/trampoline function. (Box 8)

The instrumentation function is "hooked" onto image loads through `IMG _ AddInstrument-Function()` as follows:

```
int main( INT32 argc, CHAR *argv[] ) {
// Initialize symbol processing
//
PIN_InitSymbols();

// Initialize pin
//
PIN_Init( argc, argv );
```

```
// Register ImageLoad to be called when an image is loaded
//
IMG_AddInstrumentFunction( ImageLoad, 0 );

// Start the program in probe mode, never returns
//
PIN_StartProgramProbed();

return 0;
}
```

The target program is run until completion through `PIN _ StartProgramProbed()`. Pin also supports the ability to dynamically attach and detach from a long-running process if transient tracing is needed.

Dynamic compilation and virtual machine execution incur overhead. With respect to Pin, overhead primarily stems from performing JIT-compilation, helped by the use of a code-translation cache.

Box 7.

```
typedef VOID * ( *FP_SLEEP )( unsigned int );

// This is the replacement routine.
VOID * NewSleep( FP_SLEEP orgFuncptr, UINT32 arg0, ADDRINT returnIp ) {
    // Normally one would do something more interesting with this data.
    //
    cout << "NewSleep ("
        << hex << ADDRINT ( orgFuncptr ) << ", "
        << dec << arg0 << ", "
        << hex << returnIp << ")"
        << endl << flush;

    // Call the relocated entry point of the original (replaced) routine.
    //
    VOID * v = orgFuncptr( arg0 );
    return v;
}
```

Box 8.

```
// Pin calls this function every time a new image is loaded. It is best to do probe
// replacement when the image is loaded,because only one thread knows about the image at
// this time.
VOID ImageLoad( IMG image, VOID *v )
{
    // See if sleep() is present in the image. If so, replace it.
    //
    RTN rtn = RTN_FindByName( image, "sleep" );

    if (RTN_Valid(rtn))
    {
        cout << "Replacing sleep in " << IMG_Name(image) << endl;

        // Define a function prototype that describes the application routine
        // that will be replaced.
        //
        PROTO proto_sleep = PROTO_Allocate( PIN_PARG(void *), CALLINGSTD_DEFAULT,
                                            "sleep", PIN_PARG(int), PIN_PARG_END() );

        // Replace the application routine with the replacement function.
        // Additional arguments have been added to the replacement routine.
        // The return value and the argument passed into the replacement
        // function with IARG_ORIG_FUNCPTR are the same.
        //
        AFUNPTR origptr = RTN_ReplaceSignatureProbed(rtn, AFUNPTR(NewSleep),
                                IARG_PROTOTYPE, proto_sleep,
                                IARG_ORIG_FUNCPTR,
                                IARG_FUNCARG_ENTRYPOINT_VALUE, 0,
                                IARG_RETURN_IP,
                                IARG_END);

        cout << "The original entry point to the replaced function has been moved to 0x";
        cout << hex << ( ADDRINT ) origptr << dec << endl;
```

continued on following page

Box 8. continued

```
        // Free the function prototype.
        PROTO_Free( proto_sleep );
    }
    else {
        cout << "Could not find routine in image\n";
    }
}
```

Figure 6. Pin performance test results (Luk et al., 2005)

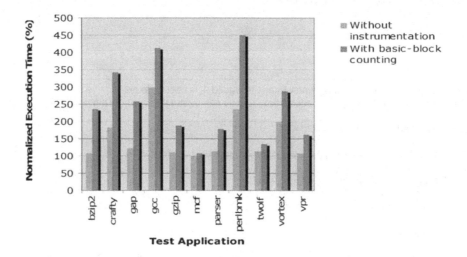

Figure 6 shows Pin performance data taken from Luk et al. (2005). These results show that the slowdown incurred by Pin is approximately four times slower than the original code without instrumentation. Even though this slowdown is significant, the Pin approach is one of the fastest JIT-based profiling solutions available today.

Summary of Compiler-Based Instrumentation Techniques

Instrumenting program code with tracing functionality is a powerful means of understanding system behavior. Modifying source code provides a straightforward means to collect trace information that must relate to application-level program functionality. It therefore enables the customization of trace insertion according to the program "features" of interest.

Alternatively, binary instrumentation is well equipped to handle complex software where the executed code cannot be identified until runtime. Binary-level modifications and execution on virtual machine architectures allow straightforward inspection of machine-level registers and data, such as the stack and caches. Conversely, because binary modification operates at such a low level, it is sometimes hard to specify what to instrument when semantics cannot be easily linked to program-level functions and basic blocks. Binary instrumentation is primarily supportive of active profiling, although the use of a virtual machine to execute code also provides a means to profile passively.

From the perspective of profiling multithreaded programs specifically, binary-code instrumentation can provide an effective means to intercept and instrument synchronization functions where source code is not available or when there is a need for very fine-grained information, such as access to cache state. Binary-code instrumentation also provides detailed access to memory and thus access to thread and process-control blocks useful in profiling multithreaded applications.

OPERATING SYSTEM AND MIDDLEWARE PROFILING TECHNIQUES

All applications rely upon services provided by the underlying operating system. These services are primarily used to coordinate access to shared resources within the system. To measure service "requests" probes can be placed directly within the operating system code that can record individual application access to provided services. Many COTS operating systems also provide a number of performance counters that explicitly track usage of shared resources. Data generated from these counters—along with data from embedded probes—can be combined to form a more complete picture of application behavior.

Another common form of shared processing infrastructure is distributed computing middleware, such as OMG's CORBA and Microsoft's .NET, which provide common services, such as location transparency and concurrency management. Distributed computing middleware often provides a number of "hook points," such as

interceptors and smart proxies that are accessible to users. These hooks provide placeholders for adding probe functionality that can be used to measure events typically hidden deeper within the middleware.

This section first discusses techniques that can be used to place probes into operating system services and how this information can be combined with data generated from operating system-level performance counters. We then discuss two approaches to profiling distribute middleware applications deployed on the CORBA platform.

Profiling System Call Interception

A typical process contains one or more threads and a shared memory space. Application code that is executed by threads within a process is free to access various operating system resources and services, such as virtual memory, files, and network devices. Access to these resources and services is facilitated through APIs that are provided by system libraries. Each thread in the system executes in either user space or kernel space, depending upon the work it is doing at that given time.

Whenever a thread makes a system call, it transitions (e.g., via a trap) from user space to kernel space (Soloman, 1998; Beck et al., 1999). Invoking system calls for thread management (e.g., thread creation, suspension, or termination) and synchronization (e.g., mutex or semaphore acquisition) often require such a transition. System call transitioning code therefore provides a useful interception point at which process activity can be monitored and a profile of system resource use can be extracted on a per-thread basis.

Figure 7 shows the use of the interpositioning technique, where libraries are built to mimic the system API. These libraries contain code that record a call event and then forward the call to the underlying system library.

The threadmon (Cantrill & Doeppner, 1997) tool uses interpositioning to insert trace code

Figure 7. Systems calls intercepted by system trap profiling library

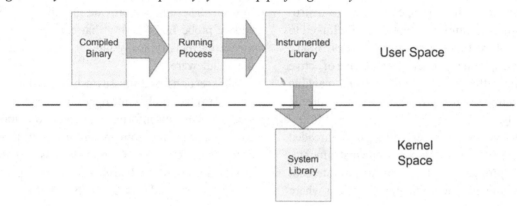

between the user-level threads library and the application by redefining many of the functions that the library uses internally to change thread state. This technique is also used by Broberg's Visualization of Parallel Program Behavior (VPPB) tool (Broberg, Lundberg, & Grahn, 1999) to gather user-level thread information. In both approaches, data obtained by user library interpositioning is integrated with data collected from other operating system services, such as the UNIX /proc file system or kstat utility. The threadmon and VPPB tools both target the Solaris operating system and therefore rely upon Solaris-specific system utilities, such as memory mapping of /dev/kmem to access the kernel.

Cantrill and Doeppner (1997) and Broberg et al. (1999) have also used another tool known as Trace Normal Form (TNF) (Murayama, 2001). This tool generates execution event traces from the Solaris kernel and user processes. Solaris provides an API for inserting TNF probes into the source code of any C/C++ program. A TNF probe is a parameterized macro that records argument values. The code excerpt below shows how C macroprobes can be inserted at the beginning and end of critical code to record the absolute (wall-clock) time required for the code to execute.

```
#include <tnf/probe.h>
```
.

```
extern mutex_t list_mutex;
```
.
.

```
TNF_PROBE_1(critical_start, "critical section start",
"mutex acquire", tnf_opaque, list_lock, &list_mutex)
```

```
mutex_lock(&list_mutex);
```
.
.

```
/* critical section code */
```
.

```
mutex_unlock(&list_mutex);
```

```
TNF_PROBE_1(critical_end, «critical section end»,
«mutex release»,
tnf_opaque, list_lock, &list_mutex)
```

These probes can be selectively activated dynamically at run time. Events are recorded each time a probe is executed. Each probe automatically records thread-specific information, such as the thread identifier, but it may also record other data related to the state of the application at the time the event was triggered. Event records are written to a binary file that is subsequently parsed and analyzed by an offline process. The Solaris kernel also contains a number of TNF probes that can record kernel activity, such as system calls, I/O operations, and thread state change. These probes can be enabled/disabled using a command-line utility known as prex (Murayama, 2001). Data records from the probes are accumulated within a contiguous portion of the kernel's virtual address space and cannot be viewed directly. Another utility that runs with administrator privileges can be used to extract the data and write it to a user file. This data can then be correlated with other user-level data to provide a clear understanding of the behavior of the application run.

The probe-based technique described above provides a detailed view of the running state of the application. Behavioral data details call counts, timing information, and resource use (thread and system state). There are some drawbacks to this approach, however, including:

- The solution is not portable because it depends on Solaris features that are not available on other operating systems.
- It requires a considerable amount of development effort because thread libraries must be modified.
- Applications must be separately built and linked for profiling.
- Tools that are used to collect the data like TNF or kstat may require lengthy setup and configuration.

Microsoft Windows Performance Counters

- Other operating systems have comparable probe-based features that can be used to get comparable data-defining application behavior. For example, Microsoft Windows provides performance counters (Microsoft, 2007a) that contain data associated to the running system. Windows provides a console that can be used to select certain specific counters related to specific processes. Once selected, the values of these counters will be displayed on the console at regular intervals. Table 5 shows example counters that are available.

Windows stores the collected values in the registry, which is refreshed periodically. Developers typically retrieve the data from the registry directly or use an API known as Performance Data Helper (Microsoft, 2007c; Pietrik, 1998). Alternatively, the Microsoft .NET framework provides the System.Diagnostics namespace that facilitates access to all the counters from within a .NET application.

Windows performance counters can be used to acquire data related to the running system, which can be correlated with a particular application run. These counters give an external view of the application, however, and there is no straightforward method of mapping counter values to logical application events. To more closely inspect a running application, therefore, instrumentation is needed within the application itself to record logical events and combine them with data generated through performance counters.

Distributed System Profiling

A distributed system consists of applications whose components are spread over a network of hosts that work together to provide the overarch-

Table 5. Performance counters provided by the Windows Operating System

Category	Description	Sample Counters
Process	Provides data related to each process	% Processor Time, % User Time, IO activity, Page Faults etc.
Processor	Provides information about the overall machine	% Processor time, % User Time, %Idle Time etc.
Memory	Provide data related to the memory of the system	Available Bytes, #Page Faults/sec, #Page Reads/sec etc.
Threads	Provides data on the threads in the system	# of Context Switches/sec, Thread State, Thread Wait Reason etc.

ing functionality. The complexity of distributed applications is often considerably greater than a stand-alone application. In particular, distributed applications must address inherent complexities, such as latency, causal ordering, reliability, load balancing, and optimal component placement, that are either absent from (or less complicated in) stand-alone applications (Schmidt, Stal, Rohnert, & Buschmann, 2000). The analysis and profiling of distributed applications involves monitoring key interactions and their characteristics along with localized functionality occurring within each component. Below we examine two approaches to profiling distributed system behavior. One approach modifies generated stubs and skeletons, whereas the other uses profiling extensibility features available in the middleware.

Monitoring of Component-Based Systems (MCBS)

MCBS (Li, 2002) is a CORBA middleware-based monitoring framework that can be used to capture application semantics, timing latency, and shared resource usage. Although the MCBS prototype is CORBA-based the solution can be extended to any distributed object architecture that generates stubs and skeletons. The MCBS approach recreates call sequences across remote interfaces. Probes are instrumented automatically through a specialized Interface Description Language (IDL) compiler, which directly modifies the generated stubs and skeletons with code that records call entry and return events, as shown in Figure 8.

Along with calls and returns, the MCBS-modified stubs and skeletons can also profile higher-level transactions (as aggregated calls), as well as parameters and return values. Event data is recorded to a log and a unique identifier assigned so that the scenario/call chain can be identified later. This identifier is generated at the start probe and is propagated through the calling sequence via thread-local storage (Schmidt et al., 2000), which is global data that is only available to the owning thread. When each new interface is invoked, the stub receives the identifier from the thread-specific storage, creates a record with it, and stores a number identifying its position in the call chain. After control returns to the caller stub, the last record is generated and the call chain record completed.

Whenever a new thread is created by the application, the parent thread identifier is stored

Figure 8. MCBS probe instrumentation

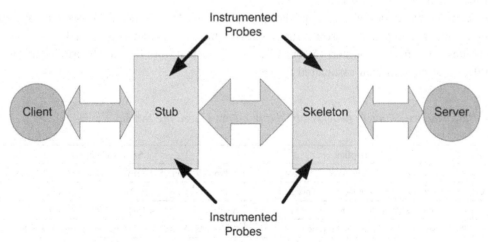

along with the new thread identifier to help identify the logical call chain in cases where threads are spawned by user-application code. Event data is stored in a memory buffer during application execution and is dumped to a file regularly as the buffer becomes full. An off-line data collector picks up the different files for the different processes and loads them into a database. The analyzer component processes the data and constructs entire call graphs. The end-to-end timing latency of call scenarios is calculated from the timestamps and latencies calculated from their deltas.

MCBS also allows the comparison of measurement overhead against normal (uninstrumented) operation. This comparison measures the instrumented execution timing with timings collected from the original application that has been manually instrumented. The manual instrumentation is restricted to a single function at a time to minimize overhead. Table 6 shows performance data for a sample application. The sample scenarios are known to have deterministic functionality, that is, they perform the same set of actions every time.

MCBS can reduce measurement overhead by profiling only specific components of the ap-

plication. Component selection can be achieved in two ways:

- Statically prior to executing, where monitored components are selected and the application is then run. The application must be stopped and restarted if the selected set of components changes.
- Dynamically while the application is running, where the monitored components can be selected at runtime. Dynamic selection helps developers focus on problem area and analyze it without incurring overhead due to measurement of other components.

Li (2002) has implemented both approaches and suggests that static selection is more straightforward (in terms of instrumentation effort) than dynamic selection. Dynamic selection is more complicated because it must avoid data inconsistency that can arise if a component process receives an off event, where monitoring is forced to stop during a run. Modifying instrumentation dynamically thus relies on the system reaching a steady state.

The current MCBS prototype is restricted to synchronous remote procedure calls. It does

Table 6. Overhead of instrumentation due to probes inserted in stubs and skeletons

Function	Average (msec)	Standard Deviation (msec)	Average (msec)	Standard Deviation (msec)	Interference
EngineController::print	1.535	0.158	1.484	1.288	3.4%
DeviceChannel::is_supplier_set	1.865	0.054	1.236	0.025	50.9%
IO::retrieve_from_queue	10.155	0.094	9.636	0.094	5.4%
GDI::draw_circle	95.066	10.206	85.866	11.342	10.7%
RIP::notify_downstream	13.831	2.377	11.557	0.381	19.7%
RIP::Insert_Obj_To_DL	2.502	0.141	1.879	0.127	33.2%
IO::push_to_queue	13.626	0.298	13.580	2.887	0.3%
UserApplication::notified	0.418	0.04	0.282	0.099	48.3%
Render::deposit_to_queue	0.529	0.097	0.358	0.010	47.8%
Render::render_object	7.138	2.104	6.280	0.074	13.6%
Render::retrieve_from_queue	0.501	0.040	0.318	0.010	57.6%

not support dynamic function invocations (e.g., through CORBA DII) nor does it support stubless colocated objects.

OVATION

OVATION (Object Computing Incorporated, 2006; Gontla, Drury, & Stanley, 2003) is a distributed monitoring framework that uses similar concepts as the MCBS framework. It is, however, specifically targeted to CORBA middleware and has been tested on both TAO (Schmidt, Natarajan, Gokhale, Wang, & Gill, 2002) and JacORB (Brose, 1997).

The OVATION tool uses CORBA Portable Interceptors (OMG, 2002) to insert probes. Portable Interceptors are based on the Interceptor pattern (Schmidt et al., 2000), which allows transparent addition of services to a framework and automatic triggering of these services when certain events occur. Whenever a CORBA client calls a server component client stub and server skeleton interceptors are invoked. Each interceptor can perform any arbitrary function, such as

timestamping an event or recording information about a call to a log file.

OVATION provides a number of predefined probes, including:

- **Snooper Probe,** which captures CORBA operation information, such as request name, arguments, request start time, end time and the threads and the processes to which an operation belongs;
- **Milestone Probe,** which permits the manual demarcation of specific events in the application code; and
- **Trace Probe,** which is used to capture information about the other non-CORBA, C++ or Java object method calls.

OVATION also allows users to add their own custom probes to the monitoring framework. This feature allows developers to profile application-specific characteristic without changing their source code. Moreover, custom probes can be dynamically enabled and disabled at run time.

Call graphs among components, along with

Figure 9. Screenshot of the OVATION visualization tool

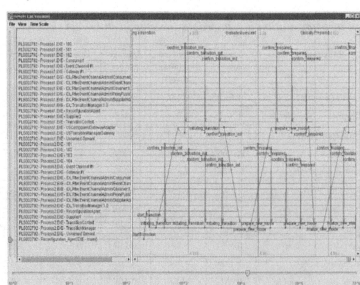

latency measurements, are reconstructed for each scenario. OVATION generates log files during program execution that contain information detailing processes, threads, and objects involved in the interaction. The OVATION visualizer transforms the log file into a graphical representation of the recorded remote object interactions. An example screenshot from the visualizer showing measured call sequences is illustrated in Figure 9.

Summary of Operating System and Middleware Profiling Techniques

All applications interact with the operating system and many interact with middleware services for distributed communication, fault tolerance, security, resource management, and so forth. Measuring behavior in the layers that supports application execution is crucial to gaining a complete understanding of the broader system because applications share resources (e.g., memory, files and devices) via these layers. Complex interactions and dependencies are often hidden and not obviously understood by the systems engineer. As large-scale systems are integrated together, these hidden dependencies result in resource conflicts and "causal chains" that lead to unexpected, and often undesirable, behavior. The tools described in this section allow profiling of execution that passes through the operating system and middleware layers. One challenge faced by these tools and their users is mapping these behaviors to higher-level application and distributed events.

VIRTUAL MACHINE PROFILING TECHNIQUES

The use of virtual machine, such as the Java Virtual Machine and the Microsoft Common Runtime Language (CLR), is becoming increasingly common in enterprise applications where portability and security are key requirements. Figure 10 illustrates a typical VM-based application architecture where each user application is independently layered above the VM.

The use of VMs to run "managed programs" lends itself to more portable profiling. For example, dynamic instrumentation of complete binaries for VM platforms is more straightforward because the bytecode represents a hardware agnostic, and more abstract representation, of the binary code (Gosling, 1995).

In general, profiling strategies for VMs, such as sampling and instrumentation, are comparable to their native counterparts; the main factors that determine effectiveness of a given approach include (1) implementation complexity, (2) incurred time/space overhead, and (3) level of detail in the output. This section describes different methods used for VM profiling and evaluates the advantages and disadvantages of each.

Sampling-Based VM Profiling

One approach to profiling applications that execute in a VM environment is to sample the execution state (i.e., program counter value and call

Figure 10. Applications running on virtual machine

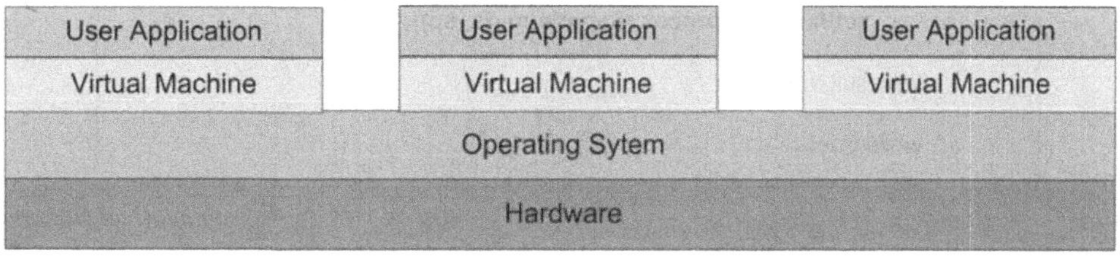

stack) at periodic timer-driven intervals. Whaley (2000) demonstrates the use of such timer-driven sampling via a "samping profiler" that examines threads within the JVM process corresponding to the Java application being profiled. The profiler then periodic traverses the operating system's thread queues, and for each active Java thread, retrieves the register state (program counter and stack pointer) as well as the current time. In effect, this is a combination of operating system level profiling with the restriction on VM processes (i.e., crossing the OS-VM boundary).

Although sampling-based profiling methods are relatively lightweight, they are susceptible to certain problems (Subramaniam & Thazhuthaveetil, 1994), including:

- **Straddling effect of counters:** the initial analysis to segregate the bytecode for dif-

ferent methods will be approximate, causing inconsistent results;

- **Short submethods:** short-lived calls that take less time than the sampling frequency may not be recorded at all; and

- **Resonance effects:** the time to complete a single iteration of a loop can coincide with the sampling period, which may sample the same point each time, while other sections are never measured.

These problems can be avoided by using techniques described in Subramaniam and Thazhuthaveetil (1994). To obtain a consistent picture of application behavior, however, a significant number of runs must be performed. This number will vary from application to application, so the sampling period may also require configuration for each application.

Box 7.

```
// Pseudo Java code illustrating Komorium re-writing. Bold represents additional
// code added by Komorium.
//
// ac = per-thread activation counter representing the upper bound of the
// number of executed bytecodes
//
// mids, sp = represents reifed method ids, stack pointer pair
//
class Foo {
    private static final MID mid_sum;
    static {
        String cl = Class.forName("Foo").getName();
        mid_sum = createMID(c1, "sum", "(II)I");
    }

    static int sum(int from, int to, AC ac, MID[] mids, int sp) {

        mids[sp++] = mid_sum;
        decrementAC(2);
        if(getValue(ac) <= 0)
            setValue(ac, processSample(mids, sp));

        int result = 0;

        while(true) {
```

continued on following page

Box 7. continued

```
                    decrementAC(3);
                    if(getValue(ac) <= 0)
                        setValue(ac, processSample(mids, sp));
                    if(from > to) {
                        decrementAC(2);
                        if(getValue(ac) <= 0)
                            setValue(ac, processSample(mids, sp));
                        return result;
                    }
                    decrementAC(7);
                    if(getValue(ac) <= 0)
                        setValue(ac, processSample(mids, sp));

                    result += f(from, ac, mids, sp);
                    ++from;
                }
            }

        static int sum(int from, int to) {
            Thread t = Thread.currentThread();
            return sum(from, to, ac, new MID[STACKSIZE], 0);
        }
    }
```

Bytecode Counting

Another instance of VM sampling-based profiling is Komorium (Binder, 2005). Komorium does not check the program counter at regular intervals. Instead, a snapshot of the call stack is recorded by each thread after a certain number of bytecodes are executed. The motivation for this approach is that bytecode counting is a platform-independent metric that does not depend upon VM-specific profiling services. Bytecode counting can also be done without on the need for low-level platform-dependent utilities to acquire resource usage data, thus making it more portable and easier to maintain.

Komorium relies on the periodic activation of a user-defined profiling agent to process samples of the call stack. Bytecode rewriting is used to pass the current call stack of the caller into the profiling function. To schedule regular activation of the custom profiling function, each thread maintains an activation counter (ac) that represents the upper bound of the number of executed bytecodes since the last invocation. The active count is decremented at given points in the code. The default behavior is to update the active count at the beginning of each basic block, which is defined as a sequence of bytecode that end with a control flow instruction. At each decrement, a consumption check is made to determine whether the custom agent (processSample) should be called. The following excerpt illustrates in pseudo-code the Komorium binary rewriting: (Box 7)

Binder, Hulaas, and Villaz (2001) evaluated the Komorium approach through experimentation. They showed that their approach could sample at an accuracy of 91% using an overlapping percentage metric (Arnold & Ryder, 2001). The best results were obtained from a profiling granularity of 5,000-10,000 bytecodes per sample, resulting in an average overhead of 47-56% for a 10,000 bytecode granularity.

VM sampling-based profiling provides an effective method of collecting temporal information relating to program control. These techniques are can be used to determine task latency, jitter, and execution quanta, as well as to identify patterns of processor migration.

Profiling via VM Hooks

A VM hook represents an access point to a previously defined event, such as method entry/exit or thread start/stop, that can occur within the context of a running application. The profiling agent implements callback methods on the profiling interface and registers them with the appropriate VM hooks. The VM then detects the events and invokes the corresponding callback method when these events occur in the application. It is straightforward to develop profilers based on VM hooks because profiler developers need only implement an interface provided by the VM, without worry-

ing about the complications that can arise from modifying the application directly.

Although the VM and profiling agent provide the monitoring infrastructure, profiler developers are responsible for certain tasks, such as synchronization. For example, multithreaded applications can spawn multiple instances of the same event simultaneously, which will invoke the same callback method on the same instance of the profiling agent. Callbacks must therefore be made reentrant via synchronization mechanisms, such as mutexes, to avoid compromising profiler internal state.

The Microsoft Common Language Runtime (CLR) profiler and the Java Virtual Machine Tool Interface (JVMTI) are two examples of VM profilers that that support VM hooks, as described below.

Figure 11. Messaging sequence of CLR profiling

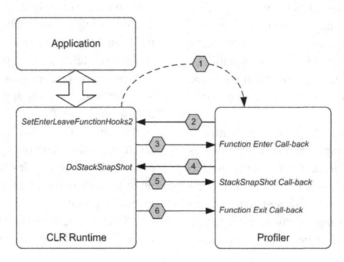

1. Profiler agent loaded (configured through environment variable).
2. Profiler agent register "events of interest" (e.g. selected function calls specified through a filter).
3. CLR makes function "enter" call-back.
4. Request a snapshot of the thread's stack.
5. StackSnapShot called back.
6. CLR makes function "exit" call-back.

CLR Profiler

The CLR Profiler (Hilyard, 2005) interface allows the integration of custom profiling functionality provided in the form of a pluggable dynamic link library, written in a native language like C or C++. The plug-in module, termed the agent, accesses profiling services of the CLR via the `ICorProfilerInfo2` interface. The agent must also implement the `ICorProfilerCallback2` interface so the CLR can call the agent back to indicate the occurrence of events in the context of the profiled application.

At startup, the CLR initializes the agent and sets the events of interest. When an event occurs, the CLR calls the corresponding method on the `ICorProfilerCallback2` interface. The agent can then inspect the execution state of the application by calling methods back on the CLR (`ICorProfilerInfo2`).

Figure 11 shows the series of communications triggered by each function entered in the CLR execution. In this example, in between processing function enter/exit call-backs, the profiling agent requests a stack snapshot so it can identify the fully qualified method name and also the call's parent, that is, the method from which the method being traced was called.

Inspecting the stack to determine parental methods (and ultimately the call-chain) is a useful technique for disambiguating system calls. For example, this approach can be used to disambiguate different lock calls so that per-lock information (e.g., hold and wait times) can be correlated with different call sites in the source code.

JVMTI Profiler

The JVMTI (Sun Microsystems Corporation, 2004) is similar to the CLR Profiler Interface in that it requires a plug-in, which is implemented as a dynamic link library using a native language that supports C. The JVM interacts with the agent

through JVMTI functions, such as `Agent_OnLoad()` and `Agent_OnUnload()`, which are exported by the agent. The JVM supplies a pointer, via the `Agent_Onload()` call, that the agent can use to get an instance of the JVMTI environment. The agent can then use this pointer to access JVMTI features, such as reading the state of a thread, stopping/interrupting threads, obtaining a stack trace of a thread, or reading local variable information. The agent uses the `SetEventCallbacks()` method to pass a set of function pointers for different events it is interested. When events occur, the corresponding function is called by the JVM, which allows the agent to record the state of the application.

Although the CLR and JVMTI profilers share many common features, such as events related to methods or threads and stack tracing ability, there are differences. For example, the JVMTI provides application-specific details, such as the method name, object name, class name, and parameters, from the calls, whereas the CLR interface provides them in a metadata format and details can only be extracted using the metadata API, which is tedious. The JVMTI also provides additional features compared to the CLR, including monitor wait and monitor waited, which provide information related to thread blocking on critical sections of code.

Research (Reiss, 2003, 2005) has shown that the JVMTI interface incurs significant runtime overhead because the profiling agent is written in a native language, so JNI calls (Sun Microsystems Corporation, 2002) are needed to call this agent. JNI calls can incur significant overhead because they perform actions such as saving registers, marshaling arguments, and wrapping objects in JNI handles (Dmitriev, 2002). This overhead may not be acceptable for some applications, so the explicit bytecode instrumentation approach described in the next section may be a less costly solution because it does not use JNI.

Application Code Instrumentation

Although sampling- and hook-based instrumentation can be performed with relatively little overhead, the breadth of the information collected is limited and often insufficient to build application-level detail. An alternative is to instrument the application's bytecode directly. Bytecode instrumentation inserts functionality (in the form of additional bytecodes) that performs application profiling within compiled code. The Komorium work discussed previously is a form of byte code instrumentation. However, we differentiate the discussion in this section by instrumentation that is driven directly by the application logic.

As a general approach, bytecode instrumentation involves redefining classes that are going to be profiled by replacing the original bytecode with instrumented code that contains logging actions triggered by specific events. This approach enables the use of application-specific events for profiling, such as transaction completion or data regarding critical sections of the application. Bytecode instrumentation has in most instances less overhead and greater flexibility than using VM-provided profiling interfaces. Nevertheless, the responsibility of implementing measurement functionality lies with the profiler user.

There are several approaches to bytecode instrumentation, including:

- Static instrumentation, which involves changing the compiled code off-line before execution that is, creating a copy of the instrumented intermediate code. Many commercial profilers, such as OptimizeIt (Borland Software Corporation, 2006), work this way. Static instrumentation has also been implemented by Reiss (2003) and later extended in Reiss (2005).
- Load-time instrumentation, which calls the agent before loading each class, and passes it the bytecode for the class that can be changed by the agent and returned. The JVMTI/CLR profiler interfaces are examples of load-time instrumentation.
- Dynamic instrumentation, which works when the application is already running and also uses a profiler interface (Dmitriev, 2002). The agent makes a call to the VM passing it the new definitions of the classes that are installed by the VM at runtime.

Like other forms of code modification, dynamic instrumentation supports "fix and continue" debugging, which avoids lengthy exit, recompile, and restart cycles. It also helps reduce application overhead by enabling developers to (1) pinpoint specific regions of code that are experiencing performance problems at runtime and (2) instrument the classes' involved, rather than instrumenting the entire application. Instrumented classes can be replaced with the original ones after sufficient data is collected.

Dynamic instrumentation of bytecode is typically more straightforward than dynamic instrumentation of low-level machine instructions because of the higher level of abstraction. Moreover, modifying bytecode provides a more portable solution that is largely agnostic to the underlying operating system and hardware platform.

Within the context of Java, the JVMTI provides a method known as `RedefineClasses()` that a profiler agent can use to insert "new" bytecode into an existing class. When this method is invoked, the JVM performs all the steps needed to load a class, parse the class code, create objects of the class, and initializes them. After these steps are complete, the JVM performs hot-swapping by suspending all threads and replacing the class, while ensuring that all pointers are updated to point to the new object (Dmitriev, 2001).

These dynamic instrumentation activities can incur significant overhead in production environments and thus must be accounted for accordingly. Some research is investigating techniques to minimize the overhead incurred by dynamic instrumentation. For example, work by Dmitriev (2002) is investigating the use of "method swapping" so that bytecode replacement can be done at a finer granularity than class-level replacement. Similar techniques are also being explored within the context of the .NET platform (Vaswani & Srikant, 2003).

A number of tools have been developed to help instrument bytecode, much like the Pin API described earlier. Examples include BIT (Lee, 1997) and IBM's Jikes Bytecode Toolkit (IBM Corporation, 2000). These tools shield application developers from the complexity of bytecode by providing an API that can be used to parse and modify it.

- The three bytecode instrument techniques (i.e., static, load-time, and dynamic) incur similar overhead. Dynamic bytecode instrumentation is more powerful, but is generally more complex and error-prone than static and load time instrumentation. Dynamic instrumentation also requires creating "new" objects of the "new" classes corresponding to all "old" objects in the application, initializing their state to the state of the old object, suspend the running threads, and switching all pointers to the "old" objects to the "new" objects. This replacement process is complicated, so application state may be inconsistent after the operation, which can cause incorrect behavior.

- Static and load-time instrumentation are generally easier to implement than dynamic instrumentation because they need not worry about the consistency of a running application. Dynamic instrumentation has a broader range of applicability, however, if done efficiently. Current research (Dmitriev, 2002, 2004) is focusing on how to make dynamic instrumentation more efficient and less complicated.

Aspect-Oriented Techniques Used for Instrumentation

Although explicit bytecode instrumentation is more flexible and incurs less overhead than VM hooks, the implementation complexity is higher because developers must be highly skilled in bytecode syntax to instrument it effectively without corrupting application code. Aspect-oriented Programming (AOP) helps remove this complexity and enables bytecode instrumenting at a higher level of abstraction. Developers can therefore focus on the logic of the code snippets and the appropriate insertion points, rather than wrestling with low-level implementation details (Davies, Huismans, Slaney, Whiting, & Webster, 2003). Relevant AOP concepts include (1) join-points, which define placeholders for instrumentation within application code, (2) point-cuts, which identify a selection of join-points to instrument, and (3) advice, which specifies the code to insert at the corresponding join-point.

AspectWerkz (Boner, 2004) is a framework that uses AOP to support static, load-time, and dynamic (runtime) instrumentation of bytecode. The advantages and disadvantages of the various techniques are largely similar to those discussed earlier. There are also aspects to consider when using an AOP-based approach, however, which we discuss below.

The AOP paradigm makes it easier for developers to insert profiling to an existing application by defining a profiler aspect consisting of point-cuts and advice. The following excerpt illustrates the use of AspectWerkz to define join-points before, after, and around the execution of the method `HelloWorld.greet()`. The annotations in the comments section of the Aspect class express the semantics, for example, "`@Before execution (* <package _ name>.<class _ name>.<method _ name>)`" means the method will be called before the execution of the `<method _ name>` mentioned.

```
/////////////////////////////////////////////////
//
package testAOP;

import org.codehaus.aspectwerkz.joinpoint.JoinPoint;

public class HelloWorldAspect {
    /**
     * @Before execution(* testAOP.HelloWorld.greet(..))
     */
    public void beforeGreeting(JoinPoint joinPoint) {
        System.out.println("before greeting...");
    }

    /**
     * @After execution(* testAOP.HelloWorld.greet(..))
     */
    public void afterGreeting(JoinPoint joinPoint) {
        System.out.println("after greeting...");
    }

/**
     * @Around execution(* testAOP.HelloWorld2.greet(..))
     */
    public Object around_greet (JoinPoint joinPoint) {
        Object greeting = joinPoint.proceed();
        return "<yell>" + greeting + "</yell>";
    }
}
```

Advice code can be written in the managed language, so there is no need to learn the low-level syntax of bytecode because the AOP framework can handle these details. The bulk of the effort therefore shifts to learning the framework rather than bytecode/IL syntax, which is advantageous because these frameworks are similar even if the target application language changes, for example, from Java to C#. Another advantage is the increased reliability and stability provided by a proven framework with dedicated support. For example, developers need not worry about problems arising with hot-swap or multiple threads being profiled because these are handled by the framework.

Some problems encountered by AOP approaches are the design and deployment overhead of using the framework. AOP frameworks are generally extensive and contain a gamut of configuration and deployment options, which may take time to master. Moreover, developers must also master another framework on top of the actual application, which may make it hard to use profiling extensively. Another potential drawback is that profiling can only occur at the join-points provided by the framework, which is often restricted to the methods of each class, that is, before a method is called or after a method returns. Application-specific events occurring within a method call therefore cannot be profiled, which means that nondeterministic events cannot be captured by AOP profilers.

Summary of Virtual Machine Profiling Techniques

Java and C# are two prominent VM-based languages that are becoming increasingly dominant in the development of enterprise-style systems. The advantage of ease-of-use, security and portability is driving their success. Nevertheless, from a run-time analysis and profiling perspective, they do pose additional challenges by executing programs in a "hidden" VM. The tools in this section can be used to extend profiling capabilities into a VM environment.

The decision to choose a particular profiling technique depends upon application requirements. The following criteria are useful to decide which approach is appropriate for a given application.

- Sampling is most effective when there is a need to minimize runtime overhead and use profiling in production deployments, though application-specific logical events may not be tracked properly.
- The simplest way to implement profiling is by using the JVMTI/CLR profiling interface, which has the shortest development time and is easy to master. Detailed logical events may not be captured, however, and the overhead incurred may be heavier than bytecode/IL instrumentation.
- Bytecode/IL instrumentation is harder to implement, but gives unlimited freedom to

the profiler to record any event in the application. Implementing a profiler is harder than using the JVMTI/CLR profiling interface, however, and a detailed knowledge of bytecode/IL is required. Among the different bytecode/IL instrumentation ways, complexity of implementation increases from static-time instrumentation to load-time to dynamic instrumentation. Dynamic instrumentation provides powerful features, such as "fix and continue" and runtime problem tracking.

- The use of an AOP framework can reduce the development complexity and increase reliability because bytecode/IL need not be manipulated directly. Conversely, AOP can increase design and deployment overhead, which may make it unsuitable for profiling. Moreover, application-level events may be hard to capture using AOP if join-points locations are limited.

HARDWARE-BASED PROFILING TECHNIQUES

Previous sections have concentrated on modifications to program code (e.g., via instrumentation) or code that implements the execution environment (e.g., VM profiling). This section describes hardware profiling techniques that collect behavioral information in multithreaded systems, focusing on two main categories of hardware-based profiling solutions: on-chip performance counters and on-chip debugging/in-circuit emulation interfaces.

On-Chip Performance Counters

On-chip debugging/profiling interfaces are specialized circuitries that are added to a microprocessor to collect events and measure time. Modern COTS processors provide on-chip performance monitoring and debugging support. On-chip, performance-monitoring support includes selectable counting registers and time stamping clocks. The Intel Pentium/Xeon family of processors and the IBM PowerPC family of processors both provide these performance monitoring features (Intel Corporation, 2006a; IBM Corporation, 1998).

For example, the Intel Xeon processor provides one 64-bit timestamp counter and eighteen 40-bit-wide Model Specific Registers (MSR) as counters (different processor models have a different number of performance counters available). Each core (in a multicore configuration) has its own timestamp counter and counter registers. The timestamp counter is incremented at the processor's clock speed and is constant (at least in later versions of the processors) across multiple cores and processors in an SMP environment. Timestamp counters are initially synchronized because each is started on the processor RESET signal. Timestamp counters can be written to later, however, potentially get them out of sync. Counters must be carefully synchronized when accessing them from different threads that potentially execute on different cores.

The performance counters and timestamp MSRs are accessed through specialized machine instructions (i.e., RDMSR, WRMSR, and RDTSC) or through higher-level APIs such as the Performance Application Programming Interface (PAPI) (London, Moore, Mucci, Seymour, & Luczak, 2001). A set of control registers are also provided to select which of the available performance monitoring events should be maintained in the available counter set. The advantages of using on-chip performance counters are: (1) they do not cost anything in addition to the off-the-shelf processor and (2) they can be used with a very low overhead. For instance, copying the current 64-bit timestamp counter into memory (user or kernel) through the Intel RDTSC instruction costs less than 100 cycles.

Countable events on the Intel Xeon processor include branch predictions, prediction misses, misaligned memory references, cache misses and transfers, I/O bus transactions, memory bus transactions, instruction decoding, micro-op execution, and floating-point assistance. These events are counted on a per-logical core basis, that is, the Intel performance counter features do not provide any means of differentiating event counts across different threads or processes. Certain architectures, however, such as the IBM PowerPC 604e (IBM Corporation, 1998), do provide the ability to trigger an interrupt when performance counters negate or wrap-around. This interrupt can be filtered on a per processor basis and used to support a crude means of thread-association for infrequent events.

On-chip performance counters have limited use in profiling characteristics specific to multi-threaded programming. Nevertheless, on-chip timestamp collection can be useful for measuring execution time intervals (Wolf, 2003). For example, measurement of context switch times of the operating systems can be easily done through the insertion of RDTSC into the operating system-kernel switching code. Coupling timestamp features with compiler-based instrumentation can be an effective way to measure lock wait and hold times.

On-chip Debugging Interfaces and In-circuit Emulators (ICE)

Performance counters are only useful for counting global events in the system. Additional functionality is therefore needed to perform more powerful inspection of execution and register/memory state. One way to provide this functionality is by augmenting the "normal" target processor with additional functionality. The term in-circuit emulator (ICE) refers to the use of a substitute processor module that "emulates" the target microprocessor and provides additional debugging functionality (Collins 1997).

ICE modules are usually plugged directly into the microprocessor socket using a specialized adapter, as shown in Figure 12. Many modern microprocessors, however, provide explicit sup-

Figure 12. Example ICE adapter and ICE module

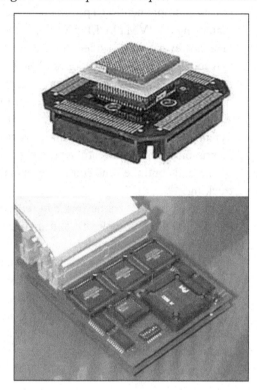

port for ICE, including most x86 and PowerPC-based CPUs. A special debug connector on the motherboard normally provides access to the on-chip ICE features.

Two key standards define debugging functionality adopted by most ICE solutions: JTAG (IEEE, 2001) and the more recent Nexus (IEEE-ISTO, 2003). The Nexus debugging interface is a superset of JTAG and consists of between 25 and 100 auxiliary message-based channels that connect directly to the target processor. The Nexus specification defines a number of different "classes" of support that represent different capability sets composed from the following sets:

- Ownership trace messaging (OTM), which facilitates ownership tracing by providing visibility of which process identity (ID) or operating system task is activated. An

OTM is transmitted to indicate when a new process/task is activated, thereby allowing development tools to trace ownership flow. For embedded processors that implement virtual addressing or address translation, moreover, an OTM is also transmitted periodically during runtime at a minimum frequency of every 256 Program/Trace messages.

- Program trace via branch trace messaging (BTM), where messages are triggered for each change in program flow discontinuity as a result of either a branch decision or an exception. Control flow can be correlated to program code, where the code is static. BTM messages include timestamp information and the full target-branch address. Thread/task ownership can be correlated from the last received OTM message.

- Data trace messaging (DTM), where a minimum of two trace windows define the start and end memory addresses that should be monitored. DTM messages are dispatched on each read and write of memory in the defined range. Depending on the type of DTM message, a timestamp, the data value read/written, the address of memory access, the current mapped page, and a control flow association are included.

- Runtime system memory substitution via memory substitution messaging (MSM), which has the ability to substitute portions of memory with new code passed from the debugging host via the Nexus interface. Triggers for substitution are exit, reset, and watchpoints.

- Signal watchpoint and breakpoint events, which are used to indicate that specific instruction addresses or data addresses (conditional) have been accessed. Watchpoints are a variation of breakpoints that do not halt the target processor. Both watchpoints and breakpoints can be set to operating system and runtime library functions of interest,

such as thread control and synchronization.

Nexus and JTAG-compatible devices can be chained together and read from the same debugging host, which is particularly useful for SMP and multi-core environments, where the profiling needs to collate events from different processors.

On-chip debugging interfaces and ICE solutions provide a primitive means for extracting low-level behavior of a program. They are particularly useful at collecting "raw" low-level details of execution, such as control flow and memory activity, that in turn can be used to assure absence of race conditions, deadlock, and so forth. For example, the following approach might be used to ensure that a program is free of race-conditions:

- Identify address ranges for memory that are shared across one or more threads.
- Identify addresses for synchronization locks and/or functions.
- Establish data-write triggers for identified memory addresses and record triggered events over the execution of the program in a test run.
- Ensure that the appropriate sequence of take lock, access memory (N times), release lock, is followed.

Of course, because this type of profiling is dynamic, the properties can only be ensured for the states the program entered during the test.

Summary of Hardware-Based Profiling Techniques

Hardware profiling is typically reserved for embedded and safety-critical system where understanding and ensuring system behavior is of utmost importance. Although hardware profiling can be relatively costly, it offers the following advantages over software profiling solutions:

- Nonintrusive data collection. Behavioral data can be collected with little or no impact on normal execution of the target system.
- Support for fine-grained data collection. High frequency data can be precisely collected at speeds commensurate with processor/bus clock speeds.
- Off-chip inspection capability. Elements of behavior, such as bus and cache interconnect activity, that do not propagate directly into a general-purpose CPU, can be inspected.

Hardware profiling is particularly advantageous for analyzing certain types of system behavior (such as memory cache hits/misses) that are not easily inspected through software means. Nevertheless, while hardware profiling excels at inspection of fine-grained system events, deriving higher-level measures can be harder. For example, using a hardware profiler to determine the level of concurrency in a system would be hard.

FUTURE TRENDS

This section discusses emerging and future technological trends in the behavioral analysis of systems.

Increased Focus on Synergies Between Static and Dynamic Analysis Techniques and Tools

Since there is no single approach to system profiling that addresses every need, we believe that the most effective approach is to use a combination of static and dynamic analysis to provide a more complete picture of system behavior. Static analysis can be used to explore all possible paths of execution and statistically proportion their execution likelihood. Likewise, dynamic analysis can be used to collect more precise information for concrete instances of a program execution.

New tools and techniques are needed, however, that strategically combine static and dynamic analysis, and that partition the system into well-defined "behavioral containers." As an example of such tools, work by Artho and Biere (2005) has developed generic analysis algorithms that can be applied in either a static or dynamic context. This solution has been demonstrated within the context of software fault detection, whereby faults identified through static analysis are subsequently verified by actual execution and dynamic analysis.

Greater Emphasis on Probabilistic Assurance of Dynamic System Behavior

Even when static and dynamic analysis techniques are combined, certain behavioral properties of large-scale dynamic software systems are still hard to measure and assure precisely, including absence of deadlock and livelock conditions, effective parallelism, and worst-case execution time. These properties can often be assured to a given statistical probability, though both dynamic and static analyses are unable to provide absolute assurance in all cases. Even techniques like explicit-state model checking can only provide assurance in very small systems, where interaction with the external environment is well understood and controlled.

A key reason these properties are hard to measure accurately stems from sources of (apparent) nondeterminism in today's software systems. Deep causal chains, multiple levels of caching, and unpredictable interactions between threads and their environment lead to an incomprehensible number of behavior patterns. The openness of operating systems in their external interactions, such as networks, devices, and other processors, and the use of throughput-efficient-scheduling strategies, such as dynamic priority queues and task preemption, are the principal cause of such behavioral uncertainty. Although real-time and safety-critical operating systems try to ensure higher levels of determinism by applying constraints on execution, such as off-line scheduling, resource reservation, and cache disabling, these solutions are often not applicable for general-purpose systems.

New tools and techniques are needed, therefore, that can assure behaviors of dynamic systems with greater probability. Examples include system execution modeling (SEM) tools (Hill, Schmidt, & Slaby, 2007) that enable software architects, developers, and systems engineers to explore design alternatives from multiple computational and valuation perspectives at multiple lifecycle phases using multiple quality criteria with multiple stakeholders and suppliers. In addition to validating design rules and checking for design conformance, SEM tools facilitate "what if" analysis of alternative designs to quantify the costs of certain design choices on end-to-end system performance. For example, SEM tools can help empirically determine the maximum number of components a host can handle before performance degrades, the average and worse response time for various workloads, and the ability of alternative system configurations and deployments to meet end-to-end QoS requirements for a particular workload. Although the results of SEM tool analysis are probabilistic—rather than absolute—they still provide valuable information to users.

Implicit Support for Measurement of infrastructure Software and Processors

Infrastructure software (such as operating systems, virtual machines, and middleware) and processors increasingly provide measurement logic that collects behavioral information during multithreaded system execution. Although these capabilities are useful, they are often provided as add-ons, rather than being integrated seamlessly into the infrastructure software and processors. As a result, the measurement hooks are often not available when needed or undue effort is required to configure and optimize them.

New tools and techniques are needed, therefore, to provide implicit support for measuring of infrastructure software and processors. In particular, the ability to measure and monitor behavior of the system should be a first class concern.

Total-System Measurement that Relates and Combines Microscopic Measurements Together to Give a Unified View of System Behavior

The nondeterministic nature of today's large-scale systems is exacerbated by the lack of integration between various microscopic measurement techniques—both in hardware and in software—and the need for a broader perspective in reasoning about and analyzing end-to-end system behavior. This problem is particularly acute in distributed real-time and embedded (DRE) systems that must combine hardware and software components to meet the following challenging requirements:

As distributed systems, DRE systems require capabilities to measure the quantity/quality of connections and message transfer between separate machines,

As real-time systems, DRE systems require predictable and efficient control over end-to-end system resources, such as memory, networks, and processors, and

As embedded systems, DRE systems have weight, cost, and power constraints that limit their computing and memory resources.

Microscopic measurements of such DRE systems often fail to provide a unified view of system behavior, which makes it hard to assure that the systems meet their functional and QoS requirements.

New tools and techniques are needed, therefore, to provide total-system measurement that provides a unified view of system behavior. An example of such a tool is Intel's VTune Performance Analyzer (REF). This tool combines behavioral information from the microprocessor (measuring on-chip counters), the operating system (OS-level context switching etc.) and the application (application-level function profiling) to provide an effective approach to application tuning.

CONCLUDING REMARKS

This chapter reviewed four approaches to analyzing the behavior of software systems via dynamic analysis: compiler-based instrumentation, operating system and middleware profiling, virtual machine profiling and hardware-based profiling. We highlighted the advantages and disadvantages of each approach with respect to measuring the performance of multithreaded and SMP systems, and demonstrated how these approaches can be applied in practice.

Table 7 summarizes our assessment of the utility of each approach with respect to key problems that arise in developing large-scale, multithreaded systems. The number of dots in each category indicates how effective the approach is for mea-

suring the corresponding characteristics (defined previously in Table 2).

The results in Table 7 show that dynamic profiling is particularly useful where fine-grained event data can be collected and used to derive characteristics of a running system. Dynamic analysis is weaker and less capable, when the behavioral characteristic depends on system-wide analysis, such as the global thread state. It is therefore clear that runtime profiling alone is insufficient to capture and predict a complete image of system behavior due to the "as observed" syndrome, that is, dynamic analysis can only assure statistical certainty of behavior because it just collects behavioral data for a given execution trace.

The alternative to dynamic analysis is static analysis, such as program analysis and model checking. The benefits of static analysis are its ability to (1) perform analysis without running the system (useful for pre-integration testing), and (2) allow the inspection of all theoretically possible (albeit less frequent) conditions. Although static analysis is promising in some areas, it also cannot capture and predict a complete image of behavior for large-scale systems. In particular,

Table 7. Summary of dynamic profiling capabilities

	Compiler-based Instrumentation	Operating System & Middleware Profiling	Virtual Machine Profiling	Hardware-based Profiling
Synchronization overhead	●●●	●●●	●●●	●●●
Task latency & jitter	●●●	●●●	●●●	●●
Task execution quanta		●●●	●●●	●●●
Unsafe memory access	●●●		●	●●●
Processor migration		●●●		●●●
Priority inversion		●●	●●	
Deadlock and livelock		●	●	●
Effective parallelism		●	●	
Worst-case execution time				●

●●●:   *Well suited to analysis of property*
●●:   *Able to partially analyze property or is typically difficult to engineer*
●:   *Approach can be used to collect relevant data, but requires additional processing/analysis capability*
No dots: *Unable to analyze property effectively*

static-analysis techniques are limited in their practical applicability (e.g., scalability) and in their ability to relate to wall-clock time.

Behavioral analysis technology will be increasingly important as the systems we build become larger, more parallel, and more unpredictable. New tools and techniques that strategically combine static and dynamic analysis—and that partition the system into well-defined "behavioral containers"—will be critical to the progression along this path.

REFERENCES

Arnold, M., & Ryder, B. G. (2001). A framework for reducing the cost of instrumented code. In *Proceedings of the SIGPLAN Conference on Programming Language Design and Implementation*, (pp. 168-179).

Artho, C., & Biere, A. (2005). Combined static and dynamic analysis. In *Proceedings of the 1st International Workshop on Abstract Interpretation of Object-oriented Language (AIOOL 2005)*, ENTCS, Paris. Elsevier Science Publishing.

Baxter, I. (2004). DMS: Program transformations for practical scalable software evolution. In *Proceedings of the 26th International Conference on Software Engineering*, (pp. 625-634).

Beck, M., Bohme, H., Dziadzka, M., Kunitz, U., Magnus, R., & Verworner, D. (1999). *Linux Kernel internals (2nd ed.)*. Addison Wesley Longman.

Binder, W. (2005). A portable and customizable profiling framework for Java based on bytecode instruction counting. In *Proceedings of the Third Asian Symposium on Programming Languages and Systems (APLAS 2005)*, (LNCS 3780, pp. 178-194).

Binder, W., & Hulaas, J. (2004, October). A portable CPU-management framework for Java. *IEEE Internet Computing, 8*(5), 74-83.

Binder, W., Hulaas J., & Villaz A. (2001). Portable resource control in Java. In *Proceedings of the 2001 ACM SIGPLAN Conference on Object Oriented Programming, Systems, Languages and Applications*, (Vol. 36, No. 11, pp. 139-155).

Boner, J. (2004, March). AspectWerkz—Dynamic AOP for Java. In *Proceedings of the 3rd International Conference on Aspect-oriented development (AOSD 2004)*. Lancaster, UK.

Borland Software Corporation. (2006). *Borland Optimize-it Enterprise Suite* (Computer software). Retrieved March 11, 2008, from http://www.borland.com/us/products/optimizeit/index.html

Broberg, M., Lundberg, L., & Grahn, H. (1999, April). Visualization and performance prediction of multithreaded solaris programs by tracing kernel threads. In *Proceedings of the 13th International Parallel Processing Symposium*, (pp. 407-413).

Brose, G. (1997, September). JacORB: Implementation and design of a Java ORB. In *Proceedings of IFIP DAIS'97*, (pp. 143-154).

Bruening, D. L. (2004). *Efficient, transparent, and comprehensive runtime code manipulation*. Unpublished doctoral dissertation, Massachusetts Institute of Technology.

Buck, B., & Hollingsworth, J. K. (2000). An API for runtime code patching. *International Journal of High Performance Computing Applications*, 317-329.

Cantrill, B., & Doeppner, T. W. (1997, January). Threadmon: A tool for monitoring multithreaded program performance. In *Proceedings of the 30th Hawaii International Conference on Systems Sciences*, (pp. 253-265).

Clarke, E. M., Grumberg, O., & Peled, D. A. (2000). *Model checking. Massachusetts Institute of Technology*. Cambridge, MA: The MIT Press.

Clauss, P., Kenmei, B., & Beyler, J.C. (2005, September). The periodic-linear model of program behavior capture. In *Proceedings of Euro-Par 2005* (LNCS 3648, pp. 325-335).

Collins, R. (1997, September). In-circuit emulation: How the microprocessor evolved over time. *Dr. Dobbs Journal*. Retrieved March 11, 2008, from http://www.rcollins.org/ddj/Sep97

Cordy, R., Halpern C., & Promislow, E. (1991). TXL: A rapid prototyping system for programming language dialects. In *Proceedings of the International Conference on Computer Languages* (Vol. 16, No. 1, pp. 97-107).

Davies, J., Huismans, N., Slaney, R., Whiting, S., & Webster, M. (2003). *An aspect-oriented performance analysis environment.* AOSD'03 Practitioner Report, 2003.

Dmitriev, M. (2001a). *Safe evolution of large and long-lived Java applications.* Unpublished doctoral dissertation, Department of Computing Science, University of Glasgow, Glasgow G12 8QQ, Scotland.

Dmitriev, M. (2001b). Towards flexible and safe technology for runtime evolution of Java language applications. In *Proceedings of the Workshop on Engineering Complex Object-Oriented Systems for Evolution* (pp. 14-18). In Association with OOPSLA 2001 International Conference, Tampa Bay, FL, USA.

Dmitriev, M. (2002). Application of the HotSwap technology to advanced profiling. In *Proceedings of the First Workshop on Unanticipated Software Evolution,* held at ECOOP 2002 International Conference, Malaga, Spain.

Dmitriev, M. (2004). Profiling Java applications using code hotswapping and dynamic call graph revelation. In *Proceedings of the 4th International Workshop on Software and Performance,* Redwood Shores, CA, (pp. 139-150).

Fernandez, M., & Espasa, R. (1999). Dixie: A retargetable binary instrumentation tool. In *Proceedings of the Workshop on Binary Translation, held in conjunction with the International Conference on Parallel Architectures and Compilation Techniques.*

Freund, S. N., & Qadeer, S. (2003). *Checking concise specifications of multithreaded software.* Technical Note 01-2002, Williams College.

Gontla, P., Drury, H., & Stanley, K. (2003, May 2003). An introduction to OVATION—Object viewing and analysis tool for integrated object networks. *CORBA News Brief, Object Computing Inc.* [Electronic media]. Retrieved March 11, 2008, from http://www.ociweb.com/cnb/CORBANews-Brief-200305.html

Gosling J. (1995, January 23). Java intermediate bytecodes. In *Proceedings of the ACM SIGPLAN Workshop on Intermediate Representations (IR'95).* (pp. 111-118), San Francisco, CA, USA.

Greenhouse, A. (2003). *A programmer-oriented approach to safe concurrency.* Unpublished doctoral dissertation, Carnegie Mellon University School of Computer Science.

Grehan, R. (1995). *BYTEmark Native Mode Benchmark*, Release 2.0, [Computer software]. BYTE Magazine.

Hollingsworth, J. K., Miller, B. P., & Cargille, J. (1994). Dynamic program instrumentation for scalable performance tools. In *Proceedings of the Scalable High-Performance Computing Conference, Knoxville, TN,* (pp. 841-850).

Hill, J., Schmidt, D.C., & Slaby, J. (2007). *System execution modeling tools for evaluating the quality of service of enterprise distributed real-time and embedded systems.* In P. F. Tiako (Ed.). *Designing software-intensive systems: Methods and principles.* Langston University, OK.

Hilyard, J. (2005, January). No code can hide from the profiling API in the .NET framework 2.0. *MSDN*

Magazine. Retrieved March 11, 2008, from http://msdn.microsoft.com/msdnmag/issues/05/01/CLRProfiler/

Hunt, G., & Brubacher, D. (1999). Detours: Binary interception of Win32 functions. In *Proceedings of the 3rd USENIX Windows NT Symposium*, (pp. 135-144).

IBM Corporation. (1998). *PowerPC 604e RISC microprocessor user's manual with supplement for PowerPC 604 microprocessor* (Publication No. G522-0330-00) [Electronic media]. Retrieved March 11, 2008, from http://www-3.ibm.com/chips/techlib/

IBM Corporation. (2000). *Jikes Bytecode toolkit* [Computer Software]. Retrieved March 11, 2008, from http://www-128.ibm.com/developerworks/opensource/

IBM Corporation. (2003). *Develop fast, reliable code with IBM rational PurifyPlus.* Whitepaper. Retrieved March 11, 2008, from ftp://ftp.software.ibm.com/software/rational/web/whitepapers/2003/PurifyPlusPDF.pdf

IEEE. (2001). *IEEE standard test access port and boundary-scan architecture.* IEEE Std. 1149.1-2001.

IEEE-ISTO. (2003). *The Nexus 5001 forum standard for global embedded processor debug interface, version 2.0* [Electronic media]. Retrieved March 11, 2008, from http://www.ieee-isto.org

Intel Corporation. (2006a). *Intel 64 and IA-32 architectures software developer's manual (Vol. 3B, System Programming Guide, Part 2).* Retrieved March 11, 2008, from www.intel.com/design/processor/manuals/253669.pdf

Intel Corporation. (2006b). Intel's tera-scale research prepares for tens, hundreds of cores. *Technology@Intel Magazine.* Retrieved March 11, 2008, from http://www.intel.com/technology/magazine/computing/tera-scale-0606.htm

Jackson, D., & Rinard, M. (2000). Software analysis: A roadmap. In *Proceedings of the IEEE International Conference on Software Engineering*, (pp. 133-145).

Kiczale, G., Hilsdale, E., Hugunin, J., Kersten, M., Palm, J., & Griswold, W. G. (2001). *An overview of AspectJ.* (LNCS, 2072, pp. 327-355).

Larus, J., & Schnarr, E. (1995). EEL: Machine-independent executable editing. In *Proceedings of the ACM SIGPLAN Conference on Programming Language Designes and Implementation*, (pp. 291-300).

Lee, H. B. (1997, July). *BIT: Bytecode instrumenting tool.* Unpublished master's thesis, University of Colorado, Boulder, CO.

Lee, E. A. (2006). The problem with threads. *IEEE Computer, 39*(11), 33-42.

Li, J. (2002). *Monitoring of component-based systems* (Tech. Rep. No. HPL-2002-25R1. HP). Laboratories, Palo Alto, CA, USA.

London, K., Moore, S., Mucci, P., Seymour, K., & Luczak, R. (2001, June 18-21). The PAPI cross-platform interface to hardware performance counters. In *Proceedings of the Department of Defense Users' Group Conference.*

Luk, C., Cohn, R., Muth, R., Patil, H., Klauser, A., Lowney, G., et al. (2005). Pin: Building customized program analysis tools with dynamic instrumentation. In *Proceedings of the ACM SIGPLAN Conference on Programming Language Design and Implementation*, (pp. 190-200).

Microsoft Corporation. (2007a). *Windows server 2003 performance counters reference.* Microsoft TechNet [Electronic media]. Retrieved March 11, 2008, from http://technet2.microsoft.com/WindowsServer/en/library/3fb01419-b1ab-4f52-a9f8-09d5ebeb9ef21033.mspx?mfr=true

Microsoft Corporation. (2007b). *Using the registry functions to consume counter data.* Microsoft

Developer Network [Electronic media]. Retrieved March 11, 2008, from http://msdn2.microsoft.com/en-us/library/aa373219.aspx

Microsoft Corporation. (2007c). *Using the PDH functions to consume counter data.* Microsoft Developer Network [Electronic media]. Retrieved March 11, 2008, from http://msdn2.microsoft.com/en-us/library/aa373214.aspx

Miller, B.P., Callaghan, M.D., Cargille, J.M., Hollingsworth, J.K., Irvin, R.B., & Karavanic, K.L. (1995, December). The Paradyn parallel performance measurement tool. *IEEE Computer, 28*(11), 37-46.

Mock, M. (2003). Dynamic analysis from the bottom up. In *Proceedings of the ICSE 2003 Workshop on Dynamic Analysis (WODA 2003).*

Murayama, J. (2001, July). *Performance profiling using TNF. Sun Developer Network.* Retrieved March 11, 2008, from http://developers.sun.com/solaris/articles/tnf.html

Nethercote, N. (2004). *Dynamic binary analysis and instrumentation.* Unpublished doctoral dissertation, University of Cambridge, UK.

Nimmer, J., & Ernst, M. D. (2001). Static verification of dynamically detected program invariants: Integrating Daikon and ESC/Java. In *Proceedings of the 1ˢᵗ International Workshop on Runtime Verification.*

Object Computing Incorporated. (2006). *A window into your systems* [Electronic media]. Retrieved March 11, 2008, from http://www.ociweb.com/products/OVATION

OMG. (2002). *Object Management Group: the common object request broker: Architecture and specification, revision 3.0.* OMG Technical Documents, 02-06-33 [Electronic media]. Retrieved March 11, 2008, from http://www.omg.org/cgi-bin/doc?formal/04-03-01

Pietrik, M. (1998, May). Under the hood. *Microsoft Systems Journal.* Retrieved March 11, 2008, from http://www.microsoft.com/msj/0598/hood0598.aspx

Reiss, S. P. (2003). Visualizing Java in action. In *Proceedings of the 2003 ACM Symposium on Software Visualization,* (p. 57).

Reiss, S. P. (2005). Efficient monitoring and display of thread state in java. In *Proceedings of the IEEE International Workshop on Program Comprehension* (pp. 247-256). St. Louis, MO.

Rinard, M. (2001). *Analysis of multithreaded programs.* (LNCS 2126, pp. 1-19).

Romer, T., Voelker, G., Lee, D., Wolman, A., Wong, W., Levy, H., et al. (1997). Instrumentation and optimization of Win32/Intel executables using Etch. In *Proceedings of the USENIX Windows NT Workshop.*

Schmidt, D. C., Natarajan, B., Gokhale, G., Wang, N., & Gill, C. (2002, February). TAO: A pattern-oriented object request broker for distributed real-time and embedded systems. *IEEE Distributed Systems Online, 3*(2).

Schmidt, D. C., Stal, M., Rohnert, H., & Buschmann, F. (2000). *Pattern-oriented software architecture patterns for concurrent and networked objects.* John Wiley & Sons.

Soloman, D. A. (1998). *Inside Windows NT (2nd ed).* Redmond: Microsoft Press.

Spinczyk, O., Lohmann, D., & Urban, M. (2005). Aspect C++: An AOP extension for C++. *Software Developer's Journal,* 68-76.

Srivastava, A., & Eustace A. (1994). *ATOM: A system for building customized program analysis tools* (Tech. Rep. No. 94/2). Western Research Lab, Compaq Corporation.

Subramaniam, K., & Thazhuthaveetil, M. (1994). Effectiveness of sampling based software profilers. In *Proceedings of the 1st International*

Conference on Reliability and Quality Assurance, (pp. 1-5).

Sun Microsystems Corporation. (2002). *The Java native interface programmer's guide and specification* [Electronic media]. Retrieved March 11, 2008, from http://java.sun.com/docs/books/jni/html/jniTOC.html

Sun Microsystems Corporation. (2004). *JVM tool interface* [Computer software]. Retrieved March 11, 2008, from http://java.sun.com/j2se/1.5.0/docs/guide/jvmti/

Sutter, H. (2005). The free lunch is over: A fundamental turn towards concurrency in software. *Dr. Dobb's Journal, 30*(3).

Sutter, H., & Larus J. (2005). Software and the concurrency revolution. *ACM Queue Magazine, 3*(7).

Vaswani, K., & Srikant, Y. N. (2003), Dynamic recompilation and profile-guided optimizations for a .NET JIT compiler. In *Proceedings of the IEEE Software Special on Rotor .NET*, (Vol. 150, pp. 296-302). IEEE Publishing.

Visser, E. (2001). *Stratego: A language for program transformation based on rewriting strategies.* (LNCS 2051, pp. 357).

Waddington, D. G., Amduka, M., DaCosta, D., Foster, P., & Sprinkle, J. (2006, February). *EASEL: Model centric design tools for effective design and implementation of multi-threaded concurrent applications* (Technical Document). Lockheed Martin ATL.

Waddington, D. G., & Yao, B. (2005). High fidelity C++ code transformation. In *Proceedings of the 5th Workshop on Language Descriptions, Tools and Applications.*

Whaley, J. (2000). A portable sampling-based profiler for Java virtual machines. In *Proceedings of ACM Java Grand* (pp. 78-87).

Wolf, F., & Mohr, B. (2003). Hardware-counter based automatic performance analysis of parallel programs. In *Proceedings of the Mini-symposium on Performance Analysis, Conference on Parallel Computing (PARCO)*. Dreseden, Germany.

ADDITIONAL READING

In addition to the references made in this chapter, we recommend the following particular reading on this subject.

"Dynamic Analysis from the bottom up" (Mock, 2003) stresses the increasing importance of dynamic analysis in view of modern software development and deployment. It discusses three main directions of research: (i) exploiting run-time information to optimize programs, (ii) applying dynamic analysis to understand, maintain and evolve software and (iii) efficient collection of run-time information.

"Static and Dynamic Analysis: synergy and duality" (Ernst, 2003) discusses the synergy between static and dynamic analysis techniques. The paper describes ways to use both these techniques in a complementary manner. It proposes the development of a hybrid analysis method and argues that static and dynamic analyses are not as different as they seem and in fact have much in common.

"The Periodic-Linear Model of Program Behavior Capture" (Clauss, Kenmei, & Beyler, 2005) presents an analysis and modeling strategy of program behavior characteristics. The approach focuses on the use of traces that are generated from instrumented code.

"Aspect C++: An AOP Extension for C++" (Spinczyk, Lohmann, & Urban, 2005) discusses the fundamental concepts of aspect-oriented programming. It specifically provides details of AOP within the context of C++ source code instrumentation.

"An Overview of AspectJ" (Kiczale, Hilsdale, Hugunin, Kersten, Palm, & Griswold, 2001) examines aspect-oriented programming for the Java programming language.

"An API for Runtime Code Patching" (Buck & Hollingsworth, 2000) presents the concepts behind the DynInst tool, which is a technique for dynamic binary-code instrumentation. This paper discusses the basic architecture and the use of trampoline functions to implant modifications to existing code.

"Windows Server 2003 Performance Counters Reference" (Microsoft, 2007a) contains a detailed description of the Windows Performance counters that can be used to profile applications. This reference includes a listing of available performance counters and a description of the APIs used to access them.

"JVM Tool Interface (JVM TI)" (Sun Microsystems Corporation, 2004) is an online resource describing the API provided by the JVM. It first explains the basic concept and architecture of the JVMTI before going into the details on the interface. In each section, there are small examples to help implement a profiler.

Chapter XI
Evaluating Quality of Service for Enterprise Distributed Systems

James H. Hill
Vanderbilt University, USA

Douglas C. Schmidt
Vanderbilt University, USA

John M. Slaby
Raytheon Integrated Defense Systems, USA

ABSTRACT

This chapter introduces the next generation of system execution modeling tools designed around model-driven engineering (MDE) coupled with domain-specific modeling languages (DSMLs). The authors discuss key design issues involved with implementing a next generation SEM tool and show how they can be applied to developing service-oriented architecture (SOA)-based applications. Finally, the authors use a real-life case study to illustrate how next generation system execution modeling tools can help understand quality-of-service (QoS) issues earlier in the development lifecycle (i.e., during design-time) instead of waiting until complete system integration.

INTRODUCTION

Integration Challenges of SOA-Based Enterprise DRE Systems

Enterprise *distributed real-time and embedded* (DRE) systems, such as supervisory control and data acquisition (SCADA) systems, air traffic control systems, and shipboard computing environments, are growing in complexity and importance as computing devices are networked together to help automate tasks previously done by human operators. These types of systems are required to provide quality of service (QoS) support to process the right data in the right place at the right time over a networked grid of computers. QoS properties required by enterprise DRE systems include the low latency and jitter expected in conventional real-time and embedded systems, and the high throughput, scalability, and reliability expected in conventional enterprise distributed systems. Achieving this combination of QoS capabilities is hard because these systems work in constrained environments with a limited amount of resources that can vary depending on the location of the system. Moreover, this level of QoS requires in depth knowledge of low-level programming techniques, for example, properly interfacing with sockets to write efficient networking protocols, which the application developers of enterprise DRE system may not possess.

To address these challenges, enterprise DRE systems are increasingly being developed using applications composed of components running on feature–rich *service-oriented architecture* (SOA) middleware frameworks. These components are designed to provide reusable services to a range of application domains that are composed into domain-specific assemblies for application (re)use. SOA middleware is intended to alleviate problems of inflexibility and reinvention of core capabilities associated with prior monolithic, functionally-designed, and "stove-piped" legacy applications developed using just the capabilities required for a specific set of requirements and operating conditions. SOA-based systems, conversely, are designed to have a more general range of capa-

bilities that enable their reuse in other contexts. Moreover, these systems are developed in layers, for example, layer(s) of infrastructure middleware services (such as naming and discovery, event and notification, security and fault tolerance) and layer(s) of application components that use these services in different compositions.

Combining stringent QoS requirements in DRE systems with the transition to SOA component frameworks has created a particularly vexing problem for researchers and developers of large and layered enterprise DRE systems: The inadequacies of system architectures may not be ascertained until years into development. At the heart of this problem is the *serialized phasing* of layered system development, shown in Figure 1, which postpones the discovery of design flaws that affect system QoS until late in the lifecycle, that is, at integration time. A hallmark of serialized phasing is that application components are not created until *after* their underlying system infrastructure components, such as naming and discovery, event and notification, security and fault tolerance, and resource management.

As shown in Figure 1, SOA-based enterprise DRE systems built using serialized phasing often do not adequately test the implementations,

Figure 1. Characteristics and complexities of serialized phasing in enterprise DRE systems

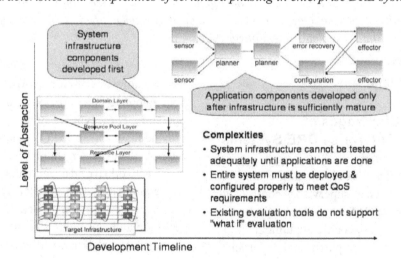

configurations, and deployments of infrastructure components under realistic workloads until the application components are done. Moreover, both application and infrastructure components are hosted on the same target platform. Each component must, therefore, be properly deployed and configured to achieve the desire QoS. As a result, it hard to know how well the system will satisfy key QoS properties due to disconnects in the phasing of infrastructure and application component development. Moreover, handcrafted software designs used in many enterprise DRE systems to address these concerns make it hard to conduct "what if" experiments on alternative system architectures and implementations to determine which valid configurations can obtain performance goals for a particular workload. Making any significant changes to these types of handcrafted systems late in their lifecycle can be costly due to the impact on the design, implementation, deployment, and (re)validation of many application and infrastructure software/hardware components.

Solution Approach: System Execution Modeling Tools

To address the problems in SOA-based enterprise DRE systems, there is a need for a methodology and an associated suite of *system execution modeling* (SEM) tools that use *model-driven engineering* (MDE) (Schmidt, 2006) technologies, such as GME (Karsai, Sztipanovits, Ledeczi, & Bapty, 2003) or GEMS (White, Gokhale, & Schmidt, 2007), to simplify the:

1. **Emulation of application component behavior** in terms of computational workloads, resource utilizations and requirements, and network communication. This step can be accomplished quickly and precisely using domain-specific modeling languages (DSMLs) (Ledeczi, Maroti, Karsai, & Nordstrom, 1999) that capture the behavior and workload

of system components (at a higher-level of abstraction than third-generation languages like C++ or Java). DSML interpreters then parse the constructed behavior and workload models to generate code that executes emulated components.

2. **Configuration, deployment, and execution** of the emulated application components atop actual infrastructure components to determine their impact on QoS empirically in actual runtime environments. These steps can also be accomplished using DSMLs that specify realistic deployments and configurations and then generate the associated metadata describing these deployments and configurations. These metadata descriptions are processed by the same deployment and configuration tools as the final system, with SEM tools providing mechanisms to record, consolidate, and collect QoS metrics (such as execution times and resource usage) from the SOA runtime environment.

3. **Process of feeding back the results** to enhance system architectures and components to improve QoS. This step can be accomplished by archiving the collected QoS metrics and providing tools that view the overall results of a deployment. SEM tools also provide histories of the collected metrics to enable engineers and architects to understand end-to-end system performance and make well-informed decisions on how to improve QoS.

As actual application components mature over time, they can replace the emulated components, thereby providing an ever more realistic evaluation environment. Figure 2 shows the relationships between the steps described above.

SEM tools enable system engineers, software architects/developers, and quality assurance (QA) engineers to address the inherent complexities that arise from properties of production systems, including communication delay, temporal phasing,

Figure 2. Evaluating the QoS of enterprise DRE system via system execution modeling tools

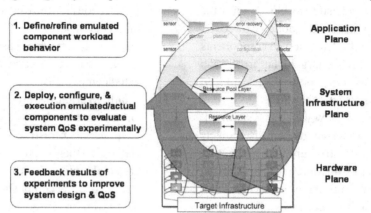

parallel execution, and synchronization. There are typically only a few execution designs that actually can satisfy the functional and performance requirements established in software and system architecture. SEM tools enable architects and engineers to discover, measure, and rectify incipient integration and performance problems early in a system's lifecycle (e.g., in the analysis or design phases). These tools help shift the focus of the software integration resources to productive activities that evaluate and validate system performance and end-user value, rather than serving as the *de facto* system design debugging activity, as is often the case today.

This chapter illustrates by example the following concepts for using MDE-based SEM tools to evaluate SOA-based enterprise DRE systems:

- The purpose of next-generation SEM tools and the limitations they address with traditional SEM tools.
- The different elements needed to construct a next-generation SEM tool, including designing the behavioral and workload DSMLs to capture emulated behavior, selecting the method(s) for configuring, deploying, and executing emulated system behavior, and un-

derstanding different analytical techniques to feedback results to users.

- The application of next-generation SEM tools to SOA-based enterprise DRE systems to evaluate system QoS to show by example how SEM tools can be used to evaluate enterprise DRE systems during the early stages of development, that is, before complete system integration.

BACKGROUND

Before we begin our discussion on MDE-based SEM tools, we first describe existing techniques and tools used to evaluate the QoS of enterprise DRE systems. This section summarizes conventional techniques and tools for evaluating enterprise DRE system performance in different phases of development.

Distributed System Emulation Testbeds

During the past several years a number of testbeds have been developed for emulating and evaluating the behavior of distributed systems in networked environments. One such testbed is Emulab (Ricci, Alfred, & Lepreau, 2003), which originated at the University of Utah to provide freely available resources and tools to configure the topology of experiments, for example, modeling the underlying communication links. The virtual topology is then mapped to ~250 physical nodes that can be accessed and managed via the Internet. Faux or real applications can be executed in this environment to evaluate the performance of both the topology and applications. As a result of Emulab's success, other institutions and organizations, such as Cornell University, Georgia Institute of Technology, and Vanderbilt University, are hosting their own Emulab for private or public use.

Another common testbed is PlanetLab (PlanetLab Consortium, 2006), which is managed by Princeton University, the University of California Berkeley, and the University of Washington. PlanetLab provides a similar user experience as Emulab, though it focuses on large-scale (Northrop, Feiler, Gabriel, Goodenough, Linger, Longstaff et al., 2006) distributed systems. PlanetLab currently consists of 726 machines, hosted by 354 sites, spanning over 25 countries. Most machines are hosted by research institutions, but regardless of where the machine is hosted, it is accessible via the Internet. Researchers can request *slices* of PlanetLab to experiment with a variety of planetary-scale services, such as content distribution networks, QoS overlays, scalable event propagation, anomaly detection mechanisms, and network measurement tools, to run experiments. The goal for PlanetLab is to grow to over 1,000 widely distributed nodes that peer with a majority of the Internet's regional and long-haul backbones.

ModelNet (Vahdat, Yocum, Walsh, Mahadevan, Kostic, Chase, & Becker, 2002) is another testbed for emulating and evaluating large-scaled distributed systems. With ModelNet, developers can emulate multiple clients and hosts using a single physical host. ModelNet provides similar functionality as Emulab, though it focuses

on resource constrained environments, that is, environments that do not have access to enough resources to scale to the deployment environment. For example, 100 Gnutella clients each with a 1 Mbps bottleneck bandwidth can be emulated on one dual processor-1 GHz machine. In addition to providing a scalable emulation environment, ModelNet facilitates the emulation of faux and real applications.

Existing distributed system emulation testbeds are useful in the early stages of development when testing functionality under various conditions/configurations, especially when the target platform is not known *a priori*. With enterprise DRE systems, however, the target platform(s) are usually known (and available) at the start of development. What is needed, therefore, are next-generation SEM tools that will help developers and testers leverage the same benefits provided by existing (public) testbeds to run as many experiments as possible on the target platform, which is usually a private-based testbed built to the specifications of the target project.

System Execution Modeling (SEM) Tools

Performance evaluation of systems has always been a research topic that has received much attention. For example, Smith (1990) and Smith and Williams (2001) has shown how variations of queuing theory (Denning & Buzen, 1978) can be applied to evaluate the performance of enterprise systems. The result of their work lead the creation of a SEM tool designed specifically for software performance evaluation (SPE) called *SPE·ED* (www.perfeng.com/sped.htm). SPE·ED allows developers to model the "business-logic" of their system and parameterize the model with performance metrics, for example, arrival rate and throughput of events, service rates of devices, and resource availability. Testers can then run simulations of their modeled system and analyze its "expected" performance. Analysis results can include determining the maximum throughput for each device, locating the bottleneck device in the system, or evaluating performance under expected, or hypothetical, system upgrades.

UPPAAL (Bengtsson, Larsen, Larrson, Pettersson, & Yi, 1995) is an integrated tool environment for modeling, simulating, and verifying real-time systems developed jointly by Basic Research in Computer Science at Aalborg University in Denmark and the Department of Information Technology at Uppsala University in Sweden. It is based on the formal language of timed automata (Subramonian, 2006), but does not require in-depth knowledge for basic usage. Similar to most SEM tools, UPPAAL provides a graphical interface to simplify the creation of timed automata models for the system under development. More importantly, the graphical interface also allows developers to visualize the simulations of the system under development. Lastly, the constructed models can be run through a model checker to check invariant and reachability properties by exploring the state-space of a system.

CPN Tools (2006) is another SEM tool that allows developers to capture the *behavior* of a component, or system under development, using color Petri nets (Kristensen, Christensen, & Jensen, 1998). Similar to UPPAAL, CPN Tools provides a graphical user interface to simplify the creation of color Petri net models. CPN Tools, however, requires some level of expertise and understanding of color Petri nets. Once models are constructed using CPN Tools, they can be simulated to verify system properties of DRE system, such as correctness and state reachability, which is similar to UPPAAL. Performance metrics, for example, service time, arrival rate, or resource utilization, can also be associated with the states and transitions in the models to run SPE simulations, which is similar to SPE·ED.

Other modeling languages, such as KLA-PER (Grassi, Mirandola, & Sabetta, 2005) and RT-UML (Bertolino & Mirandola, 2004), can be used to model system execution. KLAPER is a modeling language that facilitates workload specifications, such as resource utilization, which is then emulated in its own proprietary tool. RT-UML models and evaluates the performance of component-based systems by defining services and QoS policies for components; however, modeling system behavior is future work. RT-UML is also designed to be supported by external *simulation* tools.

Many of the tools discussed above can also be applied in the area of soft and hard real-time systems. In these types of systems, however, more focus is placed on completing tasks in a given time constraint, as opposed to verifying the state of the system, for example, the current values of attributes or utilizations of resources. In hard real-time systems, developers are concerned with achieving worst case execution time within a specified time constraint, whereas in soft real-time systems developers are concerned with achieving average execution time within a specified time constraint at a given probability (Florescu, Hoon, Voeten, & Corporall, 2006).

Tavares et al. (2005) demonstrates how time Petri nets (Merlin, 1974) can be applied to verify the scheduling of hard real-time tasks when considering multiple system constraints, such as execution time and power consumption. Likewise, Bucci, Fedeli, Sassoli, and Vicario (2003) illustrates how preemptive time Petri nets, which extend time Petri nets, can be used to verify the scheduling of hard real-time tasks set with flexible computations, such as periodic, sporadic, and nondeterministic execution times. In the domain of soft real-time systems, Florescu et al. (2006) introduces an approached called *probabilistic modeling and evaluat*ion for soft real-time systems. This approach uses a language called Parallel Object-Oriented Specification Language (POOSL) (www.es.ele.tue.nl/poosl) and involves modeling the distribution of a task's measured execution times over a given period of time. The constructed model is then analyzed to understand the probability of the task achieving a specific execution time in the future given its measured distribution curve of execution times.

It is clear that existing SEM tools are useful for understanding the state space of a system by providing high-level abstractions (i.e., conceptual models of system) that shield developers from low-level implementation details. Existing SEM tools, however, do not provide support for enterprise DRE systems developed using SOA technologies, which are developed primarily using DSML tools and not generalized tools. What is needed, therefore, are next-generation SEM tools that can provided the same functionality as existing SEM tools, but are tailored for SOA-based enterprise DRE systems, that is, provide the metadata generation capability of MDE tools and the evaluation capabilities of existing SEM tools.

Evaluation Techniques for Component Architectures

There are several techniques for evaluating the performance of component architectures, including *event tracing* and *system profiling*. Event tracing techniques are typically based on observing the performance of a single event (e.g., execution path and time) as it travels through the system (i.e., transmitted end-to-end from component to component). System profiling techniques often use external tools to monitor the performance of software and hardware while the system is executing and transcribe collected metrics to files for analysis once the system is off-line.

Mania, Murphy, and McManis (2002) discusses a technique called *trace-based analysis* for Enterprise Java Bean (EJB) components. In trace-based analysis, different execution traces, that is, function calls, are monitored and outputted to a trace file contained on the host. After the emulation, trace files are parsed and combined with the deployment descriptors to determine the different paths of execution in the system.

Hauswirth, Diwan, Sweeney, and Mozer (2005) discusses *vertical profiling* evaluation techniques in the context of EJB. In vertical profiling, performance metrics based on the types of operations and actions, for example, cache misses and CPU cycles are collected in trace files. Trace files are then fused through a process called *trace-alignment* using a common metric that occurs in the source traces. After the traces are aligned, *correlation analysis* is applied to the traces to help determine what other metrics collected in the trace may influence its behavior.

Existing techniques for evaluating the performance of component architectures are relatively complex and low-level, that is, at the middleware infrastructure level. What is needed, therefore, are next-generation SEM tools that provide the same analysis techniques, but shield the developer from the complexity of existing tools. Moreover, these tools should allow developers to leverage existing MDE tools for component architectures, but provide feedback to pinpoint how the low-level analysis correlates to the high-level component architecture's implementation.

MOTIVATING EXAMPLE AND CASE STUDY

To motivate the structure and functionality of next-generation SEM tools, this section presents a case study from the domain of enterprise DRE systems. This case study focuses on a SOA-based *multilayer resource management* (MLRM) infrastructure (Lardieri, Balasubramanian, Schmidt, Thakar, Gokhale, & Damiano, 2007) for naval shipboard computing systems and the challenges encountered while developing and evaluating it. The MLRM service architecture shown in Figure 3 forms the basis for future naval programs, which run on a coordinated grid of computers that manage many aspects of a ship's power, navigation, command and control, and tactical operations. Although our motivating example is a closed system, we believe, however, that the structure

Figure 3. SOA-based multilayer resource manager (MLRM) infrastructure for shipboard computing

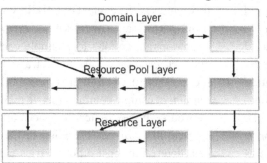

Top *domain layer* contains components that interact with the system *mission manager*

Middle *resource pool layer* is an abstraction for a set of computer nodes managed by a *pool manager*

Bottom *resource layer* contains the actual resource computing components

and functionality of next-generation SEM tools can also be applied to open systems, such as peer-to-peer applications and service providers systems (e.g., online stock applications) (Hill & Gokhale, 2007).

The MLRM, shown in Figure 3, consists of the three layers. The command and policy inputs flow in a top-down manner and correspondingly the resource status information moves in a bottom-up fashion. At the top is the *domain layer*, which contains infrastructure components that interact with the mission manager of shipboard environment by receiving command and policy inputs and passing them to the *resource pool layer*. The resource pool layer is an abstraction for a set of computer nodes managed by a *pool manager*. The pool manager is an infrastructure component that interacts with the *resource allocator* in the resource pool layer to run algorithms that deploy application components to various nodes within a resource pool. The actual computing resources reside in the third layer called the *resource layer*, which has infrastructure components called *node provisioners* that receive commands to spawn applications in every node from a pool manager.

The SOA-based MLRM services described above are designed to support the highly heterogeneous environment in which long-lived enterprise DRE systems operate. For example, the Naval

program that provides the operational context for the MLRM services is designed to support different versions of (1) component middleware, such as CIAO and OpenCCM, (2) general-purpose operating systems, such as Linux and Solaris, (3) real-time operating systems, such as VxWorks and LynxOS, (4) hardware chipsets, such as x86, PowerPC, and SPARC processors, (5) a wide range of high-speed wired interconnects, such as Gigabit Ethernet and Infiniband, and (6) different transport protocols, such as TCP/IP and SCTP.

Figure 4 shows one of the challenge problems of the MLRM case study called the *SLICE scenario*, which consists of 2 sensors, 2 planners, 1 configuration, 1 error recovery, and 2 effector components. This scenario requires the transmission of information detected by the sensors to each planner in sequence, then to the configuration component, and lastly to both effectors to perform actions that control devices in the physical world. Components in the SLICE scenario are deployed across 3 computing nodes because the workload generated by the components collectively is more than a single node can handle. The main sensor and effector (represented as sensor-1 and effector-1 in Figure 4 and in following discussions) are deployed on separate nodes to reflect the placement of physical equipment in the production shipboard system. A model of the end-to-end layout of SLICE components is shown in Figure 4, with the *critical*

Figure 4. Model of SLICE showing the MLRM components and their interconnections

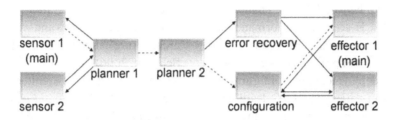

path (i.e., sequence of components that must meet a predetermined end-to-end deadline) specified by the dashed arrows.

Based on the MLRM development schedule, the integration of components that implement the SLICE scenario atop the multilayer resource management infrastructure was not projected to occur until 12 months into the program to provide sufficient time to finish developing, testing, and optimizing it. Because these components were currently under development, we understood each component's behavior and resource usage expectations in SLICE. What we did *not* know was how the overall performance of the SLICE scenario would be affected when deployed with the MLRM infrastructure.

In a conventional project developed with serialized phasing, we would have waited until final system integration to benchmark the entire system. If integration testing revealed problems with the MLRM infrastructure, the process of reconfiguring and redeploying application and infrastructure components to meet QoS requirements would have required significant effort. Moreover, developers and testers would have to use existing evaluation techniques to locate problematic areas and manually pinpoint their correlation in MLRM's implementation. Developers would also have to continuously revise *completed* infrastructure code without knowing how the changes will affect application-level performance. To prevent reimplementation late in the development cycle (e.g., at integration time) we could use the tools

like UPPAAL and CPN at early stages of development to *predict* the expected performance of the system. Although an analytic understanding of performance based on simulation is usually better than no understanding at all, these tools have the following limitations that make them inadequate for accurately evaluating the QoS of enterprise DRE systems, such as the SLICE scenario:

- They do not execute in the actual target environment, which precludes system testers from producing "realistic" performance results based the real hardware and software configuration. Moreover, existing SEM tools do not take into account nondeterministic behavior that can be introduced by component architectures, such as reliable communication and security. Subramonian (2006) has done work to extend existing SEMS tools to handle enterprise DRE systems, but these techniques require a high degree of user expertise.

- They are not designed to integrate seamlessly with contemporary SOA platforms, for example, they require developers to learn "low-level" techniques (such as observing cache misses, disk access time, or disk utilization) when they are developing at a "high-level" of abstraction (such as the application logic). Moreover, users must understand how to correlate the "low-level" performance metrics to "high-level" implementation.

The remainder of this chapter focuses on building and applying next-generation MDE-based SEM tools to help address the challenges of evaluating SLICE scenario performance at early stages of development. The goals of this case study are to: (1) simplify the process of determining which deployment and configuration strategies will meet critical path QoS deadlines, (2) create a catalog of selectable deployment strategies that meet end-to-end performance requirements, and (3) spend less time integrating and testing the actual SLICE components after they are completed, that is, to reduce time spent in system integration, which still ensuring that QoS requirements are met.

APPLYING NEXT-GENERATION SEM TOOLS TO SOA-BASED DRE SYSTEMS

In the introduction, we described the need for next-generation MDE-based SEM tools to simplify the development of SOA-based enterprise DRE systems. To address the complexities of existing tools and techniques discussed in System Execution Modeling (SEM) Tools Section requires developing the necessary MDE infrastructure for next-generation SEM tools. Figure 5 illustrates the elements and workflow of one such architecture called CUTS (Slaby, Baker, Hill, & Schmidt, 2006).

At the heart of the architecture in Figure 5 is the *Component Workload Emulator (CoWorkEr) Utilization Test Suite (CUTS)*, which is based on the CoSMIC (Gokhale et al., 2006) MDE tool chain. This figure shows the following steps:

1. In this step users (e.g., software architects, developers, and systems engineers) specify the structure of an enterprise DRE system (e.g., the component and their interconnections using CUTS DSMLs).

2. In this step users can associate the necessary QoS characteristics with individual components (e.g., CPU utilization) or the system as a whole (e.g., deadline of a critical path through the system).

3. In this step the information captured by the tools can be synthesized into executable code and configuration metadata, which the middleware then uses to deploy the emu-

Figure 5. Architecture and workflow for next-generation SEM tools

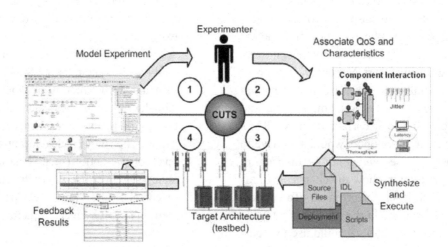

lated/actual application/system components onto the target platform.

4. In this step system developers and engineers analyze the collected metrics and explore design alternatives from multiple computational and valuation perspectives to quantify the costs of certain design choices on end-to-end system performance.

This process can be applied iteratively throughout the phases of development process.

In the context of SOA-based enterprise DRE systems, the CUTS SEM tools helps developers conduct "what if" experiments to discover, measure, and rectify performance problems *early* in the lifecycle (e.g., in the architecture and design phases), as opposed to the integration phase, when mistakes are much harder and more costly to fix. The remainder of the section discusses the elements (that is, the modeling languages, emulation methods, and analysis methods) needed to create a SEM tool chain using MDE technologies. For each element we describe the problems faced and solutions applied in the context of CUTS and the SLICE scenario.

Emulating Application Behavior Using Modeling Languages

Context

When using an MDE tool to develop a SOA-based enterprise DRE system it is necessary to capture the structure of the system, that is, the components' interfaces and attributes, the interconnections between components, and the behavior. Many MDE tools, such as Cadena (Hatcliff, Deng, Dwyer, Jung, & Prasad, 2003), PICML (Balasubramanian, Balasubramanian, Parsons, Gikhale, & Schmidt, 2005), and J2EEML (White, Schmidt, & Gokhale, 2005), capture structural aspects of SOA-based systems rather than the behavioral aspects. The emphasis on structure aspects stems from the fact that enterprise DRE systems built using SOA

technologies like J2EE, CCM, or Microsoft .NET depend heavily on XML-based descriptor files. A straightforward use of an MDE tool, therefore, is to autogenerate XML files that are tedious and error-prone to handcraft manually.

Problem: Capturing System Behavior Using Modeling Languages

Capturing the behavior of a component to perform early design-time analysis before the integration phase requires developers to rely on external tools and languages because existing MDE technologies often do not provide the same capabilities as existing behavior analysis tools and languages. For example, external tools, such as Petri nets, UPPAAL, and CPN Tools allow developers to model the behavior of the system under development and run simulations to analyze its expected performance. Likewise, languages such as SIMULA and Z allow developers to write simulations of systems for verification purposes. External dependencies on these tools and languages, however, make it hard to map the results from design-analysis tools to the respective areas in structure models provided by the MDE tool.

Existing behavior analysis tools and languages are also geared largely to software developers with deep knowledge of formal methods and advanced mathematical formalisms. In particular, it requires these developers to learn and manage multiple languages and tools, which can be hard if the knowledge base in not available. These tools and languages are generally not usable by key participants throughout the software lifecycle of enterprise DRE systems, including subject matter experts, systems engineers, and quality engineers.

Solution: Integrate Behavior Models Into Existing MDE Tools

Ideally, the DSML in a SEM tool for behavioral modeling should capture both actions and workload. The DSML interpreter should also generate the necessary files (e.g., source code and configuration files) that use proprietary methods or third-party tools to perform early design-time analysis. The advantage of this approach vs. using separate tools for capturing structure and behavior is that it reduces the number of tools the developers and experimenters have to explicitly manage. Moreover, an integrated approach can help correlate performance results with the appropriate parts of the target model. Lastly, this approach removes the complexity of manually handcrafting the source and configuration files to use existing analysis tools and languages because they can be autogenerated directly from the integrated model.

Applying the Solution to CUTS and SLICE

When developing CUTS we created two DSMLs—the *Component Behavior Modeling Language* (CBML) and the *Workload Modeling Language* (WML) (Hill & Gokhale, 2007)—and integrated them into the *Platform Independent Component Modeling Language* (PICML) in CoSMIC. CBML is a modeling language based on I/O automata (Lynch & Tuttle, 1989) (see Sidebar 1) that allows developers to capture a component's internal actions. Although CBML is based on a mathematical formalism, its users need not have expertise in the low-level details of I/O automata programming because it provides an MDE-based interface, as opposed to a traditional text-based interface. As a result CBML simplifies the use of I/O automata, such as autogenerating the model elements for modelers or generating text-based configuration files for I/O automata tools, such as the TIOA Language and Toolset (Garland, 2005).

WML is an extensible modeling language that captures the workload of different "business-logic" actions, for example, memory allocations and database operations. WML compliments CBML

Sidebar 1. Input/Output automata

Input/Output (I/O), developed by Lynch and Tuttle, is a labeled transition system model for components in asynchronous concurrent systems. The actions of I/O automata are classified as *input*, *output* and *internal* actions, where input actions are required to be always enabled. I/O automata also have "tasks." In a fair execution of an I/O automata model, all tasks are required to get turns infinitely often. The behavior of an I/O automata model is describable in terms of traces, or alternatively in terms of fair traces. Both types of behavior notions are compositional.

because the actions (operations) in CBML can be parameterized using the workloads specified in WML. When both modeling languages are used together to model the behavior of a component, developers can specify both the actions of the component and the type of workload created by these actions.

Below we discuss a method for defining a behavior and workload modeling language similar to CBML and WML in CUTS for an MDE tool. We then discuss how to integrate the standalone behavior and workload modeling languages into existing DSMLs that currently only capture structure. The goal is to create an integrated DSML that allows users to capture both structure and behavior of a system and its components, as opposed to using separate tools or languages. To help illustrate this method, we use an example behavioral specification of the *Planner-1* component from the SLICE scenario. Table 1 highlights the behavioral specification of the Planner-1 component.

As shown in Table 1, *Planner-1* has two primary behavioral specifications. The first behavior is "operations performed every second," which sends a command event to both the sensor components. The second behavioral specification is workload performed after a track event is received from a sensor component. Upon receipt of a track event, the *Planner-1* component will complete a series of operations, and then transmit an *as-*

Table 1. Behavioral specification for the Planner-1 component in the SLICE scenario

Planner-1	
Workload performed every second	Publish command of size 24 bytes
Workload performed after receipt of a track event	Allocate 30 KB; 55 dbase ops; 45 CPU ops; publish assessment of size 132 bytes; dealloc 30 KB

sessment event to the Planner-2 component. For more information on the behavior of this and other components in the SLICE scenario, see Slaby, Baker, Hill, and Schmidt (2005). The remainder of the section focuses on defining a behavior and workload modeling language, and integrating it with existing structural DSML while using the Planner-1 component as a running example.

- **Defining the behavioral modeling language:** One goal of a behavioral DSML like CBML is to provide users with the necessary elements to capture the behavior of a component that is well-defined, but does not require any expertise in understanding mathematical formalisms. The DSML should, therefore, contain elements that are familiar to modelers, yet hide the complexity of the underlying formalism used to define the language. For example, I/O automata use action-to-state sequences to define behavior where the connection between an action and state must be an *effect* and the connection between a state and action must

be a *transition*. Likewise, *preconditions* are associated with transitions and *postconditions* are associated with effects. DSMLs can help to shield modelers from low-level details of I/O automata.

Users of behavioral DSMLs are often less interested in the underlying semantics of a formal language than they are with using it effectively. DSML developers, therefore, must provide the necessary elements that represent the underlying formalism for behavior at a higher-level of abstraction, which usually entails capturing the minimal number of elements that allow the formalism to retain its semantics. For example, Figure 6 illustrates the elements in CBML that express the formal semantics of I/O automata.

In CBML, each element shown in Figure 6 corresponds to an I/O automata element. The *Input Action* element corresponds to input, which signifies the start of a behavioral specification. The *State* element represents a state in I/O automata, which must occur

Figure 6. Main modeling elements of CBML

<table>
<tr><td>▶</td><td>○</td><td>◉</td><td>▶</td><td>✦</td></tr>
<tr><td>Input Action</td><td>State</td><td>Action</td><td>Output Action</td><td>Variable</td></tr>
</table>

Figure 7. Example behavioral model using CBML

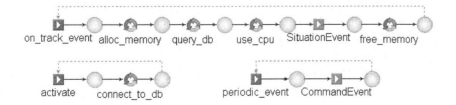

between two consecutive actions. The *Action* element corresponds to internal actions in I/O automata. *Output Action* element corresponds to output actions in I/O automata, which signify sending an event to trigger the start of another behavioral specification. The *Variable* element corresponds to variables in I/O automata, which can be used in guarded transitions between actions and states. Each element also allows developers to define the behavior (minus its workload) of a component without having prior knowledge of I/O automata semantics. Figure 7 shows a model using the elements shown in Figure 6 to define the behavior of the *Planner-1* component from the SLICE scenario in the case study. This behavior includes the input actions that start the behavior, action to state sequences, output actions, and pre-/post-conditions (not pictured).

As shown in Figure 7, each behavioral specification begins with the input action model element. Figure 7, therefore, contains three separate, and independent, behaviors in this one model:

o The *track_event* signifies the actions to perform once a track event is received on the input port of the component as specified in Table 1.

o The *periodic_event* corresponds to the actions executed on a periodic basis while the component is active as specified in Table 1.

o The *activate* behavioral specification dictates the actions to perform when the component is being activated, such as establishing a persistent connection to the target database.

In some cases, the behavioral language may contain semantics that the average user may not understand, or can be simplified. For example, in I/O automata an action element must *always* be followed by a state element. Likewise in Petri nets (Peterson, 1977), a

state element must *always* be connected to a transition element. In either case, DSML developers should provide modelers with the necessary tools to address this complexity. Most domain-specific metamodeling tools allow developers to create add-ons that can simplify the modeling process. For example, CBML contains a plug-in that will autoconnect a new action added to the model to the previous state using the correct connection type, autogenerate a new state, connect the new state to the previously added action, and set the new state as the previous state. This plug-in helps simplify the modeling effort because users need not worry about the underlying semantics of I/O automata represented in CBML.

• **Defining the workload modeling language:** When designing DSMLs for capturing component behavior, we decoupled the workload specification from the behavioral specification for several reasons. First, this decoupling allowed both languages to evolve independently of each other as long as there is a common element that bridges between the two languages. Second, this decoupling allows the behavioral modeling language to interoperate with other workload modeling languages, such as framework-specific modeling languages (Antkiewicz, 2006, Antkiewicz & Czarnecki, 2006a), as long as they use the same bridging element defined in the behavioral modeling language.

When we defined WML, we extended the action and variable elements in CBML to create an object-oriented workload modeling language. Because our focus is SOA-based systems, we wanted to model the same development paradigm (i.e., object-oriented programming) used by SOA-based systems. Figure 8 shows the high-level overview of WML.

The modeling semantics in WML represent programming semantics similar to creating

Figure 8. High-level overview of WML metamodel structure

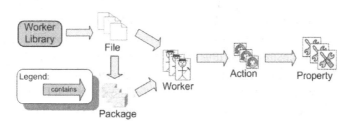

a shared library, that is, .so files on UNIX and .dll files on Windows. The top-most element of the model is the *worker library*. The worker library is a shared library assembled from a collection of files (e.g., .cpp and .h files). Each file can contain one or more *worker* elements, which represent workload generators that can be used in an emulated environment. Each *worker* contains one or more *action* elements that represent the type of operations it can perform. Action elements can contain multiple *property* elements that represent parameters for that particular action. In CBML, we defined workers and actions to have the same modeling semantics as *variables* and *actions* in CBML, respectively. Because the *workers* and *actions* use the CBML bridging elements, modelers can then use WML in their existing behavioral

models to give realistic workload parameters to the arbitrary actions. Figure 9 shows the CBML model in Figure 7 integrated with WML elements from Figure 8.

As illustrated in Figure 9, the persons in the image represent worker elements illustrated in Figure 8. Each of the circular arrows is the actions of a respective worker (as illustrated in Figure 8). Unlike the actions in Figure 7, these actions are model instances of a preexisting action contained in a WML worker element. Because the actions in WML and CBML have the same modeling semantics (i.e., act as bridging elements), it is possible it use variants of WML actions in CBML models, as illustrated in Figure 9. The remaining elements in Figure 9 are the same as the elements in Figure 7.

Figure 9. Integration of WML with CBML

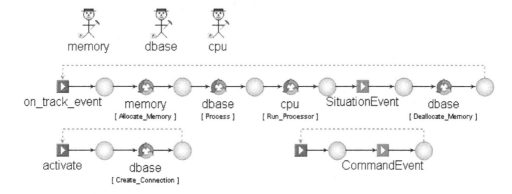

Regardless of whether WML is used to model the workload of a component, the point of decoupling the workload specification from the behavioral specification is to provide greater flexibility and extensibility. As illustrated in Figure 9, it is possible to retain the original behavioral model for a component, but interchange its "actions" as needed. If we chose to move to a different workload language or support multiple workload languages, therefore, the decoupled design of CBML and WML make it easy to integrate with other modeling languages.

- **Integrating behavioral languages with existing structural languages:** Earlier we focused on capturing component behavior using stand-alone DSMLs, namely CBML and WML. To leverage the power of the behavioral and workload DSMLs, however, they need to be integrated with existing

structural modeling languages, such as PICML or J2EEML. These DSMLs provide developers with the necessary tools to generate metadata based on structural aspects, but provide no support for modeling behavioral aspects.

The structural DSMLs for SOA-based systems usually capture a component's interfaces and attributes, which can be viewed as the beginning of a behavioral specification. Likewise, a behavioral DSML usually has an element for specifying the initial action of its specification. It is, therefore, possible to extend existing structural languages with new behavioral languages by defining a connection (or bridge) between the starting actions of both the structural and behavioral aspects, as shown in Figure 10.

As shown in Figure 10, the upper portion shows the input and output elements of

Figure 10. Conceptual model of integrating behavioral models with structural models

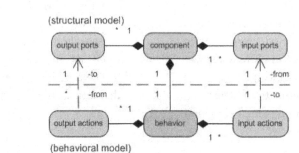

Figure 11. Integrated model of CBML and WML with PICML

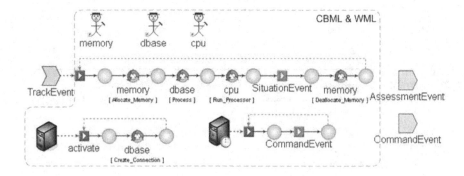

a typical structural DSML and the lower portion shows the typical input and output (I/O) elements of a behavioral DSML. The behavioral DSML contains I/O action elements that can be mapped to I/O ports, respectively, in the structural DSML. When we realize this mapping of elements from the behavioral DSML to elements in the structural DSML when integrating CBML and WML with PICML, we can create models similar to the one illustrated in Figure 11. As shown in Figure 11, the elements inside the *CBML & WML* box highlight the same CBML and WML model for the *Planner-1* component in Figure 9. Likewise, the elements outside the box are PICML elements that define the structure of the *Planner-1* component. The entire image is the result of integrating CBML and WML into PICML, and capturing behavior and structure for the *Planner-1* component using a single DSML. Now that we are able to model a component's structure and behavior, we can now define model interpreters that will parse the models and generate the necessary output so that we can emulate the components' behavior, as discussed next.

Capturing Application Behavior for Emulation

Context

Next-generation SEM tools support emulation, that is, running a variant of the system under development on the target platform. The target platform can either be a testbed that contains replicas of the real infrastructure's software and hardware or it can be the *real* infrastructure itself. In either case, next-generation SEM tools allow developers and testers to run emulations that leverage their target platform.

Problem: Determining How to Emulate Application Behavior

When developing a SEM tool, an important design decision is determining how to emulate the system being developed on the target platform. For example, should the emulated system consist of (1) XML-based configuration files that can be interpreted and executed or (2) implementation code written in third-generation languages that is generated and compiled? Should the results of performance metrics be (1) written to a file or (2) gathered and transmitted to a central location, for example, a database? The answers to these questions are important because they affect the design and usability of SEM tools.

Solution: Choose Methods of Emulation that Offers Flexibility, but Meet Application Needs

When choosing a method of emulation, it is important to evaluate its impact on the usability and flexibility of a SEM tool. For example, using a XML-based implementation offers high configurability, but has run-time performance trade-offs. Likewise, collecting and transmitting data to a central location during the experiment adds more network traffic.

Applying the Solution to CUTS and SLICE

When we designed CUTS and applied it to the SLICE scenario we evaluated the following features of a SEM tools design.

- **Component instrumentation methods:** There are two design choices to select from when trying to emulate a system. The first design choice is to use *nonreplaceable* components that mimic the behavior and workload of its realistic counterpart, but do not have the expected interface as the actual components. The motivation for using nonreplaceable components is they are straightforward to implement and generate from a model because they need not conform to any specification (i.e., use the correct interfaces or calling conventions), unlike real components.

Nonreplaceable components typically use text-based configuration files (Slaby et al., 2006). For example, an XML metadata file can contain the behavior and workload characteristics of a particular component. When the system is deployed, a generic component (or object) will read the appropriate XML metadata file and configure itself accordingly. Although this design choice offers great flexibility, it incurs the overhead of interpreting the contents of the configuration file. Morever, as the real components are developed they cannot be integrated into the emulation environment due to the disconnect between the emulated component and the real component.

The other design choice is *replaceable* components, which have the same interfaces and attributes like their real components and can be swapped out for real components once their development is complete. This design allows continuous system integration from design-time to production-time (Hill & Gokhale, 2006). It is common for replaceable components to consist of implementations generated directly from model, similar to an IDL compiler generating stubs and skeletons from an IDL file. Another advantage of this approach is that implementations can be generated on a per-component/model basis to achieve the most accurate emulation results possible. The downside of approach, however, is that it requires developers to recompile components when their behavioral model changes causing regeneration of the emulation code.

CUTS uses *replaceable* components that provide the same interfaces and attributes as their real counterparts. It processes the models specified by users and generates implementation code and project files needed to compile the complete system. In addition, CUTS implements a hybrid between purely replaceable and nonreplaceable emulation components, which generates replaceable components that use text-based configuration files to determine their behavior. The advantage of this hybrid approach is that developers and testers only regenerate and recompile implementation code if the *structure* of the system changes. If the behavior of the system changes, then only the text-based configuration file is regenerated.

- **Benchmark methods:** When emulating a system with replaceable or nonreplaceable components, it is necessary to benchmark its performance by collecting performance metrics. There are two general methods for benchmarking a component: *intrusive* (Menascé, Almeida, & Dowdy, 2004) and *nonintrusive* (Mania et al., 2002; Parsons, Mos, & Murphy, 2006). Intrusive benchmarking requires developers to annotate their existing source code with new code that collects the necessary metrics. The advantage of this approach is that developers and testers can dictate which application-level metrics to collect. The disadvantage of this approach is that testers and developers must manage the metrics collection themselves, which may involve creating a benchmarking framework or learning how to interface with an existing one.

Nonintrusive benchmarking does not require any modifications to the existing source code. Nonintrusive benchmarking, in contrast, uses external or infrastructure-level tools to monitor different aspects of the system, such as disk and memory usage or arrival of an event. It is also common to use proxies (Parsons et al., 2006) that host the real component to capture performance metrics nonintrusively. The proxies resemble the real components and record performance metrics as events enter and leave the component to which it delegates to and from. If application-level metrics, such as invoking an operation that is internal to a component, are needed, however, intrusive monitoring is necessary because nonintrusive techniques have no knowledge of application-level implementation.

CUTS provides both nonintrusive and intrusive monitoring. Nonintrusive monitoring is achieved using proxies that have the same interfaces and attributes as their hosted components. The proxy monitors all events that enter and leave the component to which it delegates to and from. If application-level metrics are needed, CUTS allows developers to log the metrics to a thread-specific logging record associated with the source event using simplified intrusive monitoring techniques.

- **Data collection methods:** Another design choice that influences system emulation is choosing the data collection method, which can either be *off-line* or *online*. In off-line collection, metrics are written to a file while the system is being emulated. After an experiment is complete the metric file is analyzed using an analysis tool. The advantage of this method is that experimenters can determine the format of the output file and what metrics are written to the file. The disadvantage is the metrics usually cannot be processed until the experiment is complete, which can pose a problem during long running experiments or when trying to monitor the progress of an experiment. In online analysis, metrics are collected and transmitted via network to a host outside the experiment environment. The advantage of this approach is that it allows analysis of metrics in an environment that does not use

the experiments resources, so the experiments will not skew the results while it is running. The disadvantage is the difficulty of devising a strategy for efficiently collecting metrics in a distributed environment and submitting them to a central location without negatively impacting the running experiment, especially in an experiment with lots of network traffic.

CUTS uses an online distributed data collection technique that collects metrics in three stages. In stage 1, each port of a component records its performance metrics, for example, number of events received, the max/min transmission and processing time, and any application-level metrics. In stage 2, an agent within the proxy collects the data from each port at a user-specified interval and resets the each port's records. In stage 3, the agent transmits the gathered data to a central location called the *Benchmark-DataCollector*, which writes the collected data to a file or database. The Benchmark-DataCollector also allows external services to query it directly to evaluate online performance. For example, a component could query the BenchmarkDataCollector for the latest execution times of each component to determine how to adjust their priority level.

Analysis of Performance Metrics for Informative Feedback of Emulation Results

Context

Analysis of performance metrics is a key part of SEM tools. Whether metrics are collected *online* or *off-line*, it is necessary to understand what the collected metrics mean so that design flaws can be located and rectified. If metrics are collected *online* the analysis tool needs to provide testers with the ability to view partial results of the collected metrics until the experiment is complete. Once the experiment is complete, the tool will then provide an overall analysis of the experiment. If metrics are collected *off-line*, then the tool needs to support joining multiple data collection files to provide a synopsis of the experiment.

Problem: Providing Meaningful Analysis of Performance Metrics

The power of an analysis tool depends on how the metrics are presented testers. Visual analysis generally works best when viewing large amounts of data because visualization helps partition (or cluster) the data so that it is intuitive to readers. Visualization also includes using charts (e.g., pie charts, bar charts, and timelines) that allow developers and testers to highlight points of interest, obtain a general or detailed view of metrics (Herman, Melancon, & Marshall, 2000), or save and correlate metrics with multiple experiments (Hauswirth et al., 2005). Achieving this goal, however, is hard because not only must performance metrics be analyzed, but visual aids must be created to present the analyzed data.

Solution: Leverage Existing Visualization Packages

Many packages—both open-source and commercial—can be used to help analyze collected metrics. With the advent of service-oriented architectures, many analysis tools, such as WebCharts (www.carlosag.net/Tools/WebChart), WebCharts3D (www.gpoint.com), and Dundas Charts (www.dundas.com), provide testers with the ability to create powerful visual aids that can integrate with Web applications and viewed online for any place that is accessible to the internet. Therefore, it is possible to provide analytical support with little effort from developers of data analyzers.

Applying the Solution to CUTS and SLICE

In CUTS, analysis is done using at tool called the Benchmark Manager Web (BMW) Utility. The BMW is a Microsoft .NET Web application that uses a third-party Web charting tool to present metrics collected during an experiment. For each experiment, the BMW provides testers with an overall synopsis of the current tests, as well as detailed information (e.g., deployment information) for each component or timeline of application-level performance metrics, as shown in two example tables from the SLICE scenario in Figure 12.

More specifically, the general view in the left-hand portion of Figure 12 shows each of the deployed components, where each component is deployed, the number of events transmitted/received by a component, and the best-, average-, and worst-case service time of an event for each component. The detailed view in the right-hand portion of Figure 12 gives a chronological timeline of the best-, average-, and worst-case execution times for a particular event in a component.

Figure 12 shows that the timing of the total workload exhibits semiperiodic behavior and much jitter. These results occur because the component from Figure 12 is deployed on the same host as other components and thus competes for resources. Likewise, as events travel from component to component in the system, the location of each component (i.e., which host contains the component) affects timing synchronization between nodes and resources. The semiperiodic behavior in Figure 12 is, therefore, illustrative of how the placement of a system component affects other component's performance in relation to the structure of the overall system. Although we do not provide this form of analysis, it is possible to use correlation analysis (see Evaluation Techniques for Component Architectures section) or *main effects screening* (Yilmaz et al., 2005)

Figure 12. General (left) and detailed (right) view of performance metrics using the BMW

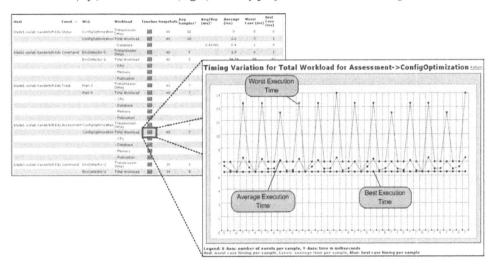

techniques to analysis collected performance metrics for these properties.

In addition to providing a detailed view of an event in a component, the BMW provides a detailed view of transmitting an event through a serious of components, which we call a *critical path*. Figure 13 shows a detailed view of analyzing a critical path using the BMW for the SLICE scenario. The upper graph in this figure depicts the average case execution time it took to transmit an event from main sensor to the main effect of the SLICE scenario as explained in the case study. The lower graph in Figure 13 depicts the worst case execution time for the same critical path. In either graph, there are two separate bar graphs. The upper bar graph is the actual time measurements collected by the nonintrusive benchmarking methods for a single event as it passes through the each component in the critical path, as shown by each block. The lower bar graph illustrates the deadline for the critical path.

If the deadline for a critical path is achieved, that is, the event passes through all the respective component before missing its deadline, the lower

bar graph will have a green strip to indicate successful completion of the critical path within its deadline, which is illustrated as "headroom" in the average-case graph. If the deadline is missed, the lower bar graph will have a red strip to indicate failure to complete deadline within specified time, which is shown as "overrun" in the worst-case graph. There graphs created by the BMW allows users to closely monitor the performance of events in the target system. Moreover, it also helps users pinpoint bottleneck components in the system and improve deployments for subsequent experiments.

The BMW is also a Web service, which means it can process SOAP requests. Support for SOAP allows CUTS to query the state of a remote experiment using any programming language that can send and receive SOAP messages. More importantly, the BMW Web service can also control the state of an experiment, including starting, stopping and pausing an experiment. The BMW, therefore, allows experimenters to manage experiments remotely for any location accessible via the Internet.

Figure 13. Detailed view of analyzing a critical path using the BMW

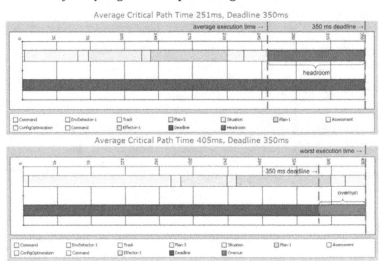

EXPERIMENTAL RESULTS

To illustrate the benefits of next-generation SEM tools, that is, those integrated with MDE technologies, we present the results of an experiment that applies CUTS to the SLICE scenario introduced in the case study. Our experiment explores the following two hypotheses:

1. The components in the SLICE scenario produce too much workload to all be deployed on the same host and still meet the 350ms deadline using the expected software and hardware configuration of the target environment.

2. It is possible to use CUTS to locate a collection of deployments (i.e., more than one) that will allow the critical path of the SLICE scenario to achieve its 350 ms deadline while meeting the deployment requirements specified in the case study.

This section discusses our process of using CUTS to evaluate the two hypotheses stated above.

It discusses using CBML and WML in CUTS to capture the behavior and workload of the components in the SLICE scenario. The CBML and WML models are then used to generate source code for replaceable emulation components. Lastly, we present the results of 11 different tests conducted in the target environments using the emulated components to analyze system performance based on the stated hypotheses. We conducted 11 tests because, after 11 different tests, we were able to answer the two hypotheses. The 11 tests, however, are *not completely exhaustive* of all possible deployment and configurations models of the SLICE scenario.

Specifying the Behavior of the SLICE Components

The first step in applying CUTS, or any other SEM tool, is to specify the behavior of each component.[1] Developers are typically given a high-level specification, which is usually a text-based document, of each component's expected behavior, or role in the system. This information must then be interpreted into a behavioral model that represents, as best as possible, the expected behavior of the system and its components. For example, Table 1 contains the behavioral specification for the *Planner-1*component of the SLICE scenario.

When we convert the behavioral specification in Table 1 into a model using CBML and WML, we get the model shown in Figure 11. Using the same method for constructing *Planner-1*'s behavioral model, we constructed models for all the remaining components in the SLICE scenario. Afterwards, we generated components for emulation from the models. The generated components had the same interface and attributes as their real components, so that as the real components were developed, they could replace the faux components. Finally, we used other structural tools in CoSMIC to generate the configuration and deployment metadata descriptor using the faux components and deployed the emulated system via the same deployment tools used in the target environment.

Emulating Application Behavior to Evaluate End-to-End QoS

One of our goals in the case study was to evaluate the end-to-end QoS of the SLICE scenario during early stages of development, as opposed to system integration time, thereby making it easier to locate and rectify performance problems as early as possible. Moreover, we wanted to locate a set of deployments, that is, placement of components onto hosts, that will allow the critical path of the SLICE scenario to run in <= 350 ms (hypothesis 2). To avoid a single point of failure, the SLICE scenario also required the deployment of components in the critical path across multiple hosts, and the main sensor and effector had to be deployed on separate hosts. We, however, wanted to determine if it was possible to meet the 350 ms critical path deadline when all the components

Table 2. System characteristics for each host in the SLICE experiment

Host	Operating System	Database
1	Fedora Core3	YES
2, 3, BDC	Fedora Core3	NO
BMW	Windows XP	YES

were deployed on a single node (hypothesis 1). We therefore, ran a series of experiments using CUTS to locate a set of deployments that satisfied the design and performance requirements.

Each host in the experiment was an IBM Blade Type L20, dual-CPU 2.8 GHz processor with 1 GB RAM with the characteristics listed in Table 2. The middleware was version 0.4.7 of CIAO/DAnCE (Deng, Balasubramanian, Otte, Schmidt, & Gokhale, 2005; Wang & Gill, 2003) and the MDE tools were version 0.4.6 of CoSMIC (Gokhale et al., 2006), which is the target middleware and MDE tool for the SLICE scenario.

Table 3 presents the results of 11 different experiments of the SLICE scenario using CUTS. Each experiment was run for 10 minutes to allow the collected performance metrics to stabilize. We were able to verify performance metric stabilization by using the online metrics analysis capabilities of the BMW. Again, we ran 11 tests because after the final test we had enough data to answer two hypotheses about the SLICE scenario. Moreover, we were able to show that CUTS could be used to analyze performance during the early stages of development to address questions about end-to-end system performance earlier in the design phase. Such questions included locating a collection of deployments that met the 350 ms critical path deadline, or determining if the SLICE scenario produced too much workload for a single host based on the current software/hardware configuration of the target environment.

Table 3. Results of SLICE scenario for different deployments

SLICE CoWorkEr Legend for Test Table			
Symbol	CoWorkEr	Symbol	CoWorkEr
A	Sensor-1 *	E	Config-Op *
B	Sensor-2	F	Error-Recovery
C	Planner-2 *	G	Effector-1 *
D	Planner-1 *	H	Effector-2
* represents CoWorkEr in the critical path			

Test	Deployment Strategy			Critical Path Execution (avg./worse) (ms)
	Host 1	Host 2	Host 3	
1	C,D,E,F	A,B	G,H	411 / 1,028
2	A,B,C,D	F	E,G,H	420 / 1,094
3	A,B,C,D,E	F	G,H	416,/ 1,085
4	A,B,C,D,E,F,G,H			463 / 1,247
5	A,B,C,D,E,G,H	F		467 / 1,219
6	A,C,D,E,G	F	B,H	323 / 844
7	A,G	C,D,E	B,F,H	363 / 887
8	D	A,B,C, F,G,H	E	405 / 975
9	A,D	C,E,G	B,F,H	235 / 387
10	A,D	E,G	B,C,F,H	251 / 395
11	A,D,E	C,G	B,F,H	221 / 343

Analyzing the Performance Results of the SLICE Scenario

Table 2 presents the results of 11 different tests we conducted for the SLICE scenario using CUTS. Only 3 of the 11 tests (Tests 9, 10, and 11) had a deployment model where the critical path components deployed across multiple nodes and, when emulated by CUTS, completed their end-to-end execution in 350 ms. From Test 9, 10 and 11, we were able to start a collection of deployments for the SLICE scenario, which addressed hypothesis 2. Of those three tests, only two tests (Test 9 and 11) had a deployment model where the critical

path was deployed on two separate nodes, and completed their end-to-end deadline in 350 ms. One experiment (test 6) completed the critical path in 350 ms, however, the critical path components were all deployed on a single host, for example, host 1. Only one of the tests (test 11) completed the critical path within the worst-case execution time of 350 ms. Although we did not exhaust all possible deployment strategies with these tests, we learned that only 27% (3 out of 11) of the current test passed on their planned infrastructure while meeting the deployment requirements, and Test 11 yielded the best performance.

- **Measuring the limitations of single host deployment:** The deployment constraints of the SLICE scenario described in the case study requires all the components in the critical path to be deployed across multiple nodes. In addition, the main sensor (Sensor-1) and the main effector (Effector-1) must be deployed on separate nodes to avoid a single point of failure. If the components are deployed across multiple hosts it is possible to simplify system recovery though redeployment (Shankaran, Koutsoukos, Schmidt, & Gokhale, 2005). Although the requirements specify that the critical path components must be deployed across multiple nodes, we wanted to determine if it was possible to deploy all the components (in the entire application and only in the critical path) on a single node and still meet the 350 ms deadline to verify hypothesis 1.

  After running Test 4 and 5, we realized that it would be impossible to meet the 350 ms deadline when all the components are deployed on the same host (i.e., the SLICE scenario produced more workload than a single host could handle as conjectured in hypothesis 1) for our current hardware and software configuration. When we deployed the components in the critical path on one host and the remaining components to a separate host (Test 6), we met the 350 ms critical path deadline for our current hardware and software configuration. We were, therefore, able to determine the possibility of achieving the 350 ms deadline when all components are deployed on a single host, and when only the components in the critical path are deployed on a same host.

- **In-depth analysis and understanding of results for hypothesis 2:** After running Test 1 through 8, only one test (Test 6) met the 350 ms end-to-end deadline. Moreover, seven of the tests had faults in their deployment specification, for example, the combination of particular components on a host generated more workload than the host could handle

Figure 14. Snapshot of timing data for Sensor-1 in test 8 obtained from the BMW test results page

Host	Event ->	WLG	Workload	Timeline	Snapshots	Avg Samples*	Avg/Rep (ms)*	Average (ms)	Worst Case (ms)	Best Case (ms)
blade5.isislab.Vanderbilt.Edu	Command	EnvDetector-1	Transmission Delay	⊞	39	5		6.19	7	6
		EnvDetector-1	Total Workload	⊞	39	5		169.6	522	54
			- CPU	⊞			2.20859	99.39	208	16
			- Memory	⊞			0.00727	0.51	1	0
			- Publication	⊞			1.40206	1.4	20	1

Figure 15. Snapshot of the critical path timing data for test 8 from the BMW analysis page

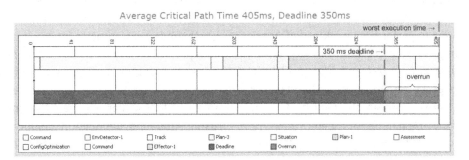

Figure 16. Snapshot of the critical path timing data for test 11 from the BMW analysis page

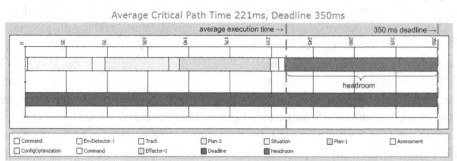

to meet 350 ms critical path deadline. To pinpoint the bottlenecks, we used CUTS graphical analysis features to investigate why these deployment strategies did not meet their QoS requirements.

Figure 14 and 15 illustrate the results provided via the BMW for Test 8, which measures the behavior when two components in the critical path handling the most workload are deployed on their own node. Figure 14 shows the time to transmit a message to the *Sensor-1* (EnvDectector-1) and how long it took to complete each type of workload (e.g., CPU, database, or memory) for the *Sensor-1*. Likewise, Figure 15 shows the average execution time of an event through each component in the critical path of the SLICE scenario. We observed that *Sensor-1* took 169.6 ms to process its workload after receiving a *command* event from *Planner-1*, *Planner-1* took 54.0 ms to perform its workload after receiving a *track* event from *Sensor-1* or *Sensor-2*; and *Planner-2* took 110.6 ms to perform its workload after receiving a *command* event from *Planner-1*. For Test 8, *Sensor-1* and *Planner-2* have the longest completion times. Based on the quantitative analysis provided by CUTS, we realized that the *Sensor-1* and *Planner-2* CoWorkEr components had a heavier work-

load than expected, and must be deployed on separate nodes. We, therefore, created a new deployment model that placed *Sensor-1* and *Planner-2* CoWorkErs on different hosts, which led to the deployment models used in Test 9, 10 and 11, all of which met the 350 ms end-to-end deadline. Of these three tests, Test 11 (shown in Figure 16) was the only test to have a worst-case execution time that met the 350 ms deadline. These deployment strategies also met the deployment requirements of placing *Sensor-1* and *Effector-1* on different nodes. We were, therefore, able to answer our second hypothesis, which was using CUTS to locate a collection of deployments that meet the 350 ms critical path deadline.

Summary of the Experimental Results

Our experience applying CUTS to the SLICE scenario showed how next-generation SEM tools can help decrease time spent resolving integration problems early in the development lifecycle. Instead of waiting until full system integration, CUTS allowed us to test multiple deployments of the SLICE scenario in the target environment using emulated application components. The results of our 11 tests for the SLICE scenario, which was not exhaustive of all possible tests, allowed us to create a collection of deployments that meet the 350 ms critical path deadline during the early stages of development. Moreover, we verified that the SLICE scenario produced more workload than a single host in our target environment could handle.

As the real components for the SLICE scenario are completed, we can integrate them into the emulation environment to achieve more realistic results because CUTS implements replaceable emulation components. This incremental replacement process allows developers to perform continuous system integration from design-time (i.e., early stages of development) to integration-time (i.e., final stages of development). As a result, the collection of deployments that meet the 350 ms deadline from the continuous system integration using CUTS will be the same deployments system engineers use when the system is in production.

FUTURE TRENDS

This section discusses emerging and future technological trends associated with developing enterprise DRE systems using SEM tools, with an emphasis on J2EE and Microsoft .NET technologies because many enterprise business applications are developed using J2EE and Microsoft .NET, so this section balances out the earlier focus on the CORBA Component Model.

Increased Use of MDE Technologies for Code Generation

MDE technologies are increasingly being applied to address many of the challenges and complexities of developing enterprise DRE system (AndroMDA, 2007; Margaria, 2004; Smith, Friese, & Freisleben, 2006; Task, Paniscotti, Roman, & Bhanot, 2006). As a result, there is a shift from the traditional development paradigm—where

developers handcraft most artifacts, such as source code and configuration files—to an MDE approach where developers use domain-specific modeling languages to develop enterprise DRE systems. A key advantage of an MDE approach is that it shields application developers from many error-prone and tedious tasks, such as manually scripting dense and complex XML files or writing redundant source code that can instead be generated from models.

For example, framework-specific modeling languages (FSMLs) (Antkiewicz, 2006, Antkiewicz & Czarnecki, 2006a), which capture the API of a framework and ensure proper usage of its building blocks, are increasingly being integrated into existing MDE tools, such as the Workbench Part Interaction (WPI) FSML prototype (Antkiewicz & Czarnecki, 2006b) or Pattern-Oriented Software Architecture Modeling Language (POSAML) (Kaul, Kogekar, Gokhale, Gray, & Gokhale, 2007). An FSML can be used to generate valid source code directly from the models. Likewise, as the underlying framework changes between versions, the FSML can capture these revisions, such as deprecated methods, new methods of an object, or modified parameters of a pre-existing method. Moreover, the FSML will enforce the changes, for example, make modelers aware of revisions in the target framework so they can correct their models accordingly via round-trip engineering.

Increased Use of Continuous Integration Servers to Improve Software Quality

Continuous integration (Fowler, 2006) environments are a form of extreme programming (XP) (Beck, 2000) where integration is accomplished by server daemons using serialized build processes. Continuous integration environments such as Build Forge (www.buildforge.com), CruiseControl (cruisecontrol.sourceforge.net), and DART (public.kitware.com/Dart) continuously exercise the complete build cycle of a product to ensure that software is of the highest quality by:

1. Performing automated builds of the system upon source code check in or successful execution and evaluation of prior events;
2. Executing suites of unit tests to verify basic system functionality;
3. Evaluating source code to ensure it meets coding standards and best practices; and
4. Executing code coverage analysis.

By utilizing continuous integration servers, developers can improve software quality because much of the manual labor required to stay abreast with large-scale software development will be handled autonomously. Moreover, instead of manually managing the software development process, more time and effort can be spent responding to development concerns (and problems) identified by continuous integration servers.

Continuous integration servers can alleviate many manually tasks introduced during the software development process, such as monitoring source code repositories to ensure the latest version of software builds successfully, or running unit tests to ensure proper functionality. Likewise, system execution modeling (SEM) tool suites provide developers with tools for testing applications in realistic environments (i.e., on the target architecture) using realistic workloads. Because system execution modeling tools offer features that continuous integration servers lack, such as realistic testing environments, and continuous integration servers offer services that SEM tool suites lack, such as management of large numbers of tests, marrying SEM tools suites with continuous integration servers will also help improve software quality. By capitalizing from the integration of both SEM tool suites and continuous integration servers, developers will also be able to improve assurance of QoS.

J2EE and Microsoft .NET Business Applications

SOA technologies such as J2EE and Microsoft .NET are commonly used by enterprises to build business applications (IDC, 2005). As a result, SEM tools are emerging to support such applications through the concept of *process modeling* (Curtis, Kellner, & Over, 1992), which is similar to behavioral modeling in SEM tools, but can operate at a higher level of abstraction. In process modeling, developers use next-generation SEM tools to capture the *workflow* (or "business-logic") of their target application. These models can then be used to run simulations/emulations to verify the application's correctness, generate a prototype of the application, or generate a production application that is integrated with the target SOA technology.

Windows Workflow Foundation (WinFX Workflow) (Box & Shukla, 2006), which is part of the Microsoft .NET 3.0 framework, allows developers to model the business processes of their enterprise business applications. WinFX Workflow contains the following parts related to process modeling and generation of business applications:

- **Activity model** that allows developers to capture the different actions, or work working units, of the business applications, for example, its operations and workloads.
- **Workflow designer** that allows developers to sequence activity models to define the behavior of the application's business logic.
- **Workflow runtime** that allows developers to execute the workflows of the business application created in the workflow designer in an emulated environment or target environment.

The Java Workflow Tooling (JWT) (Dutto & Lautenbacher, 2007) is another MDE technology for process modeling, which targets J2EE business applications. Similar to WinFX Workflow, JWT offers developers of J2EE applications the ability to capture the workflow of their business applications, and execute the workflows in the target environment. The JWT is comprised of the following parts:

- **Workflow Editor (WE)** that is a visual tool for creating, managing, and reviewing process definitions, that is, their business logic.
- **Workflow engine Administration and Monitoring tool (WAM)** that is used to execute, monitor, and analyze workflows of business applications created using the workflow editor.

The Business Process Modeling Notation (BPMN) (BPMN, 2005) is a standard developed by Business Process Management Initiative (BPMI) that allows developers to define business processes in the form of workflows. BPMN is comprised of the following parts for defining workflows:

- **Flow objects** (e.g., event, activity, and gateway) that determine how the business process behaves, or flows.
- **Connecting objects** (e.g., sequence flow, messaging flow, and association) that are used to connect one or more flow objects. This allows developers to sequence the flow objects to create workflows, or process models.
- **Swimlanes** (e.g., pool and lane) that are used to organize workflows into categories and groups within the categories, respectively.
- **Artifacts** (e.g., data objects, group, annotation) that allow developers to add information to the model that does not affect workflow, and makes it more comprehendible.

Similar to WinFX and JWT, BPMN can be transformed into an execution language called

Business Process Execution Language (BPEL) (White, 2005).

The major difference between BPMN, JWT, and WinFX Workflow is their target SOA technology. WinFX is designed for Microsoft .NET applications, whereas the JWT is designed for J2EE application. Likewise, BPMN is a technology independent graphical language for graphing business processes as workflows. Although each technology has their differences, it is clear that using MDE technologies to model business processes, that is, model their behavior, perform analysis checks, and generate the target application from the model for emulation, or production, is an important trend in future MDE technologies.

FUTURE RESEARCH DIRECTIONS

Many existing enterprise applications have been developed using traditional development techniques, that is, applications were build directly on top of operating systems and networking protocols. Consequently, many enterprises developed their own (distributed) middleware, which has become deeply embedded into—and the foundation of—many subsequent applications. Enterprises applications are now evaluating the benefits of service-oriented architectures (SOAs), such as CORBA Component Model, Microsoft .NET, and J2EE, and are increasingly migrating to this programming paradigm.

Although SOAs provide many benefits, such as encapsulation of business-logic in components for reuse, existing performance analysis techniques still rely on low-level traditional profiling techniques (Waddington, Roy, & Schmidt, 2007) because of the reliability and maturity of existing tools and techniques. For example, DTrace (Cantrill, Shapiro, & Levanthal, 2004) is a powerful profiling tool distributed with the Solaris operating system that uses low-level tracing techniques (e.g., tracing kernel- and user-level functions/variables) to locate and resolve performance issues. The Java virtual machine (JVM) profiler interface (Binder, 2005) is another example that allows developers to implement third-party profiler applications that interact with the JVM. Similar to DTrace, the JVM profiler interfaces allow profiler applications to monitor virtual machine- and user-level events while Java applications are executing.

Although tools such as DTrace and the JVM profiler interface are beneficial, SOA-based development techniques operate at higher level of abstraction than existing profiling tools support effectively. For example, a single node (such as a server) could host multiple components of the same type, that is, each component is an instance of the same component type. Consequently, low-level profiling tools will not be able to distinguish between performance issues related to each component. Next-generation system profiling to similar to CUTS can distinguish between performance issues related to each component, though they cannot provide the same low-level details as traditional profiling tools.

Future research is, therefore, needed to understand how to integrate low-level profiling tools with next-generation tools that operate at the component level. Although SOAs manage low-level implementation details, such as interaction with operating system APIs and networking protocols, the ability to profile applications using low-level tools can provide insight as to how to configure the SOA middleware properly. Moreover, profiling application behavior at the component-level will allow developers to understand how their components interact with the underlying SOA middleware (and operating system) so developers can provide the best implementation that is most beneficial to their applications.

CONCLUDING REMARKS

This chapter motivated the need for combining system execution modeling (SEM) tools with model-driven engineering (MDE) technologies to address the development and integration challenges of service-oriented architecture (SOA)-based enterprise distributed real-time and embedded (DRE) systems. To meet this need, we discussed the necessary ingredients (i.e., behavioral and structural modeling languages, emulation techniques, and analysis methods) and describe key challenges to overcome to guide in developing next-generation SEM tools in general while using our next-generation MDE-based SEM tool called CUTS as an example. We also showed how CUTS could be applied to the SLICE case study from the domain of shipboard computing to address integration challenges during early stages of development.

The following summarizes the benefits of applying CUTS to evaluate the QoS of enterprise DRE systems based on our experience thus far:

- **Early integration testing.** CUTS allowed us to emulate system components using the target hardware and software infrastructure. More importantly, we were able to emulate the system at early stages of development instead of waiting until completely implementing the real components and trying to resolve all issues during integration phase. We had attempted this is previous stages of the MLRM project described in the case study, but were unsuccessful because we missed project deadlines and had an increase in project effort.
- **Extensive QoS testing.** CUTS allowed us to rapidly create and quantitatively evaluate a range of deployment plans to see how they impacted end-to-end QoS behavior. Much more time and effort would have been required if these tests were conducted manually, that is, without the visual SEM tool functionality and automation provided by CUTS and the underlying CIAO and DAnCE QoS-enabled middleware and CoSMIC MDE tools. More importantly, CUTS

provided qualitative performance analysis to assist in locating deficiencies in current deployments so we can determine alternative deployments that meet end-to-end QoS requirements more effectively.

- **Continuous system integration testing.** The use of SEM tools enabled us to substitute real components for the emulated ones quickly, so we could incrementally evaluate QoS performance with more realistic workloads as knowledge of the application and system infrastructure evolves. This emulation enabled us to benchmark the performance of the system to evaluate QoS continuously. Moreover, it helped reduce the amount of time and effort spent during system integration trying to resolve the challenges we had addressed since the early stages of development.

Although there are many benefits to using CUTS to evaluate QoS of enterprise DRE systems, we also discovered that the following work is needed to improve the evaluation of QoS in component-based enterprise DRE systems:

- **Functional testing for (in)correctness.** It is becoming common practice to unit-test the business-logic of a component throughout the development lifecycle using continuous integration tools (Fowler, 2006). This helps increase confidence that the underlying framework used in the component is functioning correctly. When the business-logic is encapsulated inside a component, functional testing usually does not occur until integration testing (Li, Sun, Jiang, & Zhang, 2005). Future work, therefore, is needed to allow CUTS to provide unit testing for systems at the component-level (e.g., verifying input/output values are translated correctly between the components interface and business-logic, or exceptions are interpreted and handled correctly at the component-level),

while utilizing the QoS testing features already provided by CUTS.

- **Pluggable QoS analysis capabilities.** Currently, CUTS provides minimum QoS analysis, such as end-to-end execution timing analysis and worst-case scenario analysis. We are, however, learning that there are times when our analysis tools may not provide enough details in certain situations, such as correlation analysis across multiple tests based on performance metrics or analyzing proprietary systems and data. Future work is therefore needed to extend CUTS to support pluggable analysis tools (or objects) that can analyze collected metrics and collect metrics we do not collect (e.g., input/output parameter values or current state of a component) at run-time.

CUTS is currently being transitioned from the MLRM project to a production Naval shipbuilding program to assist system engineers and architects in evaluating QoS performance metrics of DRE systems. An open-source version of CUTS and the other MDE tools and QoS-enabled SOA-based middleware platforms described in this paper can be downloaded from www.dre.vanderbilt.edu/CUTS.

REFERENCES

AndroMDA. (2007). Retrieved March 22, 2008, from team.andromda.org

Antkiewicz, M. (2006, September). Round-trip engineering of framework-based software using framework-specific modeling languages. In *Proceeding of the 21st IEEE International Conference on Automated Software Engineering*, Washington, DC, (pp. 323-326).

Antkiewicz, M., & Czarnecki, K. (2006a, October). Framework-specific modeling languages with round-trip engineering. In *Proceeding of the*

9th International Conference on Model Driven Engineering Languages and Systems, Genova, Italy, (pp. 692-706).

Antkiewicz, M., & Czarnecki, K. (2006b, October). Round-trip engineering of eclipse plug-ins using eclipse workbench part interaction FSML. In *Proceedings of the International Conference on Object Oriented Programming Systems Languages and Applications (OOPSLA),* Portland, OR.

Balasubramanian, K., Balasubramanian, J., Parsons, J., Gokhale, A., & Schmidt, D. C. (2005). A platform-independent component modeling language for distributed real-time and embedded systems. In *Proceedings of the 11th Realtime Technology and Application Symposium,* San Francisco, CA, (pp. 190-199).

Beck, K. (2000). *Extreme programming explained: Embrace change.* Boston: Addison-Wesley.

Bengtsson, J., Larsen, K., Larsson, F., Pettersson, P., & Yi, W. (1995). UPPAAL: A tool suite for automatic verification of real-time systems. In *Proceedings of the Workshop on Verification and Control of Hybrid Systems III,* (Vol. 1066, pp. 232-243).

Bertolino, A., & Mirandola, R. (2004). Software performance engineering of component-based systems. In *Proceedings of the 4th International Workshop on Software and Performance,* Redwood Shores, CA, (pp. 238-242).

Binder, W. (2005, September). Portable, efficient, and accurate sampling profiling for java-based middleware. In *Proceedings of the 5th international Workshop on Software Engineering and Middleware,* Lisbon, Portugal, (pp. 46-53).

Box, D., & Shukla, D. (2006). WinFX workflow: Simplify development with the declarative model of windows workflow foundation. *MSDN Magazine, 21,* 54-62.

Bucci, G., Fedeli, A., Sassoli, L., & Vicario, E. (2003, July). Modeling flexible real time systems with preemptive time Petri nets. In *Proceeding of 15th Euromicro Conference on Real-time Systems,* Porto, Portugal, (pp. 279-286).

BPMN Information Home. (2005). Retrieved March 23, 2008, from www.bpmn.org

CPNTools: Computer tools for coloured Petri nets. (2006). Demark: University of Aarhus, CPN Group. Retrieved March 23, 2008, from wiki.daimi.au.dk/cpntools/cpntools.wiki

Cantrill, B.M., Shapiro, M.W., & Levanthal, A.H. (2004). Dynamic instrumentation of production systems. In *Proceedings of the USENIX Annual Technical Conference 2004 on USENIX Annual Technical Conference,* Boston, MA.

Curtis, B., Kellner, M., & Over, J. (1992). Process modeling. *Communications of the ACM, 35*(9), 75-90.

Deng, G., Balasubramanian, J., Otte, W., Schmidt, D., & Gokhale, A. (2005). DAnCE: A QoS-enabled component deployment and configuration engine. In *Proceedings of the 3rd Working Conference on Component Deployment,* Grenoble, France.

Denning, P.J., & Buzen, J.P. (1978). The operation analysis of queuing network models. *Computing Surveys, 10*(3), 225-261.

Dutto, M., & Lautenbacher, F. (2007). *Java Workflow Tooling (JWT) creation review.*

Retrieved March 23, 2008, from www.eclipse.org/proposals/jwt/JWT%20Creation%20Review%2020070117.pdf

Object Management Group. (2002). *Real-time CORBA specification.* OMG Document formal/02-08-02.

Florescu, O., Hoon, M., Voeten, J., & Corporall, H. (2006, July). Probabilistic modelling and evaluation of soft real-time embedded systems. In *Proceedings of Embedded Computer Systems:*

Architectures, Modeling, and Simulation (SAMOS VI), Samos, Greece.

Fowler, M. (2006). *Continuous integration*. Retrieved March 23, 2008, from www.martinfowler.com/articles/continuousIntegration.html

Gamma, E., Helm, R., Johnson, R., & Vlissides, J. (1995). *Design patterns: Elements of reusable object-oriented software*. Reading, MA: Addison-Wesley.

Garland, S. (2005). *The TIOA user guide and reference manual*. Retrieved March 23, 2008, from tioa.csail.mit.edu/public/Documentation/Guide.doc

Gokhale, A., Balasubramanian, K., Balasubramanian, J., Krishna, A., Edwards, G., Deng, G., et al. (2006). Model driven middleware: A new paradigm for deploying and provisioning distributed real-time and embedded applications. *The Journal of Science of Computer Programming: Special Issue on Model Driven Architecture*.

Grassi, V., Mirandola, R., & Sabetta, A. (2005). From design to analysis models: A kernel language for performance and reliability analysis of component-based systems. In *Proceedings of the Fifth International Workshop on Software and Performance*, Palma de Mallorca, Spain.

Hatcliff, J., Deng, W., Dwyer, M., Jung, G., & Prasad, V. (2003). Cadena: An integrated development, analysis, and verification environment for component-based systems. In *Proceedings of the 25th International Conference on Software Engineering*, Portland, OR.

Hauswirth, M., Diwan, A., Sweeney, P., & Mozer, M. (2005). Automating vertical profiling. In *Proceeding of the 19ᵗʰ Conference of Object Oriented Programming, Systems, Languages and Applications*, San Diego, CA.

Herman, I., Melançon, G., & Marshall, M.S. (2000). Graph visualization and navigation in information visualization: A survey. *IEEE Transactions on Visualization and Computer Graphics, 6*(1), 24-43.

Hill, J.H., & Gokhale, A. (2006). Continuous QoS provisioning of large-scale component-based systems using model driven engineering. In Poster preseted at *International Conference on Model Driven Engineering Languages and Systems*, Genova, Italy.

Hill, J.H., & Gokhale, A. (2007, March). Model-driven engineering for development-time QoS validation of component-based software systems. In *Proceeding of International Conference on Engineering of Component Based Systems*, Tuscon, AZ.

IDC Quantitative Research Group. (2005). *2005 Mission Critical Survey: Survey report*. Retrieved March 23, 2008, from download.microsoft.com/download/1/8/a/18a10d4f-deec-4d5e-8b24-87c29c2ec9af/idc-ms-missioncritical-ww-261005.pdf

Karsai, G., Sztipanovits, J., Ledeczi, A., & Bapty, T. (2003). Model-integrated development of embedded software, In *Proceedings of the IEEE, 91*(1), 145-164.

Kaul, D., Kogekar, A., Gokhale, A., Gray, J., & Gokhale, S. (2007). Managing variability in middleware provisioning using visual modeling languages. In *Proceedings of the Hawaii International Conference on System Sciences HICSS-40 (2007), Visual Interactions in Software Artifacts Minitrack, Software Technology Track*, Big Island, HI.

Kristensen, L.M., Christensen, S., & Jensen, K. (1998). The practitioner's guide to coloured Petri nets. *International Journal on Software Tools for Technology Transfer, 2*, 98-132.

Lardieri, P., Balasubramanian, J., Schmidt, D., Thakar, G., Gokhale, A., & Damiano, T. (2007, to appear). A multi-layered resource management framework for dynamic resource management in enterprise DRE systems. In C. C Cavanaugh (Ed.), *Journal of Systems and Software: Special Issue on Dynamic Resource Management in Distributed Real-time Systems.*

Ledeczi, A., Maroti, M., Karsai G., & Nordstrom G. (1999). Metaprogrammable toolkit for model-integrated computing. In *Proceedings of the IEEE International Conference on the Engineering of Computer-Based Systems Conference,* Nashville, TN, (pp 311-317).

Li, Z., Sun, W., Jiang, Z. B., & Zhang X. (2005). BPEL4WS unit testing: Framework and implementation. In *Proceedings of the IEEE International Conference on Web Services (ICWS'05),* Orlando, FL, (pp. 103-110).

Lynch, N., & Tuttle, M. (1989). An introduction to input/output automata. *CWI-Quarterly, 2*(3), 219-246.

Mania, D., Murphy, J., & McManis, J. (2002). Developing performance models from non-intrusive monitoring traces. In *Proceeding of Information Technology and Telecommunications (IT&T).*

Margaria, T. (2004). Modeling dependable systems: What can model driven development contribute and what likely not? In *Proceedings of IEEE International Symposium on Object-Oriented Real-Time Distributed Computing,* Vienna, Austria.

Menascé, D., Almeida, V., & Dowdy, L. (2004). *Performance by design: Computer capacity planning by example* (pp. 135-141). Upper Saddle River, NJ: Prentice Hall.

Merlin, P. M. (1974). A study of the recoverability of computing systems. Irvine: University of California, Department of Information and Computer Science.

Northrop, L., Feiler, P., Gabriel, R., Goodenough, J., Linger, R., Longstaff, T., et al. (2006). *Ultra-large-scale systems: The software challenge of the future.* Carnegie Mellon.

Parsons, T., Mos, A., & Murphy, J. (2006, August). Non-intrusive end-to-end runtime path tracing for J2EE systems. *IEEE Proceedings Software, 153,* 149-161.

Peterson, J.L. (1977). Petri nets. *ACM Computing Surveys, 9*(3), 223-252.

PlanetLab Consortium. (2006). *PLANETLAB: An open platform for developing, deploying, and accessing planetary-scale services.* Retrieved March 23, 2008, from http://www.planet-lab.org

Ricci, R., Alfred, C., & Lepreau, J. (2003). A solver for the network testbed mapping problem. *SIGCOMM Computer Communications Review, 33,* 65-81.

Shankaran, N., Koutsoukos, X., Schmidt, D.C., & Gokhale, A. (2005). Evaluating adaptive resource management for distributed real-time embedded systems. In *Proceedings of 4th Workshop on Adaptive and Reflective Middleware,* Grenoble, France.

Slaby, J., Baker, S., Hill, J., & Schmidt, D. (2005). *Defining behavior and evaluating QoS performance of the SLICE scenario* (Tech. Rep. No. ISIS-05-608). Nashville, TN: Vanderbilt University.

Slaby, J., Baker, S., Hill, J., & Schmidt, D. (2006). Applying system execution modeling tools to evaluate enterprise distributed real-time and embedded system QoS. In *Proceedings of the 12th International Conference on Embedded and Real-Time Computing Systems and Applications,* Sydney, Australia.

Schmidt, D. C. (2006). Model-driven engineering. *IEEE Computer, 39,* 41-47.

Smith, C. (1990). *Performance engineering of software systems.* Reading, MA: Addison-Wesley.

Smith, M., Friese, T., & Freisleben, B. (2006). Model driven development of service-oriented grid applications. In *Proceedings of the Advanced International Conference on Telecommunications and International Conference on Internet and Web Applications and Services*, Guadeloupe, French Caribbean.

Smith, C., & Williams, L. (2001). *Performance solutions: A practical guide to creating responsive, scalable software*. Reading, MA: Addison-Wesley.

Subramonian, V. (2006). *Timed automata models for principled composition of middleware* (Tech. Rep. No. WUCSE-2006-23). St. Louis, MO: Washington University, Computer Science and Engineering Department.

Task, B., Paniscotti, D., Roman, A., & Bhanot, V. (2006). Using model-driven engineering to complement software product line engineering in developing software defined radio components and applications. In *Proceedings of International Conference on Object Oriented Programming Systems Languages and Applications (OOPSLA)*, Portland, OR.

Tavares, E., Maciel, P., Bessa, A., Barreto, R., Barros, L., Oliveira, M., & Lima, R. (2005). A time petri net based approach for embedded hard real-time software synthesis with multiple operational modes. In *Proceedings of the 18th Annual Symposium on Integrated Circuits and System Design (SBCCI '05)* (pp. 98-103). Florianolpolis, Brazil.

Vahdat, A., Yocum, K., Walsh, K., Mahadevan, P., Kostic, K., Chase, J., & Becker, D. (2002). Scalability and accuracy in a large-scale network emulator. In *Proceedings of 5th Symposium on Operating Systems Design and Implementation (OSDI)*.

Waddington, D., Roy, N., & Schmidt, D.C. (2007). Dynamic analysis and profiling of multi-threaded systems. In P.F. Tiako (Ed.), *Designing software-intensive systems: Methods and principles*: OK: Langston University.

Wang, N., & Gill, C. (2003). Improving real-time system configuration via a QoS-aware CORBA component model. In *Proceedings of the Hawaii International Conference on System Sciences, Software Technology Track, Distributed Object and Component-based Software Systems*.

White, S. A. (2005, March). *Using BPMN to model a BPEL process*. Retrieved March 23, 2008, from www.bptrends.com

White, J., Gokhale, A., & Schmidt, D.C. (2007). Simplifying autonomic enterprise Java Bean applications via model-driven development: A case study. Submitted to the *Journal of Software and System Modeling*.

White, J., Schmidt, D.C., & Gokhale, A. (2005). Simplifying the development of autonomic enterprise Java Bean applications via model driven development. In *Proceedings of the International Conference on Autonomic Computing (ICAC)*, Seattle, WA.

Yilmaz, C., Krishna, A. S., Memon, A., Porter, A., Schmidt, D. C., Gokhale, A., & Natarajan, B. (2005). Main effects screening: A distributed continuous quality assurance process for monitoring performance degradation in evolving software systems. In *Proceedings of the 27th International Conference on Software Engineering,* St. Loius, MO, (pp. 293-302).

ADDITIONAL READING

Cascaval, C., Duesterwald, E., Sweeney, P. F., & Wisniewski, R. W. (2006). Performance and environment monitoring for continuous program optimization. *IBM Journal of Research and Development, 50*(2/3), 239-248.

Chatterjee, A. (2007). Service-component architectures: A programming model for SOA. *Dr. Dobb's Journal, 400*, 40-45.

Chilimbi, T.M., & Hauswirth, M. (2004). Low-overhead memory leak detection using adaptive statistical profiling. In *Proceedings of the 11th international Conference on Architectural Support for Programming Languages and Operating Systems*, Boston, MA.

Haran, M., Karr, A., Orso, A., Portor, A., & Sanil, A. (2005). Applying classification techniques to remotely-collected program execution data. In *Proceedings of the 10th European Software Engineering Conference held jointly with 13th ACM SIGSOFT International Symposium on Foundations of Software Engineering*, Lisbon, Portugal.

Hauswirth, M., Sweeney, P., Diwan, A., & Hind, M. (2004). Vertical profiling: Understanding the behavior of object-oriented applications. *ACM SIGPLAN Notices, 39*(10), 251-269.

Hill, J. H., & Gokhale, A. (in press). Model-driven engineering for early QoS validation of component-based software systems, *Journal of Software, 2*(2).

Huselius, J., & Andersson, J. (2005). Model synthesis for real-time systems. In *Proceedings of the Ninth European Conference on Software Maintenance and Reengineering*, Manchester, UK.

Laugelier, G., Sahraoui, H., & Poulin, P. (2005). Visualization-based analysis of quality for large-scale software systems. In *Proceedings of the 20th IEEE/ACM International Conference on Automated Software Engineering*, Long Beach, CA.

Ledeczi, A., Nordstrom, G., Karsai, G., Volgyesi, P., & Maroti, M. (2001). On metamodel composition. In *Proceedings of the 2001 IEEE International Conference on Control Applications*, Mexico City, Mexico.

Li, Z., Sun, W., Jiang, Z.B., & Zhang, X. (2005). BPEL4WS unit testing: Framework and implementation. In *Proceedings of the IEEE International Conference on Web Services*, Orlando, FL.

Kaynar, D. K., Lynch, N., Segala, R., & Vaandrager, F. (2006). *The theory of timed I/O automata, synthesis lectures on computer science*. Morgan and Claypool.

Kounev, S. (2006). Performance modeling and evaluation of distributed component-based systems using queuing Petri nets. *IEEE Transactions of Software Engineering, 32*(7), 486-502.

Kounev, S., & Buchmann, A. (2003). Performance modeling and evulation of large-scale J2EE applications. In *Proceedings of the 29th International Conference of the Computer Measurement Group (CMG) on Resource Management and Performance Evaluation of Enterprise Computing Systems*, Dallas, TX.

Memon, A., Porter, A., Nagarajan, A., Schmidt, D., & Natarajan, B. (2004). Skoll: Distributed quality assurance. In *Proceedings of the 26th IEEE/ACM International Conference on Software Engineering*, Edinburgh, Scotland.

Metz, E., Lencevicius, R., & Gonzalez, T. (2005). Performance data collection using a hybrid approach. In *Proceedings of the 10th European Software Engineering Conference held jointly with 13th ACM SIGSOFT International Symposium on Foundations of Software Engineering*, Lisbon, Portugal.

Mos, A., & Murphy, J. (2004). COMPAS: Adaptive performance monitoring of component-based systems. In *Proceedings of the 2nd ICSE Workshop on Remote Analysis and Measurement of Software Systems*, Beijing, China.

Odom, J., Hollingsworth, J. K., DeRose, L., Ekanadham, K., & Sbaraglia, S. (2005). Using dynamic tracing sampling to measure long running programs. In *Proceedings of the 2005 ACM/IEEE Conference on Supercomputing*, Seattle, WA.

Parsons, T., & Murphy, J. (in press). Detecting performance antipatterns in component-based enterprise systems. *Journal of Object Technology*.

Saff, D., & Ernst, M.D. (2004). An experimental evaluation of continuous testing during development. In *Proceedings of the 2004 ACM SIGSOFT International Symposium on Software Testing and Analysis*, Boston, MA.

Schroeder, P.J., Kim, E., Arshem, J., & Bolaki, P. (2003). Combining behavior and data modeling in automated test case generation. In *Proceedings of the 3rd International Conference on Quality Software*, Dallas, TX.

Srinivas, K., & Srinivasan, H. (2005). Summarizing application performance from a components perspective. In *Proceedings of the 10th European Software Engineering Conference held jointly with 13th ACM SIGSOFT International Symposium on Foundations of Software Engineering*, Lisbon, Portugal.

Stewart, C., & Shen, K. (2005). Performance modeling and system management for multi-component online services. In *Proceedings of the 2nd USENIX Symposium on Networked Systems Design and Implementation*, Boston, MA.

Wu, W., Spezialetti, M., & Gupta, R. (1996). Designing a non-intrusive monitoring tool for developing complex distributed applications. In *Proceedings of the 2nd IEEE international Conference on Engineering of Complex Computer Systems*, Washington, DC.

ENDNOTE

[1] We assume the structure of the system and its components have already been modeled using MDE tools.

Chapter XII
Reducing the Complexity of Modeling Large Software Systems

Jules White
Vanderbilt University, USA

Douglas C. Schmidt
Vanderbilt University, USA

Andrey Nechypurenko
Siemens AG, Germany

Egon Wuchner
Siemens AG, Germany

ABSTRACT

Model-driven development is one approach to combating the complexity of designing software intensive systems. A model-driven approach allows designers to use domain notations to specify solutions and domain constraints to ensure that the proposed solutions meet the required objectives. Many domains, however, require models that are either so large or intricately constrained that it is extremely difficult to manually specify a correct solution. This chapter presents an approach to provide that leverages a constraint solver to provide modeling guidance to a domain expert. The chapter presents both a practical framework for transforming models into constraint satisfaction problems and shows how the Command Pattern can be used to integrate a constraint solver into a modeling tool.

INTRODUCTION

Model-driven development (MDD) (Ledeczi, 2001a; Kent, 2002; Kleppe, Bast, & Warmer, 2003; Selic, 2003) is a promising paradigm for software development that combines high-level visual abstractions—specific to a domain—with constraint checking and code-generation to simplify the development of a large class of systems (Sztipanovits & Karsai, 1997). MDD tools and techniques help improve software quality by automating constraint checking (Sztipanovits & Karsai, 1997). For example, in developing a software system for an automobile, automated constraint checking can be performed by the MDD tool to ensure that components connected by the developer, such as the antilock braking system and wheel RPM sensors, send messages to each other using the correct periodicity. An advantage of model-based constraint checking is that it expands the range of development errors that can be caught at design time rather than during testing.

Compilers for third-generation languages (e.g., Java, C++, or C#) can be viewed as a form of model-driven development (Atkinson & Kuhne, 2003). A compiler takes the third-generation programming language instructions (model), checks the code for errors (e.g., syntactic or semantic mistakes), and then produces implementation artifacts (e.g., assembly, byte, or other executable codes). A compiler helps catch mistakes during the development phrase and automates the translation of the code into an executable form.

Domain-specific Modeling Languages (DSML) (Ledeczi, 2001a) are one approach to MDD that use a language custom designed for the domain to model solutions. A metamodel is developed that describes the semantic type system of the DSML. Model interpreters traverse instances of models that conform to the metamodel and perform simulation, analysis, or code generation. Modelers can use a DSML to more precisely describe a domain solution, because the modeling language is custom designed for the domain.

MDD tools for DSMLs accrue the same advantages as compilers for third-generation languages. Rather than specifying the solution in terms of third-generation programming languages or other implementation-focused terminology, however, MDD allows developers to use notations specific to the domain. With a third-generation programming language approach (such as specifying the solution in C++), high-level informa-

tion (such as messaging periodicity or memory consumption) is lost. Because a C++ compiler does not understand messaging periodicity (i.e., it is not part of the "domain" of C++ programs) it cannot check that two objects communicate at the correct rate.

With an MDD-based approach, in contrast, DSML developers determine the granularity of the information captured in the model. High-level information like messaging periodicity can be maintained in the solution model and used for error checking. By raising the level of abstraction for expressing design intent, more complex requirements can be checked automatically by the MDD tool and assured at design time rather than testing time (Sztipanovits & Karsai, 1997), as seen in Figure 1. In general, errors caught during the design cycle are much less time consuming to identify and correct than those found during testing (Fagan, 1999).

As model-based tools and methodologies have developed, however, it has become clear that there are domains where the models are so large and the domain constraints so intricate that it is extremely hard for modelers to handcraft correct or high quality models. In these domains, MDD tools that provide only solution-correctness checking via constraints provide few real benefits over the third-generation programming language approach. Even though higher-level requirements can be captured and enforced, developers must still find ways of manually constructing a model that adheres to these requirements.

Distributed real-time and embedded (DRE) systems are software intensive systems that require guaranteed execution properties (e.g., deadlines), communication across a network, or must operate with extremely limited resources. Examples of DRE systems include automobile safety and aircraft autopilot systems. Inherent complexities in DRE systems is their large model sizes and the combinatorial nature of their constraints—not code construction per se. Specifying the deployment of software compo-

Figure 1. Complexity of identifiable errors in-creases with level of abstraction

Figure 2. Number of unique deployments vs. model size

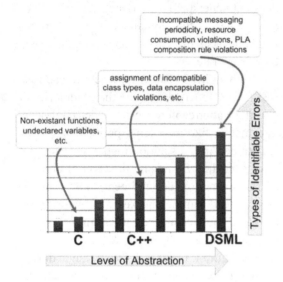

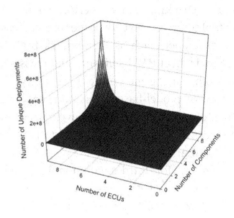

nents to Electronic Control Units (ECUs, which are the automotive equivalent of a CPU) in a car, while observing configuration and resource constraints, can easily generate solution spaces with millions or more possible deployments. For these large modeling problems, it is impractical (if not impossible) to create a complete and valid model manually.

To illustrate the complexities of scale, consider a group of 10 components that must be deployed to one of 10 ECUs within a car. There are $9^9 = 387,420,489$ *unique deployments* that could be tried. Part of the complexity of a DRE system model is how quickly the solution space grows as the number of model elements increases. Figure 2 depicts the speed at which the solution space grows for our automotive example.

Clearly, any approach to finding a deployment that observes the constraints must be efficient and employ a form of pruning to reduce the time taken to search the solution space. A manual approach may work for a model with five or so elements. As shown in Figure 2, however, the solution space can increase rapidly as the number of elements

grows, which render manual solutions infeasible for nontrivial systems.

Each component in an automobile typically has multiple constraints governing its placement. For example, an Antilock Braking System (ABS) must be hosted by a controller at least a certain distance from the perimeter of the car to enhance survivability in a crash. Moreover, the ABS will have requirements governing the CPU, memory, and bus bandwidth available on its host. When these constraints are considered for all the components, it becomes hard for modelers to handcraft correct solutions. The example in Figure 2 only has nine components and nine control units. Real automotive models typically contain 80 or more control units and hundreds of components. In models of this scale, manual approaches simply cannot handle the large numbers of possibilities and the complexity of the constraints.

The remainder of this chapter is organized as follows. The *Background* section illustrates the specific challenges of using MDD tools for these types of complex domains; The *Modeling Guidance* section presents techniques based on integrating constraint solvers into modeling environments that can be used to address these challenges; The *Future Research Directions* section describes future trends in modeling software intensive systems; and the final section presents concluding remarks.

BACKGROUND

Current Modeling Languages and Tool Infrastructure

There are a plethora of technologies and standards available for building MDD tools. This section explores some of the main frameworks, tools, and specifications that are available to develop model-driven processes for software systems.

Domain-Independent Modeling Languages

On one end of the MDD tool spectrum are Unified Modeling Language (UML) (Fowler & Scott, 2000) based tools, such as IBM's Rational Rose (Quatrani, 2003), that focus on building UML and UML-profile (Fowler & Scott, 2000) based models. When using UML, all models and languages must be specializations of the UML language. UML provides a single generic language to describe all domains. The advantage of the domain-independent approach of UML-based tools is the increased interoperability between modeling platforms that can be obtained by describing models using a single modeling language and the wide acceptance of the language. New languages can be constructed on top of UML by defining profiles, which are language extensions. UML is based on the MOF metamodel specified by the OMG.

UML is well established in software development. More recently, numerous extensions to the language based on profiles have been developed. *SecureUML* (Lodderstedt, Basin, & Doser, 2002)

provides security-related modeling capabilities to UML. *Embedded UML* (Martin, Lavagno, & Louis-Guerin, 2001) is another profile available for UML that provides DRE-specific extensions, such as timing properties of components. The UML extension approach allows developers to customize the language to meet the application domain, while still maintaining (some degree of) compatibility between tools.

Domain-Specific Modeling Languages

On the other end of the MDD tool spectrum are domain-specific modeling language (DSML) (Ledeczi, 2001a) tools. In contrast to UML, DSML tools do not necessarily share a common metamodel or language format. This freedom allows DSMLs to have greater expressivity and handle domains (such as warehouse management, automotive design, and product line configuration), that contain concepts (such as spatial attributes) that are not easily expressed and visualized using UML-based tools. The drawback of DSMLs, however, is that choosing a language generally ties a development process not only to a specific way of representing the model but also generally to a specific tool. Although the loss of interoperability can be problematic, transformations can be written to convert between model formats and still achieve tool interoperability. In many cases, the greater expressivity gained by using a DSML can greatly improve the usability of the MDD tool.

Tools for Building DSMLs

To build a DSML, a metamodeling language must be used to define the syntax of the language. A metamodel describes the rules that determine the correctness of a model instance and specifies the types that can be created in the language. The OMG's current standard is the Meta-Object Facility (MOF) (Object Management Group, 2007) language. MOF provides a metamodel language, similar to UML, that can be used to describe other new languages. MOF itself is recursively defined using MOF. MOF is a specification and therefore is not wedded to a particular tool infrastructure or language technology. Many DSMLs can be described using MOF.

Another popular metamodeling language is the Eclipse Modeling Framework's (EMF) (Moore, 2004) Ecore language. Ecore has nearly identical language constructs to MOF but is a concrete implementation rather than a standard specification. Developers can describe DSMLs using Ecore (Moore, 2004) and then leverage EMF to automatically generate Java data structures to implement the DSML. EMF also possesses the capability to generate basic tree-based graphical editing facilities for Eclipse that operate on the Java data structures produced by EMF.

Complex diagram-like visualizations of EMF-based modeling languages can be developed using the Graphical Editor Framework (GEF) for Eclipse (Moore, 2004). GEF provides the fundamental patterns and abstractions for visualizing and interacting with a model. Editors can be developed using GEF that allow modelers to draw connections to create associations, nest elements to develop containment relationships, and edit element attributes. GEF editors are based on the Model, View, Controller (MVC) pattern (Gamma, Helm, Johnson, & Vlissides, 1995). GEF, however, requires complex graphical coding.

The Graphical Modeling Framework (GMF) (Graphical Modeling Framework, 2007), is higher level framework, built on top of GEF, that simplifies the development of graphical editors. GMF automates the construction of the controller portion of GEF editors and provides a set of reusable view classes. MVC controllers are developed using GMF by creating complex XML files that map elements and their attributes to views in the model. GMF takes the XML mappings of elements to views and generates controllers that developers can use to synchronize the model and view of the MDD tool automatically.

Even with the powerful development frameworks presented thus far, developing a visual MDD tool requires significant effort. *Metaprogrammable* modeling environments (Ledeczi, 2001a) help alleviate this effort by allowing developers to specify the metamodel for a DSML visually. After the visual specification for the language is complete, the metaprogrammable modeling environment can automatically generate the appropriate code and configure itself to provide graphical editing capabilities for the modeling language.

Metaprogrammable modeling environments also provide complex remoting, model traversal, library, and other capabilities that are hard to develop from scratch. Two examples of these environments are the Generic Modeling Environment (GME) (Ledeczi, 2001b), which a windows-based metaprogrammable MDD tool, and the Generic Eclipse Modeling System (GEMS) (Generic Eclipse Modeling System, 2007), a part of the Eclipse Generative Modeling Technologies (GMT) project. The main tradeoff in using metaprogrammable modeling environments is that they tend to provide less flexibility in the visualization of the model.

Constraint Checking with OCL

Many modeling techniques rely on a constraint specification language to provide correctness checking rules that are hard to concisely describe using a graphical language. Certain types of constraints that specify conditions over multiple types of modeling elements, not necessarily related through an interface or inheritance, are more naturally expressed using a textual constraint specification language. The constraint language rules are run against instances of the UML, EMF, or other models to ensure that domain constraints are met. Constraint failures are returned to the modeler through the use of popup windows or other visual mechanisms.

The OMG Object Constraint Language (OCL) (Warmer & Kleppe, 1998) is a standard constraint specification for modeling technologies. OCL allows developers to specify invariants, preconditions, and postconditions on types in the modeling language. For example, the OCL constraint:

```
context ECU
inv: self.hostedComponents->collect(x
        | x.requiredRAM)->sum() < self.RAM
```

can be used to check that the sum of the RAM demands of the components hosted by an ECU do not exceed the available RAM on the ECU. The first line of the OCL rule defines the context or the type to which the OCL rule should be applied. The second part of the rule, beginning with "inv," defines the invariant condition for the rule. When there is a change to a property of a modeling element of the context type, the invariant conditions for the rules applicable to the element must be checked. Invariants that do not hold after the modification are flagged as errors in the MDD tool.

OCL works well for localized constraints that check the correctness of the properties of a single modeling element. As described earlier, however, the rule can only be used to check the correctness of the state of a modeling element and not to *derive valid states for a modeling element*, which is a process called **backward chaining** (Ginsberg, 1989). In a modeling context, backward chaining is a process whereby the MDD tool deduces correct modeling actions based on the domain constraints. For example, if it were possible to use the above OCL rule to backward chain, a MDD tool could not only determine whether or not an ECU was in a correct state but also, given the current state of an ECU, produce a list of components that could be hosted by the ECU without violating the rule.

For software systems with global constraints and large models, the inability of traditional modeling and constraint checking approaches, such as OCL, to not only flag errors but deduce solutions limits the utility of model-based development approaches. Backward chaining (providing modeling guidance) becomes more important as domains become more complex, and where it is thus harder to handcraft solutions.

Emerging Modeling Challenges

Deriving Solutions that Meet a Global Constraint

The increasing proliferation of DRE systems is leading to the discovery of further hard modeling problems. These domains all tend to exhibit problems, such as scheduling with resource constraints (Yuan & Nahrstedt, 2003), that are exponential in complexity because they are different types of NP problems. A key challenge in developing effective and scalable DSMLs and models for these domains is deriving the overall organization and architecture of MDD tools and software platforms that can simultaneously meet stringent resource, timing, or cost constraints.

Mobile devices are a domain that have become widely popular and typically exhibit tight resource constraints that must be considered when designing software (Forman & Zahorjan, 1994). Software design decisions, such as the CPU demand of the application, often have physical impacts on the device as well. For example, the scheduling of and workload placed on the CPU can affect the power consumed by the device. Poor scheduling or resource allocation decisions can therefore limit battery life (Yuan & Nahrstedt, 2003).

Determining the appropriate scheduling policies and application design decisions to handle the resource constraints of mobile devices is critical. Without the proper decisions, devices can have limited battery life and usability. Scheduling with resource constraints, however, is an NP problem (Cormen, Rivest, Leiserson, & Stein, 1990) and thus cannot be solved manually for nontrivial problems.

Adhering to Nonfunctional Requirements

Another challenge of DRE systems is that they often exhibit numerous types of nonfunctional QoS requirements that are hard to handle manually. For example, in automotive development, an application may have communication timing constraints on the real-time components (e.g., antilock braking control), resource constraints on components (e.g., infotainment systems), and feature requirements (e.g., parking assistance) (Weber & Weisbrod, 2002). In environments with this range of QoS requirements, a correct design must solve numerous complex problems and solve them in a layered manner so the solutions are compatible.

For example, the placement of two components on particular ECUs may satisfy a timing constraint but cause a resource constraint failure for another component, such as the infotainment system. Not only must modelers be able to solve numerous types of individually challenging problems, therefore, but they must be able to find solutions that meet all of the requirements.

Another area where complex constraints are common is in configuration management, which is key in emerging software development paradigms, such as product-lines (Jaaksi, 2002) and feature modeling (Antkiewicz & Czarnecki, 2006). In these domains, applications are built from reusable software components that interact through a common set of interfaces or framework. Applications are assembled using existing software assets for specific requirement sets. For example, in mission critical avionics product lines, such as Boeing Bold Stroke (Schmidt, 2002), the correct software component to update the HUD display is selected based on the timing, memory, and other requirements of the particular airframe to which the software is being deployed. Configuration-driven domains exhibit the same characteristics of computationally complex constraints that drive

overall system organization as other complex domains.

The remainder of this chapter presents an approach to using a constraint solver integrated into a modeling environment to address these challenges. First, the chapter introduces the types of modeling assistance that can be provided to help alleviate these challenges. Second, the chapter illustrates how a constraint solver can be used to provide these types of modeling assistance. Finally, an architecture for integrating Prolog into a modeling environment as a constraint solver is described.

MODELING GUIDANCE

This section illuminates the challenges of modeling software intensive systems and then presents an approach to providing modelers with modeling guidance from a constraint solver. Specific emphasis is placed on how modeling guidance can be used to reduce the complexity of modeling software intensive systems. Finally, the chapter illustrates how a constraint solver can be integrated into a graphical modeling tool.

Measuring Domain Complexity

The complexity of modeling an arbitrary domain can be measured along the following three axes:

- **Typical model size in elements:** Large models are harder to work with using a manual approach. Clearly, modelers are more apt to make mistakes managing—and much more likely to have trouble visualizing—a domain with hundreds of model elements than one with dozens of model elements.
- **Degree of global constraint:** Global constraints, such as resource constraints, that are dependent on multiple modeling steps or the order of modeling steps make a domain

much harder to work with. For example, a constraint requiring the deployment of an ABS component to a single ECU at a certain distance from the perimeter of the car is relatively easy to solve. It is much harder to solve constraints of an ABS component requiring its deployment to two ECUs, both a minimum distance from the outside of the car and a minimum distance from each other (for fault tolerance guarantees).

- **Degree of Optimality Required:** Optimality is hard to achieve with a manual modeling approach. In many domains, such as manufacturing, a small increase in the cost of a solution can lead to a dramatic increase in the overall cost of manufacturing when the millions of units affected by the change are considered. Many solutions must therefore be tried to find the best one. Domains that require optimal or good answers are much more challenging to model.

The three axes described above can be used to categorize and evaluate different modeling domains. The difficulty of modeling a domain can be viewed as the distance of the domain from the origin when plotted according to its degree

Figure 3. Axes of measuring modeling complexity

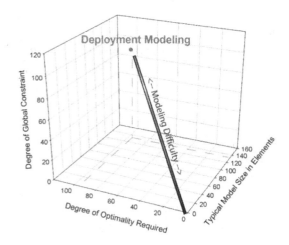

of global constraint, degree of required model optimality, and typical model size, as shown in Figure 3.

Key Challenges of Complex Domains

The key reasons that manual modeling approaches do not scale as a modeling domain moves further and further along the axes, shown in Figure 3, away from the origin is:

1. When there are thousands, millions, billions, or more possible ways that a model can be constructed and few correct ones, finding a valid solution is hard.

2. A valid solution may not be a good solution in these domains. Often, a modeler may find a solution that is valid but is far from the optimal solution. Automation and numerical methods, such as the Simplex method (Nelder & Mead, 1965), are needed to efficiently search the solution space and find good candidates. A human modeler cannot effectively search a solution space manually once it grows past a certain magnitude.

3. For large models, manual construction methods, such as pointing and clicking to intricately connect hundreds or more components, are tedious and error prone.

4. Often, global constraints rely on so much information that not all of the relevant bits of information can be seen at once. When not all of the information can be seen, modelers cannot make an informed decision.

Another difficulty of highly combinatorial domains is that although modelers may create a model that satisfies the domain constraints, the model may be considered poor in quality. For example, a modeler creating a deployment of components to ECUs could easily select a scheme that utilized far more ECUs than the true minimum number required to host the set of components.

For domains, such as automotive manufacturing, each modeling decision can have significant cost consequences for the final solution. For example, if a model can be constructed that uses three fewer control units to host the car's components and consequently saves $100 in manufacturing costs, millions of dollars in overall cost reduction for all cars of this make that are manufactured can be achieved. In these cases, it is crucial to not only find a correct solution but to find a cost effective one.

The difficulty of finding a good solution is that with large models and complex global constraints, modelers are lucky to find *any* valid solution. Because finding a single solution is incredibly challenging, it becomes infeasible or cost prohibitive to produce scores of valid solutions and search for an optimal one. Even if the set of valid solutions is large, there are numerous numerical methods to search for a solution with a given percentage of optimality. These methods, however, all rely on the ability to generate large numbers of valid solutions and are not possible without automation.

In domains with large models and intricate constraints, modelers must be able to see hundreds of modeling moves into the future to satisfy a global constraint or optimize a cost. The more localized a modelers decisions are and the less distant they peer into the future, the less chance there is that a correct or good solution will be found. Good local decisions, also known as "greedy decisions," do not necessarily produce a globally good decision.

For example, consider a simple model that determines the minimum number of ECUs needed to host a set of components. Assume that there are two types of ECUs, one that costs $10 and can host 2 components and another that costs $100 and can host 42 components. If modelers are deploying using a myopic view and not peering into the future, they will select many $10 ECUs and create a solution that costs $210, rather than looking ahead and choosing two $100 controllers

for a final cost of $200. Making a series of locally good decisions may not produce the overall best decision (Cormen et al., 1990).

Solution: Integrating Constraint Solvers and MDD Tools

An MDD tool provides a visual language for a developer to build a solution specification. An instance of a visual model contains modeling entities or elements, similar to OO classes, and different visual queues (e.g., connections, containment) specifying relationships between the elements. For example, a connection between a component and an ECU specifies deployment in the automotive modeling example from the Introduction section.

The key objective of a modeler is to add the right model entities and relationships between the entities so that they create a solution that meets the application requirements. Modelers express relationships between entities by drawing connections between them, placing entities within each other for containment, or other visual means. For each relationship that a modeler creates between entities, such as deployment, the modeler must find the right source and target for the relationship so that the relationship satisfies any constraints placed on it. In the example of deploying components to ECUs, the modeler must only draw a connection from a component to an ECU that has the OS and resource capabilities to support the component.

As has been shown in the *Introduction*, *Background*, and *Measuring Domain Complexity* sections, the large size of DRE models and their complex constraints can make manually finding the right endpoints for these relationships, such as deployment, infeasible. To address the scalability challenges of manual modeling approaches presented in the aforementioned sections, this section outlines how a constraint solver can be integrated with an MDD tool to help automate the selection of endpoints for relationships between model entities.

In the context of modeling, a constraint solver is a tool that takes as input one or more model elements, a goal that the user is attempting to achieve, and a set of constraints that must be adhered to while modifying the elements to reach the goal. As output, the constraint solver produces a new set of states for the model elements that achieves the desired goal while adhering to the specified constraints. For example, a set of components can be provided to a constraint solver along with the deployment requirements (constraints) of the components. The goal can then be set to "all components connected to an ECU." The constraint solver will in turn produce a mapping of components to ECUs that satisfies the deployment constraints.

The remainder of this section first outlines the different type of modeling assistance that an MDD tool and integrated constraint solver can provide to a user. Next, the section discusses how a user's actions in an MDD tool can be translated into constraint satisfaction problems (CSPs) so that a constraint solver can be used to automatically derive the correct endpoints for the relationships the user wishes to create. Finally, the section illustrates an architecture for integrating Prolog as a constraint solver into an MDD tool.

Modeling Assistance

There are two types of constraint solver guidance that can be used to help modelers produce solutions in challenging domains: *local guidance* and *batch processes*. Local guidance is a mechanism whereby the constraint solver is given a relationship and one endpoint of the relationship and provides a list of valid model entities that could serve as the other endpoint for the relationship. One example is that a constraint solver could be provided a deployment relationship and a component and return the valid ECUs that could be attached to the other end of the connection. This type of local guidance for deploying components is shown in Figure 4.

Figure 4. Local modeling guidance

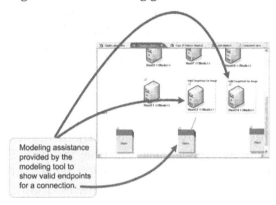

The second type of modeling guidance is for deriving endpoints for a group of relationships so that the group as a whole satisfies a global constraint. An example of a batch process would be to connect each component to an ECU in a manner such that the no ECU hosts more components than its resources can support. A batch process takes an overall goal that the modeler is trying to achieve, such as all components connected to an ECU, and creates a series of relationships on behalf of the user to accomplish that goal. By offering both local guidance and batch processes, a MDD tool can help users to accomplish both small incremental refinements to a model and large goals covering multiple modeling steps.

Local Guidance

Local guidance helps modelers correctly complete a single modeling step. A single modeling step is defined as the creation of one relationship between two modeling elements. Local guidance can be implemented as a visual queue that shows the modeler the valid endpoints for a relationship that he or she is creating. For example, when a modeler creates a connection from a component to an ECU to specify where a component is deployed, the modeler must first click on the component modeling element to initiate the connection. When the connection is initiated, the constraint solver can be used to solve for the valid deployment locations for the component and the model elements corresponding to these deployment locations can be highlighted in the model.

Challenges 3 & 4 from the section *Key Challenges of Complex Domains* can be addressed with local guidance. By identifying the model elements that are valid target endpoints of the modeling action a user is performing, a modeling tool can use visual queues (e.g., highlighting, filtering, etc.) to show the user only the information relevant to the action. Furthermore, the modeling tool can use the list of valid targets to both help the modeler identify valid solutions (helping address challenge 1 of *Key Challenges of Complex Domains*) and to prevent the user from applying an action to an invalid target endpoint (addressing challenge 3 of *Key Challenges of Complex Domains*). With a traditional MDD approach, the correctness of a user's action is checked after completion and thus the user may have to do and undo an action multiple times before the correct target endpoint is found. By finding valid solutions before a modeler completes a modeling action, the tool can preemptively constrain (e.g., veto modeling actions) what modeling elements the action can be applied to and prevent tedious and error-prone manual solution searching.

Local guidance can not only provide suggestions of correct endpoints of a relationship but can provide rankings of the local optimality of each of the endpoints. For example, deployment locations could be ranked by the resource slack available on them so that modelers are led to choose deployment targets with sufficient free resources. This manner of local guidance provides a greedy strategy to modeling guidance. At each step, modelers are led towards a solution that provides the greatest immediate benefit to the model's correctness.

Correct solutions to modeling transactions of a single modeling step can be found using local guidance. In some cases, only considering single

step transactions will not produce a solution that satisfies global constraints. For example, if modelers can add ECUs as needed to deploy components to, local guidance can produce a solution that is correct with respect to the constraints, although not necessarily optimal. If, however, ECUs cannot be added to the model and the local strategy guides the modeler to a solution where no ECU has free resources and several components are undeployed, the global constraints cannot be met.

Although a greedy strategy may not produce optimal results for certain types of CSPs, such as bin-packing, in many cases these localized strategies can provide a lower bound on the optimality of the final solution. With bin-packing, a First Fit Decreasing (FFD) (Coffman, Galambos, Martello & Vigo, 1998) packing strategy that sorts items to be placed into bins by their size and nondeterministically selects the first bin that can hold the item will guarantee that the solution never uses more than ~1.87 times as many bins as the optimal solution. Providing a lower bound on the quality of the solution that a modeler can produce can be extremely important in some domains, such as automotive manufacturing, where you want to minimize risk or cost. Although not guaranteed, a localized strategy may in fact arrive at an optimal or nearly optimal solution. Moreover, local guidance is substantially less computationally complex than providing a global maximum and can be implemented easily with a number of the approaches discussed later in this section.

Batch Processes

Global constraints require the correct completion of numerous modeling steps and are typically not amenable to user intervention. For global strategies, therefore, **batch processes** guided by constraint solvers can be used to create multiple relationships to bring the model into a correct state. The key differentiator between local guidance and a batch process is that local guidance deals with modeling transactions involving a single relationship while batch processes operate on modeling transactions containing two or more relationships. The larger the number of relationships in the transaction, generally the more complicated it is to complete.

One possible batch process for the component-to-ECU deployment tool could take each component in the model and create a connection to an ECU in the model to specify a deployment location. Local guidance would produce a single deployment connection for a single component. By increasing the size of the modeling transaction to consider the deployment locations of multiple components, the batch process can use the constraint solver to guarantee that if a possible solution is found, it utilizes only the ECUs currently in the model. By expanding the transaction size that the solver operates on, the batch process allows it to make model modifications that are not locally optimal, but lead to a globally optimal or globally correct solution.

Batch processes help address challenges 1, 2, & 3 of the section *Key Challenges of Complex Domains*. First, a batch process can correctly complete large numbers of modeling actions on behalf of the user, eliminating tedious and error-prone manual modeling (addressing challenge 3). Second, a constraint solver can create both a correct and an optimal solution that can be enacted by a batch process on behalf of the modeler (addressing challenge 1). By tuning the parameters used by the constraint solver, as is discussed in the section *Transforming Non-functional Requirements into Constraint Satisfaction Problems*, the modeler can guarantee both optimality and correctness (addressing challenge 2).

Transforming Nonfunctional Requirements into Constraint Satisfaction Problems

To integrate local and batch process guidance from a constraint solver, a model and the actions that modelers can perform on the model must be transformed into a series of constraint satisfaction problems (CSPs). This transformation allows the MDD tool to translate the actions of users into queries for a constraint solver. Valid satisfactions of the CSPs correspond to correct ways of completing a modeling action, such as creating a connection.

A CSP is a set of variables and constraints over the values assigned to the variables. For example, $X < Y < 6$ is a CSP with integer variables X and Y. Solving a CSP is finding a set of values (a labeling) for the variables such that the constraints hold true. The labeling $X = 3$, $Y=4$, is a correct labeling of $X < Y < 6$. A constraint solver takes a CSP as input and produces a labeling (if one exists) of the variables. Solvers may also produce labelings that attempt to maximize or minimize variables. For example, $X = 4$, $Y = 5$, is a labeling that maximizes the value of X.

For the deployment example, a deployment of a set of components to a set of ECUs can be viewed as a binary matrix where the cell at row i and column j is 1 if and only if the ith component is deployed to the jth ECU (and 0 otherwise). Each cell can be represented as an independent variable in a CSP. Thus, each variable D_{ij} determines if the ith component is deployed to the jth ECU. Finding a correct labeling of the values for the D variables creates a deployment matrix that can be used to determine where components should be placed.

Assume that the *ABS* (antilock braking system) component and the *WheelRPMs* components must be deployed to the same ECU. Also assume that the ABS component must be placed on an ECU at least 3 feet from the perimeter of the car. This series of deployment constraints can be translated in a CSP model. Let the ABS component be the 0th component and the WheelRPMs component be the 1st component. First, the constraint that the ABS component be deployed to the same ECU as the WheelRPMs component is encoded as $(D_{0j} = 1) \rightarrow (D_{1j} = 1)$. Next, for each ECU, a constant $Dist_j$ can be created to store the distance of the jth ECU from the perimeter of the car. Using these constants, the constraint on the placement of the ABS component relative to the perimeter of the car can be encoded as $(D_{0j} = 1) \rightarrow (Dist_j \geq 3)$. If this CSP is input into a constraint solver, the solver will label the variables and produce a deployment matrix that is guaranteed to be correct with respect to the deployment constraints.

A constraint solver can also be used to derive a solution with a certain degree of optimality. Assume that N components need to be deployed to one or more of M ECUs using as few ECUs as possible. A new variable *UsedECUs* can be introduced to store the total number of ECUs used by a solution. The constraint UsedECUs = $\sum D_{ij}$ for all i from 0..N and all j from 0..M. The solver can then be asked to produce a labeling of the variables D_{ij} that minimizes the variable UsedECUs. The solver will in turn produce a valid deployment of the components to ECUs that also minimizes the total number of ECUs used.

Constraint solvers typically offer a number of solution optimization options. The options range from maximizing or minimizing a function to using a fast approximation algorithm that guarantees a specific worst-case percentage of optimality. Depending on the constraint solver settings used, a modeler can guarantee the optimality of a model

or trade a certain percentage of model optimality for significantly reduced solving time. In contrast, a manual modeling approach provides no way to guarantee correctness, optimality, a percentage of optimality, or a tradeoff between optimality and solution time. For software intensive systems where optimality is important, allowing modelers to tune these parameters is a key advantage of using a constraint solver-integrated modeling approach.

One goal of using a constraint solver is to produce better solutions than a human modeler can create manually and to produce good solutions more reliably. When a solver uses either optimal or approximation algorithms, the solver's solution has a known and guaranteed worst case solution quality. In contrast, there is no guarantee on the solution quality with a manual approach.

As shown in Figure 5, the nonfunctional requirements for the software system must first be collected and documented (step 1). Each nonfunctional requirement must then be translated into a CSP, such as a system of linear equations (step 2). At this point, the data from the model, such as ECU distances to the car perimeter, are collected and bound to variables in the CSP produced in the previous step (step 3). Next, the CSP with some bound variables (such as resource demands) and some unbound variables (such as the D_{ij} variables in Figure 5) are input into the constraint solver (step 4). The constraint solver then produces bindings for the unbound variables and maps them back to changes in the model (step 5).

A crucial element for creating the right translation from nonfunctional requirements to a set of CSPs is the abstraction used to decompose the model into the variables and facts (i.e., bound variables) that the CSPs operate on. For example, should ECU and component be present in the formulation of the CSP to represent the bin-packing of the model's resources? The metamodel of a language, as described in *Background* section, provides the terminology and syntactic rules for a modeling language. Because the metamodel

Figure 5. Transforming a model into a constraint satisfaction problem

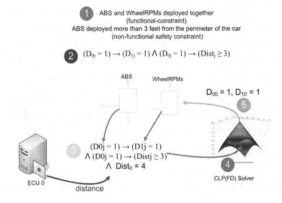

contains a precise definition of the relevant types in a modeling language it is ideal for identifying the key concepts that the CSPs should use. The metamodel of a modeling language can be viewed as a set of model entities and the role-based relationships between them. By using this abstraction based on entities and role-based relationships, a model can be conveniently decomposed for processing by a constraint solver. The idea of relationships between elements is the same as the widely used Resource Description Framework's predicate/argument format.

The role-based relationships of an entity represent both its properties (such as available CPU) and its associations (such as hosted components). Each entity can be decomposed into a unique ID and a set of role-based relationships associated with the ID. A requirement, such as "a component is only deployed to an ECU with the correct OS" can be translated into a CSP involving the *Deployment,* and *OS* relationships of a component and ECU. The variables of the CSP for this requirement would be the component and ECU that are being associated through the *Deployment* relationship. The constraint would be that the *OS* relationship of the component and the ECU had the same value (i.e., the same OS).

Associating Modeling Actions with the Constraint Solver

An important integration question is how/when to invoke the constraint solver and what CSPs and variable bindings should be passed to it. The goal is to use the constraint solver to provide local guidance and batch processes to bind the endpoints of relationships in the model. A constraint solver requires a CSP, a set of unbound variables (e.g., unbound endpoints), and a set of bound variables to produce a list of endpoints for relationships. Thus, users' actions and model state must be interpreted to find the correct CSPs, model entities, and unbound endpoints to pass to the solver. By defining the right formal model of the process by which users' actions are interpreted and translated into input data for the constraint solver, the integration process can be more cleanly defined. This section presents a formal abstraction for a user's interaction with a modeling tool and shows the point in the formal specification at which the constraint solver can be integrated and used to automate relationship endpoint binding decisions.

Modeling actions are transactions that take one or more elements of the model and modify

Figure 6. Diagram of a modeling transaction

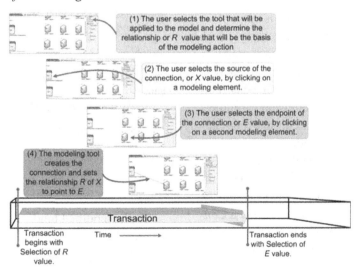

the endpoints of the selected elements' role-based relationships. Creating a deployment connection takes a component (the source of the connection) and sets the endpoint of its *TargetECU* relationship. In the *Local Guidance* and *Batch Processes* sections, a modeling action was defined as a transaction by the user that takes a relationship and sets its source and target entities. More formally, a modeling action is a function, *action(X, R, E)*, that takes a model element *X*, a relationship of the element, *R*, and produces an endpoint for that relationship *E*, as shown in Figure 6.

The goal of a traditional MDD tool is to take the input produced by the user, such as mouse clicks, and translate them into the values for *X, R,* and *E* to update the model. With a traditional MDD tool, the values for *E* are explicitly bound by modelers. A MDD tool integrated with a constraint solver not only provides this traditional explicit binding capability but also provides a constraint solver binding process, in which the constraint solver deduces the proper endpoints for relationships on behalf of the modeler.

The GEF and EMF frameworks can be used to illustrate how X, R, and E are actually implemented in a modeling framework. GEF provides an MVC framework for displaying and editing EMF models. In GEF, each possible user action, such as connecting two elements with a line in the graphical model, is represented with a *Command* object. The command object is a part of the *Command Pattern* (Gamma et al., 1995), which encapsulates actions that can affect a model in an object. When the user clicks on an element and then presses the delete key, GEF constructs a *DeleteCommand*, sets the command's argument to be the element that was click on, and then calls the command's *execute()* method, which deletes the element from the EMF model. When the user wishes to create a connection, the user selects the connection tool from a tool palette. Selecting the connection tool causes GEF to construct a *ConnectionCommand*. When the user clicks on the first element for the connection, GEF passes the

element to the ConnectionCommand as the source argument. When the user clicks on the endpoint for the connection, GEF passes the command the endpoint as the target argument and calls the command's execute() method, which creates the connection between the two elements. Tool implementers create Command objects to specify how each possible user action is translated into changes of the underlying EMF model.

With GEF's command pattern, R is determined by the type of Command object that GEF instantiates. In the deployment example, when the user selects the *DeploymentConnection* tool, GEF creates a corresponding *DeploymentConnectionCommand* object. The Command knows (because it is coded into the command object's execute method) that it is modifying the *TargetECU* relationship of its source argument. The command also knows that its source argument is the X variable in the action(X,R,E) function. Finally, the command knows that its target endpoint represents the E variable. Each Command object is used to translate a graphical user action (e.g., adding a connection) into values for X, R, and E. The Command is also responsible for modifying the R relationship between X and E in its execute method. The execute() method of a DeploymentConnectionCommand is shown in the Java code below:

```
public class DeploymentConnectionCommand extends
Command{
 ....
 //apply action(X,R,E)
 public void execute() {
  Component source = (Component)this.getSource();
//the X
  ECU target = (ECU)this.getTarget(); //the E

  //the R relationship (targetECU) between X and E is
set here
  source.setTargetECU(target);
 }
}
```

In the modified binding process for *E,* each relationship *R* is associated with a CSP specifying what is considered a correct value for *E*. For

Figure 7. A diagram of a modeling transaction with a constraint solver

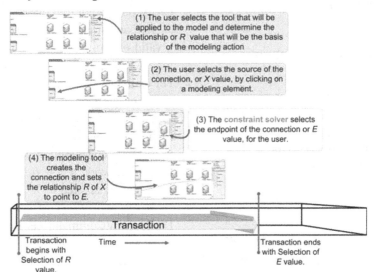

example, a component could specify that a correct value for its *TargetECU's E* value requires that the chosen *E* value and the component both have the same OS type. When a user input is translated into values for *X* and *R*, a constraint solver integrated MDD tool uses the CSP associated with *R* to automatically derive values for *E* on behalf of the user. In Figure 5, the CSP was found in step 2, the values for *X* and *R* were produced in step 4 and the bindings for *E* were delivered by the constraint solver in step 5. The modified modeling transaction process can be seen in Figure 7.

In the first step, the user selects a tool or action that will be applied to the model. The tool determines the *R* value or relationship that will be modified by the user's actions. In the second step, the user clicks on a modeling element to initiate a connection and hence modify a relationship in the underlying model. The element that the user clicks on becomes the *X* value that will be passed to the constraint solver. In the third step, the modeling environment looks up the correct CSP that must be satisfied by the endpoints of the relationship specified by the *R* value. The modeling environment then passes this CSP, the *X,* and *R* values to the solver. The solver finds the endpoints that

satisfy the CSP and returns these endpoints as possible *E* values. Finally, the *E* values are presented graphically to the user.

The GEF *DeploymentConnectionCommand* can be modified to incorporate this new process by which the constraint solver chooses the value for *E*. The Command creation and initial argument setting remains unchanged. However, after the source of the connection has been set, the constraint solver can be invoked to solve for a value for E. If a value is returned, the execute() method can be called immediately. The new *DeploymentConnectionCommand* is:

```
public class DeploymentConnectionCommand extends
Command{
    ....
public void setSource(Object obj) {
  this.source = obj;

  //the X
  Component source = (Component)obj;

  //call the solver to find valid values for E
    List  endpoints  =  this.solver.findEndpoints(source.
getId(),
              "targetECU");

  //if there is only one possible value, go ahead and
execute
```

```
if(endpoints.size() == 1){
  setTarget(endpoints.get(0));
  execute();
}
else if(endpoints.size() > 0) {
  //otherwise, show the user valid E values by
  //modifying their background color
  for(Object obj : endpoints)
    ((ECU)obj).setBackgroundColor(Color.yellow);
}
else {
 //notify the user that there are no
 //possible deployment locations for the Component
 source.setBackgroundColor(Color.red);
}
 }

//apply action(X,R,E)
 public void execute() {
  Component  source  =  (Component)this.getSource();
//the X
 ECU target = (ECU)this.getTarget(); //the E

 //the R relationship (targetECU) between X and E is
set here
 source.setTargetECU(target);
 }
 }
```

In the modified DeploymentConnectionCommand, immediately after GEF sets the source of the connection, the command invokes the constraint solver to find valid endpoints. If exactly one endpoint is found, the setTarget method is called with that endpoint and the Command is executed. If more than one valid endpoint is found, each valid target has its background color changed to yellow (a visual queue). If there is no possible deployment location for the Component, its background color is changed to red.

In a traditional process, the user would be required to click first on the source element, decide on a valid deployment location for the source, and then click on the deployment location. With the modified Command object, the object itself attempts to determine the valid targets (E) using the constraint solver. The Command can then automatically complete the action on the user's behalf, if there is exactly one possible endpoint. If there is more than one possible endpoint, the Command can highlight those endpoints for the user. If no endpoints are found, the Command

can notify the user by changing the Component's background color to red.

In many situations, the user will wish to find a valid endpoint for a specified R relationship for every member of a set of modeling elements. For example, the user may wish to select some or all of the Components and have the solver find a valid target ECU for every Component such that no global deployment constraint, such as resource consumption, is violated. Using the GEF framework, a new *BatchDeploymentCommand* can be created.

Just as with other GEF commands, the BatchDeploymentCommand can have a tool palette entry associated with it that the user can select. When the user selects the corresponding tool entry, the BatchDeploymentCommand is created. The batch command takes a group of modeling elements, which the user specifies through a group selection, and creates a connection for each member of the group to a valid ECU. The Java code for the BatchDeploymentCommand is:

```
public class BatchDeploymentCommand extends Com-
mand{
  ....

public void execute() {
//the set of Xs
 Component[] sources = (Component[])this.getSourc-
es();

//the solver deduces an E for each X
Object[] targets = this.solver.findValidTargets(sources,
          "targetECU");

if(targets != null){
 for(int i = 0; i < targets.length; i++) {
  sources[i].setTargetECU((ECU)targets[i]);
 }
}
}
}
```

Constraint Solver and MDD Tool Integration Frameworks

There are a large number of optimization, constraint solver, and inference engines available for use with local guidance and batch processes. As noted in Van Hentenryck and Saraswat (1996), however, automating the formulation of real problems in a suitable form for efficient algorithmic processing is hard. Transforming an arbitrary graphical model, a modeling action, and a set of modeling constraints into a CSP for a constraint solver is tedious and error-prone. Integrating the results of the solver back into a MDD tool and providing interactive capabilities is also hard. Each of the five steps from the section *Transforming Non-functional Requirements into Constraint Satisfaction Problems* may require substantial effort. By choosing the right approach and architecture, however, the difficulty of leveraging a constraint solver in a modeling environment can be reduced substantially.

The following are five important properties of an architecture for integrating a constraint solver with a MDD tool:

1. **Solver frameworks must respect domain-specific concepts from the MDD tool** and provide a flexible mechanism for translating nonfunctional requirements into CSPs using domain notations. MDD tool users should be able to specify constraints in a language or notation that mirrors the domain rather than a system of linear equations and makes mapping requirements to a CSP easier.

2. **The local guidance and batch processes should lead modelers toward solutions that are considered optimal** or good based on quality metrics from the domain. Whenever possible, solvers should be used to iterate through multiple valid solutions and suggest only those considered most optimal. Modelers should be able to plug-in custom formulas for measuring optimality in the target domain and the tool should be able to present multiple suggestions based on various types of optimization.

3. **The constraint solver integration should automate tedious and complex modeling tasks**, such as solving for and assigning

values for global constraints, performing repetitive localized decisions, or providing feedback to modelers to suggest valid modeling decisions.

4. **The solver framework must accommodate long-running analyses** for problem instances that cannot be solved online. For large optimization problems, such as finding the lowest cost assignment of components to ECUs, the constraint solver may need several hours or days to find a solution. In cost-critical situations, such as manufacturing, allowing the solver the extra time to find the best solution can be critical.

With a constraint-solver integrated modeling environment, a user goes through an iterative process of specifying portions of a model, adding or refining nonfunctional requirements as constraints, and using the constraint solver to automate model construction and optimization. Figure 8 illustrates the modeling processing with an integrated constraints solver.

In the first step, a user specifies the initial model entities in the solution. In the second step, the user adds constraints for the requirements of

Sidebar 1. Prolog

Prolog is a logic programming language that allows developers to specify a set of facts or Knowledge Base and then create rules specifying logical assertions or constraints on the facts. Prolog rules take one or more input variables, denoted by variable names with capital letters, and specify a series of logical assertions on these variables, other facts, or rules in the KB. When a Prolog rule is invoked with only bound variables, meaning all variables have values assigned to them, Prolog returns whether or not the logical assertions contained within the rule hold true. An important capability of Prolog is that if a rule is invoked with some unbound variables, Prolog will attempt to find bindings of those variables from the facts in the KB that satisfy the logical assertions in the rule. When constraints are implemented as Prolog rules, Prolog can deduce valid bindings for the variables that the constraints restrict.

Figure 8. A modeling cycle with constraint solver integration

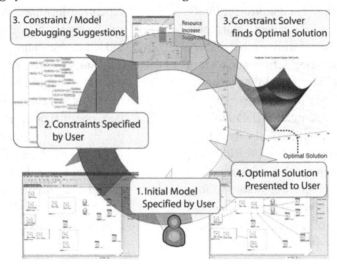

the solution into the MDD tool. During the third phase, the user invokes the constraint solver, using local-guidance or a batch process, to find valid endpoints for various relationships in the model. Finally, in the fourth step, the valid endpoints found by the constraint solver are shown to the modeler using visual queues, such as highlighting valid entities.

A Prolog-Based Approach to Constraint Solver Integration

Choosing a constraint solver is one of the driving forces in the process of transforming a set of nonfunctional requirements into a CSP. Each solver will generally have a unique representation of the problem in its native format. The choice of solver therefore affects how the transformation from nonfunctional requirements to a concrete representation of a CSP is performed. Many types of solvers are available and implemented in a number of languages. The remainder of this section presents an approach we have developed, called Role-based Object Constraints (White,

Nechypuren, Wuchner, & Schmidt, 2006), to providing local guidance and batch processes based on Prolog (Bratko, 1986).

Using ROCs, we have implemented constraint-solver integrated modeling tools for automated product line variant selection (White, 2007a), component to ECU deployment in automobiles (White et al., 2006), and aspect weaving (Nechy-purenko, Wuchner, White & Schmidt, 2007). Our implementation of ROCs is integrated with the Generic Eclipse Modeling System (GEMS) (White, 2005), a part of the Eclipse Generative Modeling Tools (GMT) project. A screenshot of a batch process executing in our GEMS- based deployment modeling tool is shown in Figure 10.

Prolog is a declarative programming language that allows programmers to define a Knowledge Base (KB) (also known as a fact set) and a group of rules that implement a set of CSPs (see Sidebar 1). Prolog can then evaluate these rules and determine if they can be satisfied by the known facts. Prolog uses a predicate syntax, where rules can be defined as predicates that resolve to the

Figure 9. Execution of a ROCs batch process shown in GEMS

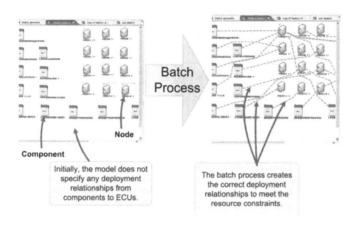

satisfaction of a conjunction of other predicates. Rules are akin to methods that check if a constraint over a set of variables holds true.

Predicate rules can be used to check constraints, by invoking the rule with all variables bound, in which case Prolog replies with whether or not the rule or CSP evaluates to true. If variables are left unbound when the rule is invoked, however, Prolog uses backward chaining to produce bindings from the KB of the unbound variables that will satisfy the CSP. Prolog therefore provides a key degree of flexibility because it can be used both to check constraints (similar to OCL described in the section *Constraint Checking with OCL*) or to derive solutions to the CSPs.

The remainder of this section presents an approach to integrating Prolog into a modeling tool. Prolog was chosen because it has a readable textual syntax as opposed to the linear-equation-based syntax of other possible solvers. Using Prolog, however, does trade some speed for readability and ease of use. Prolog also is a widely used and supported programming language for constraint solving and numerous existing solvers and libraries are available in Prolog.

Transforming Models into Prolog Knowledge Bases

Integrating Prolog as a constraint solving engine involves capturing the state of the model and translating it into a Prolog KB, as seen in Figure 11. For the deployment of components to ECUs example from the *Introduction* section, the components, ECUs, and their resources must be translated into predicate facts in Prolog. Generally, predicates are created that relate a unique key or ID of each model element to various properties that the model element possesses. This concept is similar to the use of pointers and allows the flattening of an object-oriented model into a predicate KB.

Developers must select the format of the predicates used to translate the model into a Prolog KB. One approach is to use a consistent set of Prolog predicates across modeling languages and customize them by adding domain-specific information into the variables the predicates operate on. For example:

```
self_type(1, ecu).
self_attribute(1, available_cpu, 29).
```

Figure 10. Transforming model elements into prolog facts

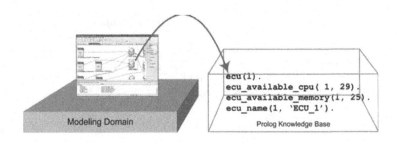

self_attribute(1, available_memory, 25).
self_attribute(1, name, 'ECU_1').

ecu_available_memory(1, 25).
ecu_name(1, 'ECU_1').

describes a set of Prolog facts that provide a general predicate format applicable to a range of model types. This set of facts asserts that the element with ID "1" is of type "ecu." The facts also assert that the element has three attributes: *available_cpu*, *available_memory*, and *name*, with values: "29," "25," and "ECU_1," respectively. Different modeling languages can be accommodated by changing the second argument of the predicates, the attribute name, which is being defined. The tradeoff of using a general format, however, is it violates the first design criterion described in the section *Constraint Solver and MDD Tool Integration Frameworks*, that is, offering a domain-specific interface. The predicates do not vary across domains, which makes it harder for a domain expert to understand how they relate the concepts from his or her domain. Rather than using terminology specific to the deployment of components to ECUs (e.g., ecu, available_memory, etc.), the predicates are based on describing the attributes and types.

A more domain-specific approach is to create custom predicates for each modeling language to mirror the notation from the domain. For example, the same set of facts can be rewritten as:

ecu(1).
ecu_available_cpu(1, 29).

which provides a more domain-specific interface. The main drawback of this format, however, is that introspection is not possible, that is, rules cannot query for all of the properties of an arbitrary element. When translating nonfunctional requirements into Prolog rules, domain-specific predicates are generally more advantageous because they allow the production of more compact and readable rules. Introspection is also typically not needed for writing CSPs in Prolog.

To identify the domain-specific predicates to use for the KB, the metamodel for a modeling language can be viewed as a set of model entities and the role-based relationships between them. For each entity, a unique id and a predicate statement specifying the type associated with the entity. For example, each ECU in the model is transformed into the predicate statement ecu(id), where id is the unique id for the ECU. For each instance of a role-based relationship in the model, a predicate statement is generated that takes the id of the first participating entity and the id of the entity to which the first entity is being related.

For example, if a component, with id 23, has a *TargetECU* relationship with an ECU, with id 25, the predicate statement targetECU(23,25) is generated. This predicate statement specifies that the entity with id 25 is a *TargetECU* of the entity with id 23. Each KB provides a domain-specific set of predicate statements. As a model is manipulated in its graphical editor, the Prolog KB is updated using assert/1 and retract/1 statements, which add and remove facts from the Prolog KB, respectively.

Mapping Nonfunctional Requirements to Prolog Rules

Using a domain-specific knowledge base, modelers can specify nonfunctional requirements in the form of Prolog rules for each type of metamodel relationship. These constraints semantically enrich the model to indicate the nonfunctional requirements of a correct model. They are used by constraint solvers to deduce solutions to local guidance and batch process problems. For example, consider the following constraint to check whether an ECU is a valid ECU of a component:

```
is_a_valid_component_targetECU(Component, ECU) :-
    component_requiredOS(Component, OS),
    ecu_providedOS(ECU, OS).
```

This constraint, which checks to ensure that the OS required by the component matches the OS provided by the ECU, can be used to check a component-ECU combination, that is:

```
is_a_valid_component_targetECU(component_23,
    ecu_25).
```

by assigning the *Component* variable the value "component_23" and the *ECU* variable the value "ecu_25." The rule can also be used to find valid ECUs that can play the *TargetECU* role for a particular component using Prolog's ability to deduce the correct solution

```
is_a_valid_component_targetECU(component_23,
    ECU)
```

by leaving the *ECU* variable unbound (unbound variables are begin with capital letters). In this example, the *ECU* variable will be bound to the ID's of the ECUs in the KB that have the same OS as the component. This example shows how the nonfunctional requirement rules can be used both to check and to deduce solutions.

The role-based relationships present in the metamodel not only produce domain-specific predicates but also serve as the glue between graphical modeling actions, such as creating connections, and the constraint solver. The nonfunctional requirement rules that developers create can be associated with role-based relationships in the metamodel as seen in Figure 12.

Figure 11. Invoking requirement rules to find relationship endpoints

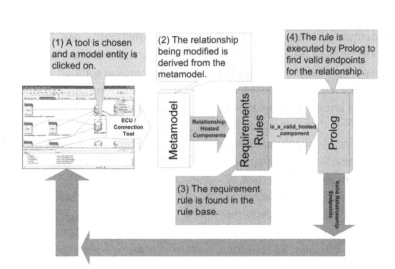

When a model element is clicked on to initiate a change (step 1), the metamodel is consulted to determine the role-based relationship (step 2) affected by the change. The corresponding nonfunctional requirement rules can then be obtained (step 3) and executed by Prolog (step 4) to check the validity of the change.

To provide local guidance, the nonfunctional requirement rules associated with metamodel relationships can be executed with unbound variables to deduce endpoints for the relationship. For example, if a user begins creating a deployment connection originating from a component, the MDD tool can deduce that the deployment connection will set the *TargetECU* relationship of the component and execute the is_a_valid_component_targetECU rule with only the originating component bound as an argument. Prolog will then return bindings for the ECUs variable of the rule that are valid deployment targets for the component.

In a graphical modeling environment that does not include a constraint solver, graphical actions, such as mouse clicking and movement, are translated into changes in the underlying object graph of the model. By adding a constraint solver, graphical actions are translated into proposed model modification transactions and then the proposed transactions are turned into CSPs and solved. Users can therefore modify the model directly as in a traditional approach and use graphical actions to initiate constraint solvers that modify the model on their behalf.

In the connection creation example from the *Local Guidance* section, a modeler's mouse-click on the source component is translated into the initiation of a connection from the component. This connection initiation proposal is then used to query the metamodel to determine the relationship that is being modified on the component. Next, the CSPs or nonfunctional requirement rules that are bound to the relationship are obtained and finally they are executed in the constraint solver to find valid bindings for the unbound variables. The bindings produced represent the valid completions of the modeling transaction. These valid bindings can be returned to the user as graphical proposals, such as highlighting model elements, or committed as changes to the underlying model.

CONCLUSION

For large-scale DRE systems, traditional modeling approaches allow developers to raise the level of abstraction used for solution specification and illuminate design flaws earlier in the development cycle. Many DRE systems, however, have exponential design constraints, extremely large model sizes, or other complexities that make it hard to handcraft a model of a solution. For these types of challenging domains, automated design guidance based on the design constraints is needed.

A constraint solver can be integrated into a modeling environment to provide design guidance for complex domains. As shown in section *Modeling Guidance*, using the concepts of *local guidance* and *batch processes* a constraint solver can help modelers perform both single and multistep modeling activities.

The lessons learned from our ROCs approach, described in the section *Modeling Guidance*, to integrating a Prolog constraint solver with the GEMs modeling environment are:

- **Constraints can be used for reasoning by a constraint solver**. A constraint solver improves solution quality not by checking manually produced solutions, but by actively guiding a user toward a correct solution. The solver helps ensure that users do not produce an incorrect solution, rather than just notifying them if their solutions are invalid.
- **User actions can be abstractly modeled as functions**. User interactions with MDD tools can be viewed as a function that takes a set of modeling elements and maps the

endpoints of a specific relationship of the elements to an endpoint explicitly provided by users. A constraint solver can be integrated into a modeling environment by dynamically choosing the endpoints for the relationships with the constraint solver rather than requiring endpoints to be explicitly enumerated by the modeler. Local guidance and batch processes can be used to produce the endpoints for relationships, as described in the section *Local Guidance*.

- **Constraint solvers should be reused**. Writing a constraint solver is hard. Developers of model-driven processes should therefore focus on integrating existing constraint solvers or constraint solving languages. Prolog is a good choice for a general purpose constraint solving language that can be integrated, as shown in the section *A Prolog-based Approach to Constraint Solver Integration*.

- **Debugging constraint conflicts or over constrained systems is hard.** When no valid solution to a CSP can be found, deriving why a solution can't be found can be complex. With global constraints, the cause of the failure can be the overall organization of the solution, and thus it is difficult to provide a meaningful explanation to the modeler.

- **Constraint solvers typically perform well in practice.** Although many optimization and constraint satisfaction problems are combinatorialy complex, constraint solvers typically can solve them in a reasonable time frame. Constraint solvers can use approximation algorithms to quickly produce solutions that are good but not optimal.

- **The complexity of a constraint satisfaction problem is dependent on each problem instance.** Certain instances of a type of constraint satisfaction problem will be easier to solve than others. Predicting which instances are challenging is hard. Although it is hard to predict which instances are challenging, constraint solvers often work well on all

instances in domains that humans manually produce solutions for.

As MDD tools continue to develop and capture more useful design decisions for larger and more complex applications, constraint solving and other design automation techniques will become more important. Design automation should not only improve design quality but should also help to allow model-driven processes to scale to handle next-generation models with significantly more complexity.

The tools and code presented in this chapter are a part of the Generic Eclipse Modeling System (GEMS). GEMS is an opensource project available from http://www.sf.net/projects/gems.

FUTURE RESEARCH DIRECTIONS

This section describes the emerging trends in the development of software intensive systems, how these trends will affect software development methodologies, and what future research will be needed to address future development problems. The future trends are presented in the context of MDD. Particular emphasis is placed on how these trends will impact the use of constraint solvers in software development.

Capturing Design Rules

Model-driven technologies are raising the level of abstraction for software development by enabling developers to express higher-level, more domain-specific intentions in the solution specifications they produce. These intentions have traditionally been captured through documentation, such as text files or MS Word documents. With MDD technologies, developers can formally specify the design goals and rules that traditionally could only be expressed in documentation, in the solution specification.

In the past, conventional tools could not document the rules that led a developer to make design decisions in a rigorous manner that could be used for automated design assistance. For example, implementation-based software development methodologies, such as coding a solution in C++, could not capture communication rate information, memory consumption, minimum distance from the car's perimeter, or other constraint information in a form that could drive application organization. With an MDD approach, however, a designer can specify that a connection needs to provide a guaranteed messaging rate rather than the type of connection that should be used, that is, designers can specify *why* one connection type should be preferred over another connection type.

Various MDD tools are developing that can utilize this design information. The Component Utilization and Test Suite (CUTS) (Hill & Gokhale, 2007) is an MDD tool that allows developers to empirically evaluate system designs before they are implemented. Other tools, such as J2EEML (White, 2007b), provide the ability to perform analysis on adaptive applications and anticipate conflicting design goals. Finally, feature modeling tools (Antkiewicz et al., 2007) provide the capability to capture software component commonality and variability requirements and enforce them during system design.

Utilizing Design Information to Provide Automated Design Assistance

Automation can be applied to help guide designers to better solutions by formally capturing the goals of the application or *why* designers chose particular design decisions. MDD tools, and specifically domain-specific modeling languages, have allowed developers to tailor the solution specification to include information pertinent to their domain. As MDD technologies increase the breadth of information that can be distilled from designers into a solution specification, a wealth of new design guidelines or constraints will become available for constraint solving.

An emerging area of research therefore involves the integration of automated reasoning systems with MDD tools. In particular, the reuse of existing constraint solver, decision assistance, and other guidance mechanisms across will be an important software development goal. These solver and decision assistance mechanisms are costly to produce and thus will benefit from greater portability between MDD tool infrastructures, such as the Eclipse Modeling Framework, Microsoft DSL tools (Microsoft, 2007), and the Generic Modeling Environment.

One challenge of leveraging constraint solvers in a modeling environment is mapping the domain requirements to CSPs that can be used for automated solving. These mappings are often complex and tightly coupled to individual solver and metamodel formats, despite the fact that requirement types, such as resource requirements, occur across multiple domains. Current solutions for transforming requirements into CSPs tightly couple the translation to a specific solver or metamodel and require costly reinvention and rediscovery of existing mappings. Additional work is needed ensure that the complex mappings from requirements to CSPs can be templatized and reused across applications.

Model transformation techniques are developing rapidly and may provide a mechanism for future decoupling of CSPs from solvers and provide portability through translation. The Atlas Transformation Language (ATL) (Jouault & Kurtev, 2005) provides powerful transformation capabilities as well as compilation to bytecode. Other emerging approaches include Open Architecture Ware (oAW) (Open Architecture Ware, 2007). Finally, templatization approaches are also viable, such as those proposed by Willans, Sammut, Maskeri, and Evans (2002).

Constraint Solver Guided Software Reuse

Significant advances in the area of software reuse will drive the need for integrating constraint solvers and MDD tools. These advances are evident in the increased use of commercial-off-the-shelf (COTS) components (Schmidt, 2002) rather than customized proprietary solutions. In particular, using COTS components in the DRE systems domain requires constraint solvers because applications in this domain often have exponential constraints that must be met by selecting and assembling COTS components together with proprietary components into a final composite application.

The selection of components is an example of a CSP. Developers must take the requirements of an application in a DRE system, the capabilities of the COTS and proprietary components, and find a set of compatible components, possibly from numerous vendors, that will satisfy both the functional and complex nonfunctional constraints. Moreover, components may have complex configuration needs, such as setting messaging policies, to enable them to function properly. Solving these challenging CSPs will require the use of constraint solvers to select components based on high-level design criteria captured in models.

COTS components will require further development and standardization in how metadata, such as messaging periodicity, is captured and disseminated to tools. Standardization will allow for greater interoperability between tools. A standard metadata format will also provide component developers with a consistent methodology for documenting component requirements, dependencies, and capabilities.

Services have seen the most standardization in metadata descriptions. The Resource Description Framework (RDF) (Lassila & Swick, 1999) and the Web Services Description Language (WSDL) are emerging as promising standards for describing services. Other approaches, such

as those presented by O'Sullivan, Edmond, and Ter Hofstede (2002), focus on capturing the nonfunctional aspects of services. Formal methods for describing components are also emerging, such as those proposed by Poizat, Royer, and Salaun (2004).

REFERENCES

Antkiewicz, M., & Czarnecki, K. (2006, October). Framework-specific modeling languages with round-trip engineering. In *Proceedings of the ACM/IEEE 9th International Conference on Model Driven Engineering Languages and Systems (MoDELS)*, Genoa, Italy.

Atkinson, C., & Kuhne, T. (2003). Model-driven development: A Metamodeling Foundation. *IEEE Software*, 20(5), 36-41.

Bratko, I. (1986). *Prolog programming for artificial intelligence*. Reading, MA: Addison-Wesley.

Coffman, E., Galambos, G., Martello, S., & Vigo, D. (1998). Bin packing approximation algorithms: Combinatorial analysis. *Handbook of combinatorial optimization*. Norwell, MA: Kluwer Academic.

Cormen, T.H., Rivest, R.L. Leiserson, C.E., & Stein, C. (1990). *Introduction to algorithms*. Cambridge, MA: MIT Press.

Fagan, M. (1999). Design and code inspections to reduce errors in program development. *IBM Systems Journal, 38(2/3)*, 258-287.

Forman, G., & Zahorjan, J. (1994). The challenges of mobile computing. *IEEE Computer*, 27(4), 38-47.

Fowler, M., & Scott, K. (2000). *UML distilled*. Reading, MA: Addison-Wesley.

Gamma, E., Helm, R., Johnson, R., & Vlissides, J. (1995). *Design patterns: Elements of reusable object-oriented software*. Reading, MA: Addison-Wesley.

Ginsberg, M. (1989). A circumscriptive theorem prover. *Artificial Intelligence, 32*(2), 209-230.

Graphical Modeling Framework. (2007). Retreived March 23, 2008, from http://www.eclipse.org/gmf

Hill, J. H., & Gokhale, A. (2007, to appear). Model-driven engineering for development-time QoS validation of component-based software systems. In *Proceeding of International Conference on Engineering of Component Based Systems*, Tuscon, AZ.

Jaaksi, A. (2002). Developing mobile browsers in a product line. *IEEE Software, 19*(4), 73-80.

Jouault, F., & Kurtev, I. (2005, October). Transforming Models with ATL. In *Proceedings of the Model Transformations in Practice Workshop at MoDELS,* Montego Bay, Jamaica.

Kent, S. (2002, May). Model driven engineering. In *Proceedings of Integrated Formal Methods: Third International Conference*, Turku, Finland.

Kleppe, A., Bast, W., & Warmer. B. (2003). *The model driven architecture: Practice and promise*. New York: Addison-Wesley.

Lassila, O., & Swick, R. (1999). *Resource description framework (RDF) model and syntax*. World Wide Web Consortium.

Ledeczi, A. (2001a). The generic modeling environment. In *Proceedings of the Workshop on Intelligent Signal Processing*, Budapest, Hungary.

Ledeczi, A., Bakay, A., Maroti M., Volgysei P., Nordstrom, G., Sprinkle, J., & Karsai, G. (2001b). Composing domain-specific design environments. *IEEE Computer, 34*(11), 44-51.

Lodderstedt, T., Basin, D., & Doser, J. (2002). SecureUML: A UML-based modeling language for model-driven security. *UML, 2460*, 426-441.

Martin, G., Lavagno, L., & Louis-Guerin, J. (2001). Embedded UML: A merger of real-time UML and co-design. In *Proceedings of the 9th International Symposium on Hardware/Software Codesign*, Copenhagen, Denmark.

Microsoft Domain-Specific Language Tools. (2007). Retrieved March 23, 2008, from http://msdn2.microsoft.com/en-us/vstudio/aa718368.aspx

Moore, B. (2004). *Eclipse development using the graphical editing framework and the eclipse modeling framework*. Boca Raton, Florida: IBM, International Technical Support Organization.

Nechypurenko, A., Wuchner, E., White, J., & Schmidt, D.C. (2007). Application of aspect-based modeling and weaving for complexity reduction in the development of automotive distributed real-time embedded systems. In *Proceedings of the Sixth International Conference on Aspect-oriented Software Development*. Vancouver, British Columbia.

Nelder, J., & Mead, R. (1965). A simplex method for function minimization. *Computer Journal, 7*(4), 308-313.

Object Management Group. (2007). *Meta object facility (MOF), version 1.4*. Retrieved March 23, 2008, from http://www.omg.org/docs/formal/02-04-03.pdf

Open Architecture Ware. (2007). Retrieved March 23, 2008, from www.openarchitectureware.org

O'Sullivan, J., Edmond D., & Ter Hofstede, A. (2002). What's in a service? Towards accurate description of non-functional service properties. *Distributed and Parallel Databases, 12*(2), 117-133.

Poizat, P., Royer, J., & Salaun, G. (2004, June). Formal methods for component description, coordination and adaptation. In *Proceedings of the 1st International Workshop on Coordination and Adaptation Techniques for Software Entities*, Oslo, Norway.

Quatrani, T. (2003). *Visual modeling with rational rose and UML*. Reading, MA: Addison-Wesley.

Schmidt, D.C. (2002). Middleware for real-time and embedded systems. *Communications of the ACM, 45*(6), 43-48.

Selic, B. (2003). The pragmatics of model-driven development. *IEEE Software, 20*(5), 19-25.

Sztipanovits, J., & Karsai, G. (1997). Model-integrated computing. *IEEE Computer, 30*(4), 110-111.

Van Hentenryck, P., & Saraswat, V. (1996). Strategic directions in constraint programming. *ACM Computing Surveys, 28*(4), 701-726.

Warmer, J., & Kleppe, A. (1998). *The object constraint language: Precise modeling with UML*. Boston, MA: Addison-Wesley.

Weber, M., & Weisbrod, J., (2002). Requirements engineering in automotive development-experiences and challenges. In *Proceedings of the IEEE Joint International Conference on Requirements Engineering,* Essen, Germany.

White, J. (2005). *The generic eclipse modeling system*. Retrieved March 23, 2008, from http://www.sf.net/projects/gems

White, J., Gokhale, A., & Schmidt, D.C. (2007a). Simplifying autonomic enterprise Java Bean applications via model-driven development: A case study. *Journal of Software and System Modeling, 7*(1), 3-23.

White, J., Schmidt, D. C., Mulligan S. (2007, June). The generic eclipse modeling system. In *Proceedings of the Model-Driven Development Tool Implementer's Forum at TOOLS '07.* Zurich, Switzerland.

White, J., Nechypurenko, A., Wuchner, E., & Schmidt, D.C. (2006). Intelligence frameworks for assisting modelers in combinatorically challenging domains. In *Proceedings of the Workshop on Generative Programming and Component Engineering for QoS Provisioning in Distributed Systems,* Portland, OR.

White, J., Schmidt, D.C., Wuchner, E., & Nechypurenko, A. (2007b). Automating product-line variant selection for mobile devices. In *Proceedings of the 11th Annual Software Product Line Conference (SPLC),* Kyoto, Japan.

Willans, J.S., Sammut, P., Maskeri, G., & Evans, A. (2002). *The precise UML group.*

Yuan, W., & Nahrstedt, K. (2003). Energy-efficient soft real-time CPU scheduling for mobile multimedia systems. In *Proceedings of the 19th ACM Symposium on Operating Systems Principles,* Bolton Landing, NY.

ADDITIONAL READING

Bast, W., Kleppe, A.G., & Warmer, J.B. (2003). *MDA explained: The model driven architecture: Practice and promise.* Boston, MA: Addison-Wesley.

Beckert, B., Keller, U., & Schmitt, P.H. (2002). Translating the object constraint language into first-order predicate logic. In *Proceedings of VERIFY,* Copenhagen, Denmark.

Bézivin, J. (2001). From object composition to model transformation with the MDA. In *Proceedings of the 39th International Conference on the Technology of Object-Oriented Languages and Systems,* Santa Barbara, CA.

Bézivin, J. (2004). In search of a basic principle for model-driven engineering. *Novatica, 5*(2).

Bézivin, J. (2005). On the unification power of models. *Software and Systems Modeling, 4*(2), 171-188.

Bézivin, J., Farcet, N., Jezequel, J.M., Langolis, B., & Pollet, D. (2003). Reflective model-driven engineering. In *Proceedings of the 6th International*

Conference on the Unified Modeling Languages and Applications, San Francisco, CA.

Budinsky, F. (2003). *Eclipse modeling framework.* Boston, MA: Addison-Wesley.

Clocksin, W.F., & Mellish, C.S. (1984). *Programming in prolog.* New York: Springer-Verlag

Coplien, J.O., & Schmidt, D.C. (1995). *Pattern languages of program design.* New York: ACM Press/Addison-Wesley.

Czarnecki, K., & Eisenecker, U.W. (2000). *Generative programming: Methods, tools, and applications.* New York: ACM Press/Addison-Wesley.

Frankel, D. (2003). *Model-driven architecture.* New York: John Wiley.

Gray, J., Bapty, T., Neema, S., Schmidt, D.C., Gokhale, A., & Natarajan, B. (2002). An approach for supporting aspect-oriented domain modeling. In *Proceedings of the Second International Conference on Generative Programming and Component Engineering,* Pittsburgh, PA.

Gray, J., Bapty, T., Neema, S., & Tuck, J. (2001). Handling crosscutting constraints in domain-specific modeling. *Communications of the ACM, 44*(10), 87-93.

Hillier, F.S. (2004). *Introduction to operations research.* New York: McGraw-Hill.

Kang, K.C., Kim, S., Lee, J., Kim, K., Shin, E., & Huh, M. (1998). FORM: A feature-oriented reuse method with domain-specific reference architectures. *Annals of Software Engineering, 5*(1), 143-168.

Mannion, M. (2002). Using first-order logic for product-line model validation. In *Proceedings of the Second International Conference on Software Product-lines.* San Diego, CA.

Mellor, S.J. (2004). *MDA distilled: Solving the integration problem with the model driven architecture.* Boston, MA: Addison-Wesley.

Northrup, L., Feiler, P., Gabriel, R.P., Goodenough, J., Linger, R., Longstaff, T., et al. (2006). *Ultra-large-scale systems: The software challenge of the future.* Pittsburgh, PA: Carnegie Mellon Software Engineering Institute.

Selic, B., & Rumbaugh, J. (1998). Using UML for modeling complex real-time systems. *Lecture Notes in Computer Science, 1474*(1), 250-260.

Sterling, L.S., & Shapiro, E.Y. (1994). *The art of prolog: Advanced programming techniques.* Cambridge, MA: MIT Press.

Van Hentenryck, P. (1989). *Constraint satisfaction in logic programming.* Cambridge, MA: MIT Press.

Vaziri, M., & Jackson, D. (2000). Some shortcomings of OCL, the object constraint language of UML. In *Proceedings of the 34th International Conference on the Technology of Object-Oriented Languages and Systems,* Santa Barbara, CA.

Warmer, J.B., & Kleppe, A.G. (2003). *Getting your models ready for MDA.* Boston, MA: Addison-Wesley.

White, J., Czarnecki, K., Schmidt, D.C., Lenz, G., Wienands, C., Wuchner, E., & Fiege, L. (2007). Automated model-based configuration of enterprise Java applications. In *Proceedings of the Enterprise Computing Conference (EDOC) 2007,* Annapolis, MD.

White, J., Schmidt, D.C., Wuchner, E., & Nechypurenko, A. (2007). Automating product-line variant selection for mobile devices. In *Proceedings of the 11th Annual Software Product Line Conference (SPLC),* Kyoto, Japan.

Section V
Best Practices and Integrations

Chapter XIII
A Domain–Specific Language for Describing Grid Applications

Enis Afgan
University of Alabama at Birmingham, USA

Purushotham Bangalore
University of Alabama at Birmingham, USA

Jeff Gray
University of Alabama at Birmingham, USA

ABSTRACT

Grid computing environments are dynamic and heterogeneous in nature. In order to realize application-specific Quality of Service agreements within a grid, specifications at the level of an application are required. This chapter introduces an XML-based schema language (called the Application Specification Language, ASL) and a corresponding modeling tool that can be used to describe applications in grid computing environments. Such application descriptions allow derivation of guided and autonomic service developments for installation and invocation routines throughout the grid. In order to promote the language and ease the application description process, a domain-specific tool is also introduced. Based on our experience, the ASL in combination with higher level models improves, simplifies and promotes the grid application deployment process while simultaneously minimizing tedious and error-prone tasks such as manual application description composition.

INTRODUCTION

Grid computing (Foster, Kesselman, & Tuecke, 2001) has gained popularity as the emerging architecture for next-generation high performance distributed computing. Grid computing provides ubiquitous access to distributed high performance computing (HPC) resources that are shared between multiple organizations through virtualization and aggregation. This is realized through a layer of software (e.g., grid middleware), thus making grid applications extremely software-intensive systems where the value of software is equivalent to the value of the underlying infrastructure. Grid middleware provides a standard set of services for authentication, authorization, resource allocation and management, job scheduling, submission, monitoring, and data transfer and management (Berman, Hey, & Fox, 2003b). Software packages and tools based on open-source/open-standard approaches such as Globus Toolkit (Foster & Kesselman, 1997) have enabled the deployment of "production quality" computational grids. Several domain-specific grids are currently operational, for example, Grid Physics Network (GriPhyN) (GriPhyN, 2006), Network for Earthquake Engineering Simulation (NEES-Grid) (NEES, 2006), International Virtual Data Grid Laboratory (IVDGL) (IVDGL, 2006), Open Science Grid (Grid, 2007), and Particle Physics Data Grid Collaboratory Pilot (Grid2003) (PPDG, 2006). Grid computing has offered researchers enormous computing and data storage capabilities by providing seamless access to geographically distributed resources through the creation of virtual organizations (VOs).

Despite the many benefits of grid computing, the grid itself does not provide a novel programming paradigm for developing new applications. Furthermore, no formal methodology exists for porting existing legacy applications to the grid. Most of the applications developed for the grid are based on traditional HPC or distributed computing principles. Typical HPC applications are developed using implicit parallel programming techniques (e.g., compiler-based automatic parallelization and directive-based parallelization) or explicit parallel programming techniques (e.g., threads and message-passing). After an HPC application is developed and tested on local resources, it is then deployed; that is, the entire application (source code, dataset, scripts) is transferred to a remote site, compiled on a remote host, and made available for execution.

Deploying an application on the grid requires additional steps that involve user intervention, great insight into the internal structure of the application, as well as familiarity with the vari-

ous grid computing technologies and toolkits. In addition, the progressive steps of application execution and job submission may involve many additional steps required from the end-user, not necessarily found in a typical application. Due to this inherent complexity and difficulty using the grid, several approaches have attempted to simplify grid deployment and configuration by developing technologies such as Web portals (Gannon et al., 2003), workflow systems (Aalst & Hee, 2002), and component assembly (Armstrong et al., 1999). The ultimate goal of such efforts is to enable the adoption of grid technologies and applications to a wider group of end-users who are not familiar with programming languages and the lower level grid infrastructure. The potential impact for improving grid accessibility to such users is significant (e.g., applied science researchers, distributed organizations, and organizations with variable computational requirements).

To tailor the complexities of a user's view of the vast amount of grid software by addressing the goals of end-user accessibility, there is a need to standardize and simplify the process of application deployment on the grid. As part of the contribution of this chapter, we present a new language called the Application Specification Language (ASL) (Afgan & Bangalore, 2007) that can be used by application developers and end-users to describe details of a given application. The ASL allows an application to be represented in the heterogeneous world of the grid by capturing its functionality, options and differences as compared with other applications found in the grid. Through the use of ASL, application descriptions can be made available for immediate use or further advancements among applications such as job schedulers, automated interface generators and application-specific on-demand help provisioning. The ASL can also be used to describe how an application is combined with other matching services and software. The ability to specify the composition of services can facilitate the creation of new and added functionality, as well as enable further advancement of existing tools that can take advantage of the provided information.

To ease the process of collecting application description data and the description generation, a domain-specific modeling language (DSML) has been designed to assist in automating the grid application description and deployment processes. We believe that higher level models will improve, simplify and promote the grid application description and deployment process while minimizing tedious and error-prone tasks such as manual composition of application descriptions. The process of using the ASL and DSML within the context of grid deployment is shown in Figure 1, which outlines the major steps required for grid application development, publication and deployment. This figure highlights the global interaction between grid components and sum-marizes the ideas presented in this chapter. Upon development of an application, the developer can provide an application-specific description of a new application in the language described in this chapter. The application is registered by a service that can subsequently be queried by users, schedulers, or other tools. Information in the application description provides necessary data to enable automated integration with other available tools and services (e.g., Grid Security Infrastructure (GSI) (Foster, Kesselman, Tsudik, & Tuecke, 1998), Monitoring and Discovery Service (MDS) (Czajkowski et al., 1998), Resource Specification Language (RSL) (Czajkowski et al., 1998), Application Information Service (AIS)) as well as services still in development (e.g., cost). The focus of this chapter is on step 2 in the figure, whose addition to the global picture

Figure 1. Architecture using existing grid middleware technologies coupled with the technologies introduced throughout this chapter to enable improved application description and deployment

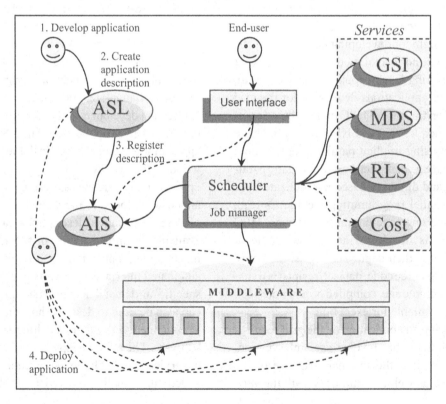

provides missing but beneficial functionality in the overall infrastructure. The dotted lines in the figure indicate possible interaction with a set of external events.

The rest of this chapter is organized as follows. The next section introduces grid computing concepts and provides a taxonomy of grid users. This is followed by a section that builds on grid technologies and provides examples of grid application development and deployment through a sample scenario outlining some of the difficulties with the current grid technologies. These issues are addressed in the section entitled *Application Specification Language*, which provides an introduction of a new language. The construction of this language is eased by a support tool based on metamodeling technology introduced and described in the *Modeling Wizards to Generate ASL* section. The end of the paper presents future trends and conclusions.

AN OVERVIEW OF GRID COMPUTING

Grid computing represents one of the new frontiers of computing. As the grid matures, many existing technologies will have to be revised and adopted to incorporate new ideas and concepts required by this evolving environment. Furthermore, many new technologies will arise as the result of emerging opportunities. This section introduces basic concepts of grid computing and presents a user categorization within this paradigm.

Grid Computing Background

The grid community has witnessed increased adoption over the past several years as the emerging architecture for next-generation high performance distributed computing. Grid computing is a culmination of distributed computing (Tanenbaum & Steen, 2002) and high-performance computing (Kumar, Grama, Gupta, & Karypis, 1994).

The grid integrates networking, communication, computation and information to provide a virtual platform for theoretically unlimited compute power and data management (Berman, Fox, & Hey, 2003a). It is designed to provide ubiquitous access to the vast number of resources and enables sharing between multiple organizations providing desired resource virtualization and aggregation. Virtual Organizations (VO) (Foster et al., 2001) represent aggregations of communities that may share national and international boundaries but have common objectives. Through VOs, grid computing is capable of aggregating heterogeneous resources that belong to different administrative domains to create a unique and valuable resource for the scientific community.

The VOs that are available in the grid are enabled through the use of middleware that provides a standard set of services for authentication, authorization, resource allocation and management, job scheduling, submission, and monitoring. Through this model, individual resources within an organization are virtualized into a common pool of accessible resources. The Globus Toolkit (GT) (Foster & Kesselman, 1997) is the most popular grid infrastructure framework for enabling the creation of grid applications. The GT offers all the basic technologies required for setting up a grid environment to support user creation, job submission and monitoring that span traditional boundaries (e.g., single institution environment setup). The technologies associated with the GT include:

- Grid Security Infrastructure (GSI) (Foster et al., 1998) is used for user authentication;
- Global Resource Allocation Manager (GRAM) (Czajkowski et al., 1998) assists in remote resource job management;
- Monitoring and Discovery System (MDS) (Czajkowski, Fitzgerald, Foster, & Kesselman, 2001) offers information discovery and state of resources; and

- GridFTP (Allcock et al., 2001) provides file transfer capabilities in the grid environment.

On top of the low-level grid middleware tools, an additional layer of grid system software packages provides an abstraction layer that hides complexities such as authentication, resource discovery, and file transfer. These intermediate layers offer direct interaction with the grid middleware allowing communication at a higher level of abstraction. Examples of such packages are portals (Gannon et al., 2003; Novotny, Russell, & Wehrens, 2004) and application schedulers (Afgan, 2004; Buyya, Abramson, & Giddy, 2000; Huedo, Montero, & Llorente, 2004) that provide a solid layer for using the grid as well as many options to develop grid applications.

The top-most layer found in grid computing is the application layer that interacts directly with an end-user. A grid application is considered to be any application that is capable of exploiting grid resources through the use of grid middleware. The possibilities for using the grid are restricted only by the usability of the system as a whole. The end-result is a highly software-intensive system where, on top of the middleware functionality,

lays the unlimited layer of application software offering a myriad of options and combinations to be explored by application developers as well as end-users. Figure 2 shows the overall layered structure of grid computing.

Because the grid is still an emerging technology, applications that were originally developed to run in more traditional environments may be adopted to take advantage of the benefits offered by grid technologies. The process of converting an existing legacy application to make use of the grid is called *application deployment* or *grid enablement*. The primary benefit an application gains, once grid-enabled, is the ability to use compute power more efficiently. Another benefit is that long running jobs can be broken up to execute in parallel on multiple resources to decrease turn-around time or increase efficiency. Additionally, larger data sets can be stored as well as processed without putting the load on any single system. By evolving a legacy application, the heterogeneity of the grid can be exploited to benefit the application as a whole by executing different application segments on separate (i.e., heterogeneous) systems making each segment take maximum advantage offered by underlying hardware, and in the end, gain maximum benefit for the application as a whole (Chase, 2005). With the diverse pool of available resources and the wider pool of available applications, ensuring mutual compatibility and maintainability becomes a major challenge. Some of the difficulties arise between the involved parties because individual requirements are not stated in a standard, clear, and concise way and thus provide no opportunities for automation or standardized reliability.

GRID USER CATEGORY CLASSIFICATION

This section provides an overview of the roles and goals of individual grid users. The section identifies the specific requirements that are imposed by

Figure 2. Layered structure of grid computing

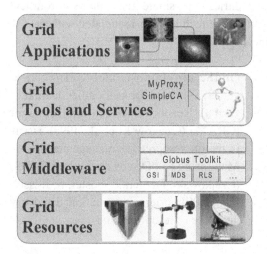

each user category, as well as the provisioning tools that accommodate their needs. The categories of users introduced in this section are middleware developer, application deployer, application developer, resource owner, and end-user. In some cases, a single person may play multiple roles (e.g., application developer and deployer).

Middleware Developer

As the interconnecting fiber of the grid, middleware represents the mechanism that facilitates the management of underlying resources as well as development of grid applications. Grid middleware is capable of delivering and sharing compute and data resources over secure channels while hiding intrinsic platform differences among the available resources. The middleware developers are key participants in the grid ecosystem and are closely connected to all other user categories. Middleware developers consider feature requests from user groups and participate in the design and implementation of the middleware standards that shape the way the grid operates. Examples of grid middleware include: the Globus Toolkit, Message Passing Interface (MPI) (Forum, 1998), Condor (Litzkow, Livny, & Mutka, 1988), Storage Resource Broker (SRB) (Baru, Morre, Rajasekar, & Wan, 1998), Web portals (GridSphere (Novotny et al., 2004), and the Open Grid Computing Environment (OGCE) (Gannon et al., 2003).

Application Deployer

An application deployer has the responsibility of performing the necessary work to grid-enable a legacy application. Due to the well-known possibility of high costs and challenges of application modification, the community focus is not on modifying the source code, but rather adopting the application through creation of wrappers that convert the entire application into a grid-enabled solution (Afgan, Sathyanarayana, & Bangalore, 2006; McConnell, 1996). The deployment process

and wrapper creation for one of the five strategies is performed using a combination of the following techniques:

- Create script interfaces for command-line tools.
- Program directly to the Globus Toolkit using an available C API.
- Use a commodity toolkit such as Java CoG kit (Laszewski, Foster, Gawor, & Lane, 2001).
- Use the Grid Application Toolkit (GAT) (Allen et al., 2005).
- Use Grid Services (Sotomayor & Childers, 2005).

Because the application deployer is working with an existing application that may have several peculiarities, as well as the heterogeneity of grid resources, many issues may arise offsetting expected application performance or even correct execution. One of the causes of the evolution problem is the lack of standardized application information (Ulrich, 2002). The application deployer must placate the existing user base and should not modify the original application requirements to address the grid-related concerns. If any modifications are required during the deployment process, to better accommodate needs of either end-user or the resource owner, currently, there is no effective way to convey the modifications that took place (as compared to the descriptive information pertinent to the original application) to either of those users categories.

Application Developer

As the grid gains acceptance, more applications will be custom tailored to take advantage of the benefits offered by the grid. Traditional programming techniques and methodologies (i.e., sequential or parallel) have their own set of challenges. Incorporating the grid into a legacy application poses a new set of accidental complexities. Most of the programming techniques and application types available when developing grid applications come from the HPC area or traditional distributed computing.

Grid services, which are based on the Service-Oriented Architecture (SOA) (Foster, Kesselman, Nick, & Tuecke, 2002a), represent the future of grid application development. However, grid services are hard to develop and deploy, as evidenced by the following steps that are required to develop a single, standalone service (Sotomayor & Childers, 2005):

1. Define and specify the service's interface so clients know how to invoke it.
2. Implement the given interface for the service; implement any related libraries.
3. Define the deployment parameters to indicate the specifics of the service.
4. Deploy the service to a grid service container.
5. Register the service so it can be discovered by other services.

In addition to coding difficulties, other issues arise when developing grid applications. These issues include security, licensing, job management, and synchronization. Another major step in application development is aggregation of newly created services or already existing ones through library calls and advanced programming techniques. Application creation will need to be tailored to extract maximum benefit from the grid for a wider community of users. Examples of such use include advertising application requirements (e.g., service name, installation instructions, license requirements), as well as minimum hardware requirements (e.g., CPU speed, underlying network infrastructure, memory consumption). Unfortunately, current methods do not provide an adequate solution to address these issues.

Resource Owner

Resource owners and providers assist in running the most basic layer of the grid multitier architecture, which consists of the resources (e.g., networks, computer, storage nodes), the middle-tier (e.g., middleware, certificate authority, portals), and the clients (e.g., GT clients, GUIs). Resource owners are responsible for maintaining their respective resources by meeting hardware requirements for individual applications, installing those applications, obtaining relevant libraries and compilers, maintaining applications, and enforcing policies. Beyond the initial cost of installing the grid environment, there is the natural cost of running individual clusters, as well as keeping licenses, subscriptions, and libraries up to date. The resource owners must also be cognizant of the Quality of Service (QoS) agreements between participating users (e.g., compatibility, application versioning, standardization). In order for grid computing to move further into the mainstream, resource providers must be able to reduce their operating costs, increase resource utilization and find a benefit in sharing their resources with the wider community.

End-User

The role of the resource owners is aligned to the bottom of Figure 2. At the top of Figure 2 are end-users who rely upon the results of a grid application. In order for the grid to become a commodity computing technology, there is a need to attract a wide variety of users. Some of the issues preventing widespread adoption are the complexities and dynamics involved in job submission and job management, which are not yet tailored for lay-persons (i.e., those who are not computer savvy). Consider the following scenario that exemplifies the manual steps needed to submit a job on the grid:

1. Select the resources needed by an application.
2. Create a proxy certificate (e.g., grid-proxy-init).
3. Copy the necessary source code and input files to a remote host (e.g., globus-url-copy).
4. Create a Resource Specification Language (RSL) (Czajkowski et al., 1998) string.
5. Submit the job for execution (e.g., globus-job-run, globus-job-submit).
6. Copy output files generated from the remote host to local machine (e.g., globus-url-copy).

Although the general concept of the above steps exists in many distributed contexts, the introduction of the grid manifests as an additional obstacle toward application usage. As such, the grid requires a level of computer expertise that is not within the skill sets of general end-users. The complexities of manual job submission, typified by the above six steps, can be ameliorated by the following user-friendly approaches:

- Write a client using a commodity toolkit (e.g., Java CoG Kit (Laszewski et al., 2001)).
- Write an interface to a grid service.
- Use a portal (e.g., OGCE (Gannon et al., 2003) or a grid-port (Thomas, Mock, Dahan, Mueller, Sutton, & Boisseau, 2001)).
- Use a workflow systems (e.g., Chimera (Foster, Voeckler, Wilde, & Zhao, 2002b)).
- Use a component framework (e.g., Armstrong et al., 1999).

All of the above techniques are viable choices and present gradual improvements in usability, customization and acceptance. Whichever layer of abstraction the above techniques provide, one common goal is to simplify job submission by abstracting grid resources from the end-user.

From the grid user classification and description, there are numerous requirements imposed by each of the user groups. This point is further complicated when user roles are combined and intertwined with a need to provide an effective way to address individual user concerns from application development and registration to application usage. By helping to solve this problem, users will be empowered to create and use grid applications while improving overall grid acceptance and resource utilization.

GRID APPLICATION DEPLOYMENT SCENARIO

Software engineering researchers have introduced many helpful principles (e.g., information hiding (Parnas, 1972)) and best practices (e.g., design patterns (Gamma, Helm, Johnson, & Vlissides, 1994)) with the goal of simplifying the development process. Despite the improvements offered by traditional software engineering principles, there still remain many open questions when it comes to new technologies such as the grid. For example, developing applications to execute in parallel computing environments changes some of the underlying assumptions; this is due to the focus of performance as the primary concern, rather than maintainability, evolution, and changeability. Parallel computing (Kumar et al., 1994) is based on a set of models primarily governed by the communication patterns between algorithmic iterations within an application. The following categories represent various types of parallel programs based on communication patterns (full details and descriptions of the individual sections are provided in the section entitled *Application name and description*):

1. Sequential applications
2. Parametric Sweep applications
3. Master-Worker applications
4. All-Worker applications
5. Loosely coupled parallel applications
6. Tightly couple parallel applications
7. Workflow applications

Development of parallel applications entails coordination between computation and communication as limited by the underlying hardware architecture. Depending on the problem type, one communication pattern may be a better choice over another based on the constraints of a specific application context. Once developed, the application is deployed on a targeted architecture. Occasionally, hardware-specific optimizations are performed to customize the code for optimal execution. Developing applications for parallel computing environments is guided by the concept of overlapping communication with computation, thus maximizing the use of resources. Although the optimal solution of any application is rarely achieved, the actuality of the application executing on a single, dedicated resource results in a reasonably understood platform to build upon. On the other hand, developing the applications for the grid under the constraints of parallel computing introduces new obstacles and complications. The execution resource becomes a virtual entity occasionally available and with a high failure rate. The communication between iterations and application modules is not only exponentially slower but also highly unstable. The development of such applications raises the complexity considerations to a higher level and introduces a whole new field of application deployment as a significant part in the application lifecycle.

Most current grid environments are based on the concepts embodied in Service-Oriented Architecture (SOA) (Foster et al., 2002a) and Web Services (Gottschalk, Graham, Kreger, & Snell, 2002). Applications deployed on existing grids are submitted as grid services, which are Web services with extended functionality to include support for stateful behavior, lifecycle management, and notifications (Foster et al., 2002a). The development of a grid service proceeds in several steps requiring expertise in many fields (Sotomayor & Childers, 2005). When developing traditional parallel applications, it is required for individual subtasks to work toward a common goal. The same idea transfers to the context of the grid, but additional difficulties arise because

many applications that already exist and conform to this subtask model are not grid-aware, which requires major reengineering. The bottom line is that many existing software applications developed by the parallel applications community will not be rewritten to comply with the grid model, but will rather be adopted by the use of wrappers. This introduces new obstacles because different user categories must interact to achieve the common goal. Originally, an application developer was able to develop an application and deploy it on a resource because they possessed the required expertise. By adopting the grid, the requirements related to application deployment have risen and require new expertise, often not readily and easily available due to the involved complexities. This implies the need for a new domain expert (i.e., a grid specialist) who possesses deep understanding of the technology and is able to transform traditional applications into grid applications. The drawback to this solution is that additional communication is necessary at the development level, which prolongs the application development. Furthermore, the delivery process is perplexed with new possibilities to introduce errors due to miscommunication or misunderstanding.

The application deployment process on a grid is a nontrivial task. The user must first determine what resources are available and then decide the most suitable resource for a particular application. It is important to differentiate the application development process from the application deployment process. As stated earlier, typical HPC applications are developed using a specific programming language and parallel programming paradigm (e.g., compiler directive-based, threads, message-passing, combination of threads and message-passing) and often the programming paradigm chosen decides the application deployment platform. If the application uses a shared-memory programming paradigm then the application can be deployed only on a shared memory system, whereas an application developed using the message-passing paradigm can be deployed on both distributed memory and shared memory systems. Furthermore, applications might have specific requirements (e.g., processor architecture, amount of memory, disk space, interconnection network, libraries, operating system) to deliver desired performance and scalability. An application developer could describe these requirements using application deployment descriptors, or hints could be added about various performance implications and space/time tradeoffs. For commercial software packages, information about licensing and subscription could also be provided by the deployment descriptors. An application scheduler may use these descriptors to select a suitable resource and schedule the application for execution.

As a concrete example showing the full process of application deployment, we will outline the options and necessary steps required to enable an application such as the Basic Local Alignment Search Tool (BLAST) (Altschul, Gish, Miller, Myers, & Lipman, 1990), a frequently used bioinformatics application to perform sequence similarity searches, to execute on a local campus grid, such as UABGrid (Gemmill & Bangalore, 2005). Portions of the following steps assume the availability of grid middleware such as the Globus Toolkit (GT) (Foster & Kesselman, 1999). This sample scenario assumes that a user authentication system is in place and that the user is able to access available resources using middleware tools. The following represents the scenario:

1. Obtain a valid user authentication proxy.
2. Manually log into each of the available resources and download BLAST.
3. Install BLAST individually on each resource.
4. Create a wrapper application that is responsible for necessary file transfers, iterative job submissions, job monitoring and notification using a grid middleware API or a commodity toolkit such as the Java CoG Kit (Laszewski et al., 2001). The wrapper developer must be aware of the method of interapplication communication and design the wrapper to accommodate for the appropriate task parallelization and communication methods with respect to the grid middleware. Also, additional levels of parallelization can be introduced at this level as is the case with a locally developed wrapper (Afgan et al., 2006). If a scheduler is not available for task scheduling among grid resources, this feature should also be included as part of the wrapper functionality.
5. Create a user interface where the application can be invoked. This can range from a set of command-line tools to a Web-based portal.

As can be seen from the given scenario, the process of enabling an application to execute on the grid requires a significant effort and high-level of expertise from the application deployer. Depending on the complexity of the wrapper, it may turn into a completely new application developed to maximize the potential of the original application in this new environment. One of the drawbacks is the requirement of the deployer to have a reasonably deep understanding of the application to ensure that the wrapper is correctly implemented.

APPLICATION SPECIFICATION LANGUAGE

Motivation and Background

A goal of an application developer is to see their solution adopted quickly by a large group of end-users. However, the typical path to adoption requires frequent interaction with end-users to address numerous questions, such as: how to install the application, how to invoke it, the purpose and function of the available options and arguments, as well as how to improve performance for a specific platform configuration. Through the lifetime of the application, additional documentation is created to address such common questions. However, with a new version of the software, much of this work needs to be discarded and redone. Avoiding this pipeline of events is challenging, but through gradual and systematic adoption of the technique proposed in this chapter, it is possible to provide more automated support for the end-user.

Computing has evolved from a user-centric context (where every detail of code execution needed human attentiveness and interaction) to a global service-driven view (such as Web Services, where complex, data dependent, goal seeking interactions and computations of independently developed components can be achieved with absolutely no human intervention). From this progression, we observe the common approach where automatic communication between programs is enabled. This is generally accomplished through definition of standard languages that specify protocols observed between applications. The following languages represent efforts within the grid community to automate specific deployment tasks:

- **Job submission description language (JSDL) (Anjomshoaa et al., 2005):** A recently completed standard from the Job Submission Working Group (JSWG, 2007) within the Open Grid Forum (OGF) (OGF, 2007). The JSDL is a specification of an abstract and independent language used for describing requirements of computational jobs in grid environments. It contains a vocabulary and normative XML schema that builds on the idea of standardizing a language to accommodate a variety of job management systems, which alleviates the problem of heterogeneity in the grid. By having a standard language available, a job submission description can enable diverse job management systems to communicate and complement job description in a more simplified manner.

- **Resource specification language (RSL) (Czajkowski et al., 1998):** Provides a common interchange language to describe resources and jobs to run on them. It is a language developed by the Globus Toolkit Project (Foster & Kesselman, 1999) and is represented by various *<name, value>* pairs that are used by the Grid Resource Allocation Manager (GRAM) (Czajkowski et al., 1998) to perform complex resource descriptions in cooperation with other components in the system. RSL preceded JSDL, so RSL can be seen as an earlier scaled-down version of JSDL.

- **Resource description language (RDL) (Anjomshoaa et al., 2005):** A language that is part of the JSDL standard document for describing underlying grid resources in terms of CPU speed, number of CPUs, and main memory. Even though not yet realized, the concept of this language has been propagated through other tools such as Condor and ClassAds (Solomon, 2004) and the necessary information (e.g., current resource status) can be obtained from MDS (Czajkowski et al., 2001) and Ganglia (Massie, Chun, & Culler, 2004).

The above mentioned languages have been developed to enable standardized exchange of information between grid resources and provide support for direct and concrete communication between these resources. By defining documents specified by these language constraints, one can rely on automated negotiation during the job submission process without regard for the heterogeneity of the underlying hardware and software. When mapping the above mentioned languages to individual grid user categories, the JSDL and RSL map most favorably to the end-user category (where the user is mainly interested in adopting the grid as a pool of resources). The JSDL and RSL enable users to limit and perform resource selection. At the same time, RDL can be classified as a language for allowing resource owners to describe the capabilities of their resources and advertise that information for wider use through mechanisms such as MDS and Ganglia. What is evidently missing is the need to support the application developer. Once an application is developed, there is no standardized way to publicize the name and capabilities of the application in a manner that can be accessed by other tools. Rather, the application developer and the end-user are forced to interact in an interrogative manner, perhaps using a wiki or similar tools to advertise the availability of an application.

By supporting a method for capturing the core purpose of the application, requirements, and options, the end-user is provided with specific information that describes the application. After successful installation, the second most important feature enabling application use is the interface that the application provides to its users. With respect to grid applications, the most appropriate way to interact with an application is through a Web-based interface that requires no local installation of the application. A Web-based interaction may also provide special tools and knowledge to access available resources (Gannon et al., 2003; Hernandez, Bangalore, Gray, Guan, & Reilly, 2006). By providing a default standardized interface to the given application automatically, a resource owner may reuse the interface rather than implement their own. The benefit for the end-user is that the interface stays constant across different providers. An additional benefit is a reduction of possible errors in interface generation originating from the resource provider due to possible misunderstanding or lack of application knowledge. The Pasteur Institute Software Environment (PISE) (Letondal, 2000) is an example of previous work where this idea has been adopted in practice. PISE is a transformation tool that receives as input a PISE-DTD compliant XML document and interprets the document to create any of the suite of interfaces ranging from HTML to CGI and IPSH (Letondal, 2000). A scalable core is

also provided by PISE that can be extended to add additional interface interpreters as needed. PISE currently contains a database of over 200 XML documents corresponding to interfaces for various applications that are primarily focused on bioinformatics. By leveraging ideas and technologies such as those provided by PISE, many of the accidental complexities associated with grid application deployment can be removed.

Description of the Language

To address the challenges raised in the previous sections, we present a new language called the Application Specification Language (ASL) (Afgan & Bangalore, 2007). As a new approach toward application specification that focuses on the needs of grid users and grid applications, the ASL is able to capture essential application information. Through standardized protocols, tools can be passed the information about an application that is specified in an ASL description. ASL is a language for describing any application's requirements, attributes, and options. The ASL directly supports the ability to capture application-specific information that is not necessarily found in the general pool of available description tags. Through the use of ASL, factors such as software and hardware requirements, data constraints, and algorithm complexity can be provided to a user. As can be seen in Figure 3, the ASL may be composed with other groups of established grid languages (e.g., JSDL/RSL, RDL). The interactions implied in the triangle connect all perspectives and user categories of a grid environment, which enable communication to take place over well-designed paths to facilitate further communication, refinement, contract creation and the possibility of higher QoS for all participants.

ASL is applicable before and during installation, during job scheduling, during job execution, and even after the job has completed. It can be complemented and modified as knowledge about an application increases. The ASL can be used

Figure 3. ASL-RDL-JSDL/RSL triangle showing direct communication paths between corresponding user categories

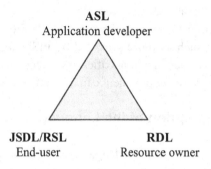

ASL
Application developer

JSDL/RSL   **RDL**
End-user   Resource owner

with legacy applications (requiring adaptation), or with newly developed applications designed specifically for the grid (often called "Smart Applications"). By providing a standardized way to describe application requirements, the ASL enables an automated capability to compare applications. Without ASL, such comparisons are very hard to perform manually because of their subjectivity. Such comparisons can be useful in numerous cases, such as application scheduling and software cost estimation (Afgan et al., 2006).

In essence, ASL is an extended application version of RSL. It provides a set of specialized tags used to capture application-specific details and thus provide a description of an application. The goal of this language is to use *application-specific descriptions* that enable deployment, maintenance, and execution of an application in a standardized and simplified way. The structure of the language is intended to describe entire, operational applications rather than individual components of an application or other software that may subsequently be composed into an application. The intent of ASL and individual ASL documents is to enable needed communication between heterogeneous resources in the grid through standard interfaces. Just like ASL's sister languages JSDL and RSL, ASL

is not a grammar-based language, but rather a specification language establishing and defining a standard interface needed for heterogeneous grid resources to communicate with each other. A grammar-based language refers to a language that is defined and constrained by a context-free grammar. A schema-based language is rooted in an XML schema and is constrained by the tags defined in the associated schema.

By providing the appropriate set of tags, ASL enables application comparison and interface generation. Because every grid application is custom built to meet a certain need, the implementation details may be difficult to describe. Many of the options available during application specification often require significant human intervention as well as use of human language descriptions that cannot be modeled and captured by a general-purpose computer language (e.g., Java or C++). Providing a standardized set of tags to capture information about an application in a concise and precise manner is difficult. The requirements imposed when selecting a given set of tags must focus on capturing the core set of characteristics describing any application and then provide an extended set of tags that allow unique application components to be specified. Our first attempt at defining this set of tags considered existing languages such as JSDL and RSL, which capture job submission requirements that map onto resource and application requirements. Examples of such tags include numerical values (e.g., CPU speed and amount of main memory required), as well as a predefined set of values (e.g., operating system and CPU architecture type).

Additional tags were created by a systematic analysis of characteristics that describe an application but were not required for application invocation (e.g., max number of CPUs an application scales to). Many of these tags are simple in nature, allowing the definition of a range of valid values that can be used to validate data entered by the end-user. The more difficult set of requirements deals with values that are dependent on each other,

Figure 4. Grouped set of elements and subelements with appropriate tags

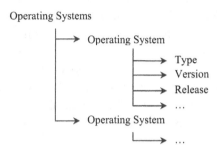

but can be viewed individually as containers of simple values. Thus, these tags were organized in groups where subelements define individual pieces of the larger component. An example is the operating system requirement. An application may be suitable for many operating systems as well as different versions of an individual operating system. Thus, creating higher level elements that contain equivalent subelements allows different version dependencies to be specified (please see Figure 4).

One concern with adopting ASL, especially when viewed from the perspective of a developer creating the ASL document, is the requirement of the document syntax to be specified correctly (i.e., equivalent tags may have a different meaning when placed in different element groups). The most difficult part of describing an application concisely occurs with tags that cannot be constrained to a set of predefined values (e.g., tags that represent a human readable text string, such as copyright policy). The obvious impediment with such tags is the lack of precision needed for formal interpretation. However, the additional information provided within these tags can benefit end-user understandability of the application. The use of the tags for all types of descriptors (e.g., simple, complex groups and natural language) helps to partition the entire document and provide guided help for natural language descriptors. A further benefit of such tags is the possibility of develop-

ing additional translators to generate application Web documentation automatically.

The completed ASL document consists of several parts (discussed in subsequent sections of this chapter) each focusing on a particular portion of an application deployment lifecycle. With the blend of the formal tags (i.e., computer readable) and informal tags (i.e., end-user understandable), the ASL assists in application description from different perspectives and provides user support in multiple formats. Examples of interpretation include an application description Web page with installation and invocation instructions, script generation for automated application installation, as well as optimal system requirements for job submission.

Structure of the Language

An ASL document consists of four distinct yet related sections that are described in XML. By dividing the document into these distinct sections, an ASL document is more modular and allows for easier initial generation and later modification. With the use of appropriate tools, each section of the document can have its own permissions, which allows the document to be modified independently and securely. As the application receives a wider user base, additional information may become available from its users. As a result of multiple executions of an application, additional information can be gathered, such as profiles of application performance, unexpected behavior, or suggestions for future enhancements. Beyond the collection of application information, the segregation of the document into appropriate sections allows for shorter search times among users allowing them to focus on sections of the document of most interest. To provide segregation of information collection and retrieval, an ASL document consists of application name and description, installation requirements, job invocation requirements, and hints.

The sections are not directly connected to each other, but the data is stored only once per ASL document. Because of this, inadvertent references to information provided in other parts of the document may exist. These sections are correspondingly mapped to XML with appropriate tags. Each of the sections is described below and the schema is provided for the given section.

Application Name and Description

The application name and description section contains the most basic information about an application and acts as the application identification component. It specifies the name and version of the application as can be found in an application repository. This section also contains subelements such as the application description describing the application in a human readable format. The description identifies the problem the application solves and maps the application to an application category. The application category element is limited to a predefined set of values as described below. It is intended to offer better understanding of the application deployment process on the grid and it is essential in classifying different types of applications deployed in a grid environment. The majority of the applications typically deployed in a grid environment can be classified into the following categories:

1. **Sequential applications:** Traditional applications developed to execute on a single node machine. For the applications that require larger resources (e.g., more memory, disk, or faster CPUs), the grid will also provide redundancy, fail-safe capability, and excess capacity.

2. **Parametric sweeps:** Multiple copies of sequential jobs using different input datasets or parameters. These applications are often submitted independently by a single user in an effort to reduce overall task execution time. Benefits of using the grid are the same

as sequential applications with the addition of multiple instance coordination performed by grid tools and middleware.

3. **Master-Worker applications:** Master-worker or bag-of-tasks model (Kumar et al., 1994), where a master process distributes work (either statically or dynamically) to a set of worker processes and aggregates the results at the end. Many financial and bioinformatics applications fall into this category, each in constant need of surplus compute resources. The main differences between parametric sweeps and master-worker applications is that the individual tasks do not have to be executing the same code, but a workflow system can be in place with the master-worker model possibly delivering a more complex application functionality. The coordination between the worker nodes and task assignment must be handled by the master process.

4. **All-Worker applications:** Similar to the master-worker model, except that each process involved, including the master, share the workload equally and data is exchanged between individual processes in some pattern (point-to-point or group communication).

5. **Loosely coupled parallel applications:** Parallel applications (e.g., coupled fluid flow and wave models) that exchange data occasionally through files during execution (e.g., beginning and ending of an outer iteration).

6. **Tightly coupled parallel applications:** A single Message Passing Interface (MPI) (Forum, 1998) application distributed across multiple systems sharing data during the execution, possibly at frequent intervals, through passed messages. It requires interoperability between different MPI libraries or an MPI library such as MPICH-G2 (Karonis, Toonen, & Foster, 2003).

7. **Workflow applications:** A model connecting many individual applications executing

at different geographically distributed locations, which are chained together to perform a complex simulation. For an application to be classified as a workflow application, additional information is needed to identify dependencies with other applications in terms of input and output data streams.

When selecting the application category for an ASL specification, the following considerations should be examined by a user composing the document. Applications that belong to categories (1) and (2) can be distributed and scheduled across any available computational resource on the grid because there is no synchronization or coordination required between individual tasks. However, applications in categories (3) and (4) must be scheduled on a single computational resource and cannot be distributed across multiple resources. This does not imply that the application may not use additional, distributed resources. If an application has been developed specifically for the grid, it can utilize middleware components to enable cross-resource task execution. In that case, task scheduling is the responsibility of the application itself because it would be deployed on a dedicated resource. Applications in categories (5) and (6) expect that the individual applications are distributed and assume that the individual tasks are scheduled to execute at the same time (through advanced reservation or mutual agreement with the resource providers). Workflow applications (category 7) assume that the scheduler can trigger the execution of one or more applications as described by the workflow. Because most of the existing schedulers (Berman et al., 2001; Casanova, Obertelli, Bernan, & Wolski, 2000; Huedo et al., 2004; Venugopal, Buyya, & Winton, 2005) do not handle advance reservation, the use of workflow applications is limited and intended mostly for future generations of applications and grid schedulers.

The remaining elements in this section are illustrated in Figure 5. *Category* element set

Figure 5. Application description section schema

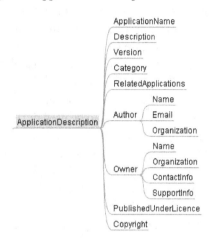

has a predefined set of values from which a user must choose. The remaining elements found in this schema section do not have their values predefined, but can be defined by the person creating the document enabling desired application description.

Installation Requirements

The installation requirements section of an ASL document contains a set of required elements that describe the pre-installation requirements as well as the installation procedure. Some of the examples of this type of element set include minimum processor speed, processor architecture, minimum amount of memory needed for installation of the application, libraries, applications required for the installation procedure (e.g., compilers, (un)packaging tools), licenses needed for application installation, network requirements, and required amount of disk space for the installation. The tags used are simple declarations that specify the value of a predefined type (e.g., string, integer). Even though this model may result in unnecessary inconsistencies between application descriptions, we believe at this stage of ASL development and definition this variability is necessary to allow for the correct words to be selected from a constrained set of choices. The full schema of the installation requirements section is given in Figure 6.

Among the elements defined in the installation category are *SoftwareDependencies* and *Applications Required* tags. The information these tags contain is intended strictly to be used during the installation procedure. The *SoftwareDependencies* tag refers to any other software that will be needed for the application execution. This can be viewed as a prerequisite for the installation; that is, in case software packages declared within this tag are not installed, the application cannot be expected to execute. Examples of such software dependencies would include Perl (Wall, Christiansen, & Orwant, 2000) with certain libraries and Postgres database (Momjian, 2000). With respect to installation, the *ApplicationsRequired* tag refers to other complete applications required to perform the installation. These applications may be invoked during the installation procedure, such as unpackaging and installation tools (e.g., Ant, make).

Job Invocation Requirements

The job invocation requirements section focuses on providing a user with the information needed to execute the application. Starting with the executable name, it also provides the available switches and minimum hardware requirements, as well as allows the developer to specify the number of input and output files with examples of their respective formats. This section does not represent a duplication of effort found in JSDL/RSL, but it is alternatively used to specify requirements for the entire application. Such specification is needed not only when executing a single job, but to describe the available options and how to use them. Rather than specifying exact input files and other job-specific parameters, the category defines application requirements, such as: the required input files, required format of those files, any output files and corresponding format of the output files, libraries required to invoke the application, and licenses needed to run the application. This capability can be viewed as a

Figure 6. Application installation section schema

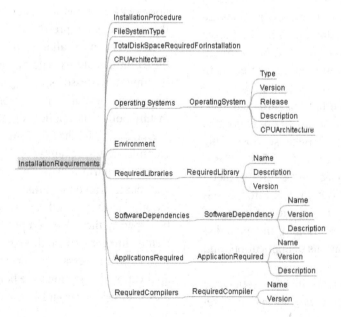

more detailed version of *man* pages in UNIX. This category allows the developer to be shielded through a contract-like document; that is, if any of the requirements are not met, the application cannot be expected to execute correctly.

The majority of the application description is provided in this section of the ASL document, so it is natural for a set of tools to be based on this category. An example tool is a translator that formats the appropriate information into a Web page allowing the information to be read through a browser, or a correct and application-specific job submission interface. Another example tool serves as a data verification tool that ensures input files are in the correct format. The complete schema is shown in Figure 8 on the next page. Similar to the installation section, the application invocation section has elements *SoftwareDependencies* and *RequiresApplications*. In this context, software dependencies refer to any software packages that are necessary and will be used as part of the application during its execution. An example would include a call to a Perl module. The description of the application requirements tag is similar to the description from the application installation section of ASL, where it specifies any other applications that may be invoked during this application's execution. This tag can be used to specify the requirements for a workflow, even though any further enforcement and coordination during execution must be done within the given application.

Hints

Due to the inherent variability of applications, information describing an application may not be adequately captured in the preceding sections of ASL due to noncompliance and uniqueness of the application. Also, the succinctness of available options in ASL tags or already existing data may prevent additional and possibly more complete application information to be stored. In order to accommodate for these possible shortcomings,

Figure 7. Hints section schema

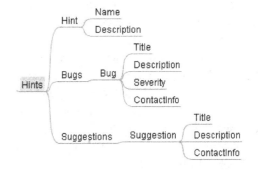

Figure 8. Application invocation section schema

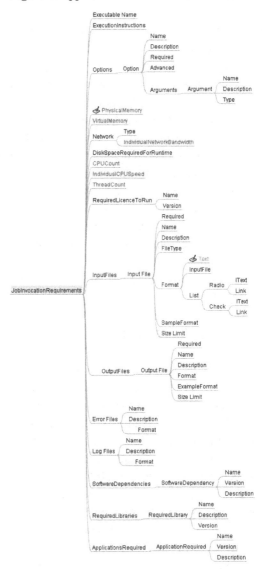

there is an additional section found in every ASL document, which is entitled *Hints*. This section contains instructions and comments, mostly in natural language, which provide additional information about the application. The purpose of this information is to allow detailed descriptions for areas of high application complexity, either for the users of the applications or other developers who may use this application as a base layer for development. Another important goal behind this section and its element set is that it can be accessed and edited by a wide user group. Performance information may be stored in this section to specify the optimal parameters on a particular hardware architecture.

Depending on application type (e.g., sequential, embarrassingly parallel, MPI-based application), certain input parameters (e.g., size of input file, input file format, number of processors) may alter application performance and thus information found here could be useful for the resource owner, end-user and even the scheduler developer. By giving permissions to a wide range of users, known bugs as well as suggestions for future advancements can be documented. A large portion of its use can be found in troubleshooting an application where expected errors can be explained. Figure 7 shows the current Hints section schema.

Example ASL Documents

This section demonstrates the use of ASL to describe an initial set of applications that show the ability of the language to specify and distinguish applications. In these examples, ASL was manually generated by providing the values associated with appropriate tags as defined in the schema. This generation is quite straightforward, which provides the user variability in selecting the tags to be defined depending on the application. The rest of this section provides snippets of ASL documents with their respective applications. Differences between applications are outlined

and the ability of ASL to capture these differences is discussed.

Application Descriptions

To show the ability of ASL to capture descriptions of applications belonging to different categories, three applications are specified, each from a different application category. The first two applications correspond to the sample scenario described in the *Grid Application Deployment Scenario* section. The first application is a sequential application implemented in Perl called *QuerySplit* that performs segmentation of the BLAST input query file (please see Figure 10). The *QuerySplit* application takes a text file as a parameter, which contains query sequences of variable length. It then proceeds to analyze the file and create several smaller files, each containing a number of queries so that the overall size of all the files is as close to each other as possible. This application is used by the second application called Dynamic BLAST, a master-worker type application (Afgan et al., 2006) (please see Figure 11 and Figure 12). Dynamic BLAST is a custom-built application intended to maximize the use of small, distributed, readily available resources found in the grid to minimize the time needed to perform BLAST searches (Altschul et al., 1990). It uses established grid protocols for communication and task coordination while the custom scheduler handles task allocation and data transfers. The final application for this chapter is a parallel implementation of matrix-matrix multiplication using Cannon's algorithm (Cannon, 1969) (please see Figure 13 and Figure 14). Figure 9 illustrates relationships between application categories, applications, and corresponding ASL documents.

ASL is a schema and tag driven language enabling a new type of communication between heterogeneous grid resources. As indicated earlier by Figure 3, ASL enables capturing of application developer specific information and subsequent communication between other existing languages.

Figure 9. Relationship between application categories, applications and shown ASL documents

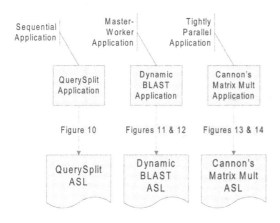

In this context, the information that needs to be communicated is the information that can be compared to information already existing in other, currently available languages. In the grid environment, the goal of such information is to mitigate inherent heterogeneity of underlying resources, and thus the information needs to be capable of representing individual components of communicating systems that are the cause of this heterogeneity.

ASL Document Snippets

This section provides selected snippets with essential parts of the application descriptions outlining the capabilities of ASL to capture application information and how dependencies can be drawn between applications, software packages and required libraries.

Figure 10 is an example of a complete ASL *JobInvocationSection* for the *QuerySplit* application described in the previous section. This description starts off by capturing all the basic application run-time information (lines 2 through 9), such as the application invocation method, the minimum amount of memory required for the application to run, as well as the minimum speed of a host CPU. The most significant part of the provided

example is to show how to describe an input file for an application. Lines 10 through 39 point out that the given application requires one input file to be provided in plain text (i.e., ASCII) and should be formatted according to the comments available in lines 17 through 33. In particular, lines 18 and 19 indicate that the properties input file must contain two plain text fields with user name and job name, respectively, followed by a pointer to another input file. The format of the contained input file is described as being in FASTA format (FASTA, 2006) whose sample is also provided in the *format* tag. The tags used for capturing necessary information (e.g., text) map favorably to individual components of a job submission interface (e.g., HTML). By analyzing the available tags and provided information, enough details are available to fully automate creation of a job submission interface by a higher level tool with items such as text boxes, radio buttons and drop-down menus with entries predefined in the ASL document. Through this approach, an application-specific job submission interface can be generated directly from the application description, thus properly directed by an application developer rather than an application deployer.

Figure 11 provides an example of how an application developer can provide all the available values for a selected application invocation option, even within an input file. The XML snippet describes an application's single input file argument options. These are listed in lines 8 through 15, which limit the user's choice to any single value when invoking the application. This is an additional example of how ASL information can be applied in dual context for automated interface generation denoting that this information belongs to a single list and can be organized into a radio button group.

Figure 12 is a continuation of the ASL document for a Dynamic BLAST application. This snippet highlights the application, library, and software dependencies that Dynamic BLAST depends on or requires. As can be seen from the

Figure 10. ASL document snippet showing Job Invocation Section for the QuerySplit application

```
1.    <asl:JobInvocationRequirements>
2.    <asl:ExecutableName>QuerySplit</asl:ExecutableName>
3.    <asl:ExecutionInstructions>Usage:  perl QuerySplit propertieFile
      </asl:ExecutionInstructions>
4.    <asl:PhysicalMemory>
5.    <asl:LowerBoundedRange>5.0</asl:LowerBoundedRange>
6.    </asl:PhysicalMemory>
7.    <asl:IndividualCPUSpeed>
8.    <asl:LowerBoundedRange>200.0</asl:LowerBoundedRange>
9.    </asl:IndividualCPUSpeed>
10.   <asl:InputFiles>
11.    <asl:NumberOfInputFiles>1</asl:NumberOfInputFiles>
12.    <asl:InputFile>
13.     <asl:Name>PropertiesFile</asl:Name>
14.     <asl:Required>true</asl:Required>
15.     <asl:Description>Job properties file whose format is described below.
        </asl:Description>
16.     <asl:FileType>ASCII</asl:FileType>
17.     <asl:Format>
18.      <asl:Text required="1">userName</asl:Text>
19.      <asl:Text required="1">jobName</asl:Text>
20.      <asl:InputFile>
21.        <asl:Name>queryInputFileName</asl:Name>
22.        <asl:Required>true</asl:Required>
23.        <asl:Description>This input file is submitted as part of the properties
24.        input file. A query input file in FASTA format containing at least one
25.        query.</asl:Description>
26.        <asl:FileType>FASTA</asl:FileType>
27.        <asl:Format>
28.        >gi|5524211|gb|AAD44166.1| cytochrome b (Elephas maximus maximus)
29.         LCLYTHIGRNIYYGSYLYSETWNTGIMLLLITMATAFMGYVLPWGQ
30.         MSFWGATVITNLFSAIPYIGTNLVEWIWGGFSVDKATLNRFFAFHFIL
31.         PFTMVALAGVHLTFLHETGSNNPLGLTSDSDKIPFHPYYTIKDFLGLL
32.        </asl:Format>
33.      </asl:InputFile>
34.      <asl:Text required="0">totalNumFragments</asl:Text>
35.     </asl:Format>
36.     <asl:SizeLimit><asl:UpperBound>0.1</asl:UpperBound></asl:SizeLimit>
37.    </asl:InputFile>
38.   </asl:InputFiles>
39.   </asl:JobInvocationRequirements>
```

Figure 11. Job Invocation Section of ASL for Dynamic BLAST application showing input file options

```
1.    ...
2.    <asl:InputFiles>
3.     <asl:NumberOfInputFiles>1</asl:NumberOfInputFiles>
4.     <asl:InputFile>
5.      <asl:Name>PropertiesFile</asl:Name>
6.      ...
7.      <asl:List>
8.       <asl:Radio>
9.        <asl:lText>blastp</asl:lText>
10.       <asl:lText>blastn</asl:lText>
11.       <asl:lText>blastx</asl:lText>
12.       <asl:lText>tblastn</asl:lText>
13.       <asl:lText>tblastx</asl:lText>
14.       <asl:lText>psiblastpn</asl:lText>
15.      </asl:Radio>
16.     </asl:List>
17.     ...
18.    </asl:InputFile>
19.    ...
20.   </asl:InputFiles>
```

Figure 12. Job Invocation Section of ASL for Dynamic BLAST application showing application, library, and software dependencies

```
1.   <asl:ApplicationsRequired>
2.       <asl:ApplicationRequired>
3.           <asl:Name>GridWay</asl:Name>
4.           <asl:Version>5.0+</asl:Version>
5.       </asl:ApplicationRequired>
6.       <asl:ApplicationRequired>
7.           <asl:Name>QuerySplit</asl:Name>
8.           <asl:Version>1.0</asl:Version>
9.       </asl:ApplicationRequired>
10.  </asl:ApplicationsRequired>
11.  <asl:RequiredLibraries>
12.      <asl:RequiredLibrary>
13.          <asl:Name>org.ggf.drmaa.*</asl:Name>
14.      </asl:RequiredLibrary>
15.  </asl:RequiredLibraries>
16.  <asl:SoftwareDependencies>
17.      <asl:SoftwareDependency>
18.          <asl:Name>GlobusToolkit</asl:Name>
19.          <asl:Version>4.0.2+</asl:Version>
20.      </asl:SoftwareDependency>
21.      <asl:SoftwareDependency>
22.          <asl:Name>java</asl:Name>
23.          <asl:Version>1.5+</asl:Version>
24.      </asl:SoftwareDependency>
25.  </asl:SoftwareDependencies>
```

Figure 13. Job Invocation Section of ASL for parallel matrix-matrix multiplication application showing and describing application invocation options and arguments

```
1.   <asl:ExecutableName>pmatmul</asl:ExecutableName>
2.   <asl:ExecutionInstructions>Usage: mpirun -np <numCPUs> pmatmul    <N> <P>
     <Q> <flag> </numCPUs>
3.   </asl:ExecutionInstructions>
4.   <asl:Options>
5.     <asl:Option>
6.       <asl:Arguments>
7.         <asl:Argument>N</asl:Argument>
8.         <asl:Description>Matrix size. Works for square matrices
             only.</asl:Description>
9.       </asl:Arguments>
10.      <asl:Required>true</asl:Required>
11.    </asl:Option>
12.    <asl:Option>
13.      …
14.    </asl:Option>
```

Figure 14. Job Invocation Section of ASL for parallel matrix-matrix multiplication application showing ability of ASL to capture memory and network requirements

```
1.   <asl:PhysicalMemory>
2.       <asl:Formula>5*N^2/sqrt(P)</asl:Formula>
3.   </asl:PhysicalMemory>
4.   <asl:Network>
5.       <asl:Type>single</asl:Type>
6.   </asl:Network>
7.   <asl:CPUCount>
8.       <asl:LowerBoundedRange>2.0</asl:LowerBoundedRange>
9.   </asl:CPUCount>
```

XML, a Dynamic BLAST application depends on being able to correctly invoke two other applications, namely GridWay (Huedo et al., 2004) and *QuerySplit*, whose description was provided in Figure 10. This idea, although simple to comprehend, has a significant potential in terms of application dependency visualization and installation tools. Through the use of this formalized method of declaring direct dependencies, much automation can be achieved. The remainder of the application description, shown in lines 11 through 15, indicates that Dynamic BLAST requires a specified library. Finally, lines 16 through 25 denote other software packages required to run Dynamic BLAST.

Figure 13 also shows the job invocation section of a parallel matrix-matrix multiplication. Line 3 specifies the format of the invocation command with several options. Lines 5 through 11 point out the necessary details about the first argument (e.g., description, whether it is required or optional). The remainder of the argument descriptions is omitted for brevity, but the information provided shows the ability of ASL to structurally and formally capture such information while allowing the user enough freedom to describe each of the arguments at the desired level of detail.

Finally, Figure 14 points out two more interesting points supported by ASL. Lines 4 through 6 deal with network requirements. Because this application is an example of a tightly coupled parallel application, the communication patterns are frequent throughout the algorithm iterations and thus the message passing requires the existence of a fast-speed, local network. Although this requirement can be built into an ASL definition and made a default requirement for all applications of this type, advances in message-passing technologies are enabling the communication to take place across administrative domains (e.g., MPICH-G2 (Karonis et al., 2003)), which would make this a possible hindrance to future applications. To avoid this limitation, the network

type tag accepts "single" as its value denoting this application can be executed only on a local network, limited to a single resource. There are other possibilities here, but these options would all require relationships to be made between parts of an ASL document. The final interesting feature found in this part of the sample ASL document is the use of formulas as part of the application description (line 2). This information can be used by a scheduler when the input data is already known to perform not only application-specific but also data-specific scheduling.

Application of ASL Documents

The previous section provided an overview of ASL, its schema, and its sample use for various application categories. The examples demonstrated the capability of ASL to capture needed information as well as provide concrete samples for its creation. The use, possibilities, extensions, and limitation of the language will be explored over time as its use becomes more widespread and tools emerge. Some examples of possible functionality and tools that can make use of ASL, either by complementing existing technologies or enabling new ones, are outlined in the *Future Trends* section of this chapter. In addition, this section introduces several projects with different goals and how adoption of ASL would improve them.

GridBench (Tsouloupas & Dikaiakos) is a project that focuses on providing a core set of benchmarks that characterize grid resources. Use of such benchmarks allows prediction of performance and scalability of compositions of applications on desired systems. The proposed framework supports collecting, archiving, and publishing collected data. The goal of GridBench is to provide a collection of kernels representative of applications and application categories that can be used to benchmark and characterize components that affect performance of applications and resources, allowing comparisons to be made. Use of ASL in this context to describe applications and subsequently include performance information into an ASL document enables automated sharing of performance associated with individual application and resources. Additional projects similar to GridBench that could use ASL are STAPL (Thomas et al., 2005), Prophesy (Taylor et al., 2000), and application performance predictors such as Downey (1997), Gibbons (1997) and Smith, Foster and Taylor (1998).

GridWay (Montero, Huedo, & Llorente, 2006) aims at supporting the "submit and forget" ideology where the user is abstracted from the grid middleware details by supporting easier and more efficient job execution on the grid. GridWay works on top of the Globus Toolkit and provides a job manager-like interface for its user where a job can be submitted, status checked, and results retrieved. Use of ASL in this context is broad and could include enablement of application-specific information to be presented to the user when selecting among several applications to execute, matching of performance of selected application to available resources, as well as fully automating application invocation parameters and options. Additional examples of grid resource brokers that could benefit from ASL in similar ways as GridWay include Nimrod/G and its parametric job description language (Steen, 2004), Condor-G (Frey, Tannenbaum, Foster, Livny, & Tuecke, 2001) and incorporation of ASL into ClassAds.

The dynamic nature of workflow systems demands the need for Grid services to be automatically generated according to the execution environment and resources available for execution. GridDeploy (Guan, Velusamy, & Bangalore, 2005) is a toolkit for automatically deploying applications as Grid services, and providing the necessary infrastructure for other applications to invoke them. Integration of ASL into GridDeploy would enable more streamlined generation of needed services because ASL provides needed

descriptions of applications and corresponding performance on various resources. Use of standardized protocols to combine information available in ASL along with information from JSDL and MDS can enable user and job-oriented service composition by tools such as GridDeploy.

MODELING WIZARDS TO GENERATE ASL

There are several accidental complexities that emerge when using XML as a specification language. For example, an XML file is embodied as linear text, which makes it difficult to capture hierarchical structures that are shared across a document. To represent hierarchy, it is often the case that an XML document contains multiple links to other parts of the document. This reduces the comprehensibility of the XML document because it requires the user to search through the whole file for the desired section link. This becomes unfeasible as the size of the XML file grows. Furthermore, the extensive tags that delineate the sections of an XML document make it very verbose, which introduces another degree for error in terms of the syntactical correctness of the document. In essence, XML serves as an excellent machine readable format due to its formal structure, but has many limitations as a human-centered language. This section introduces the approach we adopted that allows an end-user to specify properties about their grid application from higher level abstractions using a graphical modeling language. These models serve as input to a translator that assists in generating the ASL specification. An overview of domain-specific modeling is presented in the next section, followed by a description of a modeling language that generates wizards for extracting information required in an ASL specification.

Domain-Specific Modeling: Reducing the Effects of Platform Dependency

Model-driven Engineering (MDE) (Schmidt, 2006) represents a design approach that enables description of the essential characteristics of an application in a manner that is decoupled from the details of a specific technology (e.g., dependence on specific middleware or programming language). Domain-Specific Modeling (DSM) (Gray, Tolvanen, Kelly, Gokhale, Neema, & Sprinkle, 2007) is an MDE methodology that generates customized modeling languages and environments from metamodels that define a narrow domain of interest. In this context, a model corresponds to an abstraction whose concrete syntax is rendered in a graphical iconic notation that assists domain experts in constructing a problem description using concepts familiar to them. A model compiler can be associated with a specific modeling language to generate different artifacts (e.g., source code or deployment files) from a model. DSM has been shown to offer specific technical advantages in supporting rapid evolution of computer-based systems when the hardware and software configuration is tightly coupled and must frequently evolve to a new configuration schema (e.g., retooling an automotive factory (Long et al., 1998), or reconfiguring an avionics product-line (Gray, Lin, & Zhang, 2006)).

A benefit of DSM is the ability to describe properties of a system at a high-level of abstraction and in a platform-independent notation, which protects key intellectual assets from technology obsolescence. Initial research in DSM offers a contribution to end-user programming by supporting experts who may not have software development skills (e.g., physicists and avionics engineers) with a visual notation for expressing domain concepts in a specific *problem space*; thus, hiding the accidental complexities of using a general-purpose programming language. In DSM, models and model transformations are first-class

entities in the development process and represent the initial point for generation of low-level details in the *solution space*.

The goal of providing new language abstractions appropriate to the specific programming task and user has been a common objective of language researchers for several decades (Floyd, 1979) and shares a common vision with another new approach called intentional programming (Simonyi, Christerson, & Clifford, 2006). Furthermore, the DSM philosophy of narrowly defined modeling languages can be contrasted with larger standardized modeling languages, such as the UML, which are fixed and whose size and complexity (France, Ghosh, & Dinh-Trong, 2006) provide abstractions that may not be needed in every domain, adding to the confusion of domain experts. The concept of "little languages" (Bentley, 1986), or similarly named Domain-specific Languages (DSLs) (Deursen, Klint, & Visser, 2000; Wile, 2004), share the same intent of DSM, but with different concrete syntax (i.e., DSLs are typically textual languages rather than graphical).

The Generic Modeling Environment (GME) (Balasubramanian, Gokhale, Karsai, Sztipanovits, & Neema, 2006) is the metamodeling tool that we used in our approach to DSM. The next sections present our use of the GME to provide a modeling language that generates wizards for constructing an ASL specification.

ASL Wizard Metamodel

The use of a higher level graphical modeling language to create ASL specifications consists of constructing the necessary modeling elements describing an application and filling in the parameters that describe the corresponding application feature. This method would help to remove many of the errors in formatting an ASL document to ensure that the document was created correctly (i.e., the application developer would be alleviated of a lot of typing and checking the correctness of XML tags). However, ASL is a language that has a one-to-one mapping between a value and tag pair (i.e., XML tag and the associated value). Because of this, the benefits of adopting a modeling language specifically for ASL are minimized. We realized that a much more significant improvement could be offered by guiding a user in creating an ASL document through wizards. The subsequent challenge became the specific technique to generate the implementation of the wizard.

Depending on the application type, entire element sets available in ASL may not make sense for a particular application. Non-savvy users may find themselves overwhelmed with the number of available options when creating such a document, resulting in slower acceptance or rejection of the ASL. There is a need to ease this transition and provide tools enabling quick and guided creation of such documents. Unfortunately, due to the need to have many possible variations of individual wizards to handle different application categories and variations within these categories, a single wizard would fail to accommodate all the needs. Generating many wizards is prohibitive due to the possibly large number of wizard variations, as well as their temporary lifespan. To accommodate for these variable needs, we have realized a method to generate custom wizards using high-level, domain-specific models. The approach considers the desired components found in ASL and connects them into a meaningful event-driven workflow.

The result is a customized wizard that assists in creating a complete ASL document. Figure 15 shows the generation pipeline: a metamodel defines the wizard modeling language, from which specific instance configurations are created; from the instance models, the specific wizard is created (either in HTML, or some other technology); the generated wizards then create the corresponding ASL based on the user response to the wizard interaction.

There are two levels of indirection that are illustrated in Figure 15. The first level is specified in the instance models, which describe the essential elements of each wizard page and the control flow (CF) between each page based on user interaction. The instance models must handle creation of objects composing the wizard being generated and must also process all of the possible choices available to adjust the control flow of the wizard. The second level of indirection is built into the generated wizard pages. The wizards are responsible for the actual generation of the ASL document. The control flow captured by the wizards must format the output of an ASL document and store the necessary data in the ASL document. The wizards must also pass any needed information among the wizard pages. To summarize, there are two levels of generation: the generation of wizard pages from the instance models, and the generation of ASL from the wizards; in essence,

Figure 15. Three-level modeling stack used to generate ASL

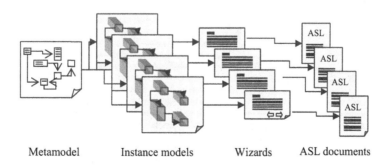

Metamodel   Instance models   Wizards   ASL documents

the process represents a generator of a generator, a unique concept within the area of DSM.

Figure 16 is a diagram showing the possible branching of the wizard pages depending on the user input. The first key observation is the possibility of any single page to be used at multiple levels of the wizard by several parent pages. The second observation is the number of required locations where automatic handling of the control flow and ASL document generation must take place. The model must allow the user accessibility and connectivity to individual pages between different stages of the wizard. This is handled through multiple levels of wizard generation within the model where the same level pages are all viewed on the same aspect within GME. Connections are allowed to be made between compatible objects at appropriate levels through the use of constraints. Connections between individual pages are then made accordingly by the user. The difficulty raised by this approach is the size of the instance model as well as the multiplicity of possible connections resulting in an instance model that is difficult to comprehend. The major obstacle

in change adoption and correct execution of the composed wizard comes from the fact that the generator needs to be capable of handling multiple instances of control flow. Each connection that is made at the instance model level must be handled automatically by the generator to provide correct execution flow. Beyond making static connections between wizard pages, additional code must be generated that is model-specific and corresponds to the choices the user is presented at each stage of the wizard.

Generating a Wizard

To highlight the challenges involved in constructing the ASL-driven wizards, this section provides a short scenario to illustrate the multiple levels of control the models must represent. From the perspective of the model user, the elements provided by the modeling language (i.e., the constructs defined in the metamodel) correspond to portions of an ASL document. These are classified as individual components ranging from high-level components (e.g., an entire job invocation section)

Figure 16. Wizard flow showing multiplicity of generated wizard pages and control flow (CF) at each junction as the ASL document is being generated

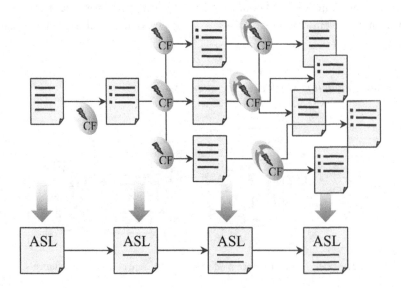

down to low-level components (e.g., tags such as the application executable name). The iconic representation of these modeling elements, as viewed from a user perspective, are shown in Figure 17.

The end-user is considered to be the domain expert who helps create a model representing the wizard control flow. This is the first difficult task to be handled by the metamodel and subsequently the code generator within the model compiler. The challenge arises from the need for the connections to be made between wizard pages when the initial wizard code is generated, as well as the additional code that needs to be incorporated to handle user choices. This implies that group components that exist in the metamodel (that correspond to equivalent structures in the ASL), such as a drop down menu with many options, must be decomposed into individual pieces and conditional connections made to subsequent pages of the wizard from each of these options. This presents an inherent burden on the model user due to the large number of possible combinations as well as coordination of model layering where complying pages can be reused. The solution is found in the composition of ASL wizard pages. Instead of coupling all of the ASL sections onto a single page, the wizard and corresponding pages can be split into a form. As such, the scope of the ASL is reduced, thus limiting the number of elements, connections and choices the user must consider in the model. The downside to this solution is that equivalent pages within the wizard may belong to a different scope and cannot be reused. Because the division is starting from the most general concepts and progressing into more detailed elements of an ASL document, this behavior should be minimized.

Figure 18 shows the skeleton of a typical ASL document with the indication of the necessary connections at this level for the generating wizard. The top-down scoping of the wizard can also be seen in this figure. Because the goal of the project is to simplify ASL generation, individual sections of the model (and thus wizard) directly map to the resulting ASL document. After a given layer of the wizard is fully generated (as shown in Figure 18), the user can provide further details on each individual section. This is accomplished by double-clicking the desired section (i.e., GME model) and opening a new set of model options. This step can be seen in Figure 19 where further details of the *ApplicationDescription* section are provided. The components used at this level map directly to the interface of the generated wizard (except the *Category* section, which is a model

Figure 17. Available model components describing ASL wizard pages

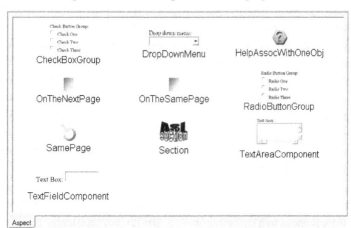

Figure 18. Model view of an ASL document skeleton

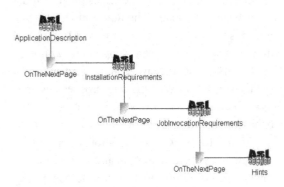

Figure 19. The details of the Application Description element set

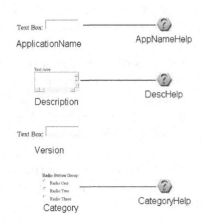

requiring individual elements to be provided by accessing the lower layer). This is primarily an example of a two-layer composition where wizard interface components were provided immediately, although additional layers could also be created requiring more pages and connections to be made, as they map to the appropriate page.

The model compiler that performs the transformation from the model to the generated wizards is presented with a challenge to deliver the requested code among the possible variations. This considerably complicates the code generator within the model compiler. The most difficult part of developing the metamodel and model compiler is the control flow component of the wizard where the connecting pages of the wizard must execute additional connection point code to handle storage and passing of the necessary information between wizard pages. The method of message passing is not defined by the user but rather implied by the generated model. This logic must be customized to the particular wizard and be completely transparent to the end-user. Beyond making the necessary connections at the page level, the generator must be capable of composing necessary code, including page scoping.

To illustrate this idea, a sample workflow can be followed: Upon generation of the wizard, a user instantiates it and provides some data to the wizard. The wizard advances to a subsequent page where the user is asked for more data, this page may branch off into several possible pages, and so forth. Selection of the subsequent page is determined from a user's input at run-time. As each page may branch into multiple subsequent pages, and even though the paths to individual pages may differ, some of the pages may be equivalent in context. At each step of the wizard, control flow code logic must be provided by the wizard generator to accommodate for this variability and workflow coordination. In addition, the code for data storage that incrementally constructs the resulting ASL document must be generated by the wizard.

We have written a model compiler that generates HTML to represent the wizard pages. This model compiler creates and formats the necessary HTML forms for each wizard page. The compiler also generates the control flow and how the data is passed between each wizard page (i.e., using CGI POST, GET). As the ASL document is being created from multiple levels within the wizard, an additional concern is the correctness of the created document with respect to the generation of proper tags for each ASL element. As discussed in the previous section, ASL contains tags that are lexicographically equivalent. If the tags are

Figure 20. Sample page of generated wizard to collect initial application information

placed outside of the correct context, an application interpreting the ASL specification would not be able to disambiguate the ASL. All of these difficulties must be handled in a generic manner within the generated code to accommodate the numerous permutations that may arise. A sample HTML-based wizard can be seen in Figure 20. The generated HTML page is part of the wizard and has been automatically created by the model compiler. The HTML is generated by the *ApplicationDescription* section of the model presented in Figure 18 and Figure 19. Each of the individual components has properties associated with them; thus, the ordering and layering of the wizard is based on the ordering property provided by the user when creating an instance model. Each of the components can also have help information, which appears as a text balloon in the generated wizard.

We have found that describing an application from a higher level of abstraction reduces the learning curve for a new technology such as ASL, but it has drawbacks in that it requires a new tool to be added in the repertoire of an application developer. The only related tool that

accomplishes a similar idea of composing wizards from a higher level specification targets the .Net platform and generates MS Windows forms wizards (Actipro, 2006). However, integration of interoperable tools that share a single interface can advance the productivity of a software developer. An example is the Grid Automation and Generative Environment (GAUGE) (Hernandez et al., 2006), which also reduces accidental complexities of grid development through adoption of DSM. Because the development process within GAUGE takes place within GME, its extension to include concepts introduced by ASL represents a possible integration opportunity. By incorporating and extending an intelligent agent used for the application development process, data can also be extracted automatically to populate sections of the corresponding ASL document, thus reducing the work required by the application developer. The integration with GAUGE represents future work that can ease the path of ASL adoption.

FUTURE TRENDS

As the general adoption of the grid moves from the research labs and campus infrastructures into mainstream industry (with the goal of offering high-levels of Quality of Service), many components (in terms of pervasive availability, secure use of systems, and seamless access) must still be provided. Many of the individual components and additional functionalities are being addressed by many researchers. The following is a list of research issues and further advancements that remain open in the context of this chapter as it fits into the larger picture of the grid:

- The initial schema and corresponding ASL documents have been constructed to ensure the language is capable of representing applications. The ASL schema should also be able to define individual components that comprise an application. The differences between two applications should also be discernable from the respective ASL specifications. Many more applications need to be described with the goal of adjusting the ASL schema to address new application categories.

- Publicizing the benefits of the ASL is necessary to promote adoption by the wider grid community. The current focus considers the standardization of the ASL within the Open Grid Forum. This is following a standardization path similar to JSDL.

- Additional tools are required to promote generation of ASL, such as the modeling approach described in this chapter.

- Tools that make use of ASL are of significant importance. Many tools can be adapted to make use of ASL documents but standardization is required before these actions can take place. Examples of such tools include the following:

  ° *Application information services* (AIS), which represent a suite of services where registration, discovery, and monitoring of an application could take place at the level of a VO. Through a set of interfaces, the users would be able to discover services and applications, and obtain help documentation.

  ° *Automated HTML application help generator,* which would be an application to interpret ASL documents and generate application-related information. This can be as simple as a static Web page being generated as the default help documentation or a more advanced on-demand search-and-match custom page generation based on user queries of problem identification to include the latest available information.

  ° *GridRPM,* would be an application to take advantage of installation and dependency information available through the mesh of ASL documents

(as available in AIS) and automatically construct descriptor files before proceeding with automatic application installation and deployment.

  ° *Grid scheduler applications* could utilize the ASL information to perform application-specific scheduling without the need to keep historical application execution data.

  ° *Accounting and software license accountability* is an area of the grid currently in its initial stages but will advance quickly in response to the high demand of grid services from industry. This area provides a vast number of options where relevant information can be stored into ASL documents and later used through automated billing and license verification.

CONCLUSION

This chapter provides an overview of developing intensive software applications in a grid computing environment along with the taxonomy of grid users. For each user category the specific responsibilities, roles, and requirements were described. A sample application scenario was provided to illustrate the interaction required among the different user categories and the grid middleware. The functionality provided by the grid middleware to accomplish the successful deployment of the sample scenario was presented and difficulties with the current solutions were also outlined. To further illustrate the complexity involved in deploying grid applications, the grid applications were categorized into seven major categories. For each deployment category the various steps involved in the deployment process were discussed. It was noted that there is no support currently available for the application developer category to describe the requirements and capabilities of an application. In order to accommodate this need, a new language was presented–the Application Specification Language (ASL)–that supports the description of applications in a grid environment. Examples outlining the capabilities of ASL were provided using the sample application scenario. Finally, the chapter described a supporting modeling language for generating ASL documents from a higher level specification, which minimizes the effort of an application developer and deployer.

ASL enables the application developer to describe the application requirements and capabilities. Using domain-specific modeling for the creation of ASL documents reduces some of the accidental complexities encountered in the grid application development and deployment process. Metamodeling techniques could be further extended to provide additional tools for applying information available in ASL to other areas of grid computing (e.g., automated user interface generation for job registration, submission, and monitoring). The work presented here takes a bottom-up approach to solving some of the problems in information availability and standardization between grid entities (e.g., applications, users, and resources) in the heterogeneous environment. Through the adoption of technology presented here, individual pieces within a complex grid system can communicate through a common language and at the appropriate level of granularity permitting context-controlled information delivery in a range or formats. Overall adoption of the domain-specific modeling ideas into the area of grid computing as an effective tool to leverage some of the grid-inherent difficulties may result in shorter application development and deployment times by reducing complexity and expertise required.

ACKNOWLEDGMENT

This was supported in part by an NSF CAREER award (CCF-0643725).

REFERENCES

Aalst, W. V. D., & Hee, K. V. (2002). *Workflow management: Models, methods, and systems.* Cambridge, MA: The MIT Press.

Actipro. (2006). *Actipro wizard - Wizard Generation.NET framework windows forms control.* Retrieved March 23, 2008, from http://www.actiprosoftware.com/Products/DotNet/WindowsForms/Wizard/Default.aspx

Afgan, E. (2004). Role of the resource broker in the grid. In Proceedings of the *42nd Annual ACM Southeast Conference,* (pp. 299-300). Huntsville, AL: ACM Press.

Afgan, E., & Bangalore, P. (2007). Application specification language (ASL)–a language for describing applications in grid computing. In *Proceedings of the 4th International Conference on Grid Services Engineering and Management - GSEM 2007,* Leipzig, Germany.

Afgan, E., Sathyanarayana, P., & Bangalore, P. (2006). Dynamic task distribution in the grid for BLAST. In *Proceedings of Granular Computing 2006,* (pp. 554-557). Atlanta, GA: IEEE.

Allcock, B., Bester, J., Bresnahan, J., Chervenak, A. L., Foster, I., Kesselman, C., et al. (2001). Data management and transfer in high-performance computational grid environments. *Parallel Computing, 28*(5), 749-771.

Allen, G., Davis, K., Goodale, T., Hutanu, A., Kaiser, H., Kielmann, T., et al. (2005). The grid application toolkit: Toward generic and easy application programming interfaces for the grid. *Proceedings of the IEEE, 93*(3), 534-550.

Altschul, S. F., Gish, W., Miller, W., Myers, E. W., & Lipman, D. J. (1990). Basic local alignment search tool. *Mol Biol, 215*(3), 403-410.

Anjomshoaa, A., Brisard, F., Drescher, M., Fellows, D., Ly, A., McGough, S., et al. (2005). *Job submission description language (JSDL) specification, version 1.0* (Tech. Rep. No. GFD-R.056). Global Grid Forum (GGF).

Armstrong, R., Gannon, D., Geist, A., Keahey, K., Kohn, S., McInnes, L., et al. (1999). Toward a common component architecture for high-performance scientific computing. In *Proceedings of the High-Performance Distributed Computing Conference (HPDC),* (pp. 115-124). Redondo Beach, CA: IEEE Computer Society.

Balasubramanian, K., Gokhale, A., Karsai, G., Sztipanovits, J., & Neema, S. (2006). Developing applications using model-driven design environments. *IEEE Computer, 39*(2), 33-40.

Baru, C., Moore, R., Rajasekar, A., & Wan, M. (1998). The SDSC storage resource broker. In *Proceedings of CASCON '98,* (pp.). Toronto, Canada: IBM Press.

Bentley, J. (1986). Little languages. *Communications of the ACM, 29*(8), 711-721.

Berman, F., Chien, A., Cooper, K., Dongarra, J., Foster, I., Gannon, D., et al. (2001). The GrADS project: Software support for high-level grid application development. *International Journal of High Performance Computing Applications, 15*(4), 327-344.

Berman, F., Fox, G., & Hey, T. (2003a). The grid: Past, present, future. In F. Berman, G. Fox, & T. Hey (Eds.), *Grid computing--making the global infrastructure a reality* (pp. 9-51). Hoboken, NJ: John Wiley & Sons.

Berman, F., Hey, A., & Fox, G. (Eds.). (2003b). *Grid computing: Making the global infrastructure a reality.* New York: John Wiley & Sons.

Buyya, R., Abramson, D., & Giddy, J. (2000). Nimrod-G: An architecture for a resource management and scheduling in a global computational grid. In *Proceedings of the 4th International Conference and Exhibition on High Performance Computing in Asia-Pacific Region (HPC ASIA 2000),* (pp. 283-289). Beijing, China: IEEE CS Press.

Cannon, L. (1969). *A cellular computer to implement the Kalman Filter Algorithm.* Bozeman, MT: Montana State University.

Casanova, H., Obertelli, G., Berman, F., & Wolski, R. (2000). The AppLeS parameter sweep template: User-level middleware for the grid. *Supercomputing 2000.* Dallas, TX: IEEE Computer Society.

Chase, N. (2005). *Grid-enable an existing Java technology application*: IBM. Retrieved March 23, 2008, from http://www.ibm.com/developerworks/edu/gr-dw-gr-javagrid-i.html

Czajkowski, K., Fitzgerald, S., Foster, I., & Kesselman, C. (2001). Grid information services for distributed resource sharing. In *Proceedings of the 10th IEEE Symposium on High Performance Distributed Computing (HPDC),* (pp. 181-195). Los Alamitos, CA: IEEE Computer Society.

Czajkowski, K., Foster, I., Kesselman, C., Martin, S., Smith, W., & Tuecke, S. (1998). A resource management architecture for metacomputing systems. In *Proceedings of the IPPS/SPDP Workshop on Job Scheduling Strategies for Parallel Processing,* (pp. 62-82). Springer-Verlag.

Deursen, A. V., Klint, P., & Visser, J. (2000). Domain-specific languages: An annotated bibliography. *ACM SIGPLAN Notices, 35*(6), 26-36.

Downey, A. (1997). Predicting queue times on space-sharing parallel computers. In *Proceedings of the International Parallel Processing Symposium (IPPS '97),* (pp. 209-218). Geneva, Switzerland.

FASTA. (2006, December 4). *FASTA format.* Retrieved March 23, 2008, from http://en.wikipedia.org/wiki/Fasta

Floyd, R. (1979). The paradigms of programming. *Communications of the ACM, 22*(8), 455-460.

Forum, M. P. I. (1998). *MPI message-passing interface standard, version 2.0*. Retrieved March 23, 2008, from http://www.mpi-forum.org/docs/docs.html

Foster, I., & Kesselman, C. (1997). Globus: A metacomputing infrastructure toolkit. *International Journal of Supercomputer Applications, 11*(2), 115-128.

Foster, I., & Kesselman, C. (1999). The Globus toolkit. In I. Foster & C. Kesselman (Eds.), *The grid: Blueprint for a new computing infrastructure* (pp. 259-278). San Francisco: Morgan Kaufmann.

Foster, I., Kesselman, C., Nick, J., & Tuecke, S. (2002a). *The physiology of the grid: An open grid services architecture for distributed systems integration*. Global Grid Forum, Open Grid Service Infrastructure Working Group.

Foster, I., Kesselman, C., Tsudik, G., & Tuecke, S. (1998). A security architecture for computational grids. In *Proceedings of the 5th ACM Conference on Computer and Communication Security Conference,* (pp. 83-92). San Francisco: ACM Press.

Foster, I., Kesselman, C., & Tuecke, S. (2001). The anatomy of the grid. *Lecture Notes in Computer Science, 2150,* 1-28.

Foster, I., Voeckler, J., Wilde, M., & Zhao, Y. (2002b). Chimera: A virtual data system for representing, querying, and automating data derivation. In *Proceedings of the 14th International Conference on Scientific and Statistical Database Management (SSDBM'02),* (pp. 37-46). Edinburgh, Scotland.

France, R., Ghosh, S., & Dinh-Trong, T. (2006). Model-driven development using UML 2: Promises and pitfalls. *IEEE Computer (Special Issue on Model-Driven Engineering, 39*(2), 41-48.

Frey, J., Tannenbaum, T., Foster, I., Livny, M., & Tuecke, S. (2001). Condor-G: A computation management agent for multi-institutional grids. In *Proceedings of the IEEE Symposium on High Performance Distributed Computing (HPDC10),* (pp. 9). San Francisco, CA.

Gamma, E., Helm, R., Johnson, R., & Vlissides, J. (1994). *Design patterns: Elements of reusable object-oriented software*. Reading, MA: Addison-Wesley.

Gannon, D., Fox, G., Pierce, M., Plale, B., Laszewski, G. V., Severance, C., et al. (2003). *Grid portals: A scientist's access point for grid services*. Global Grid Forum (GGF).

Gemmill, J., & Bangalore, P. (2005). *UABGrid--a campus-wide distributed computational infrastructure*. Birmingham, AL: UAB. Retrieved March 23, 2008, from http://uabgrid.uab.edu/

Gibbons, R. (1997). A historical application profiler for use by parallel schedulers. *Lecture Notes in Computer Science, 1291,* 58-77.

Gottschalk, K., Graham, S., Kreger, H., & Snell, J. (2002). Introduction to Web services architecture. *IBM Systems Journal, 41*(2), 170-178.

Gray, J., Lin, Y., & Zhang, J. (2006). Automating change evolution in model-driven engineering. *IEEE Computer, 39*(2), 51-58.

Gray, J., Tolvanen, J. P., Kelly, S., Gokhale, A., Neema, S., & Sprinkle, J. (2007). Domain-specific modeling. In P. Fishwick (Ed.), *Handbook on dynamic system modeling* (1st ed.). CRC Press.

Grid, O. S. (2007, Januray 19). *Open science grid*. Retrieved March 23, 2008, from http://www.opensciencegrid.org/

GriPhyN. (2006, July 30). *GriPhyN--grid physics network*. Retrieved March 23, 2008, from http://www.griphyn.org/

Guan, Z., Velusamy, V., & Bangalore, P. (2005). GridDeploy: A toolkit for deploying applications as grid services. In *Proceedings of the Interna-*

tional Conference on Information Technology Coding and Computing, Las Vegas, NV.

Hernandez, F. A., Bangalore, P., Gray, J., Guan, Z., & Reilly, K. (2006). GAUGE: Grid automation and generative environment using domain engineering and domain modeling for drafting applications for the grid. *Concurrency and Computation: Practice & Experience, 18*(10), 1293-1316.

Huedo, E., Montero, R. S., & Llorente, I. M. (2004). A framework for adaptive execution on grids. *Journal of Software: Practice and Experience, 34*(7), 631-651.

IVDGL. (2006, July 30). *International virtual data grid laboratory.* Retrieved March 23, 2008, from http://www.ivdgl.org/

JSWG. (2007). *Job submission description language WG (JSDL-WG).* Retrieved March 23, 2008, from https://forge.gridforum.org/projects/jsdl-wg/

Karonis, N., Toonen, B., & Foster, I. (2003). MPICH-G2: A grid-enabled implementation of the message passing interface. *Journal of Parallel and Distributed Computing (JPDC), 63*(5), 551-563.

Kumar, V., Grama, A., Gupta, A., & Karypis, G. (1994). *Introduction to parallel computing: Design and analysis of algorithms.* Redwood City, CA: Benjamin/Cummings.

Laszewski, G. V., Foster, I., Gawor, J., & Lane, P. (2001). A Java commodity grid kit. *Concurrency and Computation: Practice and Experience, 13*(8-9), 643-662.

Letondal, C. (2000). A Web interface generator for molecular biology programs in Unix. *Bioinformatics, 17*(1), 73-82.

Litzkow, M., Livny, M., & Mutka, M. (1988). Condor--a hunter of idle workstations. In *Proceedings of the 8th International Conference of Distributed Computing Systems,* (pp. 104-111).

Massie, M. L., Chun, B. N., & Culler, D. E. (2004). The Ganglia distributed monitoring system: Design, Implementation, and Experience. *Parallel Computing, 30*(7), 817-840.

McConnell, S. (1996). *Rapid development* (1st ed.). Redmond, WA: Microsoft Press.

Momjian, B. (2000). *PostgreSQL: Introduction and concepts* (1st ed.): Pearson Education.

Montero, R. S., Huedo, E., & Llorente, I. M. (2006). Grid scheduling infrastructures based on the GridWay meta-scheduler. *IEEE Technical Committee on Scalable Computing (TCSC) Newsletter, 8*(2).

NEES. (2006, November 6). *Network for earthquake engineering simulation.* Retrieved March 23, 2008, from http://it.nees.org/

Novotny, J., Russell, M., & Wehrens, O. (2004). GridSphere: A portal framework for building collaborations. *Concurrency and Computation: Practice & Experience, 16*(5), 503-513.

OGF. (2007). *Open grid forum.* Retrieved March 23, 2008, from http://www.ogf.org

PPDG. (2006, July). *Particle physics data grid.* Retrieved March 23, 2008, from http://www.ppdg.net/

Schmidt, D. (2006). Model-driven engineering. *IEEE Computer, 39*(2), 25-32.

Simonyi, C., Christerson, M., & Clifford, S. (2006). Intentional software. *Object oriented programming systems languages and applications (OOPSLA),* (pp. 451-464). Portland, OR: ACM Press.

Smith, W., Foster, I., & Taylor, V. (1998). Predicting application run times using historical information. In *Proceedings of the Workshop on Job Scheduling Strategies for Parallel Processing,* (pp. 122-142). Springer-Verlag.

Solomon, M. (2004, May). *The ClassAd language reference manual.* Retrieved March 23, 2008, from http://www.cs.wisc.edu/condor/classad/refman/

Sotomayor, B., & Childers, L. (2005). *Globus toolkit: Programming Java services* (1st ed.). Morgan Kaufmann.

Steen, M. V. (2004). *Nimrod-G resource broker for service-oriented grid computing.* Retrieved March 23, 2008, from http://dsonline.computer.org/0107/departments/res0107_print.htm

Tanenbaum, A. S., & Steen, M. V. (2002). *Distributed systems: Principles and paradigms.* Prentice Hall.

Taylor, V., Wu, X., Geisler, J., Li, X., Lan, Z., Stevens, R., et al. (2000). Prophesy: An infrastructure for analyzing and modeling the performance of parallel and distributed applications. In *Proceedings of the High Performance Distributed Computing (HPDC) 2000,* Pittsburgh, PA, (pp. 302-303).

Thomas, M., Mock, S., Dahan, M., Mueller, K., Sutton, D., & Boisseau, J. (2001). The GridPort toolkit: A system for building grid portals. In *Proceedings of the Tenth IEEE International Symposium on High Performance Distributed Computing (HPDC),* (pp. 216-227). San Francisco: IEEE.

Thomas, N., Tanase, G., Tkachyshyn, O., Perdue, J., Amato, N., & Rauchwerger, L. (2005). A framework for adaptive algorithm selection in STAPL. In *Proceedings of the ACM SIGPLAN 2005 Symposium on Principles and Practices of Parallel Programming (PPoPP),* Chicago, IL.

Tsouloupas, G., & Dikaiakos, M. (2003). Grid-Bench: A tool for benchmarking grids. In *Proceedings of the 4th International Workshop on Grid Computing (Grid2003),* Phoenix, AZ, (pp. 60-67).

Ulrich, W. M. (2002). *Legacy systems: Transformation strategies* (1st ed.). Prentice Hall PTR.

Venugopal, S., Buyya, R., & Winton, L. (2005). A grid service broker for scheduling e-science applications on global data grids. *Journal of*

Concurrency and Computation: Practice and Experience, 18(6), 685-699.

Wall, L., Christiansen, T., & Orwant, J. (2000). *Programming Perl* (3rd ed., Vol. 2000). O'Reilly Media.

Wile, D. (2004). Lessons learned from real DSL experiments. *Science of Computer Programming, 51*(3), 265-290.

ADDITIONAL READING

Afgan, E., & Purushotham, B. (2007). Computation cost in grid computing environments. In *Proceedings of the First International Workshop on the Economics of Software and Computation in Conjunction with International Conference on Software Engineering (ICSE) 2007,* Minneapolis, MN, (pp. 9-13).

Batory, D. (2006). Multiple models in model-driven engineering, product lines, and metaprogramming. *IBM Systems Journal, 45*(3), 451-461.

Brooks, F. P. (1987). No silver bullet-essence and accidents of software. *IEEE Computer, 20*(4), 10-19.

Buyya, R., & Murshed, M. (2002). GridSim: A toolkit for the modeling and simulation of distributed resource management and scheduling for grid computing. *The Journal of Concurrency and Computation: Practice and Experience (CCPE), 14*(13-15), 1175-1220.

Cao, F., Bryant, B. R., Raje, R. R., Auguston, M., Olson, A. M., & Burt, C. C. (2005). A component assembly approach based on aspect-oriented generative domain modeling. *Electronic Notes in Theoretical Computer Science, 114,* 119-136.

Cunha, J. C., & Rana, O. F. (2005). *Grid computing: Software environments and tools* (1st ed.). Springer-Verlag.

Foster, I., & Kesselman, C. (1998). *The grid: Blueprint for a new computing infrastructure* (1st ed.). Morgan Kaufmann.

Hernandez, F., Bangalore, P., Gray, J., & Reilly, K. (2004). A graphical modeling environment for the generation of workflows for the Globus toolkit. In *Proceedings of the Workshop on Component Models and Systems for Grid Applications, 18th Annual ACM International Conference on Supercomputing,* Saint-Malo, France.

Hey, A. J. G., Papay, J., & Surridge, M. (2005). The role of performance engineering techniques in the context of the Grid. *Concurrency and Computation: Practice & Experience, 17*(2-4), 297-316.

Horst, J., Messina, E., Kramer, T., & Huang, H.-M. (1997). Precise definition of software component specifications. In *Proceedings of the 7th Symposium on Computer-Aided Control System Design (CACSD '97),* (pp. 145-150). Gent, Belgium.

Kiczales, G., Lamping, J., Mendhekar, A., Maeda, C., Lopes, C. V., Loingtier, J., et al. (1997). Aspect-oriented programming. In *Proceedings of the European Conference on Object-Oriented Programming (ECOOP),* (pp. 220-242). Jyvoskyla, Finland: Springer-Verlag.

Kra, D. (2004). *Six strategies for grid application enablement*: IBM. Retrieved March 23, 2008, from http://www.ibm.com/developerworks/grid/library/gr-enable/

Kurtev, I., Bézivin, J., Jouault, F., & Valduriez, P. (2006). Model-based DSL frameworks. In *Proceedings of the Companion of the 21st Annual ACM SIGPLAN Conference on Object-Oriented Programming, Systems, Languages, and Applications (OOPSLA),* Portland, OR, (pp. 602-616).

Nabrzyski, J., Schopf, J. M., & Weglarz, J. (2003). *Grid resource management: State of the art and future trends. International series in operations research & management science* (1st ed.). Springer-Verlag.

Silva, V. (2005). *Grid computing for developers (Programming Series)* (1st ed.). Charles River Media.

Sodhi, S., & Subhlok, J. (2005). Automatic construction and evaluation of performance skeletons. In *Proceedings of the 19th International Parallel and Distributed Processing Symposium (IPDPS '05),* Denver, CO, (p. 10).

Song, H., Liu, X., Jakobsen, D., Bhagwan, R., Zhang, X., Taura, K., et al. (2000). The MicroGrid: A scientific tool for modeling computational grids. In *Proceedings of the IEEE Supercomputing (SC 2000),* Dallas, TX.

Chapter XIV
A Framework for Understanding the Open Source Revolution[1]

Jeff Elpern
Software Quality Institute, Inc., USA

Sergiu Dascalu
University of Nevada–Reno, USA

ABSTRACT

Traditional software engineering methodologies have mostly evolved from the environment of proprietary, large-scale software systems. Here, software design principles operate within a hierarchical decision-making context. Development of banking, enterprise resource and complex weapons systems all fit this paradigm. However, another paradigm for developing software-intensive systems has emerged, the paradigm of open source software. Although from a traditional perspective open source projects might look like chaos, their real-world results have been spectacular. This chapter presents open source software development as a fundamentally new paradigm driven by economics and facilitated by new processes. The new paradigm's revolutionary aspects are explored, a framework for describing the massive impact brought about by the new paradigm is proposed, and directions of future research are outlined. The proposed framework's goals are to help the understanding of the open source paradigm as a new economic revolution and stimulate research in designing open source software.

INTRODUCTION

The *open source revolution* is having a dramatic impact on the computer industry. Web services based on open source technologies play a major role in the Internet. The Linux® operating system has achieved the dominant position within the embedded controller segment of the telecommunication industry. Recently, open source applications have passed Mac applications in penetration into the PC market. Why is this happening? Should

we be surprised? Is this a major, self-sustaining phenomenon? This chapter proposes a framework for understanding the open source revolution by identifying a number of market forces driving the revolution and placing these forces within historical perspective. From the birth of open source–the socialism of the GNU Manifesto–to the dominance of current Web services, we show that the open source revolution is a natural response, and part of a continuing effort by users to increase their returns from technology by controlling the market power of commercial software developers. The core argument is based on economics. As users pursue optimal economic returns of their software portfolios, they gravitate toward software solutions that limit the market power of commercial developers. An example of this is the movement toward more and more standards. The adoption of open source is a natural next step for users in the battle for the control of market power. Thus, the open source revolution is the current "front line" in the battle between software developers and users on how economic returns from technologies are allocated between the two. In addition, open source is shown to be a "disruptive technology" in the sense defined by Clayton Christensen in his "The Innovator's Dilemma" (Christensen, 2003). This market force explains the "why now?" issue. As the current commercial software leaders' effort for "sustaining technology innovations" exceeds the users' ability to absorb new features and power, the seeds for the entry of a disruptive technology are sowed. Open source software fits all three criteria for a disruptive technology, which are discussed in this chapter. The disruptive technology framework is also used to provide behavioral and economic models of personal and organizational participation in open source development and delivery. It is important to note that a sweeping paradigm shift like this–the shift from proprietary code to open source–always changes the faces of winners and losers and the processes and the economic models, and, thus, will affect everyone in the industry.

Many discussions on open source software center on questions about what this "new" and "strange" idea is about. How could free source code ever work, isn't its quality poor, and who would ever work on such a project? Yet the reality is that most computer users interact with open source technologies every day as Google, Yahoo and eBay all utilize open source software. Open source is a key component of the most dynamic segment of computing, the Internet. Almost 70% of Web page accesses are provided via the over 40 million Apache™ servers (Netcraft, 2005). This is a market share two and half times greater than the nearest commercial technology.

The dominance of open source Web servers is one example of a stealth *paradigm shift* (Kuhn, 1996) taking place and discussed in this chapter. And, let us make it clear that when we say *paradigm shift,* we are referring to the full scientific revolution concept[2] defined by Kuhn.

Kuhn said that all the powerful stakeholders of the old paradigm will resist and belittle the new paradigm. It is with this insight that we start the discussion of a new, powerful force present today within the technology market. From this view we will be able to understand how the excitement of ever-growing success within the open source community co-exists with the skepticism and hostility of the established software community. This is the classic, painful process of an old paradigm being replaced by a new paradigm.

WHAT IS THE OPEN SOURCE REVOLUTION?

Any discussion of the *open source revolution* needs to begin with the observation that open collaboration, open publishing of findings, and building on the breakthrough efforts of others are at the heart of the scientific process. Society emerged from the Dark Ages and has experienced a 400-year period of accelerating technological innovation using this process.

However, in the current climate of hyper-commercialization, ever-increasing amounts of research and innovation are closed-off in proprietary technology. The *open source* movement was born as a reaction to this trend and at its core is a return to the scientific method.

There is no question that the open source paradigm shift started as a social movement. However, it is our position that the open source paradigm has evolved and now economics is the driving force. Let us quickly look at this evolution.

Social Movement

We believe that the 1984 *"GNU Manifesto"* (Stallman, 1984) is the first articulation of an *Open Source* creed. Richard Stallman's almost religious reference to the *golden rule*[3], and how it dictates his developer behavior, launched the *Free Software* movement as a social issue.

Today the GNU Project (GNU, 2008) provides the majority of components of the wildly successful GNU/Linux distributions (usually just referred to as Linux).

The GNU initial position seemed to include both the ideas of free as in *freedom of use*–ability to acquire the source code, modify and redistribute– and free as in *no economic charge*. Over time the emphasis has moved to mainly focus on *freedom of use*. The legal license that enforces Stallman's vision–the GNU Public License (GPL)–defines freedom of use terms (more details are provided in the "Open Source Characteristics" section of this chapter). The GPL license is compatible with for-profit business models.

The Free Software movement is a precursor to the Open Source movement. It is hard to distinguish one from the other except at the philosophical level. Free Software is a social movement about equality, equity, and the return to the scientific method. Open Source focuses on the power of access (no vendor lock-in), limits on market power, and accommodations for prior source code intellectual property being packaged with open source.

Thus, our starting point for the *open source revolution* is more than 30 years ago. Open source, just like a Broadway star, has worked hard to become an instant success.

Collaborative Development

Although Stallman is usually associated with free software and the GPL license, his most stunning contribution may be the *Collaborative Development* process (Williams, 2002). The concept that loosely associated, widely dispersed developers could produce complex, high-quality software was first proved in the GNU project. This was a radical departure from the structured environment, central planning, and hierarchical managed software development processes of proprietary software projects.

Many see involvement with open source projects as a developer's hobby. However, hobbies build model airplanes not jet fighters. Something more that casual "hacking" is taking place. Collaborative development is a fundamental new process.

Today the Linux environment–a huge collection of kernel modules, operating system components and application packages–is developed and tested by thousands across the world without the rigid management hierarchy of corporate software development. Clearly something interesting is happening.

The open processes–including access to the source code–consistently extend the number and the diversity of direct contributors when compared with proprietary closed processes. The new paradigm includes "users as developers." Thus, the people most knowledgeable about requirements and usage are directly impacting the code. Research is starting to quantify the advantages of diversity in the open source software development and testing process (Bosio, Little, Strigini, & Newby, 2002).

Economics Driven

From the moment the GNU Project was started economics played a certain part. However, the *tipping point* (Gladwell, 2000) where massive adoption of Open Source is driven by economics seems to have happened with a series of publications by Raymond, including the "Cathedral and the Bazaar" (Raymond, 1999), providing insight into this new paradigm. Raymond's work provided the first framework for outsiders to understand how this new process could produce world-class technology.

We believe that the open source revolution has now moved from a social statement of individuals to a mainstream economic strategy of corporate technology users. Technology users view open source as a means of controlling the *market power* of software suppliers.

Corporate users purchase technology to generate economic value. The return to the user is the generated economic value less the cost of the technology. Thus, the greater is the market power (pricing power) of the software supplier, the less is the return to the user.

The graphic in Figure 1 shows the user's return increasing at various stages of "openness." The lowest return experienced by the user happens when a software developer has a completely closed product that does not adhere to any standards.

The user increases returns by imposing standards such as SQL for data base technology, Internet RFCs set by the IETF, or XML domain schemas. Each of these provides alternatives and thus reduces the market power of the software vendor.

Open source is the next step in *openness* after standards. Access to the source reduces dependency on a single vendor. This reduces the software vendor's market power, and the return to the user increases.

We believe there is a state beyond just access to source. In the *transparent state* all the informa-

tion a user needs to make an informed decision is available from the software developer. For example, all outstanding bugs are known, the prior rate of bug fixing is provided, all benchmarks are available, performance to development schedules is provided, and so forth.

Thus, the open source approach is a key strategy available to technology users desiring to increase returns by making software more of a commodity, thus reducing the market power of technology suppliers.

OPEN SOURCE CHARACTERISTICS

The open source revolution is a concept powered by a movement and protected by a legal structure. This section outlines the legal structure.

It is imperative to understand that open source code is different from public domain source code. Public domain software can be used in any way one wishes. Open source software always has a license that grants certain rights and imposes certain restrictions, plus a copyright holder that has legal standing to enforce the license.

The initial free/open software license was the GNU Public License (GPL). The Free Software Foundation–the maintainer of the GPL license–defines free software as having four kinds of freedom as follows:

- *The freedom to run the program, for any purpose (freedom 0);*
- *The freedom to study how the program works, and adapt it to your needs (freedom 1). Access to the source code is a precondition for this;*
- *The freedom to redistribute copies so you can help your neighbor (freedom 2); and*
- *The freedom to improve the program, and release your improvements to the public, so that the whole community benefits (freedom 3). Access to the source code is a precondition for this.*

(The Free Software Foundation, 2008)

Figure 1. User's capture of economic value

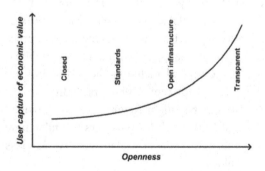

These are the core concepts that are implemented in legal language within the GPL.

Over time, many alternative open source licenses have been developed. Some deal with specific legal details and some offer very substantive differences such as the required "openness" of derivative works.

The Open Source Initiative (OSI)™ is a nonprofit corporation dedicated to managing the Open Source Definition (Open Source Initiative, 2008), a broad statement of objectives, and approving licenses as meeting the objectives. For example, Apache Software License, New BSD license, GPL, IBM Public License, MIT License, Mozilla Public License, and PHP License are all approved as OSI Certified Open Source Software.

In summary, many instances of open source licenses exist that grant the user broad powers and prevent "vendor lock-in."

BREADTH OF OPEN SOURCE

Open source is not just Linux. It is a new software paradigm that touches every segment of software development. Initial efforts focused on building the base of an open source operating system and development tools. This work was *by* computer science engineers *for* computer science engineers. This is why open source has a reputation for being very "techy" oriented.

This initial goal was achieved in the late 1990s as Linux matured into a stable and powerful operating system. Work continues on the base but the majority of open source development has shifted to the application areas. The leading collaborative development Web site alone hosts over 100,000 projects, predominately applications, and 1 million registered users (SourceForge, 2005).

One measure of the scope of open source development is to compare the above 100,000 active projects to the approximately 1,400 commercial software packages available on CompUSA's Web site (CompUSA, 2008). Table 1 presents

Table 1. Examples of breadth of open source

Domain	Technology
Core Infrastructure	Linux, Apache, Xen
Development	KDevelop IDE, Eclipse, Gcc, Gdb, PHP, Python
Direct Publishing to the Web	Slash, Twiki, PhpWiki, PostNuke, MoinMoin
Productivity	OpenOffice, OpenGroupware, openPSA
Genealogy	PhpGedView, GDBI

some examples of the breadth of open source technology.

Even very narrow market segments such as genealogy now have active open source development efforts. And, mainstream segments have so many active projects it is difficult to just stay informed.

FRAMEWORK FOR A REVOLUTION

The previous sections outlined the events and current state of open source. This section provides the fundamental framework driving the revolution. First, a business cycle theory of why technological paradigm shifts are always driven by new players is presented. The specific software forces that fit within the theory are covered.

Theory of Disruptive Innovations

The Theory of Disruptive Innovations (Christensen, 2003; Christensen & Raynor, 2003) presents the dynamics of why established firms always create an opportunity for firms with new technologies to win. In short, successful firms establish a market position around a set of technologies servicing a set of clients. Initially, the clients have needs (requirements) that are not met; the "under served" market state. The firm invests in *sustaining innovation* capabilities to close the gap between the product's capabilities and the client's requirements. Inevitably, the *sustaining innovation* closes the gap and then starts producing new features and performance faster then the clients can adopt the new product capabilities; the "over served" market state. This dynamic is presented in the chart shown in Figure 2.

The graphic presents the view of the average client. In reality clients are distributed from light to heavy users of the product's capabilities. Thus, light users would reach the "over served" state well before the average users. And, a point could exist where the majority of the clients have all their needs fulfilled, but the heavy users would still be pressuring the firm to enhance the product.

This is the point of opportunity for a disruptive innovation, usually substantially cheaper, to enter the market even though it may initially be a less capable product. The "over served" users are more than willing to trade features they do not use for cost reductions.

Of course, once established in the market the disruptive innovation establishes its own sustaining innovation rate. At every increment in capability the new, cheaper disruptive innovation eats market share.

This is one of the reasons why a framework such as the one we propose is needed to understand open source vs. proprietary source.

Figure 2. A disruptive innovation emerges

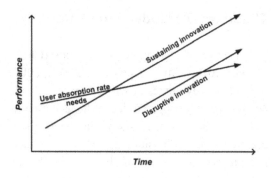

Cutting Edge to Commodity

After the quarter of a century of microcomputer technological innovation and half a century of server technology innovation, computer science algorithms that were cutting-edge at one point have become basic technology. For example, the Xerox Star pioneered graphic interfaces followed by the Apple Lisa, the Apple Mac, and finally Microsoft Windows. Each development team struggled with performance issues as the algorithms for clipping regions and stacking order were developed and matured.

In the early 1980s this knowledge was a valuable trade secret. Now, computer science graduate students around the world routinely develop graphics engines and GUI interfaces as exercises. The exotic has become the routine.

The same is true for relational databases. Oracle and IBM were cutting edge-pioneers in the 1980s. Now relational database algorithms are core computer science technology. Further, this move from exotic to routine is true across the application space as well.

In short, the value and access to technology has changed, and now the industry must follow.

Limit on Software as Intellectual Property

Proprietary software companies are structured around the concept that the source code is the company's main asset, that it has substantial intellectual property (IP) value–mostly know-how but sometimes also patents—and the user will pay premiums for access to this IP. All true in the early formation of each industry segment.

Over time each market segment experiences the following: (i) first, sustaining innovation rapidly addresses all of the needs of the less demanding users, next it addresses the average users, and soon it addresses only the most demanding segment of the market; (ii) early innovations become computer science basic knowledge, and

(iii) all users continue to pay a premium for IP and the sustaining innovation.

Thus, the least demanding users are paying for IP that is now a commodity and for sustaining innovation that they will never use. The seeds for change are thus planted.

Software as a Service

The Open Source software model moves the value from the code base to the people. This is a service model.

In the early evolution of the open source paradigm these services were *traded*. Communities formed around projects. Participants contributed services in return for access to the collective work. The larger projects, in many cases, formed non-profit organizations to co-ordinate and facilitate this *"swap of services."*

Although the collective swap has been a very successful business model for open source it is only one of many possible configurations of the business model (more details are provided in section "A New Business Model" of this chapter).

Darwin at Work

The Open Source Revolution is driven not just by the processes with each project but also by the overall force of *natural selection*. Barriers to entry are low. Barriers to trial are low. And, the programming talent can easily move. In the open source world good projects flourish and bad projects die quickly for lack of support. In economic terms, "the market is efficient."

Superior Process of Open Source

Open source is a true paradigm shift. It is not just a cheap hack of the proprietary code process. The open source model provides a diversity of coding talent, code review, testing and bug fixing that cannot be duplicated in the proprietary environment. For many software segments this may be a superior process (Bosio et al., 2002).

A NEW BUSINESS MODEL

Individuals and businesses new to open source always have the same question: "How can anyone make money when the software is free?" We see this as a larger question: "What are the open source business models?"

First, a historical viewpoint, a similar question from the 1960s: "How can anyone make money on operating system software when it comes free with the mainframe?" This is just a reminder that technology markets change rapidly and that the future product bundles will not be exactly the same as the present product bundles.

Now, about the future business models. Let us start with understanding what "buy software" really means.

Software "Derivatives"

The Black and Scholes (1973) model for pricing financial derivatives won the Noble prize in 1997 (Nobel Prize, 1997). With the model, a financial product such as a stock could be separated into "derivatives," stock without its dividends, dividends only, a call option on the stock, and so forth. These derivatives could then be sold as new financial products, either individually or in new bundles.

We can use this insight about derivatives to think about business models in the open source world. When people say they "bought some software" what do they really mean? A software package is really a bundle of derivative products:

- A set of bits on a CD (the software);
- A right-to-use license;
- An option for installation support (usually at no additional charge);
- An option to purchase software maintenance;
- An option to purchase support;
- An option to buy a future version at a reduced price (upgrade price); and
- An option to purchase training.

445

Each of these derivatives has a "stand alone" value. One analysis (Lefkowitz, 2005) places the value of the upgrade plus maintenance derivative at more than 80% of the pack cost and the software RTU license at less than 20%. In general, we make claim that the service derivatives–support, maintenance, training–exceed the value of the license derivative.

So the point is that even if the value of the license derivative was driven to zero the above package would retain more than half its value.

One of the issues with closed or proprietary source products is that of "captive" derivatives. When the source is closed, only the original developer can offer some of the derivatives: RTU license, maintenance, future versions. Third parties can offer installation, training and support derivative.

In the open source world all the derivatives are available to every firm. And, an additional derivative, customization, is available because of the access to the source.

So the process of creating an open source business model is one of deciding which of the software derivatives are bundled into the product and how to price that package.

Software as a Service Industry

The above analysis indicates that even today most of the value in a proprietary software product is the services. Thus, a service model is the natural place to start constructing open source business strategies.

A *Close to the Client Application(s) Provider* business model would include: (1) selecting an application, or portfolio of applications, as a specialty; (2) building configuration and source understanding in the application(s); and (3) packaging a yearly professional service product that includes the following derivatives: installation, training, bug fixing, maintenance and upgrades.

This business model captures the majority of the derivative value even though the firm is not the primary developer. It should be noted this model will not return the monopoly margins of a "vendor lock-in" for these derivatives but, if executed well, will return the high margins achieved by good consulting firms.

Another model for well-established and very stable technologies, for example, a Linux/Apache Web server, could be that of a *Close to the Client IT Provider*. Here the derivate set would include only installation and maintenance updates. All application expertise and bug fixing resides with the original developer organization.

Additional business models offering different sets of the software derivatives are also available.

Software as a Community Core Expertise

The open source paradigm also enables organizations banding together to produce software supporting core processes. Outstanding examples are the University portal project (JASIG, 2008) and the Collaboration and Learning Environment for higher education (Sakai Project, 2008). In both cases a number of universities have pledged resources over a number of years to the projects.

Economics and "close to the requirements" are the driving forces of the new software development paradigm. Community software has a huge potential cost advantage over proprietary software. For community software the user group is known and committed so all the sales and marketing costs associated with proprietary software are avoided, as is the profit margin. Together these average about 80% of the revenues of a proprietary software company. Thus, the members of the community are funding only the 20% of normal proprietary software costs that go to development.

OPEN SOURCE FRAMEWORK: BENEFITS PROVIDED AND SIGNIFICANCE FOR DESIGNING SOFTWARE INTENSIVE SYSTEMS

The proposed framework describes an open source revolution that is generating high quality components at every level of the software stack. From operating systems to Web services to relational databases to SOA middleware to applications, viable technologies are available. This impacts software development at both the cost and control levels.

Open Source to Reduce Costs

A design team can insert some open source components into the software stack to reduce the per user license fees. Examples of this strategy are:

* Most wireless handset manufacturers–Motorola, Nokia, Samsung, and so forth–have selected Linux for the operating system component of the software stack. The handset control application is proprietary software for each manufacturer. This "mixed stack" provides a royalty-free solution for the manufacturer.
* Most of the Web pages serviced on the Internet are from a software stack that has at least some open source components. Some large search engine providers use Linux and Apache Web servers as the operating and Web services part of the software stack. There, IP is at the application level where proprietary software is used to index the Web and generate search results.

In both examples, open source has driven the per-user or per-system royalties for third party software to zero. The use of open source is a huge economic win when manufacturing hundreds of thousands of cell phones or deploying tens of thousands of servers to crawl the Web.

Open Source to Increase Control

A design team can insert open source components into the software stack to increase their control. Examples are:

* Using an open source operating system when the application will need modifications to the kernel to perform at required levels.
* Using an open source Web server in an embedded environment of a small device such as a set top cable box. This allows the development team to fit the technology into the hardware by stripping out any functionality not used.

Both of these examples demonstrate a general principle: the higher the open source content is within the software stack, the greater end-to-end development control the team has because of the transparency of the code and the ability to modify it.

LOOKING AT ALTERNATIVES

In this chapter we present a strong case for open source as a viable development strategy. Nevertheless, in the real world, we expect to see users and corporate IT departments pursue a mixed strategy with software portfolios consisting of both proprietary and open source applications. Also, we expect new software development teams to pick the proprietary code strategy in some cases and open source in others.

Alternatives for the Users

The question of when an open source application becomes a viable alternative is driven by the maturity of the open source technology and by the skill set of the user.

Users should select proprietary software applications when at least one of the following applies:

- The software developer has a patent or other intellectual property that makes the application uniquely capable of solving specific requirements.
- The support infrastructure required by the user's technical skills–training, installation consulting, direct support, reference books and internal knowledge–is only available via proprietary software products.
- Standards such as the Structured Query Language (SQL) or the Internet IETF RFCs have imposed a level playing field for software developers and thus have generated a competitive market.

Users should select open source projects when:

- The core technology of the application category is widely understood, that is, a potential resource pool of engineering talent exists for open source projects.
- A well-established open source project meets the users' requirements.
- Users have the expertise to take advantage of the open source technology. For example, users may modify and integrate source code into a larger solution.

Stated at a higher level, users should look to proprietary software for state-of-the-art solutions. On the other hand, as any technology becomes more of a commodity, users should look toward open source applications to reduce costs.

Alternatives for the Software Developers

For software development teams the following considerations drive the proprietary vs. open source decision. Developers should select a proprietary source strategy when:

- They hold a patent of unique IP that makes it almost impossible for another development firm to directly compete.
- They have investors that require a proprietary strategy.
- They are a "first mover" and believe they will be able to defend an established market position.

Developers should select an open source strategy when:

- They plan to enter a market where the existing products are "over serving" the low-end users with a low-end disruptive technology.
- They need to build a community of outside resources to have any possibility of completing the full user requirements.
- They want to band together with similar organizations to reduce costs of "core competency" systems.

Stated at a higher level, software developers should use a proprietary source strategy to maximize returns when there is a user "lock-in." On the other hand, they should use an open source strategy to enter a market when the core technology has become a commodity and leading applications are still proprietary software.

FUTURE RESEARCH DIRECTIONS

The open source revolution has proven that large scale and complex systems such as the Linux operating system and the Apache Web server can be developed using collaborative development methodologies. At the same time many open source projects have failed to produce a lasting technology. In the section "Darwin at Work" of this chapter we presented this as an efficient market where resources quickly flowed to the best projects. However, research opportunities exist that may contribute to a systematic improvement in both the percentage of successful projects and the efficiency of the end user in selecting open source technologies.

The first research directions outlined below will provide fundamental understanding for development teams. We propose studying the impact of systems architecture and project organization on the success of open source projects. Another research direction proposed is focused on providing enhanced analysis tools for the user as he or she selects an open source project. All the research suggested is directed at improving open source effectiveness by providing insight at the early stages of development strategies and technology selection.

These research directions are supported by the availability of a resource unique to open source; access to a vast number of source code repositories. For example, SourceForge.net (www.sourceforge. net) has over 150,000 registered projects. Within the source code revision control of each open source project is information about the number of contributors, the turnover of contributors, the programming language, the growth and change rate of the code base, and interfaces with other technologies. This is a vast pool of information just waiting to be analyzed. In addition, many of the code repositories are accompanied by source and binary download services. The statistics on downloads are a good indicator of user interest and acceptance.

Impact of System Architecture on the Success of Open Source Projects

The first line of research proposed is into the effects of the core system architecture on a project's success. This is a straightforward computer science question: "Do the open source projects that utilize 'best practices,' as currently understood by the computer science community, show a

higher rate of success than projects that use other practices?"

Algorithms to extract methodology metrics from a project's source code repository can be developed. Algorithms to extract measures of project success from download statistics can also be designed. The data set could then be analyzed to identify relationships between system architecture practices and the ultimate success.

An associated research issue is how the system architecture affects the collaborative development process. For example, do object-oriented architectures and program languages—which isolate the scope of the code—make the collaborative process more effective? Or, is the open source methodology equally effective across programming languages and architectures?

Impact of Organizational Model on the Success of Open Source Projects

Another line of research could focus on the impact of the organizational model on a project's chance of success. The research could develop organizational categories (decentralized contributors, strong-core contributors, legal foundation of non-profit organization, corporate sponsor, consortium sponsor, etc.), map open source projects into these categories, and develop metrics of success. The research can then look for relationships between organizational models and the project's chances of success.

Contributor Participation as Leading Indicator of Success

The end-user or corporate information technology (IT) organization selecting an open source technology is making the decision without any of the business metrics that normally are used to assess stability because open source projects do not have income statements and balance sheets. Thus, alternative measures of viability are needed.

This line of research could focus on using the size and frequency of activity of the contributing developer community as a measure of project viability. Algorithms to extract participation measures–number of contributing developers, number of major developers, turnover of developers, coverage of multiple developers, growth of source base, and so forth–could be developed. Algorithms to extract measures of project success from download statistics could also be created. Further, the data set could be analyzed to identify relationships between developer analytics and the project's success.

Visualization could play a major role in this research direction. The focus here would be on presenting developer metrics in a form that mainstream users can understand. The goal should be to create visualizations that enable users to easily estimate the success of open source projects. Also, it would be desirable to have these projections rank-ordered close to the quantitative prediction, that is, a user projection of "very likely to succeed" will correlate with a high probability of success metric.

Along these lines, a very interesting site moving in the direction of advanced code analysis and visualization is ohloh (www.ohloh.net). This site crawls source code repositories to produce a graph of code growth, a simple rating of development activity and a list of top developers each with a contribution graphed by month. Ohloh shows Mozilla Firefox having a code history of 1 million lines in January 2000 growing to almost 2 million lines by January 2007. The contributor statistics show over 400 contributing developers with the top 10 having over 1,000 code commits each. From the above, one can see that this is clearly a large, stable project. IBM has also done very exciting and useful research in visualizing the contribution of authors to Wikipedia pages (IBM, 2008). This approach could be used to visualize source code development over time.

Thus, the market is responding to the user needs for assessing a project's stability. The majority of users would most likely assess a project of hundreds of contributing developers as stable and a project with one developer as risky. But what about the risk level of a project with 5 or 10 developers? Research in this direction could provide a deeper understanding of "risk assessment" across all sizes of developer communities. Thus, the users would be better equipped to draw the line between projects that are really "lab research" and those that are stable, commercially ready.

CONCLUSION

Open source software represents a fundamental paradigm shift in developing software. New development processes are emerging. New business models are being tested. Across technology suppliers, the open source revolution is creating new winners and losers. However, one thing is clear even in the midst of the paradigm shift chaos: technology users are, and will continue to be, the big winners.

However, while we can observe the evolution of software development driven by the market forces and we can see winning products emerge, the theory of why this new paradigm works is lacking. While many open source projects are winners, many fail. While high quality products like Linux and the Apache Web server exist and thrive, other open source projects are poorly designed and bug-ridden. Just making a project open source is not the recipe for success.

The framework proposed in this chapter describes a software development paradigm that is economically driven, long-term sustainable, and unique in terms of the processes involved. It is our hope that the framework will stimulate research into the design and development of the open source software. The open source paradigm offers a new alternative for software-intensive system development. Some of the main issues now are to build theoretical models for successful open source development and identify more precisely the application domains that open source projects can address most effectively.

REFERENCES

Black, F., & Scholes, M.S. (1973). The pricing of options and corporate liabilities. *Journal of Political Economy, 81*(3), 637-654. University of Chicago Press.

Bosio, D., Little, B., Strigini, L., & Newby, M. J. (2002, February). Advantages of open source processes for reliability: Clarifying the issues. In *Paper presented at the Workshop on Open Source Software Development,* Newcastle upon Tyne, UK.

Christensen, C. M. (2003). *The innovator's dilemma.* HarperBusiness Essentials.

Christensen, C.M., & Raynor, M. E. (2003). *The innovator's solution: Creating and sustaining successful growth.* Harvard Business School Press.

CompUSA. (2008). *Software.* Retrieved March 23, 2008, from http://www.compusa.com/products/products.asp?cmid=topnav&N=200163

Gladwell, M. (2000). *The tipping point: How little things can make a big difference.* Back Bay Books.

GNU. (2008). *The GNU operating system.* Retrieved March 23, 2008, from http://www.gnu.org

IBM. (2008). *Visualizing the editing history of wikipedia pages.* Retrieved March 23, 2008, from http://www.research.ibm.com/visual/projects/history_flow/index.htm

JASIG. (2008). *JASIG's U-Portal: Evolving portal implementations from participating universities and partners.* Retrieved March 23, 2008, from http://www.uportal.org/

Kuhn, T. S. (1996). *The structure of scientific revolutions* (3rd ed.). IL: University of Chicago Press.

Lefkowitz, R. (2005, July 21). *Calculating the true price of software.* Retrieved March 23, 2008, from http://www.onlamp.com/pub/a/onlamp/2005/07/21/software_pricing.html

Netcraft. (2005, August-October). *Market share for top servers across all domains.* Retrieved March 23, 2008, from http://news.netcraft.com/archives/2005/10/index.html

Nobel Prize. (1997). *The Nobel Prize in Economics 1997 – press release.* Retrieved March 23, 2008, from http://nobelprize.org/nobel_prizes/economics/laureates/1997/press.html

Open Source Initiative. (2008). *The open source definition.* Retrieved March 23, 2008, from www.opensource.org/docs/definition.php

Raymond, E. S. (1999). *The cathedral and the bazaar: Musings on Linux and open source by an accidental revolutionary.* O'Reilly & Associates.

Sakai Project. (2008). *About Sakai.* Retrieved March 23, 2008, from http://www.sakaiproject.org/index.php?option=com_content&task=view&id=103&Itemid=208

SourceForge. (2005). *SourceForge.net®, world's largest open source development site surpasses 100,000 projects hosted on the site.* Retrieved March 23, 2008, from http://www.ostg.com/pdfs/SourceForgeProjects_PR_Final1.pdf

Stallman, R. (1984). *GNU manifesto.* Retrieved March 23, 2008, from http://www.gnu.org/gnu/manifesto.html

The Free Software Foundation. (2008). *The free software definition.* Retrieved March 23, 2008, from http://www.fsf.org/licensing/essays/free-sw.html

Williams, S. (2002). *Free as in freedom: Richard Stallman's crusade for free software.* O'Reilly & Associates.

ADDITIONAL READING

Aberdour, M. (2007). Achieving quality in open-source software. *IEEE Software, 24*(1), 58-64.

Carrington, D., & Kim, S.-K. (2003). Teaching software design with open source software. In *Proceedings of the 33rd Annual Frontiers in Education Conference* (Vol. 3, pp. S1C/9-14). IEEE Computer Society Press.

Christley, S., & Madey, G. (2007). Analysis of activity in the open source software development community. In *Proceedings of the 40th Annual Hawaii International Conference on System Sciences,* (pp. 166b/1-10). IEEE Computer Society Press.

Crowston, K., Annabi, H., Howison, J., & Masango, C. (2004). Effective work practices for software engineering: Free/libre open source software development. In *Proceedings of the 2004 ACM Workshop on Interdisciplinary Software Engineering Research,* (pp. 18-26). ACM Press.

Dinkelacker, J., Garg, P.K., Miller, R., & Nelson, D. (2002). Progressive open source. In *Proceedings of the 24th International Conference on Software Engineering,* (pp. 177-184). IEEE Computer Society.

Ebert, C. (2007). Open source drives innovation. *IEEE Software, 24*(3), 105-109.

Edwards, J. (1998). The changing face of freeware. *Computer, 31*(10), 11-13.

Feller, J., & Fitzgerald, B. (2000). A framework analysis of the open source software development paradigm. In *Proceedings of the 21st International Conference on Information Systems,* (pp. 58-69). ACM Press.

Fink, M. (2002). *The business and economics of Linux and open source.* Prentice Hall.

Fitzgerald, B. (2004). A critical look at open source. *Computer, 37*(7), 92-94.

Fogel, K. (2005*). Producing open source software: how to run a successful free software project.* O'Reilly Media.

Fowler, D. (2000). Open season. *netWorker, 4*(2), 18-25.

Ghosh, R.A. (Ed.). (2006). *Study on the economic impact of open source software on innovation and the competitiveness of the Information and Communication Technologies (ICT) sector in the EU –final report* (Tech. Rep. contract ENTR/04/1112). Lead contractor UNU-MERIT, The Netherlands. Retrieved March 23, 2008, from http://ec.europa. eu/enterprise/ict/policy/doc/2006-11-20-flossim-pact.pdf

Ghosh, R.A., Glott, R., Wichmann, T., Spiller, D., Krieger, B., & Robles, G. (2002). *Free/libre and open source software (FLOSS): survey and study–final report* (Tech. Rep., several parts). International Institute of Infonomics, University of Maastricht, The Netherlands and Berlecon Research GmbH, Berlin, Germany. Retrieved March 23, 2008, from http://www.infonomics. nl/FLOSS/report/index.htm

Glass, R.L. (1999). The loyal opposition of open source, Linux … and hype. *IEEE Software, 16*(1), 126-127.

Golden, B. (2004*). Succeeding with open source.* Addison-Wesley.

Goth, G. (2005). Open source meets venture capital. *IEEE Distributed Systems Online, 6*(6), 1-7.

Hecker, F. (2006). Setting up shop: The business of open-source software. *IEEE Software, 16*(1), 45-51.

Hoepman, J.-H., & Jacobs, B. (2007). Increased security through open source. *Communications of the ACM, 50*(1), 89-83.

Koponen, T. (2006). Evaluation framework for open source software maintenance. In *Proceedings of the International Conference on Software Engineering Advances,* (pp. 52/1-5). IEEE Computer Society Press.

Laplante, P., Gold, A., & Costello, T. (2007). Open source software: Is it worth converting? *IT Professional, 9*(4), 28-33.

Lawton, G. (2002). Open source security: Opportunity or oxymoron? *Computer, 35*(3), 18-21.

Madanmohan, T.R., & Dé, R. (2004). Open source reuse in commercial firms. *IEEE Software, 21*(6), 62-69.

Mindel, J. L., Mui, L., & Sameer, V. (2007). Open source software adoption in ASEAN member countries. In *Proceedings of the 40th Annual Hawaii International Conference on System Sciences,* (pp. 226b/1-10). IEEE Computer Society Press.

Mockus, A., Fielding, R.T., & Herbsleb, J.D. (2002). Two case studies of open source software development: Apache and Mozilla. *ACM Transactions on Software Engineering and Methodology, 11*(3), 309-346.

Norris, J.S. (2004). Mission-critical development with open source software: Lessons learned. *IEEE Software, 21*(1), 42-49.

Neumann, P.G. (1999). Inside risks: Robust open-source software. *Communications of the ACM, 42*(2), 128.

O'Reilly, T. (1999). Lessons learned from open-source software development. *Communications of the ACM, 42*(4), 32-37.

Ousterhout, J. (1999). Free software needs profit. *Communications of the ACM, 42*(4), 44-45.

Paulson, J.W., Succi, G., & Eberlein, A. (2004). An empirical study of open-source and closed-source software products. *IEEE Transactions on Software Engineering, 30*(4), 246-256.

Rosen, L. (2004*). Open source licensing: Software freedom and intellectual property law.* Prentice Hall.

Ruffin, C., & Ebert, C. (2004). Using open source software in product development: A primer. *IEEE Software, 21*(1), 82-86.

St. Laurent, A.M. (2004*). Understanding open source and free software licensing.* O'Reilly Media.

Samoladas, I., Stamelos, I., Lefteris, A., & Apostolos, O. (2004). Open source software development should strive for even greater code maintainability. *Communications of the ACM, 47*(10), 83-87.

Scacchi, W. (2004). Free and open source development practices in the game community. *IEEE Software, 21*(1), 59-66.

Spinellis, D. (2006). Open source and professional advancement. *IEEE Software, 23*(5), 70-71.

Toth, K. (2006). Experiences with open source software engineering tools. *IEEE Software, 23*(6), 44-52.

Weber, S. (2005*). The success of open source.* Harvard University Press.

Weiss, A. (2001). The politics of free (software). *netWorker, 5*(3), 26-31.

Wikipedia®–OSS (2008). *Open-source software. Wikimedia Foundation, Inc.* Retrieved March 23, 2008, from http://en.wikipedia.org/wiki/Open_source_software

Wikipedia® – FSF (2008). *Free software foundation. Wikimedia Foundation, Inc.* Retrieved March 23, 2008, from http://en.wikipedia.org/wiki/Free_Software_Foundation

Woods, D., & Guliani, G. (2005*). Open source for the enterprise: managing risks, reaping rewards.* O'Reilly Media.

Wu, M.-W., & Lin, Y.-D. (2001). Open source software development: An overview. *Computer, 31*(10), 11-13.

ENDNOTES

1   All marks are the properties of their respective owners.

2   Kuhn (1996) defined science, in this case computer science, as taking place within a belief set, with changes accepted by a small set of authorities and with the next set of scientists selected and trained by these authorities. He termed this Web of belief, authority and acceptance a *paradigm*. From time-to-time a new scientific belief set is established–Copernicus, Newton, Einstein–that is not just a linear extension of an existing paradigm but is radically different. He calls this a *paradigm shift*. One could postulate that the paradigm of "big software projects" is well established in computer science with the many attendant issues of scaling, managing large teams, long design cycles, and so forth. One could also postulate that open source concepts and methodologies are a paradigm shift, that is, the way Apache or Linux or KDE environments are developed are not just sloppy, or underfunded, or lucky exercise of the old paradigm but the living proof of a new paradigm. From this framework it is easy to see why computer scientists using the beliefs and tools of the big-project paradigm are baffled by how the "chaotic" processes of open source can deliver short cycle, feature rich, high quality products. This is similar to the scientist using the Newtonian belief set struggling to understand Einstein's theory that distance could be relative.

3   From the "*Why I Must Write GNU*"(Stallman, 1984) section of the Manifesto: "I consider that the golden rule requires that if I like a program I must share it with other people who like it. Software sellers want to divide the users and conquer them, making each user agree not to share with others. I refuse to break solidarity with other users in this way. I cannot in good conscience sign a nondisclosure agreement or a software license agreement. For years I worked within the Artificial Intelligence Lab to resist such tendencies and other inhospitalities, but eventually they have gone too far: I could not remain in an institution where such things are done for me against my will. So that I can continue to use computers without dishonor, I have decided to put together a sufficient body of free software so that I will be able to get along without any software that is not free. I have resigned from the AI lab to deny MIT any legal excuse to prevent me from giving GNU away."

Chapter XV
Quality Metrics for Evaluating Data Provenance

Syed Ahsan
University of Engineering and Technology, Pakistan

Abad Shah
University of Engineering and Technology, Pakistan

ABSTRACT

With the proliferation of Web, a tremendous amount of data is available to researchers and scientists in computational sciences, business organizations and general public. This has resulted in an increased importance of data intensive domains such as Bioinformatics, which are increasingly using Web-based applications and service-oriented architecture which uses the data available on the Web sources. To trust the data available on Web and the results derived from it, a Data Provenance system must be devised to ensure authenticity and credibility of Web resources. In this paper we have discussed various domains which necessitate such data provenance systems. We propose a set of tangible parameters which affect the quality of data and define quality metrics to evaluate those parameters. The chapter concludes with a section on future directions in which we identify various research problems and possible applications of data provenance.

INTRODUCTION

Over the last decade, data management issues have grown in complexity owning to huge amounts of data being generated in various areas of computational sciences such as biology, meteorology, physics, astronomy, chemistry, geophysics, and weather forecasting. This has been enabled by sophisticated methods of experiments and observations in the wet labs, enabled through an ever advancing hardware technology and also through simulations in dry lab environment (Buneman,

Khanna, & Tan, 2001). These data repositories have been made available to the researchers, scientists and other consumers of this data through the Internet and Web-based applications. With the growing importance of the data intensive domains such as Bioinformatics, Geographical Information System (GIS) and Weather Forecasting, reliance on these data driven scientific Web applications has increased. The availability of these valuable assets of data has contributed immensely to the advancement of research and toward scientific discovery. However, an increased reliance on exchange and sharing of these data resources have put the notion of data quality at the forefront of research among the database community as concerns about the quality of data have been amplified (Jagadish & Olken, 2004). These applications execute complex workflows, consuming and producing data products of unknown quality. This poses serious challenges of selecting "right and correct" data for the scientists using these data products for various purposes such as *insilico* experiments and computational investigations.

Data Provenance is a kind of metadata which tracks information about the data such as its evolution, including source and authority, creation, life history including its usage history and other information about the agents of change (Wadhwa & Kamalapur, 2003). It provides a qualitative and quantitative metrics to analyze the quality and the dependability of the data. Hence, data provenance is valuable parameter to scientists working in domains such as Bioinformatics, where the quality and sources of the underlying data could play a major role in the quality of their experiments and research.

In the research, a few data quality models have been proposed to verify the quality of data that is being used (Buneman & Khanna, 2001; Simmhan et al., 2005; Ismael Caballero & Piattini, 2003). In these models, data provenance has been proposed as one of the many quality metrics to determine the quality of data. But to the best of our knowledge, so far data provenance itself has not been investigated in detail. In our opinion, data provenance is a critical and important indicator for determining and measuring the data quality and it needs further research.

In this chapter, we first explore the current understanding of the data provenance, its categorization based on the domains and where it can be applied. Then, we identify different applications of data provenance in various domains, and finally propose a set of parameters and related metrics to measure the data provenance. These proposed metrics can assist the researchers to

better understand data provenance and design provenance systems.

The remainder of the book chapter is organized as follows. In the second section, we give literature survey of the field. The issues and problems of data provinces are identified and discussed in the next section. Then, we suggest a set of metrics for the measuring data provenance. Finally, we give concluding remarks and future directions of this work.

LITERATURE REVIEW

In the last decade, the issue of quality of data that is used by researchers, scientists and other data dependent organizations has attracted the interest of the database investigators. Owning to the increased reliance of data centric organizations on distributed data sources, the data provenance has become an important quality indicator for these data sources (Searls, 2006). In this section, we also discuss how the need of the provenance primarily motivates to the scientific, business, academic and other newly identified domains. Also explained is how data provenance serves different purposes depending on the context of usage and on user perception of the appropriateness of data, and how domain and context of usage affect the mechanism of its collection.

As we mentioned, the provenance is context dependent, therefore, its various definitions are available in the literature depending on its application domain. The Oxford English Dictionary defines Provenance as "(1) the fact of coming from some particular source or quarter, origin, derivation, (2) the history or pedigree of a work of art, manuscript, rare book, and so forth; concretely , a record of to ultimate derivation and passage of item." In the context of database systems, Buneman has defined data provenance as the description of the sources of data and the process, and the work flows through which it was recorded in a databank/database (Buneman

& Khanna, 2001). Lineage refers to provenance in Geographical Information Systems as the information that describes materials and transformations applied to drive the data (Lanter, 1991). Greenwood further expands (as cited in Simmhan et al., 2005) the scope of Provenance as defined by Lanter to include not only information relating to data but also as metadata recording the process of experiment workflows and annotations and taxonomy of experimental procedure (Simmhan et al., 2005).

More generally, Data Provenance is the information about data, describing its origin and sequence of tasks (workflows/processes) that were responsible for its transformation; structurally, logically, physically or geographically. Ideally, data provenance should answer the Who, What, Where, Why, When, Which and How queries relating to a data item (Gobel, 2002), but more importantly, it replies two queries, that is, about the originating source and secondly about the derivation history of a data item. Broadly speaking, data provenance as a discipline means an area that studies the evolution of data, including the source and authority of data creation, changes to the data along with the life history of the data and the sources responsible in achieving these changes. It provides a qualitative and quantitative metric to analyze the quality and dependability of the data based on consumer trust of the source of creation and the sources that were responsible for modification (Simmhan et al., 2005).

Domains Necessitating Provenance

The mechanism of collecting metadata to establish data provenance is different for various domains, as discussed in the following sections. In literature, two domains have been identified which necessitate data provenance (Simmhan et al., 2005). We extend this list by identifying two more domains, that is, Academic Research Domain and Mass Communication. These newly identified domains, in our opinion, have gained

enough importance to be included in this literature survey and to point out new problems peculiar to them and motivate further research.

Computational Sciences Domain

Historically, data in this domain has been generated by individual researchers and small scientific communities working in universities and public or private organizations (Simmhan et al., 2005). However, with the proliferation on the Internet and the Web, various research groups with common interests have moved toward collaborative research by forming Virtual Organizations (VO) distributed all over the globe (Kesselman & Tuecke, 2001). This publishing facility has necessitated the evolution of some common standards to facilitate the sharing of disparate resources. Life Sciences Identifiers (LSID) for Biological/Life Sciences data is one such example. Despite this, the issues of trust, quality and copyright are still significant because of the greater heterogeneity of scientific data owning to incompatibility of its structure (metadata), format differences and non-uniform identifier usage conventions (Simmhan et al., 2005). Therefore, data provenance has a significant role to play for this domain in addressing the concerns of trust, quality and copyright.

Scientific domains have been using the provenance in the different forms and for various purposes, for example, research papers and other scientific publications have been one of the mostly used methods for the validating and authenticating the experimental data and results. Recently, in the Web-based environment, Digital Object Identifiers (DOIs) are used to establish the data lineage to the actual data produced and used so that the papers can be related to the experimental process and analysis (Brase, 2004). This lineage information can also be stored and recorded in the machine readable form using Resource Description Framework (RDF) and Ontologies for an efficient automated validation of results.

In GIS, Provenance information includes description of the lineage of the data product, including description of the data source, the transformations used to derive it, references to the control information and mathematical transformations of the coordinates used. Spatial Data Transfer Standard (STDS) is one such lineage recording system that helps in using the data product by deciding whether the data meets the requirements of the domain or not.

Material Scientists and Engineers use Provenance information to establish the pedigree of test data provided on the component materials of a particular product (Romeu, 1999). This is important because if substandard material is chosen based on statistical analysis on erroneous or bad data, it can lead to disastrous consequences during the use of the final product.

Data provenance is extensively used and applied in the area of Biological sciences (Buneman & Khanna, 2001). Biological data originates from wet laboratory experiments (primary sources), and then it is cured and stored in the derived databanks (secondary sources). These databanks are of varying nature due to dry laboratory (*in silico*) experiments and data curation. The perceived quality of these derived databanks depends upon the established quality of primary/source databanks. Provenance of the source data helps in establishing the trust, dependability and authenticity of the source data and in presence of the transformation history promotes the sharing of biological and biomedical data in the life sciences research (Jagadish & Olken, 2004). Through identification provenance also acknowledges the creator of the data (Searls, 2006). It keeps the history of derived data by automating the validation of the derived data and recoding changes to the source data. These changes can occur due to the incoming of new information, or the old notions are discarded as a result of new research and discoveries. In the domain of Biological Sciences, myGRID is a middleware support system which is used in the *insilico* experiments by providing services such

as resource discovery, workflow enactment, and metadata and provenance management. It also facilitates in achieving the interoperability and integration of heterogeneous databanks by making available the heterogeneous characteristics of data and providing semantic meaning.

The integrative and collaborative nature of the computational sciences increasingly demands that the authenticity and quality of the disparate databanks can be validated through some provenance mechanism tailored for specific applications. The above discussion supports this point of view. With the transparency that is achieved through complete history of the data, it is the prerogative of the user of the data to deem a data acceptable by applying their own criteria of quality.

Business Domain

In this domain, especially for E-business/E-commerce, it is easy to establish trustworthiness of data as a fairly standardized and organized data schema, and this trustworthiness can be used both ways, vertically and horizontally; that is, both within and across the organization (Hachem, Qui, Gennert, & Ward, 1993). In the case of across the organization Business to Business (B2B) scenarios, data interchange follows the established and mutually agreed schemes with the trusted partners, regulated through business rules of federal and governmental organizations (Hoven, 2004). Even then bad quality data continues to effect businesses as a result of incomplete provenance information due to temporal instability or unwillingness of competing business to share complete data and information (Hanrahan, 2004).

Another important source of data is data warehouse. Data from a data warehouse is used in the decision making in the Business domain. Data warehouses contain data from multiple resources, aggregated over time (Inmon, 1996). A process of extracting and cleansing is applied to the data that is extracted from multiple active databanks/databases and external sources to identify the relevant information, and normalization of their representation before being loaded into the warehouse (Chaudhuri & Dayal, 1997). In spite of this, data warehouses contain a huge volume of a poor quality data. As mentioned above, a poor quality data may occur when changes to a source data are not incorporated in the data warehouse (Bernstein & Bergstraesse, 1999).

Provenance information in the case of distributed data sources in e-science is used to establish a link between data in a warehouse and its source (Cui & Widom, 2003). Provenance information also helps in data mining and the pattern extraction algorithms that are used to extract semantically meaningful information and pattern from a data warehouse (Cui, Widom, & Wiener, 2000). It also helps in improving the quality of data in the warehouse by tracing erroneous data back to its source and applying relevant corrections/modifications to it (Galhardas et al., 2001).

Academic Research Domain

Previous surveys and white papers on data provenance which we have studied so far have not identified Academic Research and Publication as domains necessitating data provenance (Simmhan et al., 2005; LucMoreo, 2006). In our opinion, the academic research deserves attention and study as a separate domain due to its importance and as a major source of knowledge for academic, scientific and research community.

It is necessary for the academic and research communities to keep themselves updated with the latest research and technology, and a provenance system can help them in detecting plagiarism, falsification and fabrication of research (John, 1999). If enough metadata is provided with the research publications, the external observers or referees are able to validate the research results by repeating the experiments given in the research with the same given data set, achieving the same results. The parameters of scholarliness, that is, credibility, officialness and authoritativeness, can

be measured provided enough relevant metadata is given with the research work (John, 1999). The pattern of cited material often indicates the age and provenance of the material and aid in establishing the relevancy and currency of research (John, 1999).

Data provenance can help in semantic searches of articles and help calculate a more transparent citation impact and impact parameter for a journal (John, 1999). It can help in avoiding and detecting self plagiarism by including data related to previous work of authors as metadata. Self archiving can be made more comprehensive to detect plagiarism. It helps in giving credit to original contributors of a research work. Data provenance can be used to set standards for citation of original sources and hence discouraging plagiarism (Li & Crane, 1993). These standards should assure that all information and data relating to a particular research can be verified and traced to its original source. Because Web sources are often volatile and changing, it becomes increasingly difficult and important to have clear standards for verifying the sources of all information. Therefore, there is a need for a reference trail because of increasing use of Web sources. Publishers should also provide more data relating to publications by the same author to detect auto plagiarism. Issues of authentication of provenance of ideas, problems of joint authorship, and practice of duplicate submission of materials for publications must be addressed.

Mass Communication

The role of the Web has increased as a medium for dissemination and publication of news and all sorts of information. A huge and always increasing number of multimedia content is being hosted on the Web by freelance and amateurs journalists and authors. Capacity for error is magnified on the Internet, where information moves at greater speeds and in larger amounts. It is becoming more difficult to verify all the facts that get reported and to present a correct and objective version of the news. Also, many journalists and writers are using the Internet as a research tool and sourcing mechanism (Simon & Napolitano, 1999). Such exchanges are informal and chain-like in effect, intertwining rumor and fact. Major news agencies and channels need to authenticate the genuineness and credibility of their contents before referring to and broadcasting them. We're still in the early days of Internet journalism, but unless media organizations start taking stronger steps to defend their integrity, there will be a gradual decline in reporting standards on the Web and ultimately, a loss of the public's trust. As a first measure, existing conventional journalism ethics should be applied to online journalism. However, the Internet presents unique problems for corrections because of the many possibilities in which information can be framed (e.g., should online newspapers have a stand-alone corrections page?), in which information can be changed or revised (e.g., should online newspapers point out corrections when the Web allows them to fix errors instantaneously), and in which information can be archived (e.g., how long should online corrections stay posted and should changes be dated?). Another problem unique to the Internet world is that because the medium has become a convenient source of information, it lends itself to a kind of "journalism" where news gets passed on very quickly, with little attempt to verify all facts and correct any errors. Moreover, technical functions can have implications for the accuracy of content. For example, a trial run of a mock up story might be taken as an actual story and run on other Web sites. We suggest that the following should be provided as provenance data along with any multimedia online content to address the issue of authentication, reliability and provenance in online mass communication.

i) Link to uncensored, unedited raw data used to assemble a news story, opinion piece, or blog entry so that the problems such as misquoting, quote truncation, placing quotes out of order to arrive at an unintended meaning, quoting out of context, or manipulating interviews in the interests of a particular agenda could go away. Moreover, multiple multimedia contents can be packaged together for delivery on a subscription basis. A journalist's audience can optionally subscribe to and review some of the material that was used to assemble a story.

ii) A Journalist's electronic bibliography should be provided including journalist's background, picture and hyperlinks to verify story.

iii) Correction notices linked to original stories, time stamps for multimedia content, disclaimers for database problems, malfunctioning scripts, and technical errors.

iv) Updating archives after running corrections to avoid repetitions and requoting of errors.

In our opinion, provenance information integrated with multimedia contents can be helpful in establishing the authenticity and checking against tampering, distortion or fabrication. This provenance information should be provided through a consortium of news agencies' wide infrastructure. Individual agencies should use this infrastructure rather than creating their own verification procedures. In our future work, we intend to investigate this domain and applications in more detail.

Provenance System Frameworks

Provenance applications discussed in the previous section need to collect data about the data resources and its transformation history related to lineage, pedigree or attribution. These processes which result in these transformations are either Web-based, referred to as Web services, or part of the database itself, such as queries or the user functions. In the case of Web services, provenance data about the services involved and data sources involved in the transformations can be collected automatically by tracing the execution of the workflow, the inputs consumed and the outputs generated combined with execution time details like contextual information (Foster & Kesselman, 1998). In the case of dynamic on-need invocation of services, provenance data collection is difficult and needs to be annotated manually (Plale et al., 2005). In database domain, a derived data lineage and transformation history consists of query and stored functions executions on that particular database (Hsiao & Narang, 2000). Data warehouse present a special case of database domain where extraction and scrubbing queries are executed over multiple and layered data sources (Chiticariu, Tan, & Vijayvargiya, 2005).

These frameworks, one service driven and the other database driven, are different in the way they collect provenance information about a data source and this difference complicates the evolution of a general standardized provenance model.

More recently, script languages like Python and Perl are gaining popularity among the scientific community for their built-in support for interacting with databases and involving Web service workflows to perform complex scientific experiments (Bose & Frew, 2005). Scripts automatically generate their lineage information with additional information relating to data consumed and produced provided by the script writer (Wason, Malinari, Jiao, & Cox, 2003).

With the above discussion, two important results can be inferred.

1. Due to heterogeneity and distribution of data resources, the usability of data resource for a particular domain depends upon the provenance information attached to the data resource. The content and amount of provenance information in turn is dependent on a number of factors such as the domain of use itself, its application within a particular domain and the mechanism of collecting provenance information.

2. Differences arise in user perception about provenance information and hence data provenance itself due to the dependencies mentioned in (i). However, there are many commonalities in user perception regarding data provenance which can provide a common ground for building a more general data provenance system.

DATA PROVENANCE: ISSUES AND PROBLEMS

Existing provenance systems differ in the provenance data they collect and in methods of collecting this data. These differences arise due to the parameters discussed in the previous section. The application of provenance information discussed in previous section depends not only on the domain of use, and its application within that domain, but also the completeness of provenance data recorded. For a particular domain, Provenance data recorded for any particular application may not be sufficient for another application. In the same way, Provenance requirements for various domains are bound to differ because of user needs and experiences. Recording all the metadata parameters of a particular data source or data processing service or process are costly on memory and execution efficiency, especially if semantic, contextual and run time information is to be recorded. If the services and processes using data resources cannot record provenance information automatically, it has to be added by the user of the service (Simmhan, Plale, & Gannon, 2005). This will add an execution overhead. Therefore, it is difficult to agree upon a general provenance standard catering, because all application domains and parameters determining provenance quality for one domain may not be applicable to another domain. However, all provenance systems try to ensure that relative to a specified use, the data is used according to a code or set of values, and data fulfills the user expectation of data quality. This serves to facilitate decision making in any of the domains discussed above. We feel that using provenance as a basis for decision making depends upon the trustworthiness of provenance itself, that is, its quality, which we feel, is to be judged by the user, depending upon the completeness, extensiveness and relevance of provenance metadata (Simmhan et al., 2005). For example, Pedigree of a derived data product can only be claimed if the data source has been derived, used, modified or updated by a qualified, reputed, and trusted person or organization. Similarly, plagiarism cheats the public by presenting claims with a fake attribution through misleading provenance. Readers seeking knowledge and resources about a particular topic suffer when provenance is traced back to unreliable sources (John, 1999). Different organizations and people may have varying opinions about the quality of a data source depending upon parameters such as the domain of use and application of provenance. Web has made provenance difficult to establish and consequently makes it more important that we work harder to preserve and establish provenance. Issues such as those discussed above have to be resolved and quality of data established using and establishing provenance quality transparently and realistically.

As with Data Provenance, there can be no precise definition of data quality as it is context dependent and can have different meanings within the domains of data generators, data managers and data users. However in some application domains, the distinction between these three can be transparent, in which case it would be easier to derive a more context independent definition of data quality.

A more conventional definition of data quality simply describes it as "data that is fit for use by data consumer" or simply the "right data," and also having the following conventional characteristics (Elamsri, 2000):

- **Accuracy:** The degree of correctness and precision with which real world data of interest to a particular application domain is recorded in a databank/database.

- **Completeness:** The degree to which all data relevant to an application domain has been recorded in a databank/database. This can also means the degree to which the data is representative of a particular physical object/process.
- **Timeliness:** The degree to which the recorded data is up to date; also called temporal currency.
- **Consistency:** The degree to which the data managed in a databank/database satisfies specified integrity constraints.

From the discussion in the literature survey, it is clear that the distributed, heterogeneous and evolving nature of data sources, increasing usage of data warehouses, together with Web services and distributed queries have given new meaning to data quality and now provenance is an essential component of data quality, integrated into its every characteristic, widening its scope and constituent characteristics to define it more comprehensively. In our opinion, data provenance is a *white quality*, which should be evenly distributed and integrated in all the constituent characteristics of data quality. Later in this section, we will rewrite the above conventional characteristics of data quality in the context of provenance.

Limited Scope of Existing Data Provenance Techniques/Systems

There are only a few data provenance systems which primarily focus data provenance as an issue. These data provenance systems cater for a specific domain with the exception of Trio, which is generic only for data warehouse scenarios, has its limitations in application of use, and in representing semantics and scalability, to name a few (Yogesh, Simmhan, Plale, & Gannon, 2005). Buneman et al. (2005) has also presented a generic theoretical data provenance model for scientific databanks.

Lnater, D.P (LIP) is for GIS and is used for informational purposes, update stale data, regenerate and compare data. LIP follows a data-oriented provenance technique. Provenance data relates to spatial layers, the basic dataset of GIS, the transformation algorithm and the intended use of the data. Semantic Information is not included. Provenance is represented as annotations (Simmhan et al., 2005).

Chimera is a Process centric system based on service-oriented architecture catering for data intensive needs of Physics and Astronomy domains (Foster, Vockler, Wilde, & Zhao, 2002). Its application of use is Informational, Audit, Data regeneration and planning. Provenance information represented as annotations, relates to abstract data sets such as files. Semantic information on dataset derivation is not collected as most of the provenance collection mechanism is automatic (Foster, Vockler, Wilde, & Zhao, 2003).

MyGRID is a process centric-based service-oriented framework to support *insilico* experiments in biology (Stevens, 2003). Provenance can be stored about any data resource which is identified by an abstract LSID (Life Sciences Identifier) (Zhao, 2004). Semantically enhanced information is represented through XML/RDF annotations on cost of user overhead and execution efficiency. Its

application areas are contextual information and workflow reenactment (Goble, 2002).

Trio is a data centric system based on data-oriented framework, more specifically Relational Database (Cui & Widom, 2003) Semantic information is not recorded and provenance information relates to tuples in a database. Provenance is represented as inverse queries. Application of use is informational and update propagation in a data warehouse environment (Cui & Widom, 2000).

The provenance systems presented are domain specific and do not contain any provision to establish the quality of provenance data itself, which as we discussed in the beginning of this section, should be an integrated part of any provenance system. Moreover, increasingly, Web services are using databases and data warehouses to store and transform data, and databases, owning to their distribution and heterogeneity, are moving toward supporting service invocations within queries. In scientific domains such as bioinformatics, a derived data may have been processed and transformed by both service-oriented and database-oriented architectures, partly derived from archive data in warehouses with curated contents added at a later stage (Simmhan et al., 2005). Such common scenarios motivate the

Table 1. Some existing provenance systems (Yogesh, Simmhan, Plale, & Gannon, 2005)

	Lanter, D.P. (LIP)	**Chimera**	**MyGRID**	**Trio**
Applied domain	GIS	Physics, Astronomy	Biology	Generic (for data warehouse environment)
Data Processing Framework	Command Processing	Service-oriented	Service-oriented	Relational Database
Application of Provenance	Informational, update stale, regenerate and compare data	Informational, Audit, Data regeneration, Planning	Contextual Information, Workflow Reenactment	Informational, update propagation
Data-/Process-oriented	Data	Process	Process	Data
Representation Scheme	Annotations	Annotations	XML/RDF annotations	Inverse Queries
Granularity	Spatial Layers	Abstract datasets	Abstract Resources (LSID)	Tuples
Semantic Information	No	No	Yes	No

need of a more generic data provenance system, which can work seamlessly across different data processing architectures and user communities transparently. In the next section of this chapter, we outline the key parameters and characteristics which go into determining the quality of data provenance, starting with more general ones. This will help further research in proposing and developing a more generic provenance system. In our future work, we will focus on other domains which we have identified in this chapter.

QUALITY METRICS TO QUANTIFY DATA PROVENANCE

We have observed in literature survey that most of the quality parameters which have been proposed and discussed for metadata, also qualify for provenance data. Many of the parameters outlined are based on the parameters used by human reviewers. We feel that the boundaries between provenance data and metadata are grey and at times they merge. In this section, we have used the term Metadata and Provenance information interchangeably.

Nonmodal Parameters for Provenance Quality determination

There are a number of parameters which affect the quality of provenance and important characteristics which must be part of any provenance data to establish quality from a user perspective, such as:

1. **Provenance granularity:** Provenance data is only useful if it is collected at a level as required by the domain and the application of use. This might be at record or file level or even at a higher level of abstraction (Simmhan et al., 2005). Fine grained provenance data may result in better representation of a data set, but is costlier on memory

(Woodruff & Stonebraker, 1997). Abstract data sets like LSID (Life sciences identifiers) provide flexibility through multilevel granularity and permits identifying any resource by an LSID (Zhao, 2004). It is for the user to decide the acceptable level of granularity for a particular domain.

2. **Provenance representation:** The method of provenance representation can be a quality measure of provenance information for a certain domain. The inverse method, using the lineage information, can only find the derivation history and source of some derived resource and the processes/services that created it (Bhagwat, Chiticariu, Tan, & Vijayvargiya, 2004). However, this scheme has the advantage of low storage requirements if the source data, which is required for this scheme, is not geographically distributed (Buneman, Khanna, & Tan, 2002) and the depth of ancestral lineage tree is small.

   Annotations and descriptions, on the other hand, provide provenance information rich enough to enable reproduction of derived data by repeating the derivation process (Bhagwat et al., 2004). For this, in addition to recording information about derivation history, information about parameters passed to the derivation processes and the version of the workflow used also need to be recorded (Simmhan et al., 2005).

3. **Provenance format:** For service-based architecture, annotations written in XML format have the advantage of compatibility and portability as the *de facto* format for service-based architecture is also XML (Groth et al., 2005). More recently, annotations written in RDF and OWL are gaining popularity, as they can record semantic information by using domain ontologies. These help in information integration and help address the semantic complexity (Zhao et al., 2004). Annotations written in RDF and OWL are automatically recorded as

they have the advantage of being machine readable (Myers et al., 2004).

4. **Provenance security:** The way provenance information is stored affects provenance quality in multiple ways. If it is integrated with the data itself, it is readily available but is prone to tampering. But increasingly, especially in business and financial domains, provenance data is being separately stored in secure provenance storage where it is tamper proof and increases the trust user places in it (Morceau et al., 2006).

5. **Provenance scalability:** This parameter affects the storage and execution/access cost of provenance information. The amount of provenance information relating to a data resource increases with number of related data sources (source datasets and derived datasets), decreasing granularity, increasing user base, increased geographical distribution of source data sets and number of transformations required to derive a data source (Groth, Luck, & Moreau, 2004). The cost of recording provenance information about a derived data deeper down the lineage tree increases exponentially as the number of its ancestral data sources increase. Inverse methods suite well for scalability problem if the source data is not to be fetched/accessed from geographically distributed locations (Woodruff & Stonebraker, 1997). Annotations, however, provide a costlier solution in case of fine grained data and deep lineage trees (Woodruff & Stonebraker, 1997).

6. **Provenance data core-elements:** Quality of any metadata is dependent on the absence or presence of five core elements in a data source at any level of granularity (Ward, 2003). These core elements are title, description, subject, data and unique identifier (Spanne, 2002). Absence of any of these five core elements should result in a decline of provenance quality.

7. **Provenance completeness:** This parameter determines the extent to which provenance metadata gives an ideal representation of the data resource (Ochoa & Duval, 2006). This ideal representation varies according to the application and community use. From a human expert's perspective, provenance metadata elements will have different relevancy values in different contexts and hence, each elements affect on provenance completeness quality will vary in different contexts (Najjar, Meire & Duval, 2005).

8. **Provenance accuracy:** This parameter compares the semantic information extracted by an expert human user from provenance metadata with semantic information extracted by the same user from the document itself. Smaller differences will mean a better provenance accuracy quality (Ochoa & Duval, 2006).

9. **Provenance authority:** This parameter determines the trust a user places in the provenance information and is dependent on the user perception about the origin of provenance information. Provenance information generated by an established domain expert may be more trustworthy for some users. Others might place more trust in automated generated provenance information, as it might be more complete (Broisin, Vidal, & Duval, 2005). Determining Quality of Provenance authority should also take into consideration the user feedback about the usefulness of provenance information and about the actual usage of data sources because of provenance information.

10. **Provenance conformance (to expectations):** Provenance information can be termed of high quality if after reading it, the user can determine what the data source is about and its contents (Broisin et al., 2005). This depends upon how meaningful provenance vocabulary is and how much

semantic information can be represented by its syntax.

11. **Provenance timeliness:** The quality of provenance information depends on how current that information is determined by its current status of usefulness, what is the age of provenance data (old data tend to be more obsolete) and how often the data source is used. In certain static domains, old data sources may still have a high value for Provenance Timeliness Quality as its most recent usage still gives correct results, whereas in some evolutionary domains such as Biological Sciences, frequent updates may be needed to retain an acceptable level of Provenance Timeliness (Ochoa & Duval, 2006). To evaluate this parameter, a repository of usage history needs to be kept.

12. **Provenance accessibility:** Accessibility here means both cognitive and physical/logical accessibility. Cognitive accessibility depends on the number of spelling errors, usage of domain vocabulary, and more importantly, user feedback about the difficulty of the text (Guy, Powell, & Day, 2004). Physical/Logical accessibility of a data resource is a function of how many other data resources refer it and how easy it is to find that data resource in a repository (data warehouse, Web, distributed databases).

The parameters discussed above should be part of any provenance evaluation system irrespective of the domain and application. In our opinion, in most of the cases, to quantify any of the parameters mentioned above, weighted evaluation based on user feedback is necessary. In any provenance evaluation system, this general layer of provenance evaluation should be at an abstract level on which domain specific provenance evaluation can be built.

Quality Metrics for Quality Parameters

Many of the Quality Parameters affecting provenance as discussed above are fuzzy to a certain extent because of the user feedback and intervention, which is not quantifiable. User perception about the quality of these parameters depends upon the domain, application of use and users own competency and experiences. For example, a user may give more trust value to a human expert as compared to an AI software. The difference in user perception makes quantifying provenance a difficult task. However, we have tried to capture this subjective perception by suggesting a comprehensive system to log actual usage and ratings. This system should register the approval of the user by prompting the user if the metadata shown has been useful) or inferring that approval from the actions of the user (e.g., which metadata records have led to more downloads or actual use of objects). This information should be stored in a repository (or a group of interoperable repositories). The information that we recommend these systems should log is described in Table 1 in order of relevance for this metric. The table also

Table 2. Information needed to compute provenance metric

Recorded Information	Resulting Metric
The authority rating that the user gives to the metadata-producer	Authority Metric
The number of successful downloads	Accessibility Metric
The rating that the user gives to a metadata Record as determined by its usefulness	Timeliness Metric
The number of Web pages in a search	Accuracy Metric
Number of references by the user of the original document	Completeness Metric
User understanding of the page title	Conformance Metric

shows how to convert the log information into a provenance metric. The table does not cover all the metrics mentioned.

We have also referred to previous works on quantifying data and metadata. These works have been acknowledged by references:

1. **Provenance granularity metric:** We assign a score of 1 point for each of the metadata element appearing in the corresponding data resource. For example, if provenance is fine grained and collected at record level, all the fields of that record may appear in the metadata, resulting in a maximum score. A low level of granularity may result in a low score as compared to a higher abstract level of granularity, such as a file.

2. **Provenance representation metric:** Metric: In case of inverse method, the quality of description will be a factor of granularity and ancestral tree depth. Lower granularity and a smaller number of ancestral data resources will result in a higher score. With higher granularity and greater depth of the derivation tree, the amount of provenance information may outgrow the data resource itself.

    In case of annotations, a quantifiable metric can be the length of the textual description of the resource.

3. **Provenance format metric:** On a scale of 1 to 10, XML, RDF and OWL format will score on the higher bracket of 5 to 10 with OWL leading RDF and XML format due to increased ability of machine readable semantic representation. Moreover, an increased number of elements in data resource provenance information will increase the semantic description and allow for more targeted search.

4. **Provenance scalability metric:** Scalability in case of derived data resource depends upon the depth of ancestral lineage tree. The lineage tree is a class of rooted tree

and the number of ancestral resources at any level can be encoded by recording the level (distance from the root) at which a data resource (node) occurs in pre-order. This is called a level sequence. For example, a level sequence of 023441122 for a data resource A will show that data resource A whose node has been designated as the root (level 0) is derived from data resources at level 2,3,4,4,1,1,2 and 2. The sum of level sequence can determine the scalability factor. Lower values will result in higher scalability factor.

5. **Provenance data core-elements metric:** We assign equal weights to all the core elements. The weight of the core element absent is deducted as penalty from the maximum quality score, which is the sum of weights of all the core elements (Hughes, 2004). For a more realistic evaluation, the number of records or substructures accessed using the core elements may be considered to determine Core Element Usage.

6. **Provenance completeness metrics:** Every field of Provenance Metadata should contain a non null value (Ochoa, Cardinels, Meire, & Duval, 2005). Mathematically

$$Qcompleteness = \frac{\sum_{i=1}^{N} P(i)}{N}$$

Where P(i) is 1 if the ith field has a non null value, otherwise, N is the number of fields. Ochoa et al. (2005), in their work, have proposed including the relative importance and higher degree of completeness a human expert assigns to each metadata element according to the context of domain and usage. They have included this weighting parameter in the formula

$$Qwcompleteness = \frac{\sum_{i=1}^{N} \alpha i * P(i)}{N}$$

Where αi is the relative importance of the ith field. With this formula, a different value for provenance completeness will be calculated for different contexts.

7. **Provenance accuracy metrics:** For number and dates, we can assign a score of 1 for every 10% of the correct data accessed against the relevant provenance metadata up to a maximum score of 10 (for 100% accurate access). This score can be converted into a relative distance, or example, if we are able to obtain all the research papers submitted in the month of January from a data source, the score is 10 and the distance d= 0 up to a maximum distance of 10, which means 0% accuracy. Such distances can be calculated for all the provenance data elements and then added using a variation of Euclidean distance (Ochoa et al., 2005).

$$Qacuracy = 1 - \frac{\sqrt{\sum_{i-1}^{N} d(fieldi)2}}{\sum_{i=1}^{N} d(fieldi)}$$

(given that $\sum_{i=1}^{N} d(fieldi) \rangle 0$)

8. **Provenance conformance metrics:** It is possible for the human user to grade the ability of metadata to describe a data resource; it is not possible by some automated algorithms. However, the amount of relevant information contained in a data resource can be calculated using information theory. Ochoa et al. (2005) have proposed measuring the information content of the metadata using the following formula

$$Qconformance = \frac{\sum_{i=1}^{N} Icontent(fieldi)}{N}$$

Where N is the number of fields and Icontent (*fieldi*) is the estimation of the amount of unique information contained.

9. **Provenance timeliness metrics:** The calculation of Provenance Timeliness involves calculating the accuracy of the Provenance Metadata, age of provenance metadata and how often the metadata is used.

$$age = present\_year - publication\_year$$

$$frequency\_of\_use = \frac{times\_retrieved}{total\_records\_retrieved}$$

(Over a period of 1 year)

$$Qcurrency = Qaccuracy*age*frequency\_of\_use$$

10. **Provenance accessibility metrics:** The assessment of cognitive accessibility can be done by evaluating the difficulty of the text. That process can be automated by using one of the readability indexes available, such as Flesch Index, that access the difficulty of a text based in the characteristics of the sentences and the words used.

$$Qreadability = \frac{Fleash(description\_text)}{100}$$

11. **Provenance authority metric:** Provenance authority will depend upon the authority of the organization or person hosting the Web content and its credibility. For example, any information available online through an accredited journal of high impact factor will carry more authority. Moreover, provenance authority will also depend on its previous usage, user feedback and the sum of authority of a page's all available back links.

12. **Provenance security metric:** For some users, provenance information integrated into data will carry more weight, while for others, a secure, tamper proof separate repository of provenance information will carry more weight. This will be the case in business and financial data provenance.

The parameters and the corresponding metrics that we listed to quantify them are not exhaustive. Many of the parameters cannot be exactly measured and the measurements will remain fuzzy. However, these metrics do present a benchmark for a generic provenance quantifying frame work.

CONCLUSION AND FUTURE RESEARCH DIRECTIONS

The metrics need to be validated so as to be considered useable to assess the quality of a repository data. In order to be able to validate the metrics, we intend to have a complete comparative study, correlating the quality values assigned by human experts in metadata and the quality values generated by the metrics (in each quality parameters and combined). We will undertake this analysis in further work.

In our research work, we have identified several useful metrics which can be used in order to provide a smarter interaction with the final user. Among possible applications we can list a few:

1. **Automated quality evaluation:** To establish if the information available in the metadata record makes the Web resource useful inside a certain application;
2. **Ranking:** To assign a comparative value to a Web resource in the result list of a search tools reflecting the relevance of the Web resource;
3. **Updating Web resources:** To find similar, more recent/available, Web resources based in the characteristics or use of the original one;

4. **Recommendation:** To establish the relevance of a Web resource to a user based on usage patterns and user profiles (e.g., the information extracted from Social Software or Learning Management Systems);
5. **Measuring the usefulness of Web resources:** Calculating how useful a Web resource has been to a certain community; and
6. **Interoperability:** To find semantic-corrective calculations that will enable the exchange of information between two or more collections with the quality metrics proposed in this work demonstrate that it is possible to operationalize quality parameters.

The quality score produced could be attached to the Provenance records and used to implement interesting functions as:

- **Standardized selection:** A quality analysis using the provenance information can be carried out to determine whether the record complies with a minimum standard to be accepted. This could be especially important for automatic generators of provenance in formation.
- **Relevancy of federated search results:** A federated search across multiple repositories could establish a minimum level of quality for records to be included in search results.
- **Help in the ranking of search results:** The quality of the provenance information could be a component of the ranking algorithm used in search tools.
- **Selection of the most appropriate provenance instance:** A learning Web resource can have several provenance instances that describe it. The quality could be taken into account when selecting the most appropriate record for each situation (search, evaluation, assembly, etc).

Figure 1. A diagrammatic representation of how provenance information can be used in SOA workflow

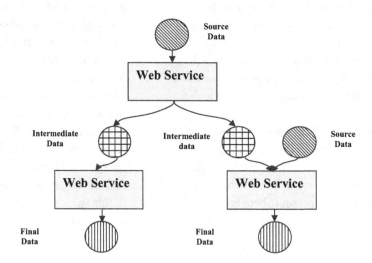

In our work, we advocated the use of a system of metrics to evaluate the quality of provenance metadata itself for a credible, realistic, trustworthy and transparent data provenance system. Such a system of Quality metrics for data provenance is difficult to realize because different users have different meanings for data provenance and data provenance quality depending upon the domain, application of use, data processing architectures, Provenance orientation, its format, presentation, scalability and even storage. This also changes the user perception of data quality itself. A brief survey of existing Data Provenance systems, which are all domain specific, revealed that not any of these systems incorporate a mechanism for establishing the quality of Provenance Metadata. We identified several generic parameters which affect the quality of Provenance metadata for establishing the quality of data irrespective of the context of usage or domain. As the boundaries between data-based and service-based architectures become grey with the convergence of database and Web technologies, we feel that these generic parameters will provide a foundation for a generic domain independent framework for quantifying quality of data derived from both databases/databanks and workflows.

We are extending our work in the future to identify parameters and metrics peculiar to the domains discussed above so that a domain specific layer of domain specific provenance quality metrics can be built on the generalized layer presented in this chapter, to constitute a generic portable framework to quantify data provenance quality seamlessly across domains. Such a framework will help enforce quality compliance on the standard of data resources that can be referred, manipulated, searched, assembled, accepted or used in any other way.

As Data Provenance is still an exploratory field, further research into its various aspects is needed. The measurement of accuracy metrics is fuzzy, as we deal with an ever increasing range of media. There is the added difficulty of measuring text accuracy, which demands an interdisciplinary research in text parsing and information theory. User feedback and evaluation about a data resource gives better and semantically relevant results, but it works only for small data resources which are static in nature. For large datasets which are constantly growing, this is not feasible and it will need complex artificial intelligence and text mining algorithms for automated recording of semantically meaningful provenance data. The organizational, legal and social issues, such as how much provenance metadata can be revealed and presented without compromising copyright or threat of plagiarism, add another dimension to the research and need to be resolved.

REFERENCES

Bernstein, P.A, & Bergstraesser, T. (1999). Metadata support for data transformations using Microsoft repository. *IEEE Data Engineering Bulletin, 22,* 9-14.

Bhagwat, D., Chiticariu, L., Tan, W.C., & Vijayvargiya, G. (2004). *.An annotation management system for relational databases* .VLDB, pp. 900-911.

Bose, R., & Frew, J. (2005). Lineage retrieval for scientific data processing: A survey. *ACM Computer Survey* (Vol. 37, pp. 1-28). New York.

Brase, J. (2004).Using digital library techniques— registration of scientific primary data. *Lecture Notes in Computer Science, 3232,* 488-494.

Broisin, J., Vidal, P., & Duval, E. (2005). A model driven approach for the management of learning object life cycle. In *Proceedings of the Intelligent, Interactive, Learning Object Repositories Network (I2LOR).*

Buneman, P., Khanna, S., & Tan, W.C. (2001). *Why and where: A characterization of data provenance.* ICDT, pp. 316-330.

Buneman, P., Khanna, S., & Tan, W.C. (2002). *On propagation of deletions and annotations through views.* PODS, pp. 150-158.

Chaudhuri, S., & Dayal, U. (1997). *An overview of data warehousing and OLAP technology.* SIGMOD Record (Vol. 26, pp. 65-74).

Chiticariu, L., Tan, W.-C., & Vijayvargiya, G. (2005). DBNotes: A post-it system for relational databases based on provenance. In L. Li & N. Crane (Eds.), *Electronic style: A guide to citing electronic information.* SIGMOD.

Cui, Y., & Widom, J. (2000). *Practical lineage tracing in data warehouses.* ICDE, pp. 367-378.

Cui, Y., & Widom, J. (2003). Lineage tracing for general data warehouse transformations. *VLDB Journal, 12,* 41-58.

Cui, Y., Widom, J., & Wiener, J.L. (2000). Tracing the lineage of view data in a warehousing environment. *ACM Transactions of Database Systems, 25,* 179-227.

Elmasri. (2000). *Fundamentals of database systems* (3rd ed.). Addison-Wesley.

Foster, I., & Kesselman, C. (1998). The grid: Blueprint for a new computing infrastructure.

Foster, I.T., Vöckler, J.-S., Wilde, M., & Zhao, Y. (2002). Chimera: *A virtual data system for representing, querying, and automating data derivation.* SSDBM, pp. 37-46.

Foster, I.T., Vöckler, J.-S., Wilde, M., & Zhao, Y. (2003). *The virtual data grid: A new model and architecture for data-intensive collaboration.* CIDR.

Galhardas, H., Florescu, D., Shasha, D., Simon, E., & Saita, C.-A. (2001). *Improving data cleaning quality using a data lineage facility.* DMDW, p. 3.

Goble, C. (2002). Position statement: Musings on provenance, workflow and (Semantic Web) annotations for bioinformatics. In *Proceedings of the Workshop on Data Derivation and Provenance,* Chicago, IL.

Groth, P., Luck, M., & Moreau, L. (2004). *A protocol for recording provenance in service-oriented Grids.* Grenoble, France: OPODIS.

Groth, P., Miles, S., Fang, W., Wong, S.C., Zauner, K.-P., & Moreau, L. (2005). *Recording and using provenance in a protein compressibility experiment.* HPDC.

Guy, M., Powell, A., & Day, M. (2004). *Improving the quality of metadata in Eprint archives.* Ariadne

Hachem, N. I., Qiu, K., Gennert, M.A., & Ward, M.O. (1993). *Managing derived data in the Gaea Scientific DBMS.* VLDB, pp. 1-12.

Hanrahan, M. (2004). *The essential ingredient: How business intelligence depends on data quality.* Dal Cais Research White Paper.

Hoven, J.V.D. (2004). *Data architecture: Standards for the effective enterprise.* Information Systems Management.

Hsiao, H.I., & Narang, I. (2000). *DLFM: A transactional resource manager.* PODS

Hughes, B. (2004). Metadata quality evaluation: Experience from the open language archives community. In *Proceedings of the 7th International Conference on Asian Digital Libraries (ICADL 2004). Lecture Notes on Computer Science, 3334,* 320-329. Springer-Verlag.

Inmon, W.H. (1996). The data warehouse and data mining. *Communications of the ACM, 39,* 49-50.

Jagadish, H.V., & Olken, F. (2004). Database management for life sciences research. *SIGMOD Record* (Vol. 33, pp. 15-20).

JEITA. (2002). *EXIF standard.* Retrieved March 24, 2008, from http://www.exif.org/

John, W.S. (1999). On the Web, plagiarism matters more than copy right piracy. *Ethics and information technology.* Netherlands: Kluwer Academic.

Lanter, D.P. (1991). Design of a lineage-based meta-data base for GIS. *Cartography and Geographic Information Systems, 18,* 255-261.

Myers, J.D., Allison, T.C., Bittner, S., Didier, B.T., Frenklach, M., Green, Jr., W. H., et al. (2004). *A collaborative informatics infrastructure for multiscale science.* CLADE, p. 24.

Najjar, J., Meire, M., & Duval, E. (2005). Attention metadata management: Tracking the use of learning objects through Attention.XML. In *Proceedings of the ED-MEDIA 2005 World Conference on Educational Multimedia, Hypermedia and Telecommunications.*

Ochoa, X., Cardinels, K., Meire, M., & Duval, E. (2005). Frameworks for the automatic indexation of learning management systems content into learning object repositories. In *Proceedings of the ED-MEDIA 2005 World Conference on Educational Multimedia, Hypermedia and Telecommunications,* (pp. 1407-1414).

Ochoa, X., & Duval, E. (2006). *Quality metrics for learning object data.* Ecuador. Retrieved March 24, 2008, from http://ariadne.cti.espol.edu.ec/M4M.

Plale, B., Gannon, D., Reed, D., Graves, S., Droegemeier, K., Wilhelmson, B., & Ramamurthy, M. (2005). Towards dynamically adaptive weather analysis and forecasting in LEAD. In *Proceedings of the ICCS Workshop on Dynamic Data Driven Applications.*

Romeu, J.L. (1999). *Data quality and pedigree.* Material Ease.

Searls, D.B. (2006). Data integration: Challenges for drug discovery. *Nature Reviews Drug Discovery, 4,* 45-58.

Spanne, J. (2002). OLAC: The state of the archives. In *Proceedings of the IRCS Workshop on Open Language Archives,* (pp. 42-46). Institute for Research in Cognitive Science, University of Pennsylvania.

Wadhwa, P.S., & Kamalapur, P. (2003). *Customized metadata solution for a data warehouse—a success story.* Wipro Technologies White Paper.

Ward, J. (2003). A quantitative analysis of unqualified Dublin core metadata element set usage within data providers registered with the open archives initiative. In *Proceedings of the IEEE/ACM Joint Conference on Digital Libraries 2003 (JDCL'03)*, (pp. 315-3).

Wason, J.L., Molinari, M., Jiao, Z., & Cox, S.J. (2003). *Delivering data management for engineers on the grid.* Euro-Par, pp. 412-416.

Woodruff, A., & Stonebraker, M. (1997). *Supporting fine-grained data lineage in a database visualization environment.* ICDE, pp. 91-102.

Yogesh, L., Simmhan, B. P., & Gannon, D. (2005). A survey of data provenance techniques. *SIGMOD Record (Special Section on Scientific Workflows), 34*(3), 31-36.

Zhao, J., Goble, C.A, Stevens, R., & Bechhofer, S. (2004). *Semantically linking and browsing provenance logs for e-science.* ICSNW, pp. 158-176.

Zhao, J., Wroe, C., Goble, C.A., Stevens, R., Quan, D., & Greenwood, R.M. (2004). Using Semantic Web technologies for representing e-science provenance. In *Proceedings of the International Semantic Web Conference*, (pp. 92-106).

ADDITIONAL READING

In addition to the material and resources mentioned in the Reference section, we are suggesting the following list of books, reports and workshop summaries which we feel can be a good source of additional reading for researchers who are interested in the specific and related areas of Data Provenance.

1. Data Quality Assessment, by Arkady Maydanchik
2. Data Quality, by Jack E. Olson
3. Universal Meta Data Models, by David Marco and Michael Jennings
4. Building and Managing Meta Data Repository: A Full Lifecycle Guide, by David Marco
5. Implementing Data Quality Through Meta Data, by David Marco and Michael Jennings
6. Psychology of Academic Cheating (2007), Edited by E.M. Anderman and T.B. Murdock
7. The Ethical Dimensions of the Biological Sciences (1993), by R.E. Bulgar, E. Heitman, and S.J. Reiser
8. A Wake Up Call: Can Trust and Quality Save Journalism? The Final Report. http://restoringthetrust.org/final_report.shtml
9. The State of the News Media 2006: An Annual Report on American Journalism
10. Provenance and Annotation of Data: International Provenance and Annotation Workshop, IPAW 2006, Chicago, Il, USA, Revised Selected Papers (Lecture Notes in Computer Science)
11. Data Mining in Bioinformatics (Advanced Information and Knowledge Processing), Edited by Jason Wang, Mohammad Zaki, Hannu Toivonen, and Dennis Shahsa
12. Data Provenance: Some Basic Issues, Lecture Notes in Computer Science
13. Report on Karma Version 0.3.
14. Bioinformatics: Converting Data to Knowledge: Workshop Summary 2006

Chapter XVI
System Integration Using Model–Driven Engineering

Krishnakumar Balasubramanian
Vanderbilt University, USA

Douglas C. Schmidt
Vanderbilt University, USA

Zoltán Molnár
Vanderbilt University, USA

Ákos Lédeczi
Vanderbilt University, USA

ABSTRACT

With the emergence of commercial-off-the-shelf (COTS) component middleware technologies software system integrators are increasing faced with the task of integrating heterogeneous enterprise distributed systems built using different COTS technologies. Although there are well-documented patterns and techniques for system integration using various middleware technologies, system integration is still largely a tedious and error-prone manual process. This chapter provides three contributions to the study of functional integration of distributed enterprise systems. First, we describe the challenges associated with functionally integrating software for these types of systems. Second, we describe how the composition of domain-specific modeling languages (DSMLs) can simplify the functional integration of enterprise distributed systems. Third, we demonstrate how composing DSMLs can solve functional integration problems in an enterprise distributed system case study by reverse engineering an existing CCM system and exposing it as Web service(s) to Web clients who use these services.

INTRODUCTION

Functional Integration of Component Middleware

With the maturation of commercial-off-the-shelf (COTS) component middleware technologies, such as Enterprise Java Beans (EJB) (Sun Microsystems, 2001), CORBA Component Model (CCM) (*CORBA Components*, 2002), and Microsoft .NET Framework (Microsoft Corporation, 2002), software developers are increasingly faced with the task of integrating heterogeneous enterprise distributed systems built using different COTS technologies, rather than just integrating proprietary software developed in-house. Although there are well-documented patterns (Hohpe & Woolf, 2003) and techniques (Britton & Bye, 2004) for integrating systems via various component middleware technologies, system integration is still largely a tedious and error-prone manual process. To improve this process, therefore, component developers and system integrators must understand key properties of the integration technologies they are applying and the systems[2] they are integrating.

There are multiple levels at which system integration is done today (TrowBridge, Roxburgh, Hohpe, Manolescu, & Nadhan, 2004), including:

- **Data integration:** which integrates systems at the logical data layer, typically using some form of data transfer/sharing. Example technologies that allow data integration include commercial databases (such as IBM DB2, Oracle, and Microsoft SQL Server) and tools (such as Microsoft BizTalk Mapper and IBM WebSphere Integration Developer) that provide database schema mapping between different databases.
- **Functional integration:** which integrates systems at the logical business layer, typically using distributed objects/components,

service-oriented architectures or messaging middleware. Examples of technologies that allow functional integration include the Java Connector Architecture and Service-oriented Integration adapters available in commercial products, such as IBM's Websphere.
- **Presentation integration:** which allows access to an application's functionality through its user interface by simulating a user's input and by reading data from the screen. This "screen scraping" is usually done via programming languages like Perl that use regular expressions to parse the screen output of legacy systems.
- **Portal integration:** which creates a portal application displaying information retrieved from multiple applications via a unified user interface, thereby allowing users to perform required tasks. Examples of technologies that allow portal integration include Microsoft ASP.NET and Java portlets combined with Java Server Pages (JSP), which provide technologies to build Web-based portals for integrating information from a variety of sources.
- **Process integration:** which defines a business process model describing the individual steps in a complex business function and coordinates the execution of long-running business functions that span multiple disparate applications. Example technologies that support process integration include implementations of Business Process Execution Language (BPEL) and its Web services incarnation (WS-BPEL).

This chapter describes technologies that help simplify the *functional integration* of systems built using component middleware. This type of integration operates at the logical business layer, typically using distributed objects/components, exposing service-oriented architectures, or messaging middleware, and is responsible for delivering services to clients with the desired quality of service (QoS). We focus on functional integration of systems in this paper because:

- Component middleware is typically used to implement the core business logic of a system. In this context it is inappropriate to use portal integration because there may be no direct user interaction and because component middleware usually resides in the second tier of a typical three-tier enterprise architecture. In contrast, the entities that make up a "portal," for example, portlets, are usually user-facing and belong in the first tier, that is, the front-end tier.

- Unlike legacy systems, component middleware technologies usually expose an API to access functionality. Employing presentation integration to integrate systems built using component middleware technologies is problematic. For example, techniques used in typical presentation integration (such as parsing the output of a system to enable integration) are *ad hoc* compared with using the well-defined APIs exposed by component middleware technologies.

- Updates to data at the business logic layer occur frequently during system execution. Due to the cost of remote data access operations and the rate at which such operations are generated by the business logic components in the second tier of a three-tier enterprise architecture, it is therefore infeasible to employ data integration to keep the data consistent among the different systems. Data integration is usually appropriate for the back-end (i.e., third tier) of a three-tier enterprise architecture, where the data is long-lived and not transient.

- The business logic of a system is often proprietary and organizations tightly control the interfaces exposed by the system. It is often unnecessary, therefore, to employ process integration, which usually applies to

interorganizational integration where loose-coupling is paramount. Process integration is a superset of functional integration, and usually relies on functional integration within autonomous organizational boundaries.

Functional integration of systems is hard due to the variety of available component middleware technologies, such as EJB and CCM. These technologies differ in many ways, including the protocol level, the data format level, the implementation language level, or the deployment environment level. In general, however, component middleware technologies are a more effective technology base than the brittle proprietary infrastructure used in legacy systems (Sharp, 2000), which have historically been built in a vertical, stove-piped fashion.

Despite the benefits of component middleware, key challenges in functional integration of systems remain unresolved when integrating large-scale systems developed using heterogeneous COTS middleware. These challenges include (1) *integration design*, which involves choosing the right abstraction for integration, (2) *interface mapping*, which reconciles different data types, (3) *technology mapping*, which reconciles various low-level issues, (4) *deployment mapping*, which involves planning the deployment of heterogeneous COTS middleware, and (5) *portability incompatibilities* between different implementations of the same middleware technology. The lack of simplification and automation in resolving these challenges today significantly hinders effective system integration.

Solution Approach: Functional Integration of Systems using (Meta)Model Composition

A promising approach to address the functional integration challenges outlined above is *Model-driven Engineering* (MDE) (Schmidt, 2006), which involves the systematic use of models as essential artifacts throughout the software life-cycle. At the core of MDE is the concept of *domain-specific modeling languages* (DSMLs) (Karsai, Sztipanovits, Ledeczi, & Bapty, 2003), whose type systems formalize the application structure, behavior, and requirements within particular domains. DSMLs have been developed for a wide range of domains, including software defined radios (Trask, Paniscotti, Roman, & Bhanot, 2006), avionics mission computing (Karsai, Neema, Abbott, & Sharp, 2002), warehouse management (Deng et al., 2003), and even the domain of component middleware (White, Schmidt, & Gokhale, 2005) itself.

Third-generation programming languages, such as C++, Java, and C#, employ *imperative* techniques for development, deployment, and configuration of systems. Imperative techniques specify the policies, for example, security, real-time QoS properties, and so forth, at the same level of abstraction (usually in great level of detail) as the mechanisms, for example, object request brokers, software services, and so forth, used to implement these policies. Thus, the policies and mechanisms are often entangled, and it is hard to separate the two.

In contrast, MDE tools and DSMLs employ a *declarative* approach using a visual notation. Declarative techniques clearly separate the specification of policies from the mechanisms used to enforce the policies. Specification of policies is usually done at a higher level of abstraction (and in less amount of detail), for example, using models, simple configuration languages, and so forth. Thus, declarative techniques relieve the user from the intricacies of how the policies are mapped onto the underlying mechanisms implementing them, thereby, allowing easy modifications to the policies.

For example, it is hard to write imperative Java or C# code that correctly and optimally deploys large-scale distributed systems with hundreds or thousands of interconnected software components. A key culprit is the significant semantic gap between design intent (such as deploy components 1-50 onto nodes A-G and components 51-100 onto nodes H-N in accordance with system resource requirements and availability) and the expression of this intent in thousands of lines of handcrafted third-generation languages. By using high-level declarative visual notations, MDE tools and DSMLs help overcome the complexity gap between the design intent and the expression of such design intent.

DSMLs are described using *metamodels*, which define the relationships among concepts in a domain and precisely specify the key semantics and constraints associated with these domain concepts. For example, a DSML might represent the different hardware elements of a radar system and the relationships between them in a component middleware technology like CCM. Likewise, it might represent the different elements, such as EJBComponent, EJBHome, EJBContainer and ApplicationServer, which are present in a component middleware technology like EJB. Developers use DSMLs to build applications using elements of the type system captured by metamodels and express design intent declaratively rather than imperatively.

A DSML is often accompanied by interpreters and generators, which analyze the models and synthesize various types of artifacts, such as source code, deployment descriptors, or input to simulators. By capturing the semantics of a domain using DSMLs and using this information to develop generators, DSMLs can be used as effective "metadata management" frameworks. DSMLs thus help automate the analysis and generation of various component middleware deployment and configuration descriptors, thereby alleviating the complexity associated with creating and exchanging metadata between different technologies.

DSMLs are an effective means to capture implicit assumptions associated with component middleware technologies. These assumptions may be specification-compliant behavior of a particular technology (such as the protocol version used when sending out the initial message in a CORBA IIOP conversation), or they may be implementation-defined behavior (such as interpretation of elements of a standard WSDL schema). In either case, representing these implicit assumptions as first-class entities of a DSML makes essential—but easily overlooked—information explicit at the modeling level. By explicitly capturing the assumptions, DSMLs allow detection of problems at an earlier stage, that is, at design time rather than final system integration time, when these problems are much more expensive to fix.

While DSMLs have been used to help software developers create homogeneous systems (Karsai et al., 2002; Stankovic et al., 2003), enterprise distributed systems are rarely homogeneous. A single DSML developed for a particular component middleware technology, such as EJB or CCM, may therefore not be applicable to model, analyze, and synthesize key concepts of Web services. To integrate heterogeneous systems successfully, therefore, system integrators need automated tools that provide a unified view of the entire enterprise system, while also allowing fine-grained control over specific subsystems and components.

Our approach to integrating heterogeneous systems is called *(meta)model composition* (Lédeczi, Nordstrom, Karsai, Volgyesi, & Maroti, 2001), where the term "(meta)model" conveys the fact that this technique can be applied to both metamodels *and* models. At the heart of this technique is a method for:

- Creating a new DSML (a composite DSML) from multiple existing DSMLs (component DSMLs) by adding new elements or extending elements of existing DSMLs,
- Specifying new relationships between elements of the component DSMLs, for example, relationships that capture the semantics of the interaction between elements of the two previously separate component DSMLs, and

- Defining relationships between elements of the composite DSML and elements of the component DSMLs, for example, relationships that define containment of elements of component DSMLs inside elements of composite DSMLs.

A key benefit of (meta)model composition is its ability to add new capabilities while simultaneously leveraging prior investments in existing tool-chains, including domain constraints and generators of existing DSMLs. A combination of DSMLs and DSML composition technologies can therefore help address the challenges outlined in § *Functional Integration of Component Middleware* that are associated with functional integration of component middleware technologies, without incurring the drawbacks of conventional approaches. Common drawbacks include (1) requiring expertise in all of the domains corresponding to each subsystem of the system being integrated, (2) writing more code in third-generation programming languages to integrate systems, (3) the lack of scalability of such an approach, and (4) the inflexibility in (re-)targeting integration code to more than one underlying middleware technology during system evolution.

This chapter describes the design and application of the *System Integration Modeling Language* (SIML). SIML is our open-source DSML that enables functional integration of component-based systems via the (meta)model composition mechanisms provided by the Generic Modeling Environment (GME) (Ledeczi et al., 2001a), which is an open-source metaprogrammable modeling environment. The SIML composite DSML combines the following two existing DSMLs:

- The CCM profile of the *Platform-independent Component Modeling Language* (PICML) (Balasubramanian, Balasubramanian, Parsons, Gokhale, & Schmidt, 2005), which supports the model-driven engineering of CCM-based systems,

- The *Web Services Modeling Language* (WSML), which supports model-driven engineering of Web services-based systems.

Because SIML is a composite DSML, it has complete access to the semantics of PICML and WSML (sub-DSMLs), which simplifies and automates various tasks associated with integrating systems built using CCM and Web services.

The remainder of this chapter is organized as follows: *§ Related Work* evaluates related work on system integration and compares it with SIML; *§ Functional Integration Case Study* describes a case study of a enterprise distributed system built using component middleware that we use throughout the paper to evaluate functional integration technologies; *§ DSML Composition using GME* describes the DSML composition framework provided by GME to simplify the integration of heterogeneous domains; *§ Integrating Systems with SIML* shows how SIML uses GME's DSML composition framework to integrate heterogeneous enterprise distributed systems; and *§ Concluding Remarks* presents concluding remarks.

RELATED WORK

This section surveys the technologies that provide the context of our work on system integration in the domain of enterprise distributed systems. We classify techniques and tools in the integration space according to the role played by the technique/tool in system integration.

Integration evaluation tools enable system integrators to specify the systems/technologies being integrated and evaluate the integration strategy and tools used to achieve integration. For example, IBM's WebSphere (IBM, 2001) supports modeling of integration activities and runs simulations of the data that is exchanged between the different participants to help predict the effects of the integration. System execution

modeling (Smith & Williams, 2001) tools, such as CUTS (Hill, Slaby, Baker, & Schmidt, 2006), help developers conduct "what if" experiments to discover, measure, and rectify performance problems early in the lifecycle (e.g., in the architecture and design phases), as opposed to the integration phase.

Although these tools help identify potential integration problems and evaluate the overall integration strategy, they do not replace the actual task of integration itself since these tools use simulation-/emulation-based abstractions of the actual systems. SIML's role is thus complementary to existing integration evaluation tools. In particular, after the integration evaluation has been done using integration evaluation tools, SIML can be applied to design the integration and generate various artifacts required for integration, as discussed in *§ The Design and Functionality of SIML*.

Integration design tools. OMG's UML profile for Enterprise Application Integration (EAI) (*UML Profile for Enterprise Application Integration (EAI)*, 2004) defines a Meta Object Facility (MOF) (*MetaObject Facility (MOF) 2.0 Core Specification*, 2003) for collaboration and activity modeling. MOF provides facilities for modeling the integration architecture, focusing on connectivity, composition and behavior. The EAI UML profile also defines a MOF-based standardized data format intended for use by different systems to exchange data during integration. Data exchange is achieved by defining an EAI application metamodel that handles interfaces and metamodels for programming languages (such as C, C++, PL/I, and COBOL) to aid the automation of transformation.

While standardizing on MOF is a step in the right direction, in practice there are various problems, such as the lack of widespread support for MOF by various tools, and the differences between versions of XML Metadata Interchange (XMI) (*MOF 2.0/XMI Mapping Specification, v2.1*, 2005) support in tools. Existing integration design tools provide limited support for interface mapping by generating stubs and skeletons, for facilitating interface mapping, and perform protocol mapping. Moreover, key activities like discovery mapping and deployment mapping must still be programmed manually by system integrators. The primary difference between SIML and integration design tools is therefore that SIML not only allows such integration design, but it also automates the generation of key integration artifacts, such as gateways. Gateways encapsulate the different adaptations required to bridge the differences in the underlying low-level mechanisms of heterogeneous middleware technologies like network protocols and service discovery, reducing the amount of effort required to develop and deploy the systems, as discussed in *§ Resolving Functional Integration Challenges using SIML* .

Integration patterns (TrowBridge et al., 2004) provides guidance to system integrators in the form of best patterns and practices, with examples using a particular vendor's products. (Hohpe & Woolf, 2003) catalogs common integration patterns, with an emphasis on system integration via asynchronous messaging using different commercial products. These efforts do not directly provide tools for integration, but instead provide pattern-based guidance to apply existing tools to achieve more effective integration. A future goal of SIML is to add support for modeling integration patterns so that users can design integration architectures using patterns. We also plan to enhance SIML's generative capabilities to incorporate integration pattern guidelines in gateway generation, as discussed in *§ Resolving Functional Integration Challenges using SIML*.

Resource adapters are used during integration to transform data and services exposed by service producers to a form amenable to service consumers. Examples include *data transformation* (mapping from one schema to another), *protocol transformation* (mapping from one network protocol to another), or *interface adaptation* (which includes both data and protocol transformation). The goal of resource adapters is to provide integrated, reusable solutions to common transformation problems encountered in integrating systems built using different middleware technologies.

Existing standards (such as the Java Messaging Specification (SUN, 2002) and J2EE Connector Architecture Specification (Microsystems, 2003)) and tools (such as IBM's MQSeries (IBM, 1999)) provide the architectural framework for performing resource adaptations. These standards and tools, however, approach the integration from a middleware and programming perspective, that is, system integrators must still handcraft the "glue" code that invokes the resource adapter frameworks to connect system components together. In contrast, SIML uses syntactic information present in the DSMLs to automate the required mapping/adaptation by generating the necessary "glue" code, as discussed in *§ Resolving Functional Integration Challenges using SIML*. Moreover, SIML relies on user input only for tool use, as opposed to requiring writing code in a programming language to configure the resource adapters.

Integration frameworks. The semantic Web and the Web Ontology Language (OWL) (Consortium, 2004) have focused on the composition of services from unambiguous, formal descriptions of capabilities as exposed by services on the Web. Research on service composition has focused largely on automation and dynamism (Ponnekanti & Fox, 2002), integration on large-scale "system-of-systems," such as the GRID (Foster, Kesselman, Nick, & Tuecke, 2002). Other work has focused on optimizing service compositions such that they are "QoS-aware" (Zeng et al., 2004); in such "QoS-aware" compositions, a service is composed from multiple other services taking into account the QoS requirements of clients. Because these automated composition techniques rely on unambiguous, formal representations of capabilities, system integrators must make their legacy systems available as Web services. Likewise, system integrators need to provide formal mappings of system capabilities to integrate, which may not always be feasible.

SIML's approach to (meta)model composition, however, is not restricted to a single domain, though the semantics are bound at design time, as discussed in § *The Design and Functionality of SIML*. While both approaches rely on metadata, SIML uses metadata to enhance the generative capabilities during integration. Automated composition techniques, in contrast, focus on extraction of *semantic knowledge* from metadata, which is then used as the basis for producing compositions that satisfy user requirements.

Integration quality analysis. As the integration process evolves, it is necessary to validate whether the results are satisfactory from functional and QoS perspectives. Research on QoS issues associated with integration has yielded languages and infrastructure for evaluating *service-level agreements*, which are contracts

between service providers and consumers that define the obligations of the parties involved and specify what measures to take if service assurances are not satisfied. Examples include (1) the Web Service-level Agreement language (WSLA) (Ludwig, Keller, Dan, King, & Franck, 2003) framework, which defines an architecture to define service-level agreements using an XML Schema, and provides an infrastructure to monitor the conformance of the running system to the desired service-level agreement, (2) (Oldham, Verma, Sheth, & Hakimpour, 2006), which allows monitoring user-specific service level agreements within the WS-Agreement framework, and (3) Rule-based Service Level Agreement (Paschke, Dietrich, & Kuhla, 2005), which is a formal multilayer approach to describing and monitoring service level agreements. Other efforts have focused on defining processes for distributed continuous quality assurance (Wang & Gill, 2004) of integrated

Figure 1. Enterprise distributed system architecture

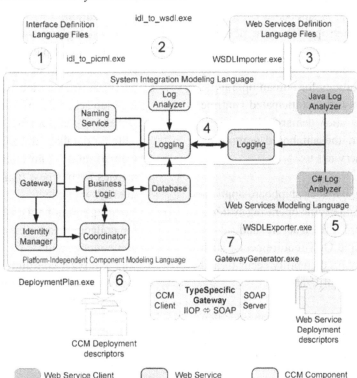

481

systems to identify the impact on performance during system evolution. Information from these analysis tools should be incorporated into future integration activities.

Although quality analysis tools can provide input to design-time integration activities, they do not support automated feedback loops. In particular, they do not provide mechanisms to modify the integration design based on results of quality analysis. SIML, in contrast, is designed to model service-level agreements to allow their evaluation before or after integration, as discussed in *§ The Design and Functionality of SIML.*

FUNCTIONAL INTEGRATION CASE STUDY

To motivate the need for MDE-based functional integration capabilities, this section describes an enterprise distributed system case study from the domain of shipboard computing environments (Hill et al., 2006), focusing on its functional integration challenges. A shipboard computing environment is a metropolitan area network (MAN) of computational resources and sensors that provides on-demand situational awareness and actuation capabilities for human operators, and responds flexibly to unanticipated runtime conditions. To meet such demands in a robust and timely manner, the shipboard computing environment uses services to:

- Bridge the gap between shipboard applications and the underlying operating systems and middleware infrastructure, and
- Support multiple QoS requirements, such as survivability, predictability, security, and efficient resource utilization.

The shipboard computing environment that forms the basis for our case study was originally developed using one component middleware

technology: OMG CCM implemented using the CIAO middleware (Institute for Software Integrated Systems, Vanderbilt University). It was later enhanced to integrate with components written using another middleware technology: W3C web services implemented using Microsoft's .NET Web services.

Shipboard Enterprise Distributed System Architecture

The enterprise distributed system in our case study consists of the components shown in Figure 1 and outlined below:

- **Gateway component**, which provides the user interface and main point of entry into the system for operators,
- **Naming Service components**, which are repositories that hold locations of services available within the system,
- **Identity Manager components**, which are responsible for user authentication and authorization,
- **Business logic components**, which are responsible for implementing business logic, such as determining the route to be taken as part of ship navigation, tracking the work allocation schedule for sailors, and so forth,
- **Database components**, which are responsible for database transactions,
- **Coordinator components**, which act as proxies for business logic components and interact with clients,
- **Logging components**, which are responsible for collecting log messages sent by other components, and
- **Log Analyzer components**, which analyze logs collected by Logging components and display results.

Clients that use the component services outlined first connect to a Naming Service to obtain the

Gateway's location. They then request services offered by the system, passing their authentication/authorization credentials to a Gateway component, which initiates the series of interactions shown in Figure 1. The system provides differentiated services depending on the credentials supplied by clients. Areas where services can be differentiated between various clients include the maximum number of simultaneous connections, maximum amount of bandwidth allocated, and maximum number of requests processed in a particular time period.

To track the performance of the system—and the QoS the system offers to different clients—application developers originally wrote Log Analyzer components to obtain information by analyzing the logs. Based on changes in the COTS technology base and user requirements, a decision was made to expose a Web service API to Logging components so that clients could also track the QoS provided by the system to their requests by accessing information available in Logging components. Because the original system was written using CCM, this change request introduced a new requirement to integrate systems that were not designed to work together, that is, CCM-based Logging components with the Web Service clients.

The flow of control—and the number and functionality of the different participants—in this case study is representative of enterprise distributed systems that require authentication and authorization from clients—and provide differentiated services to clients—based on the credentials offered by the client. Below, we examine this system from an *integration* perspective, that is, how can this system—which initially had a homogeneous, stand-alone design—be integrated with other middleware. Note that this chapter is *not* studying the system from the perspective of system functionality or the QoS provided by the Business Logic components.

Functional Integration Challenges

Functional integration of systems is hard and involves activities that map between various levels of abstraction in the integration lifecycle, including design, implementation, and use of tools. Below we describe some of the key challenges associated with integrating older component middleware technologies, such as CCM and EJB, with newer middleware technologies, such as Web services, and relate them to our experiences developing the shipboard computing case study described in *§ Shipboard Enterprise Distributed System Architecture*. The following list of challenges is by no means complete, that is, we focus on challenges addressed by our approach.

Challenge 1: Choosing an Appropriate Level of Integration

As shown in Step 1 of Figure 2, a key activity is to identify the right level of abstraction at which functional integration of systems should occur, which involves selecting elements from different technologies being integrated that can serve as conduits for exchanging information. Within the different possible levels at which integration can be performed, the criteria for determining the appropriate level of integration include:

- The number of normalizations (i.e., the conversion to/from the native types) required to ensure communication between peer entities being integrated,
- The number (and hence the overhead) and the flexibility of deployment (e.g., in-process vs. out-of-process) of run-time entities required to support functional integration,
- The number of required changes to the integration architecture corresponding to changes in the peers being integrated, and
- Available choices of platform-specific infrastructure (e.g., operating systems, pro-

Figure 2. Functional integration challenges

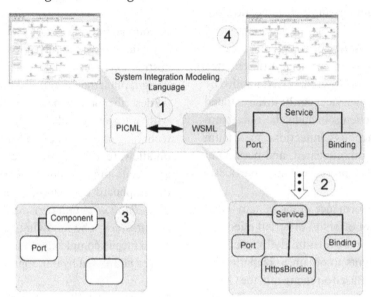

gramming languages, etc.) associated with performing integration at a particular level.

Attempting integration at the wrong level of abstraction can yield brittle integration architectures. For instance, the portions of the system implementing the integration might require frequent changes in response to changes in either the source or the target system being integrated.

In our shipboard computing case study example, we need to integrate Logging components so that Web service clients can access their services. The programming model of CCM prescribes component *ports* as the primary component interconnection mechanism. Web Services also defines ports as the primary interconnection mechanism between a Web service and its clients. During functional integration of CCM with Web services, therefore, a mapping between CCM component ports and Web services ports offers an appropriate level of abstraction for integration. Although mapping CCM and Web services ports is relatively straightforward, determining the right level of abstraction to integrate *arbitrary*

middleware technologies can be much harder because a natural mapping between technologies may not always exist. In general, it is hard for system integrators to decide the right level of abstraction, and requires expertise in all the technologies being integrated.

Challenge 2: Reconciling Differences in Interface Specifications

After the level of abstraction to perform functional integration is determined, it is necessary to map the interfaces exposed by elements of the different technologies as shown in Step 2 of Figure 2. COTS middleware technologies usually have an interface definition mechanism that is separate from the component/service implementation details, for example, CCM uses the OMG Interface Definition Language (IDL), whereas Web services use W3C Web Services Definition Language (WSDL). Older technologies (such as COBOL or C) may not offer as clear a separation of interfaces from implementations, so the interface definition itself may be tangled. Irrespective of the mechanism used to define interfaces, mapping interfaces between any two technologies involves at least three tasks:

- **Datatype mapping:** which involves mapping a datatype (both predefined and complex types) from source to target technology.
- **Exception mapping:** which involves mapping exceptions from source to target technology. Exceptions are defined separately from datatypes because the source or target technologies may not support (e.g., Microsoft's COM uses a HRESULT to convey errors instead of using native C++ exceptions).
- **Language mapping:** which involves mapping datatypes between two technologies while accounting for differences in languages at the same time. Functional integration is limited when attempting this mapping, which is often done via inter-process communication at runtime to work around limitations in hosting these technologies "in-process", that is, within the same process.

In our shipboard computing case study example, Logging components handle CORBA datatypes, (which offer a limited subset of datatypes) whereas Web service clients exchange XML datatypes (which provide a virtually unlimited set of datatypes due to XML's flexibility). Similarly, Logging components throw CORBA exceptions with specific minor/major codes containing specific fault and retry semantics. In contrast, Web service clients must convert these exceptions to SOAP "faults," which have a smaller set of exception codes and associated fault semantics. Performing these mappings is nontrivial, requires expertise in both the source and target technologies, and can incur scalability problems due to tedium and error-proneness if not automated.

Challenge 3: Managing Differences in Implementation Technologies

The interface mapping described above addresses the high-level details of how information is exchanged between different technologies being integrated. As shown in Step 3 of Figure 2, however, low-level technology details (such as networking, authentication, and authorization) are responsible for *delivering* such integration, that is, make it possible for the actual exchange of information between the different technologies being integrated. This adaptation involves a technology mapping and includes the following activities:

- **Protocol mapping**, which reconciles the differences between the protocols used for communication between the two technologies. For example, the IIOP binary protocol is used for communication in CCM, whereas the SOAP XML-based text protocol is used in Web services.
- **Discovery mapping**, which allows bootstrapping and discovery of components/services between source and target technologies. For example, CCM uses the CORBA Naming Service and CORBA Trading Service, whereas Web services use Universal Description Discovery and Integration (UDDI) to discover other Web services.
- **Quality of Service (QoS) mapping**, which maps QoS mechanisms between source and target technologies to ensure that service-level agreements are maintained. For example, CCM uses the CORBA Notification Service to enable anonymous publish/subscribe communication between components, whereas Web Services use WS-Notification and WS-Eventing to handle event-based communication between services.

In our shipboard computing case study example, Logging components only understand

IIOP. Unfortunately, IIOP is not directly interoperable with the SOAP protocol understood by Web service clients. To communicate with Logging components, therefore, requests must be converted from SOAP to IIOP and vice-versa.

There are also differences between how components and services are accessed. For example, the Logging component is exposed to CCM clients as a CORBA Object Reference registered with a Naming Service. In contrast, a Web service client typically expects a Uniform Resource Identifier (URI) registered with a Universal Description Discovery and Integration (UDDI) service to indicate where it can obtain a service. Converting from an Object Reference to a URI is not only nontrivial, but must be kept in sync if Logging components are redeployed to different hosts.

In general, mapping of protocol, discovery, and QoS technology details not only requires expertise in the source/target technologies, it also requires intimate knowledge of the implementation details of these technologies. For example, developers familiar with CCM may not understand the intricacies of IIOP, which is usually known to only a handful of middleware technology developers, rather than application developers. This expertise is needed because issues like QoS are so-called nonfunctional properties, which require inputs from domain and platform experts, in addition to application developers.

Challenge 4: Managing Deployment of Subsystems

Component middleware technologies use declarative notations (such as XML descriptors, source-code attributes, and annotations) to capture various configuration options. Example metadata include EJB deployment descriptors, .NET assembly manifests, and CCM deployment descriptors. This metadata describes configuration options on interfaces and interconnections between these interfaces, as well as implementation entities, such as shared libraries and executables.

As shown in Step 4 of Figure 2, system integrators must track and configure metadata correctly during integration and deployment. In many cases, the correct functionality of the integrated system depends on correct configuration of the metadata. Moreover, the development-time default values for such metadata are often different from the values at integration- and deployment-time. For instance, configuration of Web servers that are exposed to external clients are typically stricter, for example, they impose various limits on resource usage like connection timeouts, interfaces listened on, maximum number of simultaneous connections from a single client to prevent denial-of-service attacks, compared to the ones that developers use when creating Web applications.

In our shipboard computing case study example, Logging components are associated with CCM descriptors needed to configure their functionality, deployed using the CIAO CCM deployment infrastructure, and run on a dedicated network test bed. If Web service clients need to access functionality exposed by Logging components, however, certain services (such as a Web Server to host the service and a firewall) must be configured. This coupling between the deployment information of Logging components and the services exposed to Web Service clients means that changes to the Logging component necessitates corresponding changes to Logging Web service. Failure to keep these elements in sync can result in loss of service to clients of one or both technologies.

Challenge 5. Dealing with Interoperability Issues

Unless a middleware technology has only one version implemented by one provider (which is unusual), there may be multiple implementations from different providers. As shown in Step 5 of Figure 2, differences between these implementations will likely arise due to nonconformant extension to standards, different interpretations of the same (often vague) specification, or implementation bugs. Regardless of the reasons for incompatibility, however, problems arise that often manifest themselves only during system integration. Examples of such differences are highlighted by efforts like the Web Services-interoperability Basic Profile (WS-I) (Ballinger et al., 2006) standard, which is aimed at ensuring compatibility between Web services implementations from different vendors.

In our shipboard computing case study example, not only must Logging components expose their services in WSDL format, they must also ensure that Web service clients developed using different Web services implementations (e.g., Microsoft .NET vs. Java) are equally capably of accessing their services. Logging components therefore need to expose their services using an interoperable subset of WSDL defined by WS-I, so clients are not affected by incompatibilities, such as using SOAP RPC encoding.

Due to the five challenges described above, significant integration effort is spent on configuration activities, such as modifying deployment descriptors and configuring Web servers to ensure that system runs correctly. Significant time is also spent on interoperability activities, such as developing and configuring protocol adapters to link different systems together. Depending on the number of technologies being integrated, this activity does not scale up due to the number of adaptations required and the complexity of the adapter configuration. For example, it took several weeks to develop and configure the gateway (needed to bridge the communication between CCM and Web services) described in *§ Resolving Functional Integration Challenges using SIML.*

In general, problems discovered at integration stage often require implementation changes, thereby necessitating interactions between developers and integrators. These interactions are often inconvenient, and even infeasible (especially when using COTS products), and can significantly com-

plicate integration efforts. The remainder of this chapter shows how our GME-based (meta)model composition framework and associated tools help address these challenges.

DSML COMPOSITION USING GME

This section describes the (meta)model composition framework in the Generic Modeling Environment (GME) (Ledeczi et al., 2001b). GME is a metaprogrammable modeling environment with a general-purpose editing engine, separate view-controller GUI, and a configurable persistence engine. Because GME is *metaprogrammable*, it can be used to design DSMLs, as well as build models that conform to a DSML. Sidebar 1 describes the concepts available in GME that assist in the creation and use of DSMLs.

DSMLs are defined by metamodels, hence, DSML composition is defined by (meta)model composition. The specification of how metamodels should be composed (i.e., what concepts in the metamodels that are composed relate to each other and how) can be specified via association relationships and additional composition operators, as described in (Lédeczi et al., 2001). GME provides the following operators that assist in composition:

- The *equivalence* operator defines a full union between two metamodel components. The two are no longer separate, but instead form a single concept. This union includes all attributes and associations, including generalization, specialization, and containment, of each individual component.
- The *interface inheritance* operator does not support attribute inheritance, but does allow full association inheritance, with one exception: containment associations where the parent functions as the container are not inherited. In other words, the child inherits its parent's external interface, but not its internal structure.

- The *implementation inheritance* operator makes the child inherit all of the parent's attributes, but only the containment associations where the parent functions as the container. No other associations are inherited. In other words, the child inherits the parent's internal structure, but not its external interface. The union of interface and implementation inheritance is the normal inheritance operator of the GME metamodeling language, and their intersection is null.

Together, these three operators allow for a semantically rich composition of metamodels.

A key property of a composite DSML is that it supports the *open-closed* principle (Meyer, 1992), which states that a class should be open for extension but closed with respect to its public interface. In GME, elements of the sub-DSMLs are *closed*, that is, their semantics cannot be altered in the composite DSML. The composite DSML itself, however, is *open*, that is, it allows the definition of new interactions and the creation of new derived elements. All tools that are built for each sub-DSML work without any modifications in the composite DSML and all the models built in the sub-DSMLs are also usable in the composite DSML.

We use the following GME (meta)model composition features to support the SIML-based integration of systems built using different middle-

Figure 3. Domain-specific modeling language composition in GME

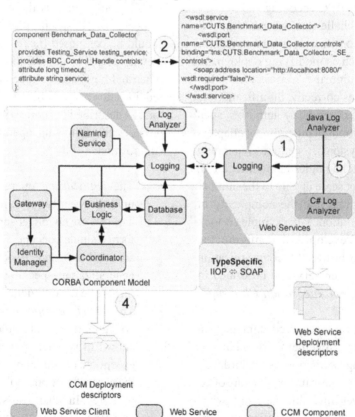

Sidebar 1. Generic modeling environment

The Generic Modeling Environment (GME) is an open-source, visual, configurable design environment for creating DSMLs and program synthesis environments, available for download from `http://escher.isis.vanderbilt.edu/downloads?tool=GME`. A unique feature of GME is that it is *metaprogrammable*, which means that it can not only build DSMLs, but also build models that conform to a DSML. In fact, the environment used to build DSMLs in GME is itself built using another DSML (also known as the *meta-metamodel*) called "MetaGME," which provides the following elements to define a DSML:

- **Project**, which is the top-level container in a DSML,
- **Folders**, which are used to group collections of similar elements together,
- **Atoms**, which are the indivisible elements of a DSML, and used to represent the leaf-level elements in a DSML,
- **Models**, which are the compound objects in a DSML, and are used to contain different types of elements like References, Sets, Atoms, Connections, and so forth (the elements that are contained by a Model are known as *parts*),
- **Aspects**, which are used to provide a different viewpoint of the same Model (every part of a Model is associated with an Aspect),
- **Connections**, which are used to represent relationships between the elements of the domain,
- **References**, which are used to refer to other elements in different portions of a DSML hierarchy (unlike Connections, which can be used to connect elements within a Model), and
- **Sets**, which are containers whose elements are defined within the same aspect and have the same container as the owner.

ware technologies, as described in *§ Integrating Systems with SIML*:

- **Representation of independent concepts.** To enable complete reuse of models and tools of the sub-DSMLs, the composition must be done in such a way that all concepts defined in the sub-DSMLs are preserved. Step 1 of Figure 3 shows how no elements from either sub-DSMLs should be merged together in the composite DSML. GME's composition

operators (Lédeczi et al., 2001) can be used to create new elements in the composite DSML, but the sub-DSMLs as a whole must remain untouched. As a consequence, any model in a sub-DSML can be imported into the composite language, and vice-versa. All models in the composite language that are using concepts from the sub-DSMLs can thus be imported back into the sub-DSML. Existing tools for sub-DSMLs can be reused as well in the composite environment. This technique of composing DSMLs is referred to as *metamodel interfacing* (Emerson & Sztipanovits, 2006) because we create new elements and relationships that provide the interface between the sub-DSMLs.

- **Supporting (meta)model evolution.** DSML composition enables reuse of previously defined (sub-)DSMLs. Just like code reuse in software development, (meta)model reuse can benefit from the concept of *libraries*, which are read-only projects imported to a host project. GME libraries ensure that if an existing (meta)model is used to create a new composite (meta)model, any changes or upgrades to the original will propagate to the places where they are used. Step 2 of Figure 3 shows how if the original (meta)model is imported as a library, GME provides seamless support to update it when new versions become available (libraries are supported in any DSML with GME, not just the metamodeling language). Components in a host project can create references to—and derivations of—library components. The library import process creates a copy of the reused project, so subsequent modifications to the original project are not updated automatically. To update a library inside a host project, a user-initiated refresh operation is required. To achieve unambiguous synchronization, elements inside a project have unique ids, which ensure correct restoration of all relationships that are established among host project components and the library elements.

- **Partitioning (meta)model namespaces.** When two or more (meta)models are composed, name clashes may occur. To alleviate this problem, (meta)model libraries (and hence the corresponding components DSMLs) can have their own names-paces specified by (meta)modelers, as shown in Step 3 of Figure 3. External software components, such as code generators or model analysis tools that were developed for the composite DSML, must use the fully qualified names. But tools that were developed for component DSMLs will still work because GME sets the context correctly before invoking such a component.

- **Handling constraints.** The syntactic definitions of a metamodel in GME can be augmented by static semantics specifications in the form of Object Constraint Language (OCL) (Warmer & Kleppe, 2003) constraint expressions. When metamodels are composed together, the predefined OCL expressions coming from a sub-DSML should not be altered. GME's Constraint Manager therefore uses namespace specifications to avoid any possible ambiguities, and these expressions are evaluated by the Constraint Manager with the correct types and priorities as defined by the sub-DSML, as shown in Step 4 of Figure 3. The composite DSML can also define new OCL expressions to specify the static semantics that augment the specifications originating in the metamodels of the sub-DSMLs.

INTEGRATING SYSTEMS WITH SIML

This section describes how we created and applied the *System Integration Modeling Language* (SIML) to solve the challenges associated with

functional integration of systems in the context of the shipboard computing scenario described in *§ Shipboard Enterprise Distributed System Architecture*. SIML is our open-source composite DSML that simplifies functional integration of component-based systems built using heterogeneous middleware technologies. First, we describe how SIML applies GME's (meta)model composition features described in *§ DSML Composition using GME* to compose DSMLs built for CCM and Web services. We then describe how the challenges described in *§ Functional Integration Challenges* are resolved using features in SIML.

The Design and Functionality of SIML

Applying GME's (Meta)Model Composition Features to SIML

To support integration of systems built using different middleware technologies, SIML uses the GME (meta)model composition features described in *§ DSML Composition using GME* as shown in Figure 4. SIML is thus a composite DSML that allows integration of systems by composing multiple DSMLs, each representing a different middleware technology. Each sub-DSML is responsible for managing the metadata (creation, as well as generation) of the middleware technology it represents.

The composite DSML produced using SIML defines the semantics of the integration, which might include reconciling differences between the diverse technologies, as well as representing characteristics of various implementations. The result is a single composite DSML that retains all the characteristics of its sub-DSMLs, yet also unifies them by defining new interactions between elements present in both DSMLs. System integrators therefore have a single MDE environment that allows the creation and specification of elements in each sub-DSML, as well as interconnecting them as if they were elements of a single domain.

For example, SIML is designed to support composite DSMLs that could represent different resource adaptations required to connect an EJB component with a Web service. Likewise, it could be used to represent the differences between implementation of Web services in the Microsoft .NET framework vs. the implementation in IBM's WebSphere. The problems with functional integration of systems outlined in *§ Functional Integration Challenges* can therefore be resolved by generating metadata directly from the composite DSML because the tools of the sub-DSMLs work seamlessly in the composite.

Applying SIML to Compose CCM and Web Services

Our initial use of SIML was to help integrate CCM with Web services in the context of the shipboard computing case study described in *§ Functional Integration Case Study*. The two sub-DSMLs we needed to integrate to support the new requirements for this case study were:

- The **Platform-independent Component Modeling Language** (PICML) (Balasubramanian et al., 2005), which enables developers of CCM-based systems to define application interfaces, QoS parameters, and system software building rules. PICML can also generate valid XML descriptor files that enable automated system deployment.
- The **Web Services Modeling Language** (WSML), which supports key activities in Web service development, such as creating a model of a Web services from existing WSDL files, specifying details of a Web service including defining new bindings, and auto-generating artifacts required for Web service deployment.

These two sub-DSMLs were developed independently for earlier projects. The case study described in *§ Functional Integration Case*

Study provided the motivation to integrate them together using GME's (meta)model composition framework.

Because SIML is a composite DSML, all valid elements and interactions from both PICML and WSML are valid in SIML. It is therefore possible to design both CCM components (and assemblies of components), as well as Web services (and federations of Web services) using SIML, just as if either PICML or WSML were used independently. The whole is greater than the sum of its parts, however, because SIML defines new interactions that allow connecting a CCM component (or assembly) with a Web service and automates generation of necessary gateways, which are capabilities that exist in neither PICML nor WSML.

Resolving Functional Integration Challenges using SIML

We now show how we applied SIML to resolve the functional integration challenges discussed in *§ Functional Integration Challenges* in the context of our shipboard computing case study example described in *§ Functional Integration Case Study*. Although we focus on the current version of SIML that supports integration of CCM and Web services, its design is sufficiently general that it can be applied to integrate other middleware technologies (such as EJB) without undue effort. Figure 5 shows how SIML resolves the following challenges to generate a gateway given an existing CCM application:

Resolving Challenge 1: Choosing an Appropriate Level of Integration

As mentioned in *§ Functional Integration Challenges*, determining the right level of integration requires expertise in all different technologies being integrated. To allow interactions between CCM components and Web services, SIML defines interactions between ports of CCM components and ports exposed by the Web services.

Figure 4. Design of system integration modeling language (SIML) using model composition

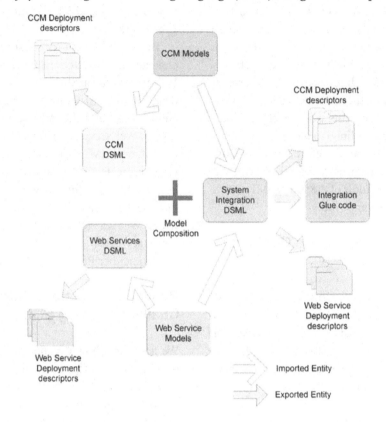

SIML also automates the generation of the glue code, so some choices with respect to the level of integration, for example, mapping of a CCM port to a Web service port, are predetermined, while other decisions, for example, aggregation of more than one CCM component into a single Web service, are customizable.

SIML thus extends the list of valid interactions of both CCM components and Web services, which is an example of a composite DSML defining interactions that do not exist in its sub-DSMLs. SIML can also partition a large system into hierarchies via the concept of "modules," which can be either CCM components (and assemblies of CCM components) or Web services.

In our shipboard computing case study example, a user of SIML needs to import the IDL

files describing the shipboard system, as show in step 1 of Figure 5. Similarly, WSDL files can also be imported into SIML, as shown in step 3 of Figure 5. After the interfaces of the systems have been imported, users can define the interactions between the subsystems, that is, the interaction between the CCM and Web Service logging capabilities can be defined by connecting the ports of the CCM Logging Component to the ports of the Logging Web service.

The connections described above automate a number of activities that arise during integration, including generation of resource adapters, such as the gateways shown in step 7 of Figure 5 and described in the resolution of Challenge 3 below. SIML thus provides a middleware technology-specific integration framework that allows system integrators to define the points of interaction in their system. SIML allows the system integration to be done in a "declarative" fashion, that is, the system integrators specify the points of integration at a high-level using connection between model elements. Using this information, SIML takes care of the translation of the integrator's intent (policy) into the low-level mechanics needed to achieve the integration. The approach taken by SIML is thus different from an "imperative" approach to integration, where the system integrator needs to specify not only the high-level integration design, but also the low-level details of the integration.

SIML's architecture can be enhanced to support integration of other middleware technologies by extending the list of interactions defined by SIML to integrate new technologies. For example, SIML could be extended to support interactions between CCM and EJB or between Web Services and EJB. Extending SIML to support EJB requires specification of a DSML that describes the elements and interactions of EJB. Once the DSML for EJB is specified, it can be imported into SIML as a library while also assigning a new namespace to it. The creation of a new namespace prevents any

clashes between the type systems, for example, between a CCM component and EJB component. Interactions between elements of CCM and EJB can then be defined in the composite DSML. From these new interactions, generative techniques (as explained in resolution to Challenge 3 below) can be applied to automate the integration tasks.

Resolving Challenge 2: Reconciling Differences in Interface Specifications

To map interfaces between CCM and Web services, SIML provides a tool called IDL2WSDL that automatically converts any valid CORBA IDL file to a corresponding WSDL file. As part of this conversion process, IDL2WSDL performs (1) *datatype mapping*, which maps CORBA datatypes to WSDL datatypes and (2) *exception mapping*, which maps both CORBA exceptions to WSDL faults. IDL2WSDL thus relieves system integrators from handling the intricacies of this mapping.

Figure 5 shows how both IDL and WSDL can be imported into the DSML environment corresponding to CCM (PICML) and Web services

Figure 5. Generating a Web service gateway using SIML

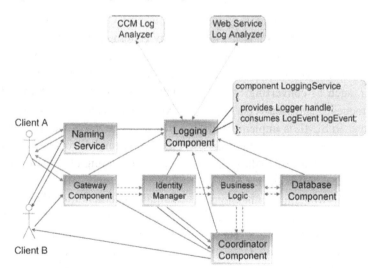

(WSML). This capability allows integrators to define interactions between CCM components and Web services as shown in step 4 of Figure 5. SIML also supports *language mapping* between ISO/ANSI C++ and Microsoft C++/CLI, which is the .NET framework extension to C++.

In our example scenario, IDL2WSDL can automatically generate the WSDL files of the Logging Web service from the IDL files of the Logging Component as shown in step 2 of Figure 5. The generated WSDL file can then be imported into SIML, and annotated with information used during deployment. As shown in step 5 of Figure 5, SIML can also generate a WSDL file back from the model, so that WSDL stubs and skeletons can be generated. SIML thus automates much of the tedious and error-prone details of mapping IDL to WSDL, thereby allowing system integrators to focus on the business logic of the application being integrated.

Resolving Challenge 3: Managing Differences in Implementation Technologies

The rules defined in SIML allow definition of interaction at the modeling level. This feature, however, is not useful if these definitions cannot be translated into runtime entities that actually perform the interactions. SIML therefore generates *resource adapters*, which automatically bridge the differences between protocol formats by performing the necessary conversions of one format into another, such as converting SOAP requests into IIOP requests, and vice-versa.

A *resource adapter* in SIML is implemented as a gateway. A gateway sits between Web service clients and encapsulates access to the CCM component by exposing it as a Web service. SIML allows system integrators to define connections between ports of a CCM component and a Web service, as shown in step 4 of Figure 5. These connections are then used by a SIML *model interpreter*, which automatically determines the opera-

tion/method signatures of operations/methods of the ports on either end of a connection, and uses this information to generate a gateway automatically. As shown in step 7 of Figure 5, the generated gateway is composed of three entities:

1. A **CCM client**, which uses the stubs (client-side proxies) generated from the IDL files and handles the communication with other CCM components using IIOP as the protocol,

2. A **SOAP server**, which uses the skeletons (server-side proxies) generated from the WSDL files and handles the communication with Web service clients using SOAP as the protocol, and

3. A **IIOP-to-SOAP translator**, which operates at the level of programming language (as opposed to the on-wire-protocol level) handling the delegation of Web service requests to the CCM client component as well as dealing with the conversion of replies from the CCM client into a Web service reply to be sent back to the Web Service clients.

The generated gateway thus encapsulates the resource adapter, which contains all the "glue code" necessary to perform datatype mapping, exception mapping, and language mapping between CCM and Web services. SIML's gateway generator is configurable and can currently generate Web service gateways for two different implementations of Web services: GSOAP (Engelen & Gallivan, 2002) and Microsoft ASP. NET. The generated gateway also performs the necessary *protocol mapping* (i.e., between IIOP and SOAP) and *discovery mapping* (i.e., automatically connecting to a Naming Service to obtain object references to CCM components). Our initial implementation does not yet support *QoS mapping*, which is the focus of future work, as described in § *Concluding Remarks*.

In our shipboard computing case study example, SIML can automatically generate the Logging

Web service gateway conforming to GSOAP or Microsoft ASP.NET, by running the SIML model interpreter as shown in step 7 of Figure 5. Auto-generation of gateways eliminates the tedious and error-prone programming effort that would have otherwise been required to integrate CCM components with Web Services. In general, given a pair of technologies to integrate, auto-generation of gateways eliminates the need for both writing code required to perform the technology mapping, as well as the repetitive instantiation of such code for each of the interfaces that need to be integrated. Auto-generation also masks the details of the configuration of the technology-specific *resource adapter*s used in the integration.

Resolving Challenge 4: Managing Deployment of Subsystems

After the necessary integration gateways have been generated, system integrators also need to deploy and configure the application and the middleware using metadata, for example, in the form of XML descriptors. Because SIML is built using (meta)model composition it can automatically use the tools developed for the sub-DSMLs directly from within SIML. For instance, PICML can handle deployment of CCM applications and WSML can handle deployment of Web services.

In our shipboard computing case study example, SIML can thus be used to automatically generate the necessary deployment descriptors for all CCM components, as well as the Logging Web service as shown in steps 5 and 6 of Figure 5. SIML therefore shields system integrators from low-level details of the formats of the different descriptors. It also shields them from manually keeping track of the number of such descriptors required to deploy a CCM component or a Web Service.

By encapsulating the required resource adapters inside a Web service or CCM component, SIML allows reuse of deployment techniques

available for both CCM and Web services. System integrators therefore need not deploy resource adapters separately. While this approach works for in-process resource adapters (such as those generated by SIML), out-of-process resource adapters need support from a deployment descriptor generator. Because SIML is a DSML itself, this support could be added to SIML so it can generate deployment support for out-of-process resource adapters.

Resolving Challenge 5: Dealing with Interoperability Issues

Because knowledge of the underlying middleware technologies is built into SIML, it can compensate for certain types of incompatibilities, such as differences in interface definition styles during design time. For example, IDL2WSDL allows generation of WSDL that supports an interoperable subset of WSDL as defined in the WS-I Basic Profile. System integrators are thus better prepared to avoid incompatibilities that would have traditionally arisen during integration testing.

SIML can also define constraints on WSDL definition as prescribed by the WS-I Basic Profile, so that violations can also be checked at modeling time. Similarly, gateway generation can automatically add workarounds for particular implementation quirks, such as defining the correct set of values for XML namespaces of the interfaces defined in WSDL files depending upon the (observed) behavior of the target middleware implementation. System integrators are once again shielded from discovering these problems during final integration testing. In our shipboard computing case study example, SIML can generate a Logging Web service gateway that either supports a WS-I subset or uses SOAP RPC encoding.

SIML's DSML composition-based approach to integrating systems therefore relieves system integrators from developing more code during integration. The automation of gateway generation allows integration of systems that have a large number of components because developers need not write system specific integration code. In addition, SIML supports evolution of the integrated system by incrementally adding more components or by targeting different middleware implementations as future needs dictate.

CONCLUDING REMARKS

The development of enterprise distributed systems increasingly involves more integration of existing commercial-off-the shelf (COTS) software and less in-house development from scratch. As the capabilities of COTS component middleware technologies grow, the complexity of integration of systems built upon such frameworks also grows. This chapter showed how a model-driven engineering (MDE) approach to functional integration of systems built using component middleware technologies enhances conventional tedious, error-prone, and nonscalable approaches to integration of enterprise distributed systems. In particular, we showed how domain-specific modeling languages (DSML) and (meta)model composition can help MDE tools address these limitations.

To demonstrate the viability of our approach, we enhanced support for composition of DSMLs in the Generic Modeling Environment (GME). Using this new capability, we developed the *System Integration Modeling Language* (SIML), which is a DSML composed from two other DSMLs: the CORBA Component Model (CCM) profile of *Platform-independent Component Modeling Language* (PICML) and the *Web Services Modeling Language* (WSML). We then demonstrated how composing DSMLs can solve functional integration problems in an enterprise distributed system case study by reverse engineering an existing CCM system and exposing it as Web service(s) to Web clients who use these services. Finally, we evaluated the benefits of our approach by

generating a Logging component gateway from the model, which automates key steps needed to functionally integrate CCM components with Web services.

The following is a summary of lessons learned thus far from our work developing and applying the SIML (meta)model composition MDE toolchain to integrate heterogeneous middleware technologies:

- **Integration tools are becoming as essential as design tools.** SIML is designed to bridge the gap between existing *component technologies* (in which the majority of software systems are built) and *integration middleware* (which facilitate the integration of such systems). SIML elevates the activity of integration to the same level as system design by providing MDE tools that support integration design of enterprise distributed systems built with heterogeneous middleware technologies.

- **Representation and evaluation of service-level agreements is a crucial aspect of integration.** Because SIML is a DSML, it can potentially be used as the infrastructure to define constraints on the integration process itself, thereby allowing evaluation of service-level agreements prior to the actual integration. For example, the MDE-based approach used in SIML allows extensions to support associating service-level agreements (SLAs) on sub-systems being integrated, and evaluate such SLAs at design-time itself. The integration can therefore be evaluated from the perspective of "quality-of-integration," in addition to evaluation for feasibility of integration from a functional perspective.

- **Automating key portions of the integration process is critical to building large-scale distributed systems.** Compared with conventional approaches, SIML's MDE approach to system integration automates key aspects of system integration, including gateway "glue code" generation, metadata management, and design-time support for expressing unique domain or implementation assumptions. It supports seamless migration of existing investment in models and allows incremental integration of new systems. SIML also helps integrate applications based on middleware technologies other than CCM and Web services.

- **Standards-based interoperability of design-time tools is key to realizing the benefits of such tools.** Although our implementation of SIML is done using GME as the underlying modeling environment, our MDE approach is general-purpose and can be applied to tool-chains other than GME. For example, by adding support for import/export for XML Metadata Interchange (XMI) (*MOF 2.0/XMI Mapping Specification, v2.1*, 2005), models developed using tools such as IBM's Rational Software Architect, Objecteering UML and MagicDraw UML, can be imported into SIML. SIML can then be used to perform the key integration activities. Application developers and integrators can therefore seamlessly realize the benefits of system development and integration using SIML's MDE-based approach.

- **QoS integration is a complex problem, and requires additional R&D advances.** Though SIML helped map functional aspects of a system from a source technology to a target technology, the nonfunctional, QoS-related aspects of a system should also map seamlessly. For example, technologies like the Real-time CORBA Component Model (RT-CCM) (Wang & Gill, 2004) support many QoS-related features (such as thread pools, lanes, priority-banded connections, and standard static/dynamic scheduling services) that allow system developers to configure the middleware to build systems with desired QoS features. When systems based on RT-CCM are integrated with other

technologies, it is critical to automatically map the QoS-related features used by an application in the source technology to the set of QoS features available in the target technology. For example, a number of specifications have been released for Web services that target QoS features, such as reliable messaging, security, and notification. The focus of our future efforts in functional integration of systems therefore involves extending SIML to map QoS features automatically from one technology to another using DSMLs, such that the integration is automated in all aspects, both functional and nonfunctional.

- **Integration design tools should become a part of the end-to-end software development cycle.** Ultimately, there is a need for integration design tools that help with functional integration, as well as other forms of integration, including data, presentation, and process integration. These design tools themselves require integration into the software development lifecycle to provide an "application integration platform," similar to how software testing tools (such as JUnit (Massol & Husted, 2003) and NUnit (Hunt & Thomas, 2004)) have gained widespread acceptance and have become an integral part of the software development lifecycle.

Instructions for downloading and building the open-source SIML and GME MDE tools are available at http://www.dre.vanderbilt.edu/cosmic.

FUTURE RESEARCH DIRECTIONS

This section discusses emerging and future technological trends in the integration of systems, with special focus on functional integration and deployment of component-middleware(such as EJB and CCM) based systems. We also discuss how MDE approaches help with functional integration of systems.

Increased Focus on Deployment and Configuration of Systems

The success of component middleware technologies like EJB and Microsoft.NET has resulted in software systems created by customizing pre-existing COTS components rather than being created from scratch. The increased use of pre-existing components shifts the focus from development to configuration and deployment of COTS components. With the increase in scale of the systems being developed, traditional approaches to deployment and configuration, (e.g., using *ad hoc* scripts) no longer suffice. To alleviate the complexity in deployment and configuration of systems with a large number of components, specifications of sophisticated deployment infrastructures (such as the OMG's Deployment and Configuration (D&C) specification (*Deployment and Configuration of Component-based Distributed Applications, v4.0,* 2006)) and implementations of these specifications (Deng, Balasubramanian, Otte, Schmidt, & Gokhale, 2005) have emerged.

Another factor contributing to the need for agile deployment and configuration of systems is the transition away from traditional versioned software releases with major upgrades in features between versions, to a more incremental upgrade process with more frequent releases with few feature updates between versions. Technologies like ClickOnce deployment (Microsoft Corporation, 2006a) and Java Web Start (Sun Microsystems, 2006c) which utilizes (Sun Microsystems, 2006b) have been developed to support rapid installation, as well as flexible upgrades of software systems onto a number of target machines.

The trend toward development and use of sophisticated and customizable deployment middleware infrastructure will continue to grow as the scale of deployed systems increases. The proliferation of such deployment middleware,

however, also motivates the need for development of design-time tools, such as PICML (Balasubramanian et al., 2005), in the commercial software product space. Tools that support the Software Factories (Greenfield, Short, Cook, & Kent, 2004) paradigm are a promising start to fill the gap present in design-time tools for deployment. Other efforts include the SOA Tools Platform project (Eclipse.Org, 2006), which aims to build frameworks that help in the design, configuration, assembly, deployment, monitoring, and management of software designed using the Service Component Architecture specification (SCA) (IBM DeveloperWorks, 2005).

Integration of Systems Using Heterogeneous Component Technologies

Large-scale distributed systems are also composed of heterogeneous competing middleware technologies, such as EJB, CCM, and Microsoft. NET. The trend towards selling software as a service has resulted in the Service-oriented Architecture (SOA) paradigm becoming a popular way to integrate and deploy in-house applications systems. The most popular implementation of SOA—Web services—leverages the ubiquitous presence of the Web to its advantage, and thus figures prominently in enterprise distributed system integration activities and standards.

An older approach is Enterprise Application Integration (EAI), which implement normalized message routers. In this approach all messages between applications that are integrated are first normalized to a canonical format before being routed to the destination. In the presence of service-oriented middleware technologies, however, such normalization might impose an unnecessary and unacceptable overhead (Vinoski, 2003) on the performance and QoS offered by the integrated system. New approaches to implementing system integration middleware, such as in IONA's Artix (IONA Technologies, 2006), Advanced Message

Queuing Protocol (Vinoski, 2006), Java Business Integration (Sun Microsystems, 2006a), and the Service Component Architecture (IBM DeveloperWorks, 2005), are designed to support pluggable architectures for system integration.

The increase in sophistication of integration middleware technologies will likely mirror the need for flexible integration architectures. Coupled with the increase in heterogeneity of the middleware technologies, the task of integration is likely to develop into a critical stage of the traditional software development lifecycle. We therefore need tools to support the design and configuration of the integration architectures based on these integration middleware platforms. Tools like SIML described in this paper are a step in this direction, and motivate the need for more R&D activities and commercial products in this area.

MDE-Based Integration

The need for design-time tools to support the integration activities highlighted above will result in the development of tools to simplify system integration. The levels of abstraction in existing software development methods, such as object-oriented programming (OOP) and aspect-oriented programming (AOP), and technologies (such as third-generation programming languages like C++, Java and C#, and application frameworks like Microsoft.NET and Java Class libraries), however, has the potential to render integration tools as complex as the software being integrated. It is therefore critical that these tools support a higher-level of abstraction, for example, models using a MDE approach, as opposed to using low-level configuration files in XML or programming language code.

A promising approach is to build MDE tools that use models with well-defined semantics to capture the design intent including the assumptions in an explicit fashion. Representing the integration architecture as models provides many benefits, including:

- Making integration design decisions explicit, supporting retargeting to multiple integration platforms and allowing domain experts to concentrate on integration activity rather than platform-specific details;
- Providing a common format for reverse engineering from pre-existing systems, which is important because integration of enterprise distributed systems typically involves integrating many pre-existing (often heterogeneous) pieces, as opposed to pieces implemented from scratch; and
- Transferring information between different integration tools than specifications written using informal notations, such as English.

Promising approaches to representation of systems using models include the OMG's Unified Modeling Language (UML) (*Unified Modeling Language (UML) v1.4*, 2001) and domain-specific languages based on OMG's Meta-object Facility (MOF) (*MetaObject Facility (MOF) 2.0 Core Specification*, 2003), as well as technologies like Microsoft's System Definition Model (SDM) (Microsoft Corporation, 2006b).

The QoS offered by systems that are integrated from a number of subsystems will likely be determined by the quality of the integration architecture. To represent complex integration architectures at a high-level of abstraction—and to support understanding of existing subsystems during integration—it is helpful to use an MDE-based integration approach. Model-driven tools like SIML are a step in dealing with the complexity of future integration technologies.

REFERENCES

Balasubramanian, K., Balasubramanian, J., Parsons, J., Gokhale, A., & Schmidt, D. C. (2005).

A platform-independent component modeling language for distributed real-time and embedded systems. In *Rtas '05: Proceedings of the 11th IEEE Real Time on Embedded Technology and Applications Symposium,* (pp. 190-199). Los Alamitos, CA, USA: IEEE Computer Society.

Ballinger, K., Ehnebuske, D., Ferris, C., Gudgin, M., Liu, C. K., Nottingham, M., et al. (2006, April). *WS-I basic profile.* Retrieved March 23, 2008, from www.ws-i.org/Profiles/BasicProfile-1.1.html

Britton, C., & Bye, P. (2004). *IT architectures and middleware: Strategies for building large, integrated systems.* Boston, MA, USA: Addison-Wesley.

Consortium, W. W. W. (2004, February). *Web ontology language.* Retrieved March 23, 2008, from www.w3.org/2004/OWL/

CORBA Components. (2002, June). Retrieved May 12, 2008 from http://www.omg.org/technology/documents/formal/components.htm

Deng, G., Balasubramanian, J., Otte, W., Schmidt, D. C., & Gokhale, A. (2005, November). DAnCE: A QoS-enabled component deployment and configuration engine. In *Proceedings of the 3rd Working Conference on Component Deployment (cd 2005),* (pp. 67-82). Grenoble, France: Springer-Verlag.

Deng, G., Lu, T., Turkay, E., Gokhale, A., Schmidt, D. C., & Nechypurenko, A. (2003, October). Model driven development of inventory tracking system. In *Proceedings of the OOPSLA 2003 Workshop on Domain-specific Modeling Languages.* Anaheim, CA: ACM Press.

Deployment and Configuration of Component-based Distributed Applications, v4.0. (2006, April). Retrieved May 12, 2008 from http://www.omg.org/technology/documents/formal/deployment.htm

Eclipse.Org. (2006). *Soa tools platform project.* Retrieved March 23, 2008, from http://www.eclipse.org/stp/index.php

Emerson, M., & Sztipanovits, J. (2006, Oct). Techniques for metamodel composition. In Proceedings of the *6th OOPSLA Workshop on Domain-specific Modeling, OOPSLA 2006,* (pp. 123-139). Portland, OR: ACM Press.

Engelen, R. van, & Gallivan, K. (2002). The gSOAP toolkit for Web services and peer-to-peer computing networks. In *Ccgrid,* (pp. 128-135). Los Alamitos, CA, USA: IEEE Computer Society.

Foster, I., Kesselman, C., Nick, J. M., & Tuecke, S. (2002). Grid services for distributed system integration. *Computer, 35*(6), 37-46.

Greenfield, J., Short, K., Cook, S., & Kent, S. (2004). *Software factories: Assembling applications with patterns, models, frameworks, and tools.* New York: John Wiley & Sons.

Hill, J. H., Slaby, J., Baker, S., & Schmidt, D. C. (2006, August). Applying system execution modeling tools to evaluate enterprise distributed real-time and embedded system QoS. In *Proceedings of the 12th International Conference on Embedded and Real-time Computing Systems and Applications* (pp. 350-362). Sydney, Australia: IEEE Computer Society.

Hohpe, G., & Woolf, B. (2003). *Enterprise integration patterns: Designing, building, and deploying messaging solutions.* Boston, MA, USA: Addison-Wesley.

Hunt, A., & Thomas, D. (2004). *Pragmatic unit testing in c# with nunit.* Raleigh, NC, USA: The Pragmatic Programmers.

IBM. (1999). *MQSeries family.* Retrieved March 23, 2008, from www-4.ibm.com/software/ts/mqseries/

IBM. (2001). *WebSphere.* Retrieved March 23, 2008, from www.ibm.com/software/info1/websphere/index.jsp

IBM DeveloperWorks. (2005). *Service component architecture.* Retrieved March 23, 2008, from http://www-128.ibm.com/developerworks/library/specification/ws-sca/

Institute for Software Integrated Systems. (Vanderbilt University). *Component-integrated ACE ORB (CIAO).* Retrieved March 23, 2008, from www.dre.vanderbilt.edu/CIAO/

IONA Technologies. (2006). *Artix -soa for the complex enterprise.* Retrieved March 23, 2008, from http://www.iona.com/products/artix/

Karsai, G., Neema, S., Abbott, B., & Sharp, D. (2002, August). A modeling language and its supporting tools for avionics systems. In *Proceedings of 21st Digital Avionics Systems Conference* (pp. 6A3-1–6A3-13). Los Alamitos, CA: IEEE Computer Society.

Karsai, G., Sztipanovits, J., Ledeczi, A., & Bapty, T. (2003, January). Model-integrated development of embedded software. *Proceedings of the IEEE, 91*(1), 145-164.

Ledeczi, A., Bakay, A., Maroti, M., Volgysei, P., Nordstrom, G., Sprinkle, J., et al. (2001a, November). Composing domain-specific design environments. *IEEE Computer 34,* 44-51.

Lédeczi Ákos, Nordstrom, G., Karsai, G., Volgyesi, P., & Maroti, M. (2001b). On metamodel composition. In *Proceedings of the 2001 IEEE International Conference on Control Applications (cca),* (pp. 756-760). Mexico City, Mexico: IEEE.

Ludwig, H., Keller, A., Dan, A., King, R. P., & Franck, R. (2003, January). *Web service level agreement language specification.* Retrieved March 23, 2008, from reseachweb.watson.ibm.com/wsla/documents.html

Massol, V., & Husted, T. (2003). *Junit in action.* Greenwich, CT, USA: Manning Publications Co.

MetaObject Facility (MOF) 2.0 Core Specification. (2003, October).

Meyer, B. (1992, October). Applying design by contract. *Computer (IEEE), 25*(10), 40-51.

Microsoft Corporation. (2002). *Microsoft .NET Development.* Retrieved March 23, 2008, from msdn.microsoft.com/net/

Microsoft Corporation. (2006a). *Clickonce deployment overview.* Retrieved March 23, 2008, from http://msdn2.microsoft.com/en-us/library/142dbbz4.aspx

Microsoft Corporation. (2006b). *System definition model overview.* Retrieved March 23, 2008, from http://www.microsoft.com/ windowsserversystem/dsi/sdmwp.mspx

Microsystems, S. (2003, November). *J2EE connector architecture specification.* Retrieved March 23, 2008, from http://java.sun.com/j2ee/connector/

MOF 2.0/XMI mapping specification, v2.1. (2005, September). Retrieved May 12, 2008, from http://www.omg.org/spec/XMI/index.htm

Oldham, N., Verma, K., Sheth, A., & Hakimpour, F. (2006). Semantic ws-agreement partner selection. In *Www '06: Proceedings of the 15th International Conference on World Wide Web,* (pp. 697-706). New York, USA: ACM Press.

Paschke, A., Dietrich, J., & Kuhla, K. (2005, November). A logic based sla management framework. In L. Kagal, T. Finin, & J. Hendler (Eds.), *Iswc '05: Proceedings of the Semantic Web and Policy Workshop, 4th International Semantic Web Conference,* (pp. 68-83). Baltimore, MD, USA: UMBC eBiquity Research Group.

Ponnekanti, S. R., & Fox, A. (2002, January). SWORD: A developer toolkit for Web service composition. In *Www '02: Proceedings of the World Wide Web Conference: Alternate Track on Tools and Languages for Web Development.* New York, USA: ACM Press. Retrieved May 12,

2008 from http://www2002.org/CDROM/alternate/786/index.html

Schmidt, D. C. (2006). Model-driven engineering. *IEEE Computer, 39*(2), 25-31.

Sharp, D. C. (2000, August). Reducing avionics software cost through component based product line development. In P. Donohoe (Ed.), *Software product lines: Experience and research directions* (Vol. 576). New York, USA: Springer-Verlag.

Smith, C., & Williams, L. (2001). *Performance solutions: A practical guide to creating responsive, scalable*. Boston, MA, USA: Addison-Wesley.

Stankovic, J. A., Zhu, R., Poornalingam, R., Lu, C., Yu, Z., Humphrey, M., et al. (2003). Vest: An aspect-based composition tool for real-time systems. In *Rtas '03: Proceedings of the 9th IEEE Real-time and Embedded Technology and Applications Symposium,* (p. 58). Washington, DC, USA: IEEE Computer Society.

SUN. (2002). *Java messaging service specification.* Retrieved March 23, 2008, from java.sun.com/products/jms/ Sun Microsystems. (2001, August). *Enterprise JavaBeans specification.* Retrieved March 23, 2008, from http://java.sun.com/products/ejb/docs.html Sun Microsystems. (2006a). *Java business integration (jbi).* Retrieved March 23, 2008, from http://www.jcp.org/en/jsr/detail?id=208 Sun Microsystems. (2006b). *Java network launching protocol and api.* Retrieved March 23, 2008, from http://jcp.org/en/jsr/detail?id=56 Sun Microsystems. (2006c). *Java Web start technology.* Retrieved March 23, 2008, from http://java.sun.com/products/javawebstart/index.jsp

Trask, B., Paniscotti, D., Roman, A., & Bhanot, V. (2006). Using model-driven engineering to complement software product line engineering in developing software defined radio components and applications. In *Proceedings of Oopsla '06: Companion to the 21st ACM SIGPLAN Conference on Object-oriented Programming Systems,*

Languages, and Applications, (pp. 846-853). New York, USA: ACM Press.

TrowBridge, D., Roxburgh, U., Hohpe, G., Manolescu, D., & Nadhan, E. G. (2004, June). *Integration patterns.* Retrieved March 23, 2008, from msdn.microsoft.com/library/default.asp?url=/library/en-us/dnpag/html/intpatt.asp

UML Profile for Enterprise Application Integration (EAI). (2004, March). Retrieved May 12, 2008, from http://www.omg.org/technology/documents/formal/eai.htm

Unified Modeling Language (UML) v1.4. (2001, September). Retrieved May 12, 2008, from http://www.omg.org/spec/UML/1.4/

Vinoski, S. (2003). Integration with Web services. *IEEE Internet Computing, 07*(6), 75-77.

Vinoski, S. (2006). Advanced message queuing protocol. *IEEE Internet Computing, 10*(6), 87-89.

Wang, N., & Gill, C. (2004). Improving real-time system configuration via a qos-aware corba component model. In *Hicss '04: Proceedings of the 37th Annual Hawaii International Conference on System Sciences (hicss'04) -track 9,* (p. 90273.2). Washington, DC, USA: IEEE Computer Society.

Warmer, J., & Kleppe, A. (2003). *The object constraint language: Getting your models ready for mda.* Boston, MA, USA: Addison-Wesley Longman.

White, J., Schmidt, D., & Gokhale, A. (2005, October). Simplifying autonomic enterprise Java Bean applications via model-driven development: A case study. In *Proceedings of MODELS 2006: 8th International Conference on Model Driven Engineering Languages and Systems.* Montego Bay, Jamacia: ACM Press.

Zeng, L., Benatallah, B., Ngu, A. H., Dumas, M., Kalagnanam, J., & Chang, H. (2004). QoS-aware middleware for Web services composition. *IEEE Transactions on Software Engineering, 30*(5), 311-327.

ADDITIONAL READING

Allen, P. (2002, January). Model driven architecture. *Component Development Strategies, 12*(1).

Balasubramanian, K., Balasubramanian, J., Parsons, J., Gokhale, A., & Schmidt, D. C. (2006). A platform-independent component modeling language for distributed real-time and embedded systems. *Elsevier Journal of Computer and System Sciences*, 171-185.

Christensen, E., Curbera, F., Meredith, G., & Weerawarana, S. (2001, March). *Web services description language (WSDL) 1.1.* Retrieved March 23, 2008, from www.w3.org/TR/wsdl

The Common Object Request Broker: Architecture and Specification. (2002, December).

DeMichiel, L., &Keith, M. (2006, May). *Enterprise Java Beans 3.0 specification: Simplified API.* Retrieved March 23, 2008, from jcp.org/about-Java/communityprocess/final/jsr220/index.html

Curbera F., Duftler M., Khalaf, R., Nagy, W., Mukhi, N., & Weerawarana, S. (2002, March-April). Unraveling the Web services Web—an introduction to SOAP, WSDL, and UDDI. *IEEE Internet Computing, 6*(2), 86-93.

Frankel, D. (2003). *Model driven architecture: Applying MDA to enterprise computing.* Indianapolis, IN: John Wiley & Sons.

Gokhale, A., Balasubramanian, K., Balasubramanian, J., Krishna, A. S., Edwards, G. T., Deng, G., et al. (2007). Model driven middleware: A new paradigm for deploying and provisioning distributed real-time and embedded applications. *The Journal of Science of Computer Programming: Special Issue on Model Driven Architecture.*

Gokhale, A., Schmidt, D. C., Natarajan, B., &Wang, N. (2002, July). Applying the model driven architecture to distributed real-time and embedded applications. In Proceedings of the *OMG Workshop on Embedded & Real-time Distributed Object Systems.* Washington, D.C.

Kleppe, A., Warmer, J., & Bast, W. (2003). *Mda explained: The model driven architecture(mdaTM): Practice and promise.* Boston, USA: Addison-Wesley Longman.

Model Driven Architecture (MDA). (2001, July).

Schmidt, D. C., & Vinoski, S. (2004a, February). The CORBA component model, part 1: Evolving towards components. *The C/C++ Users Journal.*

Schmidt, D. C., & Vinoski, S. (2004b, May). The CORBA component model, part 2: Defining components with the IDL 3.x Types. *The C/C++ Users Journal.*

Schmidt, D. C., & Vinoski, S. (2004c, September). The CORBA component model, part 3: The CCM container architecture and component implementation framework. *The C/C++ Users Journal.*

Schmidt, D. C., & Vinoski, S. (2004d, October). The CORBA component model, part 4: Implementing components with CCM. *The C/C++ Users Journal.*

Sztipanovits, J., & Karsai, G. (1997, April). Model-integrated computing. *IEEE Computer, 30*(4), 110-112.

Vinoski, S. (2002, May-June). Web services interaction models, part 1: Current practice. *IEEE Internet Computing, 6*(3), 89-91.

Wang, N., Schmidt, D. C., & O'Ryan, C. (2000). An overview of the CORBA component model.

In G. Heineman & B. Councill (Eds.), *Component-based software engineering.* Reading, MA: Addison-Wesley.

ENDNOTES

[1]   This work was sponsored in part by grants from Raytheon and Lockheed Martin Advanced Technology Laboratories.

[2]   In the remainder of this chapter, "system" or "application" refers to an enterprise distributed system built using component middleware like EJB, Microsoft .NET, or CCM.

Compilation of References

Aalst, W. (1998). The application of petri nets to workflow management. *The Journal of Circuits, Systems and Computers, 8*(1), 21-66.

Aalst, W. V. D., & Hee, K. V. (2002). *Workflow management: Models, methods, and systems.* Cambridge, MA: The MIT Press.

Aalst, W., Hee, K., & Houben, G. (1994). Modelling workflow management systems with high-level Petri nets. In G. Michelis, C. Ellis, & G. Memmi (Eds.), *Proceedings of the Second Workshop on Computer-supported Cooperative Work, Petri Nets and Related Formalisms,* (pp. 31-50).

Aalst, W., Hofstede, A. H. M. T., Kiepuszewski, B., & Barros, A. P. (2003). Workflow patterns. *Distributed Parallel Databases, 14*(1), 5-51.

Abbott, R.J. (1983, November). Program design by informal English descriptions. *Communications of the ACM, 26*(11), 882-894.

Abowd, G. (1998). Analyzing development qualities at the architecture level: The software architecture analysis method. In L. Bass, P. Clements, & R. Kazman (Eds.), *Software architecture in practice.* Addison-Wesley.

Abrahamsson, P., Warsta , J., Siponen , M. T., & Ronkainen, J. (2003), New directions on agile methods: A comparative analysis. In *Proceedings of the 25th International Conference on Software Engineering (ICSE'03),* Portland, OR, USA.

Actipro. (2006). *Actipro wizard - Wizard Generation.NET framework windows forms control.* Retrieved March 23, 2008, from http://www.actiprosoftware.com/Products/DotNet/WindowsForms/Wizard/Default.aspx

Adler, R. (1995). Emerging standards for component software. *IEEE Computer, 28*(3), 68-77.

Afgan, E. (2004). Role of the resource broker in the grid. In Proceedings of the *42nd Annual ACM Southeast Conference,* (pp. 299-300). Huntsville, AL: ACM Press.

Afgan, E., & Bangalore, P. (2007). Application specification language (ASL)–a language for describing applications in grid computing. In *Proceedings of the 4th International Conference on Grid Services Engineering and Management - GSEM 2007,* Leipzig, Germany.

Afgan, E., Sathyanarayana, P., & Bangalore, P. (2006). Dynamic task distribution in the grid for BLAST. In *Proceedings of Granular Computing 2006,* (pp. 554-557). Atlanta, GA: IEEE.

Agresti, W. (1986). *New paradigms for software development.* North Holland: IEEE Computer Society Press.

Aizenbud-Reshef, N., Nolan, B. T., Rubin, J., & Shaham-Gafni, Y. (2006). Model traceability. *IBM Systems Journal, 45*(3), 515-526.

Albert, C., & Brownsword, L. (2002). *Evolutionary process for integrating COTS-based systems (EPIC) building, fielding, and supporting commercial-off-the-shelf (COTS) based solutions* (Tech. Rep. No. CMU/SEI-2002-TR-005).

Alexander, C., Ishikawa, S., & Silverstein, M. (1977). *A pattern language—towns, buildings, construction.* New York: Oxford University Press.

Alexandre, R.J. F., & Medioni, G. G. (2001). A modular software architecture for real-time video processing. In *Proceedings of the 2nd International Workshop on Computer Vision Systems*, (pp. 35-49).

Allcock, B., Bester, J., Bresnahan, J., Chervenak, A. L., Foster, I., Kesselman, C., et al. (2001). Data management and transfer in high-performance computational grid environments. *Parallel Computing, 28*(5), 749-771.

Allen, G., Davis, K., Goodale, T., Hutanu, A., Kaiser, H., Kielmann, T., et al. (2005). The grid application toolkit: Toward generic and easy application programming interfaces for the grid. *Proceedings of the IEEE, 93*(3), 534-550.

Altschul, S. F., Gish, W., Miller, W., Myers, E. W., & Lipman, D. J. (1990). Basic local alignment search tool. *Mol Biol, 215*(3), 403-410.

Amdahl, G.M., Blaauw, G., & Brooks, F. (1964). Architecture of the IBM system/360. *IBM Journal of Research and Development, 8*(2), 87-97.

Andrews, T., Curbera, F., Dholakia, H., Goland, Y., Klein, J., Leymann, F., et al. (2003). *Specification: Business process execution language for Web services version 1.1.* Retrieved March 6, 2008, from http://www-106.ibm.com/developerworks/library/ws-bpel/

AndroMDA. (2007). Retrieved March 22, 2008, from team.andromda.org

Ang, J., Cherbakov, L., & Ibrahim, M. (2005). *SOA antipatterns.* Retrieved March 6, 2008, from http://www-128.ibm.com/developerworks/webservices/library/ws-antipatterns/

Anjomshoaa, A., Brisard, F., Drescher, M., Fellows, D., Ly, A., McGough, S., et al. (2005). *Job submission description language (JSDL) specification, version 1.0* (Tech. Rep. No. GFD-R.056). Global Grid Forum (GGF).

Antkiewicz, M. (2006, September). Round-trip engineering of framework-based software using framework-specific modeling languages. In *Proceeding of the 21st IEEE International Conference on Automated Software Engineering*, Washington, DC, (pp. 323-326).

Antkiewicz, M., & Czarnecki, K. (2006, October). Framework-specific modeling languages with round-trip engineering. In *Proceeding of the 9th International Conference on Model Driven Engineering Languages and Systems*, Genova, Italy, (pp. 692-706).

Antkiewicz, M., & Czarnecki, K. (2006, October). Round-trip engineering of eclipse plug-ins using eclipse workbench part interaction FSML. In *Proceedings of the International Conference on Object Oriented Programming Systems Languages and Applications (OOPSLA)*, Portland, OR.

Arkin, A., Askary, S., Bloch, B., Curbera, F., Goland, Y., & Kartha, N. (2005). *Web services business process execution language version 2.0.* WS-BPEL TC OASIS.

Arkley, P., Mason, P., & Riddle, S. (2002, September). Position paper: Enabling traceability. In *Paper presented at the 1st International Workshop in Traceability in Emerging Forms of Software Engineering (TFFSE)* (pp. 61-65). Edinburgh, Scotland.

Armstrong, R., Gannon, D., Geist, A., Keahey, K., Kohn, S., McInnes, L., et al. (1999). Toward a common component architecture for high-performance scientific computing. In *Proceedings of the High-Performance Distributed Computing Conference (HPDC)*, (pp. 115-124). Redondo Beach, CA: IEEE Computer Society.

Arnold, M., & Ryder, B. G. (2001). A framework for reducing the cost of instrumented code. In *Proceedings of the SIGPLAN Conference on Programming Language Design and Implementation*, (pp. 168-179).

Artho, C., & Biere, A. (2005). Combined static and dynamic analysis. In *Proceedings of the 1st International Workshop on Abstract Interpretation of Object-oriented Language (AIOOL 2005)*, ENTCS, Paris. Elsevier Science Publishing.

Arthur, L. (1988). *Software evolution—the software maintenance challenge.* John Wiley.

Atkinson, C., & Kuhne, T. (2003). Model-driven development: A Metamodeling Foundation. *IEEE Software, 20*(5), 36-41.

Atkinson, C., Bayer, J., Bunse, C., Kamsties, E., Laitenberger, O., Laqua, R., et al. (2002). *Component-based product line engineering with UML*. Addison-Wesley.

Baas, N., & Emmeche, C. (1997). *On emergence and explanation*. Retrieved March 7, 2008, from http://www.nbi.dk/~emmeche/coPubl/97d.NABCE/ExplEmer.html (2001-11-22)

Bajana, D., Borovcová, A., Čurn, J., Fojta, R., Ignáth, Š., Malohlava, M., et al. (2005). *Výstupy projektu "Hodnocení kvality škol"* (in Czech: Outputs of the project "Evaluation of the quality of schools").

Balasubramanian, K., Balasubramanian, J., Parsons, J., Gokhale, A., & Schmidt, D.C. (2005, March). A platform-independent component modeling language for distributed real-time and embedded systems. In *Proceedings of the 11th IEEE Real-Time and Embedded Technology and Applications Symposium*, San Francisco, CA, (pp. 190-199).

Balasubramanian, K., Gokhale, A., Karsai, G., Sztipanovits, J., & Neema, S. (2006). Developing applications using model-driven design environments. *IEEE Computer, 39*(2), 33-40.

Balasubramanian, K., Gokhale, A., Lin, Y., Zhang, J., & Gray, J. (2006, June). Weaving deployment aspects into domain-specific models. *International Journal on Software Engineering and Knowledge Engineering, 16*(3), 403-424.

Balasubramanian, K., Krishna, A., Turkay, E., Balasubramanian, J., Parsons, J., Gokhale, A., & Schmidt, D.C. (2005, April). Applying model-driven development to distributed real-time and embedded avionics systems *International Journal of Embedded Systems, special issue on Design and Verification of Real-Time Embedded Software*.

Ballinger, K., Ehnebuske, D., Ferris, C., Gudgin, M., Liu, C. K., Nottingham, M., et al. (2006, April). *WS-I basic profile*. Retrieved March 23, 2008, from www.ws-i.org/Profiles/BasicProfile-1.1.html

Balogh, A., & Varro, D. (2007). The model transformation of the VIATRA2 framework. *Science of Computer Programming (Special Issue on Model Transformation)*.

Balsamo, S., Bernardo, M., & Simeoni, M. (2002). Combining stochastic process algebras and queueing networks for software architecture analysis. In *Proceedings of the ACM International Workshop on Software and Performance*, (pp. 190-202).

Banerji, A. (1995). Electronic performance support systems. In *Proceedings of the International Conference on Computers in Education (ICCE '95)*.

Barais, O., Cariou, E., Duchien, L., Pessemier, N., & Seinturier, L. (2004). TranSAT: A framework for the specification of software architecture evolution. In *Proceedings of the Workshop on Coordination and Adaptation Techniques for Software Entities, ECOOP 2004*.

Barnes, J. (1980). An overview of ada. *Software—Practice and Experience, 10*, 851-887.

Baru, C., Moore, R., Rajasekar, A., & Wan, M. (1998). The SDSC storage resource broker. In *Proceedings of CASCON '98*, (pp.). Toronto, Canada: IBM Press.

Basili, V.R., & Boehm, B. (2001, May). COTS-based systems top 10 list. *Computer, 34*(5), 91-95.

Bass, L. (2007). *Reasoning about software quality attributes*. Retrieved March 7, 2008, from http://www.sei.cmu.edu/architecture/reasoning_about.html

Bass, L., Clements, P., & Kazman, P. (2003). *Software architecture in practice* (2nd ed.). Addison-Wesley.

Bauer, B., Muller J.P., & Odell, J. (2001). Agent UML: A formalism for specifying multiagent interaction. In P. Ciancarini & M. Wooldridge (Eds.), *Agent-oriented software engineering* (pp. 91-103). Berlin: Springer-Verlag.

Baxter, I. (2004). DMS: Program transformations for practical scalable software evolution. In *Proceedings of the 26th International Conference on Software Engineering*, (pp. 625-634).

Beck, K. (1999). *Extreme programming explained: Embrace change*. Boston: Addison-Wesley.

Beck, K., Beedle, M., van Bennekum, A., Cockburn, A., Cunningham, W., Fowler, M., et al. (2001). *Agile programming manifesto*. Retrieved March 6, 2008, from http://www.agilemanifesto.org/

Beck, M., Bohme, H., Dziadzka, M., Kunitz, U., Magnus, R., & Verworner, D. (1999). *Linux Kernel internals (2nd ed.)*. Addison Wesley Longman.

Becker, B., Beyer, D., Giese, H., Klein, F., & Schilling, D. (2006). Symbolic invariant verification for systems with dynamic structural adaptation. In *Proceedings of the International Conference on Software Engineering (ICSE), Shanghai, China, (pp. 21-81)*. ACM Press.

Bendraou, R., Gervais, M.-P., & Blanc, X. (2006). UML4SPM: An executable software process modeling language providing high-level abstracts. In *Proceedings of the10th IEEE International Enterprise Distributed Object Computing Conference (EDOC'06)*, Hong Kong, China.

Bengtsson, J., Larsen, K., Larsson, F., Pettersson, P., & Yi, W. (1995). UPPAAL: A tool suite for automatic verification of real-time systems. In *Proceedings of the Workshop on Verification and Control of Hybrid Systems III*, (Vol. 1066, pp. 232-243).

Bentley, J. (1986). Little languages. *Communications of the ACM, 29*(8), 711-721.

Berman, F., Chien, A., Cooper, K., Dongarra, J., Foster, I., Gannon, D., et al. (2001). The GrADS project: Software support for high-level grid application development. *International Journal of High Performance Computing Applications, 15*(4), 327-344.

Berman, F., Hey, A., & Fox, G. (Eds.). (2003). *Grid computing: Making the global infrastructure a reality*. New York: John Wiley & Sons.

Bernstein, P.A, & Bergstraesser, T. (1999). Meta-data support for data transformations using Microsoft repository. *IEEE Data Engineering Bulletin, 22*, 9-14.

Bertolino, A., & Mirandola, R. (2004). Software performance engineering of component-based systems. In *Proceedings of the 4th International Workshop on Software and Performance*, Redwood Shores, CA, (pp. 238-242).

Bhagwat, D., Chiticariu, L., Tan, W.C., & Vijayvargiya, G. (2004). *.An annotation management system for relational databases* .VLDB, pp. 900-911.

Bic, L. F., Fukuda, M., & Dillencourt, M. (1996). Distributed computing using autonomous objects. *IEEE Computer, 29*(8), 55-61.

Binder, W. (2005). A portable and customizable profiling framework for Java based on bytecode instruction counting. In *Proceedings of the Third Asian Symposium on Programming Languages and Systems (APLAS 2005)*, (LNCS 3780, pp. 178-194).

Binder, W. (2005, September). Portable, efficient, and accurate sampling profiling for java-based middleware. In *Proceedings of the 5th international Workshop on Software Engineering and Middleware*, Lisbon, Portugal, (pp. 46-53).

Binder, W., & Hulaas, J. (2004, October). A portable CPU-management framework for Java. *IEEE Internet Computing, 8*(5), 74-83.

Binder, W., Hulaas J., &Villaz A. (2001). Portable resource control in Java. In *Proceedings of the 2001 ACM SIGPLAN Conference on Object Oriented Programming, Systems, Languages and Applications*, (Vol. 36, No. 11, pp. 139-155).

Birk, A., Dingsøyr, T., & Stålhane, T. (2002, May-June). Postmortem: Never leave a project without it. *IEEE Software, 19*(3), 43-45.

Birov, D. (2004). Aspects pattern oriented architecture for distributed adaptive mobile applications. In *Proceedings of the International Conference on Computer Systems and Technologies (E-learning)*, (pp. 1-6).

Blaauw, G. (1972). Computer architecture. *El. Rechenanl., 14*(4), 154. also: Hasselmeier H., Spruth W.G. (Eds.), Rechnerstrukturen, Oldenbourg München (pp. 14-35).

Blach, R., Landauer, J., Rösch A., & Simon, A. (1998). A highly flexible virtual reality system. *Future Generation Computer Systems Special Issue on Virtual Environments 14*(3), 167-178.

Black, F., & Scholes, M.S. (1973). The pricing of options and corporate liabilities. *Journal of Political Economy, 81*(3), 637-654. University of Chicago Press.

Boehm , B. W. (1988, May). A spiral model of software development and enhancement. *IEEE Computer.*

Boehm, B. (2000). Requirements that handle IKIWISI, COTS, and rapid change. *IEEE Computer, 33*(7), 99-102.

Boehm, B., Grünbacher, P., & Briggs, B. (2001, May-June). Developing groupware for requirements negotiation: Lessons learned. *IEEE Software,* 46-55.

Boehm, B., Port, D., Abi-Antoun, M., & Egyed, A. (1998). *Guidelines for the life cycle objectives (LCO) and the life cycle architecture (LCA) deliverables for model-based architecting and software engineering (MBASE).* TR USC-CSE-98-519, USC-Center for Software Engineering.

Bollella, G., Gosling, J., Brosgol, B., Dibble, P., Furr, S., Hardin, D., & Turnbull, M. (2000). *The real-time specification for Java.* Addison-Wesley.

Bondé, L., Boulet, P., & Dekeyser, J.-L. (2006). Traceability and interoperability at different levels of abstraction in model-driven engineering. In *applications of specification and design languages for SoCs* (pp. 263-276).

Boner, J. (2004, March). AspectWerkz—Dynamic AOP for Java. In *Proceedings of the 3rd International Conference on Aspect-oriented development (AOSD 2004).* Lancaster, UK.

Booch G. (1983). *Software engineering with Ada.* Menlo Park, CA: Benjamin/Cummings.

Booch, G., Rumbaugh, J., & Jacobson, I. (2005). *Unified modeling language user guide* (2nd ed.). Addison-Wesley.

Borland Software Corporation. (2006). *Borland Optimize-it Enterprise Suite* (Computer software). Retrieved March 11, 2008, from http://www.borland.com/us/products/optimizeit/index.html

Bosch, J. (2000). *Design & use of software architectures.* Addison-Wesley.

Bose, R., & Frew, J. (2005). Lineage retrieval for scientific data processing: A survey. *ACM Computer Survey* (Vol. 37, pp. 1-28). New York.

Bosio, D., Little, B., Strigini, L., & Newby, M. J. (2002, February). Advantages of open source processes for reliability: Clarifying the issues. In *Paper presented at the Workshop on Open Source Software Development,* Newcastle upon Tyne, UK.

Bowen, J., & Hinchey, M. (1995). Ten commandments of formal methods. *IEEE Computer, 28*(4), 56-63.

Box, D., & Shukla, D. (2006). WinFX workflow: Simplify development with the declarative model of windows workflow foundation. *MSDN Magazine, 21,* 54-62.

BPMN Information Home. (2005). Retrieved March 23, 2008, from www.bpmn.org

Brase, J. (2004) .Using digital library techniques—registration of scientific primary data. *Lecture Notes in Computer Science, 3232,* 488-494.

Bratko, I. (1986). *Prolog programming for artificial intelligence.* Reading, MA: Addison-Wesley.

Bresciani, P., Perini, A., Giorgini, P, Giunchiglia, & Mylopoulos, J. (2004). Tropos: An agent-oriented software development methodology. *Journal of Autonomous Agents and MultiAgent Systems, 8,* 203-236.

Breugst, M., Choy, S., Hagen, L., Hoft, M., & Magedanz, T. (1998). Grasshopper—an agent platform for mobile agent-based services in fixed and mobile telecommunications environments. *Software agents for future communication systems.* Springer-Verlag.

Britton, C., & Bye, P. (2004). *IT architectures and middleware: Strategies for building large, integrated systems.* Boston, MA, USA: Addison-Wesley.

Broberg, M., Lundberg, L., & Grahn, H. (1999, April). Visualization and performance prediction of multithreaded solaris programs by tracing kernel threads. In *Proceedings of the 13th International Parallel Processing Symposium,* (pp. 407-413).

Broisin, J., Vidal, P., & Duval, E. (2005). A model driven approach for the management of learning object life cycle. In *Proceedings of the Intelligent, Interactive, Learning Object Repositories Network (I2LOR).*

Brooks, F. (1965). The future of computer architecture. In W. A. Kalenich (Ed.), *Information processing (Proceedings IFIP Congress)* (pp. 87-91). Washington, DC: Spartan Books, London: Macmillan.

Brooks, F. J. (1962). Architectural philosophy. In W. Buchholz (Ed.), *Planning a computer System—Project STRETCH* (pp. 5-16). McGraw-Hill.

Brooks, F. P. (1986). No silver bullet: Essence and accidents of software engineering. In *Proceedings of Information Processing'86.* North-Holland, IFIP.

Brooks, Jr., F.P., & Iverson, K.E. (1969). *Automatic data processing, System/360 edition.* New York: John Wiley & Sons.

Brose, G. (1997, September). JacORB: Implementation and design of a Java ORB. In *Proceedings of IFIP DAIS'97,* (pp. 143-154).

Brown, W. J., Malveau, R. C., McCormick, I., H.W., & Mowbray, T. J. (1998). *AntiPatterns: Refactoring software, architectures, and projects in crisis.* New York: John Wiley & Sons.

Broy, M. (2006). The 'grand challenge' in informatics: Engineering software-intensive systems. *IEEE Computer, 39*(10), 72-80.

Bruening, D. L. (2004). *Efficient, transparent, and comprehensive runtime code manipulation.* Unpublished doctoral dissertation, Massachusetts Institute of Technology.

Brügge, B. (2004). *Study on software architectures for augmented reality systems: Report to the ARVIKA Consortium* (Tech. Rep. No. TUM-I0410). Germany: Technische Universität München.

Brunner, K. (2002, April). What's emergent in emergent computing? In R. Trappl (Ed.), *Proceedings of EMCSR 2002: European Meeting on Cybernetics and Systems Research,* Vienna, Austria, (pp. 189-192).

Bucci, G., Fedeli, A., Sassoli, L., & Vicario, E. (2003, July). Modeling flexible real time systems with preemptive time Petri nets. In *Proceeding of 15th Euromicro Conference on Real-time Systems,* Porto, Portugal, (pp. 279-286).

Buck, B., & Hollingsworth, J. K. (2000). An API for runtime code patching. *International Journal of High Performance Computing Applications,* 317-329.

Buneman, P., Khanna, S., & Tan, W.C. (2001). *Why and where: A characterization of data provenance.* ICDT, pp. 316-330.

Buneman, P., Khanna, S., & Tan, W.C. (2002). *On propagation of deletions and annotations through views.* PODS, pp. 150-158.

Bureš, T., & Plášil, F. (2004). Communication style driven connector configurations. *Software engineering research and applications* (Vol. 3026 of *LNCS,* pp. 102-116). Berlin: Springer-Verlag.

Burgess, V. (2000). Changing nature of electronic performance support systems. Retrieved March 24, 2008, from *http://scholar.coe.uwf.edu/students/vburgess/ChangingEPSS/tsld001.htm*

Burmester, S., Giese, H., & Henkler, S. (2005). Visual model-driven development of software intensive systems: A survey of available tools and techniques. In *Proceedings of the Workshop of Visual Modeling for Software Intensive Systems,* (pp. 11-18).

Burmester, S., Giese, H., & Hirsch, M. (2005, October). *Syntax and semantics of hybrid components* (Tech. Rep. No. tr-ri-05-264). University of Paderborn.

Burmester, S., Giese, H., & Oberschelp, O. (2005, March). Hybrid UML components for the design of complex self-optimizing mechatronic systems. In J. Braz, H. Araújo, A. Vieira, & B. Encarnacao (Eds.), *Informatics in control, automation and robotics.* Springer-Verlag.

Burmester, S., Giese, H., & Schäfer, W. (2005, November). Model-driven architecture for hard real-time systems: From platform independent models to code. In *Proceedings of the European Conference on Model*

Driven Architecture—foundations and Applications (ECMDA-FA'05), Nürnberg, Germany, (pp. 25-40). Springer-Verlag.

Buschmann, F. (1994). *Pattern oriented software architecture—a system of patterns.* John Wiley & Sons.

Buschmann, F., Meunier, R., Rohnert, H., Sommerland, P., & Stal, M. (1996). *Pattern-oriented software architecture: A system of patterns.* New York: John Wiley & Sons.

Business Process Management Initiative. (2000). *Business process management initiative home page.* Retrieved March 6, 2008, from http://www.bpmi.org/

Business Process Management Initiative. (2004). *Business process modeling language.* Retrieved March 6, 2008, from http://www.bpmi.org/downloads/BPML-BPEL4WS.pdf

Buyya, R., Abramson, D., & Giddy, J. (2000). Nimrod-G: An architecture for a resource management and scheduling in a global computational grid. In *Proceedings of the 4th International Conference and Exhibition on High Performance Computing in Asia-Pacific Region (HPC ASIA 2000),* (pp. 283-289). Beijing, China: IEEE CS Press.

Cai, X., Lyu, M., Wong, K., & Ko, R. (2000). Component-based software engineering: Technologies, development frameworks, and quality assurance schemes. In *Proceedings of the Seventh Asia-Pacific Software Engineering Conference,* (pp. 372–379).

Cannon, L. (1969). *A cellular computer to implement the Kalman Filter Algorithm.* Bozeman, MT: Montana State University.

Cantor, M. (2003, August). Rational unified process for systems engineering--part1: Introducing RUP SE Version 2.0. *The Rational Edge: E-zine for the Rational Community.*

Cantrill, B., & Doeppner, T. W. (1997, January). Threadmon: A tool for monitoring multithreaded program performance. In *Proceedings of the 30th Hawaii International Conference on Systems Sciences,* (pp. 253-265).

Cantrill, B.M., Shapiro, M.W., & Levanthal, A.H. (2004). Dynamic instrumentation of production systems. In *Proceedings of the USENIX Annual Technical Conference 2004 on USENIX Annual Technical Conference,* Boston, MA.

Capilla, R., & Martínez, M. (2004). Software architectures for designing virtual reality applications. In *Proceedings of the European Workshop on Software Architectures* (EWSA2004) (LNCS, pp. 135-147).

Capilla, R., Nava, F., Pérez, S., & Dueñas, J.C. (2006). A Web-based tool for managing architectural design decisions. In *Proceedings of the First Workshop on Sharing and Reusing Knowledge,* ACM Digital Library, Software Engineering Notes (Vol. 31, No. 5, pp. 1-8).

Capretz, L. (2003). A brief history of the object-oriented approach. *SIGSOFT Software Engineering Notes, 28*(2), 1-10.

Carnegie Mellon University/Software Engineering Institute. (2007, June 30). *Capability maturity model integration (CMMI).* Retrieved March 7, 2008, from http://www.sei.cmu.edu/cmmi/

Casanova, H., Obertelli, G., Berman, F., & Wolski, R. (2000). The AppLeS parameter sweep template: User-level middleware for the grid. *Supercomputing 2000.* Dallas, TX: IEEE Computer Society.

Champeau, J., & Rochefort, E. (2003, October 21). Model engineering and traceability. In *Paper presented at the UML 2003 SIVOES-MDA Workshop,* San Francisco, CA, USA.

Chapin, N., Hale, J., Kham, K., Ramil, J., & Tan, W. (2001, January). Types of software evolution and software maintenance. *Journal of Software Maintenance: Research and Practice,* 3-30.

Charette, R. (2005). Why software fails. *IEEE Spektrum, 92*(9), 36-43.

Chase, N. (2005). *Grid-enable an existing Java technology application:* IBM. Retrieved March 23, 2008, from http://www.ibm.com/developerworks/edu/gr-dw-gr-javagrid-i.html

Chaudhuri, S., & Dayal, U. (1997). *An overview of data warehousing and OLAP technology.* SIGMOD Record (Vol. 26, pp. 65-74).

Chen, H., Houston, A., & Nunamaker, J. (1996). Towards intelligent meeting agents. *IEEE Computer, 29*(8), 63-70.

Chen, T. (1971, January). Parallelism, pipelining and computer efficiency. *Computer Design*, 365-372.

Chiticariu, L., Tan, W.-C., & Vijayvargiya, G. (2005). DB-Notes: A post-it system for relational databases based on provenance. In L. Li & N. Crane (Eds.), *Electronic style: A guide to citing electronic information.* SIGMOD.

Christensen, C. M. (2003). *The innovator's dilemma.* HarperBusiness Essentials.

Christensen, C.M., & Raynor, M. E. (2003). *The innovator's solution: Creating and sustaining successful growth.* Harvard Business School Press.

Chroust, G. (1971). Scope conserving expression evaluation. In *Proceedings of IFIP Congress*, (pp. 509-512).

Chroust, G. (1980). Orthogonal extensions in microprogrammed multiprocessor systems. In G. Chroust & J. R. Mühlbacher (Eds.), *Firmware, microprogramming and restructurable hardware: Proceedings of the IFIP Working Conference*, (pp. 185-190). Linz: North Holland Publishing Company.

Chroust, G. (1980). Orthogonal extensions in microprogrammed multiprocessor systems: A chance for increased firmware usage. *EUROMICRO Journal, 6*(2), 104-110.

Chroust, G. (1980). Programme chairman's preface. In G. Chroust & J. R. Mühlbacher (Eds.), *Firmware, microprogramming and restructurable hardware: Proceedings of the IFIP Working Conference*, (pp. vii-viii). Linz: North Holland Publishing Company.

Chroust, G. (1989, February). *Mikroprogrammierung und Rechnerentwurf.* Oldenbourg: Springer-Verlag.

Chroust, G. (1992). *Modelle der Software-Entwicklung—Aufbau und Interpretation von Vorgehensmodellen.* Oldenbourg: Springer-Verlag.

Chroust, G. (2000, September). Electronic performance support systems—challenges and problems. In P. Kopacek (Ed.), *Proceedings of Computer Aided Systems Theory—EUROCAST'99,* Vienna, (pp. 281-284). Springer-Verlag.

Chroust, G. (2002, September). Emergent properties in software systems. In C. Hofer, & G. Chroust, (Eds.), *Proceedings of IDIMT-2002: 10th Interdisciplinary Information Management Talks,* Zadov, (pp. 277-289). Verlag Trauner Linz.

Chroust, G. (2002, April). System properties under composition. In R. *Trappl (Ed.), EMCSR 2002: Proceedings of the European Meeting on Cybernetics and Systems Research,* Vienna, (pp. 203-208). Austrian Society for Cybernetic Studies.

Chroust, G. (2003, February). The concept of emergence in systems engineering. In C. Hofer & G. Chroust (Eds.), *The eleventh Fuschl conversation.* Vienna: ÖSGK, Reports of the Austrian Society for Cybernetic Studies.

Chroust, G. (2004). The empty chair: Uncertain futures and systemic dichotomies. *Systems Research and Behavioral Science, 21*, 227-236.

Chroust, G. (2005). Dichotomic architectural patterns in systems engineering. *IFSR 2005—the new roles of systems sciences for a knowledge-based society (Paper No. 20121).* Jaist Press (CDROM).

Chung, L., & Cooper, K. (2004, June 22). COTS-aware requirements engineering and software architecting. In *Proceedings of the International Workshop on Systems and Software Architecting,* Las Vegas, NV, (pp. 57-63).

Clarke, E. M., Grumberg, O., & Peled, D. A. (2000). *Model checking. Massachusetts Institute of Technology.* Cambridge, MA: The MIT Press.

Clauss, P., Kenmei, B., & Beyler, J.C. (2005, September). The periodic-linear model of program behavior capture. In *Proceedings of Euro-Par 2005* (LNCS 3648, pp. 325-335).

Clements, P. (1995). From subroutines to subsystems: Component-based software development (pp. 7-15). In *American Programmer, 8(*11), and A.W. Brown, (Ed.), *Component-based software engineering.* IEEE Computer Society.

Clements, P. (1995, April). Understanding architectural influences and decisions in large-system projects. In *Proceedings of the First International Workshop on Architectures for Software Systems,* Seattle, WA, (p. 13).

Clements, P. (1996). A survey of architecture description languages. In *Proceedings of the 8th International Workshop on Software Specification and Design,* (pp. 16-25).

Clements, P., & Northrop, L. (2001). *Software product-lines: Practices and patterns.* Addison-Wesley.

Clements, P., Bachman, F., Bass, L., Garlan, D., Ivers, J., Little, R., et al. (2003). *Documenting software architectures.* Addison-Wesley.

Clements, P., Bachmann, F., Bass, L., Garlan, D., Ivers, J., Little, R., et al. (2002). *Documenting software architectures: Views and beyond.* Addison-Wesley.

Clements, P., Kazman, R., & Klein, M. (2002). *Evaluating software architectures.* Addison-Wesley.

CMM. (2002, March). *Capability Maturity Model® Integration (CMMISM), Version 1.1* (Tech. Rep. No. CMU/SEI-2002-TR-012). Carnegie Mellon, Software Engineering Institute.

Coffman, E., Galambos, G., Martello, S., & Vigo, D. (1998). Bin packing approximation algorithms: Combinatorial analysis. *Handbook of combinatorial optimization.* Norwell, MA: Kluwer Academic.

Collins, R. (1997, September). In-circuit emulation: How the microprocessor evolved over time. *Dr. Dobbs Journal.* Retrieved March 11, 2008, from http://www.rcollins.org/ddj/Sep97

CompUSA. (2008). *Software.* Retrieved March 23, 2008, from http://www.compusa.com/products/products.asp?cmid=topnav&N=200163

Conradi, R., Fuggetta, A., & Jaccheri, M. L. (1998). Six theses on software process research. In *Proceedings of Software Process Technology: 6th European Workshop (EWSPT'98),* Weybridge. Springer-Verlag. LNCS 1487.

Consortium, W. W. W. (2004, February). *Web ontology language.* Retrieved March 23, 2008, from www.w3.org/2004/OWL/

Cooper, K., Cangussu, J., & Wong, E. (2007). An architectural framework for the design and analysis of autonomous adaptive systems. In *Proceedings of the 31ˢᵗ Annual International Computer Software and Applications Conference.*

Cooper, K., Dai, L., & Deng, Y. (2005). Performance modeling and analysis of software architectures: An aspect-oriented UML based approach. *Journal of Science of Computer Programming, System and Software Architectures, 57*(1), 89-108.

Cooper, K., Ramapur, C., & Chung, L. (2005). *Component aware techniques (CAT) A COTS-aware requirements engineering and software architecting approach (CARE/SA): Defining system level agents, goals, requirements, and architecture (version 4).* UTDCS-24-05. The University of Texas at Dallas, Department of Computer Science.

Coplien, J., Hoffman, D., & Weiss, D. (1998, November/December). Commonality and variability in software engineering. *IEEE Software, 15*(6), 37-45.

CORBA Components. (2002, June). Retrieved May 12, 2008 from http://www.omg.org/technology/documents/formal/components.htm

Cordy, R., Halpern C., & Promislow, E. (1991). TXL: A rapid prototyping system for programming language dialects. In *Proceedings of the International Conference on Computer Languages* (Vol. 16, No. 1, pp. 97-107).

Cormen, T.H., Rivest, R.L. Leiserson, C.E., & Stein, C. (1990). *Introduction to algorithms.* Cambridge, MA: MIT Press.

Courtney, R.E., & Gustafson, D.A. (1990). Evolution of architectural design representations. In *the Proceedings of the 1990 Symposium on Applied Computing*, (pp. 381-384).

CPNTools: Computer tools for coloured Petri nets. (2006). Demark: University of Aarhus, CPN Group. Retrieved March 23, 2008, from wiki.daimi.au.dk/cpntools/cpntools.wiki

Cugola, G., & Ghezzi, C. (1998). Software processes: A retrospective and a path to the future. *SOFTWARE PROCESS—Improvement and Practice, 4*(2), 101-123.

Cui, Y., & Widom, J. (2000). *Practical lineage tracing in data warehouses*. ICDE, pp. 367-378.

Cui, Y., & Widom, J. (2003). Lineage tracing for general data warehouse transformations. *VLDB Journal, 12*, 41-58.

Cui, Y., Widom, J., & Wiener, J.L. (2000). Tracing the lineage of view data in a warehousing environment. *ACM Transactions of Database Systems, 25*, 179-227.

Curtis, B., Kellner, M., & Over, J. (1992). Process modeling. *Communications of the ACM, 35*(9), 75-90.

Czajkowski, K., Fitzgerald, S., Foster, I., & Kesselman, C. (2001). Grid information services for distributed resource sharing. In *Proceedings of the 10th IEEE Symposium on High Performance Distributed Computing (HPDC)*, (pp. 181-195). Los Alamitos, CA: IEEE Computer Society.

Czajkowski, K., Foster, I., Kesselman, C., Martin, S., Smith, W., & Tuecke, S. (1998). A resource management architecture for metacomputing systems. In *Proceedings of the IPPS/SPDP Workshop on Job Scheduling Strategies for Parallel Processing*, (pp. 62-82). Springer-Verlag.

Dai, L. (2005). *Formal design analysis framework: An aspect-oriented architectural framework*. Doctoral dissertation, The University of Texas at Dallas.

Dang, G, Cheng, Z.Q., Jin, S.Y., Yang T., & Wu, T. (2005). A service-oriented architecture for tele-immersion. In *Proceedings of the IEEE International Conference on E-technology, E-commerce, and E-services (EEE 2005)*, Hong Kong, China, (pp. 646-649). IEEE Computer Society.

Dashofy, E.M., Hoek, A., & Taylor, R.N. (2002, May). An infrastructure for the rapid development of XML-based architecture description languages. In *Proceedings of the 24th International Conference on Software Engineering*, Orlando, FL, (pp. 266-276).

Davies, J., Huismans, N., Slaney, R., Whiting, S., & Webster, M. (2003). *An aspect-oriented performance analysis environment*. AOSD'03 Practitioner Report, 2003.

De Antonio, A., Ramirez, J., Imbert., R., & Aguilar, R.A. (2005). A software architecture for intelligent virtual environments applied to education. *Rev. Fac. Ing. Universidad de Tarapaca, 13*(1), 47-55.

de Weck, O., & Jones, M. B. (2005). Isoperformance: Analysis and design of complex systems with desired outcomes. *Systems Engineering, 9*(1), January 2006, 45-61.

DeFoe, J. (1993). *An identification of pragmatic principles of systems engineering* (Final report). *INCOSE*. Retrieved March 24, 3008, from nhp.at.fortnet.org

Dekra (2006, October 25-26). In Proceedings of the Autotest Conference, Stuttgart, Germany.

DeLoach, S. (2006). Engineering organization-based multiagent systems. In A. Garcia et al. (Eds.), *Proceedings of the 4th International Workshop on Software Engineering for Large-Scale Multi-Agent Systems, (SELMAS '05)*, (pp. 109-125). Berlin: Springer-Verlag.

Deng, G., Balasubramanian, J., Otte, W., Schmidt, D. C., & Gokhale, A. (2005, November). DAnCE: A QoS-enabled component deployment and configuration engine. In *Proceedings of the 3rd Working Conference on Component Deployment (cd 2005)*, (pp. 67-82). Grenoble, France: Springer-Verlag.

Deng, G., Lenz, G., & Schmidt, D.C. (2005, October). Addressing domain evolution challenges for model-driven software product-line architectures (PLAs). In *Proceedings of the MoDELS 2005 Workshop on MDD for Software Product-lines: Fact or Fiction?*, Montego Bay, Jamaica.

Deng, G., Lu, T., Turkay, E., Gokhale, A., Schmidt, D. C., & Nechypurenko, A. (2003, October). Model driven development of inventory tracking system. In *Proceedings of the OOPSLA 2003 Workshop on Domain-specific Modeling Languages*. Anaheim, CA: ACM Press.

Denning, P.J., & Buzen, J.P. (1978). The operation analysis of queuing network models. *Computing Surveys, 10*(3), 225-261.

Department of Defense. (1992, January). *Military standard 973: Military standard for configuration management* (Tech. Rep.). Washington, DC: Department of Defense.

Department of Defense. (1993, January). *Military standard 882c: Standard practice for system safety program requirements* (Tech. Rep.). Washington, DC: Department of Defense.

Deployment and Configuration of Component-based Distributed Applications, v4.0. (2006, April). Retrieved May 12, 2008 from http://www.omg.org/technology/documents/formal/deployment.htm

Derniame, J.-C., Baba, B.A., & Wastell, D. (Eds.). (1998). *Software process: Principles, methodology, and technology*. Berlin: Springer-Verlag LNCS 1500.

Desfray, P. (2003). *MDA–when a major software industry trend meets our toolset, implemented since 1994*: SOFTEAM.

Deursen, A. V., Klint, P., & Visser, J. (2000). Domain-specific languages: An annotated bibliography. *ACM SIGPLAN Notices, 35*(6), 26-36.

Dijkstra, E. (1968). Go to statement considered harmful. *Communications of the ACM, 11*(3), 147-148.

Dingsøyr, T., & Røyrvik, E. (2003). An empirical study of an informal knowledge repository in a medium-sized software consulting company. In *Proceedings of the 25th International Conference on Software Engineering (ICSE'03)*, Portland, OR, USA.

Dmitriev, M. (2001). *Safe evolution of large and long-lived Java applications*. Unpublished doctoral dissertation, Department of Computing Science, University of Glasgow, Glasgow G12 8QQ, Scotland.

Dmitriev, M. (2001). Towards flexible and safe technology for runtime evolution of Java language applications. In *Proceedings of the Workshop on Engineering Complex Object-Oriented Systems for Evolution* (pp. 14-18). In Association with OOPSLA 2001 International Conference, Tampa Bay, FL, USA.

Dmitriev, M. (2002). Application of the HotSwap technology to advanced profiling. In *Proceedings of the First Workshop on Unanticipated Software Evolution*, held at ECOOP 2002 International Conference, Malaga, Spain.

Dmitriev, M. (2004). Profiling Java applications using code hotswapping and dynamic call graph revelation. In *Proceedings of the 4th International Workshop on Software and Performance*, Redwood Shores, CA, (pp. 139-150).

Dobrica, L., & Niemelä, E. (2003). Using UML notational extensions to model variability in product line architectures. In *Proceedings of the International Workshop on Software Variability Management, ICSE'03*, Portland, OR, USA, (pp. 8-13).

Dörner, D. (1996). *Die Logik des Mißlingens—Strategisches Denken in komplexen Situationen*. sachbuch-9314, rororo Verlag, Hamburg.

Downey, A. (1997). Predicting queue times on space-sharing parallel computers. In *Proceedings of the International Parallel Processing Symposium (IPPS '97)*, (pp. 209-218). Geneva, Switzerland.

Drogoul, A., Vanbergue, D., & Meurisse, T. (2003). Multi-agent based simulation: Where are the agents?. *Lecture Notes in Computer Science, 2581*, 1-15.

DSM Forum. (2007). *From domain-specific modeling forum*. Retrieved March 7, 2008, from http://www.dsmforum.org/tools.html

Dueñas, J.C., & Capilla, R. (2005). The decision view of software architecture. In *Proceedings of the 2nd European Workshop on Software Architecture (EWSA 2005)*, (pp. 222-230). LNCS 3047, Springer-Verlag.

Dunham, M. H., & Kumar, V. (1998). Location dependent data and its management in mobile databases. In *Proceedings of the Database and Expert Systems Applications (DEXA) Workshop.*

Dutto, M., & Lautenbacher, F. (2007). *Java Workflow Tooling (JWT) creation review.*

Eason, K., Domodaran, L., & Stewart, T. (1974). Interface problems in man-computer interaction. In E. Mumford & H. Sackman (Eds.), *Human choice and computers* (pp. 91-105). North Holland Publishing Company.

Eclipse Modeling Project. (2007). Retrieved March 7, 2008, from http://www.eclipse.org/modeling/

Eclipse.Org. (2006). *Soa tools platform project.* Retrieved March 23, 2008, from http://www.eclipse.org/stp/index.php

Edwards, G., Deng, G., Schmidt, D.C., Gokhale, A., & Natarajan, B. (2004, October). Model-driven configuration and deployment of component middleware publisher/subscriber services. In *Proceedings of the 3rd ACM International Conference on Generative Programming and Component Engineering*, Vancouver, Canada, (pp. 337-360).

Egyed, A. (2004). Resolving uncertainties during trace analysis. In *Paper presented at the Proceedings of the 12th ACM SIGSOFT Twelfth International Symposium on Foundations of Software Engineering* (pp. 3-12). Newport Beach, CA, USA.

Elmasri. (2000). *Fundamentals of database systems* (3rd ed.). Addison-Wesley.

Elrad, T., Filman, R.E., & Bader, A. (2001). Aspect-oriented programming: Introduction. *Communications of the ACM, 44*(10), 29-32.

Emerson, M., & Sztipanovits, J. (2006, Oct). Techniques for metamodel composition. In Proceedings of the *6th OOPSLA Workshop* on *Domain-specific Modeling, OOPSLA 2006,* (pp. 123-139). Portland, OR: ACM Press.

Emmerich, W. (2000). *Engineering distributed objects.* John Wiley & Sons.

Endres, A., & Rombach, D. (2003). *A handbook of software and systems engineering—empirical observations, laws and theories.* Reading, MA: Addison-Wesley/Pearson.

Engelen, R. van, & Gallivan, K. (2002). The gSOAP toolkit for Web services and peer-to-peer computing networks. In *Ccgrid,* (pp. 128-135). Los Alamitos, CA, USA: IEEE Computer Society.

ESD Architecture Committee. (2004). The influence of architecture in engineering systems. *MIT-eds, engineering systems monograph* (p. 30).

Espinoza, A., Alarcon, P. P., & Garbajosa, J. (2006). *Analyzing and systematizing current traceability schemas* (pp. 21-32).

Evans, R., Kearney, P., Caire, G., Garijo, F., Gomez Sanz, J., Pavon, J., et al. (2001). *MESSAGE: Methodology for engineering systems of software agents.* EURESCOM.

Fadila, A., Said, G., & Nora, B. (2005). Software process modeling using role and coordination. *Journal of Computer Science, 2*(4).

Fagan, M. (1999). Design and code inspections to reduce errors in program development. *IBM Systems Journal, 38*(2/3), 258-287.

FASTA. (2006, December 4). *FASTA format.* Retrieved March 23, 2008, from http://en.wikipedia.org/wiki/Fasta

Fenelon, P., McDermid, J. A., Nicolson, M., & Pumfrey, D. J. (1994). Towards integrated safety analysis and design. *ACM SIGAPP Applied Computing Review, 2*(1), 21-32.

Ferber J. (1999). *Multi-agent systems: An introduction to distributed artificial intelligence.* Addison-Wesley.

Ferber, J., & Michel, F. (1996). Influences and reaction: A model of situated multiagent systems. In *Proceedings of the 2nd Annual Conference on Multi-agent Systems.* AAAI Press.

Fernandez, M., & Espasa, R. (1999). Dixie: A retargetable binary instrumentation tool. In *Proceedings of the*

Workshop on Binary Translation, held in conjunction with the International Conference on Parallel Architectures and Compilation Techniques.

Fernando, T., Murray, N., Tan K., & Wimalaratne, P. (1999). Software architecture for constraint-based virtual environment. In *Proceedings of the ACM International Symposium on Virtual Reality Software and Technology (VRST'99)* (pp. 147-154), London, UK.

Fiadeiro, J. (1996). On the emergence of properties in component-based systems. In *Proceedings of AMAST96*. Springer-Verlag.

Filman, R., Elrad, T., Clarke, S., & Aksit, M. (2005). *Aspect-oriented software development*. Addison-Wesley.

Finkelstein , A. (Ed.). (2000). The future of software engineering. In *Proceedings of the 22nd International Conference on Software Engineering (ICSE'2000)*, Limerick, Ireland.

FIPA. (2007). *The Foundation for Intelligent Physical Agents home page*. Retrieved March 11, 2008, from http://www.fipa.org/specs/fipa00001/SC00001L.pdf

Fishwick, P. (1996, February). Computer simulation: Growth through Extension. *IEEE Potential*, 24-27.

Flinn, J., & Satyanarayanan, M. (1999). Energy-aware adaptation for mobile applications. In *Proceedings of the Symposium on Operating Systems Principles (SOSP)*.

Florescu, O., Hoon, M., Voeten, J., & Corporall, H. (2006, July). Probabilistic modelling and evaluation of soft real-time embedded systems. In *Proceedings of Embedded Computer Systems: Architectures, Modeling, and Simulation (SAMOS VI)*, Samos, Greece.

Florio, V. D. & Deconinck, G. (2002). On some key requirements of mobile application software. In *Proceedings of the International Conference on Engineering of Computer-based Systems (ECBS 2002)*.

Floyd, R. (1979). The paradigms of programming. *Communications of the ACM, 22*(8), 455-460.

Flynn, M. H. L. (1979, February). *A theory of interpretive architectures: Ideal language machines*. CA: Stanford University Computer Systems Lab., TR 170.

Föllinger, O. (2005). *Regelungstechnik: Einführung in die Methoden und ihre Anwendung*. Hüthig.

Forman, G., & Zahorjan, J. (1994). The challenges of mobile computing. *IEEE Computer, 27*(4), 38-47.

Forum, M. P. I. (1998). *MPI message-passing interface standard, version 2.0*. Retrieved March 23, 2008, from http://www.mpi-forum.org/docs/docs.html

Foster, I., & Kesselman, C. (1997). Globus: A metacomputing infrastructure toolkit. *International Journal of Supercomputer Applications, 11*(2), 115-128.

Foster, I., & Kesselman, C. (1998). The grid: Blueprint for a new computing infrastructure.

Foster, I., & Kesselman, C. (1999). The Globus toolkit. In I. Foster & C. Kesselman (Eds.), *The grid: Blueprint for a new computing infrastructure* (pp. 259-278). San Francisco: Morgan Kaufmann.

Foster, I., Kesselman, C., & Tuecke, S. (2001). The anatomy of the grid. *Lecture Notes in Computer Science, 2150*, 1-28.

Foster, I., Kesselman, C., Nick, J. M., & Tuecke, S. (2002). Grid services for distributed system integration. *Computer, 35*(6), 37-46.

Foster, I., Kesselman, C., Nick, J., & Tuecke, S. (2002). *The physiology of the grid: An open grid services architecture for distributed systems integration*. Global Grid Forum, Open Grid Service Infrastructure Working Group.

Foster, I., Kesselman, C., Tsudik, G., & Tuecke, S. (1998). A security architecture for computational grids. In *Proceedings of the 5th ACM Conference on Computer and Communication Security Conference,* (pp. 83-92). San Francisco: ACM Press.

Foster, I., Voeckler, J., Wilde, M., & Zhao, Y. (2002). Chimera: A virtual data system for representing, querying, and automating data derivation. In *Proceedings of the 14th International Conference on Scientific and Statistical Database Management (SSDBM'02),* (pp. 37-46). Edinburgh, Scotland.

Foster, I.T., Vöckler, J.-S., Wilde, M., & Zhao, Y. (2003). *The virtual data grid: A new model and architecture for data-intensive collaboration.* CIDR.

Fowler, M. (2006). *Continuous integration.* Retrieved March 23, 2008, from www.martinfowler.com/articles/continuousIntegration.html

Fowler, M., & Scott, K. (2000). *UML distilled.* Reading, MA: Addison-Wesley.

France, R., Ghosh, S., & Dinh-Trong, T. (2006). Model-driven development using UML 2: Promises and pitfalls. *IEEE Computer (Special Issue on Model-Driven Engineering, 39*(2), 41-48.

Frankel, D.S. (2003). *Model driven architecture: Applying MDA to enterprise computing.* John Wiley & Sons.

Franz, M. (1997). Dynamic linking of software components. *IEEE Computer, 30*(3), 74-81.

Freund, S. N., & Qadeer, S. (2003). *Checking concise specifications of multithreaded software.* Technical Note 01-2002, Williams College.

Frey, J., Tannenbaum, T., Foster, I., Livny, M., & Tuecke, S. (2001). Condor-G: A computation management agent for multi-institutional grids. In *Proceedings of the IEEE Symposium on High Performance Distributed Computing (HPDC10),* (pp. 9). San Francisco, CA.

Fritsch, C., Lehn A., & Strohm, T. (2002). Evaluating variability implementation mechanisms. In *Proceedings of the International Workshop on Product Line Engineering (PLEES'02),* (pp. 59-64). IESE Report N° 056.02/E, 2002.

Fuggetta, A. (2000). *Software process: A roadmap.* In *Proceedings of the Conference on the Future of Software Engineering (ICSE 2000)* (pp. 25-34). Limerick, Ireland.

Fuxman, A. D. (2000). *A survey of architecture description languages* (Tech. Rep. No. CSRG-407).University of Toronto, Canada: Department of Computer Science.

Galhardas, H., Florescu, D., Shasha, D., Simon, E., & Saita, C.-A. (2001). *Improving data cleaning quality using a data lineage facility.* DMDW, p. 3.

Gamma, E., Helm, R., Johnson, R., & Vlissides, J. (1994). *Design patterns: Elements of reusable object-oriented software.* Reading, MA: Addison-Wesley.

Gannon, D., Fox, G., Pierce, M., Plale, B., Laszewski, G. V., Severance, C., et al. (2003). *Grid portals: A scientist's access point for grid services.* Global Grid Forum (GGF).

Garlan, D., Allen, R., & Ockerbloom, J. (1994). Exploiting style in architectural design environments. In *Proceedings of SIGSOFT'94: Foundations of Software Engineering,* (pp. 175-188).

Garlan, D., Monroe, R., & Wile, D. (1995). *ACME: An architectural interconnection language* (Tech. Rep. No. CMU-CS-95-219). Carnegie Mellon University.

Garland, S. (2005). *The TIOA user guide and reference manual.* Retrieved March 23, 2008, from tioa.csail.mit.edu/public/Documentation/Guide.doc

Gelenbe, E., Husain, K., & Kaptan, V. (2004). Simulating autonomous agents in augmented reality. *The Journal of Systems and Software, 74,* 255-268.

Gemmill, J., & Bangalore, P. (2005). *UABGrid--a campus-wide distributed computational infrastructure.* Birmingham, AL: UAB. Retrieved March 23, 2008, from http://uabgrid.uab.edu/

Georgas, J. C., Dashofy, E. M., & Taylor, R. N. (2005). Architecture-centric development: A different approach to software engineering. *Crossroads, 12*(4), 6.

Gibbons, R. (1997). A historical application profiler for use by parallel schedulers. *Lecture Notes in Computer Science, 1291,* 58-77.

Giese, H., & Burmester, S. (2004, May). Analysis and synthesis for parameterized timed sequence diagrams. In H. Giese & I. Krüger (Eds.), *Proceedings of the 3rd International Workshop on Scenarios and State Machines: Models, Algorithms, and Tools (ICSE 2003 Workshop W5), Edinburgh, Scotland,* (pp. 43-50). IEE.

Giese, H., & Henkler, S. (2006, December). A survey of approaches for the visual model-driven development of next generation software-intensive systems. *Journal of Visual Languages and Computing, 17,* 528-550.

Giese, H., & Tichy, M. (2006, September). Component-based hazard analysis: Optimal designs, product lines, and online-reconfiguration. In *Proceedings of the 25th International Conference on Computer Safety, Security and Reliability (SAFECOMP), Gdansk, Poland,* (pp. 156-169)*. Springer-Verlag.

Giese, H., Henkler, S., Hirsch, M., & Klein, F. (2006, May). Nobody's perfect: Interactive synthesis from parametrized real-time scenarios. In *Proceedings of the ICSE 2006 Workshop on Scenarios and State Machines: Models, Algorithms and Tools (SCESM'06), Shanghai, China,* (pp. 67-74). ACM Press.

Giese, H., Tichy, M., Burmester, S., Schäfer, W., & Flake, S. (2003, September). Towards the compositional verification of real-time UML designs. In *Proceedings of the 9th European Software Engineering Conference held jointly with the 11th ACM SIGSOFT International Symposium on Foundations of Software Engineering (ESEC/FSE-11),* (pp. 38-47). ACM Press.

Gilb, T., & Graham, D. (1993). *Software inspection.* Reading, MA: Addison-Wesley.

Gills, M. (2005, November 8). Survey of traceability models in IT projects. In *Paper presented at the European Conference on Model Driven Architecture - Traceability Workshop 2005*, Nuremberg, Germany.

Ginsberg, M. (1989). A circumscriptive theorem prover. *Artificial Intelligence, 32*(2), 209-230.

Gladwell, M. (2000). *The tipping point: How little things can make a big difference.* Back Bay Books.

Glaser, N., & Derniame , J.-C. (1998). Software agents: Process models and user profiles in distributed software development. In *Proceedings of the 7ᵗʰ Workshop on Enabling Technologies Infrastructure for Collaborative Enterprises* (WETICE'98), Palo Alto, CA, USA.

Glass, R. L. (2006). The standish report: Does it really describe a software crisis? *Communications of the ACM, 49*(8), 15-16.

GME. (2007). *Generic modeling environment.* Retrieved March 7, 2008, from http://escher.isis.vanderbilt.edu/downloads?tool=GME

GNU. (2008). *The GNU operating system.* Retrieved March 23, 2008, from http://www.gnu.org

Göbel, S., Pohl, C., Röttger, S., & Zschaler, S. (2004). The COMQUAD component model: Enabling dynamic selection of implementations by weaving non-functional aspects. In *Proceedings of the Third International Conference on Aspect-Oriented Software Development,* (pp. 74-82).

Goble, C. (2002). Position statement: Musings on provenance, workflow and (Semantic Web) annotations for bioinformatics. In *Proceedings of the Workshop on Data Derivation and Provenance,* Chicago, IL.

Gokhale, A., Balasubramanian, K., Balasubramanian, J., Krishna, A., Edwards, G., Deng, G., et al. (2006). Model driven middleware: A new paradigm for deploying and provisioning distributed real-time and embedded applications. *The Journal of Science of Computer Programming: Special Issue on Model Driven Architecture.*

Gomaa, H., Menasce, D. A., & Shin, M. E. (2001). Reusable component interconnection patterns for distributed software architectures. *ACM SIGSOFT Software Engineering Notes, 26*(3), 69-77.

Gontla, P., Drury, H., & Stanley, K. (2003, May 2003). An introduction to OVATION—Object viewing and analysis tool for integrated object networks. *CORBA News Brief, Object Computing Inc.* [Electronic media]. Retrieved March 11, 2008, from http://www.ociweb.com/cnb/CORBANewsBrief-200305.html

Gosling J. (1995, January 23). Java intermediate byte-codes. In *Proceedings of the ACM SIGPLAN Workshop on Intermediate Representations (IR'95).* (pp. 111-118), San Francisco, CA, USA.

Gotel, O. C. Z., & Finkelstein, C. W. (1994). *An analysis of the requirements traceability problem* (pp. 94-101).

Gottschalk, K., Graham, S., Kreger, H., & Snell, J. (2002). Introduction to Web services architecture. *IBM Systems Journal, 41*(2), 170-178.

Graphical Modeling Framework. (2007). Retrieved March 23, 2008, from http://www.eclipse.org/gmf

Grassi, V., Mirandola, R., & Sabetta, A. (2005). From design to analysis models: A kernel language for performance and reliability analysis of component-based systems. In *Proceedings of the Fifth International Workshop on Software and Performance,* Palma de Mallorca, Spain.

Gray, J., Bapty, T., Neema, S., & Tuck, J. (2001). Handling crosscutting constraints in domain-specific modeling. *Communications of the ACM, 44*(10), 87-93.

Gray, J., Lin, Y., & Zhang, J. (2006). Automating change evolution in model-driven engineering. *IEEE Computer, 39*(2), 51-58.

Gray, J., Tolvanen, J., Kelly, S., Gokhale, A., Neema, S., & Sprinkle, J. (2007). Domain-specific modeling. In P. Fishwick (Ed.), *CRC handbook on dynamic system modeling.* CRC Press.

Greenfield, J., Short, K., Cook, S., & Kent, S. (2004). *Software factories: Assembling applications with patterns, models, frameworks, and tools.* New York: John Wiley & Sons.

Greenhouse, A. (2003). *A programmer-oriented approach to safe concurrency.* Unpublished doctoral dissertation, Carnegie Mellon University School of Computer Science.

Grehan, R. (1995). *BYTEmark Native Mode Benchmark,* Release 2.0, [Computer software]. BYTE Magazine.

Grid, O. S. (2007, Januray 19). *Open science grid.* Retrieved March 23, 2008, from http://www.openscience-grid.org/

Gries, D. (1971). *Compiler construction for digital computers.* New York: John Wiley.

Grimm, K. (2003). Software technology in an automotive company: Major challenges. In *ICSE'03: Proceedings of the 25th International Conference on Software Engineering,* (pp. 498-503). Washington, DC, USA: IEEE Computer Society.

GriPhyN. (2006, July 30). *GriPhyN--grid physics network.* Retrieved March 23, 2008, from http://www.griphyn.org/

Groth, P., Luck, M., & Moreau, L. (2004). *A protocol for recording provenance in service-oriented Grids.* Grenoble, France: OPODIS.

Groth, P., Miles, S., Fang, W., Wong, S.C., Zauner, K.-P., & Moreau, L. (2005). *Recording and using provenance in a protein compressibility experiment.* HPDC.

Grundy, J. C., Apperley, M. D., Hosking, J. G., & Mugridge, W. B. (1998, September-October). A decentralized architecture for software process modeling and enactment. *IEEE Internet Computing, 2*(5), 53-62.

Grunske, L. (2003). Transformational patterns for the improvement of safety. In *Proceedings of the Second Nordic Conference on Pattern Languages of Programs (vikingplop 03).* Microsoft Buisness Press.

Grunske, L., & Neumann, R. (2002, October 6). Quality improvement by integrating non-functional properties in software architecture specification. In *Proceedings of the Second Workshop on Evaluating and Architecting System Dependability (easy),* San Jose, CA, USA.

Guan, Z., Velusamy, V., & Bangalore, P. (2005). Grid-Deploy: A toolkit for deploying applications as grid services. In *Proceedings of the International Conference on Information Technology Coding and Computing,* Las Vegas, NV.

Guy, M., Powell, A., & Day, M. (2004). *Improving the quality of metadata in Eprint archives.* Ariadne

Hachem, N. I., Qiu, K., Gennert, M.A., & Ward, M.O. (1993). *Managing derived data in the Gaea Scientific DBMS.* VLDB, pp. 1-12.

Hahn, G., Philipps, J., Pretschner, A., & Stauner, T. (2003, June). Prototype-based tests for hybrid reactive systems. In *Proceedings of the 14th IEEE International Workshop on Rapid System Prototyping (RSP'03),* (pp. 78-85).

Hampden-Turner, C., & Trompenaars, F. (2000). *Building cross-cultural competence—how to create wealth from conflicting values.* Yale University Press.

Hanrahan, M. (2004). *The essential ingredient: How business intelligence depends on data quality.* Dal Cais Research White Paper.

Hardung, B., Kölzow, T., & Krüger, A. (2004). Reuse of software in distributed embedded automotive systems. In *EMSOFT'04: Proceedings of the 4th ACM International Conference on Embedded Software,* (pp. 203-210). New York, USA: ACM Press.

Harel, D. and Marelly, R. (2002). Playing with time: On the specification and execution of time-enriched LSCs. In *Proceedings of the 10th IEEE international Symposium on Modeling, Analysis, and Simulation of Computer and Telecommunications Systems (MASCOTS'02)* (p. 193). Washington, DC: IEEE Computer Society.

Harrison, T., Levine, D., & Schmidt, D.C. (1997, October). The design and performance of a real-time CORBA event service. In *Proceedings of OOPSLA*, Atlanta, GA, (pp. 184-200). ACM.

Hatcliff, J., Deng, W., Dwyer, M., Jung, G., & Prasad, V. (2003). Cadena: An integrated development, analysis, and verification environment for component-based systems. In *Proceedings of the 25th International Conference on Software Engineering*, Portland, OR.

Hauswirth, M., & Jazayeri, M. (1999). A component and communication model for push systems. In *Proceedings of ESEC/SIGSOFT FSE*, (pp. 20-38).

Hauswirth, M., Diwan, A., Sweeney, P., & Mozer, M. (2005). Automating vertical profiling. In *Proceeding of the 19th Conference of Object Oriented Programming, Systems, Languages and Applications*, San Diego, CA.

Heineman, G.T., & Councill, W.T. (2001). *Component-based software engineering: Putting the pieces together.* Addison-Wesley.

Henry, J. W., & Stone, R. W. (1995). Computer self-efficacy and outcome expectancy: The effects on the end-user's job satisfaction. *SIGCPR Comput. Pers., 16*(4), 15-34.

Herman, I., Melançon, G., & Marshall, M.S. (2000). Graph visualization and navigation in information visualization: A survey. *IEEE Transactions on Visualization and Computer Graphics, 6*(1), 24-43.

Hernandez, F. A., Bangalore, P., Gray, J., Guan, Z., & Reilly, K. (2006). GAUGE: Grid automation and generative environment using domain engineering and domain modeling for drafting applications for the grid. *Concurrency and Computation: Practice & Experience, 18*(10), 1293-1316.

Hill, J. H., & Gokhale, A. (2007, to appear). Model-driven engineering for development-time QoS validation of component-based software systems. In *Proceeding of International Conference on Engineering of Component Based Systems*, Tuscon, AZ.

Hill, J. H., Slaby, J., Baker, S., & Schmidt, D. C. (2006, August). Applying system execution modeling tools to evaluate enterprise distributed real-time and embedded system QoS. In *Proceedings of the 12th International Conference on Embedded and Real-time Computing Systems and Applications* (pp. 350-362). Sydney, Australia: IEEE Computer Society.

Hill, J., Schmidt, D.C., & Slaby, J. (2007). *System execution modeling tools for evaluating the quality of service of enterprise distributed real-time and embedded systems.* In P. F. Tiako (Ed.). *Designing software-intensive systems: Methods and principles.* Langston University, OK.

Hill, J.H., & Gokhale, A. (2006). Continuous QoS provisioning of large-scale component-based systems using model driven engineering. In Poster preseted at *International Conference on Model Driven Engineering Languages and Systems*, Genova, Italy.

Hill, J.H., & Gokhale, A. (2007, March). Model-driven engineering for development-time QoS validation of component-based software systems. In *Proceeding of International Conference on Engineering of Component Based Systems*, Tuscon, AZ.

Hilyard, J. (2005, January). No code can hide from the profiling API in the .NET framework 2.0. *MSDN Magazine*. Retrieved March 11, 2008, from http://msdn.microsoft.com/msdnmag/issues/05/01/CLRProfiler/

Hirschheim, R. A. (1986). The effect of a priori views on the social implications of computing: The case of office automation. *ACM Computer Survey, 18*(2), 165-195.

Hoek, A., Mikic-Rakic, M., Roshandel, R., & Medvidovic, N. (2001, September). Taming architectural evolution. In *Proceedings of the 8ᵗʰ European Software Engineering Conference (held jointly with 9ᵗʰ ACM SIGSOFT International Symposium on Foundations of Software Engineering),* Vienna, Austria, (pp. 1-10).

Hofmeister, C., Nord, R., & Soni, D. (2000). *Applied software architecture.* Addison-Wesley.

Hohpe, G., & Woolf, B. (2003). *Enterprise integration patterns: Designing, building, and deploying messaging solutions.* Boston, MA, USA: Addison-Wesley.

Hollingsworth, J. K., Miller, B. P., & Cargille, J. (1994). Dynamic program instrumentation for scalable performance tools. In *Proceedings of the Scalable High-Performance Computing Conference, Knoxville, TN,* (pp. 841-850).

Holmes, N. (1997). Converging on program simplicity. *IEEE Computer, 30*(12), 134ff.

Höltta, K., Suh, E., & de Weck, O. (2005, August 15-18). Tradeoff between modularity and performance for engineered systems and products. In *Proceedings of the International Conference on Engineering Design, ICED05,* Melbourne, (p. 14). Canberra: Institution of Engineers Australia.

Holtzblatt, K. (2005). Customer-centered design for mobile applications. *Personal and Ubiquitous Computing, 9*(4), 227-237.

Hordijk, W., Krukkert, D., & Wieringa, R. (2004). *The impact of architectural decisions on quality attributes of enterprise information systems: A survey of the design space* (Tech. Rep. No. TR-CTIT-04-48). Centre for Telematics and Information Technology, University of Twente, Enschede.

Hoven, J.V.D. (2004). *Data architecture: Standards for the effective enterprise.* Information Systems Management.

Høydalsvik, G. M. (1997). *Experiences in software process modeling and enactment.* Doctoral thesis, Department of Computer and Information Science, Norwegian University of Science and Technology, Trondheim, Norway.

Hoyer, C. (2007). *ProLiSA—an approach to the specification of product line software architectures.* Doctoral thesis, J. Kepler University Linz.

Hsiao, H.I., & Narang, I. (2000). *DLFM: A transactional resource manager.* PODS

Hua, H., Brown, L.D., Gao, C., & Ahuja, N. (2003). A new collaborative infrastructure: SCAPE. In *Proceedings of IEEE Virtual Reality'03* (pp. 171-179).

Huang, A., Garlan, D., & Schmerl, B. (2004). Rainbow: Architecture-based self-adaptation with reusable infrastructure. In *Proceedings of the First International Conference on Autonomic Computing (ICAC'04),* (pp. 276-277).

Huedo, E., Montero, R. S., & Llorente, I. M. (2004). A framework for adaptive execution on grids. *Journal of Software: Practice and Experience, 34*(7), 631-651.

Hughes, B. (2004). Metadata quality evaluation: Experience from the open language archives community. In *Proceedings of the 7th International Conference on Asian Digital Libraries (ICADL 2004). Lecture Notes on Computer Science, 3334,* 320-329. Springer-Verlag.

Humphrey, W. (1989). *Managing the software process.* Reading, MA: Addison-Wesley.

Humphrey, W. S. (1997). *Introduction to the personal software process.* Information Technology for European Advancement. Addison-Wesley.

Hunt, A., & Thomas, D. (2004). *Pragmatic unit testing in c# with nunit.* Raleigh, NC, USA: The Pragmatic Programmers.

Hunt, G., & Brubacher, D. (1999). Detours: Binary interception of Win32 functions. In *Proceedings of the 3ʳᵈ USENIX Windows NT Symposium,* (pp. 135-144).

Husson, S. (70). *Microprogramming—principles and practices.* Englewood Cliffs, NJ: Prentice Hall.

IBM (Ed.). (2005). *Valeo and IBM to collaborate for automotive software development.* Retrieved March 25, 2008, from http://www-03.ibm.com/solutions/plm/doc/content/news/announcement/1346122113.html

IBM Corp. (2004). *IBM GRID computing.* Retrieved March 25, 2008, from http://www-1.ibm.com/grid/,

IBM Corporation. (1998). *PowerPC 604e RISC microprocessor user's manual with supplement for PowerPC 604 microprocessor* (Publication No. G522-0330-00) [Electronic media]. Retrieved March 11, 2008, from http://www-3.ibm.com/chips/techlib/

IBM Corporation. (2000). *Jikes Bytecode toolkit* [Computer Software]. Retrieved March 11, 2008, from http://www-128.ibm.com/developerworks/opensource/

IBM Corporation. (2003). *Develop fast, reliable code with IBM rational PurifyPlus.* Whitepaper. Retrieved March 11, 2008, from ftp://ftp.software.ibm.com/software/rational/web/whitepapers/2003/PurifyPlusPDF.pdf

IBM DeveloperWorks. (2005). *Service component architecture.* Retrieved March 23, 2008, from http://www-128.ibm.com/developerworks/ library/specification/ws-sca/

IBM Rational Unified Process Software Architecture Document Template. (2007). Retrieved March 11, 2008, from www.128.ibm.com/developerworks/rational

IBM. (1999). *MQSeries family.* Retrieved March 23, 2008, from www-4.ibm.com/software/ts/mqseries/

IBM. (2001). *WebSphere.* Retrieved March 23, 2008, from www.ibm.com/software/info1/websphere/index.jsp

IBM. (2007). *Rational software.* Retrieved March 7, 2008, from http://www-306.ibm.com/software/rational/

IBM. (2007). *Rational unified process (RUP).* Retrieved March 7, 2008, from http://www-306.ibm.com/software/awdtools/rup/

IBM. (2008). *Visualizing the editing history of wikipedia pages.* Retrieved March 23, 2008, from http://www.research.ibm.com/visual/projects/history_flow/index.htm

IDC Quantitative Research Group. (2005). *2005 Mission Critical Survey: Survey report.* Retrieved March 23, 2008, from download.microsoft.com/download/1/8/a/18a10d4f-deec-4d5e-8b24-87c29c2ec9af/idc-ms-missioncritical-ww-261005.pdf

IDS Scheer. *Aris process platform.* Retrieved March 6, 2008, from http://www.ids-scheer.com/international/english/products/31207

IEC (Ed.). (1990). *International electrotechnical vocabulary (IEV): Dependability and quality of service* (chap. 191, Tech. Rep. No. IEC 60050(191):1990). IEC: International Electronic Commission.

IEC. (1998). *ISO/IEC 61508, Part 1-7: Functional safety of electric/electronic/programmable electronic systems* (Tech. Rep.). IEC: International Electronic Commission.

IEEE IEEE-Std 830 1993 IEEE Recommended Practice for Software Requirements Specifications.

IEEE Std 1471-2000. (2000). *IEEE recommended practice for architectural description of software-intensive systems.*

IEEE. (1990). Standard glossary of software engineering terminology, IEEE standard 610.12. *IEEE software engineering standards collection (Spring ed.).*

IEEE. (2001). *IEEE standard test access port and boundary-scan architecture.* IEEE Std. 1149.1-2001.

IEEE-ISTO. (2003). *The Nexus 5001 forum standard for global embedded processor debug interface, version 2.0* [Electronic media]. Retrieved March 11, 2008, from http://www.ieee-isto.org

iLogix. (2006). *Rhapsody.* Retrieved March 7, 2008 from http://www.ilogix.com/sublevel.aspx?id=284

Inmon, W.H. (1996). The data warehouse and data mining. *Communications of the ACM, 39,* 49-50.

Institute for Software Integrated Systems. (Vanderbilt University). *Component-integrated ACE ORB (CIAO).* Retrieved March 23, 2008, from www.dre.vanderbilt.edu/CIAO/

Institute of Electrical and Electronics Engineers. (1991). IEEE standard computer dictionary. A compilation of IEEE standard computer glossaries. *IEEE Std 610.*

Intel Corporation. (2006). *Intel 64 and IA-32 architectures software developer's manual (Vol. 3B, System Programming Guide, Part 2).* Retrieved March 11, 2008, from www.intel.com/design/processor/manuals/253669.pdf

Intel Corporation. (2006). Intel's tera-scale research prepares for tens, hundreds of cores. *Technology@Intel Magazine.* Retrieved March 11, 2008, from http://www.intel.com/technology/magazine/computing/tera-scale-0606.htm

International Organization for Standarization. (2001). *ISO/IEC Standard 9126: Software engineering--product quality*, part 1, ISO.

IONA Technologies. (2006). *Artix -soa for the complex enterprise.* Retrieved March 23, 2008, from http://www.iona.com/products/artix/

Isermann, R., Matko, D., & Lachmann, K.-H. (1992). *Adaptive control systems.* Upper Saddle River, NJ, USA: Prentice Hall.

ISO/IEC. (2001). *Software engineering—product quality—part 1: Quality model* (Tech. Rep. No. ISO/IEC 9126-1:2001). International Organization for Standardization.

ISO/IEC. (2001). *Software engineering body of knowledge (SWEBOK)* (Tech. Rep. No. DTR 19759). International Organization for Standardization.

ISO/IEC. (2005, September). *Information technology—software process assessment—part 6: An exemplar system life cycle process assessment model* (Tech. Rep. No. ISO/IEC-15504-6). International Organization for Standardization.

ISO/IEC. (2006, January). *Systems engineering—system life cycle processes* (Tech. Rep. No. ISO/IEC 15288:2006, wd.1). International Organization for Standardization, ISO/IEC JTC 1/SC 7/WG 7.

ISO/IEC. (2006). *Software engineering: Software product quality requirements and evaluation (SQuaRE)*

quality model (Tech. Rep. No. ISO/IEC WD 25010). International Organization for Standardization.

ISO/IEC. (Ed.). (1996). *Information technology—vocabulary—part 14: Reliability, maintainability and availability* (Tech. Rep. No. ISO/IEC 2382-14:1996). International Organization for Standardization.

IVDGL. (2006, July 30). *International virtual data grid laboratory.* Retrieved March 23, 2008, from http://www.ivdgl.org/

Ivkovic, I., & Kontogiannis, K. (2004). Tracing evolution changes of software artifacts through model synchronization. In *Paper presented at the Proceedings of the 20th IEEE International Conference on Software Maintenance* (pp. 252-261).

J.Bank. (1993). *The essence of total quality management.* Prentice Hall.

Jaaksi, A. (2002). Developing mobile browsers in a product line. *IEEE Software, 19*(4), 73-80.

Jackson, D., & Rinard, M. (2000). Software analysis: A roadmap. In *Proceedings of the IEEE International Conference on Software Engineering,* (pp. 133-145).

Jagadish, H.V., & Olken, F. (2004). Database management for life sciences research. *SIGMOD Record* (Vol. 33, pp. 15-20).

JASIG. (2008). *JASIG's U-Portal: Evolving portal implementations from participating universities and partners.* Retrieved March 23, 2008, from http://www.uportal.org/

Jatlitebean Web pages. (2007). Retrieved March 11, 2008, from http://waitaki.otago.ac.nz/JATLiteBean

Java Community Process (JCP). (2006, May). *Enterprise JavaBean specification version 3.0.* Retrieved March 11, 2008, from www.jcp.org

JEITA. (2002). *EXIF standard.* Retrieved March 24, 2008, from http://www.exif.org/

Jennings, N.R. (2001, April). An agent-based approach for building complex software systems. *Communications of the ACM, 44*(4), 35-41.

Jensen, K. (1997). Coloured petri nets. Basic concepts, analysis methods and practical use. *Monographs in theoretical computer science* (2nd ed.). Springer-Verlag.

Jensen, K., & Rozenberg, G. (Eds.). (1991). *High-level Petri nets: Theory and application*. London, UK: Springer-Verlag.

Johansen, U., Stav, E., Walderhaug, S., & Aagedal, J. (2006). *Modelware - traceability metamodel and system solution* [D1.6-4]. Trondheim: SINTEF.

John, W.S. (1999). On the Web, plagiarism matters more than copy right piracy. *Ethics and information technology*. Netherlands: Kluwer Academic.

Jorgensen, M., & Molokken-Ostvold, K. (2006). How large are software cost overruns? A review of the 1994 CHAOS report. *Information and Software Technology, 48*(4), 297-301.

Jouault, F. (2005, November 8). Loosely coupled traceability for ATL. In *Paper presented at the European Conference on Model Driven Architecture - Traceability Workshop 2005*, Nuremberg, Germany.

Jouault, F., & Kurtev, I. (2005, October). Transforming Models with ATL. In *Proceedings of the Model Transformations in Practice Workshop at MoDELS,* Montego Bay, Jamaica.

Jouault, F., & Kurtev, I. (2006, April). On the architectural alignment of ATL and QVT. In *Proceedings of ACM Symposium on Applied Computing* (pp. 1188-1195). Dijon, Bourgogne: France.

JSWG. (2007). *Job submission description language WG (JSDL-WG)*. Retrieved March 23, 2008, from https://forge.gridforum.org/projects/jsdl-wg/

Julier, S., King, R., Colbert, B., Durbin J., & Rosenblum, L. (1999). The software architecture of a real-time battlefield visualization virtual environment. In *Proceedings of IEEE Virtual Reality* (pp. 29-36). Houston, TX, USA.

Kahkonen, T. (2004). Agile methods for large organizations—building communities of practice. *Agile Development Conference (ADC'04)*, Salt Lake City, Utah, USA.

Kaiser, B., Liggesmeyer, P., & Maeckel, O. (2003, October 9-10). A new component concept for fault trees. In *Proceedings of the 8th National Workshop on Safety Critical Systems and Software (scs 2003),* Canberra, Australia, (Vol. 33, pp. 37-46). Darlinghurst, Australia: Australian Computer Society.

Kande, M. (2003). *A concern-oriented approach to software architecture*. Doctoral dissertation, Lausanne, Switzerland: Swiss Federal Institute of Technology (EPFL).

Kangas, E., & Kinnunen, T. (2005). Applying user-centered design to mobile application development. *Communications of the ACM (CACM), 48*(7), 55-59.

Karhinen, A., & Kuusela, J. (1998, February). Structuring design decisions for evolution. In *Proceedings of the Second International ESPRIT ARES Workshop*, Las Palmas de Gran Canaria, Spain, (pp. 223-234). Springer-Verlag.

Karonis, N., Toonen, B., & Foster, I. (2003). MPICH-G2: A grid-enabled implementation of the message passing interface. *Journal of Parallel and Distributed Computing (JPDC), 63*(5), 551-563.

Karsai, G., Maroti, M., Lédeczi, A., Gray, J., & Sztipanovits, J. (2004, March). Composition and cloning in modeling and metamodeling. *IEEE Transactions on Control System Technology, Special Issue on Computer Automated Multi-paradigm Modeling, 12*(2), 263-278.

Karsai, G., Neema, S., Abbott, B., & Sharp, D. (2002, August). A modeling language and its supporting tools for avionics systems. In *Proceedings of the 21st Digital Avionics Systems Conf*erence, (Vol. 1, pp. 6A3-1-6A3-13).

Karsai, G., Neema, S., Abbott, B., & Sharp, D. (2002, August). A modeling language and its supporting tools for avionics systems. In *Proceedings of 21st Digital Avionics Systems Conference* (pp. 6A3-1–6A3-13). Los Alamitos, CA: IEEE Computer Society.

Karsai, G., Sztipanovits, J., Ledeczi, A., & Bapty, T. (2003). Model-integrated development of embedded software, In *Proceedings of the IEEE, 91*(1), 145-164.

Karsai, G., Sztipanovits, J., Ledeczi, A., & Bapty, T. (2003, January). Model-integrated development of embedded software. *Proceedings of the IEEE, 91*(1), 145-164.

Kaul, D., Kogekar, A., Gokhale, A., Gray, J., & Gokhale, S. (2007). Managing variability in middleware provisioning using visual modeling languages. In *Proceedings of the Hawaii International Conference on System Sciences HICSS-40 (2007), Visual Interactions in Software Artifacts Minitrack, Software Technology Track*, Big Island, HI.

Kazman, R., Klein, M., & Clements, P. (2000). *Atam:sm method for architecture evaluation* (Tech. Rep. No. SEI, CMU/SEI-2000-TR-004, ESC-TR-2000-004).

Keilser, S. (2006). *Software paradigms*. New York: John Wiley-Interscience.

Keller, F., & Wendt, S. (2003, April). Fmc: An approach towards architecture-centric system development. In *Proceedings of the 10th IEEE International Conference and Workshop on the Engineering of Computer-Based Systems (ECBS'03)*, (p. 173).

Keller, G., Nüttgens, M., & Scheer, A. (1992). *Semantische Processmodellierung auf der Grundlage Ereignisgesteuerter Processketten (EPK)*. Veröffentlichungen des Instituts für Wirtschaftsinformatik, Heft 89 (in German). University of Saarland, Saarbrücken.

Keller, S., Kahn, L., & Panara, R. (1990). Specifying software quality requirements with metrics. In R. Thayer & M. Dorfman (Eds.), *Tutorial: System and software requirements engineering* (pp. 145-163). IEEE Computer Society Press.

Kemper, A., & Eickler, A. (1997). *Datenbanksysteme—Eine Einführung*. Oldenbourg: Springer-Verlag.

Kent, S. (2002, May). Model driven engineering. In *Proceedings of Integrated Formal Methods: Third International Conference*, Turku, Finland.

Kiczale, G., Hilsdale, E., Hugunin, J., Kersten, M., Palm, J., & Griswold, W. G. (2001). *An overview of AspectJ*. (LNCS, 2072, pp. 327-355).

Kindler, E. (2006). On the semantics of EPCs: Resolving the vicious circle. *Data Knowledge Eng., 56*(1), 23-40.

Kivisto, K. (1999). Roles of developers as part of a software process model. In *Proceedings of the 32nd Hawaii International Conference on System Sciences*.

Kleppe, A. (2003). *MDA explained: The model driven architecture™: Practice and promise*.

Kleppe, A., Bast, W., & Warmer. B. (2003). *The model driven architecture: Practice and promise*. New York: Addison-Wesley.

Klusener, S., Laemmel, R., & Verhoef, C. (2005). Architectural modifications to deployed software. *Science of Computer Programming, 54*, 143-211.

Kolovos, D. S., Paige, R. F., & Polack, F. A. C. (2006, July). On-demand merging of traceability links with models. In *Paper presented at the European Concerence on Model Driven Architecture Traceability Workshop (ECMDA-TW)*, Bilbao, Spain.

Kopetz, H. (1997). *Real-time systems—design principles for distributed embedded application*. Boston/Dordrecht/London: Kluwer Academic.

Kopetz, H., & Bauer, G. (2003). The time-triggered architecture. *IEEE Special Issue on Modeling and Design of Embedded Software*.

Kossiakoff, A., & Seet, W. (2003). *Systems engineering—principles and practice*. New York: Wiley Series in Systems Engineering and Management, Wiley Interscience.

Král, J. (1998). *Informační Systémy*, (in Czech: *Information systems*). Veletiny, Czech Republic: Science.

Král, J., & Demner, J. (1979). Towards reliable real time software. In *Proceedings of IFIP Conference Construction of Quality Software*, North Holland, (pp. 1-12).

Král, J., & Žemlička, M. (2002). Autonomous components. In M. H. Hamza (Ed.), *Applied informatics* (pp. 125-130). Anaheim: ACTA Press.

Král, J., & Žemlička, M. (2004). Architecture and modeling of service-oriented systems. In P. Vojtáš, M. Bieliková, B. Charon-Bost, & O. Sýkora (Eds.), *Proceedings of SOFSEM 2005 Communications,* (pp. 71-80). Bratislava, Slovakia: Slovak Society for Computer Science.

Král, J., & Žemlička, M. (2004). Service orientation and the quality indicators for software services. In R. Trappl (Ed.), *Cybernetics and systems* (Vol. 2, pp. 434-439). Vienna, Austria: Austrian Society for Cybernetic Studies.

Král, J., & Žemlička, M. (2005). Implementation of business processes in service-oriented systems. In *Proceedings of 2005 IEEE International Conference on Services Computing* (Vol. II, pp. 115-122). Los Alamitos, CA, USA: IEEE CS Press.

Král, J., & Žemlička, M. (2007). Crucial patterns in service-oriented architecture. In *Proceedings of the ICDT Conference,* (p. 133). Los Alamitos, CA, USA: IEEE CS Press.

Král, J., Černý, J., & Dvořák, P. (1987). Technology of FMS control software development. In G. Menga & V. Kempe (Eds.), *Proceedings of the Workshop on Information in Manufacturing Automation*, Dresden, Germany.

Král, J., Žemlička, M., & Kopecký, M. (2006). Software confederations—an architecture for agile development in the large. In P. Dini (Ed.), *Proceedings of the International Conference on Software Engineering Advances (ICSEA'06),* (p. 39). Los Alamitos, CA, USA: IEEE CS Press.

Kramer, J. M. J. (1990). The evolving philosophers problem: Dynamic change management. *IEEE Transactions on Software Engineering, 16*(11), 1193-1306.

Krechetov, I., Tekinerdogan, B., Garcia, A., Chavez, C., & Kulesza, U. (2006). Towards an integrated aspect-oriented modeling approach for software architecture design. In *Proceedings of the Workshop on Aspect-oriented Modeling, Aspect-oriented Software Development.*

Kristensen, L.M., Christensen, S., & Jensen, K. (1998). The practitioner's guide to coloured Petri nets. *International Journal on Software Tools for Technology Transfer, 2*, 98-132.

Kroll, P., & Krutchten, P. (2003). *The rational unified process made easy.* USA: Addison-Wesley.

Kruchten, P. (1995). Architectural blueprints. The 4+1 view model of software architecture. *IEEE Software, 12*(6), 42-50.

Krueger, C.W. (2002, August). Variation management for software production lines. In *Proceedings of the Second International Conference of Software Product Lines*, SPLC 2, San Diego, CA, (pp. 37-48).

Krutchen, P. (1995). Architectural blueprints: The "4+1" view model of software architecture. *IEEE Software, 12*(6).

Kuck, D. (1977). A survey of parallel machine organization and programming. *ACM Computing Surveys, 9*(1), 29-58.

Kuhn, T. S. (1996). *The structure of scientific revolutions* (3rd ed.). IL: University of Chicago Press.

Kulesza, U., Garcia, A., & Lucena, C. (2004). Towards a method for the development of aspect-oriented generative approaches. In *Proceedings of the Workshop on Early Aspects, OOPSLA.*

Kumar, V., Grama, A., Gupta, A., & Karypis, G. (1994). *Introduction to parallel computing: Design and analysis of algorithms.* Redwood City, CA: Benjamin/Cummings.

Kurbel, K., & Schnieder, T. (1994). *Integration issues of information engineering based i-case tools.* Working Papers of the Institute of Business Informatics, University of Münster (No. 33). Retrieved March 25, 2008, from http://www.wi.uni-muenster.de/inst/arbber/ab33.pdf

Kurtev, I., Dee, M., Goknil, A., & Berg, K. V. D. (2007). Traceability-based change management in operational mappings. In *Paper presented at the ECMDA Traceability Workshop (ECMDA-TW)* (pp. 57-87). Haifa, Israel.

Lacotte, J.-P. (2004). *ITEA report on open source software* (Tech. Rep.). ITEA -

Laird, L., & Brennan, M. (2006). *Software measurement and estimation—a practical approach.* New York: Wiley Interscience, IEEE Computer Society.

Lanter, D.P. (1991). Design of a lineage-based meta-data base for GIS. *Cartography and Geographic Information Systems, 18,* 255-261.

Laplante, P., & Neill, C. (2006). *Avoiding anti-patterns at work can help you sleep at night. Centredaily.com.*

Retrieved March 25, 2008, from http://www.centre-daily.com/mld/centredaily/news/opinion/14078324.htm?template=contentModules/printstory.jsp

Laprie, J. (1990). On the assessment of safety-critical software systems. In F. R. Valette,, P. A. Freeman, & M. C. Gaudel (Eds.), *Proceedings of the 12th Internat. Conference on Software Engineering*, (p. 222). IEEE Computer Press.

Laprie, J. C. (Ed.). (1992). *Dependability: Basic concepts and terminology in English, French, German, Italian and Japanese [IFIP WG 10.4, Dependable Computing and Fault Tolerance]* (Vol. 5). Wien: Springer-Verlag.

Lardieri, P., Balasubramanian, J., Schmidt, D., Thakar, G., Gokhale, A., & Damiano, T. (2007, to appear). A multi-layered resource management framework for dynamic resource management in enterprise DRE systems. In C. C Cavanaugh (Ed.), *Journal of Systems and Software: Special Issue on Dynamic Resource Management in Distributed Real-time Systems*.

Larus, J., & Schnarr, E. (1995). EEL: Machine-independent executable editing. In *Proceedings of the ACM SIG-PLAN Conference on Programming Language Designes and Implementation*, (pp. 291-300).

Lassila, O., & Swick, R. (1999). *Resource description framework (RDF) model and syntax*. World Wide Web Consortium.

Laszewski, G. V., Foster, I., Gawor, J., & Lane, P. (2001). A Java commodity grid kit. *Concurrency and Computation: Practice and Experience, 13*(8-9), 643-662.

Le, H. N., & Nygård, M. (2005). A mobile affiliation model for supporting mobile collaborative work. In *Proceedings of the Workshop on Ubiquitous Mobile Information and Collaboration Systems (UMICS)*.

Ledeczi, A. (2001). The generic modeling environment. In *Proceedings of the Workshop on Intelligent Signal Processing*, Budapest, Hungary.

Ledeczi, A., Bakay, A., Maroti M., Volgysei P., Nordstrom, G., Sprinkle, J., & Karsai, G. (2001). Composing domain-specific design environments. *IEEE Computer, 34*(11), 44-51.

Ledeczi, A., Maroti, M., Karsai G., & Nordstrom G. (1999). Metaprogrammable toolkit for model-integrated computing. In *Proceedings of the IEEE International Conference on the Engineering of Computer-Based Systems Conference,* Nashville, TN, (pp 311-317).

Lédeczi, Á., Nordstrom, G., Karsai, G., Volgyesi, P., & Maroti, M. (2001). On metamodel composition. In *Proceedings of the 2001 IEEE International Conference on Control Applications,* Mexico City, Mexico, (pp. 756-760).

Lee, E. A. (2006). The problem with threads. *IEEE Computer, 39*(11), 33-42.

Lee, H. B. (1997, July). *BIT: Bytecode instrumenting tool*. Unpublished master's thesis, University of Colorado, Boulder, CO.

Lefkowitz, R. (2005, July 21). *Calculating the true price of software*. Retrieved March 23, 2008, from http://www.onlamp.com/pub/a/onlamp/2005/07/21/software_pricing.html

Lehman, M. (1980). Programs, life cycles, and laws of software evolution. *Proceedings of the IEEE, 68*(9), 1060-1076.

Lehman, M. B. L. (Ed.). (1985). *Program evolution—processes of software change*. APIC Studies in Data Proc. No. 27, Academic Press.

Lehman, M. M. (1996). Laws of software evolution revisited. In *Proceedings of the European Workshop on Software Process Technology,* (p. 11). IEEE Computer Society.

Lehman, M. M. (2005). The role and impact of assumptions in software development, maintenance and evolution. In *Proceedings of the 2005 IEEE International Workshop on Software Evolvability*, USA. IEEE Computer Society.

Letelier, P. (2002, September). A framework for requirements traceability in UML-based projects. In *Paper presented at the Proceedings of the 1st International Workshop on Traceability, co-located with ASE 2002* (pp. 32-41). Edinburgh, Scotland, UK.

Letondal, C. (2000). A Web interface generator for molecular biology programs in Unix. *Bioinformatics, 17*(1), 73-82.

Li, J. (2002). *Monitoring of component-based systems* (Tech. Rep. No. HPL-2002-25R1. HP). Laboratories, Palo Alto, CA, USA.

Li, Z., Sun, W., Jiang, Z. B., & Zhang X. (2005). BPEL4WS unit testing: Framework and implementation. In *Proceedings of the IEEE International Conference on Web Services (ICWS'05),* Orlando, FL, (pp. 103-110).

Limón, A. E., & Garbajosa, J. (2005, November 8). The need for a unifying traceability scheme. In *Paper presented at the European Conference on Model Driven Architecture - Traceability Workshop 2005,* Nuremberg, Germany.

Littlewood, B., & Wright, D. (1997). Some conservative stopping rules for the operational testing of safety-critical software. *IEEE Trans SwE, 23*(11), 673-683.

Litzkow, M., Livny, M., & Mutka, M. (1988). Condor--a hunter of idle workstations. In *Proceedings of the 8th International Conference of Distributed Computing Systems,* (pp. 104-111).

Lodderstedt, T., Basin, D., & Doser, J. (2002). SecureUML: A UML-based modeling language for model-driven security. *UML, 2460,* 426-441.

London, K., Moore, S., Mucci, P., Seymour, K., & Luczak, R. (2001, June 18-21). The PAPI cross-platform interface to hardware performance counters. In *Proceedings of the Department of Defense Users' Group Conference.*

Long, E., Misra, A., & Sztipanovits, J. (1998, August). Increasing productivity at Saturn. *IEEE Computer, 31*(8), 35-43.

Lucas, P., & Walk, K. (1969). On the formal description of pl/i. *Annual Review in Automatic Programming, 6,* Part 3, 105-182.

Luckham, D.C., Kenney, J.J., Augustin, L.M., Vera, J., Bryan, D., & Mann, W. (1995). Specification and analysis of system architecture using Rapide. *IEEE Transactions on Software Engineering, 21*(4), 336-354.

Lucky, R. (2006, November). Impossible trade-offs. *IEEE Spectrum,* p. 52.

Ludwig, H., Keller, A., Dan, A., King, R. P., & Franck, R. (2003, January). *Web service level agreement language specification.* Retrieved March 23, 2008, from reseach-web.watson.ibm.com/wsla/documents.html

Luk, C., Cohn, R., Muth, R., Patil, H., Klauser, A., Lowney, G., et al. (2005). Pin: Building customized program analysis tools with dynamic instrumentation. In *Proceedings of the ACM SIGPLAN Conference on Programming Language Design and Implementation,* (pp. 190-200).

Lynch, N., & Tuttle, M. (1989). An introduction to input/output automata. *CWI-Quarterly, 2*(3), 219-246.

Ma, W., Cooper, K., & Chung, L. (2006). Component-aware systems architecting: A software interoperability perspective. In *Proceedings of the 5th International Workshop on System/Software Architectures,* Las Vegas, NV, USA.

Macala, R.R., Stuckey, L., & Gross, D. (1996, May). Managing domain-specific, product-line development. *IEEE Software, 14*(13), 57-67.

Maccari, A. (1999). The challenges of requirements engineering in mobile telephones industry. In *Proceedings of the 10th International Conference and Workshop on Database and Expert Systems Applications (DEXA '99).* Springer-Verlag.

MacKenzie, C. M., Laskey, K., McCabe, F., Brown, P. F., & Metz, R. (2006, July 19). *Reference model for service-oriented architecture 1.0, committee specification 1.* Retrieved March 6, 2008, from http://www.oasis-open.org/committees/download.php/19361/soa-rm-cs.pdf

Mackrodt, W. (1981). Considerations on language interpretation for microprocessor systems. *Microprocessing and Microprogramming, 7,* 110-118.

Maier, M., Emery, D., & Hilliard, R. (2001). Software architecture: Introducing IEEE standard 1471. *Computer, 34*(4), 107-109.

Majumdar, R. K., Ramamritham, K., & Xiong, M. (2003). Adaptive location management in mobile environments. In *Proceedings of the International Conference on Mobile Data Management (MDM 2003)*. Melbourne, Australia, ACM Press.

Mania, D., Murphy, J., & McManis, J. (2002). Developing performance models from non-intrusive monitoring traces. In *Proceeding of Information Technology and Telecommunications (IT&T)*.

Margaria, T. (2004). Modeling dependable systems: What can model driven development contribute and what likely not? In *Proceedings of IEEE International Symposium on Object-Oriented Real-Time Distributed Computing*, Vienna, Austria.

Martin, G., Lavagno, L., & Louis-Guerin, J. (2001). Embedded UML: A merger of real-time UML and codesign. In *Proceedings of the 9th International Symposium on Hardware/Software Codesign*, Copenhagen, Denmark.

Martin, J., & Finkelstein, C. (1981). *Information engineering*. Carnforth, England: Savant Institute.

Maruyama, K., & Smith, S. (1977). Analysis of design alternatives for virtual memory indexes. *Communications of the ACM, 20*(4), 245-254.

Massie, M. L., Chun, B. N., & Culler, D. E. (2004). The Ganglia distributed monitoring system: Design, Implementation, and Experience. *Parallel Computing, 30*(7), 817-840.

Massol, V., & Husted, T. (2003). *Junit in action*. Greenwich, CT, USA: Manning Publications Co.

McConnell, S. (1996). *Rapid development* (1st ed.). Redmond, WA: Microsoft Press.

McDermid, J. (Ed.). (1991). *Software engineer's reference book*. Butterworth-Heinemann Oxford.

McDermid, J. A. (2003). Trends in systems safety: A European view? P. Lindsay (Ed.), *Seventh Australian Workshop on Industrial Experience with Safety Critical Systems and Software,* (Vol. 15, pp. 3-8). Adelaide, Australia: ACS.

McDermid, J., & Pumfrey, D. (1994). A development of hazard analysis to aid software design. In *Proceedings of the Ninth Annual Conference on Computer Assurance (compass94),* (pp. 17-25). Gaithersburg, MD, USA: National Institute of Standards and Technology.

McGrath, G. M. (1998, January). Behavioural issues in software engineering process modelling: A multiparadigm approach. *Hawaii International Conference on System Sciences (HICSS)*.

McGregor, J.D. (2003). *The evolution of product-line assets* (Tech. Rep. No. CMU/SEI-2003-TR-005m ESC-TR-2003-005).

Meadows, D., Meadows, D., Zahn, E., & Millig, P. (1969). *Die Grenzen des Wachstums—Bericht des Club of Rome zur Lage der Menschheit*. Bertelsmann.

Medvidovic, N., & Taylor, R. (2000). A classification and comparison framework for software architecture description languages. *IEEE Transactions on Software Engineering, 26*(1), 70-93.

Meehl, P., & Sellars, W. (1956). The concept of emergence. In H. Feigl & M. Scrive (Eds.), *Minnesota studies in the philosophy of science: The foundations of science and the concepts of psychology and psychoanalysis* (Vol. 1, pp. 239-252). University of Minnesota Press.

Mehta, N. R., & Medvidovic, N. (2005). Composing architectural styles from architectural primitives. In *ESEC/FSE-11: Proceedings of the 9th European Software Engineering Conference held jointly with the 11th ACM SIGSOFT International Symposium on Foundations of Software Engineering*, (pp. 347-350). New York: ACM Press.

Mellor, S. J. (2004). *MDA distilled: Principles of model-driven architecture*.

Menascé, D., Almeida, V., & Dowdy, L. (2004). *Performance by design: Computer capacity planning by example* (pp. 135-141). Upper Saddle River, NJ: Prentice Hall.

Mens, T., & D'Hondt, T. (2000, March). Automating support for software evolution in UML, *Automated Software Engineering, 7*(1), 39-59.

Merlin, P. M. (1974). A study of the recoverability of computing systems. Irvine: University of California, Department of Information and Computer Science.

Merriam-Webster, I. (Ed.). (1996). *Webster's new encyclopedic dictionary*. Black Doc and Leventhal.

MetaObject Facility (MOF) 2.0 Core Specification. (2003, October).

Meyer, B. (1992, October). Applying design by contract. *Computer (IEEE), 25*(10), 40-51.

Microsoft .NET Framework. (2007). Retrieved March 11, 2008, from msdn2.microsoft.com

Microsoft Component Object Model (COM). (2007). Retrieved March 11, 2008, from msdn2.microsoft.com

Microsoft Corporation. (2000). *Microsoft COM technologies DCOM.*

Microsoft Corporation. (2002). *Microsoft .NET Development.* Retrieved March 23, 2008, from msdn.microsoft.com/net/

Microsoft Corporation. (2006). *Microsoft domain-specific language (DSL) tools: Visual studio 2005 team system.* Retrieved March 7, 2008, from http://msdn.microsoft.com/vstudio/teamsystem/workshop/DSLTools

Microsoft Corporation. (2006a). *Clickonce deployment overview.* Retrieved March 23, 2008, from http://msdn2.microsoft.com/en-us/ library/142dbbz4.aspx

Microsoft Corporation. (2006b). *System definition model overview.* Retrieved March 23, 2008, from http://www.microsoft.com/ windowsserversystem/dsi/sdmwp.mspx

Microsoft Corporation. (2007). *Windows embedded CE 6.0.* Retrieved March 7, 2008, from http://www.microsoft.com/windows/embedded/

Microsoft Corporation. (2007a). *Windows server 2003 performance counters reference.* Microsoft TechNet [Electronic media]. Retrieved March 11, 2008, from http://technet2.microsoft.com/WindowsServer/en/library/3fb01419-b1ab-4f52-a9f8-09d5ebeb9ef21033.mspx?mfr=true

Microsoft Corporation. (2007b). *Using the registry functions to consume counter data.* Microsoft Developer Network [Electronic media]. Retrieved March 11, 2008, from http://msdn2.microsoft.com/en-us/library/aa373219.aspx

Microsoft Corporation. (2007c). *Using the PDH functions to consume counter data.* Microsoft Developer Network [Electronic media]. Retrieved March 11, 2008, from http://msdn2.microsoft.com/en-us/library/aa373214.aspx

Microsoft Domain-Specific Language Tools. (2007). Retrieved March 23, 2008, from http://msdn2.microsoft.com/en-us/vstudio/aa718368.aspx

Microsystems, S. (2003, November). *J2EE connector architecture specification.* Retrieved March 23, 2008, from http://java.sun.com/j2ee/connector/

Mili, R., Zalila, Z., Daescu, O., Zhang, K., Steiner, R., Oladimeji. E., & Xue, P. (2004). *Prediction and visualization of large scale distributed multi-agent systems.* The University of Texas at Dallas: Department of Computer Science.

Mili, R.Z., Steiner, R., & Oladimeji, E. (2004). Abstract architecture of agent-environment systems. *Multiagent and Grid Systems, 2*(4).

Miller, B.P., Callaghan, M.D., Cargille, J.M., Hollingsworth, J.K., Irvin, R.B., & Karavanic, K.L. (1995, December). The Paradyn parallel performance measurement tool. *IEEE Computer, 28*(11), 37-46.

Miller, C. (Ed). (2004). Human-computer etiquette: Managing expectations with intentional agents. *Communications of the ACM, 47*(4).

Miller, J., & Mukerji, J. (2003). *MDA guide version 1.0.1* [omg/2003-06-01]. Object Management Group (OMG).

Mock, M. (2003). Dynamic analysis from the bottom up. In *Proceedings of the ICSE 2003 Workshop on Dynamic Analysis (WODA 2003).*

ModelWare Project. (2006). Retrieved March 7, 2008, from http://www.modelware-ist.org/

MOF 2.0/XMI mapping specification, v2.1. (2005, September). Retrieved May 12, 2008, from http://www.omg.org/spec/XMI/index.htm

Momjian, B. (2000). *PostgreSQL: Introduction and concepts* (1st ed.): Pearson Education.

Monroe, R.T. (1998). *Capturing software architecture design expertise with Armani* (Tech. Rep. No. CMU-CS-98-163). Carnegie Mellon University: School of Computer Science.

Montero, R. S., Huedo, E., & Llorente, I. M. (2006). Grid scheduling infrastructures based on the GridWay meta-scheduler. *IEEE Technical Committee on Scalable Computing (TCSC) Newsletter, 8*(2).

Moore, B. (2004). *Eclipse development using the graphical editing framework and the eclipse modeling framework.* Boca Raton, Florida: IBM, International Technical Support Organization.

Morello, D. (2005). *The IT professional outlook: Where will we go from here?* Gartner Group.

Mössenböck, H. (2002). Automatische Speicherbereinigung. In P. Rechenberg & G. Pomberger (Eds.), *Informatik-Handbuch, 3. Auflage, Kap. D12.6.* Hanser-Verlag.

Muller, I., Braun, P., & Kowalczyk, R. (2005). Design patterns for agent-based service composition in the Web. In *Proceedings of the Fifth International Conference on Quality Software*, (pp. 425-430).

Mullins, J. (2006, July). Ring of steel. *IEEE spectrum* (pp. 5-7).

Mumford, E., & Sackman, H. (Eds.). (1974). Human choice and computers. In *Proceedings of the IFIP Conference on Human Choice and Computers*, Vienna. Amsterdam: North Holland Publishing Company.

Murayama, J. (2001, July). *Performance profiling using TNF. Sun Developer Network.* Retrieved March 11, 2008, from http://developers.sun.com/solaris/articles/tnf.html

Musa, J. (2006). *More reliable software faster and cheaper: An overview of software reliability engineering.* Osborne/McGraw-Hill.

Myers, G. (1976). *Software reliability—principles and practices.* New York: John Wiley & Sons.

Myers, G. (1977). The case against stack-oriented instruction sets. *CAN, 6*(3), 7-10.

Myers, J.D., Allison, T.C., Bittner, S., Didier, B.T., Frenklach, M., Green, Jr., W. H., et al. (2004). *A collaborative informatics infrastructure for multiscale science.* CLADE, p. 24.

Nadeau, D.R. (1999). Building virtual worlds with VRML: IEEE computer graphics and applications. *IEEE Computer Graphics (IEEECS), 19*(2), 18-29.

Najjar, J., Meire, M., & Duval, E. (2005). Attention metadata management: Tracking the use of learning objects through Attention.XML. In *Proceedings of the ED-MEDIA 2005 World Conference on Educational Multimedia, Hypermedia and Telecommunications.*

Nakajo, T. K. H. (1985). The principles of foolproofing and their application in manufacturing. *Reports of Statistical Application Research JUSE, 32*(2), 10-29.

Naur, P., & Randell, B. (Eds.). (1969). Software engineering. In *Proceedings of the NATO Conference in Garmisch-Partenkirchen, 1968.* NATO Science Committee, Scientific Affairs Division, NATO, Brussels.

Nechypurenko, A., Wuchner, E., White, J., & Schmidt, D.C. (2007). Application of aspect-based modeling and weaving for complexity reduction in the development of automotive distributed real-time embedded systems. In *Proceedings of the Sixth International Conference on Aspect-oriented Software Development.* Vancouver, British Columbia.

NEES. (2006, November 6). *Network for earthquake engineering simulation.* Retrieved March 23, 2008, from http://it.nees.org/

Nelder, J., & Mead, R. (1965). A simplex method for function minimization. *Computer Journal, 7*(4), 308-313.

Netcraft. (2005, August-October). *Market share for top servers across all domains.* Retrieved March 23, 2008, from http://news.netcraft.com/archives/2005/10/index.html

Nethercote, N. (2004). *Dynamic binary analysis and instrumentation*. Unpublished doctoral dissertation, University of Cambridge, UK.

Nguyen, M. N., & Conradi, R. (1994). Classification of meta-processes and their models. In *Proceedings of the Third International Conference on Software Process*, Washington, USA.

Nimmer, J., & Ernst, M. D. (2001). Static verification of dynamically detected program invariants: Integrating Daikon and ESC/Java. In *Proceedings of the 1ˢᵗ International Workshop on Runtime Verification*.

Nitto, E. D., & Fuggetta, A. (Eds.). (1998). Process technology. *Journal on Automated Software Engineering, 5*(Special Issue).

Nobel Prize. (1997). *The Nobel Prize in Economics 1997 – press release*. Retrieved March 23, 2008, from http://nobelprize.org/nobel_prizes/economics/laureates/1997/press.html

Noppen, J., et al. (2002). Optimizing software development policies for evolutionary system requirements. In *Proceedings of the First International Workshop on Unanticipated Software Evolution (USE'02),* Malaga, Spain, (p. 10).

Northrop, L., Feiler, P., Gabriel, R., Goodenough, J., Linger, R., Longstaff, T., et al. (2006). *Ultra-large-scale systems: The software challenge of the future.* Carnegie Mellon.

Novotny, J., Russell, M., & Wehrens, O. (2004). GridSphere: A portal framework for building collaborations. *Concurrency and Computation: Practice & Experience, 16*(5), 503-513.

O'Sullivan, J., Edmond D., & Ter Hofstede, A. (2002). What's in a service? Towards accurate description of non-functional service properties. *Distributed and Parallel Databases, 12*(2), 117-133.

Object Computing Incorporated. (2006). *A window into your systems* [Electronic media]. Retrieved March 11, 2008, from http://www.ociweb.com/products/OVATION

Object Management Group. (1995). *OMG object management architecture guide version 3.0.* Retrieved March 11, 2008, from www.omg.org

Object Management Group. (2002). *Real-time CORBA specification.* OMG Document formal/02-08-02.

Object Management Group. (2004). *OMG common object request broker architecture: Core specification version 3.0.3.* Retrieved March 11, 2008, from www.omg.org

Object Management Group. (2004). *OMG unified modeling language specification version 2.0.* Retrieved March 11, 2008, from www.omg.org

Object Management Group. (2007). *Meta object facility (MOF), version 1.4.* Retrieved March 23, 2008, from http://www.omg.org/docs/formal/02-04-03.pdf

Object Management Group. (OMG). (2002). *Request for proposal: MOF 2.0 query/views/transformations RFP* [OMG document ad/2002-04-10]. Object Management Group (OMG).

Object Management Group. (OMG). (2005). *UML 2.0 superstructure FTF Rose model containing the UML 2 metamodel.* Object Management Group (OMG).

Object Management Group. (OMG). (2006). *MOF models to text transformation language final adopted specification* [ptc/06-11-01]. Object Management Group (OMG).

Object Management Group. (OMG). (2007). *Object management group (OMG).* Retrieved March 7, 2008, from http://www.omg.org/

Ochoa, X., & Duval, E. (2006). *Quality metrics for learning object data.* Ecuador. Retrieved March 24, 2008, from http://ariadne.cti.espol.edu.ec/M4M.

Ochoa, X., Cardinels, K., Meire, M., & Duval, E. (2005). Frameworks for the automatic indexation of learning management systems content into learning object repositories. In *Proceedings of the ED-MEDIA 2005 World Conference on Educational Multimedia, Hypermedia and Telecommunications*, (pp. 1407-1414).

OGF. (2007). *Open grid forum*. Retrieved March 23, 2008, from http://www.ogf.org

Oldevik, J., & Neple, T. (2006, July). Traceability in model to text transformations. In *Paper presented at the European Conference on Model Driven Architecture Traceability Workshop (ECMDA-TW)*, Bilbao, Spain.

Oldevik, J., Neple, T., Grønmo, R., Aagedal, J., & Berre, A.-J. (2005, November 7-10). Toward standardised model to text transformations. In *Paper presented at the Model Driven Architecture (Foundations and Applications, First European Conference, ECMDA-FA 2005)* (pp. 239-253). Nuremberg, Germany.

Oldham, N., Verma, K., Sheth, A., & Hakimpour, F. (2006). Semantic ws-agreement partner selection. In *Www '06: Proceedings of the 15th International Conference on World Wide Web,* (pp. 697-706). New York, USA: ACM Press.

Oliveira, M., Crowcroft, J., Slater, M., & Brutzman, D. (1999). *Components for distributed virtual environments (VRST'99),* London, UK, (pp. 176-177).

Olsen, G. K., & Oldevik, J. (2007). Scenarios of traceability in model to text transformations. In *Paper presented at the Third European Conference on Model Driven Architecture Foundations and Applications (ECMDA'07)* (pp.144-158). Haifa, Israel.

OMG. (2001). *Unified modeling language*. Retrieved March 6, 2008, from http://www.omg.org/technology/documents/formal/uml.htm

OMG. (2002). *Object Management Group: the common object request broker: Architecture and specification, revision 3.0*. OMG Technical Documents, 02-06-33 [Electronic media]. Retrieved March 11, 2008, from http://www.omg.org/cgi-bin/doc?formal/04-03-01

OMG. (2002). *Software process engineering metamodel specification*. Formal/2002-11-14.

OMG. (2002, April). *MOF 2.0 query/views/transformations RFP*. OMG document ad/2002-04-10.

OMG. (2003, July). *The common object request broker: Architecture and specification*.

OMG. (2004a, December). *Data distribution service*. OMG document, formal/04-12-02.

OMG. (2004b).*Light-weight CORBA component model*. OMG document, ptc/04-06-10.

OMG. (2005, January). *Real-time CORBA specification*. OMG document, formal/05-01-04.

OMG. (2005, November). *MOF QVT final adopted specification*. OMG document, ptc/05-11-01.pdf.

OMG. (2006, April). *CORBA component model*. OMG Document formal/2006-04-01 ed.

OMG. (2006, February). *Business process modeling notation (BPMN) specification*. Retrieved March 6, 2008, from http://www.bpmn.org/ (Final Adopted Specification)

Ommering, R., Linden, F., Kramer, J., & Magee, J. (2002, March). The Koala Component Model for consumer electronics software. *IEEE Computer, 33*(3), 78-85.

Open Architecture Ware. (2007). Retrieved March 23, 2008, from www.openarchitectureware.org

Open Source Initiative. (2008). *The open source definition*. Retrieved March 23, 2008, from www.opensource.org/docs/definition.php

Page-Jones, M. (1988). *Practical guide to structured systems design*. Englewood Cliffs, NJ: Prentice Hall.

Paige, R., & Shaham-Gafni, Y. (2006). *D1.5 model composition: Development of consistency rules* [Modelware D1.5].

Papadopoulos, Y., McDermid, J., Sasse, R., & Heiner, G. (2001, March). Analysis and synthesis of the behaviour of complex programmable electronic systems in conditions of failure. *Reliability Engineering & System Safety, 71*, 229-247.

Parnas, D. (1972). On the criteria to be used in decomposing systems in modules. *Communication on the ACM, 15*(12), 1053-1058.

Parsons, D., Rashid, A., Telea, A., & Speck, A. (2006, February). An architectural pattern for designing component-based application frameworks. *Software—practice and Experience, 36*(2), 157-90.

Parsons, T., Mos, A., & Murphy, J. (2006, August). Non-intrusive end-to-end runtime path tracing for J2EE systems. *IEEE Proceedings Software, 153*, 149-161.

Paschke, A., Dietrich, J., & Kuhla, K. (2005, November). A logic based sla management framework. In L. Kagal, T. Finin, & J. Hendler (Eds.), *Iswc '05: Proceedings of the Semantic Web and Policy Workshop, 4th International Semantic Web Conference*, (pp. 68-83). Baltimore, MD, USA: UMBC eBiquity Research Group.

Payr, S., & Trappl, R. (Eds.). (2004). *Agent culture—human-agent interaction in a multicultural world.* Mahwah, NJ: Lawrence Erlbaum.

Pessa, E. (1998). Emergence, self-organisation, and quantum theory. In G. Minati (Ed.), *Proceedings of the First Italian Conference on Systemics, APOGEO Scientifica*, (pp. 59-79).

Peterson, J.L. (1977). Petri nets. *ACM Computing Surveys, 9*(3), 223-252.

Pettifer, S., Cook, J., Marsh, J., & West, A. (2000). DEVA3: Architecture for a large-scale distributed virtual reality system (VRST'2000). ACM Press, 33-40, Seoul, Korea.

Phillips, R. (1988). State change architecture: A protocol for executable process models. In C. Tully (Ed.), *Representing and enacting the software process: Proceedings of the 4th International Software Process Workshop, May ACM Software Engineering Notes,* (Vol. 14, No. 4., pp. 129-132).

Piatelli, M., & Bianchi, N. (1998). Maritime Etruscian cities: A systemic approach for explaining their sites. In G. Minati (Ed.), *Proceedings of the First Italian Conference on Systemics, APOGEO Scientifica*, (pp. 273-292).

Pietrik, M. (1998, May). Under the hood. *Microsoft Systems Journal.* Retrieved March 11, 2008, from http://www.microsoft.com/msj/0598/hood0598.aspx

Pinto, M., Fuentes, L., & Troya, J.M. (2005). A dynamic component and aspect platform. *The Computer Journal, 48*(4), 401-420.

Pitoura, E., & Samaras, G. (1998). *Data management for mobile computing.* Kluwer Academic.

Plale, B., Gannon, D., Reed, D., Graves, S., Droegemeier, K., Wilhelmson, B., & Ramamurthy, M. (2005). Towards dynamically adaptive weather analysis and forecasting in LEAD. In *Proceedings of the ICCS Workshop on Dynamic Data Driven Applications.*

PlanetLab Consortium. (2006). *PLANETLAB: An open platform for developing, deploying, and accessing planetary-scale services.* Retrieved March 23, 2008, from http://www.planet-lab.org

Plasser, E., & Haussteiner, I. (2005, June). *What made the Internet work—a review of interrelations, intentions and the success of the ARPA initiative and its implications for a key technology* (Rep. No. 8). Austria: Publication of the Institute for Systems Engineering and Automation, J. Kepler University Linz.

PMI Risk Management Specific Interest Group. (2002). *The new PMBOK risk management concept.* The New PMBOK Risk Management Concept. Retrieved March 25, 2008, from http://www.heartlandits.com/Newsroom/PMI/New%20PMBOK%20%20Risk%20pz#256,1

Pohl, K. (2003). Challenges for the design of software-intensive systems: Handling complexity and the two-way alignment between the business (problem) and the solution (software). In *Proceedings of the Workshop on the Science of Design*, Airlie Center, Dulles, VA, USA. Retrieved March 11, 2008, from http://www.cs.virginia.edu/~sullivan/sdsis/Program/Klaus%20Pohl.pdf

Poizat, P., Royer, J., & Salaun, G. (2004, June). Formal methods for component description, coordination and adaptation. In *Proceedings of the 1st International Workshop on Coordination and Adaptation Techniques for Software Entities*, Oslo, Norway.

Ponnekanti, S. R., & Fox, A. (2002, January). SWORD: A developer toolkit for Web service composition. In *Www '02: Proceedings of the World Wide Web Conference: Alternate Track on Tools and Languages for Web Development.* New York, USA: ACM Press. Retrieved May 12, 2008 from http://www2002.org/CDROM/alternate/786/index.html

Pour, G. (1998). Component-based software development approach: New opportunities and challenges. In *Proceed-*

ings of the Technology of Object-oriented Languages, (pp. 375-383).

PPDG. (2006, July). *Particle physics data grid*. Retrieved March 23, 2008, from http://www.ppdg.net/

Pradhan, S., Lawrence, E., & Zmijewska, A. (2005). Bluetooth as an enabling technology in mobile transactions. In *Proceedings of the International Symposium on Information Technology: Coding and Computing (ITCC 2005)*.

Project Management Institute (PMI). (2005). *A guide to the project management body of knowledge (PMBOK)* (3rd ed., Tech. Rep.). Philadelphia, PA, USA: PMI.

Quatrani, T. (2003). *Visual modeling with rational rose and UML*. Reading, MA: Addison-Wesley.

Rakotonirainy, A. (1999). Trends and future of mobile computing. In *Proceedings of the 10th IEEE International Workshop on Database and Expert Systems Applications*. Florence, Italy: IEEE CS Press.

Ramampiaro, H., & Nygård, M. (2004). CAGISTrans: Providing adaptable transactional support for cooperative work--an extended treatment. *Information Technology & Management (ITM) Journal, 5*(1-2), 23-64.

Ramampiaro, H., & Wang, A. I., et al. (2003). Requirement indicators derived from a mobile characterisation framework. In *Proceedings of the IASTED International Conference on Applied Informatics (AI'2003)*. Innsbruck, Austria: Acta Press.

Ramesh, B., & Jarke, M. (2001). Toward reference models for requirements traceability. *IEEE Transactions on Software Engineering, 27*(1), 58-93.

Ran, A., & Kuusela, J. (1996, March). Design decision trees. In *Proceedings of the Eighth International Workshop on Software Specification and Design*, (p 172).

Randell, B. (1997). *Operating systems: The problems of performance and reliability*. 40 Years of Computing at Newcastle—the first paper on dependability, SRM/311. Retrieved March 25, 2008, from http://www.cs.ncl.ac.uk/events/ anniversaries/40th/webbook/dependability/os1/os1.html

Raptis, D., & Tselios, N. K., & Avouris, N. M. (2005). Context-based design of mobile applications for museums: A survey of existing practices. In *Proceedings of the 7th Conference on Human-computer Interaction with Mobile Devices and Services*. Salzburg, Austria: ACM Press.

Rational Unified Process Workbench. (2007). Retrieved March 11, 2008, from http://www-306.ibm.com/software/rational

Ratner, D., & Reiher, P. L., Popek, G. J., & Kuenning, G. H. (2001). Replication requirements in mobile environments. *Mobile Networks and Applications (MONET), 6*(6), 525-533.

Raymond, E. S. (1999). *The cathedral and the bazaar: Musings on Linux and open source by an accidental revolutionary*. O'Reilly & Associates.

Rechenberg, P. (1993). Compilers. In D. Morris & B. Tamm (Eds.), *Concise encyclopedia of software engineering (pp. 59-64)*. Pergamon Press.

Recommended Practice for Architectural Description of Software-intensive Systems, IEEE-Std-1471-2000. (2000, October). 345 East 47th Street, New York, 10017-2394, USA.

Redmill, F. (Ed.). (1988). *Dependability of critical computer systems 1, EWICS TC7 guidelines 1 (Documentation, system requirements, development and (V&V)*. UK: Elsevier Science.

Redmill, F. (Ed.). (1989). *Dependability of critical computer systems 2: Design, assessment, maintenance and modification, EWICS TC7 Guidelines 2*. UK: Elsevier Science.

Redmill, F., & Dale, C. (Eds.). (1997). *Life cycle management for dependability*. London: Springer-Verlag.

Reicher, T., MacWilliams, A., Brügge, B., & Linder, G. (2003). Results of a study on software architectures for augmented reality systems. In *Proceedings of the 2nd IEEE and ACM International Symposium on Mixed and Augmented Reality (ISMAR'03)*. IEEE.

Reisig, W., & Rozenberg, G. (Eds.). (1998). *Lectures on petri nets I: Basic models* (Vol. 1491). Berlin: Springer-Verlag.

Reiss, S. P. (2003). Visualizing Java in action. In *Proceedings of the 2003 ACM Symposium on Software Visualization*, (p. 57).

Reiss, S. P. (2005). Efficient monitoring and display of thread state in java. In *Proceedings of the IEEE International Workshop on Program Comprehension* (pp. 247-256). St. Louis, MO.

Reitmayr, G., & Schmalstieg, D. (2001). An open software architecture for virtual reality interaction. In *Proceedings of VRST'01*, Banff, Alberta, Canada. ACM.

Ricci, R., Alfred, C., & Lepreau, J. (2003). A solver for the network testbed mapping problem. *SIGCOMM Computer Communications Review, 33*, 65-81.

Richter, L. (1980). Vertikale Migration—Anwendungen, Methoden und Erfahrungen. In K. H. Hauer & C. Seeger (Eds.), *Tagung "Hardware für Software", Konstanz* (pp 9-28). Springer-VerlagTeubner.

Rinard, M. (2001). *Analysis of multithreaded programs.* (LNCS 2126, pp. 1-19).

Roddick, J.F. (1992). Schema evolution in database systems: An annotated bibliography. *SIGMOD Record, 21*(4).

Roll, W. (2003, May). Towards model-based and CCM-based applications for real-time systems. In *Proceedings of the International Symposium on Object-oriented Real-time Distributed Computing (ISORC)*, Hokkaido, Japan, (pp. 75-82).

Romer, T., Voelker, G., Lee, D., Wolman, A., Wong, W., Levy, H., et al. (1997). Instrumentation and optimization of Win32/Intel executables using Etch. In *Proceedings of the USENIX Windows NT Workshop*.

Romeu, J.L. (1999). *Data quality and pedigree.* Material Ease.

Royce, W. W. (1987). Managing the development of large software systems: Concept and techniques. In *Proceed-*

ings of WesCon, 1970. Reprinted in Proceedings of the International Conference on Software Engineering. IEEE Computer Society Press.

Rozanski, N., & Woods. E. (2005). *Software systems architecture.* Addison-Wesley.

Russell, N., Aalst, W., Hofstede, A., & Wohed, P. (2006). On the suitability of UML activity diagrams for business process modelling. In M. Stumptner, S. Hartmann, & Y. Kiyoki (Eds.), *Proceedings of the Third Asia-Pacific Conference on Conceptual Modelling (apccm 2006)* (Vol. 53, pp. 95-104). Hobart, Australia: ACS.

Sakai Project. (2008). *About Sakai.* Retrieved March 23, 2008, from http://www.sakaiproject.org/index.php?option=com_content&task=view&id=103&Itemid=208

Satyanarayanan, M. (1996). Fundamental challenges of mobile computing. In *Proceedings of the fifteenth annual ACM Symposium on Principles of Distributed Computing* (pp. 1-7). Philadelphia.

Satyanarayanan, M. (2003). Of smart dust and brilliant rocks. *IEEE Pervasive Computing, 4*(2), 2-4.

Scacchi, W., & Noll, J. (2005). *Dynamic process enactment, discovery, and recovery.* Retrieved March 6, 2008, from http://www.ics.udi.edu/~wscacchi/Papers/New/Proposal-abridged.pdf

Schäfer, W., Prieto-Díaz R., & Matsumoto, M. (1994). *Software reusability.* Ellis Horwood.

Scheer, A. (2000). *ARIS: Business process modelling.* Berlin: Springer-Verlag.

Scheer, A.-W. (1994). *CIM—computer integrated manufacturing: Towards the factory of the future* (3rd ed., revised and enlarged). Berlin.

Schmidt, D. (2006). Model-driven engineering. *IEEE Computer, 39*(2), 25-32.

Schmidt, D. C. (1993). The ADAPTIVE communication environment: An object-oriented network programming toolkit for developing communication software. *Concurrency: Practice and Experience, 5*(4), 269-286.

Schmidt, D. C. (2002, June). Middleware for real-time and embedded systems. *Communications of the ACM, 45.*

Schmidt, D. C. (2006). Model-driven engineering. *IEEE Computer, 39*(2), 25-31.

Schmidt, D. C., Natarajan, B., Gokhale, G., Wang, N., & Gill, C. (2002, February). TAO: A pattern-oriented object request broker for distributed real-time and embedded systems. *IEEE Distributed Systems Online, 3*(2).

Schmidt, D. C., Stal, M., Rohnert, H., & Buschmann, F. (2000). *Pattern-oriented software architecture patterns for concurrent and networked objects.* John Wiley & Sons.

Schmidt, D.C. (2002). Middleware for real-time and embedded systems. *Communications of the ACM, 45*(6), 43-48.

Schmidt, D.C., Levine, D., & Mungee, S. (1998, April). The design and performance of real-time object request brokers. *Computer Communications, 21*, 294-324.

Schneiderman, R. (2002). *The mobile technology question and answer book: A survival guide for business managers.* American Management Association.

Schoitsch, E. (1997). Managing maintenance and change. In F. Redmill (Ed.), *Life cycle management for dependability* (pp. 163-188). London: Springer-Verlag.

Schoitsch, E. (2003). Dependable embedded systems—vision und roadmap. In G. Fiedler & D. Donhoffer (Eds.), *Mikroelektronik 2003, Wien.* ÖVE Schriftenreihe, Wien, Nr. 33.

Schoitsch, E. (2003, January). Embedded systems—introduction. *ERCIM News,* (52), 11.

Schoitsch, E. (2005). Design for safety and security. *Cyberspace security and defense: Research issues* (Vol. 196). Springer NATO Science Series.

Schönhage B., & Eliëns, A. (1999). From distributed object features to architectural styles. In *Proceedings of the Workshop on Engineering Distributed Objects (EDO'99), International Conference on Software Engineering (ICSE),* Los Angeles, CA, USA.

Schönhage, B., & Eliëns, A. (2000). Information exchange in a distributed visualization architecture. In *Proceedings of the Shared Concept Space of Distributed Objects Applications (DOA'00),* Antwerp, Belgium.

Schönhage, B., van Ballegooij, A., & Eliëns, A. (2000). 3D gadgets for business process visualization. In *Proceedings of the International Conference on the Virtual reality Modeling Language and Web 3D Technologies,* Monterrey, CA, USA.

Schulte, M. (2003, May). Model-based integration of reusable component-based avionics system. In *Proceedings of the Eighth IEEE International Symposium on Object-oriented Real-time Distributed Computing (ISORC'05)* (pp. 62-71). Seattle, WA.

Schulz, A. (1990). Software-Entwurf—Methoden und Werkzeuge. *2., verbesserte Aufl., Handbuch der Informatik, Oldenbourg 1990.*

Scupin, R. (1997). The KJ method: A technique for analyzing data derived from Japanese ethnology. *Human Organization, 56*(2), 33-237.

Searls, D.B. (2006). Data integration: Challenges for drug discovery. *Nature Reviews Drug Discovery, 4,* 45-58.

Selic, B. (2003). The pragmatics of model-driven development. *IEEE Software, 20*(5), 19-25.

Sendall, S., & Kozaczynski, W. (2003, September-October). Model transformation—the heart and soul of model-driven software development. *IEEE Software, 20*(5), 42-45.

Senge, P. (1990). *The fifth discipline—the art and practice of the learning organisation.* New York: Doubleday/Currency.

Sengupta, B., & Cleaveland, R. (2002, November). Triggered message sequence charts. W. G. Griswold (Ed.), *Proceedings of the Tenth ACM SIGSOFT Symposium on the Foundations of Software Engineering (FSE-10).* Charleston, SC, USA: ACM Press.

Shankaran, N., Koutsoukos, X., Schmidt, D.C., & Gokhale, A. (2005). Evaluating adaptive resource management for distributed real-time embedded systems. In

Proceedings of 4th Workshop on Adaptive and Reflective Middleware, Grenoble, France.

Sharp, D. (1999, October). Avionics product line software architecture flow policies. In *Proceedings of the 18th IEEE/AIAA Digital Avionics Systems Conference (DASC)*, St Louis, MO.

Sharp, D. C. (2000, August). Reducing avionics software cost through component based product line development. In P. Donohoe (Ed.), *Software product lines: Experience and research directions* (Vol. 576). New York, USA: Springer-Verlag.

Shaw, M., & Garlan, D. (1996). *Software architecture: Perspectives in an emerging discipline*. Prentice Hall.

Shaw, M., & Garlan, D. (2006). The Golden Age of software architecture. *IEEE Software*, 31-39.

Siemens. (2007). Retrieved March 7, 2008, from http://www.us.sbt.siemens.com/bau/products/default.asp

Silberschatz, A., Galvin, P., & Gagne, G. (2002). *Operating system concepts*. New York: John Wiley, 6. Auflage.

Simonyi, C., Christerson, M., & Clifford, S. (2006). Intentional software. *Object oriented programming systems languages and applications (OOPSLA)*, (pp. 451-464). Portland, OR: ACM Press.

Sindhgatta, R., & Thonse, S. (2005). Functional and non-functional requirements specification for enterprise applications. *Product focused software process improvement (PROFES 2005)*. Berlin/Heidelberg: Springer-Verlag.

Slaby, J., Baker, S., Hill, J., & Schmidt, D. (2005). *Defining behavior and evaluating QoS performance of the SLICE scenario* (Tech. Rep. No. ISIS-05-608). Nashville, TN: Vanderbilt University.

Slaby, J., Baker, S., Hill, J., & Schmidt, D. (2006). Applying system execution modeling tools to evaluate enterprise distributed real-time and embedded system QoS. In *Proceedings of the 12th International Conference on Embedded and Real-Time Computing Systems and Applications*, Sydney, Australia.

Smith, C. (1990). *Performance engineering of software systems*. Reading, MA: Addison-Wesley.

Smith, C., & Williams, L. (2001). *Performance solutions: A practical guide to creating responsive, scalable software*. Reading, MA: Addison-Wesley.

Smith, M., Friese, T., & Freisleben, B. (2006). Model driven development of service-oriented grid applications. In *Proceedings of the Advanced International Conference on Telecommunications and International Conference on Internet and Web Applications and Services*, Guadeloupe, French Caribbean.

Smith, W., Foster, I., & Taylor, V. (1998). Predicting application run times using historical information. In *Proceedings of the Workshop on Job Scheduling Strategies for Parallel Processing*, (pp. 122-142). Springer-Verlag.

Software Engineering Institute (Ed.). (2007). *The architecture tradeoff analysis method (ATAM)*. Retrieved March 25, 2008, from http://www.sei.cmu.edu/architecture/ata_method.html

Soloman, D. A. (1998). *Inside Windows NT (2nd ed)*. Redmond: Microsoft Press.

Solomon, M. (2004, May). *The ClassAd language reference manual*. Retrieved March 23, 2008, from http://www.cs.wisc.edu/condor/classad/refman/

Sommerville, I. (1995). *Software engineering*. Addison-Wesley. ISBN 0-2014-2765-6.

Sommerville, I. (2000). *Software engineering* (6th ed.). Reading, MA: Addison-Wesley. Sommerville, I. (2007). *Software engineering* (8th ed.). Reading, MA: Addison-Wesley. Sonneck, G., & Schoitsch, E. (2003). *AMSD deliverable D2.1., part ii: R+D top-level synthesis of DES—roadmaps—final deliverable* (Tech. Rep.). Seiberdorf, Austria: Seibersdorf Research.

Sonic Software. (2004). *Enterprise service bus*. Retrieved March 6, 2008, from http://www.sonicsoftware.com/products/sonic_esb/

Sonntag, M. V. (2002). Legal aspects of mobile agents with special consideration of the proposed Austrian e-commerce law. In *Cybernetics and Systems 2002: Pro-*

ceedings of the 16th European Meeting on Cybernetics and Systems Research, (pp. 153-158). Vienna: Austrian Society for Cybernetic Studies.

Sotomayor, B., & Childers, L. (2005). *Globus toolkit: Programming Java services* (1st ed.). Morgan Kaufmann.

SourceForge. (2005). *SourceForge.net®, world's largest open source development site surpasses 100,000 projects hosted on the site.* Retrieved March 23, 2008, from http://www.ostg.com/pdfs/SourceForgeProjects_PR_Final1.pdf

Spanne, J. (2002). OLAC: The state of the archives. In *Proceedings of the IRCS Workshop on Open Language Archives,* (pp. 42-46). Institute for Research in Cognitive Science, University of Pennsylvania.

Spinczyk, O., Lohmann, D., & Urban, M. (2005). Aspect C++: An AOP extension for C++. *Software Developer's Journal,* 68-76.

Sprinkle, J., & Karsai, G. (2004, June). A domain-specific visual language for domain model evolution. *Journal of Visual Languages and Computing, 15*(3-4), 291-307.

Sprinkle, J., Agrawal, A., Levendovszky, T., Shi, F., & Karsai, G. (2003, April). Domain model translation using graph transformations. In *Proceedings of the Conference on Engineering of Computer-based Systems,* Huntsville, AL, (pp. 159-167).

Srivastava, A., & Eustace A. (1994). *ATOM: A system for building customized program analysis tools* (Tech. Rep. No. 94/2). Western Research Lab, Compaq Corporation.

Stahl, T., & Völter, M. (2006). *Model-driven software development: Technology, engineering, management.* Chichester: John Wiley.

Stal, M. (2006, March-April). Using architectural patterns and blueprints for service-oriented architecture. *IEEE Software, 23*(2), 54-61.

Stallings, W. (Ed.). (1986). *Reduced instruction set computers—tutorial.* Computer Society Press.

Stallman, R. (1984). *GNU manifesto.* Retrieved March 23, 2008, from http://www.gnu.org/gnu/manifesto.html

Standish Group. (2006). *The chaos report 2006* (Tech. Rep.). Standish Group.

Stankovic, J. A., Zhu, R., Poornalingam, R., Lu, C., Yu, Z., Humphrey, M., et al. (2003). Vest: An aspect-based composition tool for real-time systems. In *Rtas '03: Proceedings of the 9th IEEE Real-time and Embedded Technology and Applications Symposium,* (p. 58). Washington, DC, USA: IEEE Computer Society.

Steen, M. V. (2004). *Nimrod-G resource broker for service-oriented grid computing.* Retrieved March 23, 2008, from http://dsonline.computer.org/0107/departments/res0107_print.htm

Stockenberg, J., & van Dam, A. (1978). Vertical migration for performance enhancements in layered hardware-firmware-software systems. *Computer, 11*(5), 35-50.

Straker, D. (1995). *A toolbook for quality improvement and problem solving.* Prentice Hall International (UK).

Subramaniam, K., & Thazhuthaveetil, M. (1994). Effectiveness of sampling based software profilers. In *Proceedings of the 1st International Conference on Reliability and Quality Assurance,* (pp. 1-5).

Subramonian, V. (2006). *Timed automata models for principled composition of middleware* (Tech. Rep. No. WUCSE-2006-23). St. Louis, MO: Washington University, Computer Science and Engineering Department.

Sudeikat, J., Braubach, L., Pokahr, A., & Lamersdorf, W. (2004). Evaluation of agent-oriented software methodologies—examination of the gap between modeling and platform. In *Proceedings of the Fifth International Workshop on Agent-Oriented Software Engineering, (AOSE).*

Sun Microsystems Corporation. (2002). *The Java native interface programmer's guide and specification* [Electronic media]. Retrieved March 11, 2008, from http://java.sun.com/docs/books/jni/html/jniTOC.html

Sun Microsystems Corporation. (2004). *JVM tool interface* [Computer software]. Retrieved March 11, 2008, from http://java.sun.com/j2se/1.5.0/docs/guide/jvmti/

Sun Microsystems, Inc. (1997, March). *JavaBeans 1.01 specification*. Retrieved March 11, 2008, from www.java.sun.com

Sun Microsystems. (2000). *Java remote method invocation specification*, revision 1.5, JDK 1.2, Oct. 1998.

Sun Microsystems. (2001). *Enterprise JavaBeans specification*. Retrieved March 7, 2008, from java.sun.com/products/ejb/docs.html

SUN. (2002). *Java messaging service specification*. Retrieved March 23, 2008, from java.sun.com/products/jms/ Sun Microsystems. (2001, August). *Enterprise JavaBeans specification*. Retrieved March 23, 2008, from http://java.sun.com/products/ejb/docs.html Sun Microsystems. (2006). *Java business integration (jbi)*. Retrieved March 23, 2008, from http://www.jcp.org/en/jsr/detail?id=208 Sun Microsystems. (2006). *Java network launching protocol and api*. Retrieved March 23, 2008, from http://jcp.org/en/jsr/detail?id=56 Sun Microsystems. (2006). *Java Web start technology*. Retrieved March 23, 2008, from http://java.sun.com/products/javawebstart/index.jsp

Sutcliffe, A. (1998). Scenario-based requirements analysis. *Requirements Engineering, 3*(1), 48-65.

Sutter, H. (2005). The free lunch is over: A fundamental turn towards concurrency in software. *Dr. Dobb's Journal, 30*(3).

Sutter, H., & Larus J. (2005). Software and the concurrency revolution. *ACM Queue Magazine, 3*(7).

SysML. (2006). *Systems modeling language*. Retrieved March 11, 2008, from http://www.sysml.org/

Sztipanovits, J., & Karsai, G. (1997). Model-integrated computing. *IEEE Computer, 30*(4), 110-111.

Szyperski, C. (1998). *Component software: Beyond object-oriented programming*. New York: Addison-Wesley.

Tanenbaum, A. (1995). *Distributed operating systems*. Englewood Cliffs, NJ: Prentice Hall.

Tanenbaum, A. S., & Steen, M. V. (2002). *Distributed systems: Principles and paradigms*. Prentice Hall.

Task, B., Paniscotti, D., Roman, A., & Bhanot, V. (2006). Using model-driven engineering to complement software product line engineering in developing software defined radio components and applications. In *Proceedings of International Conference on Object Oriented Programming Systems Languages and Applications (OOPSLA)*, Portland, OR.

Tavares, E., Maciel, P., Bessa, A., Barreto, R., Barros, L., Oliveira, M., & Lima, R. (2005). A time petri net based approach for embedded hard real-time software synthesis with multiple operational modes. In *Proceedings of the 18th Annual Symposium on Integrated Circuits and System Design (SBCCI '05)* (pp. 98-103). Florianolpolis, Brazil.

Taylor, V., Wu, X., Geisler, J., Li, X., Lan, Z., Stevens, R., et al. (2000). Prophesy: An infrastructure for analyzing and modeling the performance of parallel and distributed applications. In *Proceedings of the High Performance Distributed Computing (HPDC) 2000*, Pittsburgh, PA, (pp. 302-303).

Tekinerdogan, B. (2003). ASAAM: Aspectual software architecture analysis method. In *Proceedings of the Workshop on Early Aspects: Aspect-oriented Requirements Engineering and Architecture Design, held in conjunction with the AOSD Conference.*

Telelogic. *Tau home page*. Retrieved March 6, 2008, from http://www.telelogic.com/products/tau/

Tesanovic, A., Amirijoo, M., Björk, M., & Hansson, J. (2005). Empowering configurable QoS management in real-time systems. In *Proceedings of the Fourth International Conference on Aspect-oriented Software Development*, (pp. 39-50).

The Eclipse Foundation. (2007). *Eclipse model to model (M2M)*. Retrieved March 7, 2008, from http://www.eclipse.org/m2m/

The Eclipse Foundation. (2007). *Eclipse model to text (M2T)*. Retrieved March 7, 2008, from http://www.eclipse.org/modeling/m2t/

The Free Software Foundation. (2008). *The free software definition*. Retrieved March 23, 2008, from http://www.fsf.org/licensing/essays/free-sw.html

Thomas, M., Mock, S., Dahan, M., Mueller, K., Sutton, D., & Boisseau, J. (2001). The GridPort toolkit: A system for building grid portals. In *Proceedings of the Tenth IEEE International Symposium on High Performance Distributed Computing (HPDC),* (pp. 216-227). San Francisco: IEEE.

Thomas, N., Tanase, G., Tkachyshyn, O., Perdue, J., Amato, N., & Rauchwerger, L. (2005). A framework for adaptive algorithm selection in STAPL. In *Proceedings of the ACM SIGPLAN 2005 Symposium on Principles and Practices of Parallel Programming (PPoPP),* Chicago, IL.

Thome, B. (Ed.). (1993). *Systems engineering—principles and practice of computer-based systems engineering.* Chichester-New York: John Wiley.

Timesys. (2002). *Predictable performance for dynamic load and overload.* Retrieved March 7, 2008, from www.timesys.com/prodserv/whitepaper/Predictable_Performance_1_0.pdf

Tolvanen, J.P., & Kelly, S. (2005). Defining domain-specific modeling languages to automate product derivation: Collected experiences. In *Proceeding of the 9th Software Product Line Conference,* Rennes, France, (pp. 198-209).

Trask, B., Paniscotti, D., Roman, A., & Bhanot, V. (2006). Using model-driven engineering to complement software product line engineering in developing software defined radio components and applications. In *Proceedings of Oopsla '06: Companion to the 21st ACM SIGPLAN Conference on Object-oriented Programming Systems, Languages, and Applications,* (pp. 846-853). New York, USA: ACM Press.

TrowBridge, D., Roxburgh, U., Hohpe, G., Manolescu, D., & Nadhan, E. G. (2004, June). *Integration patterns.* Retrieved March 23, 2008, from msdn.microsoft.com/library/default.asp?url=/library/en-us/dnpag/html/intpatt.asp

Tsouloupas, G., & Dikaiakos, M. (2003). GridBench: A tool for benchmarking grids. In *Proceedings of the 4th International Workshop on Grid Computing (Grid2003),* Phoenix, AZ, (pp. 60-67).

Ulrich, W. M. (2002). *Legacy systems: Transformation strategies* (1st ed.). Prentice Hall PTR.

Ultra large-scale systems: The report. (2007). CMU Technical Report. Retrieved March 7, 2008, from http://www.sei.cmu.edu/uls/

UML 2.0 Superstructure. (2003). *Superstructure specification.* Document ptc/03-08-02.

UML 2.1.1 Superstructure. (2006, October). *UML 2.1.1 superstructure specification.* Document: ptc/06-10-05 (convenience document).

UML for System Engineering Request for Proposal, ad/03-03-2003 (2003), UML-RFP-03-03-28 *UML for System Engineering Request for Proposal, ad/03-03-41.* (2003, March).

UML Profile for Enterprise Application Integration (EAI). (2004, March). Retrieved May 12, 2008, from http://www.omg.org/technology/documents/formal/eai.htm

Unified Modeling Language (UML) v1.4. (2001, September). Retrieved May 12, 2008, from http://www.omg.org/spec/UML/1.4/

Vahdat, A., Yocum, K., Walsh, K., Mahadevan, P., Kostic, K., Chase, J., & Becker, D. (2002). Scalability and accuracy in a large-scale network emulator. In *Proceedings of 5th Symposium on Operating Systems Design and Implementation (OSDI).*

van der Meulen, M. (2000). *Definitions for hardware/software safety engineers.* London: Springer-Verlag.

Van Hentenryck, P., & Saraswat, V. (1996). Strategic directions in constraint programming. *ACM Computing Surveys, 28*(4), 701-726.

van, D. L. P. S. R. (1984). Development environments and run-time support in ada. In P. Depledge (Ed.), *Software engineering for microprocessor systems* (pp. 133-140). London: P. Peregrinus.

Vaswani, K., & Srikant, Y. N. (2003), Dynamic recompilation and profile-guided optimizations for a .NET JIT compiler. In *Proceedings of the IEEE Software Special on Rotor .NET*, (Vol. 150, pp. 296-302). IEEE Publishing.

VDI2206, (2004). *VDI guideline 2206—design methodology for mechatronic systems*. VDI-Verlag.

Venugopal, S., Buyya, R., & Winton, L. (2005). A grid service broker for scheduling e-science applications on global data grids. *Journal of Concurrency and Computation: Practice and Experience, 18*(6), 685-699.

Vinoski, S. (2003). Integration with Web services. *IEEE Internet Computing, 07*(6), 75-77.

Vinoski, S. (2006). Advanced message queuing protocol. *IEEE Internet Computing, 10*(6), 87-89.

Visser, E. (2001). *Stratego: A language for program transformation based on rewriting strategies*. (LNCS 2051, pp. 357).

Vizhanyo, A., Agrawal, A., & Shi, F. (2004, October). Towards generation of efficient transformations. In *Proceeding of the ACM International Conference on Generative Programming and Component Engineering*, Vancouver, Canada, (pp. 298-316).

W3 Consortium. (1999). *XSL transformations (XSLT)*. Retrieved March 6, 2008, from http://www.w3c.org/TR/xslt. W3C Recommendation

W3 Consortium. (2007). *XSL transformations (XSLT) Version 2.0*. Retrieved March 6, 2008, from http://www.w3c.org/TR/xslt20/. W3C Recommendation

Waddington, D. G., & Yao, B. (2005). High fidelity C++ code transformation. In *Proceedings of the 5th Workshop on Language Descriptions, Tools and Applications.*

Waddington, D. G., Amduka, M., DaCosta, D., Foster, P., & Sprinkle, J. (2006, February). *EASEL: Model centric design tools for effective design and implementation of multi-threaded concurrent applications* (Technical Document). Lockheed Martin ATL.

Waddington, D., Roy, N., & Schmidt, D.C. (2007). Dynamic analysis and profiling of multi-threaded systems.

In P.F. Tiako (Ed.), *Designing software-intensive systems: Methods and principles*: OK: Langston University.

Wadhwa, P.S., & Kamalapur, P. (2003). *Customized metadata solution for a data warehouse—a success story*. Wipro Technologies White Paper.

Walderhaug, S., Stav, E., Johansen, U., & Aagedal, J. (2006, July). Towards a generic solution for traceability in MDD. In *Paper presented at the European Conference on Model Driven Architecture Traceability Workshop (ECMDA-TW)*, Bilbao, Spain.

Walk, K., Alber, K., Bandat, K., Bekic, H., Chroust, G., Kudielka, V., et al. (1968, June). *Abstract syntax and interpretation of pl/i* (Tech. Rep. 25.082). Vienna, Austria: IBM Laboratory.

Wall, L., Christiansen, T., & Orwant, J. (2000). *Programming Perl* (3rd ed., Vol. 2000). O'Reilly Media.

Wang , A. I., Conradi, R., & Liu, C. (2000). Integrating workflow with interacting agents to support cooperative software engineering. In *Proceedings of the 4th IASTED International Conference on Software Engineering and Applications (SEA'2000)*, Las Vegas, NV, USA.

Wang, A. I. (2000). Using software agents to support evolution of distributed workflow models. In *Proceedings of the International ICSC Symposium on Interactive and Collaborative Computing (ICC'2000) at International ICSC Congress on Intelligent Systems and Applications (ISA'2000)*, Wollongong, Australia.

Wang, A. I. (2001). *Using a mobile, agent-based environment to support cooperative software processes*. Doctoral thesis, Norwegian University of Science and Technology. ISBN 82-7984-172-5.

Wang, A. I. (2002). An evaluation of a cooperative process support environment. In *Proceedings of the 6th IASTED International Conference on Software Engineering and Applications (SEA2002)*, Cambridge, MA, USA.

Wang, A. I., & Sørensen, C.-F., et al. (2005). Using the MOWAHS characterisation framework for development of mobile work applications. *Product focused software process improvement (PROFES 2005)*. Berlin/Heidelberg: Springer-Verlag.

Wang, A. I., Larsen, J.-O., Conradi, R., & Munch, B. (1998). Improving cooperation support in the EPOS CM System. In *Proceedings of the 6th European Workshop on Software Process Technology (EWSPT'98),* Weybridge (London), UK.

Wang, N., & Gill, C. (2003). Improving real-time system configuration via a QoS-aware CORBA component model. In *Proceedings of the Hawaii International Conference on System Sciences, Software Technology Track, Distributed Object and Component-based Software Systems.*

Wang, N., & Gill, C. (2004). Improving real-time system configuration via a qos-aware corba component model. In *Hicss '04: Proceedings of the 37th Annual Hawaii International Conference on System Sciences (hicss'04) -track 9,* (p. 90273.2). Washington, DC, USA: IEEE Computer Society.

Ward, J. (2003). A quantitative analysis of unqualified Dublin core metadata element set usage within data providers registered with the open archives initiative. In *Proceedings of the IEEE/ACM Joint Conference on Digital Libraries 2003 (JDCL'03),* (pp. 315-3).

Warmer, J., & Kleppe, A. (1998). *The object constraint language: Precise modeling with UML.* Boston, MA: Addison-Wesley.

Wason, J.L., Molinari, M., Jiao, Z., & Cox, S.J. (2003). *Delivering data management for engineers on the grid.* Euro-Par, pp. 412-416.

Wasserman, A.I. (1996, November). Toward a discipline of software engineering. *IEEE Software, 13*(6), 23-31.

Weber, M., & Weisbrod, J., (2002). Requirements engineering in automotive development-experiences and challenges. In *Proceedings of the IEEE Joint International Conference on Requirements Engineering,* Essen, Germany.

Weyns, D., Parunak, H. V. D., & Michel, M. (Eds.). (2005). Environments for multiagent systems: State-of-the-art and research challenges. In *Post-Proceedings of the First International Workshop on Environments for Multiagent Systems, Lecture Notes in Computer Science,* (Vol. 3374).

WfMC. (1999, February). *Workflow management coalition—terminology & glossary* (Tech. Rep. No. WFMC-TC-1011). The Workflow Management Coalition. Retrieved March 6, 2008, from http://www.wfmc.org/standards/docs/TC1011_term_glossary_v3.pdf

Whaley, J. (2000). A portable sampling-based profiler for Java virtual machines. In *Proceedings of ACM Java Grand* (pp. 78-87).

White, J. (2005). *The generic eclipse modeling system.* Retrieved March 23, 2008, from http://www.sf.net/projects/gems

White, J., Gokhale, A., & Schmidt, D.C. (2007). Simplifying autonomic enterprise Java Bean applications via model-driven development: A case study. *Journal of Software and System Modeling, 7*(1), 3-23.

White, J., Nechypurenko, A., Wuchner, E., & Schmidt, D.C. (2006). Intelligence frameworks for assisting modelers in combinatorically challenging domains. In *Proceedings of the Workshop on Generative Programming and Component Engineering for QoS Provisioning in Distributed Systems,* Portland, OR.

White, J., Schmidt, D. C., Mulligan S. (2007, June). The generic eclipse modeling system. In *Proceedings of the Model-Driven Development Tool Implementer's Forum at TOOLS '07.* Zurich, Switzerland.

White, J., Schmidt, D.C., & Gokhale, A. (2005). Simplifying the development of autonomic enterprise Java Bean applications via model driven development. In *Proceedings of the International Conference on Autonomic Computing (ICAC),* Seattle, WA.

White, J., Schmidt, D.C., Wuchner, E., & Nechypurenko, A. (2007). Automating product-line variant selection for mobile devices. In *Proceedings of the 11th Annual Software Product Line Conference (SPLC),* Kyoto, Japan.

White, S. A. (2005, March). *Using BPMN to model a BPEL process.* Retrieved March 23, 2008, from www.bptrends.com

Wieringa, R. (1998, December). A survey of structured and object-oriented software specification methods and techniques. *ACM Computing Surveys, 30*(4), 459-527.

544

Wikipedia-English. (2005). *Wikipedia, the free encyclopedia.* Retrieved March 25, 2008, from http://en.wikipedia.org/wiki/

Wile, D. (2004). Lessons learned from real DSL experiments. *Science of Computer Programming, 51*(3), 265-290.

Willans, J.S., Sammut, P., Maskeri, G., & Evans, A. (2002). *The precise UML group.*

Williams, F., & Steven, G. (1990). How useful are complex instructions?—a case study using the Motorola M68000. *Microprocessing and Microprogramming, 29*(4), 247-259.

Williams, S. (2002). *Free as in freedom: Richard Stallman's crusade for free software.* O'Reilly & Associates.

Wimmer, M. A. (2000, October). *Designing interactive systems: Key issues for a holistic approach.* Doctoral thesis, Kepler University Linz, Austria.

Wind River Systems. (1998). *VxWorks 5.3.* Retrieved March 7, 2008, from ww.wrs.com/products/html/vxworks.html

Wirsing, M. (Ed.). (2004, May). *Report on the EU/NSF Strategic Workshop on Engineering Software-Intensive Systems.* Edinburgh, GB.

Wohed, P., Aalst, W., Dumas, M., Hofstede, A., & Russell, N. (2006). On the suitability of BPMN for business process modelling. In S. Dustdar, J. Faideiro, & A. Sheth (Eds.), *International Conference on Business Process Management (BPM 2006)* (Vol. 4102, pp. 161-176). Springer-Verlag.

Wolf, F., & Mohr, B. (2003). Hardware-counter based automatic performance analysis of parallel programs. In *Proceedings of the Mini-symposium on Performance Analysis, Conference on Parallel Computing (PARCO).* Dreseden, Germany.

Wood, W., & Agogino, A. (2005). Decision-based conceptual design: Modeling and navigating heterogeneous design spaces. *Transactions of the ASME, 127*, 2-10.

Woodruff, A., & Stonebraker, M. (1997). *Supporting fine-grained data lineage in a database visualization environment.* ICDE, pp. 91-102.

Wooldridge, M. (2002). An introduction to multi-agent systems. *An introduction to multi-agent systems.* John Wiley.

Wooldridge, M. (2004). America's school on agents and multiagent systems. In *Proceedings of AAMAS'04.*

Workflow Management Coalition. (2004). Workflow specification. Retrieved March 6, 2008, from http://www.wfmc.org/standards/docs/Wf-XML-11.pdf

Wymore, W. A. (1993). *Model-based systems engineering.* Boca Raton, London, Tokyo: CRC Press.

Yau, S.S., & Tsai, J. (1986, June). A survey of software design techniques. *IEEE Transactions On Software Engineering, SE-12*(6), 713-721.

Yeomans, B. (1996). *Enhancing the World Wide Web* (Tech. Rep.). Computer Science Department, University of Manchester.

Yilmaz, C., Krishna, A. S., Memon, A., Porter, A., Schmidt, D. C., Gokhale, A., & Natarajan, B. (2005). Main effects screening: A distributed continuous quality assurance process for monitoring performance degradation in evolving software systems. In *Proceedings of the 27th International Conference on Software Engineering,* St. Louis, MO, (pp. 293-302).

Yogesh, L., Simmhan, B. P., & Gannon, D. (2005). A survey of data provenance techniques. *SIGMOD Record (Special Section on Scientific Workflows), 34*(3), 31-36.

Yourdon, E., & Constantine, L. (1979). *Structured design.* Englewood Cliffs, NJ: Prentice Hall.

Yuan, W., & Nahrstedt, K. (2003). Energy-efficient soft real-time CPU scheduling for mobile multimedia systems. In *Proceedings of the 19th ACM Symposium on Operating Systems Principles,* Bolton Landing, NY.

Zambonelli F., Jennings N., & Wooldridge, M. (2003, September). Developing multiagent systems: The Gaia methodology. *ACM Transactions on Software Engineering and Methodology,* 12(3).

Zandy, V. C., & Miller, B. P. (2002, September). Reliable network connections. In *Proceedings of the Eighth Annual International Conference on Mobile Computing and Networking*, (pp. 95-106).

Zdun, U., & Avgeriou, P. (2005). Modeling architectural patterns using architectural primitives. In*OOPS-LA '05: Proceedings of the 20th Annual ACM SIGPLAN Conference on Object Oriented Programming, Systems, Languages, and Applications*, (pp. 133-146). New York: ACM Press.

Zemanek, H. (1980). Abstract architecture: General concepts for systems design. In D. Bjoerner (Ed.), *1979 Copenhagen Winter School, Proceedings*, (pp. 1-42). Berlin: Springer-Verlag, Lecture Notes in Computer Science (No. 86).

Zemel, T. R. W. (1994). The role of software architectures in mega-system development. In M. M. Tanik, W. Rossak, & D. E. Cooke (Eds.), *Software systems in engineering* (pp. 74-85). New Orleans, LA/New York: The American Society of Mechanical Engineers Engineers.

Zeng, L., Benatallah, B., Ngu, A. H., Dumas, M., Kalagnanam, J., & Chang, H. (2004). QoS-aware middleware for Web services composition. *IEEE Transactions on Software Engineering, 30*(5), 311-327.

Zhao, J., Goble, C.A, Stevens, R., & Bechhofer, S. (2004). *Semantically linking and browsing provenance logs for e-science.* ICSNW, pp. 158-176.

Zhao, J., Wroe, C., Goble, C.A., Stevens, R., Quan, D., & Greenwood, R.M. (2004). Using Semantic Web technologies for representing e-science provenance. In *Proceedings of the International Semantic Web Conference*, (pp. 92-106).

Zimmerman, J. B. (1999). *Mobile computing: Characteristics, business benefits, and the mobile framework* (Tech. Rep. No. INSS 690 CC). University of Maryland European Division.

Zoebel, D., & Albrecht, W. (1995). *Echtzeitsysteme—Grundlagen und Techniken.* Bonn, Germany: Internat. Thomson Publ.

About the Contributors

Enis Afgan is currently a PhD candidate in the Department of Computer and Information Sciences at the University of Alabama at Birmingham, under the supervision of Dr. Purushotham Bangalore. His research interests focus around Grid Computing with the emphasis on user-level scheduling in heterogeneous environments with economic aspects. His other interests include distributed computing, optimization methods, and performance modeling. He received his BS degree in computer science from the University of Alabama at Birmingham in 2003.

Syed Muhammad Ahsan is an associate professor at the Department of Computer Science and Engineering, University of Engineering and Technology, Lahore, Pakistan, where he is involved in teaching and research for the last 14 years and has supervised more than 20 MS dissertations. He is doing his PhD in Bioinformatics at U.E.T., Lahore under the supervision of Dr. Abad Ali Shah. He has a bachelor in engineering and a masters in computer science, both form U.E.T., Lahore. Syed Ahsan has more then 15 journal and international research papers to his credit, including this book chapter. He has also refereed five international research papers and has chaired a technical session at IKE, 07, USA. His research interests include Bioinformatics, Semantic Web, Data Provenance and Agile methodologies. He is also the coprincipal investigator for Bioinformatics Resource Facility at U.E.T., Lahore, Pakistan.

Krishnakumar Balasubramanian is a PhD candidate at the Institute of Software Integrated Systems at Vanderbilt University. His research interests include distributed, real-time, and embedded systems; model-driven engineering; the application of MDE to deploy and configure component middleware for DRE systems, and patterns and frameworks for DRE systems development. He received an MS in computer science from Washington University in St. Louis.

Purushotham Bangalore is an assistant professor in the Department of Computer and Information Sciences at the University of Alabama at Birmingham (UAB) and also serves as the Director of Collaborative Computing Laboratory. He has a PhD in computational engineering from Mississippi State University where he also worked as a research associate at the Engineering Research Center. His area of interest includes programming environments for parallel and grid computing, scientific computing, and bioinformatics.

Rafael Capilla is a graduate in computer science and holds a PhD in computer science by the Universidad Rey Juan Carlos of Madrid (Spain). He worked as a senior analyst for 2 years in a telecommunication company and more than 8 years as a Unix system administrator. Currently, he is an assistant professor in the same university teaching software architecture and Web programming. He is coauthor of one book, two book chapters, one journal article, and more than 25 referred conference papers. His research focuses on software architecture, product-line engineering, software variability, and internet technologies.

Gerhard Chroust holds a Diplom-Ingenieur and a PhD from the Technical University of Vienna and a MS from the University of Pennsylvania. From 1966 to 1991 he conducted research and development at the IBM Laboratory Vienna on the Formal Definition of PL/I, on microprogramming, on compiler construction, and on software engineering environments. In 1992, he became a full professor for Systems Engineering at the Kepler University Linz, Austria. He authored and edited several books and numerous articles on systems engineering. His research focuses on the design of socio-technical systems, with respect to theory, methods and process models with special emphasis on systemic, human and cultural aspects.

Reidar Conradi was born in Oslo in 1946. He received his MS in 1970 and his PhD in 1976, both from the Norwegian University of Science and Technology in Trondheim (NTNU, previously called NTH), and has been at NTNU since 1975. He is now a professor at the Department of Computer and Information Science (IDI) at NTNU. Conradi was a visiting scientist at Fraunhofer Center for Experimental Software Engineering in Maryland and at Politecnico di Milano in 1999/2000. His interests are process modeling, software process improvement, software engineering databases, versioning, object-orientation, software architectures for distributed systems, and programming languages.

Kendra Cooper received a BASc, MASc and PhD in electrical and computer engineering from The University of British Columbia. Dr. Cooper has worked in the early phases of the software development lifecycle for over 10 years in industrial and academic settings. She is an assistant professor of computer science at the Erik Jonsson School of Engineering and Computer Science, The University of Texas at Dallas. Her research interests focus on modularization and reuse techniques (component-based, aspect-oriented, product line), with an emphasis on requirements engineering and software architecture. Dr. Cooper has over 70 peer reviewed publications and serves on the editorial boards of four journals. She is a member of the IEEE.

Lirong Dai is an assistant professor in the Department of Computer Science and Software Engineering at Seattle University. She received a BSc in computer science from Sichuan University; and a MSc and PhD from The University of Texas at Dallas. Dr. Dai's research areas include the specification and verification of software architecture design, nonfunctional requirements realization, design and analysis, with a specialization in aspect-oriented architectural design and analysis techniques.

Sergiu Dascalu is an assistant professor in computer science and engineering with the University of Nevada, Reno, which he joined in July 2002. He has published over 80 peer-reviewed papers on computer-related topics and has been actively involved in organizing scientific international conferences and workshops. His main research interests are in software specification and design, software environments and tools, human-computer interaction, and computer-aided education. Sergiu received a PhD in computer science from Dalhousie University, Halifax, Nova Scotia, Canada, and a master's degree in Automatic Control from the Polytechnic University of Bucharest, Romania.

Gan Deng is a PhD candidate at the Institute for Software Integrated Systems (ISIS) at Vanderbilt University. His research interests include distributed, real-time, and embedded systems; quality-of-service (QoS)-enabled component middleware; deployment and configuration of ultra large scale distributed systems, and model-driven engineering. He is a student member of the IEEE and ACM.

Jeff Elpern is a high-tech executive and entrepreneur. Currently, he is the V.P. of Software for a Silicon Valley telecommunications component manufacturer, founder and CEO of SQI, Inc.,–a software-as-a-service company based in Reno, Nevada,–and founder of the nonprofit Open Source Nevada Web site. Jeff has over 25 years of high-tech experience at senior levels, including CEO. He developed his classical marketing skills on Madison Avenue and in the automotive industry. Jeff earned a master of science degree, with distinction, from Carnegie-Mellon University's Graduate School of Industrial Administration and a bachelor of science degree in business from the University of Nevada.

Holger Giese is an assistant professor for object-oriented specification of distributed systems in the Software Engineering Group of the University of Paderborn since 2001. Currently, he is a visiting professor at the Hasso Plattner Institute for Software Systems Engineering in Potsdam. He studied technical computer science at the University Siegen and received his engineering degree in October 1995. He received a doctorate in computer science at the Institute of Computer Science at the University of Münster in February 2001. He is a member of the collaborative research center for "Self-optimizing Concepts and Structures in Mechanical Engineering" and one of the directors of the B1 subproject for software design techniques His research interests are software engineering for distributed, component-based and real-time systems. This includes techniques and tools for the modeling, analysis, validation, and verification of safety-critical distributed real-time systems with mechatronic components using design patterns, components, and software architecture modeling. He authored or coauthored over 80 internationally reviewed publications.

Aniruddha Gokhale is an assistant professor of computer science and engineering at Vanderbilt University, Nashville, TN. His research focuses on model-driven engineering of middleware systems to manage QoS properties of distributed real-time and embedded systems. Prior to his current position, he was with Bell Labs in New Jersey. Dr. Gokhale received his PhD in computer science from Washington University in St. Louis. He is a member of the IEEE and ACM.

Jeff Gray is an associate professor of computer and information sciences at the University of Alabama at Birmingham, where he codirects research in the Software Composition and Modeling (SoftCom) laboratory. Jeff received a PhD in computer science from Vanderbilt University where he also served as a research assistant at the Institute for Software Integrated Systems (ISIS). His research interests include model-driven engineering, model transformation, aspect-oriented development, and generative programming. Dr. Gray's research has been funded recently by DARPA, IBM and NSF, including an NSF CAREER.

Stefan Henkler received his BCSc in 2003 and his master degree in 2005 from the University of Paderborn. Since then, he is working in the collaborative research centre "Self-Optimizing Concepts in Mechanical Engineering" at the University of Paderborn. His research interests are in the area of modeling, analysis, and code generation of mechatronic systems. He authored or coauthored over 20 internationally reviewed publications.

Martin Hirsch received his BCSc in 2002 and his master degree in 2004 from the University of Paderborn. From 2004 until 2007 he was a PhD student on a scholarship at the University of Paderborn. Since 2007, he is a PhD student in the collaborative research centre "Self-Optimizing Concepts in Mechanical Engineering" at the University of Paderborn. His research interests are in the area of the compositional verification of mechatronic systems. He authored or coauthored over 20 internationally reviewed publications.

Ulrik Johansen is a research scientist at SINTEF ICT in Trondheim, Norway. He holds a Master of Science degree from the Norwegian Institute of Technology, Division of Telecommunications, in Trondheim. He has been working at SINTEF since 1979.
His main fields of compenetnce are within software engineering concerning: software specification, design and implementation; system developing methodologies; software architecture design. He has also competence within security and safety concerning safety assessment of safety critical systems, and security analysis and improvements of communication networks.

Jaroslav Král graduated in 1959 at Faculty of Mathematics and Physics of the Charles University, Prague, Czech Republic. He has been working in computer science at Czech Academy of Sciences and several Czech universities. He is now a full professor at the Faculty of Mathematical Physics of Charles University Prague and a visiting professor at the Faculty of Informatics of Masaryk University Brno, Czech Republic. His current research interests include: theory of formal languages and compilers, service-oriented systems engineering, education of software experts. He published more than 160 scientific papers.

Hien Nam Le received the BSc in computer science from La Trobe University, Australia, and the master degree in information technology from University of Queensland, Australia in 1996 and 2001, respectively. He received his PhD in computer science in 2006 from Norwegian University of Science and Technology (NTNU), Norway. Currently, he is working as a postdoc at the Department of Telematics, NTNU where he teaches courses on Self Configuring Systems and Networked Services. His research interests include mobile transactions, situated mobile services and service-oriented computing.

Akos Ledeczi is a Senior Research Scientist at the Institute for Software Integrated Systems and a Research Associate Professor at the Electrical Engineering and Computer Science Department at Vanderbilt University. He holds a MSc degree from the Technical University of Budapest and a PhD from Vanderbilt University, all in electrical engineering. His research interests include model integrated computing as well as embedded systems in general and wireless sensor networks (WSN) in particular. The group he is leading has produced some well known results including the Generic Modeling Environment, a widely used software engineering tool, the first WSN-based countersniper system, several time synchronization protocols and different radio interferometric localization and tracking techniques.

Gunther Lenz works for Siemens Corporate Research in Princeton, New Jersey. The goal of his work is to identify innovative techniques and technologies that enable systematic reuse and automation of the software development process. Therefore, he currently focuses on Model-driven Software Development (MDSD), automated guidance in context and Software Factories. Gunther is the author of the books „Practical Software Factories in .NET" and „.NET-A Complete Development Cycle."

He is an invited member of an expert advisory board for Microsoft, and received the Microsoft MVP Solution Architect award. Gunther frequently presents at international conferences on subjects related to software engineering.

Yuehua (Jane) Lin is a consultant at Precision Resources, Birmingham, Alabama. Her research interests include model transformation and supporting tools. She received a PhD from the University of Alabama at Birmingham.

Margartita Martínez holds MS and PhD degrees in computer science by the Universidad Politécnica de Madrid. She started as lecturer in the Universidad Politécnica de Madrid in 1986, and she became an associate professor in 1994. In 1998 she moved to the Universidad Rey Juan Carlos, where she teaches user interface design and development. She is coauthor of two book chapters, two journal articles and 15 referred conference papers. Her research area is human computer interaction.

Rym Mili is an Associate Professor of Computer Science at the Erik Jonsson School of Engineering and Computer Science. She holds a PhD in computer science from the University of Ottawa (Canada), and the Doctorat de Spécialité in Computer Science from the University of Tunis (Tunisia). Her research interests are in software engineering and multi-agent system development. Dr. Mili is the head of the Visualization and Agent Technology laboratory. Her research has been funded by the National Science Foundation, Sandia National Laboratories and Rockwell-Collins. She is the author of over 40 journal and conference papers, and served on numerous international program committees.

Zoltán Molnár received the MSc degree in computer science from the University of Szeged, Hungary, in 1999. His work experience includes telecommunication systems software development for 3rd generation GSM networks and Linux platform development. Currently as a staff engineer at Vanderbilt University he is responsible for developing and maintaining the GME toolset. Among his main contributions is the domain specific API generator, which allows GME interpreter authors to express their code in domain specific terms. He has experience in software design with UML, metamodeling with GME, and development with C++, C# languages.

Cristina Muñoz received a degree in computer science by the University Rey Juan Carlos (Madrid). She worked in the development of a virtual reality church system, and currently is PhD student in the Universidad Politécnica of Madrid under the HESPERIA project. Her research focuses on digital signature recognition and voice analysis.

Francisco Nava is a graduate in computer science by the Universidad Politécnica of Madrid (Spain). He has more than 25 years experience as a senior system analyst, project manager, and freelance consulting, as well as Director of the Information Systems Department at L'Oreal. Currently, he is an associate professor in the Universidad Rey Juan Carlos of Madrid (Spain) teaching Programming Methodology and Information Systems Audit. He is coauthor of one book, and 12 referred conference papers. His research focuses on software architecture and computer based patient record.

Andrey Nechypurenko is a senior software engineer in Siemens AG CorporateTechnology (CT SE2). Mr. Nechypurenko provides consulting services for Siemens business units focusing on distributed real-time and embeddedsystems. Mr. Nechypurenko also participates in research activities on model driven development and parallel computing. Before joiningSiemens AG, he worked in the Ukraine on high performance distributedsystems in the telecommunications domain.

Mads Nygård is a full professor in the Department of Computer and Information Science at the Norwegian University of Science and Technology (NTNU) in Trondheim, Norway. There he teaches courses on Operating Systems and Distributed Systems. He received his Dr. Techn. degree in Distributed Databases from NTNU in 1990, and his main research interests are Distributed Systems, Transaction Processing and Mobile Environments. He has published more than 65 international scientific papers of all types and has served as both General Chair and Organization Committee Chair at international scientific conferences. Earlier, he has worked for both the United Nations Development Program (UNDP) and the Organization for Economic Cooperation and Development (OECD).

Gøran K. Olsen is a reasearch scientist at SINTEF ICT in Oslo, Norway. He holds a master of science degree in informatics from the University of Oslo where he specialised in model-driven development. He has been involved in several European reasearch projects e.g. MODELWARE and ELLECTRA-WEB. He is currently involved as leader of the traceability task in the European research project MODELPLEX. He was a member of the organizing commitee for the 3rd ECMDA-Traceability Workshop held in conjunction with ECMDA-FA 2007.

Heri Ramampiaro is associate professor at the Department of Computer and Information Science, Norwegian University of Science and Technology (NTNU) in Trondheim, Norway. Ramampiaro's research interests include information retrieval, advanced databases, cooperative work, mobile computing, Internet, software agents, digital image processing and multimedia. He is currently engaged in projects such as applying databases and information retrieval in Bioinformatics, and one of the principal investigators for the CAIM (Context-aware Image Management) research project.

Nilabja Roy is a graduate student in the Department of Electrical Engineering and Computer Science with Computer Science major at Vanderbilt University. His main research interests are middleware, patterns, domain specific modelling languages, reliability and performance modeling of systems. He is currently working on developing a highly sophisticated dynamic monitoring and profiling service framework for use in distributed real-time and embedded (DRE) middleware domain. Previous to joining Vanderbilt, he was involved in software development in the telecom field, designing a distributed mediation application communicating over large geographical distances, which required extensive benchmarking and astute designing skills to maintain reliability, performance for the end-users. He got his bachelors from Jadavpur University, India, in electrical engineering.

Vladimir Rubin received his diploma in computer science from the Moscow State University of Railway Transport. From 1999 to 2001, he worked as a software developer at the Keldysh Institute of Applied Mathematics (Moscow, Russia). From 2001 to 2003, he worked as a system engineer in the NetCracker Technology Corp. (2001, 2002–Moscow, Russia; 2003–Boston, USA). From 2004 to 2007, he was a PhD student of the International Graduate School of Dynamic Intelligent Systems and stayed with the Software Engineering Group, Department of Computer Science, University of Paderborn (Paderborn, Germany). Since 2007, he is a Senior Software Engineer at the sd&m AG (Frankfurt, Germany).

Douglas C. Schmidt is a Professor of Computer Science and Associate Chair of the Computer Science and Engineering program at Vanderbilt University. He has published 9 books and over 350 technical papers that cover a range of research topics, including patterns, optimization techniques, and empirical analyses of software frameworks and domain-specific modeling environments that facilitate the development of distributed real-time and embedded (DRE) middleware and applications running over high-speed networks and embedded system interconnects. Dr. Schmidt has also led the development of ACE, TAO, CIAO, and CoSMIC, which are widely used, open-source DRE middleware frameworks and model-driven tools that contain a rich set of components and domain-specific languages that implement patterns and product-line architectures for high-performance DRE systems.

Erwin Schoitsch, born in 1944 (Vienna), received his master degree in technical physics and a bachelor degree in computer science (1962-1969) at the University of Technology in Vienna. He has worked at Austrian Research Centres (ARC) for more than 35 years, focusing on industrial and research projects dealing with systems of high dependability or software process improvement, including many European projects (ESPITI, OLOS, SPIRE, ENCRESS, ACRuDA, ECUA, ISA-EuNet, AMSD, COOPERS, DECOS).
He is active in international working groups (EWICS TC7, ERCIM) and standardization of functional safety (IEC 61508, ISO WD 26262). His main interest is the holistic approach to system dependability.

Abad Ali Shah is a Foreign Professor of Higher Education Commission (HEC) of Pakistan, and placed in the Department of Computer Science & Engineering of University of Engineering & Technology (UET), Lahore, Pakistan. He spent 12 years in the computer science department, King Saud University, Riyadh, KSA before joining HEC on July 2004. He received his BSc in mathematics and physics from Punjab University, Lahore, Pakistan in 1967, a MSc in applied mathematics from Quaid-I-Azam University, Islamabad, Pakistan in 1981, with a Quaid-I-Azam Award, a MS in computer science from Rensselaer Polytechnic Institute, Troy, New York, in 1986, and a PhD in computer science from Wayne State University, Detroit, Michigan, USA, in 1992. His current research interests include object-oriented databases, temporal databases, Web databases, Web services, information retrieval (IR) software engineering, Semantic Web, Web engineering and Bioinformatics. He has more than 90 research articles on his credit, including three book chapters including this one. Currently, he is supervising many PhD and MS dissertations. He is a member of ACM.

Carl-Fredrik Sørensen is currently working as senior research scientist at SINTEF Fisheries and Aquaculture working with electronic traceability and tracking of goods. He received his PhD in software engineering in 2006 at the Department of Computer and Information Science at the Norwegian University of Science and Technology (NTNU). His research interests include mobile/pervasive computing, CSCW, peer-to-peer computing, software architecture, open source, and software engineering. He has published more than 20 international scientific papers.

Erlend Stav is a senior research scientist at SINTEF ICT in Trondheim, Norway. His current research interests include software architecture, component software, model driven development, visual development environments and tools, and assistive technology for elderly and disabled users. In 2006, he received his PhD in computer science from the Norwegian University of Science and Technology, in the topic of developing extensible application composition environments for end users.

Renee Steiner is a Senior Software Engineer in Research and Development at Intervoice, Inc., and an adjunct professor at the Erik Jonsson School of Engineering and Computer Science, The University of Texas at Dallas. She received a BS, MS, and PhD in computer science with a specialization in software engineering. Dr. Steiner's interests include software engineering, multi agent system engineering and visualization. She is a member of the ACM and the IEEE.

Matthias Tichy received his diploma degree in business computing from the University of Paderborn in 2002. Since then, he is working in the collaborative research centre "Self-Optimizing Concepts in Mechanical Engineering" at the University of Paderborn. His research focuses on dependability issues in software-intensive systems. His main research area is the analysis and improvement of the safety of component-based system architectures. He authored or coauthored over 25 internationally reviewed publications.

Daniel G. Waddington is a principal researcher at Lockheed Martin Advanced Technology Laboratories (ATL), Cherry Hill, New Jersey. He originally completed his PhD in middleware support for managed Quality-of-Service at Lancaster University, UK, in 1999. After leaving Lancaster in 2000, he spent 5 years with Bell Laboratories developing languages and tools for metaprogramming and software maintenance of IPv6-based telecommunication applications. He now leads a number of ATL research projects in the field of building military applications for next generation multicore processing architectures.

Ståle Walderhaug is a PhD student at the Department of Computer Science at the University of Tromsø, and a research scientist at SINTEF ICT in Trondheim, Norway. His doctoral studies are on model-driven development techniques to improve the interoperability of information systems in health care. He holds a master of science degree from the Norwegian University of Science and Technology and has been working as a research scientist at SINTEF since 2000. Ståle Walderhaug was the Norwegian representative in the NATO MEDCIS Working Group Telemedicine Expert Panel from 2002-2005 and has experience from several of the European research projects.

Alf Inge Wang is currently working as an associate professor at the Department of Computer and Information Science at the Norwegian University of Science and Technology (NTNU) where he teaches courses on programming, software architecture, mobile application development and game development. He received his PhD in software engineering in 2001. His research interests are game development, game concept development, computer support for mobile collaborative work, peer-to-peer computing, software architecture, and software engineering education. He has published more than 50 scientific international papers, including journal papers, book chapters and being editor for a book.

Jules White is a researcher in the Distributed Object Computing (DOC) group at Vanderbilt University's Institute for Software Integrated Systems (ISIS). Mr. White's research focuses on reducing the complexity of modeling complex domains. Before joining the DOC group, he worked in IBM's Boston Innovation Center. Mr. White is the head of development for the Generic Eclipse Modeling System (GEMS) (http://www.sf.net/projects/gems).

Egon Wuchner works as a researcher and consultant in the Coporate Technology SE2 department of Siemens AG in Munich, Germany. He is an expert in software architecture and distributed systems.

His research focuses on concepts, technologies and tools to improve the development of large distributed systems, for example, their handling of operational requirements, their comprehensibility and maintanability. His recent research has been in Aspect-oriented Software Development and Model-driven Development.

Michal Žemlička is a senior assistant professor at the Faculty of Mathematics and Physics of Charles University, Prague. He graduated in 1996. His current research interests are extensible compilers, theory of parsing, the design of large software systems, data structures, and computational linguistics. He has published more than 50 scientific papers.

Index